INSPIRING SCIENCE

JIM WATSON AND THE AGE OF DNA

INSPIRING SCIENCE

JIM WATSON AND THE AGE OF DNA

With a Foreword by Matt Ridley

EDITED BY

John R. Inglis
Cold Spring Harbor Laboratory

Joseph Sambrook
Peter MacCallum Cancer Centre

Jan A. Witkowski
Banbury Center, Cold Spring Harbor Laboratory

COLD SPRING HARBOR LABORATORY
Cold Spring Harbor, New York

INSPIRING SCIENCE

JIM WATSON AND THE AGE OF DNA

Publisher	John Inglis
Managing Editor	Jan Argentine
Project Manager	Maryliz Dickerson
Illustration Coordinator	Elizabeth Powers
Permissions Coordinator	Nora Rice
Production Editor	Dorothy Brown
Desktop Editor	Susan Schaefer
Production Manager	Denise Weiss
Cover Designer	Ed Atkeson

Front Cover: The drawing of Jim Watson is by American sculptor Robert Berks; photograph courtesy of Jim Strong.

Library of Congress Cataloging-in-Publication Data

Inspiring science : Jim Watson and the age of DNA / edited by John R.
Inglis, Joseph Sambrook, Jan A. Witkowski.
    p. cm.
Includes bibliographical references and index.
  ISBN 0-87969-698-2 (hc : alk. paper)
 1. Watson, James D., 1928– 2. Molecular biologists--United
States--Biography. 3. DNA. I. Inglis, J. R. (John R.) II. Sambrook,
Joseph. III. Witkowski, J. A. (Jan Anthony), 1947– IV. Title.
  QH506.W4I55 2003
  572.8'092--dc21   2003013791

10 9 8 7 6 5 4 3 2

All Cold Spring Harbor Laboratory Press publications may be ordered directly from Cold Spring Harbor Laboratory Press, 500 Sunnyside Boulevard, Woodbury, New York 11797-2924. Phone: 1-800-843-4388 in Continental U.S. and Canada. All other locations: (516) 422-4100. FAX: (516) 422-4097. E-mail: cshpress@cshl.org. For a complete catalog of all Cold Spring Harbor Laboratory Press publications, visit our World Wide Web Site http://www.cshlpress.com

Contents

PREFACE

WHEN THE THREE OF US HAD DECIDED to put together a celebration of Jim Watson's achievements, we went to get his permission. Expecting a rebuff, we had already prepared the obvious arguments—50 years of DNA, a half century as a scientist, best-selling author, 35 years at Cold Spring Harbor—that sort of thing. But, to our surprise, far from being put off by a project that was to include reminiscences of him, Jim was slightly pleased and placed only a few restrictions: He wanted to know nothing at all about the book before it appeared and stipulated that it should contain nothing too worshipful and certainly nothing boring.

The first of Jim's conditions has been met in its entirety. As to the second and third, throughout the editing process, we have tried our best to achieve them without compromising the style or content of the essays. We have eliminated duplications as far as possible, but have retained overlaps between contributions when authors had different views of the same events. A couple of essays were shortened, and in a few cases, we have reduced the number of superlatives to a respectable level. Otherwise, however, the editing has been carried out with a light hand.

Because Jim has not yet seen any of the contributions, there may be a few things that he would not have wished said. We have tried to correct errors of fact, but the book may nevertheless contain stories, apocrypha, or other embroidery that Jim may wish to disown. He will no doubt take up these matters himself with the contributors concerned.

Our aim was to assemble a number of essays by Jim's friends and colleagues, covering as much of his scientific life as possible but avoiding events that have already been the focus of much public interest and publicity—the prelude to the discovery of DNA, for example. There are two noticeable gaps. There is nothing here about young Jim—his childhood or his undergraduate career at the University of Chicago. And there is very little about his sabbatical return to Cambridge in 1956. We might have obtained information to fill these lacunae, but the main purpose of this book is not to reconstruct an academic history or an authoritative biography, but to record friendship and appreciation.

Although most of the book has been written especially for the occasion, we realized from the outset that it would be unnecessarily dogmatic to exclude material simply on the grounds that it has already appeared elsewhere. Out of the total of 43 essays in the book, one—that of Edward O. Wilson—has been published in the book *Naturalist* while another (Avrion Mitchison's) has recently appeared on the web. We have also included facsimiles of scientific papers that were the foundation of Jim's scientific career.

Reading these contributed essays, one realizes that Jim's behavior—sometimes regarded as mercurial and unpredictable—has in fact been remarkably constant. Some of the reminiscences of Jim could be transposed by 50 years without appearing anachronistic. Now, as then, Jim makes fools suffer and still makes no pretense of being an equal among equals. In these essays, he is not recognizably different when old and young, and nothing of his youthful enthusiasm has been lost to age or conceded to diplomacy.

Most of the people who read this book will be too young to know how it felt to live in a world where DNA was a minor chemical and a gene was a metaphysical concept. Jim and Francis Crick changed all that during the course of a Saturday morning in the late winter of 1953. In retrospect, the events of that day have an inevitability. If it was Jim's destiny to travel to Cambridge to discover the structure of DNA, it became his responsibility over the course of 50 years to direct the consequences of that discovery to their scientific and ethical conclusions. What no one could have expected was that Jim, in doing so, would open a world of such lasting beauty and brilliant light.

John Inglis
Joe Sambrook
Jan Witkowski

ACKNOWLEDGMENTS

We are most grateful to the book's contributors for working so hard to meet our request for something that was brief and interesting and for gracefully accepting our editorial suggestions. Several contributors provided us, in addition, with photographs from their private archives. We also thank, in many cases, the contributors' assistants who helped keep us in touch over the two-year course of the project.

Two contributors, James Eisenman and Dr. Alfred Tissières, wrote essays during their final illnesses. We wish to thank Mrs. Jan Eisenman and Mme. Virginia Tissières for their kindness in seeing the essays through the final stages of editing.

Dr. Max Perutz died before being able to contribute to the book. Knowing his days were numbered, he sent letters of private farewell to people he valued and we are most grateful to Dr. Vivien Perutz and Professor Robin Perutz for permission to reproduce the letter Max wrote to Jim.

The book contains a large number of documents and images owned or originally published by others. For permission to reproduce these items, often without charge, we thank the following: Dr. Philip Campbell, editor of *Nature*, and the Nature Publishing Group; Annika Ekdahl, The Nobel Foundation; Dr. Kenneth Rose, The Rockefeller Foundation Archive Center; Dr. Derek Chadwick, The Novartis Foundation; Maggie Bartlett, the National Human Genome Research Institute; Sandra Rux, the Connecticut Academy of Arts and Sciences; Gloria Sandler, *Newsday*; Peter Sloggatt, *The Long Islander*; Rick Stafford, photographer; and Robert Berks, sculptor and artist.

The Archives of Cold Spring Harbor Laboratory were an essential resource and we are grateful to the Director of Libraries and Archives Mila Pollock, and librarians Claudia Zago, Gail Sherman, Leigh Johnson, Margaret Henderson, Ellen Brenner, Kiryn Haslinger, and Paula Abisognio. Our special thanks and appreciation go to archivists Clare Bunce, Teresa Kruger, and Cara Brick, who helped locate many of the illustrations that accompany the text.

It is also a pleasure to acknowledge the assistance of people working in other departments at Cold Spring Harbor Laboratory: Philip Renna, Cat Eberstark, and Marco Cheung (Media Arts and Visualization); Miriam Chua and Laura Hyman (Public Affairs); and Maureen Berejka (the Office of the President).

This book would not have become a reality without the many skills of our colleagues at Cold Spring Harbor Laboratory Press: Jan Argentine, Managing Editor; Elizabeth Powers, Illustration Coordinator; Mary Cozza and Inez Sialiano, Editorial Assistants; Nora Rice, Editorial Assistant and Permissions Coordinator; Denise Weiss, designer and Production Manager; Dorothy Brown, Production Editor; Susan Schaefer, Desktop Editor; and above all, Maryliz Dickerson, Project Manager, whose dedication and diligence was critical to the endeavor.

The Editors
July 2003

FOREWORD

I
T IS OFTEN SAID THAT SCIENTISTS ARE CULTURALLY dispensable. If a particular scientist had not lived, his discovery would have been made by someone else, but if a great artist had not lived, his masterpiece would not have been created at all. Gravity, relativity, and natural selection would have been understood almost as soon without Newton, Einstein, or Darwin. Genetics was indeed (re)founded without Mendel. But the Mona Lisa, Hamlet, and the Ninth Symphony would never have been imagined without Leonardo, Shakespeare, and Beethoven.

This axiom is especially true of the double helix and the genome, the towering bookends of Jim Watson's remarkable career. Had Watson never lived, any one of a number of candidates would have stepped forward to claim the base-pairing insight that is the key to unraveling DNA's structure. Rosalind Franklin was almost there; Maurice Wilkins was about to start model building; Linus Pauling would have evaded McCarthyism to see the X-ray data soon enough; Francis Crick might have done it on his own. Chargaff, Donohue, Hershey, Gosling, Furberg, Bernal—any one of them could have snatched the prize if they had shared Watson's urgency and vision. But that is what makes Watson's achievement all the more remarkable. It was precisely because the prize was ripe, and so many brilliant minds were after it, that his grasping it equal-first was an act of genius. He may have shaved only months, perhaps a year, off the timetable of history, but he won the race, something Shakespeare and Beethoven never had to do.

The same is true of the genome. If Watson had not led the Human Genome Project, somebody else would have done it. Somebody else did do it, after Watson was forced from the post in 1992. But it would probably have taken longer, been less international, neglected the ethical and social sides, and resulted in even more of a gold rush of gene patenting and monopoly. The urgency and almost reckless ambition of the early years of the Genome Project were quintessentially Jim. In some ways, Watson's decision to hold out against the speculative patenting by the National Institutes of Health of gene sequences of unknown function—the stance that led to his dismissal—may be one of his most far-reaching legacies. Had the Human Genome Project followed that route not only would patents have slowed down research, but science would have suffered a massive blow to its reputation.

What a much duller—and safer—history DNA would have had without Watson stirring things up. From the first friction with Rosalind Franklin to the battle against regulation in the 1970s to the confrontations with Craig Venter in the 1990s, it was Watson's ability to live dangerously that made history. Without it we would now, 50 years

MATT RIDLEY

Satisfying public fascination with the nature of genes and their influence on human character and behavior has been a motivating force for many book authors. None have been as consistent or successful as Matt Ridley, whose international best sellers include *The Red Queen: Sex and the Evolution of Human Nature* (1994, Macmillan); *The Origins of Virtue* (1996, Viking); *Genome: The Autobiography of a Species in 23 Chapters* (1999, HarperCollins); and most recently, *Nature vs. Nurture: Genes, Experience, and What Makes Us Human* (2003, HarperCollins). Trained in zoology at Oxford University, he was science editor and American editor of *The Economist* from 1983 to 1992, and a columnist for the *The Sunday Telegraph* and *The Daily Telegraph* between 1993 and 2000. He has also written articles and book reviews for a host of other publications. An enthusiastic promoter of public discourse on science, Ridley shares with Jim Watson a commitment to science education and is Chairman of The International Centre for Life, a science park and educational facility in Newcastle Upon Tyne that, like the Dolan DNA Learning Center of Cold Spring Harbor Laboratory, enables children of all ages to explore genetics and DNA science through hands-on experiments and state-of-the-art audiovisual technology.

on, be looking back with the self-satisfied hindsight of sober grandees, instead of looking forward into the giddy future with awkward and ambitious questions. There is little doubt that Watson's life, like his most famous book, is a work of art, by which I mean something creative, dangerous—and irreplaceable.

The Double Helix (1968, Atheneum) would certainly not have been written if Watson had not written it. It was a book that revolutionized the way science would be portrayed in nonfiction books thereafter and defined the seminal events of 1951–1953 for good and ill. In its ground-breaking iconoclasm and scandalous honesty, "Honest Jim" (as it was originally called) was at least as great a literary event as "Lucky Jim," or "Lord Jim." The pen portrait of Francis Crick that is the first chapter of the book is simultaneously hilarious, rude, and admiring, but it establishes in just three pages an unforgettable character, as the next chapter establishes the characters of Wilkins and Franklin. The reader gets the sense, within eight pages, of having entered a play with a strong cast and the omens of a thrilling plot. Just because it is factual should not detract from its being art.

Like many people, I can remember reading the book for the first time at school and finding it a revelation. I understood only bits of the science, but the human side was clear enough. I had no idea that scientists, or for that matter adults, behaved like this—that science is made by "very human events in which personalities and cultural traditions play major roles" (the words are from Watson's Preface). Here at last was science as the messy exploration of ignorance, not the tidy recitation of facts that I was used to in the classroom. The teachers had somehow omitted from my courses the news that "a goodly number of scientists are not only narrow-minded and dull, but also just stupid."

If only Newton had left us such an account, replete with diatribes at Leibnitz and patronizing swipes at Halley. If only Archimedes had told us who else was in that bath. *The Double Helix* is both a vital piece of history and a literary masterpiece precisely because it is the first time that a person present at a great event has attempted to recapture it without the benefit of hindsight. Although he was writing 15 years later, Watson deliberately eschewed the chance to polish history, or to correct his own errors and misinterpretations, even to be magnanimous to his defeated rivals. He wanted to "convey the spirit of an adventure characterized both by youthful arrogance and by the belief that the truth, once found, would be simple as well as pretty." In a sense, the book is therefore the truest history of the discovery that will ever be written. As Sir Peter Medawar perceptively noted in his review of *The Double Helix*, "Many of the things Watson says about the people in his story will offend them, but his own artless candour excuses him, for he betrays in himself faults far graver than those he professes to discern in others" (March 28, 1968, *New York Review of Books*, pp. 3–5).

Yet in unsparingly portraying himself as naïve, ambitious, prejudiced, and lustful, Watson was to ensure that his own reputation would forever be flawed in the eyes of those who love to judge. It is a decision few great men with an eye on history have taken, but it is one that future generations will treasure.

Today, *The Double Helix* has lost some, but not all, of its power to shock. Even Francis Crick, who campaigned successfully against its publication by Harvard University Press, later admitted that "I come out rather well in the book." The scale of this change is testament to the book's influence over nonfiction prose. Not only do today's science writers depict their characters as human beings, they also avoid patronizing (or educating) their readers about scientific facts—they take them by the hand to embark on a tour of discovery. They do what Watson did: Show them the ignorance that came first, not the established facts that came later. They convey the excitement of chipping away at mystery, rather than compiling knowledge. It is a subtle change, but widespread. Consider this from the Preface to Richard Dawkins's *The Selfish Gene* (1976, Oxford University Press): "I have long felt that biology ought to seem as exciting as a mystery story, for a mystery story is exactly what biology is." Or this, from James Gleick's *Chaos: Making a New Science* (1987, Viking): "Professional scientists, given brief, uncertain glimpses of nature's workings, are no less vulnerable to anguish and confusion when they come face to face with incongruity." This is post-Watsonian science literature.

Genes, Girls, and Gamow: After The Double Helix (2001, Alfred A. Knopf), Watson's much later account of life after DNA, broke new ground again, abandoning smooth prose to tell a scientific saga with the clumsy style and hesitant uncertainty of a young man's mind. Had it been a novel, it would have been praised for its post-modern, innovatory syntax. But once again the world was not ready for Watson, and many literal-minded reviewers gave him no quarter.

Watson's other achievements—his extraordinarily influential textbooks, his eye for picking talent, his ability to shape the agenda of molecular biology, his fund-raising and administrative skills—would be enough for most careers in science. But history will soon forget all that. To future generations, Watson will be the person who, with Crick, discovered the linear, digital information at the heart of life. It is hard, these days, to recall just how unexpected this discovery was. Friedrich Miescher, the discoverer of DNA itself, suggested in 1892 that DNA might convey the hereditary message "just as the words and concepts of all languages can find expression in 24–30 letters of the alphabet," but in the following 50 years nobody returned to the idea that the secret of the gene would be a linear, digital message. Even after 1953, it took Watson and Crick years to persuade people that what they had discovered was not chemistry, but language.

The double helix was an unusual scientific discovery, because it was so pregnant with future implications. Saturday, February 28, 1953 stands alone in the history of science not just for the surprise that it sprang upon the world, but for the infinite opportunities for future discovery that suddenly became not just possible but unavoidable. It was already inevitable, by lunch time that day, that one day a species of living creature would read its own complete genetic recipe, compare it with that of its closest relative, drink deep draughts of knowledge from the comparison, and then begin to edit the text. It might take ten years to crack the code, 20 to learn to edit it, 30 to learn to amplify it, 40 to learn to read it rapidly and cheaply, 50 to understand the full machinery of switches by which it is expressed, and more to pluck up the courage to alter it. But those breakthroughs would surely come. We are simply playing out the script that Watson and Crick wrote that morning before retiring to The Eagle pub. The reading of the human genome was already inevitable by the middle of that day—with all its medical, ethical, and philosophical implications. Nobody, not even Watson and Crick, realized that they would see it in their lifetime. But Watson more than anybody else seems to have realized just how inevitable the progress would be, to have seen just how long a shadow they had cast upon the future. It might have been possible to discover the double helix and not see the implications, not immediately realize that base-pairing meant genetic engineering. After all, there were scores of biochemists and biologists who refused to recognize that their subject had just changed forever. Perhaps even Watson might have held back from such bold insights without the confident and penetrating Crick at his side. But with both of them in possession of this knowledge, the digital, editable future was ineluctable. Had the double helix been discovered by somebody else, wrote Crick, "it might not have been pushed as Jim and I pushed it." People make history.

Richard Dawkins once wrote that "What is truly revolutionary about molecular biology in the post-Watson-Crick era is that it has become digital...the machine code of the genes is uncannily computer-like." Organisms can in theory now be transmitted, weightless and at the speed of light, in the form of their digital code. Today at the flick of a cursor, I can call up the sequence of any one of tens of thousands of genes on the Ensembl browser, and I can use a computer to find substitutions, common motifs, insertions or deletions between species or individuals. You can spend a whole scientific career discovering digits of DNA without ever getting your hands dirty. All this digital biology would have been impossible without digital technology. The parallel development of the two, starting in the 1950s and flowering in the 1990s, has to be a coincidence. The transistor and the double helix did not have to emerge within a decade of each other. Either one could have come a decade earlier or later. But it is a remarkably fortunate coincidence. Without massive computer power, assembling the fragments of code into a complete human genome sequence would have been beyond the capabilities of even an army of clerks.

Much of the revolution sparked by Watson and Crick was wholly unpredictable. Who would have thought that the first and boldest application of DNA in everyday life would be forensic? Digital DNA has acquitted and convicted criminals, impeached a president, traced many a father, exposed a fake Tsar's daughter. Who would have predicted its extraordinary revelations about the origin of life? DNA uses a universal code unexpectedly implying a single, common ancestry for all life. And it carries echoes of an earlier RNA world inaccessible to paleontology. Who would have believed that DNA would become the main tool of taxonomy? It thereby demoted the human species from a special ape to merely a third species of chimpanzee, a humiliation as large as that visited upon us by Copernicus and Darwin. Who could have foreseen the digitization of genealogy that allowed me to send off my Y chromosome for comparison with that of others with my surname? Who could have imagined DNA's impact on archaeology and anthropology, with its revelation of whose genes triumphed after invasions or which kinds of people left Africa and when? Who could have predicted the discovery by DNA fingerprinting of a scandalous epidemic of infidelity in the animal kingdom and thereby given birth to the theory of sperm competition? Who would have guessed that the digital sequences of body-plan and memory genes from flies and people would reveal profound ancestral similarities inherited from a common ancestor that lived before the first fossils of animals? Who would have dared to suggest just how ordinary a human's genome would prove to be? It is shorter than a newt's, has fewer genes than a simple weed's, and contains much more repetitive junk than a fly's.

All this in DNA's first few decades. What comes next? Ask Jim.

Matt Ridley

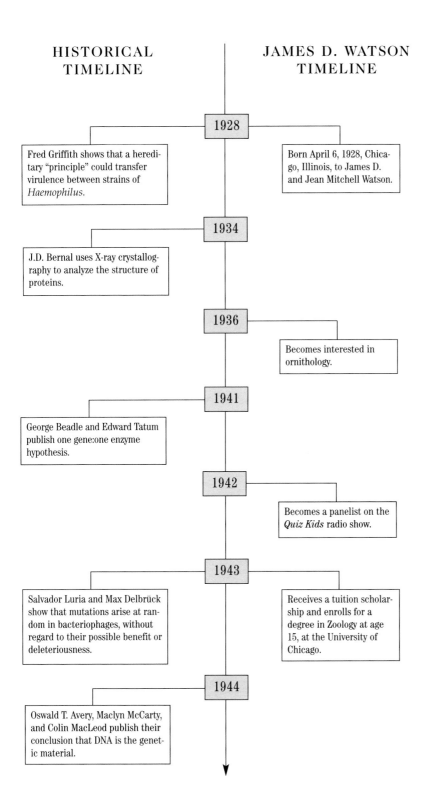

HISTORICAL TIMELINE

JAMES D. WATSON TIMELINE

1928

Fred Griffith shows that a hereditary "principle" could transfer virulence between strains of *Haemophilus*.

Born April 6, 1928, Chicago, Illinois, to James D. and Jean Mitchell Watson.

1934

J.D. Bernal uses X-ray crystallography to analyze the structure of proteins.

1936

Becomes interested in ornithology.

1941

George Beadle and Edward Tatum publish one gene:one enzyme hypothesis.

1942

Becomes a panelist on the *Quiz Kids* radio show.

1943

Salvador Luria and Max Delbrück show that mutations arise at random in bacteriophages, without regard to their possible benefit or deleteriousness.

Receives a tuition scholarship and enrolls for a degree in Zoology at age 15, at the University of Chicago.

1944

Oswald T. Avery, Maclyn McCarty, and Colin MacLeod publish their conclusion that DNA is the genetic material.

Please note that the listing of Jim Watson's honors and awards may not be complete and that certain prizes awarded to Jim were shared with others.

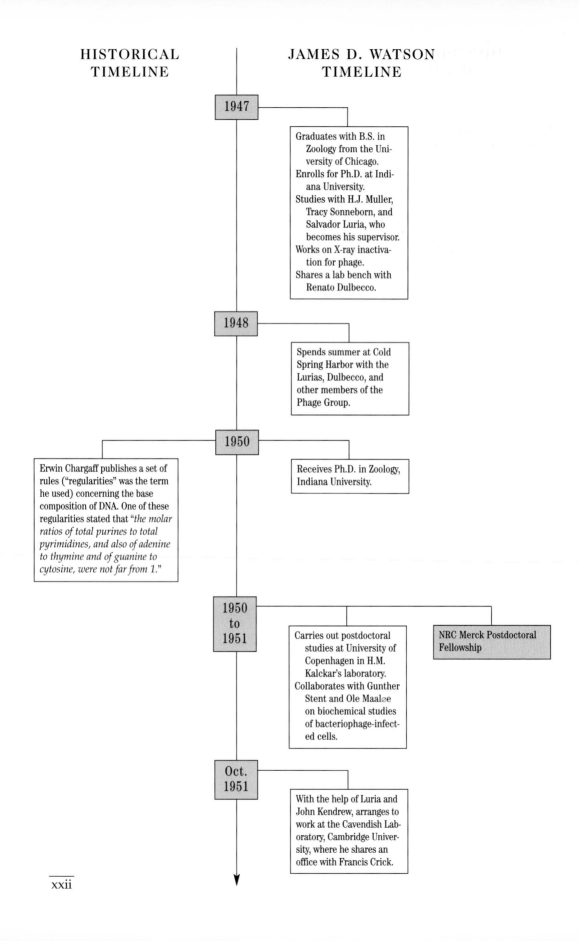

HISTORICAL
TIMELINE

JAMES D. WATSON
TIMELINE

1947

Graduates with B.S. in
Zoology from the Uni-
versity of Chicago.
Enrolls for Ph.D. at Indi-
ana University.
Studies with H.J. Muller,
Tracy Sonneborn, and
Salvador Luria, who
becomes his supervisor.
Works on X-ray inactiva-
tion for phage.
Shares a lab bench with
Renato Dulbecco.

1948

Spends summer at Cold
Spring Harbor with the
Lurias, Dulbecco, and
other members of the
Phage Group.

1950

Erwin Chargaff publishes a set of
rules ("regularities" was the term
he used) concerning the base
composition of DNA. One of these
regularities stated that *"the molar
ratios of total purines to total
pyrimidines, and also of adenine
to thymine and of guanine to
cytosine, were not far from 1."*

Receives Ph.D. in Zoology,
Indiana University.

**1950
to
1951**

Carries out postdoctoral
studies at University of
Copenhagen in H.M.
Kalckar's laboratory.
Collaborates with Gunther
Stent and Ole Maaløe
on biochemical studies
of bacteriophage-infect-
ed cells.

NRC Merck Postdoctoral
Fellowship

**Oct.
1951**

With the help of Luria and
John Kendrew, arranges to
work at the Cavendish Laboratory, Cambridge University, where he shares an
office with Francis Crick.

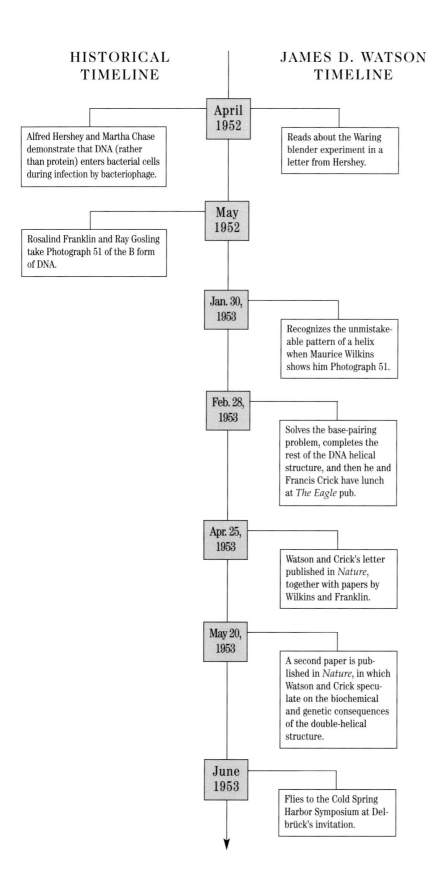

HISTORICAL TIMELINE

JAMES D. WATSON TIMELINE

April 1952

Alfred Hershey and Martha Chase demonstrate that DNA (rather than protein) enters bacterial cells during infection by bacteriophage.

Reads about the Waring blender experiment in a letter from Hershey.

May 1952

Rosalind Franklin and Ray Gosling take Photograph 51 of the B form of DNA.

Jan. 30, 1953

Recognizes the unmistakeable pattern of a helix when Maurice Wilkins shows him Photograph 51.

Feb. 28, 1953

Solves the base-pairing problem, completes the rest of the DNA helical structure, and then he and Francis Crick have lunch at *The Eagle* pub.

Apr. 25, 1953

Watson and Crick's letter published in *Nature*, together with papers by Wilkins and Franklin.

May 20, 1953

A second paper is published in *Nature*, in which Watson and Crick speculate on the biochemical and genetic consequences of the double-helical structure.

June 1953

Flies to the Cold Spring Harbor Symposium at Delbrück's invitation.

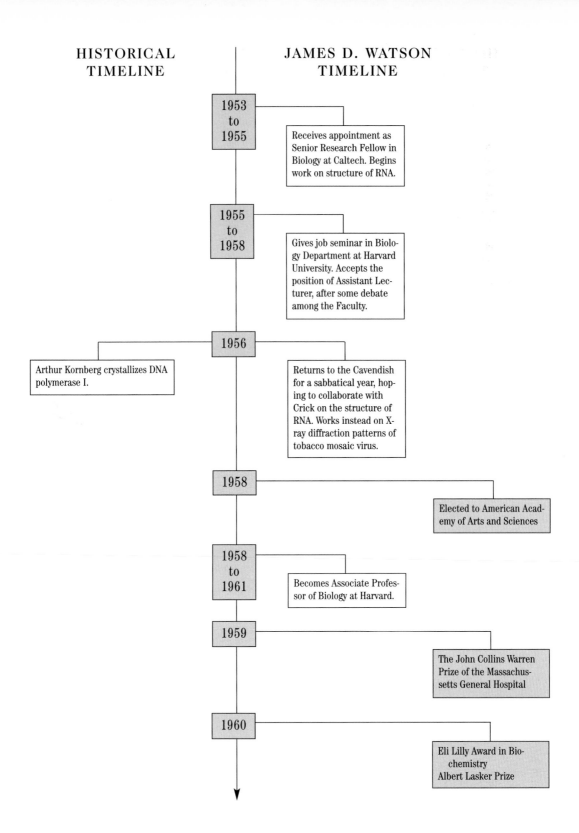

HISTORICAL
TIMELINE

JAMES D. WATSON
TIMELINE

1953
to
1955

Receives appointment as
Senior Research Fellow in
Biology at Caltech. Begins
work on structure of RNA.

1955
to
1958

Gives job seminar in Biology Department at Harvard
University. Accepts the
position of Assistant Lecturer, after some debate
among the Faculty.

1956

Arthur Kornberg crystallizes DNA
polymerase I.

Returns to the Cavendish
for a sabbatical year, hoping to collaborate with
Crick on the structure of
RNA. Works instead on X-
ray diffraction patterns of
tobacco mosaic virus.

1958

Elected to American Acad-
emy of Arts and Sciences

1958
to
1961

Becomes Associate Profes-
sor of Biology at Harvard.

1959

The John Collins Warren
Prize of the Massachus-
setts General Hospital

1960

Eli Lilly Award in Bio-
chemistry
Albert Lasker Prize

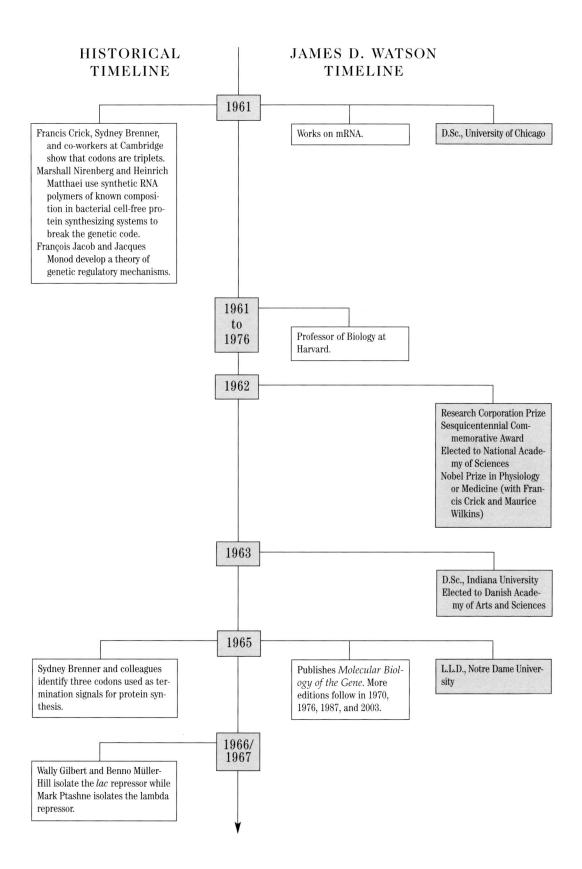

HISTORICAL TIMELINE

JAMES D. WATSON TIMELINE

1961

Francis Crick, Sydney Brenner, and co-workers at Cambridge show that codons are triplets.
Marshall Nirenberg and Heinrich Matthaei use synthetic RNA polymers of known composition in bacterial cell-free protein synthesizing systems to break the genetic code.
François Jacob and Jacques Monod develop a theory of genetic regulatory mechanisms.

Works on mRNA.

D.Sc., University of Chicago

1961 to 1976

Professor of Biology at Harvard.

1962

Research Corporation Prize
Sesquicentennial Commemorative Award
Elected to National Academy of Sciences
Nobel Prize in Physiology or Medicine (with Francis Crick and Maurice Wilkins)

1963

D.Sc., Indiana University
Elected to Danish Academy of Arts and Sciences

1965

Sydney Brenner and colleagues identify three codons used as termination signals for protein synthesis.

Publishes *Molecular Biology of the Gene*. More editions follow in 1970, 1976, 1987, and 2003.

L.L.D., Notre Dame University

1966/ 1967

Wally Gilbert and Benno Müller-Hill isolate the *lac* repressor while Mark Ptashne isolates the lambda repressor.

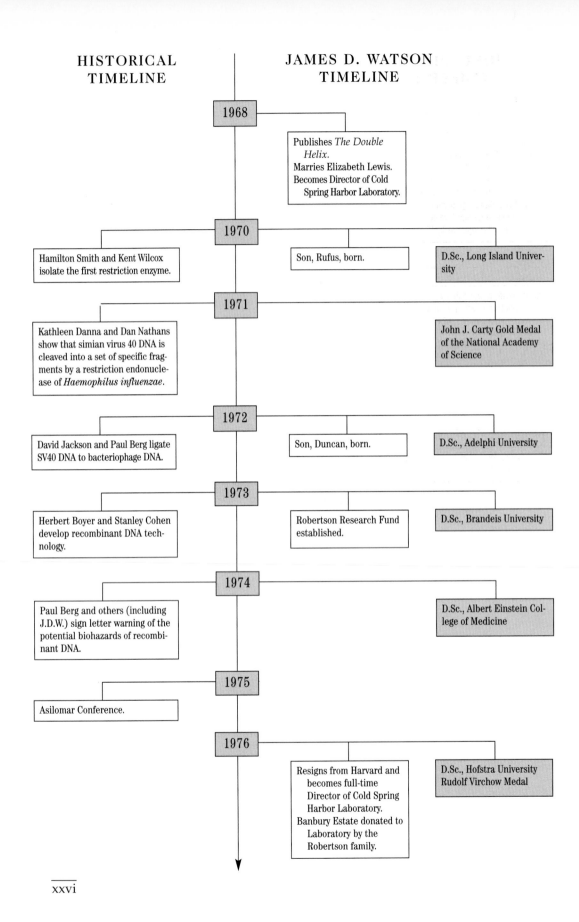

HISTORICAL
TIMELINE

JAMES D. WATSON
TIMELINE

1968

Publishes *The Double Helix*.
Marries Elizabeth Lewis.
Becomes Director of Cold Spring Harbor Laboratory.

1970

Hamilton Smith and Kent Wilcox isolate the first restriction enzyme.

Son, Rufus, born.

D.Sc., Long Island University

1971

Kathleen Danna and Dan Nathans show that simian virus 40 DNA is cleaved into a set of specific fragments by a restriction endonuclease of *Haemophilus influenzae*.

John J. Carty Gold Medal of the National Academy of Science

1972

David Jackson and Paul Berg ligate SV40 DNA to bacteriophage DNA.

Son, Duncan, born.

D.Sc., Adelphi University

1973

Herbert Boyer and Stanley Cohen develop recombinant DNA technology.

Robertson Research Fund established.

D.Sc., Brandeis University

1974

Paul Berg and others (including J.D.W.) sign letter warning of the potential biohazards of recombinant DNA.

D.Sc., Albert Einstein College of Medicine

1975

Asilomar Conference.

1976

Resigns from Harvard and becomes full-time Director of Cold Spring Harbor Laboratory.
Banbury Estate donated to Laboratory by the Robertson family.

D.Sc., Hofstra University
Rudolf Virchow Medal

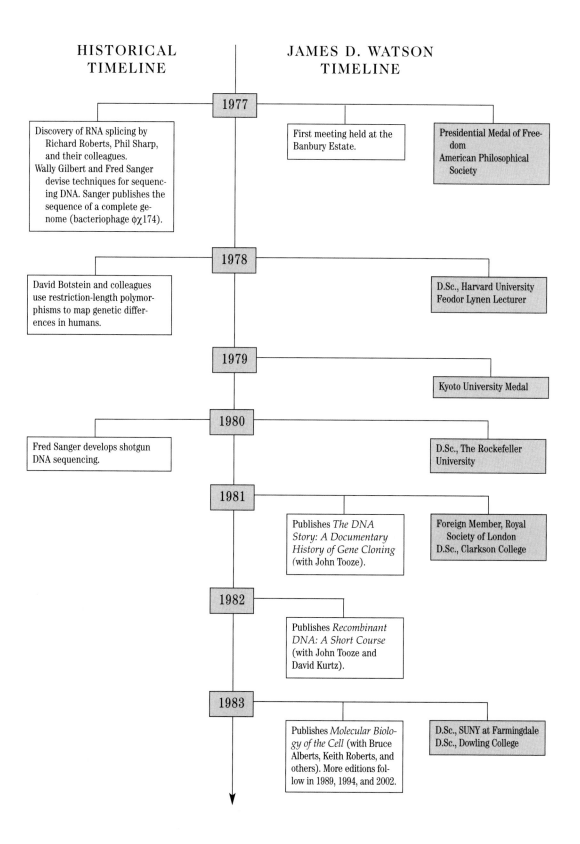

HISTORICAL
TIMELINE

JAMES D. WATSON
TIMELINE

1977

Discovery of RNA splicing by
Richard Roberts, Phil Sharp,
and their colleagues.
Wally Gilbert and Fred Sanger
devise techniques for sequencing DNA. Sanger publishes the
sequence of a complete genome (bacteriophage φχ174).

First meeting held at the
Banbury Estate.

Presidential Medal of Free-
dom
American Philosophical
Society

1978

David Botstein and colleagues
use restriction-length polymorphisms to map genetic differences in humans.

D.Sc., Harvard University
Feodor Lynen Lecturer

1979

Kyoto University Medal

1980

Fred Sanger develops shotgun
DNA sequencing.

D.Sc., The Rockefeller
University

1981

Publishes *The DNA
Story: A Documentary
History of Gene Cloning*
(with John Tooze).

Foreign Member, Royal
Society of London
D.Sc., Clarkson College

1982

Publishes *Recombinant
DNA: A Short Course*
(with John Tooze and
David Kurtz).

1983

Publishes *Molecular Biology of the Cell* (with Bruce
Alberts, Keith Roberts, and
others). More editions follow in 1989, 1994, and 2002.

D.Sc., SUNY at Farmingdale
D.Sc., Dowling College

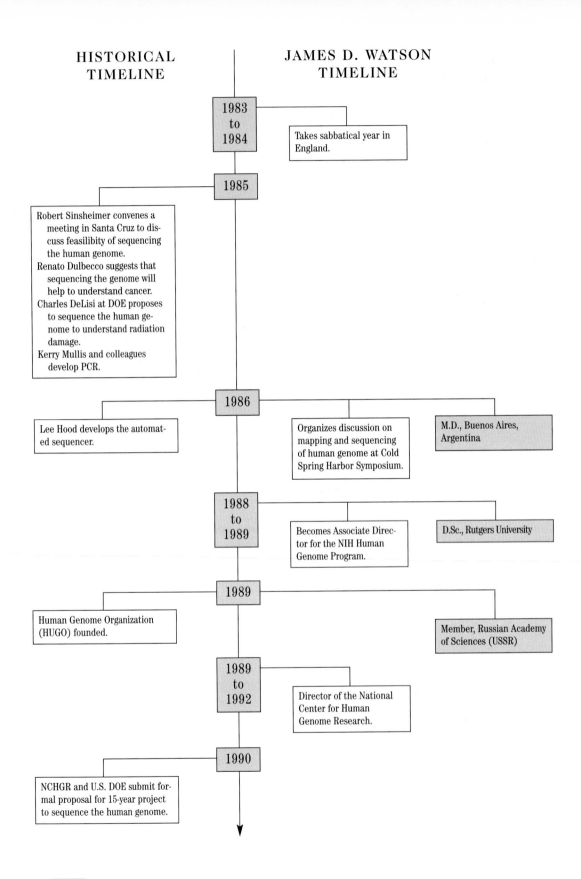

HISTORICAL
TIMELINE

JAMES D. WATSON
TIMELINE

1983 to 1984

Takes sabbatical year in England.

1985

Robert Sinsheimer convenes a meeting in Santa Cruz to discuss feasilibity of sequencing the human genome.
Renato Dulbecco suggests that sequencing the genome will help to understand cancer.
Charles DeLisi at DOE proposes to sequence the human genome to understand radiation damage.
Kerry Mullis and colleagues develop PCR.

1986

Lee Hood develops the automated sequencer.

Organizes discussion on mapping and sequencing of human genome at Cold Spring Harbor Symposium.

M.D., Buenos Aires, Argentina

1988 to 1989

Becomes Associate Director for the NIH Human Genome Program.

D.Sc., Rutgers University

1989

Human Genome Organization (HUGO) founded.

Member, Russian Academy of Sciences (USSR)

1989 to 1992

Director of the National Center for Human Genome Research.

1990

NCHGR and U.S. DOE submit formal proposal for 15-year project to sequence the human genome.

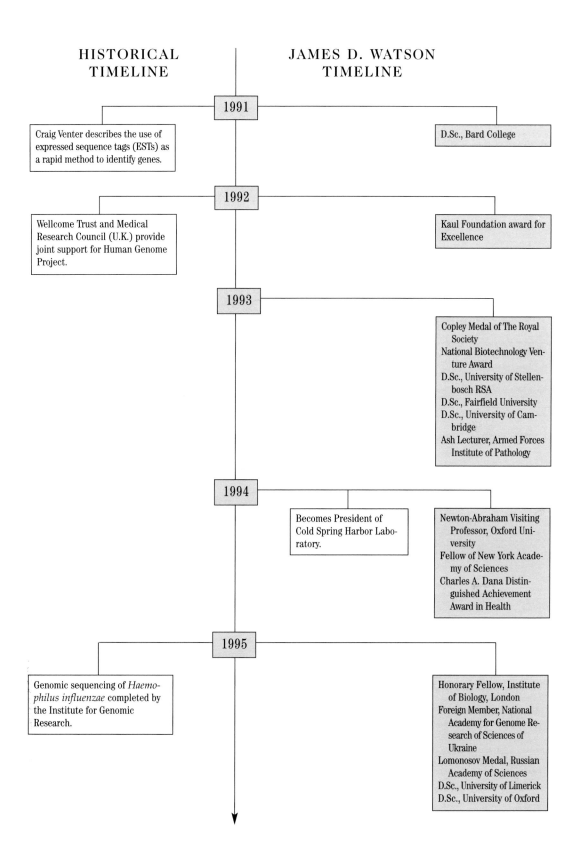

1991

Craig Venter describes the use of expressed sequence tags (ESTs) as a rapid method to identify genes.

D.Sc., Bard College

1992

Wellcome Trust and Medical Research Council (U.K.) provide joint support for Human Genome Project.

Kaul Foundation award for Excellence

1993

Copley Medal of The Royal Society
National Biotechnology Venture Award
D.Sc., University of Stellenbosch RSA
D.Sc., Fairfield University
D.Sc., University of Cambridge
Ash Lecturer, Armed Forces Institute of Pathology

1994

Becomes President of Cold Spring Harbor Laboratory.

Newton-Abraham Visiting Professor, Oxford University
Fellow of New York Academy of Sciences
Charles A. Dana Distinguished Achievement Award in Health

1995

Genomic sequencing of *Haemophilus influenzae* completed by the Institute for Genomic Research.

Honorary Fellow, Institute of Biology, London
Foreign Member, National Academy for Genome Research of Sciences of Ukraine
Lomonosov Medal, Russian Academy of Sciences
D.Sc., University of Limerick
D.Sc., University of Oxford

HISTORICAL TIMELINE

JAMES D. WATSON TIMELINE

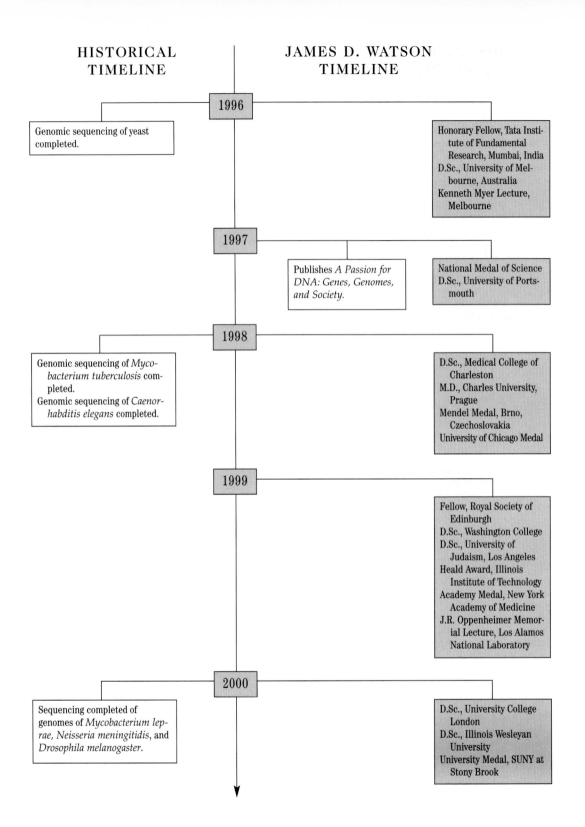

1996

Genomic sequencing of yeast completed.

Honorary Fellow, Tata Institute of Fundamental Research, Mumbai, India
D.Sc., University of Melbourne, Australia
Kenneth Myer Lecture, Melbourne

1997

Publishes *A Passion for DNA: Genes, Genomes, and Society.*

National Medal of Science
D.Sc., University of Portsmouth

1998

Genomic sequencing of *Mycobacterium tuberculosis* completed.
Genomic sequencing of *Caenorhabditis elegans* completed.

D.Sc., Medical College of Charleston
M.D., Charles University, Prague
Mendel Medal, Brno, Czechoslovakia
University of Chicago Medal

1999

Fellow, Royal Society of Edinburgh
D.Sc., Washington College
D.Sc., University of Judaism, Los Angeles
Heald Award, Illinois Institute of Technology
Academy Medal, New York Academy of Medicine
J.R. Oppenheimer Memorial Lecture, Los Alamos National Laboratory

2000

Sequencing completed of genomes of *Mycobacterium leprae, Neisseria meningitidis,* and *Drosophila melanogaster.*

D.Sc., University College London
D.Sc., Illinois Wesleyan University
University Medal, SUNY at Stony Brook

HISTORICAL TIMELINE

JAMES D. WATSON TIMELINE

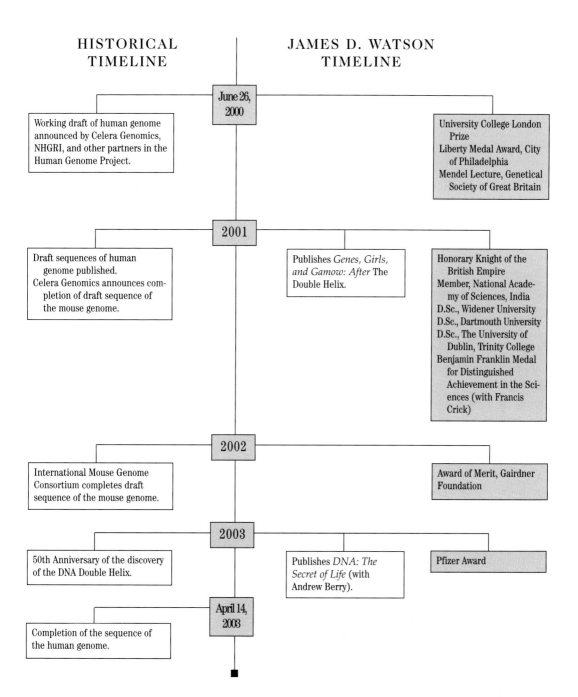

June 26, 2000

Working draft of human genome announced by Celera Genomics, NHGRI, and other partners in the Human Genome Project.

University College London Prize
Liberty Medal Award, City of Philadelphia
Mendel Lecture, Genetical Society of Great Britain

2001

Draft sequences of human genome published.
Celera Genomics announces completion of draft sequence of the mouse genome.

Publishes *Genes, Girls, and Gamow: After* The Double Helix.

Honorary Knight of the British Empire
Member, National Academy of Sciences, India
D.Sc., Widener University
D.Sc., Dartmouth University
D.Sc., The University of Dublin, Trinity College
Benjamin Franklin Medal for Distinguished Achievement in the Sciences (with Francis Crick)

2002

International Mouse Genome Consortium completes draft sequence of the mouse genome.

Award of Merit, Gairdner Foundation

2003

50th Anniversary of the discovery of the DNA Double Helix.

Publishes *DNA: The Secret of Life* (with Andrew Berry).

Pfizer Award

April 14, 2003

Completion of the sequence of the human genome.

ORIGINS

Section I photograph: *Jim Watson at Indiana University at Bloomington, 1950. (Courtesy of the James D. Watson Collection, CSHL Archives.)*

STUDENT DAYS

JAMES DEWEY WATSON WAS ADMITTED TO THE UNIVERSITY OF CHICAGO as a teenager, in 1943. Robert Hutchins, who had become President of the University in 1929, was an educational innovator who felt that the education provided by American high schools was inadequate or perhaps even worse. He developed a four-year program at Chicago that covered the last two years of high school and the first two years of college, thus bringing bright students into the university environment at the earliest possible age. It is not clear why Jim was among the chosen few. His performance at school was satisfactory but not stellar—he wrote later that his IQ was but a respectable 120. Jim had made his mark on a wider audience when he took part in the *Quiz Kids* radio show, but, as he tells it, he took part in the program primarily because the show's producer lived next door. And it was not likely that his performance played a significant part in the University's decision to accept him—he did not last long on the show, being beaten by a precocious nine-year-old girl. Perhaps those interviewing him caught some glimpse of his potential.

That potential was not altogether realized while he was at the University of Chicago. Rather like his high school days, Jim performed well, but he was not an outstanding student, getting mainly Bs. But it is clear that Jim's experiences at Chicago shaped his general intellectual approach to the world. He wrote many years later that he learned to go to original sources, that theory was important, and that it was more important to know how to think than to memorize facts. Most striking to all who have come to know him in later years, one of his major personal traits appears to have developed in this period: "...crap was best called crap. Offending someone was always preferable to avoiding the truth... . But being honest about what is bad and false leads nowhere unless you hold equally strong values about what is right."

Jim's interests changed from bird watching to genetics while at Chicago. It was there that he read the newly published *What is Life?* (1945, The Macmillan Co.) by the theoretical physicist Erwin Schrödinger and decided that the gene was where the action was, or should be. His new-found enthusiasm for genetics was reinforced when he sat in on the course taught by Sewall Wright who, together with Ronald Fisher and J.B.S. Haldane, laid the foundations of population and evolutionary genetics.

So it was that when Jim, now 19 years old, graduated in the summer of 1947, his mind was on genes rather than birds. His first choice of graduate school was the Department of Biology at the California Institute of Technology, then a powerhouse of genetics. Thomas H. Morgan (Nobel Laureate, 1933) had been Professor of Biology from 1928 to 1945, and Morgan's closest colleague, Alfred Sturtevant, was still active. George Beadle (Nobel Laureate, 1958) had taken over from Morgan, and Max Delbrück (Nobel Laureate, 1969) was carrying out phage research. But Caltech rejected Jim as did Harvard, so instead he followed the recommendation of his advisor and went to Indiana University at Bloomington.

As regards genetics, Indiana University might be thought of as the Caltech of the Midwest. The Department of Zoology had its genetics Nobel Laureate in Hermann Muller (1946) and the eminent protozoan geneticist Tracy Sonneborn, and Salvador Luria (Nobel Laureate, 1969) was in the Department of Bacteriology. Jim soon realized that *Drosophila*'s position as the genetic subject par excellence had faded and that Luria's phages were much more promising for an ambitious young man seeking the gene. Luria accepted him as a graduate student and assigned a project examining the effects of mutation-inducing X-rays on phage. Renato Dulbecco (Nobel Laureate, 1975), a newly arrived postdoctoral fellow from Italy, was already carrying out similar work using ultraviolet light.

It was not long before Jim began moving in the highest circles of the newly emerging field of molecular genetics. Soon after Jim's arrival, Max Delbrück visited Bloomington and Jim was thrilled to meet a legendary figure and was entranced by Delbrück's personality. (Erwin Schrödinger had made Delbrück's work on the gene the core of *What Is Life?*) In the summer of 1948, Luria took Jim and Dulbecco to Cold Spring Harbor where he met two other young men, Gunther Stent and Seymour Benzer. It was a formative experience for them all—Seymour Benzer wrote later that he changed from a solid-state physicist to a geneticist in the course of one morning.

By the summer of 1949, Jim had done sufficient work for his Ph.D. thesis, but he did not write it up until early in 1950. It was not, he felt, a particularly exciting piece of work, which Delbrück thought was just as well. As Jim describes it, Delbrück told him "...that I was lucky that I had not found anything as exciting as Dulbecco had, thereby being trapped in a rat race where people wanted you to solve everything immediately." (Dulbecco had discovered photoreactivation of phage that had been inactivated by irradiation with ultraviolet light.) Jim defended his thesis—The Biological Properties of X-ray-inactivated Bacteriophage—on May 26, 1950; his examiners included Muller, Sonneborn, Luria, and the biochemist Irwin C. Gunsalus. The defense was successful and the examiners wrote to Dean Stith Thompson of the Indiana University Graduate School that Jim had passed his final exam. The degree was conferred officially on October 15, 1950, but by then Jim had moved to new pastures, far from the plains of Indiana.

Phage Days in Indiana

Renato Dulbecco

The Salk Institute for Biological Studies

I first met Jim Watson in 1948 when I was a postdoctoral fellow in Salvador Luria's laboratory at Indiana University in Bloomington, Indiana. I had been there for a short time, recently arrived from Italy, when Salva came one day to the lab with a radiant face, and announced the appointment of a graduate student, a Whiz Kid from the University of Chicago. I didn't know what the expression meant, and Salva explained that it refers to very bright young people; he was also very happy because the new student came from an excellent university, where he had received very good training. Salva needed good young collaborators to expand his work on multiplicity reactivation of bacteriophage T2.[1]

When he arrived, Jim took a desk near to mine in the small lab, under the eaves of the building. Our proximity allowed us to establish a good rapport, with many discussions about the work in the lab and the state of biology in general. I rapidly realized that Jim, although ready to discuss any idea, had his own ideas, and would not give them up. I developed a considerable respect for Jim's judgment in scientific issues. When, the following year, Max Delbrück offered me the possibility of moving to the California Institute of Technology as Senior Research Fellow, I asked Jim whether I should go, whether Caltech was a good place to do the type of research I was doing. He answered without hesitation and briefly, saying that Caltech was the best place in the country to do research.

Our friendship reached a high peak when we both attended a meeting at Oak Ridge, Tennessee. We drove there in my car. At the end of the meeting, we decided to go visit the Tennessee Valley Authority, a development that interested me as an example for the future. We spent some time going from one dam to another, in the beautiful landscape of the Tennessee valley. We were toward the end of our trip, driving toward a power station, which was in sight, quite close to us. But suddenly the air was filled with debris. The wall of the power station had collapsed toward the street. Certainly a picture not easily forgotten. A generator had blown up, demolishing part of the station. It was a memorable trip, which reinforced our friendship and allowed Jim to explain to me his ideas about science, and especially about the people active in the field.

Jim became well known among young people at the University for his facial expressions, with the most incredible distortions of his mouth and wild eye movements. Only when he had to consider something serious could he maintain a normal expression. I remember especially two occasions on which he did so. One was when I

RENATO DULBECCO

The first eukaryotic genes to be intensively studied at the molecular level were those of the small DNA tumor viruses SV40 and polyomavirus. Renato Dulbecco provided the quantitative systems and the rational ideas that catapulted these to the forefront of molecular biology in the early 1970s.

Born in Catanzaro in Southern Italy, Renato Dulbecco moved as a child to his father's native Liguria. During high school, his strengths were in mathematics and physics, but on entering the University of Turin at the age of 16, Dulbecco decided to train as a physician. During World War II he served in the Italian army as a medical officer, first in France and then on the Russian front. After the Mussolini government fell, Dulbecco joined the resistance in Piedmont as a physician for local partisans.

Practicing medicine was never Dulbecco's first choice. After a brief fling in the volatile world of postwar Italian politics, he returned to the University of Turin, first to study physics and then to work in Giuseppe Levi's laboratory, where he hoped to use radiation to study the genetics of a simple organism. At this point, Salvador Luria re-entered Dulbecco's life. The two of them had been in the same medical school class but had lost contact during the war, which Luria had spent in the United States. Luria, just two years older than Dulbecco but already well-established in prokaryotic genetics, offered Dulbecco a postdoctoral position in his laboratory at Bloomington, Indiana. There, as Dulbecco describes, his colleague was Jim Watson, 14 years his junior and a graduate student.

Dulbecco moved to the California Institute of Technology in 1949, and in the early 1950s, developed quantitative techniques to assay and study animal viruses. Using these techniques, Dulbecco isolated the first poliovirus mutant, which was subsequently used by Albert Sabin to prepare a vaccine against poliomyelitis.

In 1958, Dulbecco started working on the small oncogenic viruses, polyomavirus and SV40. His most important discovery was that the DNA of this virus (and its close relative, SV40) integrates into the chromosomal DNA of a cell, causing the cell to display a transformed phenotype.

In 1964, Dulbecco received the Lasker Award for his work on poliovirus, and in 1975, the Nobel Prize in Physiology or Medicine for his elegant work on SV40 and polyomavirus. He was an early and fervent proponent of the Human Genome Project. Renato Dulbecco is President Emeritus of the Salk Institute, La Jolla, California, where much of his best research work was carried out.

showed that bacteriophages exposed to ultraviolet light undergo photoreactivation in the infected cells. I had been trying to understand why two plates used in an assay of the infectivity of an irradiated phage sample always showed different numbers of plaques. The two plates were routinely prepared together and left on the bench one on top of the other for some time to allow the agar to solidify; the upper plate always had more plaques. Jim knew about the difference. Finally, I showed that the effect was caused by a powerful fluorescent light situated over the bench: The upper plate got more light. I called Jim and pointed at the light, saying it was the culprit. He looked for a while, thinking seriously, but made no comment.[2]

The other occasion was when Jim and I took a course in genetics taught by Hermann Muller, at the time one of the most important geneticists. After an exam, Muller had the habit of stacking the tests in a pile, in order of merit, with the best on top. After the final exam, Jim and I were approaching the pile together. I noticed that my test was on top. Jim said nothing, but I remember his saddened, serious face when he retrieved his test, just underneath mine.

Jim had few filters between his mental processes and verbal expression of his opinions: He would tell what he thought openly and without any special kindness. On one occasion—I don't remember exactly what it was, perhaps a picnic—my wife offered him a hamburger that she had cooked. He looked at it, tasted it, made a horrified face, and rejected it, saying it was no good. On another occasion, years later, Jim and I were in London for a meeting. At the time, I was moving from Caltech to what later became the Salk Institute. I was explaining to him that we were looking for some good people to join us, people who had already obtained some important results. He interrupted me by saying, when have you done something important? I was taken aback, I did not try to counteract his statement. I took it seriously, obviously that was his judgment, and in subsequent years, that statement made me consider many times what I had achieved in the past and what I should be doing in the future.

At Bloomington, Jim was taking an advanced course in mathematics, and we often talked about his thesis problem, because I had good training in that field before leaving Italy. One day he came with a tough assignment, which, it turned out, neither he nor I could solve. The following day, he got the answer in class, and when he came to the lab he showed it to me with a tone that made me well aware of my limitations. For me it was a useful warning. I recognized that his candid and tough judgments were useful for me. I always respected him and was grateful to him for them. His open attitude contributed to the development of a strong bond between us, at least in me toward him.

Those were the days of competition, which stimulated Jim's toughness. Many years later, when his position in modern biology was fully established, Jim was quite different. I remember an episode at a meeting in the early time of the development of the Genome Project. At the end of the meeting, when most people were leaving the hall, a few (including Sydney Brenner, Victor McKusick, and Jim) gathered together, while I was collecting my papers. They were talking about starting a new organization, the Human Genome Organization, HUGO. I noticed that at a certain point, Jim interrupted the conversation, and, pointing in my direction, said I should be included among the founders—the others agreed. This time, Jim may have recognized that I had done something, perhaps not important, but significant.

In later years, when he was the head of Cold Spring Harbor Laboratory, he showed much consideration for me personally when he invited me to the Laboratory, rendering more comfortable my travel and my staying there. I greatly enjoyed those visits, as well as the kindness of Jim's wife, Liz. This kind attitude, however, did not stop Jim from raiding my laboratory, taking all the most significant people, to start a new lab at Cold Spring Harbor.

The last time I had the occasion of spending some time with Jim was in La Jolla on the occasion of the 30th anniversary of his marriage to Liz. They had been married in La Jolla, where the Salk Institute is located. He gathered a few friends to celebrate the anniversary there along with his sons, Rufus and Duncan. On that occasion, he gave a little speech in which he mentioned our Indiana years. It was, for me, a moving occasion.

What stays in my mind as the most impressive memory of Jim is something that happened when we were at Indiana. Jim became interested in the role of DNA in phage inheritance on the basis of information deriving from the work of Putnam, Kozloff, and Maaløe, which showed the transfer of a considerable proportion of the phage DNA from parent to progeny during replication.[3] Jim followed the developments with great attention, and talked about them. He was considering the possibility that DNA was the genetic material of the virus and told me that he would pursue the idea after he took his degree at Indiana. He pointed out that to understand the role of DNA, it would be important to determine its structure, and that to get started in that direction, he would go to work in Maaløe's lab in Copenhagen. He in fact did, and from there moved to Cambridge, where he could realize his dream. In subsequent years, as the knowledge about DNA, its biological meaning, and its structure became clearer and clearer, the ideas that Jim was expressing in Bloomington became in my mind more and more significant: They were the key to these discoveries.

Thinking back over the 50-odd years of my knowing Jim, only one episode comes to mind where, quite independently, we both showed bad judgment. In the early 1970s, I had bought a Rover 2000TC. It was a great car, but it had one disadvantage— it frequently broke down.[4] I had spent many hours fixing it and had got to the point of traveling with the shop manual and endless spare parts and tools in the trunk. During that period, I spent some time in Boston with my family, and Jim and Liz invited us to come to their house for lunch. The lunch was delayed for a bit while a tow truck arrived and hauled Jim's Rover 2000TC away forever. He had enough of its unreliability and was junking it. I had gotten rid of mine just a few months before.

Quiz Kids

Gunther S. Stent

University of California, Berkeley

I entered a charmed world when I turned into the Cold Spring Harbor Laboratory from New York State Route 25A on June 4, 1948. Twenty-four years old, I had driven East in my decrepit 1942 Ford jalopy, quitting Champaign-Urbana forever on the very afternoon that I received my Ph.D. in Physical Chemistry from the University of Illinois. I was going to take Max Delbrück's Phage Course in preparation for spending the next two years in his laboratory at the California Institute of Technology as a Merck Postdoctoral Fellow of the National Research Council.

Shortly after my arrival at the Lab, Delbrück introduced me to a summer classmate, Jim Watson, a 20-year-old graduate student who had recently joined Salvador Luria's research group at Indiana University. We had attended rival high schools on Chicago's South Side, and he had starred in NBC's Chicago-originated, nationally broadcast *Quiz Kids* radio program (Feldman 1982) as its ornithology expert, able to identify any bird species by its song.[1] Although I had been an avid listener, I did not remember Jim, no doubt because I was not interested in his subject. The Quiz Kid whose expertise (as well as person) *did* interest me was Cynthia Cline, the show's glamorous musicology expert. Not only could she identify scene and act of any opera from a few bars, but she could also play Chicago-style boogie-woogie. I, too, had appeared on a kids radio quiz program in Chicago, on a strictly local, third-rate show called *Young America Answers*.

The similarities and differences between Jim and myself in our high school days foreshadowed our later careers. Both of us became molecular biologists before that calling even existed, and both of us received prizes in Stockholm for our work. But my award was Stockholm University's Runström Medal for Developmental Biology, while Jim's was the Nobel Prize in Physiology or Medicine.

At first, I was not very enthusiastic about Jim. Despite his being my junior by four years, a mere graduate student, he treated me, the august Doctor of Philosophy, as an equal, acting as if his opinions were just as good as mine. But before long, I came to terms with the annoying fact that, whenever we disagreed about some scientific matter, Jim's opinions were almost always right and mine were almost always wrong. And so we became lifelong friends.

GUNTHER S. STENT

Gunther Stent, born in Berlin and trained in physical chemistry at the University of Illinois, moved to Max Delbrück's laboratory at the California Institute of Technology as a postdoctoral fellow in the fall of 1948.

After the events described in this memoir, Stent moved from the Institut Pasteur to the University of California, Berkeley, where he has spent almost all of his subsequent working life. For several years, Stent worked on the molecular biology of bacterio-phages and, in 1963, published the *Molecular Biology of Bacterial Viruses* (W.H. Freeman), an elegant and exciting book that was as formative to younger scientists of the time as was Jim Watson's the *Molecular Biology of the Gene* (1965, W.A. Benjamin) to later generations. With Jim and John Cairns, Stent edited *Phage and the Origins of Molecular Biology* (1966, Cold Spring Harbor Laboratory) the famous *homage* to Delbrück, and also assembled the Norton critical edition of *The Double Helix* (1980, W.W. Norton). By the end of the 1960s, Stent had lost interest in molecular biology, and began working on the structure and embryological development of the leech nervous system, particularly the neural circuits involved in the control of movement. To many people, however, Stent remains best known from his books, which range from the philosophical (*Morality as a Biological Phenomenon* [1978, Abakon-Verlagsgesellschaft; 1980, University of California] and *Paradoxes of Free Will* [2002, American Philosophical Society]) to the factual (*Molecular Genetics: An Introductory Narrative* [1971, 1978, W.H. Freeman] and *Neurobiology of the Leech* [1981, Cold Spring Harbor Laboratory]).

PASADENA

Caltech lived up to my fantasy of a palm-tree studded Academic Nirvana, peopled by such brilliant minds as Linus Pauling and Max Delbrück. The research project that Max assigned to me was one of the few he could have picked for which my training as a physical chemist happened to have eminently qualified me. One of the phage strains that Max was studying fails to attach to its bacterial host cell unless it has been previously "activated" by contact with the amino acid tryptophan. Max suspected (or maybe hoped) that the hitherto known facts about this activation process were not compatible with ordinary physicochemical principles. So he thought that, maybe, there was a paradox hidden here which might lead us to one of those "other laws of physics," which, as Max's teacher, Niels Bohr (1933) had suggested in his famous lecture "Light and Life," might be needed to understand the behavior of living matter. I was to have a partner in my research project, Elie Wollman, a young French bacteriologist on leave from André Lwoff's Department of Microbial Physiology at the Institut Pasteur in Paris.

As I had feared at the very start, there was no need to invoke "other laws of physics" to explain the seemingly bizarre dynamics of the tryptophan activation phenomenon. During our two years at Caltech, Elie and I manage to devise a model based on conventional physicochemical principles that accounted for all of the data (Stent and Wollman 1950). Our model turned out to be a forerunner of the "cooperative" theories of the complex interactions between small metabolite molecules and large proteins put forward a few years after our papers appeared. These theories would provide a physicochemical understanding of the regulation of enzyme function in metabolic reactions. Yet, as far as I know, despite Max's prophecy that our papers would become classics, none of the later cooperative theorists ever cited them.

COPENHAGEN

My Merck Postdoctoral Fellowship at Caltech was coming to an end in June, 1950, and Max suggested that I go to Copenhagen to work in the lab of the Danish biochemist Herman Kalckar. He made the same proposal to Jim, who was finishing his Ph.D. dissertation with Luria at Indiana and had just been awarded his Merck Fellowship. Max told us that it might do us some good to learn DNA chemistry from Kalckar, because, maybe, DNA *does* have something to do with genetics. He didn't realize that Kalckar actually knew very little about DNA. His specialty was adenosine triphosphate (ATP) and its provision of free energy for driving biochemical reactions. I suspect Max thought at the time that being composed of ATP-like nucleotides, DNA provides the free energy for driving self-replication of proteinaceous genes, in chromosomes as well as in phage.

After Jim and I turned up in Kalckar's lab at the University of Copenhagen in September, 1950, it didn't take us long to realize that, in view of his lack of interest in DNA, we were not going to learn much about it from him. So we moved over to Ole Maaløe's lab at the Danish State Serum Institute. There we carried out radioactive

In Kalckar's Laboratory, Copenhagen, Fall 1950. (Seated) Herman Kalckar, two technical assistants, Eugene Goldwasser, Walter McNutt, Rikke Hoff-Jörgensen. (Standing) Gunther Stent, Nils Ole Kjeldgaard, Hans Klenow, James Watson, Vincent Price. (Courtesy of Gunther S. Stent.)

tracer studies on the fate of the parental phage DNA and on the synthesis of the progeny phage DNA in the infected bacterial host cell. Our results were not exactly world-
shaking, but they helped bring into focus the intracellular transactions of phage DNA
that were in want of understanding (Maaløe and Watson 1951; Stent and Maaløe 1953).

In the late fall of 1950, Jim and I attended an afternoon lecture given by Sir
Lawrence Bragg at the House of the Royal Danish Science Society.[2] Bragg began his
presentation by saying that he had actually meant to report on the progress of his colleagues Max Perutz and John Kendrew at the Cavendish Laboratory in Cambridge in
their X-ray crystallographic determination of the three-dimensional structure of hemoglobin and myoglobin.[3] A few days before his departure for Copenhagen, however, he
received a manuscript from Linus Pauling, in which Pauling announced his solution
of the problem of the secondary structure of protein molecules in terms of what he
called the "alpha helix." So—in a spirit of true nobility—Bragg decided to report on
the tremendous breakthrough that had been made at Caltech in the analysis of protein
structure. He said that he thought that this would be of more interest to his Danish
hosts than the work that was presently going on at the Cavendish.

I noticed that as Jim was listening to Bragg, he became more and more agitated.
After Bragg had finished, Jim turned to me and said, "THAT'S what we've got to do,
Gunther! Get the 3-D structure of DNA, instead of farting around with phage DNA
metabolism!" I thought Jim had gone off his rocker. What did he think an ornithologist
could do about working out the 3-D structure of DNA, when a physical chemist like
me wouldn't dare to wrestle with that problem?

PARIS AND CAMBRIDGE

At the end of our Copenhagen year, I moved to Paris, to spend the last of my four postdoctoral *Wanderjahre* in André Lwoff's Department of Microbial Physiology at the
Institut Pasteur. I didn't accomplish much in Paris (except marrying Inga Loftsdottir,
an Icelandic pianist, to whom Jim had introduced me in Copenhagen). My intellectual development, however, benefited from my close contacts with the brilliant crowd
that hung out in the famous "Attic of Monsieur Lwoff" on the top floor of the Institut
Pasteur. They included Jacques Monod, Elie Wollman, François Jacob, Alvin Pappenheimer, and Melvin Cohn, in addition to the *grand patron* himself (who always referred
to my former Copenhagen partner as *"le grand Jim"*).[4]

As for *le grand Jim*, he moved to Cambridge to try to work out the structure of DNA.
He did so against the advice of many friends (including myself) and in defiance of Paul
Weiss, the Chairman of the Merck Fellowship Board, who cut off Jim's fellowship. Max
and Luria too didn't expect that Jim would actually succeed in his ambitious project,
but they managed to persuade the March of Dimes to support Jim's stay in Cambridge.

In the spring of 1952, Jim and I both attended the annual meeting of the British
Society for General Microbiology held in Oxford. Luria had been invited to give one of
the plenary addresses, whose text he had submitted to the organizers a week or two
before the meeting. When Luria was denied a US passport because of his leftwing politics, the British organizers asked Jim to read his absent teacher's paper.

One of its main points was that Luria's and Cyrus Levinthal's electron micrographic images of phage-infected bacteria strongly suggested that its *protein* is the

Microbial Genetics Meeting, Copenhagen, Spring 1951. (Seated) Ole Maaløe, Raymond Latarjet, Elie Wollman. (Standing) Niels Bohr, Nicolo Visconti, Gösta Ehrensvard, Wolfhard Weidel, Carl-Göran Hedén, Valentin Bonifas, Gunther Stent, Herman Kalckar, James Watson, Barbara Wright, Mogens Westergaard. (Courtesy of Gunther S. Stent.)

genetic material of the phage.[5] So they proposed that the phage DNA is some kind of "glue" that holds the phage protein together when the progeny phage particles are "baked" at the end of the eclipse period of the intracellular reproductive cycle.

Shortly before the meeting, some exciting news from Cold Spring Harbor had reached Jim in Cambridge. Alfred Hershey and his young assistant, Martha Chase, had shown that when phage infects its bacterial host, only its DNA enters the cell. The phage protein remains outside devoid of any further function in the reproductive drama about to ensue within. What was poor Jim to do? He decided to present Luria's text in its full original version and merely mentioned at the very end that a minor revision of Luria and Levinthal's main conclusion is actually called for. The genes of the infecting phage that are responsible for directing the synthesis of progeny phages happen to reside in its DNA rather than in its protein.

According to Jim's memoir, *The Double Helix* (Watson 1968), it was learning of the Hershey-Chase experiment in the spring of 1952 that drove him and Francis Crick to intensify their efforts to work out the structure of DNA, leading to the epic discovery whose 50th anniversary this volume commemorates.

REFERENCES

Bohr N. 1933. Light and life. *Nature* **131:** 421–423, 457–495.
Feldman R.D. 1982. *Whatever happened to the Quiz Kids? Perils and profits of growing up gifted.* Chicago Review Press, Chicago.

Maaløe O. and Watson J.D. 1951. The transfer of radioactive phosphorus from parental to progeny phage. *Proc. Natl. Acad. Sci.* **37**: 507.

Stent G.S. and Maaløe O. 1953. Radioactive phosphorus tracer studies on the reproduction of T4
bacteriophage. *Biochim. Biophys. Acta* **10**: 55–59, 84–93.

Stent G.S. and Wollman E.L. 1950. Studies on activation of T4 bacteriophage by cofactor. *Biochim.
Biophys. Acta* **6**: 292–306, 307–316, 374–383.

Watson J.D. 1968. *The double helix: A personal account of the discovery of the structure of DNA.*
Atheneum, New York.

Some Early Recollections of Jim Watson

Seymour Benzer

California Institute of Technology

My earliest recollection of Jim dates back more than half a century to 1948, when he was 20, and I was a student in the Phage Course at Cold Spring Harbor. Salvador Luria had urged me to take the course, as I had expressed interest in shifting from solid-state physics to biology, being inspired by Delbrück's model of gene mutations, which resembled electron transitions between energy levels in a semiconductor. Although Delbrück had initiated the course, in an attempt to recruit people into the field, he had by then passed the baton to Mark Adams. In the traditional dress-up mock graduation ceremony at the end of the course, Max Delbrück, not present to do his usual comic performance, was represented by a portrait hanging on the wall. At the appropriate moment, however, the spirit of Delbrück appeared. That was Jim Watson, covered by a white sheet, a halo over his head. In those days, Jim sometimes earned his way by serving tables in Blackford. Little did anyone imagine that, one day, he would be running the place.

Luria recounted to me that Jim had been enrolled in a course he taught at the University of Indiana in Bloomington. Jim, who fancied himself as possibly the world's outstanding ornithologist, sat in the back of the room, his eyes (as they still do) rolling over the ceiling, hardly seeming to pay attention. But, at the end of the course, he approached Luria to become his thesis advisor. It was a wise choice, especially as Renato Dulbecco, who was also a stimulating presence at Cold Spring Harbor that summer, was a postdoctoral fellow in Luria's laboratory.

The following year, I met Jim again at Oak Ridge National Laboratory, Tennessee, where I had gone for a first year of work on phage. By that time, both Delbrück and Luria had offered me postdoctoral positions at Caltech or Bloomington, respectively. I consulted with Jim. He explained that Luria offered the advantage that he would ask me each day what I had done, whereas Delbrück might disappear into the library for weeks at a time. Jim thus played a key role at a branch point in my career: I chose Caltech. Besides, Pasadena was an easier place to keep warm. Another recollection from that meeting was Delbrück's enunciation of the principle of limited sloppiness[1] for scientific discovery, as exemplified by the phenomenon of photoreactivation discovered by Kelner[2] for bacteria, and Dulbecco for phage.

Jim would visit Caltech from time to time during my stay (1949–1951) in Max Delbrück's group. Desert camping and mountain climbing were more or less *"de*

Jim serving tables at Blackford (circa late 1940s). (Courtesy of Seymour Benzer.)

SEYMOUR BENZER

Seymour Benzer is one of the group of physicists who turned to biology after reading Erwin Schrödinger's *What Is Life?* (1945, The Macmillan Co.). As a graduate student at Purdue University during World War II, Benzer carried out defense research on germanium semiconductor devices that contributed to the development of the transistor, and received his Ph.D. in physics in 1947. He took the Cold Spring Harbor Phage Course in 1949 and was transformed into a biologist by the end of the first morning. After postdoctoral studies with Delbrück at Caltech and with Jacob, Monod, and Lwoff at the Pasteur Institute, he returned to set up a laboratory in the Biology Department at Purdue, where he undertook his classic work on the fine structure of the gene and its relation to DNA.

Before Seymour Benzer, the gene was regarded as the elementary unit of inheritance; recombination was believed to occur exclusively in intergenic spaces. Benzer's genetic map of mutations in the *r*II region of bacteriophage T4 made nonsense of all this. His map of the *r*II region expanded progressively over the succeeding ten years and its resolution became ever finer. Jonathan Weiner in his book *Time, Love, Memory: A Great Biologist and His Quest for the Origins of Behavior* (1999, Knopf) describes how Benzer would appear at conferences in the 1950s, carrying his map onstage and unrolling it like a Torah scroll. Eventually, the map reached the point where recombination could be detected between (what later turned out to be) adjacent base pairs. The map of *r*II mutants was the basis of studies on relating chemical mutagenesis to the structure of DNA and later was used by Crick and Brenner to prove the triplet nature of the genetic code.

His second career in biology has been as distinguished as his first. After moving his laboratory to Caltech in 1967, he turned to the behavioral genetics of *Drosophila*, and, using a counter-current machine, isolated and characterized a rich variety of single-gene mutants with an amazing spectrum of phenotypes, ranging from defects in phototaxis and chemotaxis, to altered circadian clocks, to the inability to perform courtship rituals. Now 80 years old, Benzer's interests have in recent years expanded to include, appropriately enough, longevity.

Cold Spring Harbor Phage Course graduation ceremony, 1948. Jim, seated at the blackboard, represents the ghost of Max Delbrück, who did not teach the course that year because Manny, his wife, was pregnant. Salva Luria is at second left of picture. Mark Adams, the course leader, is holding forth, presumably examining a putative graduate. (Courtesy of Seymour Benzer.)

Jim, the ornithologist, at Brown County State Park (1950), near Bloomington, Indiana. At left is George Streisinger. At right is Giuseppe Bertani. (Courtesy of Seymour Benzer.)

rigueur." One of the less excruciating outings was a climb up the trail from the town of Sierra Madre to the top of Mount Wilson. My most vivid memory is of Jim almost running up the trail like a gazelle, as I dragged my ass behind (but I did, eventually, make it to the top). Once, Jim and I went out to a Chinese dinner at Sang's Inn in Pasadena, along with Max and others in the research group, which, at that time, included Renato Dulbecco, Gunther Stent, Jean Weigle, and Elie Wollman. Jim and I, being curious types and interested in food, scrutinized the menu in the hope of finding something beyond chow mein and chop suey. But Max overruled us, ordering "Six Caltech specials." It is a testament to Max's charisma that we gave in. At a later dinner out with Max, I discovered that he was essentially taste blind; he failed to distinguish the lobster from the chicken.[3]

One outstanding memory of the Caltech period was a seminar presented by Linus Pauling, at which he (literally) unveiled his model of the α-helix. With great showmanship, he repeatedly moved toward the wrapped model as if to lift the veil, but then would return to the blackboard to make just "one more point." Finally, the beautiful structure was revealed. The same seminar room (119 Kerckhoff) is still in use over fifty years later, and has seen many such landmarks, including notable lectures by Jim. On one occasion, some years later, while having lunch together at the Caltech "Greasy Spoon" (which was then a wooden shack), Jim complained that he had been unable to get permission from Pauling to use his X-ray diffraction equipment, because Pauling considered him a competitor. I wonder why.

From 1951 to 1952, I was at the Institut Pasteur in Paris, working with Jacques Monod and François Jacob in André Lwoff's laboratory. Jim put in an appearance, which I believe was at the time when he was fleeing Herman Kalckar's laboratory in Copenhagen to move (over Paul Weiss' severe objection)[4] to Cambridge. Jim, with a glint in his eye, was carrying around a book on phosphate chemistry. This seemed to me a bit bizarre at the time. I did not realize what he was up to.

That same year, at a meeting at Oxford, Jim reported on the famous "Waring blender" experiment of Alfred Hershey and Martha Chase, which provided evidence that the DNA component of the phage particle, not the protein, carries the genetic information. That summer, Hershey told the story himself at a meeting at the Abbaye de Royaumont outside Paris. Jim was conspicuous by his attire, which featured sneakers with dangling, untied laces, much to the chagrin of André Lwoff, who would have preferred somewhat better decorum in the setting of a medieval monastery. One of the great pranks at that meeting was Manny Delbrück's[5] hanging a large W.C. sign on the door of Nicolai Visconti's room. When asked the next morning how well he had slept, he complained bitterly that all night long, people kept coming in, saying "Oh, excuse me!" and going out again.

Jim in typical attire and attitude at the 1953 Symposium. (Courtesy of Seymour Benzer.)

A conversation between Jim and Seymour (circa 1960). (Courtesy of Seymour Benzer.)

The following year, of course, was the big bang at the Cold Spring Harbor Symposium, where Max arranged for Jim to present the double-helix structure. Strangely enough, there were some people who responded, "So what?" It was a vicarious treat for me, years later, to work for awhile with Francis Crick on the structure of poly(A) in the tower of the Cavendish lab, handling the same metal molecular model pieces that he and Jim had used in solving DNA.

In 1959, Jim led an effort to recruit me to Harvard, actually throwing a party in his apartment. Much of the conversation had to do with liberating (the new) molecular biology from the entrenched influence of the classical museum biologists in the same department. One more vote would make a difference. But it was January, and the temperature was 20 degrees below zero. I chickened out.

In 1965, I again took a course in preparation for another switch of field, this time Stephen Kuffler's course on neurobiology at Woods Hole, Massachusetts. I will not forget the high-speed ride Jim gave me to Boston in his open MG, which, fortunately, had a hand grasp to prevent me from being ejected. Jim gave me a copy of his manuscript for *The Double Helix* (Watson 1968). He was not so much interested in my opinion, but my wife's, since he calculated that popular books are mostly bought by housewives. In any case, I couldn't put it down. It created quite a stir among the biologists at Woods Hole, some feeling that it painted an unsavory picture of scientists' behavior. I recall Jim's phoning me, later on, with suspiciously slurred speech, bemoaning the fact that a certain party was trying to block its publication. Now, of course, it is read by young scientists as a primer on how to succeed in research.

Throughout the subsequent years, I have had many encounters with Jim. The conversations, albeit dominated by his restless mind and (still) roving eyes, have always been stimulating, informative, and warm with fond remembrance. I look forward to more of them.

REFERENCES

Watson J.D. 1968. *The double helix: A personal account of the discovery of the structure of DNA.* Atheneum, New York.

The Properties of X-ray-inactivated Bacteriophage. I. Inactivation by Direct Effect

James Dewey Watson

Reprinted, with permission, from Journal of Bacteriology, Vol. 60, No. 6, December, 1950.

Reprinted from JOURNAL OF BACTERIOLOGY
Vol. 60, No. 6, December, 1950

THE PROPERTIES OF X-RAY-INACTIVATED BACTERIOPHAGE[1]

I. INACTIVATION BY DIRECT EFFECT

JAMES DEWEY WATSON[2]

Departments of Bacteriology and Zoology, Indiana University, Bloomington, Indiana

Received for publication August 7, 1950

The potentialities of inactive viruses as a tool in virus research have been shown by Luria and Dulbecco (1949) in their study on the interactions between several ultraviolet-inactivated bacteriophage particles adsorbed to the same bacteria. Their finding that active phage may be produced in bacteria infected with two or more inactive particles indicated that inactivation occurs as the result of partial damage that blocks a specific step in virus multiplication.

It is probable that inactivating agents other than ultraviolet light can cause partial damage. More interesting is the possibility that these agents will cause different types of damage, which will block virus reproduction at different stages. We might therefore be able to reconstruct the successive steps in host-virus interaction by studying the stages in the synthesis at which the multiplication of the inactive phage is blocked. To test these possibilities we have begun to study bacteriophage inactivated by X-rays.

The inactivation of bacteriophage by X-rays was first studied by Wollman and Lacassagne (1940), who found that the X-ray sensitivity of different phages suspended in broth increased with the particle size as determined by ultrafiltration and centrifugation. These and later experiments on X-ray inactivation have been analyzed from the viewpoint of the "target theory" of radiation action, according to which ionizing radiation acts by producing ionizations ("hits") in localized structures or targets, within the biological object itself. Various authors (Wollman, Holweck, and Luria, 1940; Luria and Exner, 1941; Lea and Salaman, 1946) calculated the target volumes ("sensitive volumes") from the inactivation rates of bacteriophage suspended in broth and found them to agree relatively well with the sizes of the actual particles.

Because of concern with the validity of the target theory, little attention has been paid to the analysis of the properties of the inactive phage. The present work represents an attempt to determine the stages in phage multiplication that are blocked by X-ray damage.

MATERIALS AND METHODS

Cultures: All experiments employed the coli phages T1–T7 and their common host *Escherichia coli* strain B (Demerec and Fano, 1945). Use has also been made

[1] Contribution No. 440 from the Department of Zoology, Indiana University. Submitted to the faculty of the Graduate School in partial fulfillment of the requirements for the degree Doctor of Philosophy in the Department of Zoology, Indiana University. Funds for the research have been provided by a grant from the American Cancer Society to Dr. S. E. Luria as recommended by the Committee on Growth of the National Research Council.

[2] A. E. C. predoctoral fellow during 1949–1950. Present address: Universitetets Institute for Cytofysiologi, Copenhagen Ø, Denmark.

of their h mutants (Luria, 1945) and r mutants (Hershey, 1946), as well as of bacterial mutants resistant to one or more phages, as indicators for one phage in the presence of another (Delbrück, 1946). Phage stocks were lysates in broth or in synthetic medium M-9. Purified phages were prepared by differential centrifugation, using the multispeed attachment of an International refrigerated centrifuge, followed by resuspension in the M-9 medium, solution A, with the addition of 10^{-3} M Mg^{++} to stabilize the phage activity (Adams, 1949).[3] The general methodology used in work with these phages has been summarized by Adams (1950).

Media: Synthetic medium M-9, solution A—KH_2PO_4, 3 g; $MgSO_4$, 0.2 g; NH_4Cl, 1 g; anhydrous Na_2HPO_2, 6 g, dissolved in 900 ml of distilled water, Solution B—4 g of glucose dissolved in 100 ml of distilled water. Solutions A and B are sterilized separately and mixed in a 9:1 ratio before use. The pH of the final solution is 7.0.

The nutrient broth contained 0.8 per cent Difco nutrient broth plus 0.5 per cent NaCl. The nutrient agar contained 1.1 per cent Difco agar in 0.8 per cent Difco nutrient broth plus 0.5 per cent NaCl. Unless otherwise indicated, all experiments were done at 37 C and the plates were incubated at the same temperature.

Irradiation techniques: Two sources of X-rays have been used. One was an X-ray machine at the Memorial Hospital, New York City, which was kindly placed at our disposal by Miss E. Focht. The source consisted of two tubes placed face to face 30 cm apart, operating under 180 kV peak and 25 mA. The beam was filtered only by the glass wall of the tubes. The intensity of radiation at a point equidistant between the anticathodes was 1,940 r per minute. The second source was the X-ray machine at Indiana University, consisting of one tube operating under 200 kV peak and 20 mA. The beam was filtered only by the glass wall of the tube. The intensity of radiation was estimated indirectly as follows: With the X-ray machine at Memorial Hospital, the inactivation dose (e^{-1} survival; Lea, 1946) for phage T2 was determined to be 40,000 r. With the tube at Indiana University 30 minutes' irradiation at a distance of 13 cm from the anticathode gave one inactivation dose for T2. The intensity at this distance was therefore taken as 1,330 r per minute.

The phage was exposed to the X-rays in a cylindrical lucite container. The thickness of the phage layer was usually less than 5 mm; hence adsorption by the liquid was for all purposes negligible.

Ultraviolet light was provided by a General Electric germicidal bulb, 15 watts, alimented through a Sola stabilizer. The beam contains mainly radiation of wave length 2537 A. At a distance of 50 cm, the flux is 7.5 erg mm^{-2} sec^{-1}. For the photoreactivation experiments, the light source was represented by two parallel fluorescent lamps, 40 watts each, at a distance of 20 cm from the exposed material.

---

[3] In all experiments reported in this paper, the concentration of Mg^{++} added to synthetic media was 10^{-3} M.

Influence of the Suspending Medium on the Inactivation of Bacteriophage

The rate of bacteriophage inactivation by X-rays depends on the medium in which the phage is suspended (Luria and Exner, 1941). Figure 1 shows that bacteriophage T2 is inactivated at a faster rate in M-9 synthetic medium than in nutrient broth. The inactivation of phage in synthetic medium is interpreted (Luria and Exner, 1941) as being largely an indirect effect caused by agents produced in the surrounding medium by ionizations outside the phage. When phage is suspended in broth, the inactivation is not due to indirect agents, since these are neutralized by "protective substances" present in broth. The chemical basis for the protective action has been recently analyzed by Dale *et al.* (1949) for the indirect X-ray inactivation of enzymes and by Latarjet and Ephrati (1948) on bacteriophage.

The initial inactivation rate in nutrient broth cannot be decreased by increasing the concentration of broth or by adding other protective substances. There exists, therefore, an X-ray effect on phage against which no protection is given by foreign substances in the medium. This "unprotectable" inactivation is considered as due to a direct effect of X-rays (Luria and Exner, 1941), that is, to acts of absorption of X-ray energy within the phage articles.

In our investigation of the biological properties of X-ray-inactivated phage we have analyzed phage inactivated under various conditions of the surrounding medium. This paper is concerned with the properties of phage inactivated in broth ("direct effect"). Later papers will deal with the properties of phage inactivated by the "indirect effects."

Biological Properties of Phage Inactivated by "Direct Effect"

Survival curves. X-ray inactivation of T2 suspended in nutrient broth follows the pattern observed earlier by Luria (1944) and Latarjet (1948). The exponential inactivation curve (figure 2) indicates that the inactivation process is due to a one-hit mechanism (Wollman, Holweck, and Luria, 1940), which we assume consists of the production of one successful ionization.

When the average number of hits per particle is r, the proportion of active to total phage is e^{-r}. The dose necessary to give on the average 1 hit per particle ($e^{-1} = 37$ per cent survival) has been called the "inactivation dose" (Lea, 1947). The dose can be expressed in multiples of the inactivation dose, these values giving the average "number of hits" per particle. For T2 the inactivation dose is 40,000 r. This value is unchanged if the phage is suspended in 5 per cent gelatin instead of nutrient broth, gelatin being a "protective substance" (Luria and Exner, 1941).

For survivals lower than 10^{-2}, a downward bend becomes noticeable in the inactivation curve, suggesting the presence of a second inactivating mechanism. This bend almost disappears if the broth concentration is doubled, suggesting that the extrainactivation is caused by toxic agents produced by the radiation in the surrounding medium.

The inactivation rate of phage mutants T2r and T2hr was found to be identical with that of wild type T2. T4 and T6 showed equal radiosensitivity as T2, in agreement with earlier observations of Luria (1944). Exponential inactivation was also found for T1 and T7, with the "inactivation dose" for both being

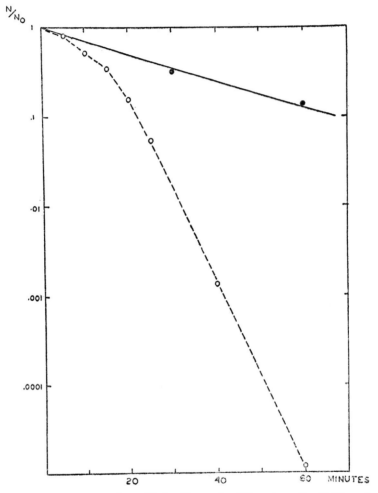

Figure 1. Inactivation of phage T2 by X-rays in different media. N/N₀ = fraction of active phage after irradiation. The X-ray dose is expressed in minutes of exposure. Solid line: Phage in nutrient broth. Broken line: Phage suspended in M-9, solution A.

approximately 85,000 *r*, confirming earlier experiments of Luria and Exner (1941) with T1 and of Luria (1944) with T7.

The probability that one ionization produces inactivation (ionic yield) can be determined by calculating how many ionizations occur within the phage particle for one successful hit. For these calculations it is necessary to know the particle size; from electron micrographs this has been estimated for phages T2,

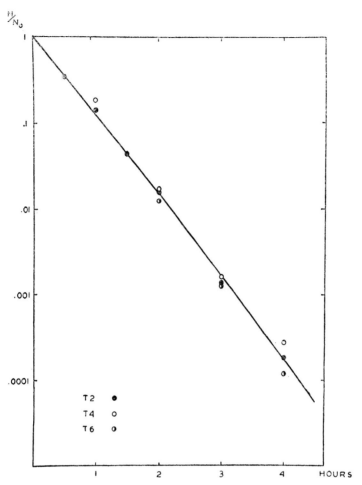

Figure 2. X-ray inactivation of various phages in nutrient broth. N/N_0 = fraction of active phage after irradiation. The X-ray dose is expressed in hours of exposure.

T4, and T6 to be 2.5×10^{-16} cm³. Since the inactivation dose is 40,000 r, corresponding to 8×10^{16} ionizations per cm³, the ionic yield is 0.05.[4]

[4] Earlier investigations have expressed ionization efficiency in terms of ionization clusters instead of individual ionizations. This was done because ionizations are not distributed at random but tend to occur on the average in groups of 3, so that when one ionization occurs within the phage, several others are also likely to occur. The use of clusters to express efficiency is justified only when a large fraction of the ionizations are effective. Then only one in a cluster is effective, the others being wasted. If, however, only 1/20 of the ionizations are effective, practically all of the ionizations in the cluster may have a chance of inactivating the phage and the probability of inactivation should be expressed in terms of single ionizations. This reasoning is valid only if all portions of the phage particle are equally radiosensitive; if the radiosensitivity is limited to a restricted region of the phage particle, then overlapping of "effective" ionizations should be taken into consideration.

The value 0.05 is considerably lower than the ones estimated for similar phages by earlier workers (see Lea, 1946), ranging between 1 in 3 to 1 in 6. This difference is due to the way in which the phage volume has been determined. We have used electron micrographic data, whereas earlier results were obtained using size determinations by ultrafiltration, which may be less accurate.

Adsorption. The adsorption of X-ray-inactivated phage (XRP) by bacteria cannot be measured directly by titrating the free particles after contact with bacteria, since the inactive phage cannot be titrated. We have determined whether inactive particles can be adsorbed by testing their ability to interfere with the adsorption of active phage by heat-killed bacteria (HKB), a method that permits the study of adsorption uncomplicated by virus multiplication.

Schlesinger (1932) showed that some phage strains are adsorbed by HKB, on which they cannot multiply, so that the adsorbed phage is lost and for all practical purposes inactivated. The adsorption of active phage on HKB is therefore measured as a loss of free phage. Schlesinger also showed that only a limited number of phage particles can be adsorbed by a bacterium before the available surface becomes saturated.

We prepared HKB by heating broth cultures of bacteria in the logarithmic phase of growth at 65 C for 1 hour. No viable bacteria remained, and all ability to support phage growth was lost. After heat treatment the HKB were stored at 4 C; the adsorptive capacity remained constant, permitting use of the same preparation of HKB over a period of months.

The ability of active phage to adsorb on HKB was utilized to test the adsorption of XRP in the following way: The adsorption of active phage T2 by HKB was first measured, and a logarithmic rate of adsorption was obtained, approximately equal to the adsorption rate of T2 on living bacteria in the logarithmic phase of growth. The adsorption rate of T6 upon HKB was then tested and found to be logarithmic and equal to that of T2.[5] Next, the number of T2 particles adsorbed, before saturation of the bacterial surface manifests itself as a flattening of the adsorption curve, was measured and found to be approximately 300. Bacteria thus saturated with active T2 were then mixed with T6, and the adsorption of T6 was measured. T2 and T6 can be differentiated easily by plating on the bacterial indicator strain B/2, on which only T6 grows, and on B/6, on which only T2 grows. No adsorption of T6 was detected, indicating that saturation of HKB with T2, besides preventing further T2 adsorption, also prevented T6 adsorption.

Finally, we replaced the active T2 with XRP T2, to see whether the inactive particles could absorb on the HKB and prevent T6 adsorption. The results of such an experiment, shown in table 1, indicate that XRP T2 is as effective a coating agent as active T2, thus demonstrating the adsorption ability of XRP T2.

Bacterial killing ability of XRP. Following X-ray irradiation in broth, a fraction of the inactive T2 particles is still able to kill sensitive bacteria. The ability

[5] Of the seven phages of the T group, only T1 is not adsorbed by HKB. T2, T4, and T6 are adsorbed by HKB approximately as fast as by living bacteria. T3 and T7 are adsorbed by HKB at a slower rate.

of one inactive particle to kill was demonstrated by mixing various amounts of XRP with a constant amount of bacteria. If one particle is sufficient to kill, the fraction of surviving bacteria in the different mixtures should be e^{-x}, where x is the mean number of killing particles adsorbed per bacterium. The values of e^{-x} in different mixtures from an experiment of this type are shown in table 2.

TABLE 1

Prevention of T6 adsorption by XRP T2

HKB at a concentration of 2×10^7 cells per ml. The XRP T2 had received 8 hits. Platings were done on B/2 so that only T6 would form plaques.

TUBE NO.	CONTENTS AFTER FIRST INPUT	SECOND INPUT 2 HOURS LATER	T6 COUNT AT VARIOUS TIME INTERVALS			
			0	20 min	40 min	60 min
1	Active phage T2 plus HKB (300 phage particles per bacterium)	T6 (0.005 phage particles per bacterium)	272	267	261	242
2	Active phage T2 plus HKB (30 phage particles per bacterium)	T6 (0.005 phage particles per bacterium)	253	138	76	44
3	XRP T2 plus HKB (300 phage particles per bacterium)	T6 (0.005 phage particles per bacterium)	295	266	251	265
4	HKB alone	T6 (0.005 phage particles per bacterium)	251	120	62	26

TABLE 2

Survival of bacteria following infection with different amounts of XRP T2

Various amounts of XRP T2 (4 hits) were added to different portions of a bacterial suspension. After 9 minutes the mixtures were diluted and plated for colony count.

TUBE NO.	(a) CONCENTRATION OF XRP RELATIVE TO TUBE NO. 1	SURVIVING BACTERIA (e^{-x})	(b) x	(c) (b)/(a)
1	1	0.62	0.48	0.480
2	2	0.35	1.05	0.525
3	4	0.12	2.12	0.530
4	6	0.054	2.95	0.492
5	12	0.0061	5.10	0.425

The values of x (column b) are proportional to the amount of inactive phage (column c). In this regard, XRP behaves like ultraviolet-inactivated phage (UVP; Luria and Delbrück, 1942), since in both cases a bacterium can be killed by the action of one inactive particle.

A marked difference, however, between XRP and UVP is that the ability of the inactive particles to kill disappears quite rapidly with increasing X-ray doses. In figure 3 the fraction of killing particles remaining after various doses is plotted as a function of the dose. It is seen that the killing ability of a particle, like the ability to reproduce, is destroyed exponentially with the dose. The ratio of the two slopes is 1:3, indicating that for every three inactivating hits there is one hit that destroys the killing ability.

No difference with regard to the loss of killing ability was found between T2 and its mutants T2r and T2hr. Likewise the ability of T2h to kill B/2 was destroyed by one-third of the inactivating hits. T4 and T6 also behaved like T2, with one-third of the inactivating hits destroying the ability to kill. The same was true for T2 irradiated in 5 per cent gelatin.

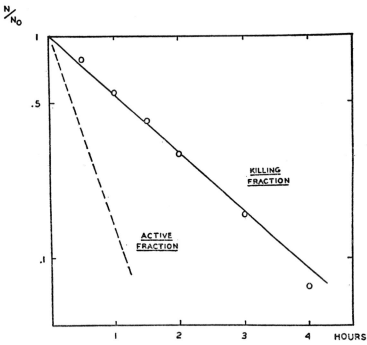

Figure 3. Loss of the bacterial killing ability of T2 as a function of X-ray dose. N/N_0 = fraction of phage able to kill bacteria after irradiation. The X-ray dose is expressed in hours of exposure. In order to compare the relative rates at which reproducing and killing abilities are lost the inactivation curve from figure 2 is also plotted (broken line). For this curve, N/N_0 = fraction of active phage after irradiation.

Since T2, T4, and T6 are genetically very similar (Delbrück, 1946), we wished to see how genetically unrelated phages behaved. The phages T1 and T7 were therefore investigated. Exponential loss of killing ability was again found, with approximately 1 out of 2.5 hits destroying killing ability. It thus appears probable that exponential loss of killing ability is a general characteristic of X-ray-irradiated phage.

We conclude, therefore, that the X-ray irradiation produces two distinct types of inactive phage, one that can kill bacteria and one that cannot. Since both types of particles can adsorb on sensitive bacteria, irradiation by X-rays provides a method for separating the ability to adsorb from the ability to kill bacteria.

Mutual exclusion of T1 by XRP T2. Delbrück and Luria (1942) found that, following infection of a bacterial cell with two unrelated phages, only one phage type can multiply. This "mutual exclusion" (Delbrück, 1945b) is well illustrated by the unrelated phages T1 and T2; if a bacterium is infected simultaneously by both phages, only T2 grows and T1 multiplication is completely suppressed; even the infecting T1 particles are lost. Luria and Delbrück (1942) also found that the T2 particle does not have to multiply in order to exclude T1; ultraviolet-inactivated T2, which had lost its ability to reproduce, was still able to exclude T1 completely.

TABLE 3

Exclusion of T1 by XRP T2

Culture of *E. coli* B in logarithmic phase = (B).

Four minutes at 37 C were allowed for adsorption of phage. An intermediate dilution was then made into anti-T1 serum and kept 4 minutes at 37 C. This serum treatment gives 7 per cent survival of the unadsorbed phage. All plaque counts below are corrected for this fraction. After further dilutions samples were plated on B/2 before lysis.

The multiplicity of infection for active T2 was determined from the survival of bacteria, assuming a Poisson distribution. Multiplicity of T2 = x.

The "expected" values are based on the assumption that T1 is liberated only by cells without any "killing" T2.

TUBE NO.	CONTENTS	T1 COUNT ON B/2					
		Exp. 74—x = 1.75		Exp. 77—x = 3.2		Exp. 82—x = 3.0	
		Found	Expected	Found	Expected	Found	Expected
1	Active T1 + (B)	330		332		390	
2	Active T1 + active T2 + (B)	66	58	15	14	52	20
3	Active T1 + inactive T2 (3 hits) + (B)	104	172	96	104	141	143
4	Active T1 + inactive T2 (6 hits) + (B)	206	234	160	205	160	240
5	Active T1 + inactive T2 (8 hits) + (B)	285	298	198	264	290	320

We have tested for this excluding ability in XRP. Bacteria were mixedly infected with active T1 and XRP T2. Anti-T1 serum was added to neutralize unadsorbed phage (Delbrück, 1945a), and the infected bacteria were plated before lysis on B/2. Under these conditions, T1 plaques are produced only by infected bacteria that liberate T1. Exclusion of T1 is detected by a decrease in T1 count below the value in a control without XRP. We found that exclusion of T1 by XRP T2 was less complete than with active T2, as shown in table 3. This means that some of the irradiated T2 particles had lost the ability to exclude T1. The fraction of particles able to exclude T1 decreases with increasing dose at a rate approximately equal to the rate at which the frequency of particles with bacterial killing ability decreases. This can be demonstrated by calculating the number of bacteria that are expected to liberate T1 if T1 multiplies only in bacteria that lack any "killing" T2 particle. Comparison of these expected values with the experimental data reveals a relatively close agreement (table 3). Although this agreement does not prove that the excluding ability is limited to those particles that kill, since the results are compatible with the assumption that the two properties are inactivated independently at equal rates, the latter interpretation seems unlikely.

Thus XRP consists of two classes of particles differing in interfering ability, the noninterfering particles being probably those that also have lost their bacterial killing ability.

Suppression of active T2 multiplication by mixed infection with XRP T2. When bacteria are mixedly infected with active phage and XRP, with low ratios of either phage to bacteria, no suppression of active phage reproduction results. This was shown by experiments in which bacteria were infected with one active particle, one inactive "killing" particle, and several inactive "nonkilling" particles, and were plated before burst to determine the number of bacteria that

TABLE 4

Liberation of T2r+ by bacteria infected with active T2r+ plus XRP T2r

Bacteria (B) were mixedly infected with T2r+ active and XRP T2r and then plated before lysis. The number of plaques containing T2r+ was determined and compared with a control containing bacteria infected with T2r+ only.

TUBE CONTENTS	MULTIPLICITY OF ACTIVE T2r+	MULTIPLICITY OF XRP T2r		T2r+ COUNT
		"Killing"	"Non-killing"	
Active T2r+ + (B)......................	0.06	—	—	198
Active T2r+ + XRP (4 hits) + (B).........	0.06	0.12	0.36	196
Active T2r+ + XRP (6 hits) + (B).........	0.06	0.50	2.50	206
Active T2r+ + XRP (8 hits) + (B).........	0.06	0.50	5.50	210

yield active phage. This number was compared with the number of bacteria that liberated phage in a control mixture with active phage only. The results of such an experiment, shown in table 4, indicate that one or several XRP particles, either "killing" or "nonkilling," do not suppress active phage production.

The result is different, however, when large numbers of inactive phage particles are adsorbed by each bacterium. Bacteria were mixed simultaneously with active T2r (ratio of phage to bacteria = 0.02) and with inactivated T2r+ (ratios of phage to bacteria ranging from 1 to 100). The XRP had received 8 hits; under these conditions 7 per cent of the particles retained killing ability. Following adsorption, antiserum against T2 was added to neutralize unadsorbed phage (Delbrück, 1945a), samples were plated before lysis, and the number of bacteria that yielded T2r was determined; suppression of active T2r was detected by a decrease in the number of bacteria yielding T2r, the plaques of which are easily recognizable.

The results of a typical experiment are given in table 5 and indicate that the degree of suppression increases with increase in the multiplicity of infection with XRP. The amount of suppression varies from 20 per cent when 10 XRP particles are adsorbed per bacterium to 94 per cent when 100 XRP particles are adsorbed.

The degree of suppression is not strongly influenced by the multiplicity of the active phage T2r; an increase from 0.9 to 9 did not markedly change the result. This suggests that the active and inactive particles are not competing with each other and that the suppression is due to an unspecific effect of a large excess of adsorbed phage. Suppression might, therefore, be related to the "lysis from without" phenomenon (Delbrück, 1940), in which adsorption of a large number of phage particles per bacterium causes prompt lysis of bacteria without permitting phage growth.

To test this possibility, XRP T2 was mixed with bacteria at a ratio of phage to bacteria of 200. The mixture was incubated at 37 C, and the degree of bacterial turbidity was observed. Within 5 minutes the turbidity decreased markedly,

TABLE 5
Suppression of active T2r by mixed infection with high multiplicities of XRP T2r+

The XRP T2r+ had received 8 hits. Ten minutes of adsorption on bacteria (B) give 80 per cent adsorption of the active phage. Adsorption of the XRP was assumed equal to that of the active. Following adsorption, an intermediate dilution was made into anti-T2 serum to neutralize unadsorbed phage. Platings were made before lysis and the T2r plaques were counted.

TUBE CONTENTS	MULTIPLICITY OF ACTIVE T2r	MULTIPLICITY OF XRP T2r+		T2r COUNT	SUPPRESSION OF T2r, %
		"Killing"	"Non-killing"		
Active T2r + (B)	0.02	—	—	260	0
Active T2r + XRP T2r+ (1:10²) + (B)	0.02	0.07	0.93	259	0
Active T2r + XRP T2r+ (1:10) + (B)	0.02	0.7	9.3	190	23
Active T2r + XRP T2r+ (1:2) + (B)	0.02	3.5	46.5	54	79
Active T2r + XRP T2r+ pure + (B)	0.02	7.0	93	16	94

indicating that the bacteria were being lysed; by 10 minutes the turbidity was reduced to that of the suspending broth. Surprisingly, XRP particles are much more effective than active phage in causing this type of lysis. Over 3 to 4 times as many active particles are necessary to produce a comparable amount of lysis.

At lower multiplicities of XRP the bacteria do not lyse immediately; instead, a number of them assume a spherical shape, detectable by microscopic observation. If a 20-fold excess of XRP is added to bacteria, the following picture is observed: The cells retain their normal shape for about 5 minutes; then some begin to assume a spherical shape, approximately 25 per cent of the cells being rounded at 20 minutes. Longer observations indicated no increase in the proportion of swollen cells, lysis of which then occurs gradually.

A 25 per cent fraction roughly corresponds to the fraction of bacteria in which active phage production by the amount of XRP used in this experiment would be suppressed. These experiments thus suggest that the suppression of active phage reproduction by XRP is due to lysis from without of some of those bacteria that adsorb large numbers of inactive phage.

The inactive samples used in these experiments contained a small fraction (7 per cent) of phage particles that retained the ability to kill bacteria by single infection, and it was possible that the suppression was caused either by the adsorption of a large number of particles, both "killing" and "nonkilling," or by the adsorption of a small number of "killing" particles. It was shown above, however, (see table 4) that one "killing" particle does not suppress reproduction of active phage of the same type. Since with a large number of "nonkilling" particles some suppression occurs even when the multiplicity of "killing" particles is less than one (table 5), it is likely that suppression can be caused by "nonkilling" particles.

In summary, infection of a bacterial cell with 10 or more XRP particles can cause "lysis from without." If a bacterium is infected with both active and inactive particles, "lysis from without" results in the suppression of active phage production. Following adsorption of a large number of XRP particles, the bacteria swell, assume spherical shapes, and lyse. The time interval before lysis is a function of the number of adsorbed particles, decreasing to less than 5 minutes with a multiplicity of 200. The ability to lyse bacteria from without is not destroyed by an X-ray dose sufficient to destroy the "killing" ability.

Cytological observations on bacteria infected with XRP. Using preparations stained by the HCl-Giemsa technique (Robinow, 1944) to study "chromatinic" material, Luria and Human (1950) have investigated the cytology of bacteria infected with UVP. They observed bacteria infected with phage T2 that had received heavy UV doses, so that little multiplicity reactivation (Luria, 1947) occurred. Following infection, the "nuclear bodies" break down and the chromatinic material becomes distributed throughout the bacterial cell. At the same time the cells become swollen, though they retain their normal rod shape. It was suggested that the inactive phage killed the bacteria by destroying their genetic apparatus.

The cytology of bacteria infected with XRP was studied in collaboration with Mrs. Mary L. Human. Bacteria were infected with XRP T2, and, after various incubation times, stained for "chromatinic" material. A multiplicity of 2 "killing" particles was employed, so that the majority (85 per cent) of bacteria would be killed. Since the inactive phage had received 8 hits, very few bacteria would liberate active phage either because of multiplicity reactivation (see below) or of residual actual phage.

Within five minutes after infection, the nuclear bodies began to lose their clear outline, and by 20 minutes the chromatinic material was distributed throughout the cell. The intensity of the chromatinic staining gradually decreased, and the cells became markedly swollen in appearance. Thus the cytological picture of bacteria killed by low multiplicities of XRP is similar to that of bacteria killed by UVP.

Although a multiplicity of two "killing" particles was used, the total number of particles adsorbed per bacterium, both "killing" and "nonkilling," was 25.

Some of the cells should, therefore, be "lysed from without." This expectation was confirmed by finding a second type of infected bacteria in addition to the type described above. These cells are easily distinguished by their spherical shape in contrast to the normal rod shape of the other infected cells. Lysis from without occurs without phage liberation. It was of interest, therefore, to find that these cells, though they become spherical in shape, still contain distinct "nuclear bodies" 20 minutes after infection. This observation supports the hypothesis of Delbrück (1940) that "lysis from without" is basically different from normal lysis.

Lysis inhibition by XRP. Phages T2, T4, and T6 differ from their r mutants in that the latter produce rapid lysis of turbid bacterial cultures, whereas the wild type (r+) produces very delayed lysis. Doermann (1948) has shown that this lysis inhibition is caused by the phage particles themselves. The r+ phages liberated from the first lysed bacteria are adsorbed by the remaining bacteria and inhibit their lysis. One r+ particle added as early as 3 minutes following primary infection by r+ can cause lysis inhibition. T2r+, T4r+, and T6r+ can cross-inhibit lysis; for instance, following primary infection by T6r+, a secondary infection with T2r+ causes lysis inhibition. The r mutants do not inhibit lysis by second infection.

We wished to see whether XRP that had lost the ability to kill bacteria could still inhibit lysis. If so, this would dissociate lysis inhibition from the phage mechanisms directly connected with synthesis of new phage.

Bacteria were mixed with active T6 at a low ratio of phage to bacteria, so that single infection would result. After 3 minutes had been allowed for adsorption, the mixture was diluted to stop further adsorption. A second infection with XRP T2 (12 hits) was made 4 minutes later. The multiplicity of the secondary infection was 5, so that less than 1 per cent of the bacteria remained uninfected. Since only 2 per cent of the XRP retained "killing" ability, less than 10 per cent of the bacteria were infected with "killing" T2 particles. Five minutes were allowed for the second infection, after which the mixtures were again diluted to stop adsorption. At various intervals aliquots were plated on B/2, to obtain a one-step growth curve of T6 (Ellis and Delbrück, 1939).

This curve was compared with a curve obtained when the second infection was with active T2, and with a curve obtained with primary infection with T6 only. Two experiments showed that T6 liberation from bacteria also infected with XRP T2 was delayed 8 minutes beyond the normal latent period of T6 (26 minutes), and that this delay was equal to that produced by active T2. We conclude, therefore, that XRP T2 can inhibit lysis as effectively as active phage T2.

Thus, phage particles do not need the ability to reproduce in order to inhibit lysis; this was confirmed by the finding that UVP also can inhibit lysis. Moreover, the "killing" ability is apparently not necessary in order to inhibit lysis; the ability to adsorb is probably the only requirement.

Photoreactivation (PHTR). Dulbecco (1949b, 1950) observed reactivation of UVP by exposure to visible light in the presence of bacterial cells (photoreactivation = PHTR). His observation represented an extension of the original finding of Kelner (1949*a,b*) that visible light could reactivate spores of actinomycetes and cells of *Escherichia coli* killed by ultraviolet light. We have tested whether PHTR of X-ray damage occurs by exposing XRP to visible light. Since Dulbecco (1950) has shown that the UVP must be adsorbed to bacteria for PHTR to occur, we have applied the photoreactivating light to XRP in the presence of bacteria. XRP was plated with bacteria, and the plates were immediately incubated under fluorescent light at room temperature. The dose of visible light was sufficient to cause maximum PHTR of UVP (Dulbecco, 1950).

Table 6 summarizes experiments with phage T2, which definitely show the existence of some PHTR of XRP. In contrast to UVP, the amount of PHTR is small; in the dark, there remains an inactivation corresponding to 7.6 hits with an X-ray dose that gives 8 hits after maximum PHTR. As a result, the difference between plaque counts before and after PHTR is very small, necessitating many repetitions of each experiment to demonstrate PHTR beyond doubt. Our data are still too incomplete to determine the ratio of the damage in maximum light to the damage in the dark.

Experiments to determine the influence of variables such as the amount and wave length of photoreactivating light have not been attempted, because of the very small amount of PHTR. Storage of inactive phage for weeks at 4 C has no effect on its susceptibility to photoreactivation. XRP T4 and T6 are also capable of PHTR, with T4 showing about half as much PHTR as T2, whereas T6 slightly exceeds T2

Since PHTR of XRP is so small and can be detected only under optimum experimental conditions, assays of XRP done under ordinary laboratory light are indistinguishable from those done in the absence of photoreactivating light. It has therefore been possible to do experiments with XRP without taking special precautions to exclude visible light.

In summary, we can say that PHTR of XRP exists but is very small in amount. Concerning the difference between X-rays and ultraviolet light, we should not forget that approximately one-half of the energy of X-rays is dissipated in the form of excitations (similar to those produced by ultraviolet) as opposed to ionizations. It is therefore possible that the small amount of photoreactivable damage in XRP corresponds to damage similar to that produced by ultraviolet light.

Multiplicity reactivation. In 1947, Luria reported that assays of UVP are dependent on the concentration of the inactive phage when first mixed with bacteria. Bacteria were mixed with various concentrations of UVP, and after a few minutes the mixtures were diluted enough to bring the total dilution of the irradiated phage samples to a constant value, after which aliquots were plated for phage count. Since plating was done before lysis, each plaque represented an infected bacterium liberating active phage. The plaque counts were found to be higher when bacteria had first been mixed with more concentrated phage. Luria showed that this increase in plaque count is due to the production of active phage in a fraction of the bacteria infected with two or more inactive particles (multiplicity reactivation).

We have repeated this experiment using XRP instead of UVP. XRP T4 at various dilutions was mixed with bacteria and allowed to adsorb. Before lysis, the samples were diluted and plated with an excess of sensitive bacteria. Following incubation, plaque counts were made to determine the number of bacteria that liberated active phage. The results shown in table 7 indicate that the number of

TABLE 6

Photoreactivation of XRP T2

All experiments were performed with the same irradiated samples, whose residual titers remained constant throughout the series of experiments. After plating, all plates were incubated for 15 hours at room temperature, some in light, some in darkness.

NO. OF X-RAY "HITS" FROM PLAQUE COUNTS IN DARKNESS	EXPERIMENT NO.	PLAQUE COUNT IN LIGHT (a)	PLAQUE COUNT IN DARKNESS (b)	(a)/(b)
0	64	260	246	1.06
	68	391	441	0.87
	70	328	339	0.97
	76	2,266	2,279	0.99
	Σ	3,245	3,305	0.98
3	64	277	285	0.97
	68	313	280	1.12
	70	246	243	1.01
	81	1,488	1,419	1.05
	Σ	2,324	2,227	1.04
6	64	310	241	1.29
	68	339	269	1.26
	70	301	214	1.41
	79	1,661	1,328	1.25
	84	1,160	908	1.28
	Σ	3,771	2,960	1.28
8	64	278	196	1.48
	68	336	254	1.32
	70	265	202	1.31
	73	2,131	1,574	1.35
	83	1,520	1,097	1.39
	Σ	4,540	3,323	1.37

bacteria yielding active phage is greater than the number of bacteria infected with the residual active phage. Experiments with T2 and T6 gave results similar to those with T4. This indicates that XRP, like UVP, can be reactivated by multiple infection.

In order to compare results with those obtained with UVP, we should know how many bacteria contain two or more inactive particles that can be reactivated by multiple infection. Evidence is not yet available, however, as to whether the XRP particles that have lost the ability to kill bacteria can be reactivated. We have decided to consider only the "killing" particles as reactivable, since we feel that quantitative analysis based on the alternative assumption, i.e., that all particles are reactivable, is more likely to be misleading. In the following discussion the "multiplicity" of XRP will therefore refer to the average number of adsorbed particles with killing ability.

It is seen in table 7 that the probability that a multiple-infected bacterium would liberate active phage increases with increasing multiplicity up to a multiplicity of approximately 2. Beyond this point the probability rapidly falls off. This is in marked contrast to the situation with UVP, with which the probability increases up to a multiplicity of 10 or 20. We believe that this difference is related to the fact that when XRP is used, in addition to the inactive particles that can kill, there are also adsorbed a number of particles that cannot kill.

TABLE 7

Probability of reactivation of XRP T4 as a function of the multiplicity of infection

Experiment no. 26. XRP T4, 6 hits per particle. Each mixture contained a constant amount of bacteria and various amounts of irradiated phage.

MIXTURE NO.	PHAGE INPUT*	MULTI-PLICITY* OF INFECTION	(a) BACTERIA WITH RESIDUAL ACTIVE PARTICLES	(b) BACTERIA WITH TWO OR MORE INACTIVE PARTICLES	(c) BACTERIA THAT LIBERATE ACTIVE PHAGE	(d) EXCESS (c) − (a)	RATIO (d)/(b)
1	2.54×10^8	3.6	9.20×10^5	3.6×10^7	9.5×10^5	3×10^4	0.00083
2	1.27×10^8	1.8	4.60×10^5	2.9×10^7	9.0×10^5	4.4×10^5	0.015
3	6.30×10^7	0.9	2.30×10^5	1.4×10^7	4.0×10^5	1.7×10^5	0.012
4	3.15×10^7	0.45	1.15×10^5	5×10^6	1.6×10^5	4.5×10^4	0.009

* Only particles able to kill bacteria are included in these calculations. For every killing particle there are 6 nonkilling ones.

For an irradiated sample with 6 hits, there are six particles that cannot kill for one that can. We have shown earlier that those particles, though unable to kill by single particle action, can, if adsorbed in large numbers, suppress active phage production. It is, therefore, probable that our failure to detect increased reactivation at high multiplicities (table 7) is due to the suppression of active phage production by the large excess of particles unable to kill.

At low multiplicities the number of adsorbed particles unable to kill is too small to influence the amount of detectable reactivation. We can, therefore, use reactivation results employing low multiplicities for a comparison with reactivation of UVP. The comparison can be made on the basis of the probability of reactivation, which is the ratio between the number of bacteria that liberate active phage and the number of multiple-infected bacteria. The fraction of bacteria containing 2 or more "killing" particles is: $1 - (x + 1)e^{-x}$, where x is the multiplicity of infection. For all phages so far tested, T2, T4, and T6, the probability of reactivation, for equal percentage of active survivors and equal multiplicity, is much lower for XRP than for UVP. For example, when the average multiplicity is 1, the probability that a multiple-infected bacterium liberates active phage is 0.3 for UVP T4 with 2×10^{-2} survival. With XRP T4 with 2×10^{-2} survival, this probability is only 0.01. Since reactivation of XRP is very slight and experimentally difficult to ascertain, confirmation of the phenomenon was desired by other methods.

Luria (1947) reported cross reactivation of UVP T2 by mixed infection with active T4 or T6. Cross reactivation of XRP T2 by mixed infection with active T6 was tested and found to occur. Table 8 shows the results of two typical experiments, which indicate that active T6 increases the number of bacteria liberating T2.

TABLE 8

Cross reactivation of XRP T2 by active T6

Bacteria were mixedly infected with XRP T2 (6 hits) and active T6. The multiplicity of XRP T2 was 0.1, that of active T6 was 1.8. Platings were done on B/6 before burst.

EXPERIMENT NO.	COUNT ON B/6 WITH T6 ALONE	COUNT ON B/6 WITH XRP T2 ALONE	COUNT ON B/6 WITH XRP T2 PLUS ACTIVE T6
30	0	1.7×10^6	3.1×10^6
32	0	1.0×10^6	1.9×10^6

TABLE 9

Cross reactivation between XRP T2r+ and UVP T2r

Bacteria were mixedly infected with XRP T2r+ (6 hits) and UVP T2r (5×10^{-3} survival). The multiplicity of the inactive phages was 0.05, so that almost all of the mixed infections resulted from one particle of XRP and one particle of UVP. Plating was done before burst and the number of mixed bursts ("mottled plaques") counted.

EXPERIMENT NO.	MAXIMUM NUMBER OF MIXED BURSTS EXPECTED FROM BACTERIA WITH RESIDUAL ACTIVE T2r+	NUMBER OF MIXED BURSTS ("MOTTLED PLAQUES") FOUND
35	6.3×10^2	6.3×10^3
36	1.1×10^3	4.6×10^3
37	9.6×10^2	2.8×10^3

Dr. A. H. Sturtevant suggested (personal communication to S. E. Luria) that cross reactivation might occur between XRP and UVP. To facilitate detection of such cross reactivation, genetic markers were employed, and bacteria were mixedly infected with XRP T2r+ and UVP T2r. In this way, the UVP alone gives only r progeny, the XRP alone gives only r+ progeny; bacteria in which cross reactivation occurs between XRP and UVP may give a mixed burst containing T2r+ and T2r. The bacteria giving mixed yields of r and r+ are detected by plating before burst and determining the number of "mottled plaques" (Hershey, 1946; Dulbecco, 1949). The results of a series of such experiments are tabulated in table 9 and demonstrate beyond doubt the existence of cross reactivation, since in all cases the number of mixed bursts was much greater than was expected from residual active phage.

Experiments employing the genetic markers r and r+ were also used to show that XRP can contribute genetic characters in mixed infection with active phage. Bacteria were infected with one particle of active T2r+ and one particle of XRP T2r. Not only were all the mixedly infected bacteria able to liberate active T2r+, but in addition some of the bacteria produced mixed yields containing T2r+ and T2r. As table 10 indicates, the number of these bacteria greatly exceeds the number expected from the residual active T2r; this shows the ability of the XRP particles to participate in genetic recombination.

In summary, our experiments show that XRP particles can take part in reactivation leading to the production of active phage particles. The probability of reactivation for particles with a given survival is lower for XRP than for UVP. This difference may be due to the fact that X-rays produce in the phage particles some type of damage that cannot be reactivated. An alternative explanation is that each adsorption of X-rays results in damage to a larger portion of the phage particle. As yet we cannot rule out either of these possibilities, though the much lower photoreactivability of XRP suggests that these two inactivating

TABLE 10

Reactivation of XRP T2r by active T2r+

Bacteria were mixedly infected with XRP T2 (3 hits) and active T2r+. The multiplicity of infection of both phages was 0.05, so that almost all the mixed infections resulted from one particle of each type. Plating was done before burst and the number of mixed bursts ("mottled plaques") counted.

EXPERIMENT NO.	NUMBER OF MIXED BURSTS EXPECTED FROM RESIDUAL ACTIVE T2r	NUMBER OF MIXED BURSTS FOUND
41	5.8×10^4	2.1×10^5
42	4.2×10^4	1.7×10^5
43	5.6×10^4	1.4×10^5
44	7.2×10^4	2.0×10^5

agents may differentially damage different portions of the phage. Experiments testing the effect of X-rays on specific genetic determinants should be useful in answering this question.

DISCUSSION

By means of X-ray irradiation we have been able to obtain phage particles that have lost some of their specific properties, such as the abilities to kill the host bacterium or to exclude another phage type. Some of these properties are lost at different rates, which fact suggests that they depend on the integrity of different parts of the phage particle. It is probable that these parts function at different stages during phage-host interaction, so that phage growth will be blocked at different stages depending on which part is damaged.

By examining the rates at which the different properties are lost, it should be possible to draw a tentative sequence of the various events in phage growth. For instance, if a certain type of inactive particle can accomplish steps a, b, and c, another type can go through steps a and c, and still another can accomplish only step c, we may conclude that the order of these events in reproduction is c, a, b. This type of analysis, utilizing XRP and UVP, permits identification of the following two stages of phage growth:

Adsorption. The distinctness of this stage is shown by finding a phage, the nonkilling XRP, that can adsorb but cannot progress further in reproduction. The adsorption stage must involve a rather deep change in the bacterial cell, since nonkilling XRP can cause both lysis from without and lysis inhibition. In turn, the latter processes are ascribed to an early step in phage-host interaction. As expected, UVP can also lyse from without and inhibit lysis.

Lysis from without occurs under three main conditions: (1) infection of a bacterium by a great excess (100 or more) of phage particles; (2) infection by several phage particles in the absence of nutrients or in the presence of metabolic "inhibitors" (Cohen, 1949); (3) infection by several particles of nonkilling XRP in nutrient medium. A possible clue to its understanding comes from the fact that UVP does not cause lysis from without at low multiplicities in the presence of nutrients. This suggests that lysis from without is the result of an inability to progress to further steps in reproduction. Under this hypothesis, in the absence of nutrients the phage cannot go beyond the adsorption stage and tends instead to cause lysis from without. Supporting this viewpoint is the observation that lysis from without can occur without breakdown of the bacterial "nuclei" (see below).

Invasion. This stage is illustrated by UVP and killing XRP. These particles possess the ability to kill bacteria by single infection but are unable to reproduce. In cells infected with UVP the "chromatinic bodies" disintegrate, suggesting that the UVP kill bacteria by destroying their nuclear apparatus (Luria and Human, 1950). Similar changes have been observed with killing XRP. This stage is further characterized by a blocking of DNA synthesis (Cohen, 1948), inability to form adaptive enzymes (Monod and Wollman, 1947; Luria and Gunsalus 1950), and suppression of increase in respiratory rate (Cohen, 1949).

Mutual exclusion is apparently established in this stage, since we find that the ability to exclude is destroyed by X-rays at the same rate as the ability to kill. In agreement with this idea is the observation (Delbrück, personal communication) that when cells are infected in buffer, that is, in the absence of a nutrient source, mutual exclusion is not established by giving one phage type a head start, presumably due to failure of the process to go beyond the "adsorption" stage.

Such a complete reorganization of the bacterial cell suggests a deep intromission of the infecting phage in the bacterial affairs. We therefore call this stage "invasion" and characterize it as the stage following adsorption during which the infecting phage particle destroys the nuclear apparatus of the host bacterium. Electron micrographs of cells infected with killing particles, compared with others of nonkilling particles, should be of interest in deciding whether after adsorption the former type disappears from the bacterial surface, while the latter does not.

Our picture admittedly presents many gaps. For instance, the stage at which multiplicity reactivation occurs is still unknown. Since all UVP particles can kill and reactivate excellently by multiple infection, it seems plausible to believe that this reactivation occurs either during or following invasion. Photoreactivation, on the other hand, can occur by exposure to light of bacteria infected in buffer, where invasion presumably does not take place, and may take place both before and after invasion.

Further progress in this type of analysis will be dependent on the availability of additional types of inactive phage. It may be possible through the use of chemical inactivating agents acting in more specific ways to subdivide reproduction into finer steps. For instance, we might be able to obtain phage that can adsorb but not inhibit lysis nor lyse bacteria from without; or we might obtain phage that can kill but not exclude another phage. In any case, the present success with UVP and XRP offers strong incentive for further work with inactive phage.

ACKNOWLEDGMENTS

This investigation has been done under the supervision of Dr. S. E. Luria, to whom the author is deeply indebted for advice and encouragement. Many useful suggestions have also been given by Drs. G. Bertani, M. Delbrück, A. H. Doermann, and R. Dulbecco. Some of these experiments were performed at the Biological Laboratory, Cold Spring Harbor, New York, using facilities kindly provided by its director, Dr. M. Demerec, and at the California Institute of Technology in the laboratory of Dr. M. Delbrück.

SUMMARY

The inactivation by X-rays of bacteriophages of the T group suspended in broth has been investigated, and the properties of the inactive viruses have been studied. Inactivation is a simple exponential function of the dose, indicating a one-hit inactivating mechanism. All the inactive particles are able to adsorb on sensitive bacteria, but only a fraction of them retain the ability to kill bacteria or to exclude another phage type. The ability to inhibit lysis or to lyse bacteria from without is not lost when the ability to kill bacteria is destroyed. Multiplicity reactivation and photoreactivation of X-ray-inactivated phage are observed in slight amounts. The results have been used to distinguish two stages in the early period of phage reproduction, the first stage being called "adsorption," the second "invasion."

REFERENCES

ADAMS, M. H. 1949 The stability of bacterial viruses in solutions of salts. J. Gen. Physiol., **32**, 579–594.

ADAMS, M. H. 1950 Methods of study of bacterial viruses. *In* Methods in Medical Research, vol. II. Year Book Publishers, Chicago.

COHEN, S. S. 1948 The synthesis of bacterial viruses. 1. The synthesis of nucleic acid and protein in *Escherichia coli* B infected with $T2r^+$ bacteriophage. J. Biol. Chem., **174**, 281–293.

COHEN, S. S. 1949 Growth requirements of bacterial viruses. Bact. Revs., **13**, 1–24.

DALE, W. M., DAVIES, J. V., AND GILBERT, C. W. 1949 The kinetics and specificities of deamination of nitrogenous compounds by X-radiation. Biochem. J., **45**, 93–99.

DELBRÜCK, M. 1940 The growth of bacteriophage and lysis of the host. J. Gen. Physiol., **23**, 643–660.

DELBRÜCK, M. 1945a Effects of specific antisera on the growth of bacterial viruses. J. Bact., **50**, 137–150.

DELBRÜCK, M. 1945b Interference between bacterial viruses. III. The mutual exclusion and the depressor effect. J. Bact., **50**, 151–170.

DELBRÜCK, M. 1946 Bacterial viruses or bacteriophages. Biol. Rev. Cambridge Phil. Soc., **21**, 30–40.

DELBRÜCK, M., AND LURIA, S. E. 1942 Interference between bacterial viruses. I. Interference between two bacterial viruses acting upon the same host, and the mechanism of virus growth. Arch. Biochem., **1**, 111–141.

DEMEREC, M., AND FANO, U. 1945 Bacteriophage-resistant mutants in *Escherichia coli*. Genetics, **30**, 119–136.

DOERMANN, A. H. 1948 Lysis and lysis inhibition with *Escherichia coli* bacteriophage. J. Bact., **55**, 257–276.

DULBECCO, R. 1949a The number of particles of bacteriophage T2 that can participate in intracellular growth. Genetics, **122**, 126–132.

DULBECCO, R. 1949b Reactivation of ultraviolet-inactivated bacteriophage by visible light. Nature, **163**, 949–950.

DULBECCO, R. 1950 Experiments on photoreactivation of bacteriophages inactivated with ultraviolet radiation. J. Bact., **59**, 329–347.

ELLIS, E. L., AND DELBRÜCK, M. 1939 The growth of bacteriophage. J. Gen. Physiol., **22**, 365–384.

HERSHEY, A. D. 1946 Spontaneous mutations in bacterial viruses. Cold Spring Harbor Symposia Quant. Biol., **11**, 67–77.

KELNER, A. 1949a Effect of visible light on the recovery of *Streptomyces griseus* conidia from ultra-violet irradiation injury. Proc. Nat. Acad. Sci. U. S., **35**, 73–79.

KELNER, A. 1949b Photoreactivation of ultraviolet-irradiated *Escherichia coli* with special reference to the dose-reduction principle and to ultraviolet-induced mutations. J. Bact., **58**, 511–522.

LATARJET, R. 1948 Intracellular growth of bacteriophage studied by roentgen irradiation. J. Gen. Physiol., **31**, 529–546.

LATARJET, R., AND EPHRATI, E. 1948 Influence protectrice de certaines substances contre l'inactivation d'un bactériophage par les rayons X. Compt. rend. soc. biol., **142**, 497–499.

LEA, D. E. 1946 Actions of radiations on living cells. Cambridge University Press, Cambridge, Eng.

LEA, D. E., AND SALAMAN, M. H. 1946 Experiments on the inactivation of bacteriophage by radiations, and their bearing on the nature of bacteriophage. Proc. Roy. Soc. (London), B, **133**, 434–444.

LURIA, S. E. 1944 *Unpublished observations*.

LURIA, S. E. 1945 Mutations of bacterial viruses affecting their host range. Genetics, **30**, 84–99.

LURIA, S. E. 1947 Reactivation of irradiated bacteriophage by transfer of self-reproducing units. Proc. Nat. Acad. Sci. U. S., **33**, 253–264.

LURIA, S. E., AND DELBRÜCK, M. 1942 Interference between bacterial viruses. II. Interference between inactivated bacterial virus and active virus of the same strain. Arch. Biochem., **1**, 207–218.

LURIA, S. E., AND DULBECCO, R. 1949 Genetic recombinations leading to production of active bacteriophage from ultraviolet inactivated bacteriophage particles. Genetics, **34**, 93–125.

LURIA, S. E., AND EXNER, F. M. 1941 The inactivation of bacteriophages by X-rays—influence of the medium. Proc. Nat. Acad. Sci. U. S., **27**, 370–375.

LURIA, S. E., AND GUNSALUS, I. C. 1950 *Unpublished experiments*.

LURIA, S. E., AND HUMAN, M. L. 1950 Chromatin staining of bacteria during bacterio-
    phage infection. J. Bact., **59,** 551–560.
MONOD, J., AND WOLLMAN, E. 1947 L'inhibition de la croissance et de l'adaptation
    enzymatique chez les bactéries infectées par le bactériophage. Ann. inst. Pasteur,
    73, 937–957.
ROBINOW, C. F. 1944 Nuclear apparatus and cell structure of rod-shaped bacteria.
    Addendum to R. J. Dubos. The bacterial cell. Harvard University Press, Cambridge,
    Mass.
SCHLESINGER, M. 1932 Über die Bindung des Bakteriophagen an homologe Bakterien.
    Z. Hyg. Infektionskrankh., **114,** 136–175.
WOLLMAN, E., HOLWECK, F., AND LURIA, S. 1940 Effect of radiations on bacteriophage
    C$_{16}$. Nature, **145,** 935.
WOLLMAN, E., AND LACASSAGNE, A. 1940 Recherches sur le phénomène de Twort-d'Hér-
    elle. VI. Evaluation des dimensions des bactériophages au moyen des rayons X.
    Ann. inst. Pasteur., **64,** 5–39.

CAMBRIDGE

Section II photograph: *Francis Crick and Jim Watson during a walk along The Backs at Cambridge University (ca. 1952–1953). In the distance is King's College Chapel. (Courtesy of the James D. Watson Collection, CSHL Archives.)*

Talking and Thinking

A FTER A MONTH OF WRITING WHICH HE DESCRIBED AS "torture," Jim successfully defended his Ph.D thesis on "The Biological Properties of X-ray-inactivated Bacteriophage," in late May, 1950. What to do next had been under discussion since the previous summer, which Jim had spent under the vigilant authority of Max Delbrück in Pasadena. From reading Erwin Schrödinger's *What Is Life* (1945, The Macmillan Co.) as an undergraduate in Chicago, Jim had learned that genes were the keys to life, but his years in Indiana had convinced him that phage genetics could not provide a clarifying and elucidative physical description of genes. By 1950, then, Jim was convinced that his goal of understanding how genes function could not be achieved without knowing what genes are; i.e., what chemicals they are made of. Salvador Luria recognized this but disliked—Jim uses "abhorred"—chemists, and it was clear that Jim was not going to learn what genes were made of by staying any longer in Indiana. Jim had also acquired a taste for European manners from Luria and Delbrück and from the Europeans whom he had met at meetings and during the summers at Cold Spring Harbor:

> Europe seemed the natural place since, in the Luria-Delbrück circle, the constant reference to their early lives left me with the unmistakable feeling that Europe's slower paced traditions were more conducive to the production of first-rate ideas.

Jim writes in the *The Double Helix* (1968, Atheneum) that there was the issue of what sort of chemistry he should learn. For most biologists who thought about these things, proteins were the strongest candidates for the material of heredity; their 20 amino acids led to a complexity of molecular structure that nucleic acids with a mere four nucleotides could not match. However, Luria and Delbrück believed that Oswald Avery's work demonstrated that genes were made of nucleic acids and so it was to a nucleic acid chemist that Jim should go. There was one European biochemist who, in Luria's eyes, was not entirely beyond the pale. Herman Kalckar from Copenhagen had first made a name working on oxidative phosphorylation, but when in New York in the 1940s, he became interested in nucleoside and nucleotide metabolism. Before returning to Copenhagen in 1946, Kalckar had been a student in the first Cold Spring Harbor Phage Course, taught by Delbrück and Luria in 1945. That Kalckar was a biochemist and showed some interest in biology was hopeful; perhaps, Jim thought, learning some biochemistry from Kalckar would not be so bad. Jim applied for a Merck Fellowship, worth $3000 per year, from the National Research Council.

Jim was not the only phage researcher to go to Kalckar's laboratory. Gunther Stent who was a postdoctoral fellow with Delbrück was also going there to learn nucleic acid biochemistry. Unfortunately, things did not go well. Jim had met Kalckar in Chicago in November 1949 when it appeared that Kalckar was keen to study phage replication using isotopes and wanted phage researchers to bring a biological and genetical slant to his laboratory. However, any hope that Luria and Delbrück might have had that their protégé would advance an understanding of genetics through chemistry was, as Jim put it "...a complete flop. Herman [Kalckar] did not stimulate me in the slightest."

Fortunately for Jim and Stent, Kalckar's friend, Ole Maaløe, had just returned from Caltech where he had become a passionate convert to phage research. Maaløe worked at the State Serum Institute, and the two Americans began experiments there, Jim making his way by bicycle. The experiments with Maaløe were successful, and they produced a respectable, if not earth-shattering, paper.[1] This success notwithstanding, the fact remained that Jim was not doing what he was supposed to be doing—learning biochemistry with Kalckar. He was forced to face this uncomfortable fact when the National Research Council asked him to outline his plans for the coming year. Not prepared to risk losing the Fellowship through confessing to a boredom with biochemistry, Jim asked to stay in the "stimulating" environment of Copenhagen for another year, thinking that he would ask permission to move after the renewal had been granted.

Kalckar was to spend April and May, 1950, at the Stazione Zoologica in Naples and suggested that Jim accompany him. This was an opportunity not to be missed—the experiments with Maaløe were complete and the prospect of sunshine of Naples was attractive after the long winter in Copenhagen.

Unfortunately, the weather was not what Jim expected, and biochemistry in Naples was no more exciting than in Copenhagen. "Sometimes," Jim "daydreamed about discovering the secret of the gene...," but not once did he have "...the faintest trace of a respectable idea." The only thing to look forward to was a meeting on the structures of biological macromolecules that was to include some papers on nucleic acids. But most of these were "hot air," except that of Maurice Wilkins, who was substituting for his boss, J.T. Randall, Director of the Biophysics Unit at King's College, London. In his talk, Wilkins said that when living matter is prepared in crystal form, the arrangement of its molecules can be seen and may lead to an understanding of the gene,[2] and then he showed an X-ray diffraction picture of DNA, recently taken by Raymond Gosling.

> ...Maurice's X-ray diffraction picture of DNA...was flicked on the screen near the end of his talk. Maurice's dry English form did not permit enthusiasm as he stated that the picture showed much more detail than previous pictures and could, in fact, be considered as arising from a crystalline substance. And when the structure of DNA was known, we might be in a better position to understand how genes work. Suddenly I was excited about chemistry.[3]

That the three-dimensional structure of any biologically interesting macromolecule had not yet been solved did not dampen Jim's excitement. Jim engaged Wilkins in conversation but failed, even with the added attraction of Elizabeth, his sister, to arouse much enthusiasm in Wilkins for the idea that Jim should be his colleague in London.

But Jim was now a convert to X-ray crystallography, a transformation made stronger by the revelatory derivation of the α-helix motif in proteins by Linus Pauling. What attracted Jim was that Pauling had relied on model building, constrained by bond angles and other parameters of the atoms. Jim was convinced he could use the same method to solve the structure of DNA if only he could have access to X-ray crystallographic data. Three laboratories were possibilities. He quickly whittled these down to one by reasoning that Pauling at Caltech would not be interested in a "mathematically deficient biologist," and as his interaction with Wilkins in Naples had been less than dazzling, it left only Max Perutz at the Cavendish Laboratory in Cambridge. Jim wrote to Luria who, by chance, met John Kendrew, also of the Cavendish and reported back to Jim that Kendrew was "...quite anxious to have somebody like you." The Cambridge group was, Luria thought, "...sounder than Astbury and Bernal," who were the other world leaders in X-ray crystallography.[4]

Jim's intended move into X-ray crystallography at Cambridge did not sit well with Paul Weiss, Chairman of the Merck Fellowship of the National Research Council. To add to the complications, Jim took up residence in Cambridge before contacting the NRC. Weiss was not pleased that Jim was changing both fields and countries, and perhaps in the back of his mind were his ambivalent memories of Jim as a student in his zoology course at Chicago. Weiss recollected many years later that Jim "was (or appeared to be) completely indifferent to anything that went on in class; he never took any notes and yet at the end of the course he came [out] on top of the class." In January 1952, it seemed that Jim's Fellowship was to be treated as a new application and would be granted, but by March, it was clear that this was not going to happen. It took hard work and string-pulling on Luria's part to finesse the change. "As for Paul Weiss," wrote Luria to Jim, "I incline to agree with your definition, although being less British than you are, I would call him a 'damn son-of-a-bitch' rather than a 'bloody bastard'."

It took only some six months for Jim to develop his life-long Anglophilia, for he rapidly fell under the spell of Cambridge, the most beautiful place he had ever seen: "From my first day in the lab I knew I would not leave Cambridge for a long time..." But it was not the beauty of the place that kept him "...for I had immediately discovered the fun of talking to Francis Crick." The two of them, according to Crick, "...hit it off immediately..." and so the most famous partnership in biology—perhaps in all of science—was under way.

Jim's Cool Reception among the British Geneticists

Avrion Mitchison

Windeyer Institute of Medical Science

Jim Watson's travels in the UK during the 1950s brought him into contact with eminent geneticists, whom he found disappointing for their lack of enthusiasm for DNA (Olby 2003). He mentions visiting Conrad Waddington (1905–1975) in Edinburgh in 1953 and remarks that he was surprised to find Waddington "indifferent to the double helix" (Watson 2001). I don't recall him mentioning my uncle J.B.S. Haldane (1902–1964) whom he might also have met, well known among Jim's Cambridge set for having published a book titled *The Biochemistry of Genetics* in 1954 without mentioning DNA. These were men whom I much admired, and the reasons for their lack of interest intrigue me. I give the dates to make clear that these were not old dodderers, but rather at that time were at the peak of their activities and influence. Nor were they alone in their unsatisfactory response to Jim's great discovery. Other eminent figures in the landscape of British genetics who more or less shared their view were R.A. Fisher (1890–1962) at Cambridge; E.B. "Henry" Ford (1901–1988) at Oxford; the eminent evolutionist Julian Huxley (1887–1975); leading experts in cytogenetics Cyril Darlington (1903–1981) and Michael White (1910–1983); and Fisher's ex-colleague Robert Race (1907–1984), who remained in London and, with his wife Ruth Sanger, studied the genetics of human blood groups. All of them were Fellows of the Royal Society, whose lives and discoveries are written up in the Society's Biographical Memoirs (http://www.royalsoc.ac.uk/library/obitspage.htm). To catch the tone of that generation, I recommend Bryan Clarke's delicious account of "Henry" Ford (Clarke 1995).

My credentials for writing about these men are that I was raised in a nest of biologists: Grandfather John Scott Haldane was a physiologist (for further particulars, *vide* Aldous Huxley's caricature of him in *Antic Hay* [1923]); of my two elder brothers, one became an authority on tuberculosis and the other on the cell cycle; and Aldous and Julian Huxley were family friends. From this promising material, I early developed an obsessive interest in scientific instances of the human comedy. What is now called a gap year was spent in my uncle's (J.B.S. Haldane) department in University College London, where the principal entertainment in that gray war time was to listen to him and Fisher bashing one another at meetings of the Genetical Society. Ostensibly they argued about statistical calculations, but really it was about Marxism versus eugenics (Fisher proposed that the family allowance be directly rather than inversely proportional to income!).[1] Fisher dined with me in Magdalen College, where the dons were

AVRION MITCHISON

Avrion Mitchison grew up in an atmosphere saturated with science. His grandfather was the physiologist John Scott Haldane, and his maternal uncle was J.B.S. Haldane. His mother, Naomi, who studied science at Oxford, wrote extensively and prolifically and, as she put it, "throughout my life,...kept bumping into scientists"—including the young Jim Watson, who during his time at Cambridge was a visitor to Carradale, the Mitchison house in Argyll, Scotland.

Such early and deep immersion in science could be regarded as unsophisticated brainwashing or sophisticated stimulation. Either way, it had the intended effect: Av Mitchison, like his two older brothers, became a scientist. At Oxford, his tutor was Peter Medawar who guided him to immunology, still a box of infinite blackness in the late 1940s. In the years following his postdoctoral work in the Sonneborn laboratory at Indiana, Mitchison worked, taught, and lectured at Edinburgh, Harvard, Stanford, and University College London, where from 1971 to 1991, he was Professor of Zoology. During this period, he discovered that transplantation immunity could be transferred by sensitized cells, so providing the key evidence relating transplantation immunity to delayed-type hypersensitivity. He devised a method for identifying mixtures of cells of different genotypes in vivo and used it to show that the "radiation recovery factor" is a graft of living cells and not a humoral agent. Finally, he showed that persistence of immune tolerance depends on persistence of antigen. From 1991 until his retirement in 1996, Av Mitchison was the Founding Director of the Deutches Rheuma-Forschungs Zentrum in Berlin.

disappointed to find that this giant of the mathematical intellect would admit only to keeping numerous mice.

I assisted Michael White, whom I much admired for his harvesting of elm branches in central London for the sake of the midge whose chromosomes he studied in such minute detail. Later, at Oxford, I went to Ford's lectures on ecological genetics, which placed evolution at the center of science and convinced us that evolution was not just in the past but going on all around us. He must be the last man (and possibly the first) to walk through the passages of a science department in full morning dress, announcing that he was required to attend the Privy Council. I also began my research career with Race, learning how to type blood, the starting point of immunogenetics.

Why did these men take so cool a view of DNA? It surely cannot be that they were simply too busy with their own tasks—the prior-engagement theory of sluggishness—and it certainly was not because they were not bright enough. My belief is that they differed from Jim more deeply, in style of thought and consequently in choice of objectives and means of approach. In summary, they were particularists, and Jim is a generalist. Their style of work was to choose a particular problem, to work on it for a limited period of time, and then to move on. In contrast, Jim chose to work on the most general problem in biology, the nature of genetic material. He was lucky to choose DNA, as genes could easily have turned out to be made of RNA or even protein, and the simplicity and generality would have been lacking. As it is, DNA has turned out to be far the most general material in biology. The manner in which it replicates and translates constitutes biology's ground rules. These rules have had a hugely unifying effect, cutting across the division of biology into separate areas of animals, plants, and microorganisms. They allow us to think in much the same way about areas as diverse as development of shape, resistance to infection, and physical versus cultural inheritance. The structure of DNA has had as broad an impact as Darwin's theory of evolution.

Jim's life work has been to foster these developments. One can only speculate whether it was a generalist character that made him follow this path, or whether it was the other way round, with a choice of subject that molded his life. Probably a bit of both. Mulling over those British geneticists, one is struck by the influence of upbringing: respect for learning acquired by upbringing in a rectory (Fisher, Ford), and late entry in science after a classical education (Ford, Haldane). Late entry seems to be a recipe for subsequent flexibility, the ability to move on from subject to subject.

A bunch of true English eccentrics, then, set the tone of the British genetics outside the privileged domain of the Cavendish Laboratory where Jim worked, where, of course, there were no geneticists. (It was one of Jim's contributions that he introduced an approach to genetics based on Delbrück, Luria, and Hershey and the Phage Group, rather than the British model.) So what do they tell us about sociology of particularism and its contrast with generalism?

- *Vision.* Generalists tend to denounce the particularists for lack of vision. In defense, the particularists plead that far from lacking vision, they need a special sort of vision that the generalists lack. They have to be able to pick a worthwhile problem out of the multitude offered by nature. Every important question, they argue, can best be answered by picking the right biological system (this is sometimes called the comparative method). White picked his midge not in the spirit of a stamp collector, but as a test case for how little genetic material is needed to support somatic cell life.

- *Strategy.* The happy hunting grounds of particularists are wild nature and medical science, and both invite the same sort of case-by-case investigation, for example, the work of Race and Fisher on the blood groups of humans. Right now, the application of mathematics to biology is at an interesting stage. Fisher and Haldane tended to develop particular methods for particular problems (the latter more than the former). My guess is that use of the Hopf bifurcation may transcend the particular.[2]

- *The Darwinian tradition.* British geneticists pride themselves on following in the tradition of "treasure your exceptions," a style of research that is necessarily particularist. They enthuse about the beauty of the English countryside, and the rich opportunity offered by the flora and fauna of its hedgerows, meadows, and streams. The same sort of thing is heard in the United States, although wild nature is altogether more formidable there.

- *Personality.* The Genetical Society used to be a quarrelsome place because it attracted really difficult personalities. My view is that particularist research is an excellent occupation for such people, as the damage that they can do there is limited. They are no good in generalist areas, as there they need to inspire a team.

- *Life on the plateau.* These personality traits are highly adapted to working in a part of science that has reached a funding plateau and has come, perhaps, something of a backwater. Most of the papers published by those British geneticists had no more than two authors because the particularist takes one student at a time, and so needs less money. Nor do they leave a trail of postdocs searching for a job in a static field. By contrast, a generalist operating at full tilt can be quite destructive.

- **Periodicity.** Do periodic events spur fresh outbursts of generalism? I have in mind new developments like the bond angles and lengths that made possible the Crick-Watson approach to DNA, or the sequencing methods that have changed the face of genetics. Possibly, but my guess is that "breaking the paradigm" has more to it than that.

- **Wisdom.** Senior faculty do not welcome the prospect of their ideas being relegated to the attic, particularly when their junior's mission of simplifying the subject strikes them as a cheap trick to wow the students.

The contrast between the British geneticists and the Jim that I knew at Cambridge was enormous. What struck me were his warmth and enthusiasm, the lack of boastfulness, and the vision of where the miraculous structure of DNA would take biology. At the same time, I found it hard to imagine anyone among all those eminent geneticists who would share that enthusiasm, particularly as I walked past Henry Ford's closed door back in Oxford. All my family liked Jim a lot, but found him something of an innocent abroad, interested in British life but a bit baffled. Later, we were amused by his efforts in *The Double Helix* to paint himself, quite misleadingly, as a villain (Watson 1968).

Let me mention a specific difficulty that Conrad Waddington and Peter Medawar had with DNA. In those days, both of them were keen on plasmagenes. These were imagined to be some kind of cytoplasmic genetic material that would be inherited from cell to cell, which could explain long-term differentiation of proliferating cells. Medawar thought they could explain cell-to-cell spread of pigmentation in guinea pig

Jim Watson as best man at Avrion Mitchison's wedding, Isle-of-Skye, July 1957. (From left) Caroline Stewart (bridesmaid), Annabel McPherson (bridesmaid), Avrion Mitchison, Lorna Martin (bride), Jim Watson, Patricia McPherson (bridesmaid). (Courtesy of N. Avrion Mitchison.)

skin. The model was Sonneborn's killer-determinant particles in *Paramecium*. I too loved this idea, and decided to postdoc with Tracy Sonneborn, with encouragement from Jim who had enjoyed his time in Indiana University. The model collapsed when Ruth Dippel isolated and characterized mutants of the killer-determinant particles (Dippell 1950). After Judith Dilts found DNA in the cytoplasmic killer-determinant particles, they were relegated to the status of parasitic bacteria (Dilts 1976). The collapse of plasmagenes was a disappointment, although for me, knowing Sonneborn, experience with *Paramecium* and life at Indiana University were all well worthwhile.[3]

Waddington had a second preoccupation, with the canalization of development and its counterpart "genetic assimilation." The latter term has a sinister ring of Lamarkism, but that wasn't what Waddington meant. He was testing the hypothesis that gross perturbation, for instance, growing *Drosophila* on semitoxic salt concentrations, might shake embryos out of their normal strictly regulated development and reveal new genetic possibilities, a possibility of practical importance in animal breeding. He made some progress, but the real breakthrough occurred only recently, when knockout of heat shock proteins in *Drosophila* was found to reveal new evolutionary possibilities (McLaren 1999). Here again, Waddington was interested in unconventional forms of heredity. I wonder whether Jim missed out on something during his visit to Edinburgh, although admittedly, Waddington required patience in the listener.

Where in Europe might Jim's ideas have found a warmer welcome? In Paris, chez Monod, goes without saying. A more challenging question concerns Germany, where Norbert Hilschmann (now at Goettingen) and H.-J. Rheinberger (Berlin) have told me the history. Adolf Butenandt (1903–1995) became Director of the KWI (Kaiser-Wilhelm-Institut) for Biochemistry in Berlin in 1936, a feat that reflects his Nazi sympathies. He was a steroid chemist who received the Nobel Prize for Chemistry in 1939 for his work on the structures of androsterone and progesterone. His achievements in molecular biology are less widely known. At the KWI, he started work together with Alfred Kuhn on the one gene:one protein rule (please see Endnote 2 to Francis Crick's contribution), taking a pigment polymorphism in the eyes of the moth *Ephestia* as material. They showed that the ommochromes obey the one:one rule, prior to the work of Boris Ephrussi and George Beadle in *Neurospora*. Another line was to start work on TMV (tobacco mosaic virus), which led after the war to the structure of TMV protein as determined by Gerhard Schramm and Gerhardt Braunitzer. In the same period, Nicolai Timoféeff-Ressovsky at the KWI for Brain Research in Berlin-Buch, jointly with Lise Meitner, and K.G. Zimmer and Max Delbrück at the KWI for Chemistry in Berlin used radiation mutagenesis to estimate by target theory the size of the gene. Taken as a piece, this work represents a root of molecular biology as valid as the bacteriophage genetics that Delbrück started in the United States; in both cases, the aim was to determine the complete structure of a minimal genetic organism. Jim began his research career in phage genetics, and there is some irony in the fact that he never got around (so far as I know) to visiting molecular biology's other starting place.

The story has a happy ending. Now that DNA technology is so widely used to explore evolution, the schism between DNA-based generalism and Darwinian particularism is closing. As a participant in this enterprise, I take pleasure in noting that genetics is again a unified subject.

REFERENCES

Clarke B.C. 1995. Edmund Brisco Ford. *Biographical memoirs of the royal society.* **41:** 145–168.

Dilts J.A. 1976. Covalently closed, circular DNA in kappa endosymbionts of *Paramecium. Genet. Res.* **27:** 161–170.

Dippell R.V. 1950. Mutation of the killer cytoplasmic factor in *Paramecium aurelia. Heredity* **4:** 165–187.

Haldane J.B.S. 1954. *The biochemistry of genetics.* Allen & Unwin, London.

Huxley A. 1923. *Antic hay.* Chatto & Windus, London.

McLaren A. 1999. Too late for the midwife toad: Stress, variability and Hsp90. *Trends Genet.* **15:** 169–171.

Olby R. 2003. Quiet debut for the double helix. *Nature* **421:** 402–405.

Watson J.D. 1968. *The double helix: A personal account of the discovery of the structure of DNA.* Weidenfeld and Nicolson, London.

Watson J.D. 2001. *Genes, girls, and Gamow: After* The Double Helix. Alfred A. Knopf, New York.

NAOMI MITCHISON'S RECOLLECTIONS OF JIM WATSON

Naomi Mitchison, the mother of Av Mitchison, presided over Carradale, a rather grand house in Scotland. An early feminist, she was a vocal campaigner for women's rights and actively lobbied for birth control. She wrote books of poetry, biographies, and more than 70 novels, the most controversial of which, *We Have Been Warned* (1935, Constable & Co. Ltd.), explored aspects of sexual behavior (rape, seduction) and abortion that were not topics for public discussion in Britain at the time. The manuscript was rejected by several publishers and was ultimately published in a censored form.

Jim visited Carradale in 1956 and almost 40 years later, Naomi wrote of her memories of him.

> *Jim was a gentle & affectionate man. They were all here in this house talking about the double helix (is that the word I mean?). In a corner of this house there is an old pouffe that I sat on while the young men argued & occasionally I interrupt[ed] to say that they must make a better way of explaining what they think... . I remember this well & how I would sit in the middle of the excitement & say "Yes, but-." The house here is much the same (in spite of a fire some years after that) & I still have the thing I sat on near the floor but arguing with the men standing round. It was all quite difficult to accept at that time, an entirely new way of looking at being alive.*

> *Yes, Jim was happy here. He liked the house full of books and babies, when anything might go if it was for learning or happiness. And I think he knew that was the world I tried to make real.*

> *We were all so young (though we didn't think we were) and dear Jim was a nice young man whom anyone would like to flirt with. And I suppose I was also an attractive young female. If you come here you would sit on the same sofa that Jim liked to flop into. And how they talked!*

> *I remember that Jim was more or less in love with me, &, though I always liked him, I got rather irritated by his wanting to come close—Where is Jim now? I hadn't been in touch with him.*

Extracts of letters from Naomi Mitchison to Joe Sambrook

Naomi Mitchison died in 1999 at the age of 101. Below is a portion from the letter above.

April 28

I remember this well & how I would sit in the middle of the excitement & say "Yes, but—" The house here is much the same (in spite of a fire some years after that) & I still have the thing I sat on near the floor but arguing with the men standing round. It was all quite difficult to ~~accept~~ accept at that time, an entirely new way of looking at being alive.

Our Work on Virus Structure

Francis Crick

Salk Institute for Biological Studies

In 1935 (when Jim was about 7 and I was an undergraduate), Wendell Stanley published a remarkable paper about tobacco mosaic virus (TMV) (Stanley 1935). He reported that he had obtained very thin, elongated crystals of TMV. The virus was pure and highly infectious. A small amount rubbed on the back of a tobacco plant (or certain other plants) produced large amounts of infectious virus. Moreover, there were slightly different strains of TMV that bred true. It seemed highly reasonable that the virus was, at least in some sense, alive and yet it could form crystals. At the time, a crystallized virus seemed almost a contradiction in terms. Remember the old question—animal? vegetable? or mineral?—and minerals are crystalline.

Stanley claimed that his TMV crystals were pure protein, but this was not surprising because almost everyone at that time thought that genes would turn out to be made of protein, and although it was not then strictly known that viruses had genes, it seemed only too plausible that the key to "life" might involve pure protein. Stanley's paper was greeted with astonishment—How could a living thing be crystallized?

The two leading British TMV workers were Fred Bawden and William Pirie. Bawden was a cheerful, extroverted character, easy to get along with. Pirie was just the opposite. They were naturally skeptical of Stanley's claims, but in a paper published in *Nature* in 1936, together with two well-known crystallographers, J.D. Bernal and I. Fankuchen, they confirmed that TMV crystallized, although the crystals were strictly paracrystalline (Bawden et al. 1936). The X-ray diffraction pattern suggested that the virus consisted of a large number of similar subunits, and extended to fairly small spacings. More importantly, Bawden and Pirie showed that TMV was not pure protein but contained several percent by weight of RNA. In turn, Stanley confirmed this finding.[1]

By 1947, when I had stopped working for the British Admiralty and had gone to Cambridge to start on biological research, things were a little different. There was George Beadle and Edward Tatum's one gene:one enzyme hypothesis[2] and, more important, the claim by Avery, MacLeod, and McCarty published in 1944 that the factor that could transform the appearance of bacterial colonies from rough to smooth was pure DNA, not protein (Avery et al. 1944). They made no broad claims in print, but, in a letter to his brother, Avery had written, "sounds like a virus, may be a gene." Their result was widely known but not entirely believed. Was transformation really due to a protein impurity (as Alfred Mirsky quite wrongly insisted) or was it really DNA, but some sort of freak case?[3] In any event, the evidence suggested that DNA was a specific part of transforming factor, not necessarily the whole. Perhaps, as Mirsky believed, *part* of the specificity was carried by protein and part by DNA.

Francis H.C. Crick

Francis Crick's family moved from sleepy Northampton to cosmopolitan London after World War I, when the family's shoe factory was forced to close down. Francis studied physics at University College, London, as an undergraduate in the 1930s. His graduate studies on the viscosity of water were interrupted by World War II, during which Francis worked for the Admiralty, mostly researching and designing magnetic and acoustic mines. By 1947, he had become fascinated by the line "between the living and the nonliving" and, with financial support from his family and a studentship from the Medical Research Council, moved to the Strangeways Laboratory, Cambridge, where he attempted to measure the properties of cytoplasm by using magnets to move small particles of magnetic core taken up by cultured chick embryo fibroblasts. By 1949, Francis had completed the migration from physics into chemistry and biology and joined the X-ray crystallographic unit at the Cavendish Laboratory of the Medical Research Council. The unit was to study protein structure, and Francis' new colleagues included Max Perutz and John Kendrew. Francis again enrolled as a research student, obtaining a Ph.D. in 1954 while at Gonville and Caius College with a thesis "X-ray Diffraction: Polypeptides and Proteins."

Jim Watson's arrival at the MRC Unit in 1952 concentrated Francis' attention onto the structure of nucleic acids. Like prospectors for gold a century earlier, the pair shared a certain intellectual *joie de vivre*, an indifference to social boundaries and to scientific convention. Above all, they believed that the structure of DNA would be the key to understanding the replication of genes.

Francis' collaboration with Jim Watson lasted only a few years, as their scientific interests quickly diverged: Jim wanted to understand the "riddle of RNA structure," while Francis worked on solving the genetic code. In 1961, he, Leslie Barnett, and Sydney Brenner provided genetic proof that amino acid sequences of proteins were stored in DNA in a triplet code (Crick, *Nature 192:* 1227–1232 [1961]). Earlier, however, Francis had proposed the adaptor hypothesis, which explained how small RNA molecules could act as intermediaries between nucleic acids and amino acids. This was described in a paper written in January 1955 for private circulation (On Degenerate Templates and the Adaptor Hypothesis: A Note for the RNA Tie Club) but not published in the formal scientific literature. Crick states in his book *What Mad Pursuit* (1988, Basic-Books) that "it is my most influential unpublished paper." But there are many other ideas as well: the Wobble hypothesis, which explains why transfer RNAs recognize more than one codon through non-Watson-Crick base pairings in the third position of a triplet (Crick, *J. Mol. Biol. 19:* 548–555 [1966]), and directed panspermia, which made the controversial suggestion that microorganisms from elsewhere in the universe were the source of life on earth (Crick and Orgel, *Icarus 19:* 341–346 [1973]).

In the late 1960s, Francis left genetics, working on gradients in embryos and then, after moving to the Salk Institute in 1976, on cognitive science, particularly the nature of consciousness and the memory of visual images.

A voluble man with a booming voice, a braying double-forte laugh, and a keen eye for beautiful women, Crick is a man of immense charm, sharp intellect, and wit.

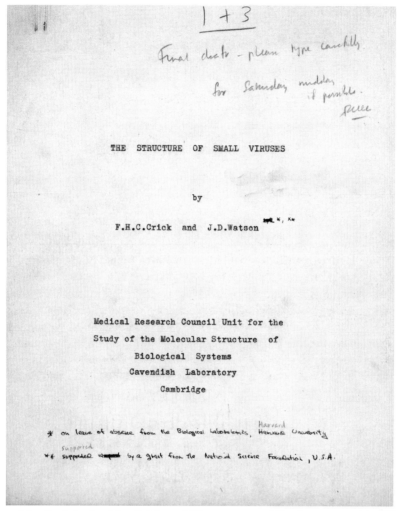

Title page of the final draft of the Crick and Watson paper, "The Structure of Small Viruses," published in Nature, *1956. (Courtesy of the James D. Watson Collection, CSHL Archives.)*

Very careful work by Rollin Hotchkiss showed that, as had been claimed, the transforming factor was indeed pure DNA[4] (Hotchkiss et al. 1952). The much dirtier blender experiment by Alfred Hershey and Martha Chase on bacteriophage infection made transforming factor seem less like a freak, and in 1953, the proposed double-helical structure of DNA, together with better knowledge about the base composition and typical size of DNA, made it obvious that DNA alone might be the genetic material.

So why bother about the exact structure of viruses? It now seemed that the way to think of the simpler viruses was as a small collection of genes, as DNA or RNA, packed in a protein box. From this point of view, the exact structure of the box was only of secondary importance, since the nucleic acid was where most of the action was. But this assumes that all these ideas were by then firmly established, which was far from being the case, so it was not unreasonable to ask questions about all aspects of virus structure.

By 1953, several other viruses had been crystallized, including bushy stunt virus and turnip yellow mosaic virus. Both these viruses crystallized in a unit cell that had the shape of a cube. From this very fragmentary data could one say anything about the general principles underlying the structures of small viruses?

Partly because of the α-helix of proteins, proposed by Linus Pauling,[5] Jim was convinced that many biological structures were helical, i.e., based on a screw axis. Jim learned how to take X-ray diffraction photographs, and in a paper published in 1954 (Watson 1954), he presented suggestive evidence that the rods of TMV (visible in the electron microscope) had a screw axis, although he could only determine the parameters of the screw approximately. In 1955, Rosalind Franklin confirmed Jim's suggestion, and obtained a better estimate of the screw. She also proposed that the RNA was not on the axis of the virus, but about 40 Å (Franklin 1955, 1956) from the center, probably in a groove in the protein shell.

All this implied that the rods of TMV consisted of a helical arrangement of fairly small protein subunits. An obvious generalization was that the same would be broadly true for small, round viruses, except that in those cases, the symmetry would be cubic. Crystallographers were familiar with cubic symmetry, and they knew that mirror planes and center of symmetry were not allowed for biological molecules such as protein and nucleic acids, as they would have turned a D-residue into an L-residue, and vice versa.[6]

There are just three cubic point groups with rotation axes only, described as 23, 432, and 532, but crystallographers had somewhat neglected 532 because (apart from freak cases) a crystal cannot itself have a fivefold axis. The number of "asymmetric units" in these three point groups is 12, 24, and 60, respectively. Jim and I realized that a virus possessing cubic symmetry must necessarily be built from a regular aggregation of smaller symmetric building blocks (i.e., proteins) and this can only be done in a number of ways (Watson and Crick 1956). Jim and I thought that the 532 looked the most likely shape, as it allowed the greatest number of asymmetric units.

We invented a general argument as to why the shell of the virus would not be just one very large protein, but must consist of multiple subunits. Even if the RNA (or DNA) was packed in the center, as compactly as possible, it had to have a certain minimum volume. To encase this in a protein shell, the protein would have to be at least 10 Å thick, and probably more, and so would need to have a considerable mass. If we then made the (at that time) unwarranted assumption that all this protein had to be encoded by the viral nucleic acid, and that at least three nucleotides would be needed to code for each amino acid, then it was easy to show that only protein of a limited size could be coded in this way, and so the only way to build a protein shell was to use multiple copies of the protein (or proteins). Such a shell could most easily be built as helical rods, or fairly spherical polyhedra, the protein subunits being related by symmetry, so that the same packing was used over and over again. In short, small viruses were either rods or "spheres" because those were the shapes most easily obtained by packing together identical subunits to form a box.[7]

It is difficult to realize now how these fairly obvious arguments seemed at that time to be highly speculative. Was the RNA in TMV really its genetic material? There was just one small clue. Harris and Knight (1952) had examined the carboxy end-groups of TMV protein and found that the virus particle had about 2500 terminal groups, all threonine. When they infected tobacco leaves with this modified virus, to their surprise (but not to ours) the viral particles produced all had terminal threonine again. Obviously, as we saw it, this was because it was the RNA that was coding for the protein.

After a year at Caltech, and after his appointment to Harvard, Jim took a year's leave of absence and returned to Cambridge for the academic year 1955 to 1956. Jim had hoped that he and I would work together on the three-dimensional structure of RNA, as Alex Rich was also visiting us. As it turned out, Alex and I stumbled on the structure of polyglycine II (Crick and Rich 1955) and then went on to propose a structure for collagen (Rich and Crick 1955), so we never got round to working on RNA structure. Later on, Jim did take X-ray pictures of polyadenylic acid and produced convincing evidence that it was a double helix, but of a different type from DNA.

Jim and I had decided to write a lengthy review of our ideas on virus structure, even though the experimental evidence supporting them was rather thin. My son Michael made model polyhedra for us out of cardboard. We got as far as a first draft of this review, a copy of which I still have.

At about the same time, Don Caspar was analyzing crystals of tomato bushy stunt virus by X-ray diffraction. His photographs showed that the crystals had a cubic space group. By good fortune, one of his crystals was somewhat disordered. It had a pattern of diffuse reflections that contained ten symmetrically arranged spots. This suggested that the virus particle had fivefold as well as two- and threefold symmetry and that the virus probably had the point group 532.[8]

This fortunate observation convinced Jim and me that our ideas were indeed on the right lines. We decided to abandon the review we were writing. Instead, we wrote up a shorter outline of our ideas. This was published in *Nature*, in March 1956 (Watson and Crick 1956) together with a letter from Don Caspar (1956) describing his results on tomato bushy stunt virus. We also published a short account in a CIBA Foundation Symposium, held in London in March 1956 (Crick and Watson 1957).

There was still no strong evidence that the RNA of TMV coded for its protein. The obvious experiment was to take two strains of TMV apart and combine the RNA of one strain with the protein of the other. I tried to persuade Roy Markham and John Smith, working on viruses at the Molteno Institute in Cambridge, to try this, but they obvi-

Michael Stoker, Jim Watson, Milton Sarton, and Francis Crick at the 1956 Ciba Foundation Symposium, "The Nature of Viruses." (©The Novartis Foundation, formerly the Ciba Foundation. Reproduced with permission.)

ously thought I was some kind of crackpot. Fortunately, exactly this experiment was carried out by Fraenkel-Conrat and Singer (1956, 1957) at Berkeley. Almost simultaneously, Gerhard Schramm in Tübingen (Gierer and Schramm 1956) showed that the RNA of TMV was infectious by itself. At last, there were really key experiments to support our ideas.

Jim has recounted in his book, *Genes, Girls, and Gamow* (Watson 2001), how he and André Lwoff played a practical joke on Robley Williams who was reporting the Berkeley results at the CIBA Symposium in London in March 1956. They sent him a faked telegram that read "TMV PROTEIN INFECTIOUS—BE CAUTIOUS—WENDELL," supposedly from Wendell Stanley, the head of the Berkeley Virus Laboratory. But they relented and told Robley the telegram was a fake before he had to speak on the topic.

A virus with 532 symmetry is made up of 60 identical asymmetric units, but it soon became apparent that small viruses had many more identical protein subunits than that. The key idea was beautifully laid out by Don Caspar and Aaron Klug. They proposed that there is some flexibility in the way the protein subunits of the viral shell can fit together, and enumerated all the more probable ways that this might happen. Almost all small viruses fit into this framework.

Jim had proposed a plausible mechanism for the assembly of TMV, but by careful measurements of the partly assembled protein, Klug was able to show that the actual mechanism was rather more complicated.

In April 1956, Rosalind Franklin, Aaron Klug, and I attended the International Conference of Crystallography in Madrid. Caspar's paper "The Molecular Viruses as Point-Group Crystals" (Caspar et al. 1956) described how his experimental results and our theories could be harmonized. After the conference, Rosalind, my wife Odile, and I toured Southern Spain together, travelling by bus and train. Jim meanwhile journeyed to Israel, and then on to Egypt, where he went by night sleeper up the Nile to Luxor. He seems to have had a wonderful time visiting all these exotic places. Despite all these travels, Jim felt at home in England, so much so that he forgot to renew his visa in time, and was fined 5 pounds by Lady Adrian.[9] Looking back, one can see that the structure of the protein shell is of much less importance than the exact nature of the viral genes and how they act. This had to wait for new technologies for sequencing nucleic acid. What Jim and I did was to provide a framework of ideas for coping with the various problems, a framework which at the time seemed almost revolutionary but now seems completely obvious.

REFERENCES

Avery O.T., MacLeod C.M., and McCarty M. 1944. Studies on the chemical nature of the substance inducing transformation of pneumococcal types: Induction of transformation by a desoxyribonucleic acid fraction isolated from pneumococcus Type III. *J. Exp. Med.* **79:** 137–158.

Bawden F.C., Pirie N.W., Bernal J.D., and Fankuchen I. 1936. Liquid crystalline substances from virus-infected plants. *Nature* **138:** 1051–1052.

Caspar D.L.D. 1956. Structure of bushy stunt virus. *Nature* **177:** 475–476.

Caspar D.L.D., Crick F.H.C., and Watson J.D. 1956. The molecular viruses considered as point-group crystals. In *International union of crystallography symposium* at Madrid. (Publisher and editor not stated.)

Crick F.H.C. and Rich A. 1955. Structure of polyglycine-II. *Nature* **176:** 780–781.

Crick F.H.C. and Watson J.D. 1957. Virus structure: General principles. In *CIBA Foundation Symposium on the nature of viruses* (ed. G.E.W. Wolstenholme and E.C.P. Millar), pp. 5–13. Churchill, London.

Fraenkel-Conrat H. 1956. The role of the nucleic acid in the reconstruction of active tobacco mosaic virus. *J. Am. Chem. Soc.* **78:** 882–883.

Fraenkel-Conrat H. and Singer B.A. 1957. Virus reconstruction, Part 2. Combination of protein and nucleic acid from different strains. *Biochim. Biophys. Acta* **24:** 540–548.

Franklin R.E. 1955. Structure of tobacco mosaic virus. *Nature* **175:** 379–381.

Franklin R.E. 1956. Location of the ribonucleic acid in the tobacco mosaic particle. *Nature* **177:** 928–930.

Gierer A. and Schramm G. 1956. Infectivity of ribonucleic acid from tobacco mosaic virus. *Nature* **177:** 702–703.

Harris J.I. and Knight C.A. 1952. Action of carbonoxypeptidase of tobacco mosaic virus. *Nature* **170:** 613–614.

Hotchkiss R.D. 1952. The biological nature of the bacterial transforming factors. *Exp. Cell Res.* (suppl.) **2:** 383–389.

Rich A. and Crick F.H.C. 1955. Structure of collagen. *Nature* **176:** 915–916.

Stanley W.M. 1935. Isolation of a crystalline protein possessing the properties of tobacco mosaic virus. *Science* **81:** 644–645.

Watson J.D. 1954. The structure of tobacco mosaic virus. Part 1. X-ray evidence of a helical arrangement of sub-units around the longitudinal axis. *Biochim. Biophys. Acta* **13:** 10–19.

Watson J.D. 2001. *Genes, girls, and Gamow:* After The Double Helix, p. 217. Alfred A. Knopf, New York.

Watson J.D. and Crick F.H.C. 1956. Structure of small viruses. *Nature* **177:** 473–475.

One Day in the Cavendish *(April 1, 1953)*

Some details of the discovery of the structure of DNA have been described by Jim Watson in *The Double Helix* and by Francis Crick in his autobiography *What Mad Pursuit*, but neither are contemporary accounts—Jim's was written 12 years and Francis' 20 years after the event.[1] We do not have even a contemporary scientific commentary since *Nature*'s "News and Views" section in the 1950s did not include commentaries on published papers. However, a contemporary account, written by Gerard Pomerat to Warren Weaver, Director of the Natural Sciences division of the Rockefeller Foundation, has been found in the Rockefeller Archives.

The Rockefeller Foundation played a major part in promoting molecular biology and has been described as acting as "...midwife at what was later seen to be its [molecular biology's] birth."[2] Warren Weaver[3] supported projects dealing with the "mathematics, physics, and chemistry of vital processes", including Linus Pauling's work on proteins, Theodor Svedberg's development of the ultracentrifuge, Dorothy Wrinch's doomed mathematical approach to protein structure, and William Astbury's X-ray crystallographic studies of proteins and DNA. It is not surprising, then, that the Rockefeller Foundation funded the structural studies of proteins by Lawrence Bragg, Max Perutz, and John Kendrew in the Cavendish Laboratory in the Department of Physics of the University of Cambridge.

Pomerat, Warren Weaver's Assistant Director, was there to learn how the work on hemoglobin was going (not very well), but his visit on April 1, 1953, just five weeks after the discovery of the double helix, incidentally provides a vivid description of the two young men who "bubble over about their new structure." They were putting "the finishing touches on a huge model about six feet tall," presumably the model that appears in the famous photographs by Antony Barrington Brown. (There is considerable confusion about what model was built when.[4] The first model was very small, just a single turn, built to measure the bond lengths and to check that it made sense stereochemically. There was another small model that Jim took with him to the 1953 Cold Spring Harbor Symposium and is shown in Plate 2 of the *Proc. Roy. Soc. A* paper at the end of this section. It featured 45 years later in the Apple "Think Different" advertising campaign.)

Pomerat wrote that he advised Bragg that Alexander Todd (later Lord Todd of Trumpington) should inspect the model for chemical accuracy. (Todd was the premier organic chemist in Britain—he won the Nobel Prize in Chemistry in 1957 for his work on nucleic acids, including the synthesis of ATP and ADP.) Bragg, Kendrew, and Perutz had suffered considerable embarrassment in April, 1951, when Pauling and Corey published the structure of the α-helix motif of proteins. Not only had the Cavendish team failed to come up with the α-helix, but in 1950, Bragg, Kendrew, and Perutz had published a long but inconclusive paper on protein structure, inconclusive because they had failed to realize that peptide bond is planar.[5] Bragg later called the work "...the most ill-planned and abortive in which I have ever been involved."[6] Todd may have seen their models (there is some confusion about this), but in any case, he was not asked specifically about the nature of the peptide bond. Todd later reconstructed the conversation he had with Bragg, writing that he had asked Bragg: "Don't you take any chemical advice when you do this kind of work?"[7] It explains, perhaps, the contrast noted by Pomerat between the response of Bragg and Perutz to the double helix: "Sir L. has some small reservations about it all (DNA), but the usually cautious Perutz is quite enthusiastic." Perhaps the 1950 paper was still weighing on

Bragg's mind at the time of Pomerat's visit. (Pomerat's account differs from those of Watson and Crick, who write, more plausibly, that it was Bragg who insisted on Todd's review of what they had done.)

Pomerat noted that Bragg that day told Watson and Crick that the manuscript of "A Structure for Deoxyribose Nucleic Acid" could be sent to *Nature*. The manuscript had been completed three days earlier, typed by Elizabeth, Jim's sister, while Odile Crick, Francis' wife drew the iconic, ribbon-diagram of the double helix.[8]

Gerard Roland Pomerat retired in 1967, and while the Rockefeller Foundation noted that he had "...played a significant and highly effective part in virtually all of the major advances which have occurred in the biological science since the war," he has been an obscure figure in the history of molecular biology. Now his memorandum provides us with a Rosencrantz and Guildenstern perspective of two young men who knew that they had discovered the secret of life.

EXTRACT FROM GERARD POMERAT'S DIARY

1 April 1953 (Cambridge)

[Deleted paragraph]

There was at the Cavendish today a great air of excitement for Perutz, and two of the younger men in the department were anxious to show Sir Lawrence (and GRP) what they have been up to in the last week. They believe they have really got the structure of nucleic acid from a crystallographic rather than a chemical standpoint. Their clue came out of the beautiful X-ray diagrams produced in Randall's lab and some of the work which had meanwhile been going on at Cambridge. They are just putting the finishing touches on a huge model about six feet tall which shows that the molecule is made up of two helical chains running parallel to each other and repeating at a distance of 34 Å. The two coils run one above the other, at equal distances from the center, and centripetal to them are a series of direct linkages between pyrimidine and purine rings which in turn are liked to the helices. They have discussed their model with Wilkins of Randall's group and have written up a description of it as a note for *Nature* (which would probably appear in early May) which Sir L. today authorizes them to send. They are particularly excited about the possibility of showing it to Pauling, who will be here this week, but GRP also persuades them to show it to Todd first (and to this Sir L. gives full approval). If this structure were the correct one it would present a very good skeleton on which to affix some of the modern theories of chromosome duplication. Sir L. has some small reservations about it all, but the usually cautious Perutz is quite enthusiastic.

The two other chaps who have been associated with Perutz on the nucleic acid structure are J.D. Watson and F.H.C. Crick. Watson was trained in genetics and biochemistry at the University of Chicago and got his Ph.D. under Luria. He went to Copenhagen on a Merck fellowship and has been at the Cavendish since September 1951. At present is on a Polio Foundation fellowship and in September will return to the USA to work with Delbrück at Caltech. Crick is a physicist trained in chemistry by Andrade at University College. He worked on Navy problems during the war, then in 1946 got an MRC studentship to work with Hughes at the Strangeways. He was too quantitatively minded for Hughes's type of work and came to the Cavendish four years ago. Will get his Ph.D. in X-ray crystallography this summer and is then going to the USA to spend six months with Harker and six months with Pauling. Both young men are somewhat mad hatters who bubble over about their new structure in characteristic Cambridge style and it is hard to realize that one of them is an American. Having in mind the lot that one sees in Bernal's lab it is hard to comprehend why crystallography should show such a sex bias in selecting out good-looking and apparently very stable and well-adjusted young women. The two chaps here are certainly not lacking, however, in either enthusiasm or ability.

[Deleted paragraphs]

Reprinted with permission of Rockefeller Archive Center.

Jim and Syd

Sydney Brenner

The Salk Institute

I have never seen Jim in a restful mood. When I first met him—now more than 50 years ago in the Cavendish Laboratory in Cambridge—we had come to see the DNA model.[1] Francis talked animatedly about it, while Jim hovered behind us most of the time, occasionally uttering a remark, opening letters, rearranging his desk. Later, when I went for a walk with Jim, he strode out at a tremendous pace and I almost had to run to keep up with him. He left the impression with me of a large irritated bird stamping about, pecking here, there, and everywhere. This ornithoscopic view of Jim became much reinforced in later years, especially when Jim stood up to talk. He transfixes the audience with one of those beady-eyed stares before delivering one of those pronouncements for which he is famous. He did this recently at a meeting on cloning and genetic improvement of humans and announced that everything he had heard was "pure crap." It took me a little while to realize what was wrong with this statement; it is that crap must surely be the most impure substance in the entire universe and trying to define the ideal form of crap in terms of purity was not the right way to go!

Although I count myself as one of Jim's friends, we have not spent much time together during the past 50 years. My relationship with Francis and Jim has been very different. I spent many years in what was a scientific partnership with Francis and our scientific interaction continues to this day.[2] My relationship with Jim has been more like that of an ally. On the few times we have talked about science, Jim has told me that I was doing the wrong thing or that the time was not ripe for it. In much the same way as we treated Max Delbrück's disbelief in a theory as the best evidence that it was right, I came to see Jim's admonishments as a sign that I had chosen the correct path.

Jim and I traveled together from Cold Spring Harbor to Pasadena in the late summer of 1954. We spent one night in Boston in sleeping bags in the house that Boris Ephrussi was going to use on his sabbatical at Harvard.[3] There was a tremendous downpour which I later learned was Hurricane Caroline, and I have a distinct memory of getting up early to let some workmen into the house. Jim remained in his sleeping bag with only his head showing, lying absolutely motionless and with such a blank stare on his face that one made a mental note to check up later that he was still alive. The workmen were clearly impressed by the sight and as each passed by with a sidelong look at the body in the bag on the bed, the last man asked me, "Is he OK?" How could one tell them that they were in the presence of one who would be recognized as a giant of twentieth century science and that he was going to be very OK.

After I came to Cambridge, I saw Jim on many occasions when he returned there. And, of course, I saw him on many of my visits to Harvard in the 1960s. These were

SYDNEY BRENNER

Sydney Brenner was born in Germiston, South Africa, and seems to have had science in his genes. He carried out experiments to extract pigments from plants when he was ten years old and published his first paper (in *Nature*) when he was 18 years old. Although his doctorate, like Jim's, was not inspiring, his exposure to the double helix, and more particularly to Jim and Francis Crick, determined his switch to molecular genetics. Brenner has made important contributions in many areas, notably in molecular genetics (mutations, the genetic code, and messenger RNA); the development of *Caenorhabditis elegans*, an hermaphroditic nematode worm, as one of the most important model organisms; and to genomics, again through the use of a model organism, *Fugu*, the Japanese puffer fish. Brenner is famous as a wit and coiner of words, as his essay makes clear. His 2002 Nobel Prize in Physiology or Medicine was long overdue.

Sydney Brenner (right, front) at the 1954 Cold Spring Harbor Phage Meeting, standing in front of Francis Crick and Milislav Demerec. To Sydney's right is Al Hershey. (Photograph by Norton Zinder. Courtesy CSHL Archives.)

the Kennedy years and the beginning of the cult of the celebrity, as extended beyond money and Hollywood to the sciences and the arts. In those years, it was *de rigueur* for Harvard scientists to take up advisory roles in Washington. At one party, I was asked whether I was doing anything like this in England. I hastily invented a job for myself as Scientific Advisor to Princess Margaret.[4] Jim had got himself a job consulting with the Army, and we had a discussion on the advisability of spraying bacteriophage T1 all over the United States. I was worried about laboratories using *E. coli* as this phage was a well-known scourge that survived drying, grew at a prodigious rate, and was impossible to eradicate. For years after this conversation, I studied newspapers to see if any *E. coli* labs had succumbed to the pestilence.

On one of my visits to Harvard, Jim excitedly told me that he was arranging a dinner party for Melina Mercouri and Jules Dassin.[5] She had recently been featured in Ethel Kennedy's swimming pool in a magazine and it fitted with the spirit of the times. After regaling me with details of the menu and his screening of Radcliffe girls who were going to serve at the dinner, Jim said, "You are not invited." No reason was given for this formal disinvitation, and I was left to speculate for years whether it was simply because there was no room for additional guests or because I was not the proper sort of person to be present with the glitterati. There was also the possibility that Jim was worried that I may misbehave and say something to bring discredit on him. He once sent me to a dinner with one of the Trustees of Cold Spring Harbor and said that Alan Hodgkin[6] would be going as well to make sure that I would behave. Actually, Alan got a bit tipsy during the dinner and it was the other way around.

I have seen a lot of Jim after he moved to Cold Spring Harbor and we had extensive interactions during the Recombinant DNA saga and later on the Human Genome Sequencing Project. When we gathered at Asilomar in 1975, Jim announced, after pecking angrily at the committee, that the whole business was a lot of nonsense. However, he had been one of the signatories of the letter proposing the moratorium on the deployment of the technology, and lending his name in this way made the problem of ending the moratorium politically very difficult. I thought Jim was politically naïve, but standing outside everything and saying the unsayable for someone of his stature was very important. It did, however, expose him to the risk of being seen as a weird crank. When he was asked why he signed the moratorium he replied, "I was a jackass," and this opened the possibility that he still was one. Anyway, reason (if it can be called that) triumphed and we were able to declare unanimously that the moratorium was over.

So much has been written on the human genome sequencing and on Jim's role not only in getting it going, but in becoming the first Director of the Human Genome Project at the National Institutes of Health. I recently heard it said that it was a most unlikely role for Jim to assume; many people see him still as an ivory tower research scientist. However, Jim is a very skilled administrator who understands the politics of getting things done. Everything he has done in Cold Spring Harbor testifies to his accomplishments. He knows that you must reach the hearts and minds of people before you go for their pockets and how important it is to convince people that they are direct participants in a collaboration.

I had different views on how we should sequence the human genome, believing that we should do expressed genes first. Jim asked me what such a cDNA project would cost. I replied, "Twenty million, but for you, Jim, I will give a special price of ten million." Jim looked at me, turned his head and said that it wasn't enough money and that nobody will take me seriously. I asked him what he thought the right sum was. "Two hundred million," came the reply, and he was right.

In the last few years and especially as we survive the celebrations of DNA50, Jim has taken to making pronouncements on the genetic improvement of humans. I have heard him say that the Irish could do with genetic improvement, adding quickly that he was half-Irish himself. I think Jim makes these pronouncements because he feels that only he can utter the unutterable. To the extent that we should never say never, I agree with him, but when I contemplate what humanity has achieved by cultural evolution, the idea of trying to do this by outdated biological evolution seems particularly ludicrous. The brain is mightier than the genome. Both Jim and I believe that we are entering upon a new phase of the human sciences where we will, as he put it recently, discover the basis of human nature. Worrier and Warrior, Jim has been the guardian of DNA for the past 50 years. For human beings, we now need to place DNA in the correct context, and only through the interactions of our biology and our histories will we come to understand what makes us what we are and how we can become what we might be.

A Letter to Jim

During the course of a career that lasted for 66 years, Max Perutz came to epitomize all that is best in science. His death, on February 6, 2002, just three weeks after his final letter to Jim (see following page), was followed by a flood of tributes.

From the obituary published in the issue of *Nature* of February 21, 2002.

> It would be difficult to overestimate Perutz' influence on modern biology. His pioneering work solving protein structures, his inspiration of others and his founding and directing the Laboratory of Molecular Biology in Cambridge where he worked until the end of 2001, 22 years after his official retirement, shaped what we know as molecular biology.

From the obituary published in *The Independent* (London) on February 7, 2002.

> Max Perutz was a deeply humane man, loved and admired by his colleagues, who combined that gift with exceptional powers of analysis, planning and leadership. His domed forehead suggested a mighty brain, but his small fingers were neat and dextrous. A robust and confident mountaineer, he studied glacier flow early in his career, so as to work in the Alps. A back injury in middle life ended his skiing, but he retained his love of mountains. While his achievements were crowned with many honours, they rode lightly on his shoulders. He refused any honour that would give him a title, and was known, and invariably addressed by colleagues, as "Max." He lived a quiet and unostentatious life, walking from his home to the laboratory almost daily until a few months before his death. His brain remained razor-sharp, he gave thrilling lectures, and his research continued. Within the last year he had made important contributions to the understanding of Huntington's disease, based on ideas of crystal nucleation.

Linus Pauling, Max Delbrück, and Max Perutz in Pasadena (1976). (Press photograph. Source unknown. Courtesy of Vivien and Robin Perutz.)

Max and Jim were awarded the Nobel Prize in the same year: 1962. However, the two were very different scientists. Max himself remained a committed experimentalist to the end of his life. By contrast, in Horace Judson's *The Eighth Day of Creation* (1996, Cold Spring Harbor Laboratory Press) Max describes Jim "lounging around, arguing about problems instead of doing experiments." He went on to say that Jim's form of idleness allowed him to solve "the greatest of all biological problems: the structure of DNA." Max concludes "There is more than one way of doing good science."

Max was a marvellous speaker. At a dinner held in Peterhouse College in 1994 to celebrate Max's 80th birthday, he summarized his career as follows:

> There are...things to be thankful for: to have lived in a country free from oppression and also from war—Falklands apart—these 49 years; to have worked among the British scientific community where you are judged, not by your origins, nor by your religion, nor by your politics, nor by your connections in high places, nor by your wealth, but solely by the quality of your work; to have enjoyed and to be still enjoying generous support for my work from both sides of the Atlantic; to be tolerated by my colleagues at the laboratory and here (Peterhouse) with affection and without being made to feel a burden, and finally for having received so many honours which in my youth I never expected to come my way, though I used to tease my son when he was little and when peerages were still hereditary that one day I would become Lord Haemoglobin, and he would inherit the title whether he wants to or not.

MRC
Medical Research Council

MRC Laboratory of Molecular Biology
Hills Road
Cambridge, CB2 2QH
England
Dr. M.F. Perutz

14 January 2002

Prof. Jim Watson
President, Cold Spring Harbor Laboratory
P.O. Box 100
Cold Spring Harbor NY 11724-0100

Dear Jim,

My days are numbered, and I just wanted to let you know how much fun dealing with you gave me in the early days. In 1950 or so, you poked your head through the door and asked shyly: "Can I come and work here?" I had a quick think and recalled that Luria had written to John about a young postdoc of his, so I said yes without a moment's hesitation. I then asked you what made you decide to join us and expected to hear how much interesting reports of our work had aroused in you. Instead, you said: "Because Kalckar is getting divorced." When it was all settled, we agreed that you should try to get into a College, but it was already at the beginning of Term. With great difficulty I persuaded Denis Wilkinson, a physicist friend of mine who was a Fellow, to take you into Jesus. After a while, I asked you if it was alright there. You replied that they were only interested in rowing and you wanted to get out. Another diplomatic effort of mine got you out of Jesus and into Clare, hoping you would be happy there. When I tried to sound you out about it, you replied: "The food is awful!" You were awkward and not a model of tact, but your arrival had an electrifying effect on our small group, because all our thoughts had been focussed on proteins, that we thought contained the riddle of life, but you convinced us that it was in DNA. Then one Monday morning in March 1953, Francis asked me to come to your room, and there stood your atomic model of the double helix! I realized at once that it must be right. It was the most dramatic moment in my scientific life.

I was sorry not to appear at your launching party at Clare the other day, but I had a very good excuse. I had been working on Huntington's Disease for some years which also got me interested in the amyloid structure, because fibres of poly-L-glutamine with the same cross beta X-ray pattern has amyloid. That pattern was first seen by Bill Astbury in 1935 and has been a riddle ever since. Last September I had an idea what the structure responsible for it might be. The more I thought about it, the more apparent did it become, that it was the only possible solution, so I dropped everything else, replied to no letters, went to no meetings and concentrated on that one problem. I finished two papers about the structure of amyloid at 12.50 on 20th December, and Alan Fersht, now an editor, sent them straight to PNAS. At 13.00 I had to be admitted to hospital for an operation on my bile duct which was blocked by a tumor of a cancer that started with a pimple under my nose last January, and is now out of control. I have enjoyed 65 years of productive research here at Cambridge and what more can anyone expect of life? Please give my regards to Liz and tell her that I am sorry I never got to know her better.

Yours ever,

Max

Monday Morning Quarterback

Elof Carlson

Emeritus, State University of New York, Stony Brook

In 1968, I was in the Department of Zoology at the University of California, Los Angeles, and I was asked to be in charge of the seminar program. This included picking up visitors and taking them to dinner with appropriate faculty guests. I was told that Linus Pauling would be in the University Guest House for a 5-day visit and I should pick him up for breakfast. The date was the day that Jim Watson's *The Double Helix* first went on sale. I had read a shorter version of the book in the *Atlantic Monthly* and was so intent on getting the book that I had reserved a copy at Campbell's Bookstore in Westwood Village near the campus. That morning, I waited for the store to open, obtained my copy, and went to the guest house to pick up Dr. Pauling. When he saw my copy of *The Double Helix*, he asked if he could see it, flipped through the pages, saw his own photograph, and broke out in a smile.

I then asked Pauling a question. "If you had seen Franklin's X-ray photograph of DNA that was shown to Watson, would you have interpreted the structure that Watson and Crick presented?" Pauling immediately replied, "You know, that's not the way science works. Sometimes your mind is so set you don't see the obvious."

I admired Pauling for that honesty because many historians and scientists do have a "Monday Morning Quarterback" view of science and are convinced that they saw in hindsight what was not there in their original interpretations.

Pauling gave five lectures on five different topics that week, a virtuoso performance. Four were on science and one was his protest of America's involvement in the Vietnam War. He advised graduate students not to drop out of their studies to fight the war because he felt their contributions in the long run would be of more benefit to humanity.

On his last day, no senior faculty member wanted to host Pauling and his wife for dinner, so my wife Nedra and I invited him to our modest home and almost all our guests were graduate students. Such was the political climate at the time that my faculty colleagues feared their careers would be hampered if they attended a dinner with Linus Pauling.

Elof Axel Carlson

Elof Axel Carlson is a Distinguished Teaching Professor in the Department of Biochemistry and Cell Biology at the Stony Brook campus of the State University of New York. He did his undergraduate work at New York University, and received his Ph.D. from Indiana University, where he studied genetics. His interests in the history of science are reflected by his books, *The Gene: A Critical History* (1966, W.B. Saunders) and *Genes, Radiation, and Society: The Life and Work of H.J. Muller* (1982, Cornell University Press), and most recently *The Unfit: A History of a Bad Idea* (2001, Cold Spring Harbor Laboratory Press). His interest in eugenics dates from his high school years, and he has followed its controversies ever since.

"The Night before Crickmas"

In June 1966, Rollin Hotchkiss wrote the following poem to celebrate Francis Crick's 50th birthday. To honor his birthday, a party was held on the lawn behind Blackford Hall at Cold Spring Harbor. The event was enlivened by a stripper, specially hired for the occasion, who emerged on cue from a large birthday cake, much to Francis' delight. For further details, see essay by Jim Eisenman in Section IV.

Many years later, at a banquet to celebrate the 40th anniversary of the double helix, Hotchkiss described that earlier occasion: "On that sunny June day, Crick, co-inventor of the double-helix model, was challenged with an alternative model. After graciously and enthusiastically welcoming it, he signaled that he did not feel obliged in the least to alter his basic philosophy."

THE NIGHT BEFORE CRICKMAS

T'was the night before Crickmas, and all through the colleges
Not a scientist was thinking—they were only adding to knowledges
Save Monod in his think-cap, explaining induction for the ages
Without a mutation in the whole forty pages—
When out of X-ray there arose such a clatter:
A new explanation of the arrangement of matter.

It explained to Franklin the sense of her data
Which she would have seen too, sooner or later,
And aroused Maurice Wilkins to earnest debates
On the need to have more data updates.

—Well, in seeking to balance the base pair budget
And predict some sure facts without having to fudge it,
They almost did pull an *il faut ne pas gaffe*[a]
By rifling the pockets of Erwin Chargaff,
Who promptly responded in jest and in choler
As on the fence, off-the-cuff, writer and scholar.

Also sifting these fragments of jetsam and flotsam
Was that wraith-like young drifter, J. Dewey Watson—
Who translated Crick's lore of X-ray diffraction
Into everyday language to our great satisfaction.

So—the theory caught on, among those interested,
Who forgot for some time it had still to be tested.
By the time it had come, more or less, to be proved,
Our young crystallographer was theoretically grooved

So he read and he traveled to pick up fresh news
And so solve the code: choose and pick, pick and choose,
Selecting the best, sometimes hard, sometimes lenient,
And rejecting the worst—or the plain inconvenient.

So theories, ideas and dogmas were fathered,
Dividing his colleagues into the hot and the bothered.
But the point of it all, I am glad to relate,
He told us all how—and it really was great:

Kiss and tell, kiss and tell, the double strands move,
Then along comes an enzyme in linear groove:
Spread the word, spread the word, to proline or glycine,
But hold on to the end, and avoid puromycin.
Go ahead, have some fun, shift your frame, kiss and tell:
You can get it all back maybe, after a spell.

How good that we had someone who could read it
When all of the rest of us quite failed to heed it!
Merry Crickmas, then!—all of us, we've been lucky, it's true,
And congratulate all—you and me, me and you,
And toast high to heaven for sending this boon—
—and let's celebrate Crickmas each forthcoming June!

[a]I am sure someone with a tidy mind will bristle at the apparent infraction of school book French usage: the "*il faut ne pas. . . .*" (when *il ne faut pas* is satisfactory for "one mustn't ... .")!).

Ring it up to poetic license—or "all gall, but not all Gallic"—or my willful occupation of a French island colony in a dream world—BUT I ask the privilege: my own hearing of the line insists on a broad "il faut. . . .," a pause, then a shift to a savage, eyes-narrowed "*ne pas!*," squeezed out through tensely clenched teeth! [This gaffe is . . .something that one must . . .just never do!]

(Neither my poetic, nor my dramatic, license has been renewed, by the way.)

R.D.H. May 1994

Reprinted, with permission, from Hotchkiss 1995. The night before Crickmas: A poem and deliverance. *Ann. NY Acad. Sci.* **758**: 205–207 (©1995 New York Academy of Sciences, U.S.A.).

A Structure for Deoxyribose Nucleic Acid

J.D. Watson and F.H.C. Crick

Reprinted, with permission, from *Nature*, Vol. 171, p. 737, April 25, 1953.

(Reprinted from Nature, Vol. 171, p. 737, April 25, 1953)

A Structure for Deoxyribose Nucleic Acid

WE wish to suggest a structure for the salt of deoxyribose nucleic acid (D.N.A.). This structure has novel features which are of considerable biological interest.

A structure for nucleic acid has already been proposed by Pauling and Corey[1]. They kindly made their manuscript available to us in advance of publication. Their model consists of three intertwined chains, with the phosphates near the fibre axis, and the bases on the outside. In our opinion, this structure is unsatisfactory for two reasons: (1) We believe that the material which gives the X-ray diagrams is the salt, not the free acid. Without the acidic hydrogen atoms it is not clear what forces would hold the structure together, especially as the negatively charged phosphates near the axis will repel each other. (2) Some of the van der Waals distances appear to be too small.

Another three-chain structure has also been suggested by Fraser (in the press). In his model the phosphates are on the outside and the bases on the inside, linked together by hydrogen bonds. This structure as described is rather ill-defined, and for this reason we shall not comment on it.

We wish to put forward a radically different structure for the salt of deoxyribose nucleic acid. This structure has two helical chains each coiled round the same axis (see diagram). We have made the usual chemical assumptions, namely, that each chain consists of phosphate di-ester groups joining β-D-deoxyribofuranose residues with 3′,5′ linkages. The two chains (but not their bases) are related by a dyad perpendicular to the fibre axis. Both chains follow right-handed helices, but owing to the dyad the sequences of the atoms in the two chains run in opposite directions. Each chain loosely resembles Furberg's[2] model No. 1; that is, the bases are on the inside of the helix and the phosphates on the outside. The configuration of the sugar and the atoms near it is close to Furberg's 'standard configuration', the sugar being roughly perpendicular to the attached base. There is a residue on each chain every 3·4 A. in the z-direction. We have assumed an angle of 36° between adjacent residues in the same chain, so that the structure repeats after 10 residues on each chain, that is, after 34 A. The distance of a phosphorus atom from the fibre axis is 10 A. As the phosphates are on the outside, cations have easy access to them.

The structure is an open one, and its water content is rather high. At lower water contents we would expect the bases to tilt so that the structure could become more compact.

The novel feature of the structure is the manner in which the two chains are held together by the purine and pyrimidine bases. The planes of the bases are perpendicular to the fibre axis. They are joined together in pairs, a single base from one chain being

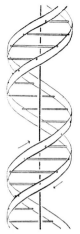

This figure is purely diagrammatic. The two ribbons symbolize the two phosphate—sugar chains, and the horizontal rods the pairs of bases holding the chains together. The vertical line marks the fibre axis

hydrogen-bonded to a single base from the other chain, so that the two lie side by side with identical z-co-ordinates. One of the pair must be a purine and the other a pyrimidine for bonding to occur. The hydrogen bonds are made as follows: purine position 1 to pyrimidine position 1; purine position 6 to pyrimidine position 6.

If it is assumed that the bases only occur in the structure in the most plausible tautomeric forms (that is, with the keto rather than the enol configurations) it is found that only specific pairs of bases can bond together. These pairs are: adenine (purine) with thymine (pyrimidine), and guanine (purine) with cytosine (pyrimidine).

In other words, if an adenine forms one member of a pair, on either chain, then on these assumptions the other member must be thymine; similarly for guanine and cytosine. The sequence of bases on a single chain does not appear to be restricted in any way. However, if only specific pairs of bases can be formed, it follows that if the sequence of bases on one chain is given, then the sequence on the other chain is automatically determined.

It has been found experimentally[3,4] that the ratio of the amounts of adenine to thymine, and the ratio of guanine to cytosine, are always very close to unity for deoxyribose nucleic acid.

It is probably impossible to build this structure with a ribose sugar in place of the deoxyribose, as the extra oxygen atom would make too close a van der Waals contact.

The previously published X-ray data[5,6] on deoxyribose nucleic acid are insufficient for a rigorous test of our structure. So far as we can tell, it is roughly compatible with the experimental data, but it must be regarded as unproved until it has been checked against more exact results. Some of these are given in the following communications. We were not aware of the details of the results presented there when we devised our structure, which rests mainly though not entirely on published experimental data and stereochemical arguments.

It has not escaped our notice that the specific pairing we have postulated immediately suggests a possible copying mechanism for the genetic material.

Full details of the structure, including the conditions assumed in building it, together with a set of co-ordinates for the atoms, will be published elsewhere.

We are much indebted to Dr. Jerry Donohue for constant advice and criticism, especially on interatomic distances. We have also been stimulated by a knowledge of the general nature of the unpublished experimental results and ideas of Dr. M. H. F. Wilkins, Dr. R. E. Franklin and their co-workers at King's College, London. One of us (J. D. W.) has been aided by a fellowship from the National Foundation for Infantile Paralysis.

J. D. Watson
F. H. C. Crick

Medical Research Council Unit for the
   Study of the Molecular Structure of
            Biological Systems,
   Cavendish Laboratory, Cambridge.
            April 2.

[1] Pauling, L., and Corey, R. B., *Nature*, **171**, 346 (1953); *Proc. U.S. Nat. Acad. Sci.*, **39**, 84 (1953).
[2] Furberg, S., *Acta Chem. Scand.*, **6**, 634 (1952).
[3] Chargaff, E., for references see Zamenhof, S., Brawerman, G., and Chargaff, E., *Biochim. et Biophys. Acta*, **9**, 402 (1952).
[4] Wyatt, G. R., *J. Gen. Physiol.*, **36**, 201 (1952).
[5] Astbury, W. T., Symp. Soc. Exp. Biol. 1, Nucleic Acid, 66 (Camb. Univ. Press, 1947).
[6] Wilkins, M. H. F., and Randall, J. T., *Biochim. et Biophys. Acta*, **10**, 192 (1953).

Printed in Great Britain by Fisher, Knight & Co., Ltd., St. Albans.

Genetical Implications of the Structure of Deoxyribonucleic Acid

J.D. Watson and F.H.C. Crick

Reprinted, with permission, from *Nature*, Vol. 171, p. 964, May 30, 1953.

(*Reprinted from Nature, Vol. 171, p. 964, May 30, 1953*)

GENETICAL IMPLICATIONS OF THE STRUCTURE OF DEOXYRIBONUCLEIC ACID

By J. D. WATSON and F. H. C. CRICK

Medical Research Council Unit for the Study of the Molecular Structure of Biological Systems, Cavendish Laboratory, Cambridge

THE importance of deoxyribonucleic acid (DNA) within living cells is undisputed. It is found in all dividing cells, largely if not entirely in the nucleus, where it is an essential constituent of the chromosomes. Many lines of evidence indicate that it is the carrier of a part of (if not all) the genetic specificity of the chromosomes and thus of the gene itself.

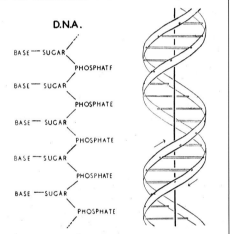

Fig. 1. Chemical formula of a single chain of deoxyribonucleic acid

Fig. 2. This figure is purely diagrammatic. The two ribbons symbolize the two phosphate-sugar chains, and the horizontal rods the pairs of bases holding the chains together. The vertical line marks the fibre axis

Until now, however, no evidence has been presented to show how it might carry out the essential operation required of a genetic material, that of exact self-duplication.

We have recently proposed a structure[1] for the salt of deoxyribonucleic acid which, if correct, immediately suggests a mechanism for its self-duplication. X-ray evidence obtained by the workers at King's College, London[2], and presented at the same time, gives qualitative support to our structure and is incompatible with all previously proposed structures[3]. Though the structure will not be completely proved until a more extensive comparison has been made with the X-ray data, we now feel sufficient confidence in its general correctness to discuss its genetical implications. In doing so we are assuming that fibres of the salt of deoxyribonucleic acid are not artefacts arising in the method of preparation, since it has been shown by Wilkins and his co-workers that similar X-ray patterns are obtained from both the isolated fibres and certain intact biological materials such as sperm head and bacteriophage particles[2,4].

The chemical formula of deoxyribonucleic acid is now well established. The molecule is a very long chain, the backbone of which consists of a regular alternation of sugar and phosphate groups, as shown in Fig. 1. To each sugar is attached a nitrogenous base, which can be of four different types. (We have considered 5-methyl cytosine to be equivalent to cytosine, since either can fit equally well into our structure.) Two of the possible bases—adenine and guanine—are purines, and the other two—thymine and cytosine—are pyrimidines. So far as is known, the sequence of bases along the chain is irregular. The monomer unit, consisting of phosphate, sugar and base, is known as a nucleotide.

The first feature of our structure which is of biological interest is that it consists not of one chain, but of two. These two chains are both coiled around a common fibre axis, as is shown diagrammatically in Fig. 2. It has often been assumed that since there was only one chain in the chemical formula there would only be one in the structural unit. However, the density, taken with the X-ray evidence[2], suggests very strongly that there are two.

The other biologically important feature is the manner in which the two chains are held together. This is done by hydrogen bonds between the bases, as shown schematically in Fig. 3. The bases are joined together in pairs, a single base from one chain being hydrogen-bonded to a single base from the

2

85

other. The important point is that only certain pairs of bases will fit into the structure. One member of a pair must be a purine and the other a pyrimidine in order to bridge between the two chains. If a pair consisted of two purines, for example, there would not be room for it.

We believe that the bases will be present almost entirely in their most probable tautomeric forms. If this is true, the conditions for forming hydrogen bonds are more restrictive, and the only pairs of bases possible are :

adenine with thymine ;
guanine with cytosine.

The way in which these are joined together is shown in Figs. 4 and 5. A given pair can be either way round. Adenine, for example, can occur on either chain ; but when it does, its partner on the other chain must always be thymine.

This pairing is strongly supported by the recent analytical results[5], which show that for all sources of deoxyribonucleic acid examined the amount of adenine is close to the amount of thymine, and the amount of guanine close to the amount of cytosine, although the cross-ratio (the ratio of adenine to guanine) can vary from one source to another. Indeed, if the sequence of bases on one chain is irregular, it is difficult to explain these analytical results except by the sort of pairing we have suggested.

The phosphate-sugar backbone of our model is completely regular, but any sequence of the pairs of

Fig. 3. Chemical formula of a pair of deoxyribonucleic acid chains. The hydrogen bonding is symbolized by dotted lines

3

(see Fig. 2) for a polypeptide chain to wind around the same helical axis. It may be significant that the distance between adjacent phosphorus atoms, $7 \cdot 1$ A., is close to the repeat of a fully extended polypeptide chain. We think it probable that in the sperm head, and in artificial nucleoproteins, the polypeptide chain occupies this position. The relative weakness of the second layer-line in the published X-ray pictures[3a,4] is crudely compatible with such an idea. The function of the protein might well be to control the coiling and uncoiling, to assist in holding a single polynucleotide chain in a helical configuration, or some other non-specific function.

Our model suggests possible explanations for a number of other phenomena. For example, spontaneous mutation may be due to a base occasionally occurring in one of its less likely tautomeric forms. Again, the pairing between homologous chromosomes at meiosis may depend on pairing between specific bases. We shall discuss these ideas in detail elsewhere.

For the moment, the general scheme we have proposed for the reproduction of deoxyribonucleic acid must be regarded as speculative. Even if it is correct, it is clear from what we have said that much remains to be discovered before the picture of genetic duplication can be described in detail. What are the polynucleotide precursors ? What makes the pair of chains unwind and separate ? What is the precise role of the protein ? Is the chromosome one long pair of deoxyribonucleic acid chains, or does it consist of patches of the acid joined together by protein ?

Despite these uncertainties we feel that our proposed structure for deoxyribonucleic acid may help to solve one of the fundamental biological problems— the molecular basis of the template needed for genetic replication. The hypothesis we are suggesting is that the template is the pattern of bases formed by one chain of the deoxyribonucleic acid and that the gene contains a complementary pair of such templates.

One of us (J. D. W.) has been aided by a fellowship from the National Foundation for Infantile Paralysis (U.S.A.).

[1] Watson, J. D., and Crick, F. H. C., *Nature*, **171**, 737 (1953).
[2] Wilkins, M. H. F., Stokes, A. R., and Wilson, H. R., *Nature*, **171**, 738 (1953). Franklin, R. E., and Gosling, R. G., *Nature*, **171**, 740 (1953).
[3] (*a*) Astbury, W. T., Symp. No. 1 Soc. Exp. Biol., 66 (1947). (*b*) Furberg, S., *Acta Chem. Scand.*, **6**, 634 (1952). (*c*) Pauling, L., and Corey, R. B., *Nature*, **171**, 346 (1953) ; *Proc. U.S. Nat. Acad. Sci.*, **39**, 84 (1953). (*d*) Fraser, R. D. B. (in preparation).
[4] Wilkins, M. H. F., and Randall, J. T., *Biochim. et Biophys. Acta*, **10**, 192 (1953).
[5] Chargaff, E., for references see Zamenhof, S., Brawerman, G., and Chargaff, E., *Biochim. et Biophys. Acta*, **9**, 402 (1952). Wyatt, G. R., *J. Gen. Physiol.*, **36**, 201 (1952).

Printed in Great Britain by Fisher, Knight & Co., Ltd., St. Albans

The Complementary Structure of Deoxyribonucleic Acid

F.H.C. Crick and J.D. Watson

Reprinted, with permission, without change of pagination from the *Proceedings of the Royal Society, A.*, volume 223, pp. 80–96, 1954.

Reprinted without change of pagination from the
Proceedings of the Royal Society, A, *volume* 223, pp. 80–96, 1954

The complementary structure of deoxyribonucleic acid

By F. H. C. Crick and J. D. Watson*†

Medical Research Council Unit for the Study of the Molecular Structure of
Biological Systems, Cavendish Laboratory, University of Cambridge

(*Communicated by Sir Lawrence Bragg, F.R.S.—Received* 24 *August* 1953)

[Plate 2]

This paper describes a possible structure for the paracrystalline form of the sodium salt of deoxyribonucleic acid. The structure consists of two DNA chains wound helically round a common axis, and held together by hydrogen bonds between specific pairs of bases. The assumptions made in deriving the structure are described, and co-ordinates are given for the principal atoms. The structure of the crystalline form is discussed briefly.

Introduction

The basic chemical formula of DNA is now fairly well established. It is a very long chain molecule formed by the joining together of complex monomeric units called nucleotides. Four main types of nucleotides are found in DNA, and it is probable that their sequence along a given chain is irregular. The relative amounts of the four nucleotides vary from species to species. The linkage between successive nucleotides is regular and involves 3′-5′-phospho-di-ester bonds.

Information about the three-dimensional shape is much less complete than that about its chemical formula. Physical-chemical studies, involving sedimentation, diffusion and light-scattering measurements, have suggested that the DNA chains exist in the form of thin rather rigid fibres approximately 20 Å in diameter and many thousand of ångströms in length (Jordan 1951; Sadron 1953). Very recently these indirect inferences have been directly confirmed by the electron micrographs of Williams (1952) and of Kahler & Lloyd (1953). Both sets of investigators have presented very good evidence for the presence in preparations of DNA of very long thin fibres with a diameter of 15 to 20 Å, and so there now appears little doubt about the general asymmetrical shape of DNA.

The only source of detailed information about the configuration of the atoms within the fibres is X-ray analysis (Astbury 1947; Wilkins, Stokes & Wilson 1953; Franklin & Gosling 1953 a). DNA's from various sources can be extracted, purified and drawn into fibres which are highly birefringent and give remarkably good X-ray diagrams. The same type of X-ray pattern is obtained from all soures of DNA, and the unit cell found is many times larger than that of the fundamental chemical unit, the nucleotide.

It seems improbable that the structure can be solved solely by modern crystallographic methods such as inequalities or vector superposition. These methods have so far been successfully used with relatively simple compounds. The DNA unit cell, however, is very large, and in fact contains a larger number of atoms than in any

* Aided by a Fellowship from the National Foundation for Infantile Paralysis (U.S.A.).

† Present address, Biology Division, California Institute of Technology, Pasadena 4, California.

structure, crystalline or fibrous, so far determined. Moreover, the number of X-ray reflexions is small, as there are few reflexions at spacings less than 3 Å, and so the classical method of trial and error seems the most promising approach.

It has therefore seemed worth while for us to build models of idealized poly-nucleotide chains to see if stereochemical considerations might tell us something about their arrangement in space. In doing so we have utilized interatomic distances and bond angles obtained from the simpler constituents of DNA and have only attempted to formulate structures in which configurational parameters assume accepted dimensions. We have only considered such structures as would fit the preliminary X-ray data of Wilkins, Franklin and their co-workers. Our search has so far yielded only one suitable structure. This structure, of which a preliminary account has already appeared (Watson & Crick 1953*a*), consists of two intertwined polynucleotide chains helically arranged about a common axis. The two chains are joined together by hydrogen bonds between a purine base on one chain and a pyrimidine base on the other. This structure appears to us most promising, and in fact we believe that its broad features are correct. In this paper we shall present the assumptions used in formulating this structure and give precise co-ordinates for the principal atoms. We shall make no attempt to test the structure with the experimental X-ray evidence as this is being done by others.

Chemical background

The DNA molecule can be formally divided into two parts, the backbone and the side groups. The backbone, as shown in figure 1, is very regular and is made up of alternate sugar (2-deoxy-D-ribose) and phosphate groups joined together in regular, 3′, 5′-phosphate-di-ester linkages (Brown & Todd 1952; Dekker, Michelson & Todd 1953). The side groups consist of either a purine or a pyrimidine base, only one of which is attached to any given sugar. Two purines, adenine and guanine, and two pyrimidines, cytosine and thymine, are commonly present. In addition, a third pyrimidine 5-methyl-cytosine (Wyatt 1952) occurs in small amounts in certain organisms, while in the *T*-even phages cytosine is absent and is replaced by a fourth pyrimidine, 5-hydroxy-methyl-cytosine (Wyatt & Cohen 1952).

The glycosidic combination of the base and the sugar is known as a nucleoside, while the phosphate ester of a nucleoside is called a nucleotide. The deoxyribose residue in each of the nucleotides is in the furanose form (Brown & Lythgoe 1950) and is glycosidically bound to N_3 in the pyrimidine nucleosides and to N_9 in the purine nucleosides (for a review, see Tipson 1945). The configuration at the glyco-sidic linkage has been shown to be β in deoxyadenosine and deoxycytidine (Todd *et al.* unpublished) and is considered by analogy to be the same in the other natural deoxyribonucleosides.

A DNA chain may contain thousands of nucleotides and is thought in view of the regular internucleotide linkage to be unbranched. Very little is known about the precise sequence of the different nucleotides, but as far as can be now ascertained the order is irregular and any sequence of nucleotides is possible.

At pH values > 2, the primary phosphoryl groups are ionized, and so most in-vestigations have utilized the sodium salt. The crystallographic analysis has so far dealt exclusively with this salt, and our structural suggestions are correspondingly limited to this form.

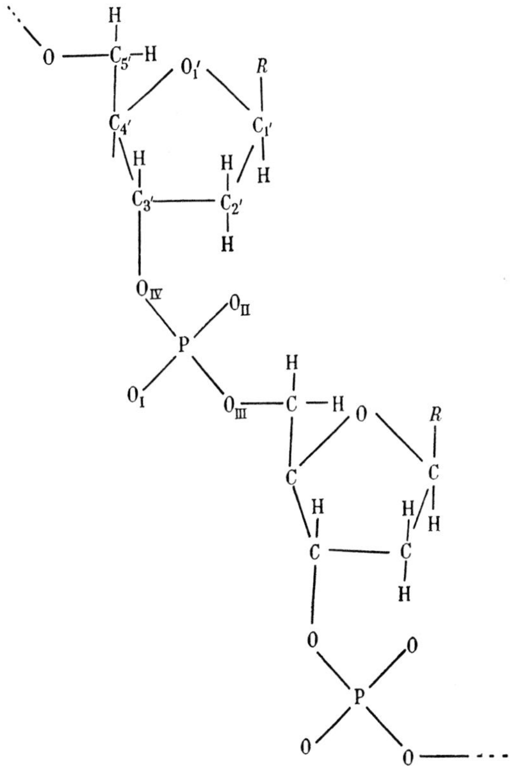

FIGURE 1. The general formula of DNA. R is a purine or pyrimidine base.

CRYSTALLOGRAPHIC CONSIDERATIONS

X-ray photographs of DNA fibres were obtained in 1938 by Astbury & Bell (1938) and more recently by Wilkins & Franklin and their collaborators at King's College, London (Wilkins *et al.* 1953; Franklin & Gosling 1953 *a, c*). The photographs were taken of purified samples which had been drawn into birefringent fibres in which the DNA molecules are orientated approximately parallel to the fibre axis. The photographs of Wilkins & Franklin and their collaborators are appreciably sharper than those of Astbury & Bell, and we shall restrict our discussion to their work.

It is observed* that DNA can exist in two different forms†, a crystalline form structure A, and a paracrystalline form structure B. The crystalline form occurs at

* The information reported in this section was very kindly reported to us prior to its publication by Drs Wilkins and Franklin. We are most heavily indebted in this respect to the King's College Group, and we wish to point out that without this data the formulation of our structure would have been most unlikely, if not impossible. We should at the same time mention that the *details* of their X-ray photographs were not known to us, and that the formulation of the structure was largely the result of extensive model building in which the main effort was to find any structure which was stereochemically feasible.

† The existence of the two forms was first suggested by powder photographs of DNA gells (Riley & Oster 1951).

75 % relative humidity and contains about 30 % water by weight. Its repeat distance along the fibre axis is 28 Å. At higher humidities this form takes up more water, increases in length by about 30 % and assumes the alternative paracrystalline form. In contrast to the crystalline form which lacks any strong meridional reflexion the paracrystalline form gives a very strong meridional reflexion at 3·4 Å. In conjunction with the increase in fibre length, the repeat along the fibre axis increases to 34 Å. Both forms give equatorial reflexions corresponding to sideways repeats of 22 to 25 Å, and it appears that their diameters are approximately the same. The transition between the two forms is freely reversible, and it seems likely that they are related in a simple manner.

They have further shown (Wilkins *et al.* 1953) that the X-ray pattern of both the crystalline and paracrystalline forms is the same for all sources of DNA ranging from viruses to mammals. At first sight this seems surprising, as the ratios of the various nucleotides vary from one source to another and it might have been expected that the size and shape of the structural unit would vary correspondingly. On the other hand, we should recall that the sequence of nucleotides within a given DNA chain is irregular, and so the fact that DNA forms a repetitive structure (much less a crystalline structure!) is itself unusual.

It seemed to us that the most likely explanation of these observations was that the structure was based upon features common to all nucleotides. This suggested that in the first instance one should consider mainly the configuration of the phosphate-sugar chain, with an 'average' base attached to each sugar. In other words, an idealized polynucleotide with all the monomers the same.

For such a model it is stereochemically plausible to assume that all the sugar and phosphate groups are in equivalent positions and have identical environments irrespective of which nucleotide is being considered. This implies that one nucleotide is related to another by a symmetry operation, and in the case of a single optically active chain, this operation is necessarily a rotation about an axis accompanied by a translation along the axis. This corresponds to a screw axis, and the operation if repeated leads in general to a helix, as pointed out before by Pauling, Corey & Branson (1951) and by Crane (1950).

The idea that the DNA structure is helical* is supported by two general features of the experimental data. First, it provides a simple explanation of the fact that the fibre axis repeat ($\simeq 30$ Å) is many times longer than the probable axial spacing between nucleotides ($\simeq 3$ Å), since a helical structure composed of identical monomers will give a spacing related to the pitch of the helix (Cochran, Crick & Vand 1952). Secondly, the unit-cell dimensions of the crystalline form (Franklin & Gosling 1953*c*) are pseudo-hexagonal in cross-section, as one might expect if the structure was based on helical bundles approximately cylindrical in shape.

We have therefore attempted to build helical structures in which the repeat distance along the fibre axis is that reported by Wilkins, Franklin and co-workers. Before doing so, however, it was necessary to decide whether to build models of the

---

* We should mention that on several occasions Dr Wilkins in personal conversation indicated that the paracrystalline X-ray pattern had helical features. Our postulation of a helical structure was, however, the consequence of the above reasons, and we feel independent of Dr Wilkins's suggestion.

crystalline form structure A or the paracrystalline form structure B. We had no hesitation in choosing the latter, mainly because of its extremely strong 3·4 Å meridional reflexion (discussed below), since this gives information which can be of direct help in building models.

FORMULATION OF A STRUCTURE FOR THE PARACRYSTALLINE FORM

The X-ray pattern of structure B is dominated by a very strong reflexion on the meridian at a spacing of 3·4 Å (Wilkins *et al.* 1953; Franklin & Gosling 1953 a). This distance, as first pointed out by Astbury, corresponds to the thickness of a purine or pyrimidine base, and suggests that the nucleotide bases on a given chain are arranged at right angles to the fibre axis and spaced 3·4 Å above each other. The idea that the bases are roughly perpendicular to the fibre axis is supported qualitatively by the ultra-violet dichroism (Wilkins, Gosling & Seeds 1951).

It is difficult to imagine any other arrangement producing such a strong reflexion. This reflexion corresponds to a spacing approximately twice that of the covalent bonds present in DNA, and so most probably arises from a regular arrangement of internucleotide van der Waals contacts. It is worth noting why this reflexion cannot arise from a staggered arrangement of chains containing successive nucleotides spaced 6·8 Å above each other. This distance is approximately the internucleotide length of an extended polynucleotide chain, and if present in DNA should result in reversibly inextensible fibres. Now, Wilkins *et al.* (1951) have reported that DNA fibres can be reversibly stretched by a factor 1·5, and so the fibre axis per nucleotide must be considerably less than the fully extended internucleotide length. We thus have little doubt that the fibre axis translation per nucleotide is 3·4 Å, and (assuming equivalence) that a given polynucleotide chain contains 10 nucleotide residues per 34 Å fibre axis repeat.

It is difficult, nevertheless, to account for the rather high density (Astbury 1947) of DNA on the basis of a helical structure containing but 10 nucleotides within the unit cell. In fact, density consideration suggests the presence of a structure containing two to three times as many residues.

The most plausible way to explain this is to assume that the DNA molecule contains several polynucleotide chains and that they are helically coiled about a common axis. Density considerations immediately rule out the presence of more than three chains, and so we are left to decide between two or three chains. At first sight it appears that three chains is the correct answer, as the density of DNA is generally reported (Astbury 1947) as about 1·65 g cm^{-3}, a value corresponding to approximately 30 nucleotides within a cylinder of radius 10 Å and height 34 Å. We must remember, however, that the density measurements are generally reported from dry specimens (from which only very disordered X-ray patterns can be obtained; Wilkins, personal communication) and that as yet we do not know the effective density of the paracrystalline form.

The density of structure A, however, has been measured by Franklin & Gosling (1953 c), and indicates the presence of approximately 24 nucleotides per lattice point, a value which superficially is incompatible with either two or with three chains. This incompatibility disappears, however, when we consider that the translation from structure B to structure A is accompanied by a visual shortening of the fibre by roughly 30 % (Franklin & Gosling 1953 a). The longitudinal component is thus no longer 3·4 Å but 3·4 Å × 0·70 = 2·4 Å. The unit cell of structure A, therefore, contains two polynucleotide chains each of which contains about 12 nucleotides per fibre axis repeat, since 2·4 × 12 ≃ 28. As the transformation from A to B is readily reversible, it seems most improbable that the chains would be grouped in threes in structure B, and we believe that in this form also the fundamental structural unit contains two helically arranged polynucleotide chains.

It is necessary to decide what part of the nucleotide to place in the centre of the helix. Initially, it seemed reasonable to believe that the basic structural arrangement would be dictated by packing consideration at the centre and that the core would contain atomic groups common to all the nucleotides. Our first attempts, therefore, involved possible models with the phosphate groups in the centre, the sugar groups further out and with the bases on the outside (the alternative arrangement of placing the sugar in the centre, is very improbable due to the irregular shape of the deoxyribofuranose group.)

Now the phosphate group carries a negative charge which is neutralized by the presence of a Na^+ ion. We thought it possible that this electrostatic attraction might dominate the structure and that the correct solution to DNA structure might fall out if we found a satisfactory way of packing the charged groups. We decided momentarily to ignore the sugar and base constituents and to build up regular patterns of co-ordination for the Na^+ and phosphate groups. In particular, we tried arrangements in which both of these ions were at the same distance from the fibre axis. No difficulty was found in obtaining repeat distances of 3·4 Å in the fibre direction as long as we considered only the charged groups. When, however, we attempted the next step of joining up the phosphate groups with the sugar groups we ran into difficulty. The phosphate groups tended to be either too far apart for the sugars to reach between them, or to be so close together that the sugars would fit in only by grossly violating van der Waals contacts. At first this seemed surprising, as the sugar-phosphate backbone contains, per residue, five single bonds, about all of which free rotation is possible. It might be thought that such a backbone would be very flexible and compliant. On the contrary, we came to realize that because of the awkward shape of the sugar, there are relatively few configurations which the backbone can assume. It therefore seemed that our initial approach would lead nowhere and that we should give up our attempt to place the phosphate groups in the centre. Instead, we believe it most likely that the bases form the central core and that the regular sugar-phosphate backbone forms the circumference.

Before building models of this type, it is necessary to know the approximate radius at which to place the backbone. As mentioned before, both the crystalline and paracrystalline forms give equatorial reflexions corresponding to sideways spacings of 22 to 24 Å (Wilkins *et al.* 1953; Franklin & Gosling 1953 a), and so it seems very likely that both have effective radii of approximately 10 Å. This imposes a severe restriction on the types of models, for the polynucleotide chain has a maximum length. The distance between successive phosphorus atoms in a fully extended chain is only about 7 Å, and so the maximum length of the ten nucleotide repetitive unit is but 70 Å. This is almost exactly the length of one repeat of a helical chain of radius 10 Å and pitch 34 Å, and so we can immediately conclude that the polynucleotide chain can have at most one revolution per fibre axis repeat. If the DNA molecule contained only one chain we could be more definite and conclude that the X-ray evidence demands one turn in 34 Å. As the molecule, however, contains two chains, the possibility remains that they are related by a diad parallel to the fibre axis and that each chain makes only half a revolution in 34 Å.

These possibilities can be differentiated by building models. We find that we can build models of one chain with a rotation of approximately 40° per residue but that it is difficult, if not impossible, with a rotation of only 20°. The van der Waals contacts in this latter case are much too close, and it appears probable that no structure of this type can exist. It, therefore, seems probable that each chain is in a nearly fully extended condition and makes one revolution every 34 Å. It should be noted that this argument rules out the possibility that the two intertwined chains are related by a diad parallel to the fibre axis, for if true, the fibre axis repeat would be halved to 17 Å.

It seems most likely that the two chains will be held together by hydrogen bonds between the bases. Both the purine and pyrimidine bases can form hydrogen bonds at several places on their periphery, and such instability would result from their absence that we may be confident of their presence. These bonds are strongly directional in character and can form only in the plane of the bases. They cannot be formed, however, between bases belonging to the same chain, since successive bases are located approximately on top of each other, and if we would draw a vector joining their centres, it would lie almost perpendicular to the plane in which they can form hydrogen bonds. Instead, we may expect the hydrogen bonds to be formed between bases belonging to the opposing chains and in doing so to unite the bases in pairs. This can be done in a regular manner only if we always join a purine with a pyrimidine. This is accomplished more suitably by forming two hydrogen bonds per pair; one from purine position 1 to pyrimidine position 1, the other from purine position 6 to pyrimidine position 6.

We should note the reason why the two chains cannot be linked together by two purines or by two pyrimidines. It arises from our postulate that each of the sugar-phosphate backbone chains is in the form of a regular helix. This implies that the glycosidic bonds (the link between the sugar and the base) always occur in identical orientation with regard to the helical axis. The two glycosidic bonds of a pair will therefore be fixed in space and have a constant distance between them. This distance, however, is different for each of the three possible types of pairs, purine with purine, pyrimidine with pyrimidine and purine with pyrimidine. The only way, therefore, to keep this distance fixed and to insert both types of bases into the structure is to restrict the pairing to the mixed variety.

We believe that the bases will most likely be present in the tautomeric forms shown in figure 2, and so in general only specific pairs of bases will bond together. These pairs are adenine with thymine (figure 3), and guanine with cytosine (figure 4).

When 5-methyl cytosine is present it should also pair with guanine as the methyl group is located on the side opposite to that involved in the pairing process. For similar reasons, 5-hydroxy-methyl-cytosine should likewise pair with guanine. It is easy to see why the other types of pairs will not occur. If, for instance, adenine is paired with cytosine, there are two hydrogen atoms between the amino nitrogens and none between the two ring nitrogens. For similar reasons guanine cannot be paired with thymine.

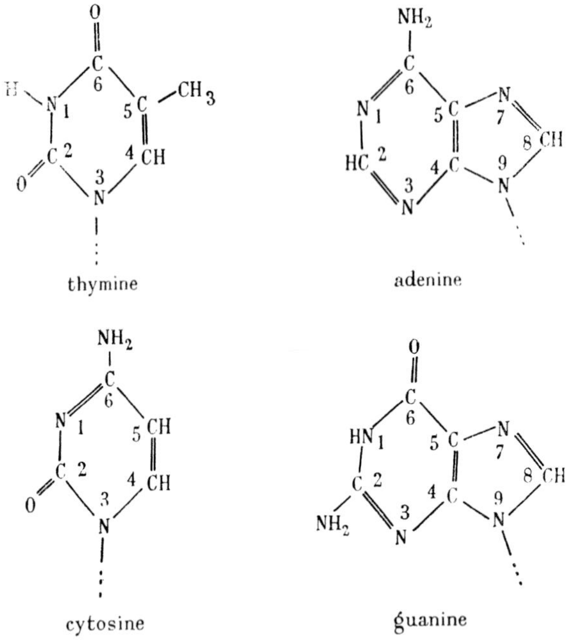

thymine

adenine

cytosine

guanine

FIGURE 2. The formulae of the four common bases of DNA, showing the tautomeric forms assumed.

When models employing this pairing arrangement are built, several additional structural features become apparent. In the first place, we find by trial that the model can only be built in the right-handed* sense. Left-handed helices can be constructed only by violating the permissible van der Waals contacts. Secondly, in order to maintain the equivalence of the sugar and phosphate groups it is necessary to have the two chains (but not the bases) related by a diad perpendicular to the fibre axis. This is possible because the two glycosidic bonds of a purine-pyrimidine pair are not only the same distance apart in both of our chosen pairs, but are found to be related to each other by a diad, and can thus be fitted into the structure either way round (see figures 3 and 4). It is this feature which allows all four bases to occur on both chains. The insertion of the perpendicular diad requires the chains to run in opposite directions (a chain has a direction determined by the sequence of the atoms in it) and places the sugar-phosphate backbone

* The Fischer convention has recently been shown to be correct (Bijvoet, Peerdeman & van Bommel 1951).

of each chain in identical orientations with regard to the purine and pyrimidine side groups.

The structure can be built with any sequence of bases on a given chain. We should note, however, that the postulate of specific pairs introduces a definite relationship between the sequence of bases on the opposing chains. For instance, if on one chain we find at some point the sequence adenine, cytosine, thymine and adenine, then the corresponding sequence on the other chain must be thymine, guanine, adenine and thymine. The two chains thus bear a complementary relationship to each other.

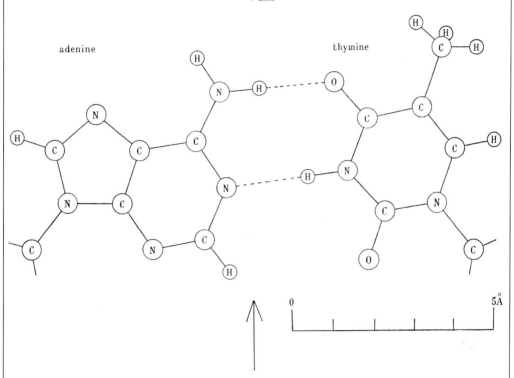

FIGURE 3. The pairing of adenine and guanine. Hydrogen bonds are shown dotted. One carbon atom of each sugar is shown. The arrow represents the crystallographic diad.

The structure appears to satisfy all of the requirements which we initially postulated for the DNA molecule. The arrangement of the sugar-phosphate backbone which occupies the outer regions of the molecule is extremely regular, and it is possible to imagine it forming a crystalline pattern with neighbouring molecules. On the other hand, it permits an irregular sequence of nucleotides to exist on a given chain and thus allows for a large variety of DNA molecules. This fusion of regular and irregular features is achieved admittedly only at the expense of the additional restrictive postulate of complementary chains. The necessity for this postulate might be considered a severe, if not fatal objection to our structure, but as mentioned later, it is strongly supported by the recent analytical data.

DETAILED CONFIGURATION OF THE DOUBLE HELIX

We shall refer first to the specific pairs of bases. Adenine and thymine are shown paired in figure 3, while guanine and cytosine are shown paired in figure 4. These drawings are to scale and have been constructed as far as possible by utilizing bond angles and bond lengths which have been reported to occur in these compounds.

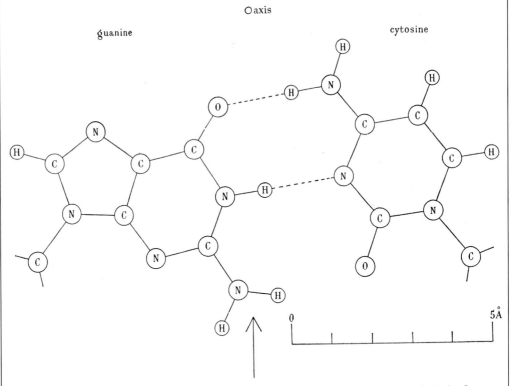

FIGURE 4. The pairing of guanine and cytosine. Hydrogen bonds are shown dotted. One carbon atom of each sugar is shown. The arrow represents the crystallographic diad.

The crystal structures of both adenine and guanine have been studied by Broomhead (1948, 1951), while the structure of cytosine is known through Furberg's (1950) analysis of the crystal structure of cytidine. More recently Broomhead's data on adenine have been refined by Cochran (1951) and the atomic parameters of this compound are now accurate to within 0·02 Å.

As yet, no determination has been made of the structure of thymine, but it seems unlikely that its ring configuration will differ markedly from cytosine. Any deviations which might occur would have only a negligible effect on the pairing configuration, and we have utilized the idealized thymine configuration of figure 3. We also lack information about the exact angles at the β-glycosidic bond. There is no reason, however, to believe that they should differ significantly from those in cytidine or in the cyclic adenosine nucleoside studied by Zussman (1953), and they likewise have been assigned symmetrically.

The configuration of the adenine-thymine pair is stereochemically most satisfactory. The direction of the vector from the amino nitrogen to the keto oxygen lies exactly in the NH direction, as does the vector from the purine nitrogen atom 1 to the pyrimidine nitrogen atom 1. Both of the hydrogen bonds should therefore be of maximum stability (Donohue 1952). In addition, the two glycosidic bonds of the pair are related by a diád to within 1°, which is less than the accuracy to which the configuration of the bases is known. The distance apart of the $C_{1'}$ carbon atoms of the two sugars is close to 11 Å.

There is more ambiguity about the guanine-cytosine pair. This arises largely from doubt about the exact structure of guanine (Broomhead 1951). In particular, we are doubtful about the exact position of the keto oxygen atom. In figure 4 we have used the published position, and this makes the relative positions of the glycosidic bonds different from the adenine-thymine pair by about 2°. This difference would be negligible if the guanine keto oxygen was symmetrically placed. It is also uncertain as to whether this pair might form a third hydrogen bond between the amino group of guanine and the keto oxygen of cytosine. This point is unlikely to be settled until the configurations of both these bases are known to a greater accuracy. It seems clear, nevertheless, that these uncertainties are only of second-order importance, and that for all practical considerations the two pairs should be considered structurally equivalent.

The phosphate-sugar backbones were constructed utilizing a sugar configuration reported for ribose by Furberg (1950). A similar configuration for a pentose ring has also been reported by Beevers & Cochran (1947) in the fructofuranoside ring of sucrose. It seems probable that the furanose ring is puckered, and we have tentatively placed the $C_{3'}$ atom out of the ring in such a direction that its oxygen atom $O_{3'}$ is brought closer to the common plane. A tetrahedral arrangement has been assumed for the bond angles around the phosphorus atom. The bond lengths about the phosphorus have been assigned unsymmetrically following the suggestion of Pauling & Corey (1953), the two P—O bonds in the backbone have lengths of 1·65 Å while the remaining non ester P—O bonds are thought to have the shorter length of 1·45 Å. As a result of Furberg's analysis of cytidine (1950) there seems little doubt that the glycosidic bond is a single bond. We can thus be sure that the sugar group instead of being coplanar with the nitrogen base, as postulated by Astbury (1947), is more nearly perpendicular to it.

The paired bases are arranged so as to be approximately perpendicular to the fibre axis. This places the glycosidic bonds in a similar arrangement, while the puckered plane of the sugar ring assumes a position nearly parallel to the fibre axis. Each backbone chain completes one revolution after 10 residues in 34 Å, and so the rotation per residue is 36°. The phosphorus atoms are at radii of 10 Å, and the backbone has a configuration roughly similar to that described by Furberg (1952) in his paper dealing with suitable configurations for single helically arranged polynucleotide chains.

General views of the structure are shown in the photographs of figures 5 and 6, plate 2, which illustrate the salient features of a scale model. The drawings in figures 7 and 8 are given to demonstrate more accurately the exact configuration

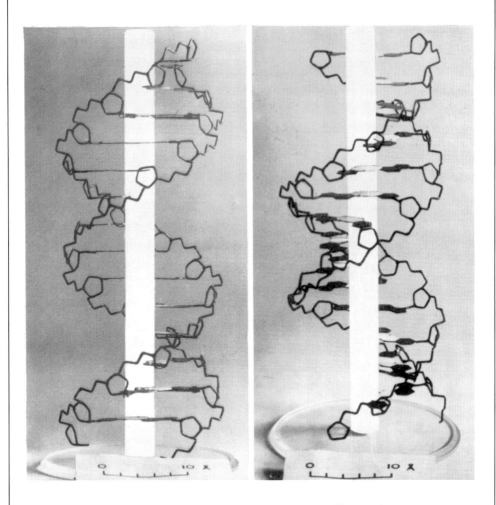

FIGURE 5.   FIGURE 6.

FIGURE 5. Photograph of a rough scale model of the structure. The chemical bonds in the phosphate sugar backbone are represented by wire. (All the hydrogen atoms and the two oxygen atoms of the phosphate group not in ester linkage have been omitted.) The pairs of bases are represented by metal plates. The fibre axis is represented by a Perspex rod.

FIGURE 6. Another view of the model shown in figure 5. The white plates represent the area between the bases in which hydrogen bonding takes place.

(See pg. 90)

of the backbone. Figure 7 shows two successive residues on the same chain pro-jected on to a plane perpendicular to the fibre axis, while in figure 8 is shown a projection of a sugar-phosphate residue on to a plane whose normal is perpen-dicular to the fibre axis. It can be seen that the atoms forming the sequence

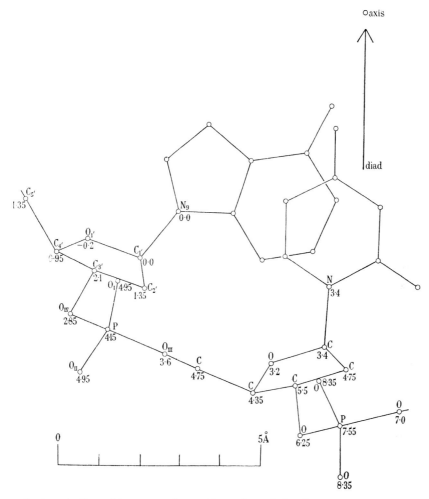

FIGURE 7. A projection of two successive residues of *one* chain of the structure. The direction of projection is parallel to the fibre axis. The figures show the height of each atom (in ångströms) above the level of the lower base.

$C_{4'}$—$C_{5'}$—$O_{5'}$—P—$O_{3'}$ all lie in such a plane; co-ordinates of the principal backbone atoms are given to 0·05 Å in table 1. No attempt has been made to place the sodium ion or the water molecules, though it is possible that some of these groups are located in relatively constant positions.

Because the two backbones are related by a diad, the distance between their effective 'centres of gravity' is much greater than might be imagined from the location of the glycosidic bonds. Instead of being separated by only $\frac{1}{4}$ of the fibre axis repeat (the angle of the pair of glycosidic bonds is close to 90°), they are separated by approximately $\frac{3}{8}$ of the 34 Å repeat. In contrast to the outside of the molecule, the centre tends to give the impression of a one-stranded helix. This is a consequence of the intimate pairing of the bases.

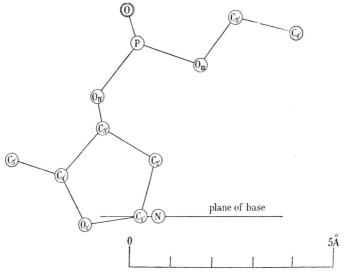

FIGURE 8. A projection of one residue in a direction perpendicular to both the fibre axis and to the plane containing the atoms $C_{4'}$—$C_{5'}$—O_5—P—$O_{3'}$.

TABLE 1. CO-ORDINATES FOR THE ATOMS OF THE BACKBONE,
FOR A SINGLE RESIDUE

atom	ρ (Å)	ϕ	Z (Å)
P	10·0	0·0°	0·0
O_I	8·95	$-$ 3·6°	$+0·8$
O_{II}	11·25	$+$ 0·7°	$+0·8$
O_{III}	9·65	$+$ 8·9°	$-0·5$
O_{IV}	10·35	$-$ 5·3°	$-1·3$
$C_{5'}$	9·6	$-22·2°$	$-2·8$
$C_{4'}$	9·65	$-13·2°$	$-3·2$
$C_{3'}$	9·2	$-$ 7·3°	$-2·05$
$C_{2'}$	8·65	$+$ 0·4°	$-2·8$
$C_{1'}$	8·2	$-$ 3·5°	$-4·15$
$O_{1'}$	8·8	$-11·8°$	$-4·35$
N	6·7	$-$ 4·2°	$-4·15$
diad	—	$+39·0°$	$-4·15$

Each of the van der Waals contacts appears to be acceptable. They are five relatively short contacts between the phosphate oxygen atoms and hydrogen atoms. None, however, is less than 2·5 Å, a quite acceptable length for side-by-side contacts. The position of the plane of the bases with respect to the sugar does not appear to be the optimum, but it is nevertheless within the range stated by Furberg as possible. Another short contact is found between the hydrogen atoms attached to the $C_{3'}$ and $C_{5'}$ atoms of the sugar. This contact, however, is also side by side, and so the postulated length (2·1 Å) appears permissible. The stagger of hydrogen atoms between the $C_{4'}$—$C_{5'}$ bond is not optimal, but the deviation is only 25° and so allowable.

We can therefore conclude that the model is stereochemically feasible. Nevertheless, it is certainly not ideal, and it is possible that it could be improved by slightly altering the assumptions made about the configuration of the phosphorus atoms, especially its bond lengths, and by altering the configuration of the sugar. We have assumed that the puckering of the sugar ring is achieved by throwing the $C_{3'}$ atom out of the plane of the ring; a better model might result by choosing a different shape. Alternatively, it may be that an attraction between the rings of the bases is pulling the backbone out of its potential minimum.

THE CRYSTALLINE FORM

The transition to the crystalline form is accompanied by a decrease in water content (Franklin & Gosling 1953 a), and it seems very probable that this form exists in a more tightly packed condition than the paracrystalline form. It is thus

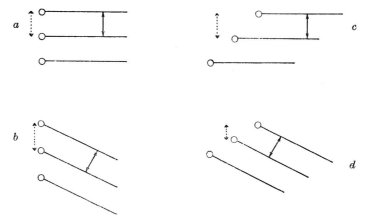

FIGURE 9. To show that if the bases are staggered, tilting will reduce the translation in the axis direction (represented by a dotted arrow). The solid arrow represents the perpendicular distance between the bases, which remains constant. a and b, not staggered; c and d, staggered; a and c, before tilting; b and d, after tilting.

not surprising to observe that the change to the crystalline state is characterized by a visual shortening of the fibre length of about 30 % (Franklin & Gosling 1953 a). There is little if any change in the diameter of the fibre, and so it seems likely that the fibre axis translation per nucleotide is reduced from 3·4 to approximately 2·5 Å. This conclusion might appear difficult to believe, as the van der Waals separation of the rings of the bases must remain the same and thus might appear to oppose a fibre shortening, but in fact the vertical translation can be reduced if the paired bases are tilted anti-clockwise (when viewed from the fibre axis).

The manner in which this might occur is shown in figure 9. It can be seen that shortening will only take place if successive pairs of bases are not stacked directly on top of one another, but are displaced to one side. In fact, if the bases are **not** displaced, tilting will result in an increase of the fibre-axis translation. Of course, in our structure the successive pairs are displaced helically, not simply sideways as in figure 9, but this in no way destroys the general argument.

We should note that the hydrogen bonding arrangement remains unchanged by the tilting, as both members of a pair are similarly rotated about the perpendicular diad between the bases. This would not be so if the bases were instead related by a diad *parallel* to the fibre axis. In this latter case, the configuration of the backbone could be made equivalent only by tilting the two members of a pair in opposite directions and thus by effectively destroying the hydrogen bonds. Thus, if tilting is shown to occur in the crystalline state, we should have strong reasons for believing that the backbones are related by perpendicular diads.

We have not attempted to construct a detailed model with tilted bases, as we feel that this could be done more suitably in conjunction with the detailed X-ray evidence. Nevertheless, for the reasons outlined above, we believe that such a model can be built and that it will involve the same basic structural features proposed here for the paracrystalline form.

DISCUSSION

Our structure bears only superficial resemblances to the majority of structures previously suggested. Most of these earlier formations (Astbury 1947; Furberg 1952) have involved single stranded structures and must be rejected on the basis of the density considerations outlined in the beginning of this paper. The only multi-stranded structure which previously has been seriously proposed is that of Pauling & Corey, who very kindly sent their manuscript to us prior to its publication. Their structure involved three intertwined helical chains in which the core of the molecule was formed by phosphate groups. Their proposal was submitted without knowledge of the work at King's College, London, by Wilkins and Franklin and their co-workers, and appears in the light of their experimental results to be untenable. The main objection to their proposal involves the number of chains. As indicated earlier the density of the crystalline form (Franklin & Gosling 1953 c) strongly suggests the presence of two chains, and we find it difficult to imagine that any three-chained proposal can be made which will fit the experimental evidence.

The structure accounts in a nice way for the analytical data on the composition of DNA. By requiring specific pairing of purine and pyrimidine groups, it provides for the first time a suitable explanation for the recent chemical data (Chargaff 1951; Wyatt 1952; Chargaff, Crampton & Lipschitz 1953), which indicated not only a molar equivalence of the purines and pyrimidines, but also the molar equivalence of adenine and thymine, and of guanine and cytosine. The ratio of adenine to guanine varies greatly in DNA's from different sources, and it is difficult to imagine a structural explanation for the equivalence of adenine with thymine and of guanine with cytosine which does not involve specific pairing.

As far as we can tell our structure is compatible with the X-ray evidence of Wilkins and Franklin and their co-workers (Wilkins *et al.* 1953; Franklin & Gosling 1953 a). In a preliminary report on their work, they have independently suggested that the basic structure of the paracrystalline form is helical and contains two intertwined chains. They also suggest that the sugar-phosphate backbone forms the outside of the helix and that each chain repeats itself after one revolution in 34 Å.* Nevertheless, these crystallographic conclusions are tentative, and the structure can in no sense be considered proved until a satisfactory solution to the structure of the crystalline form is obtained.

In conclusion, we may mention that the complementary relationship between the two chains is very likely related to the biological role of DNA. It is generally assumed that DNA is a genetic substance and in some way possesses the capacity for self-duplication. It seems to us that the presence of a complementary structure strongly suggests that the self-duplicating process will be found to involve the alternative formation of complementary chains, and that each chain will be found capable of serving as a template for the formation of its complement. A fuller exposition of these latter ideas is given elsewhere (Watson & Crick 1953*b,c*).

We are most indebted to Dr M. H. F. Wilkins both for informing us of unpublished experimental observations and for the benefit of numerous discussions. We are also grateful to Dr J. Donohue for constant advice on the problems of tautomerism and van der Waals contacts, and to Professor A. R. Todd, F.R.S., for advice on chemical matters, and for allowing us access to unpublished work.

One of us (J.D.W.) wishes in addition to acknowledge the very kind hospitality provided during his stay at the Cavendish Laboratory by Sir Lawrence Bragg, F.R.S., and by the members of the Medical Research Council Unit located there. He is especially grateful to the encouragement provided by Dr J. C. Kendrew and Dr M. F. Perutz. In conclusion he would like to mention Professor S. E. Luria of the University of Illinois to whom he is indebted for both the opportunity to come to and to remain in Cambridge.

REFERENCES

Astbury, W. T. 1947 *Symp. Soc. Exp. Biol.* **1**, Nucleic Acid, p. 66. Cambridge University Press.
Astbury, W. T. & Bell, F. O. 1938 *Nature, London*, **141**, 747.
Beevers, C. A. & Cochran, W. 1947 *Proc. Roy. Soc.* A, **190**, 257.
Bijvoet, J. M., Peerdeman, A. F. & van Bommel, A. J. 1951 *Nature, Lond.*, **168**, 271.
Broomhead, J. M. 1948 *Acta Cryst.* **1**, 324.
Broomhead, J. M. 1951 *Acta Cryst.* **4**, 92.
Brown, D. M. & Lythgoe, B. 1950 *J. Chem. Soc.* p. 1990.
Brown, D. M. & Todd, A. R. 1952 *J. Chem. Soc.* p. 52.
Chargaff, E. 1951 *J. Cell. Comp. Physiol.* **38**, 41.
Chargaff, E., Crampton, C. F. & Lipschitz, R. 1953 *Nature, Lond.*, **172**, 289.
Cochran, W. 1951 *Acta Cryst.* **4**, 81.
Cochran, W., Crick, F. H. C. & Vand, V. 1952 *Acta Cryst.* **5**, 581.
Crane, H. R. 1950 *Sci. Mon.* **70**, 376.

* More recently, Franklin & Gosling (1953*b*) have suggested that the X-ray data for the crystalline form also supports a structure of this general type. They also mention that the equatorial reflexions for the paracrystalline form suggest that the diameter of our model is a little too large. *Note added in proof*: Wilkins, Seeds, Stokes & Wilson (1953) have also presented X-ray evidence for the crystalline form being a pair of helices.

Dekker, C. R., Michelson, A. M. & Todd, A. R. 1953 *J. Chem. Soc.* p. 947.
Donohue, J. 1952 *J. Phys. Chem.* **56**, 502.
Franklin, R. E. & Gosling, R. G. 1953*a* *Nature, Lond.*, **171**, 740.
Franklin, R. E. & Gosling, R. G. 1953*b* *Nature, Lond.*, **172**, 156.
Franklin, R. E. & Gosling, R. G. 1953*c* *Acta Cryst.* **6**, 673, 678.
Furberg, S. 1950 *Acta Cryst.* **3**, 325.
Furberg, S. 1952 *Acta chem. scand.* **6**, 634.
Jordan, D. O. 1951 *Progr. biophys.* **2**, 51.
Kahler, H. & Lloyd, B. J. 1953 *Biochim. Biophys. Acta*, **10**, 355.
Michelson, A. M. & Todd, A. R. 1953 *J. Chem. Soc.* p. 951.
Pauling, L., Corey, R. B. & Branson, H. R. 1951 *Proc. Nat. Acad. Sci., Wash.*, **37**, 205.
Pauling, L. & Corey, R. B. 1953 *Proc. Nat. Acad. Sci., Wash.*, **39**, 84.
Riley, D. P. & Oster, G. 1951 *Biochim. Biophys. Acta*, **7**, 526.
Sadron, C. 1953 *Progr. biophys.* **3**.
Tipson, R. S. 1945 *Advanc. Carbohyd. Chem.* **1**, 238. New York: Academic Press Inc.
Watson, J. D. & Crick, F. H. C. 1953*a* *Nature, Lond.*, **171**, 737.
Watson, J. D. & Crick, F. H. C. 1953*b* *Nature, Lond.*, **171**, 964.
Watson, J. D. & Crick, F. H. C. 1953*c* *Cold Spr. Harb. Symp. Quant. Biol.* (in the Press).
Wilkins, M. H. F., Gosling, R. G. & Seeds, W. E. 1951 *Nature, Lond.*, **167**, 759.
Wilkins, M. H. F., Seeds, W. E., Stokes, A. R. & Wilson, H. R. 1953 *Nature, Lond.*, **172**, 759.
Wilkins, M. H. F., Stokes, A. R. & Wilson, H. R. 1953 *Nature, Lond.*, **171**, 738.
Williams, R. C. 1952 *Biochim. Biophys. Acta*, **9**, 237.
Wyatt, G. R. 1952 *The chemistry and physiology of the nucleus.* New York: Academic Press.
Wyatt, G. R. & Cohen, S. S. 1952 *Nature, Lond.*, **170**, 846.
Zussman, J. 1953 *Acta Cryst.* **6**, 504.

PRINTED IN GREAT BRITAIN AT THE UNIVERSITY PRESS, CAMBRIDGE
(BROOKE CRUTCHLEY, UNIVERSITY PRINTER)

1953 SYMPOSIUM

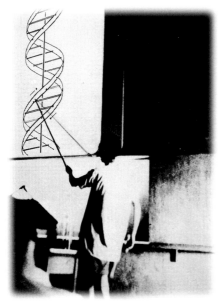

*(Top) Jim Watson speaking at the 1953 Symposium on Quantitative Biology on "Viruses,"
where the double-helical structure of DNA was described. (Courtesy of the James D. Watson
Collection, CSHL Archives.)*
*(Bottom) Bush Auditorium, circa 1962. The new Bush Auditorium was first used for the 1953
Symposium. (Courtesy CSHL Archives.)*

A Day in June

JIM WATSON PRESENTED A PAPER ON THE DOUBLE-HELICAL structure of DNA at the 18th Cold Spring Harbor Symposium on "Viruses" in early June, 1953, six weeks after the publication of the Watson-Crick paper in *Nature*. In the days when journals were transported by sea, many at the meeting had not yet heard of the discovery; others knew the basic facts but little more; and a select few, particularly the members of the Phage Group, were well aware of the structure and had already partly embraced its biological implications. For all, however, the 1953 Cold Spring Harbor Symposium was the first opportunity to see the model.

Jim was potentially facing a fairly sceptical audience. Even as late as 1953, a good many people, in particular the biochemists, remained unconvinced that DNA was the genetic material. They were unwilling to acknowledge the importance of the key experiments preceding the Watson-Crick model, in particular the transformation experiments of Oswald Avery and his Rockefeller colleagues. The Waring blender experiment of Al Hershey and Martha Chase, much more to the liking of the biochemists and immediately convincing to the Phage Group, was in fact far from conclusive since the phage DNA associated with the infected cell was accompanied by 20% protein.

Max Delbrück, who had a major hand in the organization of the Symposium, had invited Jim to speak at the meeting soon after receiving Jim's letter of March 12 containing a hand-drawn sketch of a base pair (see page 117). Max was excited by, and immediately accepting of, the model, although he could not see how bases located internally to the phosphate-sugar backbone could carry information; nor could he see how the two strands could unwind during replication. Nevertheless, with great enthusiasm, he set about proselytizing the Watson-Crick structure, both at Caltech and elsewhere.

So the members of Phage Group arrived at the Cold Spring Harbor Symposium fully primed to accept the model. But how would it be received by others?

In 1993, people who had attended the 1953 Symposium were asked to record their memories of the occasion and their impressions of Jim. A few people left the meeting unaware of the significance of what they had heard; others had vague recollections of Jim's talk but could not recall details. Others had clear and crisp memories. Extracts from some of their letters are printed on the following pages, together with photographs of the Symposium participants.

MEMORIES OF THE 1953 SYMPOSIUM

Having been at Caltech during this period, I was privy to the Watson letters to Delbrück, prior to the *Nature* paper and was therefore not startled by the presentation of the structure at the CSH meeting. I do believe, however, that most of the virologists and geneticists were—very pleasantly—astonished. In general, they had not paid much attention to the field of DNA research. Also, either they had not seen the *Nature* paper or they had not grasped its significance. At the meeting, they did and its genetic implications were obvious and overwhelming.

...Aside from his talk itself, my recollections of conversations with Watson are mostly of anecdotes about evenings in the pub, hassles with the Director (Bragg),[1] etc. Curious, and likely an unfair impression.

Robert L. Sinsheimer
Professor Emeritus
Department of Biological Sciences
University of California, Santa Barbara
January 30, 1993

Watson's (and Crick's) model was argued about its logic (how can the bases, in their sequence, have information if the are *inside* the helix)? Also, Aaron Bendich[2] said that in his chemical analysis (carried out in Chargaff's [3] laboratory) A ≠ T and G not quite equal to C. Bendich said that Chargaff was against the model in part for the discrepancies in the base analysis.

Julius Marmur
Department of Biochemistry
Albert Einstein College of Medicine of Yeshiva University
March 2, 1993

...However, at the time, neither Avery's findings nor those of Hershey/Chase were considered absolute proof that genetic material was DNA... .

...I believe the scientific community did not readily accept theoretical extrapolations from their model, although its simplicity, elegance, and probable correctness were appreciated. Everyone awaited experimental results that would establish it beyond any doubt.

Charles Yanofsky
Department of Biological Sciences
Stanford University
March 2, 1993

My sense of the 1953 meeting was that there was already a great deal of acceptance and excitement about Watson-Crick before Jim spoke. It's hard to dissociate the impact of the papers themselves and Max's role in distributing them. But I doubt whether his imprimatur was necessary.

Louis Siminovitch
Director of Research
Samuel Lunenfeld Research Institute
Mount Sinai Hospital
February 3, 1993

My memory of Jim then was of a gangling young man, casually dressed in shorts and T shirt, with rather wild staring eyes and with one sandshoe and one slipper. I don't recall speaking with him, because I would have felt that I had nothing to say. My most vivid memory of that meeting is of Delbrück getting up in the middle of a talk on bacterial chromosomes by high-power light microscopy by a man called Lanni and telling him to stop; which he promptly did and fled the meeting.

Concerning acceptance of the idea that DNA was the genetic material, I had spent 1948–1949 working in Dubos' lab, where one of the staff was Rollin Hotchkiss, whose main effort over the previous several years was to show that the pneumococcus transforming principle was pure DNA, with no protein contamination. So I had been brought up on the Avery idea. As I remember it, there was general acceptance by the phage and animal virologists at that meeting of the idea that DNA was the genetic material of viruses (but for good reason, not by the few plant virologists). The revolutionary part was that the double helix structure provided a picture of how it might replicate.

Frank Fenner
The John Curtin School of Medical Research
The Australian National University
February 1, 1993

...One thing I remember was a sense of shock at the attempt (and I presume success) at bulldozing. Any suggestion that alternative or more complex ideas besides the central role of DNA were treated pejoratively. I wish I could reconstruct the phrase with which an exploratory question was answered, but it was brutal. Personal style and heavy self-confidence floated in the air and I did not like it at all.

There is no doubt that the model was widely discussed outside the sessions and in my presence fully appreciated, and certainly the immediate biological implications were seen.

Roy J. Britten
Kerckhoff Marine Laboratory
California Institute of Technology
February 4, 1993

...Yes, I was at the famous CSH meeting, having been brought there by Szilard.[4] I had already been in the Biochemistry Department at the University of Chicago for several years, but had little idea of what was going on in molecular biology. Szilard undertook to provide me with some education at CSH and he certainly did; I was bowled over by the visit. Yes, I remember Jim Watson carrying around the model on the terrace outside the auditorium after his lecture. I remember asking him something and had the feeling he thought I wasn't worth talking to (quite right).

During that meeting I knew I was confronting something new and important, but I was unable to digest it or place it in perspective, as many of those present were no doubt able to do. The only other thing I remember was some sort of square-dancing that Jim seemed to enjoy.

Howard Green
George Higginson Professor
Chairman of the Department
Department of Cellular and Molecular Physiology
Harvard Medical School
February 16, 1993

...there was appreciable resistance in an important segment of the biological community to acceptance of the idea that DNA was the genetic material as well as the structure of DNA presented by Watson and Crick.

I think this represents simply an example of cultural lag. In the middle of this century, biology was still strongly under the influence of the philosophical position that molecular events would explain only a relatively small part of life processes. I think many biologists felt threatened by the idea that specific molecular structures and interactions would provide the logic to explain all or most of the cellular phenomena.

...While some of us felt that a new era in biology had begun which would revolutionize medicine as well, others insisted on caution. Still, I believe everyone was deeply stirred.

...Jim...was then as he is today—deeply introspective, impatient with sloppy thinking, and interested only in experiments and logical analysis that would open up new vistas in science.

Theodore T. Puck
Senior Fellow, Eleanor Roosevelt Institute for Cancer Research
Distinguished Professor, Department of Medicine
University of Chicago Health Sciences Center
March 11, 1993

...I noticed Jim at the first summer evening seminar I attended, because he was sitting in the front row on the floor, not on the chair, with his back to the speaker, with his head between his knees. After the seminar, I could not resist to ask Jim why he was not facing the speaker like everybody else, and Jim's reply was: "Because I cannot concentrate on the subject when I watch this idiot."...

In 1951–1952, Demerec succeeded to secure funds for building the new Carnegie laboratories and a new lecture hall, and these were completed just before the 1953 Cold Spring Harbor Symposium devoted to viruses (June 5–11, 1953). That was supposed to be a really great Symposium since it was organized by Max Delbrück. Jim was scheduled as one of the speakers, and the scientist who was supposed to pick Jim up at the airport had asked me to drive to the Idlewild (now JFK) airport. Thus, on the way back from the airport I listened to many details about the double helix. Sometime before the Symposium, somebody (I guess not Jim, but I do not remember who) gave a summary of the double-helix work just before it was published in *Nature* (in the small seminar room in Blackford Hall, roughly where the bar is at present, which also served as a temporary dormitory in the late 1940s). We all just loved the results. It was all so clear and obvious—I was sure it to be so! Just after the (Jim's) presentation, Max Delbrück got up and said "Gentlemen, hats off, for the first time I understand how DNA replicates. It is not like-begets-like, but like-begets-complementary. Niels Bohr would be happy to hear that."...

Jim gave a superb lecture at the Symposium, but for me it was already a "déjà vu" since the excitement of hearing for the first time was already some weeks or months old. Isn't it strange? I accepted 100% the double-helix gospel from the first time I heard about it, so it was so surprising and disconcerting that for quite a few years to come, when lecturing or visiting many U.S. and European universities, that I learned that many faculty members in biology and biochemistry either did not hear about the double helix or greeted it with remarks like: "One of these theoretical models to which nobody pays attention," or "Oh that gossip." I even heard one prominent faculty member of an eastern university make the following comment in 1955 or 1956: "It is not even worthwhile to read all this DNA literature anymore; it is all trash." Moreover, I also recently looked over the 1953–1954 Annual Report of the Biological Laboratory in Cold Spring Harbor, where the highlights of this Symposium were mentioned, but there was nothing about the double helix.

Waclaw Szybalski
Department of Oncology
McArdle Laboratory for Cancer Research
University of Wisconsin-Madison Medical School
February 16, 1993

The thing that I remember most vividly about the Symposium in 1953 was the appearance of Jim with a magnificent three-dimensional model of the double helix encased in a transparent Lucite cylinder. He sat on the steps of Blackford Hall and explained in detail about the intricacies of the model to all who gathered around, and believe me, he did draw a crowd. I don't remember the details of his formal presentation, but I do remember the discussions that it engendered, particularly those by Max Delbrück and Gunther Stent glowing over the elegance of the model and how it could explain the mechanism of DNA replication by the complementarity generated by Chargaff's ratios.

It was all very exciting, but I don't agree with Seymour Cohen that the Watson-Crick model was what created unusual insight on the role of DNA. I think that most of us at that time accepted DNA as the major genetic element when in 1944, Avery, MacLeod, and McCarty identified the pneumococcal transforming factor to be DNA. That followed a good 10 years of confirmation by a number of people (Hotchkiss, Alexander, Leidy, Lerman, etc.). We also were pretty much convinced by the Hershey-Chase experiment that DNA was the critical ingredient in phage replication. The Watson-Crick model was the clinching factor to explain self-replication, even before Kornberg found the polymerase.

...My impressions of young Jim was that he was a bit shy, but highly opinionated and intolerant of lesser intellects. I also remember his practical joke antics, particularly when he and Nick Visconti raided a sedate cocktail party at the Demerec house wearing Halloween masks and bombarding the guests with a machine gun that shot ping-pong balls. I don't remember Jim participating in the extracurricular activities that kept most of the other young people busy when not in the labs, such as the softball games alongside of Barbara McClintock's corn field (many balls landed in her fields) or MacDowell's evening square dances on Carnegie lawn.

Joseph S. Gots
Emeritus Professor
Department of Microbiology
University of Pennsylvania
February 26, 1993

✛ ✛ ✛

...I being aware of the work, accepted the implications immediately. There was a general commotion among virologists but I do not think that everybody realized the real significance of the discovery. This always happens. A new discovery has to penetrate, through osmosis, to the brains of a multitude of scientists before it is fully recognized.

Hillary Koprowski
Department of Microbiology and Immunology Center for Neurovirology
Jefferson Medical College
Thomas Jefferson University
March 1, 1993

Stephen Zamenhof, Jim Watson

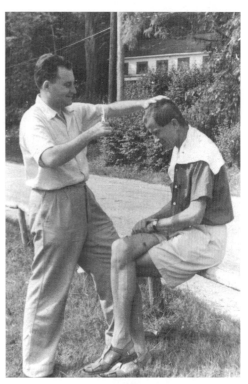

Seymour Benzer, Max Delbrück

François Jacob, André Lwoff,
Louis Siminovitch

Gunther Stent

Photographs from the 1953 Cold Spring Harbor Symposium on Quantitative Biology. (Courtesy CSHL Archives.)

Martha Chase, Alfred Hershey

Cyrus Levinthal, Salvador Luria

Max Delbrück, Aaron Novick, Leo Szilard, Jim Watson

Photographs from the 1953 Cold Spring Harbor Symposium on Quantitative Biology. (Courtesy CSHL Archives.)

270 SCIENTISTS TAKE PART IN SYMPOSIUM HERE ON 'VIRUSES'

During the week from June 5 to 11 American and foreign scientists in the field of virus research attended the Cold Spring Harbor Symposium at the Biological Laboratory. More than 270 scientists took part in the meetings, which were held in the new lecture hall dedicated two week ago by Dr. Vannevar Bush.

This was the eighteenth annual meeting of the Cold Spring Harbor Symposia on Quantitative Biology, which bring together scientists working on different phases of some broad problem. The subject this year was "Viruses." These are the smallest and simplest of living organisms known to man. They are so small that they can be observed only with the electron microscope; and some plant viruses are so simple in their chemistry that they can be crystallized. But in spite of their small size and simple chem-

(Continued on Page Two)

270 SCIENTISTS

(Continued from Page One)

istry the viruses are very important to man, not only because some of them are responsible for diseases but also because they perform complex functions characteristic of higher forms of life, and therefore are valuable for the study of these functions. Viruses reproduce, and pass through a stage comparable to mating in higher organisms. During this stage the hereditary traits of two viruses are exchanged and assorted in accordance with the well-known Mendelian law which applies to plants, animals, and men.

At this year's conference biologists, biophysicists, biochemists, and pathologists reported and discussed the results of their experiments with bacterial, plant, and animal viruses. For more than ten years scientists have been working out techiques for studying the multiplication, heredity, and chemistry of the viruses that attack bacteria. In the past two years a good start has been made on adapting similar methods to investigate the viruses that attack animal cells and cause many diseases still uncontrolled by medical science — such as poliomyelitis, influenza, and the common cold. Dr. R. Dulbecco of the California Institute of Technology gave a review of his pioneer work in growing animal viruses in the laboratory under conditions suitable for the quantitative determination of their multiplication.

Other discussions dealt with the different stages in the growth of viruses, their heredity, and their chemical structure. Dr. J. D. Watson, a Fellow of the National Foundation for Infantile Paralysis working in the Cavendish Laboratory at Cambridge University, England, reported his work with Dr. F. H. C. Crick on the molecular pattern of a substance known as desoxyribonucleic aeid, which is believed to be the carrier of inherited traits and the material that links organic life with inorganic matter. A detailed account of this research, received by cable from London, appeared in the New York Times last Saturday.

By far the greatest portion of the conference was spent in discussion of the basic discoveries of research scientists, since these are the foundation for applied and clinical reasearch. However, the questions of transmission, virulence, immunity, and control — all important in

the medical field — were treated often in the discussions.

Cooperating with the Laboratory in the organization of this meeting was the National Foundation for Infantile Paralysis, which supports an extensive virus research program in the effort to find a means of controlling polio. Since the Foundation invited a large number of key participants, it was possible for more foreign visitors than usual to be present at the meeting. Participants from abroad totaled 17, including four from Canada, six from England and Scotland, three from France, two from Germany, one from Australia, and one from Switzerland. The 255 other scientists came from 23 states.

Article from The Long-Islander, *June 1953, about the Symposium on "Viruses." (Reprinted, Courtesy Long Islander Newspapers, Inc., Huntington, N.Y.)*

UNIVERSITY OF CAMBRIDGE   DEPARTMENT OF PHYSICS

TELEPHONE
CAMBRIDGE 55478

CAVENDISH LABORATORY
FREE SCHOOL LANE
CAMBRIDGE

March 12, 1953

Dear Max

Thank You very much for your recent letters. We were quite interested in your account of the Pauling Seminar. The day following the arrival of your letter, I received a note from Pauling, mentioning that their model had been revised, and indicating interest in our model. We shall thus have to write him in the near future as to what we are doing. Until now we preferred not to write him since we did not want to commit ourselves until we were completely sure that all of the van der Walls contacts were correct and that all aspects of our structure were stereochemically feasible. I believe now that we have made sure that our structure can be built and today we are laboriously calculating out exact atomic coordinates.

Our model (a joint project of Francis Crick and myself) bears no relationship to either the original or to the revised Pauling-Corey-Shoemaker models. It is a strange model and embodies several unusual features. However since DNA is an unusual substance we are not hesitant in being bold. The main features of the model are (1) The basic structure is helical - it consists of two inter-twining helices - the core of the helix is occupied by the purine and pyrimidine bases. - The phosphates groups are on the outside (2) the helices are not identical but complementary so that if one helix contain a purine base, the other helix contains a pyrimidine. This feature is a result of our attempt to make the residues equivalent and at the same time put the purines and pyrimidine bases in the center. The pairing of the purine with pyrimidine is very exact and dictated by their desire to form hydrogen bonds - Adenine will pair with Thymine while Guanine will always pair with Cytosine. For example

Adenine—sugar

(next page)

Jim Watson's letter to Max Delbrück, March 12, 1953. (Continued on following pages.)
(Reprinted courtesy of the Archives, California Institute of Technology.)
See transcribed letter following Jim's letter above.

UNIVERSITY OF CAMBRIDGE   DEPARTMENT OF PHYSICS

TELEPHONE
CAMBRIDGE 55478

CAVENDISH LABORATORY
FREE SCHOOL LANE
CAMBRIDGE

Thymine   with   Adenine

Or

Cytosine   with   Guanine

While my diagram is crude, in fact these pairs form 2 very nice hydrogen bonds in which all of the angles are exactly right. This pairing is based on the effective existence of only one out of the two possible tautomeric forms — in all cases we prefer the Keto form over the enol, and the amino over the imino. This is a definitively an assumption but Jerry Donohue and Bill Cochran tell us that, for all organic molecules so far examined, the keto and amino forms are present in preference to the enol and imino possibilities.

The model has been derived almost entirely from stereochemical considerations with the only x-ray consideration being the spacing between the pair of bases 3.4Å which was originally found by Astbury. It turns to build itself with approximately 10 residues per turn in 34Å. The screw is right handed.

The x-ray pattern approximately agrees with the model, but since the photographs available to us are poor and negative (we have no photographs of our own and like Pauling must use Astbury's photographs) this agreement in no way constitutes a proof of our model. We are certainly a long way from proving its correctness. To do this we must obtain collaboration from the group at Kings College London who possess very excellent photographs of a crystalline phase in addition to rather good photographs of a paracrystalline phase. Our model has been made in reference to the paracrystalline form and as yet we have no clear ideas as to how these helices can

Jim Watson's letter to Max Delbrück, March 12, 1953. (Continued.)
Jim's letter is transcribed on facing page.

March 12, 1953

Dear Max

Thank you very much for your recent letters. We were quite interested in your account of the Pauling seminar. The day following the arrival of your letter, I received a note from Pauling, mentioning that their model had been revised, and indicating interest in our model. We shall thus have to write him in the near future as to what we are doing. Until now we preferred not to write him since we did not want to commit ourselves until we were completely sure that all of the van der Waals contacts were correct and that all aspects of our structure were stereochemically feasible. I believe now that we have made sure that our structure can be built and today we are laboriously calculating out exact atomic coordindates.

Our model (a joint project of Francis Crick and myself) bears no relationship to either the original or to the revised Pauling-Corey-Shoemaker models. It is a strange model and embodies several unusual features. However since DNA is an unusual substance we are not hesitant in being bold. The main features of the model are (1) the basic structure is helical—it consists of two intertwining helices—the core of the helix is occupied by the purine and pyrimidine bases—the phosphate groups are on the outside (2) the helices are not identical but complementary so that if one helix contains a purine base, the other helix contains a pyrimidine. This feature is a result of our attempt to make the residues equivalent and at the same time put the purines and pyrimidine bases in the center. The pairing of the purine with pyrimidines is very exact and dictated by their desire to form hydrogen bonds. Adenine will pair with Thymine while Guanine will always pair with Cytosine. For example [see Jim's handwritten letter for the example]

While my diagram is crude, in fact these pairs form 2 very nice hydrogen bonds in which all of the angles are exactly right. This pairing is based on the effective existence of only one out of the two possible tautomeric forms—in all cases we prefer the keto form over the enol and the amino over the imino. This is definitively an assumption but Jerry Donohue and Bill Cochran tell us that, for all organic molecules so far examined, the keto and amino forms are present in preference to the enol and imino possibilities.

The model has been derived almost entirely from stereochemical considerations with the only x-ray consideration being the spacing between the pair of bases 3.4A which was originally found by Astbury. It tries to build itself with approximately 10 residues per turn in 34A. The screw is right handed.

The x-ray pattern approximately agrees with the model, but since the photographs available to us are poor and meager (we have no photographs of our own and like Pauling must use Astbury's photographs) this agreement in no way constitutes a proof of our model. We are certainly a long way from proving its correctness. To do this we must obtain collaboration from the group at Kings College London who possess very excellent photographs of a crystalline phase in addition to rather good photographs of a paracrystalline phase. Our model has been made in reference to the paracrystalline form and as yet we have no clear ideas as to how these helices can pack together to form the crystalline phase.

In the next day or so Crick and I shall send a note to *Nature* proposing our structure as a possible model, at the same time emphasizing its provisional nature and the lack of proof in its favor. Even if wrong I believe it to be interesting since it provides a concrete example of a structure composed of complementary chains. If by chance it is right then I suspect we may be making a slight dent into the manner in which DNA can reproduce itself. For these reasons (in addition to many others) I prefer this type of model over Pauling's which if true would tell us next to nothing about manner of DNA reproduction.

I shall write you in a day or so about the recombination paper. Yesterday I received a very interesting note from Bill Hayes. I believe he is sending you a copy.

I have met Alfred Tissieres recently. He seems very nice. He speaks fondly of Pasadena and I suspect has not yet become accustomed to being a Fellow of Kings.

My regards to Manny

Jim

P.S. We would prefer your not mentioning this letter to Pauling. When our letter to *Nature* is completed we shall send him a copy. We should like to send him coordinates.

The Structure of DNA

J.D. Watson and F.H.C. Crick

Reprinted from the 1953 Cold Spring Harbor Symposium on Quantitative Biology. (Courtesy CSHL Press.)

THE STRUCTURE OF DNA

J. D. WATSON[1] AND F. H. C. CRICK

Cavendish Laboratory, Cambridge, England

(Contribution to the Discussion of Provirus.)

It would be superfluous at a Symposium on Viruses to introduce a paper on the structure of DNA with a discussion on its importance to the problem of virus reproduction. Instead we shall not only assume that DNA is important, but in addition that it is the carrier of the genetic specificity of the virus (for argument, see Hershey, this volume) and thus must possess in some sense the capacity for exact self-duplication. In this paper we shall describe a structure for DNA which suggests a mechanism for its self-duplication and allows us to propose, for the first time, a detailed hypothesis on the atomic level for the self-reproduction of genetic material.

We first discuss the chemical and physical-chemical data which show that DNA is a long fibrous molecule. Next we explain why crystallographic evidence suggests that the structural unit of DNA consists not of one but of two polynucleotide chains. We then discuss a stereochemical model which we believe satisfactorily accounts for both the chemical and crystallographic data. In conclusion we suggest some obvious genetical implications of the proposed structure. A preliminary account of some of these data has already appeared in Nature (Watson and Crick, 1953a, 1953b).

I. EVIDENCE FOR THE FIBROUS NATURE OF DNA

The basic chemical formula of DNA is now well established. As shown in Figure 1 it consists of a very long chain, the backbone of which is made up of alternate sugar and phosphate groups, joined together in regular 3' 5' phosphate di-ester linkages. To each sugar is attached a nitrogenous base, only four different kinds of which are commonly found in DNA. Two of these—adenine and guanine—are purines, and the other two—thymine and cytosine—are pyrimidines. A fifth base, 5-methyl cytosine, occurs in smaller amounts in certain organisms, and a sixth, 5-hydroxy-methyl-cytosine, is found instead of cytosine in the T even phages (Wyatt and Cohen, 1952).

It should be noted that the chain is unbranched, a consequence of the regular internucleotide linkage. On the other hand the sequence of the different nucleotides is, as far as can be ascertained, completely irregular. Thus, DNA has some features which are regular, and some which are irregular.

A similar conception of the DNA molecule as a long thin fiber is obtained from physico-chemical analysis involving sedimentation, diffusion, light scattering, and viscosity measurements. These techniques indicate that DNA is a very asymmetrical structure approximately 20 A wide and many thousands of angstroms long. Estimates of its molecular weight currently center between 5×10^6 and 10^7 (approximately 3×10^4 nucleotides). Surprisingly each of these measurements tend to suggest that the DNA is relatively rigid, a puzzling finding in view of the large number of single bonds (5 per nucleotide) in the phosphate-sugar back-

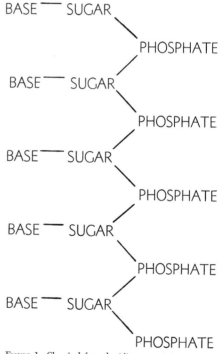

FIGURE 1. Chemical formula (diagrammatic) of a single chain of desoxyribonucleic acid.

[1] Aided by a Fellowship from the National Foundation for Infantile Paralysis.

[123]

bone. Recently these indirect inferences have been confirmed by electron microscopy. Employing high resolution techniques both Williams (1952) and Kahler *et al.* (1953) have observed, in preparations of DNA, very long thin fibers with a uniform width of approximately 15-20 A.

II. EVIDENCE FOR THE EXISTENCE OF TWO CHEMICAL CHAINS IN THE FIBER

This evidence comes mainly from X-ray studies. The material used is the sodium salt of DNA (usually from calf thymus) which has been extracted, purified, and drawn into fibers. These fibers are highly birefringent, show marked ultraviolet and infrared dichroism (Wilkins *et al.*, 1951; Fraser and Fraser, 1951), and give good X-ray fiber diagrams. From a preliminary study of these, Wilkins, Franklin and their co-workers at King's College, London (Wilkins *et al.*, 1953; Franklin and Gosling 1953a, b and c) have been able to draw certain general conclusions about the structure of DNA. Two important facts emerge from their work. They are:

(1) *Two distinct forms of DNA exist.* Firstly a crystalline form, Structure A, (Figure 2) which occurs at about 75 per cent relative humidity and contains approximately 30 per cent water. At higher humidities the fibers take up more water, increase in length by about 30 per cent and assume Structure B (Figure 3). This is a less ordered form than Structure A, and appears to be paracrystalline; that is, the individual molecules are all packed parallel to one another, but are not otherwise regularly arranged in space. In Table 1, we have tabulated some of the characteristic features which distinguish the two forms. The transition from A to B is reversible and therefore the two structures are likely to be related in a simple manner.

(2) *The crystallographic unit contains two polynucleotide chains.* The argument is crystallographic and so will only be given in outline. Structure B has a very strong 3.4 A reflexion on the meridian. As first pointed out by Astbury (1947), this can only mean that the nucleotides in it occur in groups spaced 3.4 A apart in the fiber direction. On going from Structure B to Structure A the fiber shortens by about 30 per cent. Thus in Structure A the groups must be about 2.5 per cent A apart axially. The measured density of Structure A, (Franklin

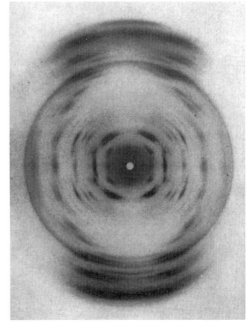

FIGURE 2. X-ray fiber diagram of Structure A of desoxyribonucleic acid. (H. M. F. Wilkins and H. R. Wilson, unpub.)

and Gosling, 1953c) together with the cell dimensions, shows that there must be *two* nucleotides in each such group. Thus it is very probable that the crystallographic unit consists of two distinct polynucleotide chains. Final proof of this can only come from a complete solution of the structure.

Structure A has a pseudo-hexagonal lattice, in which the lattice points are 22 A apart. This distance roughly corresponds with the diameter of fibers seen in the electron microscope, bearing in mind that the latter are quite dry. Thus it is probable that the crystallographic unit and the fiber are the one and the same.

III. DESCRIPTION OF THE PROPOSED STRUCTURE

Two conclusions might profitably be drawn from the above data. Firstly, the structure of DNA is

TABLE 1.
(From Franklin and Gosling, 1953a, b and c)

	Degree of orientation	Repeat distance along fiber axis	Location of first equatorial spacing	Water content	Number of nucleotides within unit cell
Structure A	Crystalline	28 A	18 A	30%	22-24
Structure B	Paracrystalline	34 A	22-24 A	> 30%	20 (?)

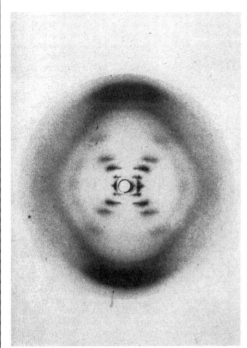

FIGURE 3. X-ray fiber diagram of Structure B of desoxyribonucleic acid. (R. E. Franklin and R. Gosling, 1953a.)

regular enough to form a three dimensional crystal. This is in spite of the fact that its component chains may have an irregular sequence of purine and pyrimidine nucleotides. Secondly, as the structure contains two chains, these chains must be regularly arranged in relation to each other.

To account for these findings, we have proposed (Watson and Crick, 1953a) a structure in which the two chains are coiled round a common axis and joined together by hydrogen bonds between the nucleotide bases (see Figure 4). Both chains follow right handed helices, but the sequences of the atoms in the phosphate-sugar backbones run in opposite directions and so are related by a dyad perpendicular to the helix axis. The phosphates and sugar groups are on the outside of the helix whilst the bases are on the inside. The distance of a phosphorus atom from the fiber axis is 10 A. We have built our model to correspond to Structure B, which the X-ray data show to have a repeat distance of 34 A in the fiber direction and a very strong reflexion of spacing 3.4 A on the meridian of the X-ray pattern. To fit these observations our structure has a nucleotide on each chain every 3.4 A in the fiber direction, and makes one complete turn after 10 such intervals, i.e., after 34 A. Our

structure is a well-defined one and all bond distances and angles, including van der Waal distances, are stereochemically acceptable.

The essential element of the structure is the manner in which the two chains are held together by hydrogen bonds between the bases. The bases are perpendicular to the fiber axis and joined together in pairs. The pairing arrangement is very specific, and only certain pairs of bases will fit into the structure. The basic reason for this is that we have assumed that the backbone of each polynucleotide chain is in the form of a regular helix. Thus, irrespective of which bases are present, the glucosidic bonds (which join sugar and base) are arranged in a regular manner in space. In particular, any two glucosidic bonds (one from each chain)

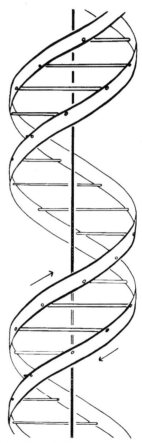

FIGURE 4. This figure is diagrammatic. The two ribbons symbolize the two phosphate-sugar chains and the horizontal rods. The paths of bases holding the chain together. The vertical line marks the fiber axis.

which are attached to a bonded pair of bases, must always occur at a fixed distance apart due to the regularity of the two backbones to which they are joined. The result is that one member of a pair of bases must always be a purine, and the other a pyrimidine, in order to bridge between the two chains. If a pair consisted of two purines, for example, there would not be room for it; if of two pyrimidines they would be too far apart to form hydrogen bonds.

In theory a base can exist in a number of tautomeric forms, differing in the exact positions at which its hydrogen atoms are attached. However, under physiological conditions one particular form of each base is much more probable than any of the others. If we make the assumption that the favored forms always occur, then the pairing requirements are even more restrictive. Adenine can only pair with thymine, and guanine only with cytosine (or 5-methyl-cytosine, or 5-hydroxy-methyl-cytosine). This pairing is shown in detail in Figures 5 and 6. If adenine tried to pair with cytosine it could not form hydrogen bonds, since there would be two hydrogens near one of the bonding positions, and none at the other, instead of one in each.

A given pair can be either way round. Adenine, for example, can occur on either chain, but when it does its partner on the other chain must always be thymine. This is possible because the two glucoside bonds of a pair (see Figures 5 and 6) are symmetrically related to each other, and thus occur in the same positions if the pair is turned over.

It should be emphasized that since each base can form hydrogen bonds at a number of points one can pair up *isolated* nucleotides in a large variety of ways. *Specific* pairing of bases can only be obtained by imposing some restriction, and in our

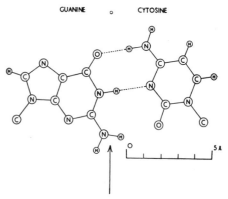

FIGURE 6. Pairing of guanine and cytosine. Hydrogen bonds are shown dotted. One carbon atom of each sugar is shown.

case it is in a direct consequence of the postulated regularity of the phosphate-sugar backbone.

It should further be emphasized that whatever pair of bases occurs at one particular point in the DNA structure, no restriction is imposed on the neighboring pairs, and any *sequence* of pairs can occur. This is because all the bases are flat, and since they are stacked roughly one above another like a pile of pennies, it makes no difference which pair is neighbor to which.

Though any sequence of bases can fit into our structure, the necessity for specific pairing demands a definite relationship between the sequences on the two chains. That is, if we knew the actual order of the bases on one chain, we could automatically write down the order on the other. *Our structure therefore consists of two chains, each of which is the complement of the other.*

IV. EVIDENCE IN FAVOR OF THE COMPLEMENTARY MODEL

The experimental evidence available to us now offers strong support to our model though we should emphasize that, as yet, it has not been proved correct. The evidence in its favor is of three types:

(1) The general appearance of the X-ray picture strongly suggests that the basic structure is helical (Wilkins *et al.*, 1953; Franklin and Gosling, 1953a). If we postulate that a helix is present, we immediately are able to deduce from the X-ray pattern of Structure B (Figure 3), that its pitch is 34 A and its diameter approximately 20 A. Moreover, the pattern suggests a high concentration of atoms on the circumference of the helix, in accord with our model which places the phosphate sugar backbone on the outside. The photograph also indicates that the two polynucleotide chains are not

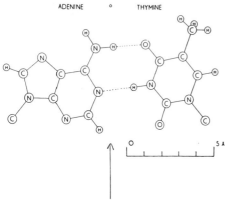

FIGURE 5. Pairing of adenine and thymine. Hydrogen bonds are shown dotted. One carbon atom of each sugar is shown.

spaced equally along the fiber axis, but are probably displaced from each other by about three-eighths of the fiber axis period, an inference again in qualitative agreement with our model.

The interpretation of the X-ray pattern of Structure A (the crystalline form) is less obvious. This form does not give a meridional reflexion at 3.4 A, but instead (Figure 2) gives a series of reflexions around 25° off the meridian at spacings between 3 A and 4 A. This suggests to us that in this form the bases are no longer perpendicular to the fiber axis, but are tilted about 25° from the perpendicular position in a way that allows the fiber to contract 30 per cent and reduces the longitudinal translation of each nucleotide to about 2.5 A. It should be noted that the X-ray pattern of Structure A is much more detailed than that of Structure B and so if correctly interpreted, can yield more precise information about DNA. Any proposed model for DNA must be capable of forming either Structure A or Structure B and so it remains imperative for our very tentative interpretation of Structure A to be confirmed.

(2) The anomolous titration curves of undegraded DNA with acids and bases strongly suggests that hydrogen bond formation is a characteristic aspect of DNA structure. When a solution of DNA is initially treated with acids or bases, no groups are titratable at first between pH 5 and pH 11.0, but outside these limits a rapid ionization occurs (Gulland and Jordan, 1947; Jordan, 1951). On back titration, however, either with acid from pH 12 or with alkali from pH 2½, a different titration curve is obtained indicating that the titratable groups are more accessible to acids and bases than is the untreated solution. Accompanying the initial release of groups at pH 11.5 and in the range pH 3.5 to pH 4.5 is a marked fall in the viscosity and the disappearance of strong flow birefringence. While this decrease was originally thought to be caused by a reversible depolymerization (Vilbrandt and Tennent, 1943), it has been shown by Gulland, Jordan and Taylor (1947) that this is unlikely as no increase was observed in the amount of secondary phosphoryl groups. Instead these authors suggested that some of the groups of the bases formed hydrogen bonds between different bases. They were unable to decide whether the hydrogen bonds linked bases in the same or in adjacent structural units. The fact that most of the ionizable groups are originally inaccessible to acids and bases is more easily explained if the hydrogen bonds are between bases within the same structural unit. This point would definitely be established if it were shown that the shape of the initial titration curve was the same at very low DNA concentrations, when the interaction between neighboring structural units is small.

(3) The analytical data on the relative proportion of the various bases show that the amount of adenine is close to that of thymine, and the amount of guanine close to the amount of cytosine + 5-methyl cytosine, although the ratio of adenine to guanine can vary from one source to another (Chargaff, 1951; Wyatt, 1952). In fact as the techniques for estimation of the bases improve, the ratios of adenine to thymine, and guanine to cytosine + 5-methyl cytosine appear to grow very close to unity. This is a most striking result, especially as the sequence of bases on a given chain is likely to be irregular, and suggests a structure involving paired bases. In fact, we believe the analytical data offer the most important evidence so far available in support of our model, since they specifically support the biologically interesting feature, the presence of complementary chains.

We thus believe that the present experimental evidence justifies the working hypothesis that the essential features of our model are correct and allows us to consider its genetic possibilities.

V. GENETICAL IMPLICATIONS OF THE COMPLEMENTARY MODEL

As a preliminary we should state that the DNA fibers from which the X-ray diffraction patterns were obtained are not artifacts arising in the method of preparation. In the first place, Wilkins and his co-workers (see Wilkins *et al.*, 1953) have shown that X-ray patterns similar to those from the isolated fibers can be obtained from certain intact biological materials such as sperm head and bacteriophage particles. Secondly, our postulated model is so extremely specific that we find it impossible to believe that it could be formed during the isolation from living cells.

A genetic material must in some way fulfil two functions. It must duplicate itself, and it must exert a highly specific influence on the cell. Our model for DNA suggests a simple mechanism for the first process, but at the moment we cannot see how it carries out the second one. We believe, however, that its specificity is expressed by the precise sequence of the pairs of bases. The backbone of our model is highly regular, and the sequence is the only feature which can carry the genetical information. It should not be thought that because in our structure the bases are on the "inside," they would be unable to come into contact with other molecules. Owing to the open nature of our structure they are in fact fairly accessible.

A MECHANISM FOR DNA REPLICATION

The complementary nature of our structure suggests how it duplicates itself. It is difficult to imagine how like attracts like, and it has been suggested (see Pauling and Delbrück, 1940; Friedrich-Freksa, 1940; and Muller, 1947) that self duplication may involve the union of each part with an opposite or complementary part. In these discussions it has generally been suggested that protein and nucleic acid are complementary to each other and that self replication involves the alternate syntheses of these two components. We should like to propose instead that the specificity of DNA self replication is accomplished without recourse to specific protein synthesis and that each of our complementary DNA chains serves as a template or mould for the formation onto itself of a new companion chain.

For this to occur the hydrogen bonds linking the complementary chains must break and the two chains unwind and separate. It seems likely that the single chain (or the relevant part of it) might itself assume the helical form and serve as a mould onto which free nucleotides (strictly polynucleotide precursors) can attach themselves by forming hydrogen bonds. We propose that polymerization of the precursors to form a new chain only occurs if the resulting chain forms the proposed structure. This is plausible because steric reasons would not allow monomers "crystallized" onto the first chain to approach one another in such a way that they could be joined together in a new chain, unless they were those monomers which could fit into our structure. It is not obvious to us whether a special enzyme would be required to carry out the polymerization or whether the existing single helical chain could act effectively as an enzyme.

DIFFICULTIES IN THE REPLICATION SCHEME

While this scheme appears intriguing, it nevertheless raises a number of difficulties, none of which, however, do we regard as insuperable. The first difficulty is that our structure does not differentiate between cytosine and 5-methyl cytosine, and therefore during replication the specificity in sequence involving these bases would not be perpetuated. The amount of 5-methyl cytosine varies considerably from one species to another, though it is usually rather small or absent. The present experimental results (Wyatt, 1952) suggest that each species has a characteristic amount. They also show that the sum of the two cytosines is more nearly equal to the amount of guanine than is the amount of cytosine by itself. It may well be that the difference between the two cytosines is not functionally significant. This interpretation would be considerably strengthened if it proved possible to change the amount of 5-methyl cytosine in the DNA of an organism without altering its genetical make-up.

The occurrence of 5-hydroxy-methyl-cytosine in the T even phages (Wyatt and Cohen, 1952) presents no such difficulty, since it completely replaces cytosine, and its amount in the DNA is close to that of guanine.

The second main objection to our scheme is that it completely ignores the role of the basic protamines and histones, proteins known to be combined with DNA in most living organisms. This was done for two reasons. Firstly, we can formulate a scheme of DNA reproduction involving it alone and so

from the viewpoint of simplicity it seems better to believe (at least at present) that the genetic specificity is never passed through a protein intermediary. Secondly, we know almost nothing about the structural features of protamines and histones. Our only clue is the finding of Astbury (1947) and of Wilkins and Randall (1953) that the X-ray pattern of nucleoprotamine is very similar to that of DNA alone. This suggests that the protein component, or at least some of it, also assumes a helical form and in view of the very open nature of our model, we suspect that protein forms a third helical chain between the pair of polynucleotide chains (see Figure 4). As yet nothing is known about the function of the protein; perhaps it controls the coiling and uncoiling and perhaps it assists in holding the single polynucleotide chains in a helical configuration.

The third difficulty involves the necessity for the two complementary chains to unwind in order to serve as a template for a new chain. This is a very fundamental difficulty when the two chains are interlaced as in our model. The two main ways in which a pair of helices can be coiled together have been called plectonemic coiling and paranemic coiling. These terms have been used by cytologists to describe the coiling of chromosomes (Huskins, 1941; for a review see Manton, 1950). The type of coiling found in our model (see Figure 4) is called plectonemic. Paranemic coiling is found when two separate helices are brought to lie side by side and then pushed together so that their axes roughly coincide. Though one may start with two regular helices the process of pushing them together necessarily distorts them. It is impossible to have paranemic coiling with two regular simple helices going round the same axis. This point can only be clearly grasped by studying models.

There is of course no difficulty in "unwinding" a *single* chain of DNA coiled into a helix, since a polynucleotide chain has so many single bonds about which rotation is possible. The difficulty occurs when one has a pair of simple helices with a common axis. The difficulty is a topological one and cannot be surmounted by simple manipulation. Apart from breaking the chains there are only two sorts of ways to separate two chains coiled plectonemically. In the first, one takes hold of one end of one chain, and the other end of the other, and simply pulls in the axial direction. The two chains slip over each other, and finish up separate and end to end. It seems to us highly unlikely that this occurs in this case, and we shall not consider it further. In the second way the two chains must be directly untwisted. When this has been done they are separate and side by side. The number of turns necessary to untwist them completely is equal to the number of turns of one of the chains round the common axis. For our structure this comes to one turn every 34 A, and thus about 150 turns per million molecular weight of DNA, that is per 5000

A of our structure. The problem of uncoiling falls into two parts:

(1) How many turns must be made, and how is tangling avoided?

(2) What are the physical or chemical forces which produce it?

For the moment we shall be mainly discussing the first of these. It is not easy to decide what is the uninterrupted length of functionally active DNA. As a lower limit we may take the molecular weight of the DNA after isolation, say fifty thousand A in length and having about 1000 turns. This is only a lower limit as there is evidence suggesting a breakage of the DNA fiber during the process of extraction. The upper limit might be the total amount of DNA in a virus or in the case of a higher organism, the total amount of DNA in a chromosome. For T2 this upper limit is approximately 800,000 A which corresponds to 20,000 turns, while in the higher organisms this upper limit may sometimes be 1000 fold higher.

The difficulty might be more simple to resolve if successive parts of a chromosome coiled in opposite directions. The most obvious way would be to have both right and left handed DNA helices in sequence but this seems unlikely as we have only been able to build our model in the right handed sense. Another possibility might be that the long strands of right handed DNA are joined together by compensating strands of left handed polypeptide helices. The merits of this proposition are difficult to assess, but the fact that the phage DNA does not seem to be linked to protein makes it rather unattractive.

The untwisting process would be less complicated if replication started at the ends as soon as the chains began to separate. This mechanism would produce a new two-strand structure without requiring at any time a free single-strand stage. In this way the danger of tangling would be considerably decreased as the two-strand structure is much more rigid than a single strand and would resist attempts to coil around its neighbors. Once the replicating process is started the presence, at the growing end of the pair, of double-stranded structures might facilitate the breaking of hydrogen bonds in the original unduplicated section and allow replication to proceed in a zipper-like fashion.

It is also possible that one chain of a pair occasionally breaks under the strain of twisting. The polynucleotide chain remaining intact could then release the accumulated twist by rotation about single bonds and following this, the broken ends, being still in close proximity, might rejoin.

It is clear that, in spite of the tentative suggestions we have just made, the difficulty of untwisting is a formidable one, and it is therefore worthwhile re-examining why we postulate plectonemic coiling, and not paranemic coiling in which the two helical threads are not intertwined, but merely in close apposition to each other. Our answer is that with paranemic coiling, the specific pairing of bases would not allow the successive residues of each helix to be in equivalent orientation with regard to the helical axis. This is a possibility we strongly oppose as it implies that a large number of stereochemical alternatives for the sugar-phosphate backbone are possible, an inference at variance to our finding, with stereochemical models (Crick and Watson, 1953) that the position of the sugar-phosphate group is rather restrictive and cannot be subject to the large variability necessary for paranemic coiling. Moreover, such a model would not lead to specific pairing of the bases, since this only follows if the glucosidic links are arranged regularly in space. We therefore believe that if a helical structure is present, the relationship between the helices will be plectonemic.

We should ask, however, whether there might not be another complementary structure which maintains the necessary regularity but which is not helical. One such structure can, in fact, be imagined. It would consist of a ribbon-like arrangement in which again the two chains are joined together by specific pairs of bases, located 3.4 A above each other, but in which the sugar-phosphate backbone instead of forming a helix, runs in a straight line at an angle approximately 30° off the line formed by the pair of bases. While this ribbon-like structure would give many of the features of the X-ray diagram of Structure B, we are unable to define precisely how it should pack in a macroscopic fiber, and why in particular it should give a strong equatorial reflexion at 20-24 A. We are thus not enthusiastic about this model though we should emphasize that it has not yet been disproved.

Independent of the details of our model, there are two geometrical problems which *any* model for DNA must face. Both involve the necessity for some form of super folding process and can be illustrated with bacteriophage. Firstly, the total length of the DNA within T2 is about 8×10^5 A. As its DNA is thought (Siegal and Singer, 1953) to have the same very large M.W. as that from other sources, it must bend back and forth many times in order to fit into the phage head of diameter 800 A. Secondly, the DNA must replicate itself without getting tangled. Approximately 500 phage particles can be synthesized within a single bacterium of average dimensions $10^4 \times 10^4 \times 2 \times 10^4$ A. The total length of the newly produced DNA is some 4×10^8 A, all of which we believe was at some interval in contact with its parental template. Whatever the precise mechanism of replication we suspect the most reasonable way to avoid tangling is to have the DNA fold up into a compact bundle as it is formed.

A POSSIBLE MECHANISM FOR NATURAL MUTATION

In our duplication scheme, the specificity of replication is achieved by means of specific pairing between purine and pyrimidine bases; adenine with thymine, and guanine with one of the cytosines. This specificity results from our assumption that each of the bases possesses one tautomeric form which is very much more stable than any of the other possibilities. The fact that a compound is tautomeric, however, means that the hydrogen atoms can occasionally change their locations. It seems plausible to us that a spontaneous mutation, which as implied earlier we imagine to be a change in the sequence of bases, is due to a base occurring very occasionally in one of the less likely tautomeric forms, at the moment when the complementary chain is being formed. For example, while adenine will normally pair with thymine, if there is a tautomeric shift of one of its hydrogen atoms it can pair with cytosine (Figure 7). The next time pairing occurs, the adenine (having resumed its more usual tautomeric form) will pair with thymine, but the cytosine will pair with guanine, and so a change in the sequence of bases will have occurred. It would be of interest to know the precise difference in free energy between the various tautomeric forms under physiological conditions.

GENERAL CONCLUSION

The proof or disproof of our structure will have to come from further crystallographic analysis, a task we hope will be accomplished soon. It would be surprising to us, however, if the idea of complementary chains turns out to be wrong. This feature was initially postulated by us to account for the crystallographic regularity and it seems to us unlikely that its obvious connection with self replication is a matter of chance. On the other hand the plectonemic coiling is, superficially at least, biologically unattractive and so demands precise crystallographic proof. In any case the evidence for both the model and the suggested replication scheme will be strengthened if it can be shown unambiguously that the genetic specificity is carried by DNA alone, and, on the molecular side, how the structure could exert a specific influence on the cell.

REFERENCES

ASTBURY, W. T., 1947, X-Ray Studies of nucleic acids in tissues. Sym. Soc. Exp. Biol. 1:66-76.

CHARGAFF, E., 1951, Structure and function of nucleic acids as cell constituents. Fed. Proc. 10:654-659.

CRICK, F. H. C., and WATSON, J. D., 1953, Manuscript in preparation.

FRANKLIN, R. E., and GOSLING, R., 1953a, Molecular configuration in sodium thymonucleate. Nature, Lond. 171:740-741.

1953b, Fiber diagrams of sodium thymonucleate. I. The influence of water content. Acta Cryst., Camb. (in press).

1953c, The structure of sodium thymonucleate fibers. II. The cylindrically symmetrical Patterson Function. Acta Cryst., Camb. (in press).

FRASER, M. S., and FRASER, R. D. B., 1951, Evidence on the structure of desoxyribonucleic acid from measurements with polarized infra-red radiation. Nature, Lond. 167:760-761.

FRIEDRICH-FREKSA, H., 1940, Bei der Chromosomen Konjugation wirksame Krafte und ihre Bedeutung für die identische Verdopplung von Nucleoproteinen. Naturwissenshaften 28:376-379.

GULLAND, J. M., and JORDAN, D. O., 1946, The macromolecular behavior of nucleic acids. Sym. Soc. Exp. Biol. 1: 56-65.

GULLAND, J. M., JORDAN, D. O., and TAYLOR, H. F. W., 1947, Electrometric titration of the acidic and basic groups of the desoxypentose nucleic acid of calf thymus. J. Chem. Soc. 1131-1141.

HUSKINS, C. L., 1941, The coiling of chromonemata. Cold Spr. Harb. Symp. Quant. Biol. 9:13-18.

JORDAN, D. O., 1951, Physiochemical properties of the nucleic acids. Prog. Biophys. 2:51-89.

KAHLER, H., and LLOYD, B. J., 1953, The electron microscopy of sodium desoxyribonucleate. Biochim. Biophys. Acta 10:355-359.

MANTON, I., 1950, The spiral structure of chromosomes. Biol. Rev. 25:486-508.

MULLER, H. J., 1947, The Gene. Proc. Roy. Soc. Lond. Ser. B. 134:1-37.

PAULING, L., and DEDBRÜCK, M., 1940, The nature of the intermolecular forces operative in biological processes. Science 92:77-79.

SIEGAL, A., and SINGER, S. J., 1953, The preparation and properties of desoxypentosenucleic acid. Biochim. Biophys. Acta 10:311-319.

VILBRANDT, C. F., and TENNENT, H. G., 1943, The effect of

ADENINE   THYMINE

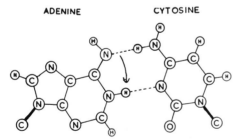

ADENINE   CYTOSINE

FIGURE. 7. Pairing arrangements of adenine before (above) and after (below) it has undergone a tautomeric shift.

pH changes upon some properties of sodium thymonucleate solutions. J. Amer. Chem. Soc. 63:1806-1809.

WATSON, J. D., and CRICK, F. H. C., 1953a, A structure for desoxyribose nucleic acids. Nature, Lond. 171:737-738. 1953b, Genetical implications of the structure of desoxyribose nucleic acid. Nature, Lond. (in press).

WILKINS, M. H. F., GOSLING, R. G., and SEEDS, W. E., 1951, Physical studies of nucleic acids—nucleic acid: an extensible molecule. Nature, Lond. 167:759-760.

WILKINS, M. H. F., and RANDALL, J. T., 1953, Crystallinity in sperm-heads: molecular structure of nucleoprotein in vivo. Biochim. Biophys. Acta 10:192 (1953).

WILKINS, M. H. F., STOKES, A. R., and WILSON, H. R., 1953, Molecular structure of desoxypentose nucleic acids. Nature, Lond. 171:738-740.

WILLIAMS, R. C., 1952, Electron microscopy of sodium desoxyribonucleate by use of a new freeze-drying method. Biochim. Biophys. Acta 9:237-239.

WYATT, G. R., 1952, Specificity in the composition of nucleic acids. In "The Chemistry and Physiology of the Nucleus," pp. 201-213, N. Y. Academic Press.

WYATT, G. R., and COHEN, S. S., 1952, A new pyrimidine base from bacteriophage nucleic acid. Nature, Lond. 170:1072.

Jim Watson's Nobel Banquet Speech

Just nine years after the discovery of the structure of DNA, Jim Watson, Francis Crick, and Maurice Wilkins were awarded the 1962 Nobel Prize in Physiology or Medicine for "their discoveries concerning the molecular structure of nucleic acids and its significance for information transfer in living material." At the Nobel Banquet, Jim gave a speech on behalf of all three of them. It is short—less than 500 words—as is required by the protocol of the occasion, and Jim would no doubt have wished to have said more. He could have opted for a safe, bland recitation of events. But remarkably, the entire second half of the speech becomes a highly personal statement, a credo almost, of how science can overcome human fallibility. A statement of belief, but also a statement of purpose.

Despite its extemporaneous style, Jim worked hard on this speech, going through several drafts (see draft on following page) before being satisfied he had it right.

Jim Watson at Nobel Banquet. (Courtesy of the James D. Watson Collection, CSHL Archives.)

Francis Crick and Maurice Wilkins have asked me to reply ~~jointly for them.~~ *for all three of us.*

~~This is very difficult so I shall have to reply for myself.~~ This *is* certainly

the second most wonderful moment in my life. The first was our discovery of

the structure of DNA. At that time we knew that a new world had been opened

and that an old world which seemed rather mystical was gone. The ~~second thing~~

~~I want to say was that This~~ *Our* discovery was done using the methods of physics

and chemistry to understand biology. I am a biologist while my friends Maurice

and Francis are physicists. I am very much the junior one and my contribution

to this work could have only happened with the help of Maurice and Francis.

The ~~third thing I want to say is that~~ At that time we ~~were doing this work,~~

some biologists were not very sympathetic with us because we wanted to solve

a biological truth by physical means. But fortunately some physicists thought

that through using the techniques of physics and chemistry a real contribution

to biology could be made. The wisdom of these men *in* encouraging us was tremendously

important in our success. Prof. Bragg, our director at the Cavendish and Prof.

Niels Bohr ~~very~~ often expressed their belief that physics would be a help in

biology. The fact that these ~~very~~ great men believed in this approach, made it

much easier for us to go forward. ~~And the last~~ thing I would like to say is that,

that science is a very difficult thing; it's not very easy and ~~much of the time~~

~~we are discouraged.~~ To stay in the ~~game~~ we often tend to be rather unusual

and ~~difficult people.~~ I knew many people, at least when I was young, who

thought I was quite unbearable. Some also thought Maurice was very strange,

and others, including myself, thought that Francis was at times difficult.

Fortunately we were working among ~~humanely~~ wise and tolerant people who under-

stood the spirit of scientific discovery and the conditions necessary for its

INSERT A

INSERT B

Typescript draft of Jim Watson's 1962 Nobel Banquet Speech. (Courtesy of the James D. Watson Collection, CSHL Archives.)

YOUR MAJESTIES, YOUR ROYAL HIGHNESSES, YOUR EXCELLENCIES, LADIES AND GENTLEMEN.

Francis Crick and Maurice Wilkins have asked me to reply for all three of us. But as it is difficult to convey the personal feeling of others, I must speak for myself. This evening is certainly the second most wonderful moment in my life. The first was our discovery of the structure of DNA. At that time we knew that a new world had been opened and that an old world which seemed rather mystical was gone. Our discovery was done using the methods of physics and chemistry to understand biology. I am a biologist while my friends Maurice and Francis are physicists. I am very much the junior one and my contribution to this work could have only happened with the help of Maurice and Francis. At that time some biologists were not very sympathetic with us because we wanted to solve a biological truth by physical means. But fortunately some physicists thought that through using the techniques of physics and chemistry a real contribution to biology could be made. The wisdom of these men in encouraging us was tremendously important in our success. Professor Bragg, our director at the Cavendish, and Professor Niels Bohr often expressed their belief that physics would be a help in biology. The fact that these great men believed in this approach made it much easier for us to go forward. The last thing I would like to say is that good science as a way of life is sometimes difficult. It often is hard to have confidence that you really know where the future lies. We must thus believe strongly in our ideas, often to [the] point where they may seem tiresome and bothersome and even arrogant to our colleagues. I knew many people, at least when I was young, who thought I was quite unbearable. Some also thought Maurice was very strange, and others, including myself, thought that Francis was at times difficult. Fortunately we were working among wise and tolerant people who understood the spirit of scientific discovery and the conditions necessary for its generation. I feel that it is very important, especially for us so singularly honored, to remember that science does not stand by itself, but is the creation of very human people. We must continue to work in the humane spirit in which we were fortunate to grow up. If so, we shall help insure that our science continues and that our civilization will prevail. Thank you very much for this very deep honor.

Courtesy of James D. Watson Collection (CSHL Archives).
Reprinted, with permission, from Les Prix Nobel 1962 (©The Nobel Foundation 1962).

CAREER SCIENTIST

Section III photograph: *Jim Watson at Harvard, 1963 (Courtesy of the James D. Watson Collection, CSHL Archives.)*

CALTECH, CAMBRIDGE, AND HARVARD

I
N MAY, 1953, EXACTLY THREE YEARS AFTER COMPLETING his lackluster Ph.D, Jim boarded a BOAC Constellation bound for New York, to tell the world about the structural basis of heredity. That year, the topic of the Cold Spring Harbor Symposium
was "Viruses" and almost all of the phage group had assembled on the bucolic North
Shore of Long Island. Milislav Demerec, the Director of the Biological Laboratory at
Cold Spring Harbor, was the chief organizer of the Symposium. However, Jim's invitation came from Max Delbrück, to whom Jim had written regularly during his time in
Cambridge. His letter first describing the discovery of the double helix, complete with
a sketch of the base pairs, had been sent to Delbrück on March 12, just three weeks
after the model of DNA had been completed and a few days before the final version of
the Watson and Crick paper was typed. Delbrück was convinced by the model and distributed copies to the participants at the Symposium of the three structural papers
published in the April 25th issue of *Nature* (Watson and Crick, *Nature 171:* 737 [1953];
Wilkins et al., *Nature 171:* 738 [1953]; Franklin and Gosling, *Nature 171:* 740 [1953]).

Although Jim's presentation at the Symposium went well, there is a photograph of
a rather pensive Watson sitting with Max Delbrück, Aaron Novick, and Leo Szilard
(see page 115) on the porch of Blackford Hall. Jim was right to be thinking about his
future; his time at Cambridge was coming to a close and he was due to continue
research on phage with Delbrück at Caltech. But Cambridge had changed his scientific interests and he had achieved his goal of determining the structure of the genetic
material. His next goal was to understand the process by which DNA directed protein
synthesis, and this meant understanding the role of RNA. The strategy Jim intended to
follow was the same as with DNA, that is, he expected that the function of RNA would
be revealed by its structure.

Jim arrived in Pasadena in September, 1953. It was not an auspicious start as "the
acrid stench" which greeted him when he left the plane "...grew even viler as the taxi
ascended the Pasadena Freeway." Things did not improve and by the end of September "...the full horror of being in Pasadena hit me." Jim found himself at odds with the
society and with the political outlook of the Caltech faculty, and at odds with the scientific interests of Delbrück's group. Even as Jim and Francis were working away in
Cambridge, Delbrück had abandoned phage genetics. His new love was the mold *Phycomyces* and his new hope was that an analysis of its phototropic responses would lead
to insights into the interactions of organisms with their environment. Jim had lost his
interest in phage in Kalckar's laboratory, and his new way of thinking was much more

appropriate for Linus Pauling's empire. Not surprisingly, he did not want to be under the authority of the autocratic Pauling and, instead, remained in Delbrück's group and formed a collaboration with Alex Rich in Pauling's laboratory. Together they began X-ray diffraction studies of RNA.

Unfortunately, their pictures of RNA were at best fuzzy, and while different from those of DNA, the diffraction images of RNA had no clearly defined pattern that would lend itself to structural analysis. Although Rich and Watson published a couple of papers on their findings (Rich and Watson, *Nature 173*: 995–996 [1954]; Rich and Watson, *Proc. Natl. Acad. Sci. 40*: 759–764 [1954]), and Leslie Orgel, a British chemist, joined in modeling possible DNA-RNA interactions, it was a depressing time scientifically. Even entertaining discussions with George Gamow, a rather manic Russian-American physicist, about the genetic code and the formation of an organization called the RNA Tie Club were not enough to compensate for the lack of attractive young women on the Caltech campus. But a visit to Paul Doty in July, 1954, had already implanted in Jim's mind the thought that Harvard might be the place to be, and not only for the girls he saw in Harvard Yard. Doty had high hopes that changes were on their way which would transform the old-fashioned Harvard Biology Department into something far more exciting. Further conversations with Doty and the evolutionary biologist Ernst Mayr led to a job seminar at Harvard in January, 1955, which was well-received. Two months later, Jim was offered an Assistant Professorship to begin on July 1, 1955. But, with a panache that many will recognize, Jim persuaded the Chairman of the Harvard Biology Department to grant him a one year leave of absence, so that he would spend the first year of his appointment in Cambridge on the other side of the Atlantic!

The year in Cambridge was devoted to ridding himself of the Los Angeles smog, if Jim's account in *Genes, Girls, and Gamow* (2002, Knopf) is to be taken at face value. He seems to have spent much time on the continent and at college dinners in Cambridge, not to mention a visit to Naomi Mitchison's grand house in Scotland, where Christa Mayr, Ernst Mayr's daughter, revealed that their long-standing friendship could not be more than that. But it was not all play and Jim did two important pieces of work, often overlooked, in his premature sabbatical year. The first was an X-ray structural study of tobacco mosaic virus in which he showed that the arrangement of protein subunits on TMV was helical (Watson, *Biochim. Biophys. Acta 13*: 10–19 [1954]). However, he was unable to calculate the number of subunits per turn of the helix—a problem that was eventually solved by Rosalind Franklin. The second study, a theoretical one with Crick, was on the assembly of small viruses (Crick and Watson, *Nature 177*: 473–475 [1956]).

So it was, with his intellectual batteries recharged, that Jim left Cambridge, England, for Cambridge in the United States. He was now determined to work out the steps by which the information in DNA is turned into the order of amino acids along a protein, and he recognized that this had to be done experimentally—his laboratory was going to have to do biochemistry. Fortunately, while in Cambridge, Jim had met, and become friendly with, Alfred Tissières, a Swiss biochemist working on the constituents of the bacterial cell-free extracts used to study protein synthesis. Jim invited him to Harvard and so the Watson laboratory's first projects dealt with the ribosome.

It is notable that Jim's publication record was not stellar, averaging two papers per year while at Harvard. This did not reflect the output of the laboratory, nor Jim's intellectual contributions to the work published by his graduate students and postdoctoral fellows. Rather, his name was included with the authors only when he felt that his contributions were substantive. (Later, some of his graduate students felt deprived of the honor of appearing on the same paper as a discoverer of the double helix.) But the publications that did bear his name were important and included papers on the ribosome and the discovery of messenger RNA.

It was in his Harvard period that Watson emerged as a writer in two quite distinct areas and made unique contributions in both. The first was in scientific autobiography, with the publication of *The Double Helix* in 1968 (Atheneum). It was highly controversial, with threats of law suits from Francis Crick and Maurice Wilkins, and Harvard University Press reneging on its commitment to publish the book. It was published and evoked responses ranging from outright condemnation to acclamation as a new and honest form of scientific autobiography (see "The Reviews" section of the Norton Critical edition of *The Double Helix* [1980; ed. Gunther S. Stent]). It became a best seller and was translated into many languages. The second was in textbook publishing. Jim found that there was no textbook that covered the topics in molecular biology and genetics that he was teaching to the Harvard undergraduates. He set out to correct this deficiency and with *Molecular Biology of the Gene* (1965, W.A. Benjamin) created a new style of textbook with declamatory subheadings and stylized diagrams (drawn by Keith Roberts). This felicious style was rapidly adopted by textbooks of all genres and is Jim Watson's enduring contribution to education.

Jim's legacy to Harvard was equally great, although it was not appreciated as such by the Biology Department. Paul Doty, John Edsall, Konrad Bloch, and George Wald were leaders in a push to revitalize the Department and, as a first step, formed the Committee on Higher Degrees in Biochemistry. Watson was openly contemptuous of the fuddy-duddy Biology faculty and fought savagely for every new faculty position that came open. The dedicated myrmecologist E.O. Wilson found him "the most unpleasant human being I ever met," and called him the "Caligula of Biology." Nevertheless, Jim helped to attract a remarkable set of scientists—Matt Meselson, Wally Gilbert, Mark Ptashne, Guido Guidotti—to the Committee and eventually, in 1967 just before Jim became Director of Cold Spring Harbor Laboratory, the Committee was transformed into the Department of Biochemistry and Molecular Biology.

Remembering Delbrück

Biology is a very interesting field ...[because of] the vastness of its structure and the extraordinary variety of strange facts...but to the physicist it is also a depressing subject, because...the analysis seems to have stalled around in a semidescriptive manner without noticeably progressing towards a radical physical explanation...we are not yet at the point where we are presented with clear paradoxes and this will not happen until the analysis of the behavior of living cells has been carried into far greater detail.

Max Delbrück
(A Physicist Looks at Biology,
Trans. Conn. Acad. Arts Sci. 38: 173–190 [1949,
Reprinted with permission of the Connecticut
Academy of Arts and Sciences])

In his search for the "radical physical explanation" Max Delbrück brought to biology a fiercely reductionist style, a quantitative analytic approach, and an ability to distill simple rules from complex phenomena. In the early 1930s, he had been a student of Niels Bohr, who had been a powerful proselytizer for biology. Persuaded by Bohr's lecture, *Light and Life* (later published in *Nature 131:* 421–423; 457–459 [1933]), and, more importantly, Erwin Schrödinger's book, *What Is Life?* (1956, Doubleday) (based in large part on Delbrück's work, with Timoféeff-Ressovsky and Zimmer, on the nature of mutations), other physicists (Szilard, Crick, Wilkins, for example) were drawn to biology. By the late 1940s, Delbrück had become the acknowledged leader of a group of very bright scientists, "intent on discovering how [a] background in physical sciences could be productively applied to biological problems" (*Emory Ellis*).[1]

Jim was introduced to Delbrück in Salvador Luria's apartment in Bloomington in 1948. Many years later, in an interview with Horace Judson, Jim said, "His visit excited me, for the prominent role of his idea in *What Is Life* made him a legendary figure in my mind. My decision to work under Luria had, in fact, been made so quickly because I knew that he and Delbrück had done phage experiments together and were close friends."

Jim was quickly absorbed into phage group and formed a relationship with Delbrück that was both enduring and close. Max could be domineering, but not with Jim. Their association became one of intellectual equals, which over the years, gave each of them immense pleasure.

After Max died in 1981, Jim spoke at a memorial service for Max in Dabney Hall at Caltech. His speech, full of emotion, is reproduced on the following page.

Max Delbrück (1906–1981)

I first knew Max from his writings and sensed he was very special. The hero of Schrödinger's *What Is Life* and the physicist most close to the gene, he wrote with a youthful, logical joy about the tiny phages with which he hoped to lead us to the essence of life. My reading of his 1946 Harvey Lecture made his one-step growth curves and single-burst experiments seem the only way to grow up, and I entered Salva Luria's lab to work on phage never doubting there might be another way to the truth.

Two months later, on one spring evening at the Luria flat, I caught my initial glimpse of Max. Instantly my hero worship became adoration, and soon I wanted to be as much like Max as possible, including someday marrying a girl as perfect as his Manny. For Max was no ordinary exceedingly bright mortal, but a youthful, graceful god. Through him the world of Biology was to be rescued from its complexity by placing in its hands the marvelous replicating powers of the phages that Max would have us call T1, T2, and T4.

My approach to science, as well as to people, became indelibly fixed during the following summer when many of the Phage Group assembled at Cold Spring Harbor. In addition to the Delbrücks and Lurias, there were Gunther Stent and Seymour Benzer with whom to eat, talk, or swim in an atmosphere that I could never describe as less than perfect. Now I realize that most of the personality that I then, and still now, find so wonderfully unique about Cold Spring Harbor was given to it by Max.

He abhorred the petty, and in searching for the deepest of theories he insisted that we work together in a collective, generous fashion. The selfish and the avaricious were not tolerated, and those unfortunate souls who could only so survive were not for Max. And those of us who without ever being formally ordained, knew that we were the Apostles of Phage.

Stuffiness or protocol had no place in his life and he never was Professor or Dr. Delbrück but Max to all who would learn with him. There was no hierarchy into which to fit, and the informality with which ideas were accepted or rejected gave us all the chance to do our best. And to dream that later we might find out the ultimate of answers.

Never did Max divert toward his own glorification the talents of his disciples. He knew that one day we would have to stand on our own and always made sure that when we claimed a decisive experiment, he also became convinced, and that we had not been led astray by the hastiness of youth. When thus reassured, he then would share with us the simple pleasures that came from canoeing into the harbor, or going on a treasure hunt, or the playing of tennis.

Even now I cannot accept that Max is not still here and worry that my words today will not please him. I want badly to be with him yet one more time to say what I never had the courage to reveal to him, that save now for my wife and children, he, Max, meant more to me than anyone else, and I hope I did not too often needlessly disappoint him.

Jim Watson

Does RNA Form a Double Helix?

Alexander Rich

Massachusetts Institute of Technology

Jim Watson and I started working together in the fall of 1953. At the time, I was a post-doctoral fellow working with Linus Pauling and had been at Caltech since 1949. Jim and I met briefly there in 1949, but he then took off initially to Copenhagen and later to Cambridge, England. Linus Pauling had organized a Conference on Proteins held in Pasadena in September 1953. The meeting had a large number of people who had made important contributions to the structure of proteins, including the older investi-gators Sir Lawrence Bragg, William Astbury, and David Harker, as well as a somewhat younger group including Max Perutz, John Kendrew, and Hugh Huxley. In addition, Jim Watson and Francis Crick as well as Maurice Wilkins attended.[1] It was at this meet-ing that Max Perutz announced his breakthrough discovery of using heavy atoms to solve phase problems for the Fourier component in the X-ray diffraction analysis of protein crystals.[2]

Although most of the papers concerned proteins, work on DNA was presented as well. Early in 1953, Linus Pauling had asked me to take some X-ray diffraction patterns of DNA fibers. The available equipment was much less than optimal; nonetheless, I was able to get some diffraction patterns from oriented fibers, but the patterns con-tained a mixture of both the A and the B forms, and they were not readily interpreted. Shortly afterward, in the spring of 1953, the Watson-Crick paper was published, and it was clear to me that their structure was essentially correct. Linus Pauling felt the same way and had discarded his earlier triple-stranded model. It was clear to me that work-ing further on DNA was not a useful enterprise, especially in view of the superb dif-fraction patterns obtained by Rosalind Franklin and Maurice Wilkins. My presentation to the conference dealt with how proteins and the DNA double helix might interact. The ideas were not very productive since not enough was known about the structure to recognize the important possibility of having a protein α-helix lodge in the major groove of DNA.

During the meeting, Jim and I talked a great deal about RNA, which was then a rel-atively unknown molecule. In particular, it was not known whether RNA would form a double helix in a manner similar to that seen with DNA. Although the nucleotide components of DNA and RNA were very similar, they had an important and signifi-cant difference, namely, the presence of a hydroxyl group at the 2′ position on the ribose ring of RNA. This not only changed the chemistry of the molecule, but was like-ly also to influence its three-dimensional conformation. Indeed, Watson and Crick pointed out in their first *Nature* paper (Watson and Crick 1953) that it was unlikely RNA could form the double helix; the presence of the 2′ hydroxyl group would prob-

ALEXANDER RICH

Alex Rich and Jim Watson have known each other for 54 years and their lives have crossed and twined many times. Their collaboration was most intense in the mid 1950s when they together tried to understand the structure of RNA. In hindsight, it is hardly surprising that they were unsuccessful. Even the basic facts about the physical properties of RNA were unknown and no one had a clue about what it did in the cell or how it did it. In addition, the RNA preparations of that era were almost certainly degraded and the analytical tools that were available were completely inadequate. Jim consequently found himself stuck in smoggy Pasadena, bored with bacteriophage genetics, frustrated with RNA and with an unsatisfactory social life. It should make for depressing reading. But what shines through from Alex Rich's account is the camaraderie of the small group, the intensity of their conversations, and their openness to new ideas. The work may not have gone well but at least science was done as it should be.

Alex and Jim migrated independently to jobs on the East Coast and never worked together again. But their varied interactions over the course of half a century make for a long and interesting tale.

Alex Rich was the first to show that RNA, like DNA, could form a double helix and, when head of the Section on Physical Chemistry at the National Institutes of Health (1954–1958), carried out the first RNA-RNA hybridization reactions. In 1958, he moved to the Biology Department at the Massachusetts Institute of Technology, where he discovered the first DNA-RNA hybridization and later obtained the first images of the double-stranded DNA at atomic resolution (Wang et al., *Nature 282:* 680–686 [1979]).

He is celebrated for solving the three-dimensional structure of transfer RNA (Kim et al., *Science 185:* 435–439 [1974]) and for his discovery of Z-DNA, a high-energy form of DNA with a left-hand twist (Wang et al., *Nature 282:* 680–686 [1979]). During his long career, Alex Rich has been awarded many honors and has published more than 500 papers in fields ranging from molecular structure to the origin of life.

ably prevent RNA from taking up a double-stranded configuration. Jim's evident interest in RNA structure and my looking around for a new project made for a natural joint effort by the two of us to investigate the conformation of RNA.

Jim was a postdoctoral fellow with Max Delbrück, whose laboratories were in a building adjacent to the chemistry building at Caltech. Delbrück had worked for many years analyzing bacteriophages and their growth, collaborating most summers with Salvador Luria at Cold Spring Harbor. Jim had become highly skilled in that type of work in Indiana, and his responsibilities in the Delbrück lab included assisting the more junior in their bacteriophage studies. However, Max himself had already started a new thrust dealing with the mold *Phycomyces* and the way it bent its fruiting stalks in response to light. I had spent a great deal of time talking with Max during my early years at Caltech. He was an extremely bright person, a physicist by training with a keen analytical mind, but he had a certain unease with chemistry and a discomfort in working with molecules. At that stage, people were beginning to analyze proteins by electrophoresis, which produced a series of bands that could be visualized on a gel. Half jokingly, Max told me that he did not mind working with these because he regarded them as similar to lines in a spectrum and felt comfortable with that analysis.

Jim and I planned our RNA research to essentially repeat what had worked successfully with DNA. Jim had a number of contacts, and he wrote to several people asking for samples of RNA that usually arrived in the form of a lyophilized white powder. A typical experiment involved putting a small amount of the white powder on a glass slide and adding a very small droplet of distilled water. The ratio of RNA to water was such that the solution was quite sticky. A thin glass fiber attached to the objective lens of a microscope would be poked into the sticky droplet and slowly withdrawn. The process of drawing fibers was very much an art form. One had to draw fast enough to orient the elongated molecules, but not so fast that the material on the glass fiber would separate from the material on the glass slide. After the fiber was drawn, sometimes a centimeter or so in length, it was dried in air and then examined in the microscope to measure its birefringence. It routinely had negative birefringence, which was consistent with the purines and the pyrimidines lying at right angles to the fiber axis in a manner analogous to that seen in DNA fibers. However, it was extremely difficult to get well-oriented RNA fibers. Furthermore, the X-ray camera used to generate the diffraction pattern had been designed for a study of inorganic molecules and was only marginally useful for our studies. Work in the laboratory consequently proceeded very slowly, and the diffraction patterns improved only to a limited extent. What we found quite interesting was that all of the preparations seemed to give fairly similar diffraction patterns even though the base ratios of the RNA molecules differed widely. This was, of course, in marked contrast to DNA where the ratios of bases were quite fixed as a consequence of Watson-Crick base pairing. We knew that it was likely that something was fundamentally different about RNA, but it was difficult to get information that would allow us to understand the origin of the diffraction pattern.

Social life in Pasadena was for us essentially a continuation of our scientific life. Quite often, Jim Watson would come over to our house for dinner. It was clear to both me and my wife Jane that he was quite lonely and was looking for a suitable female companion, but few candidates were available. Jim and I would talk a bit about science, but he would then talk to Jane and explain at great length how difficult it was for him to find a girlfriend. Jane was a sympathetic listener, and they became fast friends. A photograph taken outside our house on South Grand Oaks early in 1954 shows the three of us as well as Jack Dunitz and Giovanni Giacometti, postdoctoral fellows also working with Linus Pauling.

There was a great sense of camaraderie among the postdoctoral fellows and the faculty at Caltech. It was a fairly small school, and it was possible to know almost everyone on the campus. We took advantage of the easy access to the mountains, the sea, and the desert, and many trips were made on weekends. Max Delbrück and his wife Manny often went on these explorations, together with Jim, myself, and Jane. What was significant was the great sense of informality that existed at Caltech. The weekend outings provided an opportunity to talk at length with different colleagues, faculty, and student alike, which resulted in many productive interactions.

Postdoctoral days at Caltech in Pasadena, California, 1954. (Left to right) Jack Dunitz, Giovanni Giacometti, Jim Watson, Alex Rich, Jane Rich. (Photograph courtesy of Alex Rich).

The flow of visitors to Caltech was continuous. A good friend of Max Delbrück's was George Gamow, a theoretical physicist from Washington, D.C., who had read Watson and Crick's paper and immediately began addressing the problem of how DNA could code for proteins. He published an article in *Nature*, presenting a coding scheme (Gamow 1954). Although it was wrong, it was the first explicit statement of the fact that one needed a code to relate the nucleotide sequences of DNA to the amino acid sequences of proteins. Gamow's ideas were immediately understood largely by workers on the nucleic acids, but at that time, we could not conceive of how such information transfer took place. Gamow had written to Francis Crick in the summer of 1953 suggesting how a linear sequence of nucleotides in DNA might specify a particular order of amino acids by assembling the amino acids directly on a double helix. However, the thought entertained by many of the workers in the field was that RNA was likely to be an intermediate. This hypothesis was encapsulated in the familiar statement at the time that "DNA makes RNA makes proteins." It was not based on any experimental data, but was more a hopeful thought, reinforced by the knowledge that many viruses contain only RNA. When they infected cells, specific proteins were made. It was for this reason that Jim Watson, at a later stage, started seriously studying the tobacco mosaic virus, which consisted only of RNA and proteins in an attempt to learn something about the conformation of the RNA in the virus.

Gamow, "Geo" to his friends, was a lively personality, with a sharp exuberant wit, a large repertoire of jokes, and a penchant for drink. When he visited Pasadena in February 1954, the group of us spoke at great length about possible ways of approaching the problem of protein synthesis, and he obtained information from Jim about the dimensions of a DNA model so that he could play with the possibility of assembling amino acids directly on it. He also organized the RNA Tie Club, one member for each of the 20 amino acids, each member having a specially designed tie and an interest in the coding problem.[3]

Early in 1954, Leslie Orgel arrived in Pasadena to work with Linus Pauling. His wife Alice, a physician, was then interning in Los Angeles. Orgel had a keen mind and an ability to ask penetrating questions and soon joined in the many discussions that Jim and I had about RNA, its possible conformations, and its role in biological systems. Orgel's specialty was theoretical inorganic chemistry, and he had worked on ferrocene, a newly discovered molecule in which an iron atom resided in the center between two benzene rings stacked around it. In the spring of that year, Jack Dunitz, Orgel, and I solved the single crystal three-dimensional structure of ferrocene, which was a laborious effort considering the primitive state of computing at that time. In our publication, we thanked my wife Jane for her work in measuring the intensities of the hundreds of spots on an X-ray film, all of which was done by visual comparison.

On one occasion, a particular RNA sample produced a diffraction pattern that was somewhat better oriented than the others and seemed to have some similarity to DNA patterns. A series of meridional reflections near 3–3.5 Å were clearly due to the stacking of purine and pyrimidine bases and an area devoid of diffraction in the region below it, suggesting that the RNA was helical. As we looked at that pattern, Leslie Orgel came to the firm conclusion that it was probably a DNA sample mistakenly sent to us by someone who thought it was RNA. I felt that the pattern was sufficiently different from DNA and thought it was likely to be RNA. This formed the basis of a bet. The resolution of the bet came when Jim carried out Feulgen staining to distinguish ribose from deoxyribose. The analysis proved that the sample was indeed RNA, and I won the bet. The wager consisted of an ice cream cone with two scoops, but for some reason I never collected it. Leslie believes he probably now owes me several gallons of ice cream, considering the rate of inflation since the bet was made almost 50 years ago.

Because of the Korean War, the military draft was in place, and Jim Watson was eligible. He had taken an induction physical examination and was judged suitable for the military. Even though he had a series of temporary waivers (painfully extracted from his draft board in Chicago by George Beadle, the Head of Caltech's Biology Division) he was apprehensive that he might have to join the service. During this time at Caltech, I was actually a member of the U.S. Public Health Service. I had enlisted in 1952, as soon as the doctor's draft law was passed. Serving in the U.S. Public Health Service, a uniformed service, fulfilled the requirements of the draft. I joined at that time what was widely described as the "Yellow Berets." We ended up working at the National Institutes of Health, rather than going directly into the military. My appointment at NIH was that of a Section Chief, and one of my responsibilities was to hire people who would then work in the Section. I looked about among the people at Caltech and offered Jim the possibility of joining the Public Health Service and coming to NIH, as that certainly was preferable to joining the military. He was keen to do this because it provided him with a certain psychological protection against the possibility of having his career wrecked by military service. I also recruited my colleague Jack Dunitz, a skilled crystallographer who eventually moved with me to NIH in the fall of 1954. In addition, I offered a position to Matt Meselson, who was just completing his Ph.D. with Linus Pauling and was eligible for the draft. Jim had made a trip to Bethesda to visit the NIH campus and was relieved to find that there was nothing military there; it was simply a very large center for biological and medical research. As the year progressed, a decision was made in Washington not to draft men above a certain age. Jim was just above that age, so he was able to remain at Caltech.

At the time of his physical examination, in early February 1954, Jim and I published the first of our two papers dealing with RNA. The *Nature* paper, entitled "Physical Studies on Ribonucleic Acid" (Rich and Watson 1954a) described the results of our X-ray diffraction studies of RNA fibers. We discussed the changes in the X-ray powder pattern of RNA at various relative humidities and the birefringence of the fibers and also described the phenomenon that occurred when one pulled the fiber too rapidly. A region of the fiber "necked down"; it became thinner and was then positively birefringent by contrast to the rest of the fiber which had negative birefringence. This phenomenon, which was similar to that observed by Maurice Wilkins with DNA fibers, suggested that it is possible to distort the fibrous molecules so that they change their conformation. The bases would then lie in an orientation parallel to the fiber axis, rather than perpendicular as in the relaxed state.

Jim's social life at Caltech was quite active during this period. The Delbrücks had parties quite often, and Jim, Jane, and I were frequently in attendance. At one point, the Delbrücks suggested a costume party, and I was quite impressed to see Dale Kaiser, a graduate student of Delbrück's, coming to the party as a pipette. He had ingeniously made a cylinder of thin cardboard with the gradations of a pipette. The cylinder extended over his head, and he could see through eye holes, and his arms came out on either side of the cylinder. It made it a bit difficult to dance, but was otherwise quite striking.

When Jim Watson arrived at Caltech, we introduced him to Richard Feynman at about the time that Dick had become quite interested in molecular biology. His interest was great enough that he started doing some research in Delbrück's lab on bacteriophage with considerable assistance from Jim. He learned very quickly, and it was clear that he could switch to molecular biology if he chose. However, as he told me later, he decided not to continue because he thought he could do theoretical physics better than biology. Late in the spring of 1954, the Delbrücks organized a camping trip to Joshua Tree National Monument. As usual, these trips were a mixture of exploring the wilderness and talking about science, and Jim and I had several discussions on the trip about what we would include in a second paper that we were going to write on the X-ray fiber diffraction studies of RNA. On the way back, we made a detour through Palm Springs and Jane and Jim went walking, visiting posh stores in Palm Springs while I continued to talk about science with other members of the party. After they returned, they told me that they had gone into fancy dress shops and Jane had tried on a number of different dresses with Jim explaining to the sales people that they were planning to attend very elegant garden parties. I wondered what the sales people thought about Jane coming in with blue jeans and scuffed camping boots to try on all these fancy clothes. She found it difficult to keep a serious face while Jim described the many different parties that they were planning to attend.

The paper we sent to the *Proceedings of the National Academy of Sciences* in May 1954 (Rich and Watson 1954b) was communicated by Linus Pauling and contained a general discussion of the similarities and differences between DNA and RNA, with particular emphasis on structural consequences of the hydroxyl group on the 2′ position of ribose in RNA. The important thing about the DNA structure was that it had complementary paired bases in which adenines were equal to thymine and guanine was equal to cytosine. In the paper, we assembled a table of the published compositions of different RNA preparations analyzed by a number of different workers. Some of the RNA molecules seemed to have base compositions that mirrored the complementary composition of DNA, whereas others had compositions that deviated strongly. However, our fiber diffraction studies clearly showed that all of these specimens produced the same diffraction pattern. It clearly presented a dilemma.

On a functional level, we discussed the supposition which many people were considering that RNA was a link between DNA and proteins, such that DNA could make RNA, and RNA could make protein. However, there was no experimental basis for this, and no indications from our diffraction studies as of yet.

In the article, we reproduced the fiber diffraction patterns of one of the better RNA fibers and had next to it copies of the published DNA diffraction pictures of both Maurice Wilkins and Rosalind Franklin. What was clear from the RNA diffraction patterns was that there were a series of strong reflections near the meridian of the pattern between 3.3 and 4 Å, similar in many ways to the patterns seen in highly oriented DNA fibers. This was undoubtedly due to the stacking of the bases which was consistent with negative birefringence of the fibers. We commented on the notable absence of reflections near the meridian between 13 and 4 Å, clearly indicating that there was a helical arrangement. A repeat distance along the fiber axis was 25–28 Å, and the equatorial reflections suggested a diameter of 21–25 Å. Changes in humidity resulted in small changes in the intensities of the various reflections, but no significant change such as that found in going from the low-humidity A form to the high-humidity B form of DNA. The conclusion of the papers was that although it looked as if it had a helical organization with some similarity to DNA, the patterns were not sufficiently detailed to draw a firm conclusion.

Furthermore, the fact that the same pattern appeared—even though the base ratios varied widely in different preparations—clearly indicated that there was something profound that we did not understand. With the benefit of hindsight, it is clear that what we were looking at in these preparations were largely segments of ribosomal RNA that had both single-stranded and double-stranded components. We were unable to get high degrees of orientation from these materials, and of course, the single-stranded components in the preparations could explain the variation in base composition.

BETHESDA, MARYLAND

In June 1954, Jane and I left Pasadena and settled in a house near the Chesapeake Canal, not far from NIH. In a short time, the laboratory at NIH was functioning. Jack Dunitz joined me from Caltech, and shortly afterward I was able to induce David Davies, who had also been a postdoctoral fellow at Caltech, to return from England and join us at NIH. The thrust of the research work was still related to questions of RNA structure: Could it form a two-stranded helix?

Our lifestyle continued in the same way, with many dinner parties and social events that wove science into them. Jim Watson visited NIH several times during this period, partly due to the fact that Christa Mayr[4] whom he was courting went to college at Swarthmore. In addition, Jim frequently visited Cambridge, Massachusetts, as he was actively pursuing the possibility of joining the Harvard Biology Department.

Near the end of 1954, Jim came to dinner at our cottage, together with Christa Mayr and George Gamow. Gamow and I were busy at the time, writing our review of the coding problem (Gamow et al. 1956). Later in the spring of 1955, when Jim again visited with Christa, we were able to continue our discussions of RNA structure, but we could not see a clear way forward.

During that spring, Severo Ochoa of New York University came to give a seminar at NIH, and he described the enzyme that Marianne Grundberg-Manago had isolated in his laboratory. The enzyme used ribonucleoside diphosphates as substrate and synthesized polymers of ribonucleotides.[5] I immediately saw that this could provide useful information about RNA conformation, and Severo kindly provided me with samples. I was able to use these samples to obtain much better orientation than was possible with RNA from natural sources.

At the meeting in Pasadena in September 1953, Francis Crick told me about the powerful rotating anode that had been developed in the MRC laboratories in Cambridge, England, and which was capable of producing an intense beam of X-rays. He told me that if I ever had a need for a high-intensity beam, he would be happy to have me come over to use it. Accordingly, with these new X-ray diffraction patterns, I wrote to Francis in the late spring of 1954 to arrange a visit to Cambridge to examine these fibers with their more sophisticated apparatus.

During that period, Jim was offered an Assistant Professorship in the Harvard Biology Department. He had obtained a traveling fellowship from the National Science Foundation that allowed him to take a year off and return to Cambridge, before assuming his position at Harvard. Thus, it was in July 1955 that we were all together again in England.

A "BRIEF" VISIT TO CAMBRIDGE, ENGLAND

On my arrival in Cambridge, Francis graciously offered to put me up in his house on Portugal Place while I was collecting diffraction data. The diffraction patterns produced by the various synthetic RNA polymers were of varied interest. A copolymer containing both adenine and uracil residues produced X-ray diffraction patterns very much like those that we had seen at Caltech and NIH with the naturally occurring RNA preparations. Since we knew that the synthetic polymers were not likely to have branches in the RNA, it seemed reasonable to assume that there were few if any branches in the naturally occurring RNA fibers. The fiber of polyuridylic acid did not have much orientation. However, the fiber produced by polyadenylic acid sometimes began to show a distinctly different pattern, which was clearly helical and was worth probing in greater detail. Jim Watson was also preparing fibers, and he began to get even better diffraction photographs from polyadenylic acid.

By then, Leslie Orgel and his wife Alice had left the United States and settled in Cambridge, so that we were able to resume the kind of discussions that we had begun a year earlier when we were all together at Caltech. The sense of recreating the Caltech environment was enhanced by the arrival of Linda Pauling, the daughter of Linus Pauling, who also stayed in the Crick household for part of the summer.

My work then took an unexpected turn away from RNA to protein. Francis told me one Saturday morning that he had just read in *Nature* of a new form of glycine polymer called polyglycine II. It seemed to us that it should be possible to work out the structure of this new form of polyglycine II because the number of variables was quite limited. We went to the Cavendish Laboratory later in the morning and started working with brass wire skeletal molecular models of a glycine polymer. After building the model carefully and making measurements, we were reasonably confident that the major X-ray reflections produced by this conformation would account for the X-ray powder diagram of polyglycine II and we sent a paper off to *Nature* (Crick and Rich 1955). On studying the model further, I realized that the three chains from the polyglycine II lattice might be a model for the structure of collagen. Francis and I worked intensively to make a molecular model for collagen, studying different conformations with the polyglycine II hydrogen-bonding pattern. This led to a proposal for the structure of collagen (Rich and Crick 1955) which, many years later, was shown by others to be correct by single-crystal X-ray diffraction. The net result of these discoveries was that my planned "brief" visit extended to over six months.

This work was carried out in the context of many social interactions with people in the Cambridge community. At one point in the summer, Jane received a letter from her aunt, her father's sister, who was visiting London and invited Jane and me to come to see a Chinese opera and visit with her. Her aunt and uncle lived in Cold Spring Harbor, a short distance from the Laboratory, and they were very active in the Biological Association, which supported the Cold Spring Harbor Laboratory. My work with Francis was too intense for me to break off and go to London, and Jim gallantly offered to take Jane in my place, so off they went. On the ride there, Jim told Jane that he was interested in accomplishing two things. The first was to write a best-selling book and the second was to become Director of the Cold Spring Harbor Laboratory, where he had spent many summers. The latter goal stimulated him to meet Jane's relatives. At the time, Jane made a mental note of Jim's future plans. Of course, Jim accomplished both of these goals within the space of ten years.

When I came to England, I brought with me a very good Rolex camera and was keen to take photographs of local English life. At one point, we had a meeting in the Cricks' upstairs sitting room of the RNA Tie Club that George Gamow had organized the previous year. One of these photographs showed the four of us, Francis, Leslie, Jim and myself, looking very somber, wearing our flamboyant RNA ties that had a black background and a wavy green single strand of RNA containing golden colored purines and pyrimidines.

During this period, Jim was under considerable emotional stress since his relationship with Christa remained unresolved. Although he was very much interested in other young ladies, he had difficulty finding an appropriate companion. It was characteristic of Jim that he confided in women who were good listeners and were sympathetic to his plight. Jane played this role at Caltech and later in Cambridge, England. His other sympathetic listeners included Max Delbrück's wife Manny and later Celia Gilbert, the wife of his Harvard colleague, Walter Gilbert. These discussions no doubt helped Jim achieve a certain emotional equilibrium. However, this topic was mentioned only tangentially with male colleagues; it was clear that there was a strong emotional life simmering beneath the surface.

Meeting of the RNA Tie Club in Francis Crick's house, Cambridge, England, 1955. (Left to right) Francis Crick, Alex Rich, Leslie Orgel, Jim Watson. Note the ties! (Photograph courtesy of Alex Rich.)

As the fall of 1955 progressed, we continued working on the possibilities of RNA conformation, largely trying to develop new ideas and testing them with wire molecular models to see if we could make conformations that made some sense in explaining how RNA might be involved in protein synthesis. This effort was stimulated by informal manuscripts that were distributed among the members of the RNA Tie Club. The effort received a strong jolt in early November 1955 while Jim and I were still in England. Jane and I received a chatty letter from Max Delbrück, who had been visiting the East Coast. He wrote about many things but then mentioned the great interest that had been stimulated by the recent structure published by Robert E. Rundle. Rundle was an inorganic crystallographer working at Ames, Iowa, and I knew him to be a very clever man. According to Max's description, the conformation completely explained the manner in which amino acids were assembled in protein synthesis. Delbrück went on to state that Robert Corey, a co-worker of Pauling's at Caltech, had checked the coordinates and they were acceptable. I also received a letter from George Gamow, mentioning Rundle's work. A few hours later I learned from Jim that Gamow had written to him as well, making inquiries about Rundle's structure.

The letter mentioned that the material had been published in a recent note to the *Journal of the American Chemical Society* (*JACS*) and we made great efforts to see if someone in Cambridge had the most recent issue. Unfortunately, although most chemists received the journal, the volume was very heavy and it invariably was sent to subscribers by sea rather than air-mail, and was nowhere to be found.

There followed a rather intense morning during which we worked with our molecular models, frantically trying to imagine different ways that RNA chains could be assembled to make sites specific for amino acid binding. Francis worked with great vigor, and Jim had a cloudy expression on his face throughout. At one point in late morning, Don Caspar, an American scientist visiting from Boston, came into the room. We told him what we were trying to do. I have a vivid picture in my mind of Caspar perched on top of a tall stool with his legs crossed, looking thoughtfully at the Delbrück letter. After a time, he wondered out loud whether this could be a joke. Immediately, everyone in the room stopped what they were doing. All of a sudden, this seemed like a very plausible possibility. At that point, we checked with Peter Pauling,[6] who had received a recent letter from his father, and nothing was mentioned of this "breakthrough." He certainly would have known if his father's colleague Robert Corey had been working on the coordinates. By lunchtime, it seemed highly probable that Caspar was right especially because Max Delbrück, as well as George Gamow, had a great penchant for practical jokes. The fact that they had been together in Bethesda reinforced this possibility.

We still had some lingering doubts, and it was later decided that in the afternoon, I would take a drastic step and actually make a trans-Atlantic telephone call to co-workers in my laboratory at NIH. At that time, of course, trans-Atlantic telephone calls were very uncommon. We all gathered around a telephone in the Cavendish Laboratory, and I got through to my associate Jack Dunitz, who not only knew Rundle very well, but also had followed the RNA work with some interest. I asked Jack if he had heard about the Rundle publication in the *JACS*. Dunitz's reply relieved our anxiety in an unusual way. Speaking in his clipped Scottish accent and mentioning that trans-Atlantic calls were very expensive, he suggested that I should speak very rapidly into the telephone. He would tape my call and play it back later at a slower rate, so that he would get the whole message in a most economical way. The absurdity of his suggestion was apparent, and the conclusion was that we had been the butt of a practical joke.

It turned out that there had been a party in Bethesda, attended by Delbrück and Gamow, as well as people from my laboratory, and the elaborate scheme had been developed at that time. It was carried out with great precision and coordination, and we all fell for it.

Francis Crick and I had concluded most of our work on the collagen structure by the end of the year. Jim had been in the lab for most of the fall, but toward the end of the year, he went off to Scotland. In early January 1956, I left to return to Bethesda and NIH. I thanked Francis and Odile Crick for extending their hospitality to Jane and me for such a long period. Indeed, I felt a bit like the main character in the movie "The Man Who Came To Dinner," who came to dinner and ended up living in the household for an extended period.

RETURN TO NIH

Within two months of my return to NIH, David Davies and I found that mixing polyadenylic acid and polyuridylic acid led to a significant change in the viscosity of the droplet that we were using for withdrawing fibers. Furthermore, long fibers could be drawn that produced a diffraction pattern that was totally different from those of its components. The pattern clearly showed that these two polymeric molecules had wrapped around each other to form a double helix! In addition, the characteristic pattern with a strong first layer line and a weak second layer line near the meridian showed that it was essentially the same kind of pattern that Jim and I had observed with naturally occurring RNA fibers. Now, however, they were well-oriented, and we could obtain information about the geometry of the helix. We were also aware that this was the first of a special type of chemical reaction in which long molecules would form helical complexes in solution, depending on the specificity of the hydrogen bonds between the constituent parts. Although we did not use the name, this was indeed the first nucleic acid hybridization.

These results were conveyed to Jim and Francis, who were still in Cambridge, and elicited a fair amount of excitement. David Davies and I sent off a short note to *JACS* (Rich and Davies 1956), describing the X-ray diffraction pattern and its geometry. We concluded that the molecules had interacted to form specific pairs of hydrogen bonds between adenine and uracil residues, analogous to the bonds previously described between adenine and thymine residues in DNA. The major conclusion from this work, as cited in the brief note, was that we showed for the first time that it was possible for the RNA backbone to assume a configuration somewhat similar to that found in DNA using the same complementarity in its base pairs. Furthermore, the fact that the molecule made an RNA duplex suggested that this could be the form in which RNA carries out its implied molecular duplication in the plant and smaller animal RNA viruses. Finally, we suggested that this method of forming a two-stranded helical molecule by mixing two substances together might be used for a variety of studies directed toward an understanding of the formation of helical molecules utilizing specific interactions (Rich and Davies 1956). In short, we suggested the possibility that this method might become more general, which has subsequently proven to be the case.

Although these results seemed eminently reasonable to those of us who had been thinking about the structural problems of nucleic acids, our interpretation was not widely accepted. At one point, I was walking along a long corridor at NIH and bumped into Herman Kalckar, the Danish biochemist with whom Jim had worked in Copenhagen a few years earlier. I mentioned to Herman that we had just discovered that polyadenylic acid and polyuradylic acid form a double helix when added together in solution. Kalckar was incredulous. "What," he said, "without an enzyme?" His surprise stemmed from the fact that all previous experiments in which a double helix was formed involved an enzyme, as in experiments that Arthur Kornberg had carried out. The idea that helices could simply form spontaneously in solution struck him as somewhat improbable. Another type of objection raised was that these were extremely long molecules, containing thousands of nucleotide bases. The feeling was that they would become hopelessly entangled when trying to wrap around each other to form a double helix. These objections came from people who failed to appreciate the highly energetic nature of segmented molecular movement in polymers due to Brownian motion. The RNA duplexes would continually change their conformations until a lowest-energy configuration was formed, as represented by the double helix.

In the early fall of 1956, a McCollum Pratt meeting was organized at Johns Hopkins University in Baltimore around the subject of the "Chemical Basis of Heredity." It was an excellent meeting with all of the major research workers in the field. Jim and Francis attended; others in attendance included Erwin Chargaff, George Beadle, and Arthur Kornberg. Francis Crick gave a talk about the conformation of DNA while wearing his RNA Tie Club tie. Jim Watson presented the work that had been carried out on polyadenylic acid fibers. In that case, the evidence clearly showed a helical diffraction pattern which suggested that there were two parallel chains. It required a protonated molecule, and the full details of that work took some time for us to unravel (Rich et al. 1961).

When it was my time to talk, I described the experiments on the interaction between polyadenylic acid and polyuridylic acid. By then, I had a large amount of data on the changes in the diffraction pattern with alterations in humidity, showing how the molecules, packed in a hexagonal lattice, would float apart with an increase in humidity and come together as they dried. Unlike DNA, an RNA double helix did not change its conformation with changes in humidity and had only a single form, unlike DNA with its A and B forms (Rich 1957). This was subsequently found to be very similar to the A form of DNA. Another person attending the meeting was Julian Huxley, a prominent writer who had a keen interest in science.[7] He came up to me after the meeting and warmly congratulated me for having discovered "molecular sex," i.e., two molecules that wrapped around each other with great specificity. It seemed to me that this was a fair description.

In a sense, these observations started to answer the question that Jim and I began to study some two years earlier, namely, can RNA form a double helix? But because fiber X-ray diffraction diagrams can illustrate only general things about a molecule, they cannot "prove" the structure because there are too many unknown variables. Proof required a single-crystal X-ray diffraction study, and it was not until 1973 that we solved the first fragments of an RNA double helix in crystals of the dinucleoside phosphates ApU with adenosine and uridine (Rosenberg et al. 1973) and GpC with guanosine and cytidine (Day et al. 1973). These were solved at a resolution of 0.8 Å, so that we could visualize all the details of the structure, including its ions and water molecules.

By 1956, we were beginning to realize that it was unlikely we would find an RNA structure which would "solve" the coding problem in protein synthesis. The simple idea that RNA could form convenient pockets into which amino acids would fit seemed less and less likely. At the meeting in Baltimore, some evidence was presented of an unstable RNA made after bacteriophage T2 infection that had a base composition very similar to that of T2 DNA. It took another four years or so before it was understood that this was what we later called messenger RNA.

In a sense, the solution of the RNA problem in protein synthesis was really obtained by Francis Crick, who had written a note a year earlier to the RNA Tie Club in which he described the "adapter hypothesis"—the idea that small RNA molecules might be attached to amino acids and that these would line up on DNA (or RNA) in a way that would arrange the amino acids in their correct sequence. Only in subsequent years would it be realized that the discovery by Mahlon Hoagland and Paul Zamecnik of what was later called transfer RNA made it possible to understand that this was in fact the way information passed from nucleic acid sequences to amino acid sequences. The effort that Jim and I put toward understanding RNA structure was the beginning of an appreciation of the fact that RNA could adopt many different conformations, both in protein synthesis and in regulating other biological phenomenon. It was the opening step in what has become a large segment of current molecular biology.

REFERENCES

Crick F.H.C. and Rich A. 1955. Structure of polyglycine II. *Nature* **176:** 780–781.

Day R.O., Seeman N.C., Rosenberg J.M., and Rich A. 1973. A crystalline fragment of the double helix: The structure of the dinucleoside phosphate guanylyl-3′,5′-cytidine. *Proc. Natl. Acad. Sci.* **70:** 849–853.

Gamow G. 1954. Possible relation between DNA and the protein structure. *Nature* **137:** 318.

Gamow G., Rich A., and Ycas M. 1956. The problem of information transfer from the nucleic acids to proteins. In *Advances in biological and medical physics, IV*, pp. 23–68. Academic Press, New York.

Rich A. 1957. The structure of synthetic polyribonucleotides and the spontaneous formation of a new two-stranded helical molecule. In *The chemical basis of heredity* (ed. W.D. McElroy and B. Glass), pp. 557–562. The Johns Hopkins University Press, Baltimore.

Rich A. and Crick F.H.C. 1955. The structure of collagen. *Nature* **176:** 915–916.

Rich A. and Davies D.R. 1956. A new two-stranded helical structure: Polyadenylic acid and polyuridylic acid. *J. Am. Chem. Soc.* **78:** 3548.

Rich A. and Watson J.D. 1954a. Physical studies on ribonucleic acid. *Nature* **173:** 995–996.

Rich A. and Watson J.D. 1954b. Some relations between DNA and RNA. *Proc. Natl. Acad. Sci.* **40:** 759–764.

Rich A., Davies D.R., Crick F.H.C., and Watson J.D. 1961. The molecular structure of poly-adenylic acid. *J. Mol. Biol.* **3:** 71–86.

Rosenberg J.M., Seeman N.C., Kim J.J.P., Suddath F.L., Nicholas H.B., and Rich A. 1973. Double helix at atomic resolution. *Nature* **243:** 150–154.

Watson J.D. and Crick F.H.C. 1953. Molecular structure of nucleic acids. *Nature* **171:** 737–738.

Flowers and Phage

Joan Steitz

Yale University School of Medicine

Jim Watson burst into my life with a beaker of golden daffodils. It mysteriously appeared on my desk one day in the winter of 1961. As an undergraduate at Antioch College in Ohio, my co-op job assignment was to work in the lab of Alex Rich at the Massachusetts Institute of Technology. There, I was assisting graduate student Jon Warner and postdoc Paul Knopf in attempts to denature and renature ribosomes. (If DNA could be taken apart and reannealed, why not ribosomes?) Apparently, while visiting Alex to discuss their common interest in ribosomes, Jim had noticed me standing in front of the Beckman DU spectrophotometer, where I spent endless hours watching the absorbance increase as I raised the temperature on the water-jacketed cell holder. I never, however, succeeded in obtaining the hoped-for return to lower optical density when the cell cooled back to room temperature. Nonetheless, I had been smitten by my first exposure to molecular biology (not yet a subject treated in college textbooks or courses). The idea that there was a molecular basis for the genetic phenomena that had intrigued me in high school was entrancing. I was thrilled to learn that the basis of life was somehow encoded in the sequence of bases in the elegant double-stranded DNA structure that had been proposed by Jim and Francis Crick only eight years earlier.

I returned to Antioch for the spring quarter of 1961, but in the summer was back working in the Rich lab (this time isolating DNA from a variety of organisms chosen for their varying GC content). I saw Jim several times, including a memorable dinner at an intimate restaurant in Harvard Square—followed by a ballet performance in a huge tent somewhere on the banks of the Charles River. He still owned his MG convertible with rightside steering wheel and delighted in tooling around Cambridge exposed to the elements. I felt privileged to meet dignitaries such as Matt Meselson and Peter Pauling in Jim's company.

In the fall of 1961, I boarded a transatlantic steamer to spend my junior year abroad, first learning German in Bavaria and then studying in Tübingen. Work was also an integral part of Antioch education abroad and Alex and Jim arranged for me to work in the laboratory of Alfred Gierer[1] in the relatively new Max-Planck Institut für Virusforschung in Tübingen. There, I again assisted more senior scientists, this time in experiments on phage, including the newly discovered single-stranded DNA phage. Jim visited the laboratory once in the spring of 1962 and, in his seminar, excitedly conveyed the Harvard side of the discovery of messenger RNA.[2] We took a long walk in the woods, and later in my attic rooms in a four-century-old house in the Haagasse, Jim learned that I did not know how to make a proper cup of tea. I hadn't brought the water to a complete boil!

JOAN STEITZ

After graduating in 1967 with a Ph.D. from Harvard, Joan Steitz worked for three years at the MRC, Cambridge, sequencing the three ribosome-binding sites of R17 RNA where protein synthesis initiates. This type of work continued to expand for several years after her own lab was established at Yale. By early 1980s, however, Steitz had begun to work on small ribonucleoproteins—snRNPs or snurps—protein:RNA complexes that are required for accurate splicing of messenger RNAs in mammalian cells. She has dominated this field for many years with work of unimpeachable quality.

Steitz has been a Professor of Molecular Biophysics and Biochemistry at Yale since 1978. She was elected to the National Academy of Science in 1983, has been a Howard Hughes Medical Institute investigator since 1986, and was awarded the National Medal of Science in the same year. Joan Steitz received the first Weizmann Women in Science Award in 1994.

In the account that follows, Joan Steitz gives the feeling that Jim Watson's laboratory at Harvard in the early 1960s was the center of the world. Perhaps it was in a way: Jim had attracted the brightest and best to work there, and he himself was in transition from Nobel Prize-winning scientist to best-selling author. It is hardly surprising that Joan was slightly overwhelmed when the doors of the Biology Department opened, perhaps for the first time, to a talented young woman. Molecular biology at that time was fuelled by testosterone and it was a good few years before women were to achieve the same entry rights as men to the club.

My experiences working as a technician for others convinced me that I was not sufficiently devoted to science to pursue a graduate degree in molecular biology. After all, the graduate students and postdocs in the labs I saw in Boston and Germany worked nights and weekends, more than I believed I was willing to do. Moreover, I had not laid eyes on a female science professor (because there were virtually none in any American research university in the early 1960s); women worked as research associates, usually in their husband's lab. Thus, when I returned to the United States to complete my senior year at Antioch, I applied to medical school and was admitted to Harvard.

But the summer of 1963 transformed my future. Because I wanted to spend the summer in Minneapolis with my parents before departing for medical school, I had obtained a job in the lab of Joe Gall, who began his academic career at the University of Minnesota but had just been hired by Yale. Joe set me up with my own independent project and then went about packing the lab for his move to New Haven. My goal was to determine whether ciliary basal bodies from *Tetrahymena pyriformis* contained nucleic acid—a reasonable question to ask since mitochondria had just been shown to possess their own complement of DNA. Suddenly, I found myself working nights and weekends! By August and with Joe's encouragement, I decided that I did not really like sick people, and perhaps I should change my plans. I contacted Jim to ask whether I might be able to switch from Harvard Medical School to the graduate program in Biochemistry and Molecular Biology. At the time, a department by that name did not exist; degrees were granted instead by a committee made up of selected faculty from the

Biology and Chemistry Departments in Cambridge. Fortunately, an accepted student had just dropped out of the entering class for the fall, and Jim (no doubt after consultation with Joe Gall and Alex Rich) engineered my insertion into the open slot. It came with a fellowship in the grand amount of $1700 per annum! Since I was a known quantity, at least the faculty could be assured that they would not suffer the same surprise as a few years earlier when a female applicant from India submitted the picture of an Indian movie star and was therefore admitted; she did not last long in the program.

In September, 1963, I thus became the sole woman in a class of 10 to embark on graduate studies in Biochemistry and Molecular Biology at Harvard. The first year comprised only coursework and was perhaps the hardest period of my life. Even though I had been a chemistry major at Antioch, I struggled with the qualifying exams in physical and organic chemistry, which were the same as those required of the entering chemistry graduate students. Luckily, several tries were permitted and by spring I managed to pass both.

One of the highlights of the year was Jim's course in molecular genetics. It was crammed with intriguing questions about the functioning of DNA and RNA. We were spared neither the most recent unpublished data nor the latest rumors. The genetic code had not yet been cracked. Suppression was purely a genetic phenomenon, not yet known to involve mutant tRNAs. Factors enabling the elongation steps in protein synthesis had just been discovered, but translation initiation and termination were still black boxes. How did it all work? I was enthralled (and did well on the final exam).

Yet, when it came time to choose a lab for my thesis work in the spring of 1964, Jim was not my first choice! My summer with Joe Gall had not resolved whether basal bodies truly contained nucleic acid; I was further intrigued by the question of how these complex structures arose, especially since the pairing of centrioles (which appeared structurally comparable to basal bodies) suggested that they might self-duplicate—just like DNA. The architecture of basal bodies was at that time emerging from ultrastructural studies using the electron microscope, so I went along to ask the Biology Department's premier microscopist whether I might work on this problem in his lab. He conceded that he did reserve a small bench in the corner of the lab for "biochemistry," but then interrogated me on how I anticipated I would manage to combine a career in science with marriage and children. I managed to escape from his office before I burst into tears. Next, I approached Jim, proclaiming my interest in ribosomes. He omitted the embarrassing questions and said yes!

There were two major projects in Jim's lab when I arrived, one focusing on protein synthesis and the ribosome, the other on the newly discovered RNA phage, R17. The more senior graduate students included Peter Moore, Mario Capecchi, and Jerry Adams (working on translation) and Ray Gesteland and Gary Gussin (working on RNA phage); John Richardson was somewhat of an outlier, working on RNA polymerase. The lab was run jointly with Wally Gilbert, who was still formally affiliated with the Physics Department and was only beginning to have graduate students and postdocs of his own.

In the summer of 1964, because of inadequate space in the main laboratory complex, I worked in an old class lab down the hall and around the corner, but on the same floor of the Biolabs (the third floor). My initial assignment was to help Ray Gesteland isolate ribonuclease-negative mutants of *E. coli*—identifying the "messengerase" that conferred short half-lives on mRNAs was a Holy Grail at the time. Dick Roblin, the other first-year student who joined the Watson lab that summer, was my companion in this outpost. Notably, his eventual thesis comprised the sequence of one nucleotide—determining that the R17 phage RNA had pppGp at its 5´ end—remarkable in contrast to the 10^9 base pairs of the human genome first announced in 2000! Only near the end of my second year were Dick and I accommodated with the rest of the lab. Jim begrudgingly acknowledged that his days at the bench were over and allowed me to move into the one-bay lab that adjoined his office.

I learned only after a few months that I was the first woman ever to be accepted by Jim as a graduate student. Yet, there was no dearth of women in the lab. Jim often stated his belief that pretty faces would encourage the graduate students and postdocs to spend time in the lab (and therefore be productive). Especially during the summers, a bevy of female undergraduates, mostly "Cliffies," appeared; they are much in evidence in the "rhino pictures," the annual photographic portrait of Jim's group at Harvard. Even I was assigned an undergraduate helper, one who boasted the shortest miniskirt and heaviest eye make-up of all of that summer's decorative additions. Jim also believed that students and postdocs would become more accomplished if they had to write protocols and supervise an assistant.

The atmosphere in the lab mirrored that in the field at the time—fiercely competitive, but paradoxically remarkably collegial. Jim let it be known how disgusted he was that Norton Zinder would not share with others the RNA phage (called f2) isolated in his lab at Rockefeller; thus, we worked with its close relative R17, which Jim had obtained from Paranchych.[3] Nonetheless, Jim seemed to make frequent visits to the Zinder lab, and when he returned, we would all crowd around in the hallway to learn the latest from the competition. Jim would pop in occasionally, especially if he had been away and ask "What's up?" But if I needed detailed advice on an experiment, I would go to Wally or later to Klaus Weber, who, after he became an Assistant Professor, made the Watson/Gilbert lab a triumvirate. Yet, Jim had uncanny insight into where each problem was going and was very much in charge of shaping the scientific direction of the lab.

Afternoon tea was a daily affair in the lab and usually involved lively scientific conversation, as well as gossip. Visiting speakers were paraded from one graduate student to another. Students were invariably included in dinner outings. Parties at Jim's apartment on Apian Way were all-inclusive affairs with faculty and students from the Medical School as well as the Harvard and MIT Cambridge campuses. Afterward, Jim would grumble about how so-and-so was so crass as to have leaned against one of his growing collection of artwork.

Jim made it no secret that he preferred graduate students over postdocs (even including future notables such as Benno Müller-Hill, John Tooze, Mary Osborn, and Maxime Schwartz, with whom I overlapped). His principles for the training of graduate students were clearly enunciated and reinforced by repetition so that there could be no misunderstanding. They are important operational guidelines that have stood the test of time in my lab, as well as Jim's.

- *Giving talks.* At the weekly group seminars, which also included visitors from other Boston labs working on molecular biology, Jim was fearsome. After uttering only half a dozen sentences, a student (or postdoc) would be interrupted by Jim.

"Stop right there! Go back to the beginning and tell us what you are going to talk about." It did not take long to learn Jim's prescription for giving a talk: Tell them what you are going to tell them; tell them; then tell them what you told them.

- *Writing papers.* Likewise, when you handed a draft of a paper to Jim, having already consulted others in the lab, you could expect that it would come back with the introduction (at least) completely rewritten. Nonetheless, Jim did not attach his name to the publications from his lab, even those of graduate students. In the first paper I wrote after I married (1966), Jim urged me not to abandon my maiden name. But, it was an era in which I felt it more important to know who was connected to whom, and insisted on taking on my husband's name. Only several years later, even nonprofessional women were retaining their own names after marriage.

- *Choosing problems.* If the question wasn't important, why waste your time pursuing it? Only problems that could provide molecular understanding were worth undertaking. Thus, until the mid 1960s, the project had to involve bacteria or phage. Anyone who worked on higher cells was either misguided or (more likely) stupid: With such complexity, there was no hope of true understanding.

- *Lab organization.* Everyone had his (or her) own project. And it was preferred that the student establish ownership by "finding" the project initially. Thus, as a second-year student, I tried out four or five different projects before settling on my ultimate thesis subject—characterization of the A protein of the R17 phage particle. Only when the situation became dire, did Jim rescue students by telling them what they should do.

While I was in the lab, Jim was engaged in two major writing projects. One was the first edition of *Molecular Biology of the Gene*, the landmark text that defined the fledgling field of molecular biology and set a new standard for how textbooks should be written (Watson 1965). In the preface, Jim credited me for my "consistently intelligent comments" during the preparation of the manuscript, whereas I recall being embarrassed that most of my questions simply reflected basic ignorance of what Jim was writing about. The second project was *The Double Helix*, Jim's enchanting account of the discovery of the DNA structure (Watson 1968). Jim's proposals for the name of the book were *Honest Jim* or *The Base Pair*, both of which were rejected by the publisher. Jim forwarded versions of the text to Francis and others in Cambridge for comment. The scathing letters that came back were posted on the lab bulletin board. Since at the time I was negotiating to go to the Cambridge Medical Research Council lab for post-doctoral studies, I fretted that my future might be adversely affected. I simply did not realize that the relationship between Jim and Francis was more than strong enough to survive the havoc caused by *The Double Helix*.

During my second and third years in Jim's lab, I shared an apartment with three other female graduate students from various departments at Harvard and MIT. We ate dinner together and frequently entertained guests. Once, when Francis was to visit Harvard for a week or so, Jim suggested that he might "enjoy a respite from faculty wife dinners." We wrote our invitation on pink perfumed stationery and Francis accepted. One of my roommates was Nancy Rogerson, a South Carolinian who claimed to believe in ghosts and was studying theoretical physics at MIT. She was always concerned with details like whether the pickle dish was positioned at the correct angle relative to the forks on a properly set dinner table. Another roommate was Ann Baker, later to become Ann Burgess. Ann was the sole woman in the graduate class admitted the year after mine. Only several years later did the ratio of women to men entering the Biochemistry and Molecular Biology program rise above 10%. Francis did not take issue with the angle of the pickle dish and regaled us with wonderful stories. It was a delightful dinner.

During my second year at Harvard, I became involved with my future husband, Tom Steitz. He was a student in the same graduate program working in the lab of chemist Bill Lipscomb on the crystal structure of carboxypeptidase. The enzyme was isolated by lab personnel from the pancreatic juice of Alice the cow, who was catheterized and resided somewhere outside of Cambridge. While battling with Harvard's President Nathan Pusey,[4] Jim threatened to move Alice to the President's lawn on the central Harvard campus—he had read in the ancient statutes of the University that faculty had the right to graze their animals there. Unfortunately, Alice stepped on her catheter and met her demise about the time that Jim's dispute with Pusey simmered down.

Also while I was at Harvard, the Committee on Biochemistry and Molecular Biology made the unorthodox decision to offer a faculty position to a woman! Ann Norris had done groundbreaking work on aminoacyl-tRNA synthetases with Paul Berg at Stanford. At the last moment, she decided to marry Buzz Baldwin and remain in Palo Alto. Jim was disgusted, and Ann's act seriously set back the attitude of the Harvard faculty about the wisdom of including women in their ranks.

Joan Steitz and Fritz Lipmann at the 1969 Cold Spring Harbor Symposium. (Courtesy CSHL Archives.)

Being a woman determined the two most important decisions of my early scientific career. The first was ending up in Jim's lab for my Ph.D. The second was my choice of a postdoctoral project, which ultimately led to a faculty position at Yale. Since there were no female science professors at major research universities, I never imagined myself becoming one, assuming instead a future career as a research associate. Thus, when I arrived at the Cambridge MRC in late 1967 (Jim had written to Francis), I decided to take on an extremely challenging project. It had been widely discussed in the lab beforehand, but was too risky to be grabbed by any of my (male) postdoctoral contemporaries. They would have to produce something concrete in order to succeed on the American job market in a few years time. In contrast, I had nothing to lose (since I did not anticipate ever competing for a faculty position), and the project clearly fit Jim's criterion of importance. After a year of frustration, I began to obtain the hoped-for results. Meanwhile, during our absence in England, the academic landscape in the United States had changed. With the first wave of the Women's Movement in full swing, universities were suddenly clamoring for promising young women faculty. I was flabbergasted to receive several offers, and finally my husband and I settled on assistant professor positions at Yale.

But I, however, had not psychologically prepared myself to become a professor and was exceedingly fearful of failing, only to add to the Ann Norris example and provide more evidence that women should not be offered positions at major universities. Shortly before we were to move to Yale, I broke down while attending the 1970 Cold Spring Harbor Symposium. I ended up in tears in Jim's office. Jim comforted me by revealing that he had had nightmares of standing before a class totally unprepared when he lectured for the first time at Harvard. His support convinced me that I must take on the challenge that confronted me.

Once again, Jim's instincts proved correct. In the ensuing years, trying to emulate what I saw of Jim's stewardship of his lab at Harvard has provided the wonder and joy of watching my own students learn to succeed at science.

REFERENCES

Watson J.D. 1965. *Molecular biology of the gene*. W.A. Benjamin, New York.
Watson J.D. 1968. *The double helix*. Atheneum, New York.

On the Edge: My Time in Jim Watson's Lab

Benno Müller-Hill

Genetics Institute of Cologne University

Jim Watson's lab was the best possible in the world, so I thought when I worked there, and ever since, I have not changed my mind. Before I describe what it was that made it so outstanding, I have to tell briefly how I came there.

I had studied chemistry in Germany. Inorganic chemistry seemed boring, organic chemistry laborious, biochemistry seemed most interesting. I did my Ph.D. work with Kurt Wallenfels, an organic chemist who was interested in sugars and enzymes. I worked on the binding sites of β-galactosidase. Wallenfels got a NATO grant with Howard Rickenberg, Bloomington, Indiana, who had discovered Lac permease. The goal was to show that Lac permease and β-galactosidase were identical. I thought that this was nonsense, but it was a unique opportunity to go to America. So I accepted the offer and went there in the beginning of 1963. I had with me samples of various glycosides that had been synthesized in the Wallenfels laboratory. I wanted to test them for their inducer or anti-inducer capacity of the *lac* system of *E. coli*.

François Jacob and Jacques Monod had proposed in 1960 in a brief French language paper (Jacob et al. 1960) the essence of their model of gene control: A repressor binds to an operator (a genetic switch that controls the activity of a nearby gene) and thus inhibits gene expression. We had read this paper in the Wallenfels seminar, and I

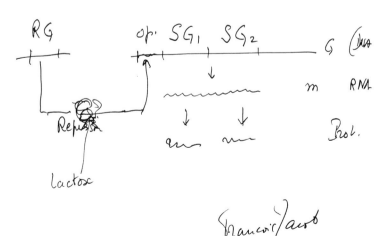

The lac *operon, drawn by François Jacob in 2002. (Courtesy of Jan Witkowski.)*

Benno Müller-Hill

Benno Müller-Hill was born in 1933 in Freiburg, Germany. He studied chemistry in Freiburg and Munich and in the mid 1960s worked for three years in Jim's Watson laboratory at Harvard. In 1966, he and Wally Gilbert isolated the Lac repressor in a series of tour-de-force experiments. In 1968, Benno became full professor at the Genetics Institute of Cologne University. His main scientific interests are protein-DNA interaction and gene control. In addition to many scientific papers, Benno has written two books: a monograph entitled *The lac Operon: A Short History of a Genetic Paradigm* (1996, Walter de Gruyter, Berlin), and a history of human genetics in Nazi Germany published in German in 1984 (*Tödliche Wissenschaft. Die Aussonderung von Juden, Zigeunern und Geisteskranken 1933–1945*; Rowohlt Verlag, Reinbeck), and in English in 1988 (*Murderous Science: Elimination by Scientific Selection of Jews, Gypsies, and Others in Germany 1933–1945*; Oxford University Press). A paperback edition with an afterword by Jim Watson was published by Cold Spring Harbor Laboratory Press in 1998.

If Benno and Wally Gilbert had not isolated the Lac repressor, someone else certainly would have done so. But no one other than Benno could have written a book such as *Murderous Science*. In it he describes how German geneticists in the 1930s used their scientific knowledge to identify thousands of "undesirables," who were then sterilized. This brutality became the ghastly proof-of-principle for the subsequent Holocaust.

Many years later, Benno continues to tell the story despite a frigid silence from some of his German colleagues. In 2000, he gave a lecture at Harvard Medical School, which ended with a rhetorical question: "What is the bottom line?" His answer: *"...that science produces only one value and this is honesty and truth and nothing but that...The major mistake is that scientists think their science produces more...that science allows them to distinguish between good and bad... but good and bad, these are questions which are only answered by religion and not science."*

Benno argues that scientists must try to anticipate how society will interpret (and perhaps misuse) their findings: *"It is the duty of human geneticists to predict the possible social consequences of genetic research and to act accordingly."*

The extracts in italics are taken from an article written by Harvard graduate student Robin Lucas Orwant, which appeared in the Bulletin of the Biological and Biomedical Sciences Ph.D. program at Harvard Medical School. The article is available in full on the Web at: http://www.hms.harvard.edu/dms/bbs/bulletin/0600_june/murderous.html.

became fascinated by it. My interest grew when Jacob and Monod published in 1961 two extensive papers (Jacob and Monod 1961a,b) on the subject. The evidence now seemed overwhelming. There was just one detail which seemed unlikely: Lac repressor was supposedly RNA and not a protein (Jacob and Monod 1961b). If it were RNA, how should it then interact specifically with glycosides?[1]

The isolation of Lac repressor seemed to me the most challenging problem of the 1960s. When in Bloomington, I analyzed all of the sugars I had received in the Wallenfels lab for their inducer and anti-inducer capabilities. This knowledge could be used to select various types of *lac* mutants. In my second year in Bloomington, I tried to isolate the Lac repressor and failed. My time was running out. I had to find a new job. For this, I went to the International Congress of Biochemistry which was held in the summer of 1964 in New York. I wanted to ask Jim Watson whether he had a postdoctoral

Benno Müller-Hill at work in the Watson-Gilbert group at the Harvard Biolabs in the 1960s. (Photograph courtesy of Benno Müller-Hill.)

position for me. So I went to the lecture that he was announced to give there. There was such a crowd that I could not even enter the lecture hall. So I left the place and drifted through the building in despair. Suddenly I saw Jim in front of me. I recognized him from pictures. He was all alone. I immediately went to him and told him I was interested in isolating Lac repressor and that I was looking for a job as a postdoc. He told me that he had no such job, but that Wally Gilbert (I had never heard of him), who worked in his lab, possibly might be interested and might possibly have such a job. A meeting was arranged. So I met Wally in the Harvard Biolabs. We both had tried and failed to isolate Lac repressor.[2] We both thought that this was the most challenging problem of molecular biology. Wally offered me the one postdoctoral position he had. So began my life in Jim's lab.

When I arrived in the Biolabs in the beginning of 1965, about half a dozen graduate students were working in Jim's lab: I remember Jerry Adams, Joan Argetsinger, Dick Burgess, Mario Capecchi, Gary Gussin, Bill Haseltine, and Bob Kamen. In the Watson-Gilbert group there was one postdoc, Klaus Weber. Wally Gilbert was in the lab each day from 11 a.m. to midnight. He always had time to talk about experiments or ideas. He loved novel techniques. Jim Watson in contrast was rarely seen. He had no bench. Was he in his office? Possibly, but I would not have dared to disturb him there. He had solved the DNA structure. Thus, one could only talk to him when one had something important to tell him. It took about a year until I reached this situation. I had isolated two nonsense mutants in the *lacI* gene.[3] This proved that active Lac repressor is a protein and not RNA. So I told Jim that in two sentences. "Very good" he said smilingly, and that was that. Later I gave him the manuscript I had written about this experiment. "Heavy and Teutonic" was his comment, when he gave me back the manuscript with his extensive corrections (Müller-Hill 1966).

Klaus Weber, the German postdoc, seemed to be closer to Jim than I was. Klaus and I had a competition to see who had the longest conversations with Jim. We added up the minutes. After one year, Klaus had together about 22 minutes; I had about 15 minutes. So one may ask of what good is this? The answer is that it provided a tremendous challenge to produce something new which was worth announcing. This pressure was most productive. Jim and Wally's students (it was unclear to me whose students they were) *were* most productive. Would the lab have worked without Wally? I doubt it. Would it have worked without Jim? I doubt it. Both were unique. Both complemented each other in a perfect manner.

It was life on the edge. If Wally and I did not succeed in isolating the Lac repressor, we both would fall a long way. We would either win or lose. That I had learned from Jim. Not all of the experiments Jim's students did were based on their own ideas. Wally's influence was heavy. There was tea every day at 4 p.m. where everybody talked to everybody, mainly about experiments. During this break, the excellence and the absence of Jim exerted its pressure. Most important was the general practice that neither Jim nor Wally were ever co-authors of the papers of their students! This lone authorship gave every student a tremendous feeling of having accomplished something. The outside world concluded—I have heard this many times—that Jim did not do any science when in Harvard. How utterly wrong! The policy of not becoming co-author of students' papers was old. It went back to Salvador Luria, Jim's teacher, who had followed this policy from the beginning of his career. He had learned it from Thomas Hunt Morgan who had followed it all his life, in particular when he began to analyze the genetics of *Drosophila*.

When I started my career as a professor in Cologne in 1968, I tried to follow Jim's example: I was not co-author of my students' and postdocs' papers, unless I had performed a significant part of the experiments reported in the paper. Again this stimulated my students tremendously. These were the years of student revolt. My policy had encouraged them to attack me. They told me several times that I exploited them when I talked about their results at conferences. After eight years I capitulated. Jim's model no longer worked. I could no longer continue. I was alone in Germany and Europe. When I look at the situation of today I become slightly nauseated. Groups may be as large as 50 collaborators who compete against each other. The chief is almost always co-author. What a different world!

Back to the Biolabs. In the summer of 1966 my situation changed. Wally Gilbert and I isolated the Lac repressor (Gilbert and Müller-Hill 1966). I had isolated a *lacI* mutant which bound inducer two- to threefold more tightly than the wild type.[4] Wally had used commercially available radioactive IPTG and equilibrium dialysis (an idea of Klaus Weber) to test for the presence of LacR. Now we had real success. We had won our gamble. It had paid off. Mark Ptashne, who was at our heels with Lambda (λ) repressor, announced his success soon after (Ptashne 1967).

During this time, I met Barbara Lohse, an elegant American woman who knew Jim. I saw with amazement that at parties, Barbara was able to talk with Jim for over half an hour, more than Klaus and I had ever talked to him during a whole year. How did she do it? She was no scientist and so they could not be talking about science. So when I began to talk with him about paintings and literature, conversations suddenly became easier. He showed me the paintings he had bought, I remember particularly a drawing by Klee. Things had changed.

Jim was so different. Sitting in the lecture hall, before a lecture began, he often read *The New York Times*. Sometimes, he continued reading when the speaker had started.

On one occasion, he continued reading for almost the entire lecture. I think it was Ethan Signer, a geneticist working at MIT, who gave the lecture. It was the first day of the Tet offensive, which was the beginning of the end of the superiority of the U.S. Army in Vietnam. I agreed with Jim. The news that day was more important than the content of the lecture.

For Wally and me, science went on well. Although I failed with the experiment to get the repressor to work in a test tube,[5] Wally succeeded in demonstrating the binding of the Lac repressor to the *lac* operator. Magnanimous, he made me co-author of the paper (Gilbert and Müller-Hill 1967). I then succeeded in isolating an *I* gene mutant that produced tenfold more Lac repressor. When placed on a suitably engineered strain of *E. coli*,[6] the amount of Lac repressor could be increased a hundredfold: Lac repressor was now as trivial a protein to purify as any housekeeping enzyme (Müller-Hill et al. 1968). Around this time, in the autumn of 1967, I got the offer of a full professorship at the University of Cologne. When I showed the letter to Jim, he said "you have to accept it," and so I did the same day.

During this time Jim showed me—for one night!—the manuscript of *The Double Helix* (Watson 1968); I loved it and told him so. I could not understand why Crick was about to sue him over this text. At that time, Jim got married. He later sent me the text of the second part of his biography describing the years after the discovery of the double helix. *Calculated Madness* was the first title he told me he wanted to give to this text. It contained too little sex to assure large sales for his U.S. publisher. So initially it was refused. I am most glad that this excellent book has now been published by Oxford University Press[7] (Watson 2001).

During the 35 years I have spent in Cologne, I have tried to keep in contact with Jim. In 1969 and 1970, I taught the Bacterial Genetics course at Cold Spring Harbor Laboratory. I saw Jim then; I visited him when he stayed in London, he came to Cologne, and we both went to Davos. I liked to hear what he had to say on any subject. His yes and no decisions were always illuminating. He sent me a copy of the article in the *New Republic* where he is described on a full page as insane, and I shared his feelings against this abominable type of free press. While Jim has influenced me in many ways, there is one issue where I may have influenced his thinking. This is the past of eugenics and the future of human genetics.

In the late 1970s, I discovered that very little had been written about the history of human genetics ("race hygiene") in Germany. I investigated and wrote a short book about it, *Tödliche Wissenschaft*. The book appeared in 1984 (Müller-Hill 1984) and was first reviewed in *Nature*. It was translated into English (Müller-Hill 1988). I sent Jim a copy. In the book's historical chronicle, I mention Charles Davenport from Cold Spring Harbor Laboratory who had proposed in 1932 that Eugen Fischer, the great anthropologist of Nazi Germany, become President of the International Federation of Eugenic Organisations.[8] I ended the chronicle with:

> 25 April 1953 Watson and Crick define the three-dimensional structure of DNA, the hereditary material first identified in 1944. Rapid, almost explosive, advances in the science of genetics begin. Soon, semisynthetic hereditary material engineered for specific purposes can be introduced into plant and animal tissues, even in the germ line, where it is inherited by the next generation. Has anything been learned from the outbreak of barbarism in Germany or will it be repeated on a worldwide scale in a yet more dreadful form and to a yet more dreadful degree?

After reading my book, Jim arranged for a new edition published in 1998 by Cold Spring Harbor Laboratory Press (Müller-Hill 1998). He wrote a piece on Eugenics in the Cold Spring Harbor Laboratory (Watson 1997). He arranged that a substantial amount of money for the Human Genome Project be earmarked for ethical studies. He quoted extensively from my book in a speech at an international congress on Molecular Medicine in Berlin and he described the days in Berlin (Müller-Hill 1998) in an Afterword to my book.

The story has come to an end. Is there a bottom line? What is it? Allow me to summarize it: In order to understand the world, one has to risk disorder; one lives then on the edge in calculated madness. If this process gets out of hand, one may lose and never come back. So let's congratulate Jim—how astonishingly well he has done in the 75 years of his life.

REFERENCES

Gilbert W. and Müller-Hill B. 1966. Isolation of the *lac* repressor. *Proc. Natl. Acad. Sci.* **56:** 1891–1898.

Gilbert W. and Müller-Hill B. 1967. The *lac* operator is DNA. *Proc. Natl. Acad. Sci.* **58:** 2415–2421.

Jacob F. and Monod J. 1961a. Genetic regulatory mechanisms in the synthesis of proteins. *J. Mol. Biol.* **3:** 318–356.

Jacob F. and Monod J. 1961b. On the regulation of gene activity. *Cold Spring Harbor Symp. Quant. Biol.* **26:** 193–211.

Jacob F., Perrin D., Sanchez C., and Monod J. 1960. L'opéron: groupe de gènes á expression coordineé par un opérateur. *Comptes Rendus Acad. Sci.* **250:** 1727–1729.

Müller-Hill B. 1966. Suppressible regulator constitutive mutants of the lactose system in *Escherichia coli. J. Mol. Biol.* **15:** 374–375.

Müller-Hill B. 1984. *Tödliche Wissenschaft. Die Aussonderung von Juden, Zigeunern und Geisteskranken 1933–1945.* Rowohlt Verlag, Reinbek.

Müller-Hill B. 1988. *Murderous science. Elimination by scientific selection of Jews, Gypsies, and others in Germany 1933–1945.* (English translation.) Oxford University Press, Oxford.

Müller-Hill B. 1998. *Murderous science: Elimination by scientific selection of Jews, Gypsies, and others in Germany 1933–1945.* (With an Afterword by James Watson.) Cold Spring Harbor Laboratory Press, Cold Spring Harbor, New York.

Müller-Hill B., Crapo L., and Gilbert W. 1968. Mutants that make more Lac repressor. *Proc. Natl. Acad. Sci.* **59:** 1259–1264.

Ptashne M. 1967. Isolation of the λ phage repressor. *Proc. Natl. Acad. Sci.* **57:** 306–313.

Watson J.D. 1968. *The double helix: A personal account of the discovery of the structure of DNA.* Atheneum, New York.

Watson J.D. 1997. Genes and politics. *J. Mol. Med.* **75:** 615–617.

Watson J.D. 2001. *Genes, girls, and Gamow: After* The double helix. Oxford University Press, Oxford.

When Ribosomes Were King

Alfred Tissières

Emeritus, University of Geneva

When and where did I first meet Jim Watson? On returning to Cambridge from Pasadena where I had spent one year as a postdoctoral fellow at Caltech, Jim Watson came one evening early in 1953 to see me at the Molteno Institute where I was working.[1] Manny Delbrück, Max's wife, had recommended that he look me up. The following day, a nucleic acid chemist who was working at the Molteno said: "Alfred, I saw you last night with this character Jim Watson, an eccentric American. He and Francis Crick are proposing a model for the structure of DNA. I can tell you one thing: They are wrong."

After this encounter, I saw Jim quite frequently, as he used to come to my rooms in King's College to talk about Cambridge, the work going on at the Medical Research Council Lab headed by Max Perutz, and the structure of DNA. I was at that time working with bacterial cell-free preparations and had examined these extracts in the analytical centrifuge. Two major symmetrical peaks were seen with the Schlieren optics, strikingly similar to the ribonucleoprotein particles known today as large and small ribosomal subunits.[2]

Jim came one day to my rooms in the summer of 1956 and said: "We have similar interests. I am moving to Harvard next year. Why don't you join me to work on these ribosomal particles?" A few months later, I accepted Jim's suggestion and I arrived at Harvard in February 1957. For the next five years, Jim, David Schlessinger, a graduate student, and I worked on *E. coli* ribosomes.[3]

When I was back in Cambridge, England, after my stay in Harvard, some of my Swiss colleagues asked me whether I would consider going back to organize a Department of Molecular Biology in Geneva. The conditions appeared to be adequate and I accepted the offer. A temporary building was set up and we were able to start working in 1964. Jim decided that he would spend some time in our new lab and he suggested to some of his students at Harvard who had just graduated to join us. This is how Peter Moore, John Richardson, Raymond Gesteland, and Gary Gussin joined our new lab. Bruce Alberts, having graduated from Paul Doty's lab, also came and so did John Collier and Dick Burgess. Thus, starting our new lab was made remarkably easy.

Jim's interactions with others have not always been easy. At Harvard, he even sometimes generated a certain amount of tension among colleagues and others. He regarded some people in the Biology Department where he was working as old fashioned. Jim, however, was backed by some of the chemists who were important (in particular, Paul Doty, John Edsall, and Konrad Bloch). With time, Jim became not only

ALFRED TISSIÈRES

Alfred Tissières, born in 1917 in Matigny, Switzerland, held a medical degree from the University of Lausanne, and a Ph.D. from Cambridge, for work carried out at the Molteno Institute under the supervision of David Keilin. After a postdoctoral fellowship at Caltech, Alfred returned to the Molteno Institute, where as he describes, Jim sought him out at the urging of Manny Delbrück and brought him to Harvard in 1957 to work on ribosomes. For the next ten years, Jim and Alfred were close collaborators. They were an oddly matched pair: Jim the more mercurial, Alfred the steadier and more perseverant bench scientist. But they remained firm friends and, after Jim became Director of Cold Spring Harbor Laboratory, Alfred and his family were regular summer visitors.

He was a very good mountain climber, who reached the summit of Abi Gamin in India in 1950 and was a member of an unsuccessful Cambridge University expedition to climb Rakaposhi (7,788 m/25,551 ft) in 1954. Alfred Tissieres died of pneumonia on June 7, 2003. In a remembrance read at Alfred's funeral, Jim noted:

> No one walked faster than Alfred, and I'm sure he slowed himself down to let me accompany him on walks into the higher Alps. Always telling me that getting to the top of a real mountain was interesting, Alfred had the good sense to never see himself on a rope with me when real voids lay below.

Gary Gussin and Alfred Tissières at Cold Spring Harbor Laboratory in the 1960s. (Courtesy CSHL Archives.)

accepted but recognized as someone unique and very valuable. Jim's relationships with some of his scientific colleagues was sometimes rough in the early days, for instance, with Francis Crick at the time of the publication of *The Double Helix* (1968, Atheneum). But today, as far as I know, Francis, and even some of Jim's old adversaries in the Biology Department, recognizes his unique qualities and fully appreciates what he has achieved.

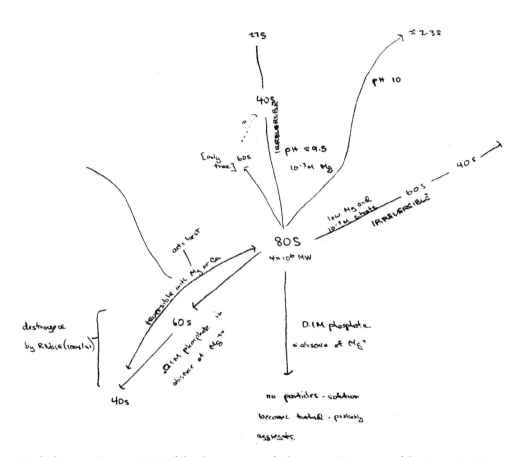

Jim's diagram (circa 1960) of the dissociation of ribosomes. (Courtesy of the James D. Watson Collection, CSHL Archives.)

It Smells Right...

Lionel Crawford

Emeritus, Imperial Cancer Research Fund

Over the years, I have come to the conclusion that Jim has an unusually acute sense of smell. Often, at a pause in an otherwise rather rambling discussion of results from the lab and elsewhere, things would be brought to an abrupt halt by Jim's comment that "It smells right" without any further expansion or explanation. It seems to be a very useful shorthand for what, in some of our more voluble colleagues, would be a long and inconclusive rehearsal of all the arguments for and against and the reservations about the interpretation of the relevant experimental results. Sometimes rather frustrating for me, since I would like to have heard what was in Jim's mind as it raced ahead of mine and reached a reasonable conclusion, one that in the long run would turn out to be right.

Of course not everything smelled right. On the contrary, there were occasions when it was equally useful that things smelled wrong. One time I remember when Jim was puzzling over the direction of transcription to go into the corrected proofs of an early version of *Molecular Biology of the Gene* (1965). There were results indicating that both of the alternatives (5′ to 3′ and 3′ to 5′) were correct. This was clearly unsatisfactory for the book and a decision had to be made. However, one more result came at the critical moment from someone whom Jim felt was reliably wrong and that decided it—the 5′ to 3′ direction must be the right one.

There were also times when things smelled a lot and very bad. One summer, when we were visiting the Biological Laboratories in Harvard, Jim fished out a large Mason jar of cottontail rabbit papillomas that had been collected by Earl Johnson in Rago, Kansas. There was a rather plaintive letter on the noticeboard asking when he was going to be paid $25, I think, for collecting the entire bunch of warts. Warts were cheap in those days before rampant inflation hit the market, after which rabbit skins were fetching more like $25 each. Probably the same jar had provided the material for the Watson and Littlefield (1960) paper.[1] It was the year that Jim finally gave up having a lab bench (1965), and the bench he had been using, in the lab next to his office, was where I set up to process the warts and extract the Shope papillomavirus from them. All went well for a while, but then I noticed that there was a congregation of blowflies around the rather ill-fitting windows of the lab and, very soon after that, the sound of Jim's voice in the corridor enquiring loudly what the terrible smell was. The warts were fine in their glycerol preservative, but as soon as that was removed, the amines from the decaying tissue were soon widely distributed and pretty disgusting. Still, it was well worth it and the results were fascinating, although we did not get as far as

LIONEL V. CRAWFORD

In the 1960s and 1970s, the fifth floor at the Imperial Cancer Research Fund in Lincoln's Inn Fields, London, was an amazing place. Incredibly crowded, its narrow corridors were lit by the weakest of fluorescent lights and whatever sunlight could penetrate the grime-encrusted windows. The well-established lab heads (Lionel, Alan Smith, Bob Kamen, Beverly Griffin, and Mike Fried) watched each other as carefully as birds of prey. Somehow, however, the place became an incubator for future stars: Richard Treisman from Bob Kamen and Tony Pawson from Alan Smith, while Lionel, remarkably and to his great credit, produced Ed Harlow, David Lane, and Bruce Ponder within the space of a couple of years.

Lionel had come to ICRF after seven years in Glasgow at the Institute for Virology. During this time, he and his wife Elizabeth were frequent summer visitors first to Harvard and later, after Jim became Director, to Cold Spring Harbor, where he taught the first Tumor Virus Workshop in 1969. Lionel loved the swing and speed of American science: "Coming back to the U.K, I miss the excitement which is so characteristic of the molecular scene in the U.S. now." But he could never be tempted to stay for more than the odd sabbatical or a couple of summer months.

Lionel holds a Ph.D. from Cambridge, and in later years, returned there to work with great distinction on human papillomaviruses. He was elected as a Fellow of the Royal Society in 1988.

Jerry Vinograd did later. The fact that Jim had given up his lab bench in no way reduced his feel for experimental data; it could be quite irritating on occasion to have him look at a collection of preliminary results and be able to make more sense of them than you could yourself.

Summers in Jim's lab were always hectic. Apart from the fact that there was a fixed date for leaving (economy air fares naturally), there was no telling when Jim would drop into the lab and want to know what interesting things had been going on since he last had an update. This was bad enough when you were struggling with recalcitrant experimental systems and sometimes equipment gremlins too, but even worse for my wife. Jim liked pictures and one summer it was arranged that Elizabeth would borrow an electron microscope in Keith Porter's lab.[2] It was sometimes easier for visitors from abroad to circumvent the internal politics in the Biolabs where space was at a premium and territorial borders were fiercely defended. Jim had managed to annoy a lot of people by suggesting, for example, that a lot of space could be freed up in the museum by throwing out the great accumulation of jars of pondwater that had been collected by eminent natural historians in the dim and distant past. Anyway, it was an arrangement that worked well and Elizabeth was soon producing pictures of R17 phage and pili (Crawford and Gesteland 1964). One evening, Jim had been looking at some of her pictures, eventually leaving us rather late at night. The following morning while we were blearily discussing the state of the world and planning the next experiment, Jim came in and wanted some excitement. She showed him more of the same set of pictures only to be told "...but I saw those yesterday." Clearly, the electron microscope fairy should have been busy while we were asleep. Overall, it is true to say that

Jim was rather impatient, he knew where we were experimentally, he knew where he wanted to be, and he knew when he wanted to be there—yesterday!

It was not only in the lab that patience was in short supply, it was also true of the seminar room. In a seminar by Julian Davies,[3] I remember Jim suddenly standing up about halfway through and saying "That's enough of that crap Julian, you've got another ten minutes and just give us the facts." Rather daunting to hear this when you yourself would soon be caught in the same spotlight, and very different from the deferential attitude of the seminar audiences that I had been used to in England. Together with the impatience came a great deal of encouragement and enthusiasm. This is what made our summers in Jim's lab exciting, sometimes exhilarating, and finally exhausting. It was always difficult to know what answer to give to the usual question greeting our return to the UK: "Did you have a nice holiday in the States or wherever it was you went?"

Not all the time was spent in the lab—we got invited to go for walks with Jim. "With" is something of an exaggeration. We would all start out together, but Jim's preferred pace was significantly faster than ours, and we would still be on our way up by the time he had reached the top of the climb. One hike in the White Mountains followed this pattern and turned out to pass near the nest of a large hawk. We missed the trail on the way down and had to go through the hawk's territory twice. Jim had done the same and the hawk was pretty irate by the time we came through, attacking us with considerable ferocity and impressive sound effects. When we met up again at the car and compared our experiences, they were very much the same, except that while

Annual photograph of the Watson-Gilbert Laboratory (1963). Wally Gilbert is at the top left; Lionel Crawford is sitting crosslegged on the rhinoceros's back; Jim is leaning against the shoulder. (Courtesy of the James D. Watson Collection, CSHL Archives.)

Jim was being dive bombed by the hawk, being a true ornithologist, he had noted the pattern and coloration of its plumage and could tell us that it was a goshawk. I can't remember whether he determined its gender as well, but it was a good example of careful observation even under difficult circumstances. Summers were also enlivened with occasions such as the lab photograph, posed on and around the rhinoceros at the front entrance of the Biological Laboratories. Getting up on the animal was de rigueur for the younger and more agile members of the lab and did not present too many difficulties. Getting down after the picture had been taken was not quite as easy but greatly enjoyed as a spectator sport. Skirts were fashionably short in the 1960s and there seemed to be a good correlation between the shortness of the skirt and the amount of "help" that Jim felt the young ladies needed in the dismount.

There was usually something to show for our summer of hard work and the push would then be to get it written up. Jim liked to write the first and last sentences and it must be admitted that he did have a certain flair for writing. The bit in between also had to be written while frantically trying to get the data and pictures to make it all hold together. Writing was not all done in the tranquility of offices or orderly desks; in fact, there were seldom desks at all to write at. One paper on RNA polymerase had still not been completed by the time we had to be back on our way to England, so John Richardson[4] was detailed to accompany us to the Boston airport in the taxi back to Harvard to tidy up the manuscript and give it to Jim for his approval. Under the circumstances, the paper (Crawford et al. 1965) made pretty good sense.

One place where Jim was conspicuous by his absence was the bit just below the title of the paper where the authors were listed. The current obsession with citations and numbers of publications seems to have generated a culture where it is expected

Jerry Adams and Lionel Crawford, 1970, at the Cold Spring Harbor Symposium for Quantitative Biology. (Courtesy CSHL Archives.)

that the most minor contribution to a paper merits inclusion as an author—but not in Jim's lab. For junior visitors to the lab, this was important as it meant that the credit for the work and the responsibility for its reliability was left squarely with them. There must have been times when foreign visitors from some countries would have been very keen to include Jim as an author so that, when they went home, they could point out to the authorities (who had little idea of the content of the paper) a name that they would instantly recognize. This certainly happened in other labs, but not in Jim's. In comparison to the professors who seemed to publish a paper a month or even more, he must have seemed very unproductive. As so often is the case, just basing judgments on numbers without anything else would be very misleading, and the opposite was in fact the case. It would be interesting to know if this influence carried on with people who had been through Jim's lab and whether they in turn kept to the strict requirement of being an author only when a significant amount of work had been done hands-on, or major ideas contributed, or both. Perhaps the average number of authors on papers from people who had been through the lab would turn out to be on the low side compared with the international average as it increases year by year.

Probably everyone who has spent time in Jim's lab was affected by their stay and, of course, his influence extended far beyond the lab with his books and other writing. This influence seemed particularly valuable when the populist fringe of the scientific community was having one of its periodic fits of political correctness. Jim's contributions would introduce a much needed element of common sense that made people think, instead of just going along with the party line. He certainly made me think a good deal, and I am sure I am not the only one who has reason to be grateful for that.

REFERENCES

Crawford E.M. and Gesteland R.F. 1964. Absorption of bacteriophage R17. *Virology* **22:** 165–167.
Crawford L.V., Crawford E.M., Richardson J.P., and Slayter H.S. 1965. The binding of RNA polymerase to polyoma and papilloma DNA. *J. Mol. Biol.* **14:** 593–597.
Watson J.D. 1965. *Molecular biology of the gene*. W.A. Benjamin, New York.
Watson J.D. and Littlefield J.W. 1960. Some properties of DNA from Shope papillomavirus. *J. Mol. Biol.* **2:** 161–165.

Excerpt from *Naturalist*

Edward O. Wilson

Harvard University

The following is excerpted from Edward O. Wilson's *Naturalist* (Island Press/ Shearwater Books, c1994; Chapter 12, "The Molecular Wars," pp. 218–225) and is used by permission of the author and publisher.

Without a trace of irony I can say I have been blessed with brilliant enemies. They made me suffer (after all, they were enemies), but I owe them a great debt, because they redoubled my energies and drove me in new directions. We need such people in our creative lives. As John Stuart Mill once put it, both teachers and learners fall asleep at their posts when there is no enemy in the field.

James Dewey Watson, the codiscoverer of the structure of DNA, served as one such adverse hero for me. When he was a young man, in the 1950s and 1960s, I found him the most unpleasant human being I had ever met. He came to Harvard as an assistant professor in 1956, also my first year at the same rank. At twenty-eight, he was only a year older. He arrived with a conviction that biology must be transformed into a science directed at molecules and cells and rewritten in the language of physics and chemistry. What had gone before, "traditional" biology—*my* biology—was infested by stamp collectors who lacked the wit to transform their subject into a modern science. He treated most of the other twenty-four members of the Department of Biology with a revolutionary's fervent disrespect.

At department meetings Watson radiated contempt in all directions. He shunned ordinary courtesy and polite conversations, evidently in the belief that they would only encourage the traditionalists to stay around. His bad manners were tolerated because of the greatness of the discovery he had made, and because of its gathering aftermath. In the 1950s and 1960s the molecular revolution had begun to run through biology like a flash flood. Watson, having risen to historic fame at an early age, became the Caligula of biology. He was given license to say anything that came to his mind and expect to be taken seriously. And unfortunately, he did so, with a casual and brutal offhandedness. In his own mind apparently he was *Honest Jim*, as he later called himself in the manuscript title of his memoir of the discovery—before changing it to *The Double Helix*. Few dared call him openly to account.

Watson's attitude was particularly painful for me. One day at a department meeting I naively chose to argue that the department needed more young evolutionary biologists, for balance. At least we should double the number from one (me) to two. I informed the listening professors that Frederick Smith, an innovative and promising population ecologist, had recently been recruited from the University of Michigan by Harvard's Graduate School of Design. I outlined Smith's merits and stressed the impor-

Edward O. Wilson

Coming from the improbable beginnings of a strict upbringing in Alabama as a Southern Baptist, Edward O. Wilson has been a Harvard professor for nearly five decades. He has distinguished himself as Professor of Zoology, Curator in Entomology at the Museum of Comparative Zoology, and researcher. His accomplishments include pioneering work on chemical communication in ants, and (with William H. Bossert) the first evolutionary analysis of the physical and chemical properties of pheromones; the creation (with Robert H. MacArthur) of the theory of biogeography, a basic part of modern ecology and conservation biology; the creation of the discipline of sociobiology; and the first modern syntheses of knowledge of social insects (1971) and (with Bert Hölldobler) of ants (1990). Wilson writes "I was a senior in high school when I decided I wanted to work on ants as a career. I just fell in love with them, and have never regretted it."

Wilson has written more than 370 articles, mostly for scientific journals, and 2 of his 21 books have been awarded Pulitzer Prizes: in 1979, for *On Human Nature* (1978, Harvard University Press) and in 1991, for *The Ants* (co-authored with Bert Hölldobler; 1990, Belknap Press of Harvard University Press). Wilson's awards include the U.S. National Medal of Science (1976), Japan's International Prize for Biology (1993), the Crafoord Prize from the Royal Swedish Academy of Sciences (1990), the French Prix du Institut de la Vie (1990), Germany's Terrestrial Ecology Prize (1987), Saudi Arabia's King Faisal International Prize for Science (2000), and the Franklin Medal of the American Philosophical Society (1999).

In 1959, the English physicist and novelist, C.P. Snow first wrote about the differences between scientific and literary intellectuals, and what these differences tell us about the behavior of groups, communities, and nations. In *Consilience: The Unity of Knowledge* (1998, Knopf), Wilson notes that not only does the gap between the two cultures of the sciences and the humanities continue to exist today, but its very origin is unexplained.

> There is only one way to unite the great branches of learning and end the culture wars. It is to view the boundary between the scientific and literary cultures not as a territorial line but as a broad and mostly unexplored terrain awaiting cooperative entry from both sides. The misunderstandings arise from ignorance of the terrain, not from a fundamental difference in mentality. The two cultures share the following challenge. We know that virtually all of human behavior is transmitted by culture. We also know that biology has an important effect on the origin of culture and its transmission. The question remaining is how biology and culture interact, and in particular how they interact across all societies to create the commonalities of human nature. What, in final analysis, joins the deep, most genetic history of the species as a whole to the more recent cultural histories of its far-flung societies? That, in my opinion, is the nub of the relationship between the two cultures. It can be stated as a problem to be solved, the central problem of the social sciences and the humanities, and simultaneously one of the great remaining problems of the natural sciences.

It seems odd that Wilson, after such as stellar career, continues to worry about the intellectual chasm defined by C.P. Snow. He himself is living proof that the sciences and the humanities can not only be reconciled, but merged into a coherent and swelling theme.

tance of teaching environmental biology. I proposed, following standard departmental procedure, that Smith be offered joint membership in the Department of Biology.

Watson said softly, "Are they out of their minds?"

"What do you mean?" I was genuinely puzzled.

"Anyone who would hire an ecologist is out of his mind," responded the avatar of molecular biology.

For a few moments the room was silent. No one spoke to defend the nomination, but no one echoed Watson either. Then Paul Levine, the department chairman, jumped in to close the subject. This proposal, he said, is not one we are prepared to consider at this time. With documentation, we might examine the nomination at some further date. We never did, of course. Smith was elected a member only after the molecular biologists split off to form a department of their own.

After this meeting I walked across the Biological Laboratories quad on my way to the Museum of Comparative Zoology. Elso Barghoorn hurried to catch up with me. A senior professor of evolutionary biology, he was one of the world's foremost paleobotanists, the discoverer of Pre-Cambrian microscopic fossils, and an honest man. "Ed," he said, "I don't think we should use 'ecology' as an expression anymore. It's become a dirty word." And sure enough, for most of the following decade we largely stopped using the word "ecology." Only later did I sense the anthropological significance of the incident. When one culture sets out to erase another, the first thing its rulers banish is the official use of the native tongue.

The molecular wars were on. Watson was joined to varying degrees in attitude and philosophy by a small cadre of other biochemists and molecular biologists already in the department. They were George Wald, soon to receive a Nobel Prize for his work on the biochemical basis of vision; John Edsall, a pioneering protein chemist and a youngish elder statesman who smiled and nodded a lot but was hard to understand; Matthew Meselson, a brilliant young biophysicist newly recruited from the California Institute of Technology; and Paul Levine, the only other assistant professor besides Watson and myself promoted to tenure during the 1950s. Levine soon deserted population biology and began to promote the new doctrine aggressively on his own. Zeal of the convert, I thought to myself.

At faculty meetings we sat together in edgy formality, like Bedouin chieftains gathered around a disputed water well. We addressed one another in the old style: "As Professor Wetmore has just reminded us..." We used Robert's Rules of Order. Prestige, professorial appointments, and laboratory space were on the line. We all sensed that our disputes were not ordinary, of the academic kind that Robert Maynard Hutchins once said are so bitter because so little is at stake. Dizzying change and shifts of power were in the air throughout biology, and we were a microcosm. The traditionalists at Harvard at first supported the revolution. We agreed that more molecular and cellular biology was needed in the curriculum. The president and several successive deans of the Faculty of Arts and Sciences were also soon persuaded that a major shift in faculty representation was needed. The ranks of molecular and cellular biologists swelled rapidly. In one long drive, they secured seven of eight professorial appointments made. No one could doubt that their success was, at least in the abstract, deserved. The problem was that no one knew how to stop them from dominating the Department of Biology to the eventual extinction of other disciplines.

My own position was made more uncomfortable by the location of my office and laboratory in the Biological Laboratories, the bridgehead from physics and chemistry into which the richly funded molecular biologists were now pouring. I found the atmosphere there depressingly tense. Watson did not acknowledge my presence as we passed in the hall, even when no one else was near. I was undecided whether to respond in kind by pretending to be unaware of his own existence (impossible) or to humiliate myself by persisting with southern politesse (also impossible). I settled on a mumbled salutation. The demeanor of Watson's allies ranged from indifferent to chilly, except for George Wald, who acquired an Olympian attitude. He was friendly indeed, but supremely self-possessed and theatrically condescending. On the few occasions we spoke, I could not escape the feeling that he was actually addressing an audience of hundreds seated behind me. He would in fact adopt political and moral oratory before large audiences as a second calling during the late 1960s. At the height of the campus turmoil at Harvard and elsewhere, Wald was the speaker of choice before cheering crowds of student activists. He was the kind of elegant, unworldly intellectual who fires up the revolution and is the first to receive its executioner's bullet. And on the future of our science he agreed completely with Watson. There is only one biology, he once declared, and it is molecular biology.

My standing among the molecularists was not improved by my having been granted tenure several months before Watson, in 1958. Although it was an accident of timing—I had received an unsolicited offer from Stanford and Harvard counteroffered—and in any event I considered him to be far more deserving, I can imagine how Watson must have taken the news. Badly.

Actually, I cannot honestly say I knew Jim Watson at all. The skirmish over Smith's appointment was only one of a half-dozen times he and I spoke directly to each other during his twelve years at Harvard and in the period immediately following. On one occasion, in October 1962, I offered him my hand and said, "Congratulations, Jim, on the Nobel Prize. It's a wonderful event for the whole department." He replied, "Thank you." End of conversation. On another occasion, in May 1969, he extended his hand and said, "Congratulations, Ed, on your election to the National Academy of Sciences." I replied, "Thank you very much, Jim." I was delighted by this act of courtesy.

At least there was no guile in the man. Watson evidently felt, at one level, that he was working for the good of science, and a blunt tool was needed. Have to crack eggs to make an omelet, and so forth. What he dreamed at a deeper level I never knew. I am only sure that had his discovery been of lesser magnitude he would have been treated at Harvard as just one more gifted eccentric, and much of his honesty would have been publicly dismissed as poor judgment. But people listened carefully, and a few younger colleagues aped his manners, for the compelling reason that the deciphering of the DNA molecule with Francis Crick towered over all that the rest of us had achieved and could ever hope to achieve. It came like a lightning flash, like knowledge from the gods. The Prometheans of the drama were Jim Watson and Francis Crick, and not just by a stroke of good luck either. Watson-Crick[1] possessed extraordinary brilliance and initiative. It is further a singular commentary on the conduct of science that (according to Watson in a later interview) no other qualified person was interested in devoting full time to the problem.

For those not studying biology at the time in the early 1950s, it is hard to imagine the impact the discovery of the structure of DNA had on our perception of how the world works. Reaching beyond the transformation of genetics, it injected into all of biology a new faith in reductionism. The most complex of processes, the discovery implied, might be simpler than we had thought. It whispered ambition and boldness to young biologists and counseled them: Try now; strike fast and deep at the secrets of life. When I arrived at Harvard as a graduate student in 1951, most outside the biochemical cognoscenti believed the gene to be an intractable assembly of proteins. Its chemical structure and the means by which it directs enzyme assembly would not, we assumed, be deciphered until well into the next century. The evidence nevertheless had grown strong that the hereditary substance is DNA, a far less complex macromolecule than most proteins. In 1953 Watson and Crick showed that pairing in the double helix exists and is consistent with Mendelian heredity. ("It has not escaped our notice," they wrote teasingly at the end of their 1953 letter to *Nature*, "that the specific pairing we have postulated immediately suggests a possible copying mechanism for the genetic material.") Soon it was learned that the nucleotide pairs form a code so simple that it can be read off by a child. The implication of these and other revelations rippled into organismic and evolutionary biology, at least among the younger and more entrepreneurial researchers. If hereditary can be reduced to a chain of four molecular letters—granted, billions of such letters to prescribe a whole organism—would it not also be possible to reduce and accelerate the analysis of ecosystems and complex animal behavior? I was among the Harvard graduate students most excited by the early advances of molecular biology. Watson was a boy's hero of the natural sciences, the fast young gun who rode into town.

More's the pity that Watson himself and his fellow molecularists had no such foresights about the sector of biology in which I had comfortably settled. All I could sift from their pronouncements was the revolutionary's credo: Wipe the slate clean of this old-fashioned thinking and see what new order will emerge.

I was of course disappointed at this lack of vision. When Watson became director of the Cold Spring Harbor Laboratory in 1968 (he kept his Harvard professorship by joint appointment until 1976) I commented sourly to friends that I wouldn't put him in charge of a lemonade stand. He proved me wrong. In ten years he raised that noted institution to even greater heights by inspiration, fund-raising skills, and the ability to choose and attract the most gifted researchers.

A new Watson gradually emerged in my mind. In October 1982, at a reception celebrating the fiftieth anniversary of Harvard's Biological Laboratories, he pushed his way across a crowded room to compliment me on a throwaway remark I had made during a lecture earlier that afternoon. "The history of philosophy," I had said, "consists largely of failed models of the brain." Afterward I realized that my phrasing was the kind of preemptive dismissal he would have made twenty years earlier. Had I been corrupted in the meantime? Yes, a little perhaps. I had never been able to suppress my admiration for the man. He had pulled off his achievement with courage and panache. He and other molecular biologists conveyed to his generation a new faith in the reductionist method of the natural sciences. A triumph of naturalism, it was part of the motivation for my own attempt in the 1970s to bring biology into the social sciences through a systemization of the new discipline of sociobiology.

Successful or not, I was infected by the virus. During a visit to the Cold Spring Harbor Laboratory not long ago, I asked Jim offhandedly what he thought makes great science. He replied without a breath of hesitation, "Great goals." In that he agrees with Tenzing Norgay, who with Edmund Hillary first climbed Earth's greatest mountain. "It is Everest," Tenzing said, "that makes men great."

Growing Up Around Jim

Jeffrey H. Miller

University of California, Los Angeles

I first met Jim Watson when I arrived at Harvard in the fall of 1966 to begin graduate work in biochemistry and molecular biology. This discipline had not yet been granted full departmental status, so the program I enrolled in was administered by the "The Committee on Biochemistry and Molecular Biology," and Jim was one of the professors on the committee. I have since come to know Jim in various roles as a mentor, receiving valuable advice on course work, teaching, writing, and career placement. However, in the beginning, I was just another eager and ambitious student newly arrived on the Cambridge scene. What were the times like? It was 13 years after the publication of the DNA structure, only 4 years after Watson had won the Nobel Prize, and just 5 years after the first code word of the genetic code was deciphered. Now, the last of the code words were being elucidated. The technologies that have come to dominate molecular biology had not yet been invented. It was still 8–10 years before cloning and DNA sequencing would revolutionize molecular biology, and of course even longer before PCR amplification, genomic sequencing, and microarrays would appear on the scene.

THE CAMBRIDGE SCENE

The high level of anxiety in being a graduate student in Cambridge in the sciences in the mid 1960s resulted from a mixture of excitement and fear. The excitement emanated from the scientists who were there or who just passed through. Just imagine the effect on a beginning student. During my first year, I took courses from three people who had won or would win the Nobel Prize (Konrad Bloch, Jim Watson, and Walter Gilbert). Jacques Monod, Sydney Brenner, Francis Crick, John Cairns, Richard Lewontin gave seminars. In my later years, at dinners of The Harvard Society of Fellows, I would sit next to guests such as John Kenneth Galbraith and B.F. Skinner. The anxiety came from the possibility of not succeeding in the eyes of these people or those of our peers.

Many students arrived on the scene somewhat full of themselves, having no clue as to the grilling that was in store for them from established scientists eager to mold new scientists in a rigorous fashion. My own comeuppance began even before I set foot in one of the Harvard labs. I arrived in Cambridge, somewhat awkward and unsure of myself, driving my new yellow and white Pontiac—a present from my parents to mark my graduation from the University of Rochester. As I drove through an outlying resi-

JEFFREY H. MILLER

Jim's interactions with people can be tangential, explosive, and brief or, as with Jeffrey Miller, spread out over a scientific lifetime. Sometimes Jim pushes and heaves people in new directions, but, as Jeffrey's contribution shows, he can also encourage scientists to stick with what they are good at. At the back of Jim's mind, perhaps, was the thought that *E. coli* genetics was in danger of extinction or, even worse, would fall by default into the hands of the mediocre. Jim certainly saw Jeffrey as the best person, through summer courses and laboratory manuals, to maintain Cold Spring Harbor's tradition in prokaryotic genetics.

Jeffrey is a third-generation geneticist by intellectual descent from François Jacob and Jacques Monod in the late 1950s, Sydney Brenner in the 1960s, and finally Jon Beckwith, Benno Müller-Hill, and Ethan Signer. Benno apart, all these had an aversion to biochemistry and could get by handsomely without it, as could Jim. For several years, so did Jeffrey. During his early years in Geneva, Jeffrey's work remained focused on the *lac* system, particularly the repressor. However, more recently, and particularly since moving to the University of California at Los Angeles, his interests have expanded to include large-scale DNA sequencing and genomic analysis, the enzymology of DNA repair, protein structure, and the role of DNA repair enzymes in the onset and progression of human cancer.

Jeffrey Miller on the beach at Cold Spring Harbor (circa 1969). Children: Andrew Sambrook on right and Joanna Sambrook second from right. (Courtesy CSHL Archives.)

dential section I ran out of gas. After hiking the customary couple of miles to the gas station and returning on foot with a two gallon container of gas, I was startled to realize that I could not immediately locate the gas tank in the rear of the car. It was fashionable at that time to hide the gas tank in different places in different model cars. My previous Pontiac had its gas tank cunningly hidden in the taillight, and you had to unscrew the light to reveal it. Of course it wasn't there this time. All gas stations at the time were "Full Serve," so you normally just said "fill'er up" to the attendant, and never paid attention to what they were doing. After about a half hour of searching, I gave up. The gas tank simply wasn't there. So, defeated, I hiked back to the gas station and sheepishly admitted that I couldn't find my gas tank. At first the attendants didn't believe me, and thought they were on Candid Camera. Finally, they drove me back to the car, charging me $8 for a service call (not a trivial amount of money for a graduate student in 1966 when the yearly stipend was $2400). To reveal the gas tank, you had to lift the license plate, which may be common now, but if one didn't know this, it wasn't so easy. As I left the gas station, after settling my bill, I heard one mechanic saying to another, "Can you believe it? Couldn't find his gas tank! I suppose the next thing he'll be telling us is that he goes to Harvard." Having endured this ignomy and been reduced to size, I was now ready to begin my graduate career.

Excited by the work of Jacob and Monod, I had become interested in the lactose operon and the search for the repressor. Wally Gilbert and Benno Müller-Hill had just reported at meetings the apparent isolation of the Lac repressor. Wally gave a seminar at Harvard to a packed house near the end of the year with definitive results. The atmosphere was electric. At the end of the seminar, a graduate student who already had his M.D. and was completing a Ph.D. in Konrad Bloch's laboratory got up and in an emotional voice asked a question about the ethical implications of the use of the results of the type Wally and others would get, and challenged Wally to use the new knowledge in a humane and thoughtful way. The student's name was Leon Kass, who was recently named to head President Bush's advisory committee on stem cell research, following a prominent career in bioethics.

Choosing a research advisor was on my mind during the first few months while taking four courses. Jonathan Beckwith had just come to Harvard Medical School, and his papers and preprints with Ethan Signer on transposing the *lac* region of *Escherichia coli* to other parts of the chromosome and then cloning *lac* by putting it onto specialized transducing phage excited me because of the artful and creative genetics they represented. So I spoke with Beckwith about possibly working in his laboratory. Even though he was at the Medical School and I was in a campus program across the river in Cambridge, this was still allowed according to the rules of the Committee, although no one had actually done it up until then. However, I was still investigating other possibilities and was a potential candidate to work in the Watson-Gilbert group. In December, I wandered by Jim Watson's office on the third floor of the Biolabs, only to have someone bump into me from behind. It was none other than Jim himself. As he left, I thought I heard him say, "I'm having a party at my house Saturday night. Come at nine." All week I was walking on cloud nine, waiting with bottled-up anticipation. It was a thrill for a first-year graduate student to be able to socialize with famous scientists.

Saturday night was a cold winter night, and as I walked up the outside steps to Jim's second floor apartment at 10 Appian Way, I was puzzled by the lack of sounds coming from the apartment. Had I heard Jim correctly? Meekly, I knocked on the door. No answer. I knocked again. Still no answer. Now I was sure I had made a mistake. I knocked one more time. Suddenly the door opened, and there was Jim Watson. "What are you doing here?" he glowered. I stuttered out that he had told me there was a party at his house Saturday at nine. He then looked at me and proclaimed, in what I was later to learn was Watsonian logic, "Everyone in Cambridge knows that when I say nine I mean ten!" Reluctantly, he let me in, and I had to wait 30 minutes until Dave Denhardt proved he was the second least cool guy in Cambridge, arriving at 9:30. Then, at exactly 10:00, a herd of 70 people appeared at the door and the party began. The occasion was Mario Capecchi's thesis party, and when Mario arrived, glasses were passed around and the champagne was poured. The scenes were classic, with Mark Ptashne, Benno Müller-Hill, and Wally Gilbert engaged in a heated discussion about repressors. Jon Beckwith came and it was there that he gave me a green light to work in his research group.

TEACHING

The first semester I was at Harvard, Jim Watson gave a lecture course on nucleic acids, DNA replication, and bacteriophages. It was during this first real exposure to him that I and the other students were confronted with the classic Watsonian enigma. At first glance, his lectures seemed rambling, with no clear direction. But as time went on, we realized how penetrating and insightful his intellect was. When he showed us electron micrographs that had just been published of RNA polymerase that revealed symmetric hexamers made up of identical subunits, he admonished it was possible that the hexamers were a contaminant and that the real RNA polymerase was quite different. We were skeptical of his seemingly off-handed dismissal of what looked like a valid scientific paper. But, sure enough, a few months later, someone else produced pictures of the true RNA polymerase, an asymmetric protein. The hexamers had indeed been contaminants. After spending several lectures on DNA replication, virtually all of which had been worked out by Arthur Kornberg's group, Jim added a cautionary note, pointing out that a drawback of the excellence of Kornberg's group's work was that it left no room for competitors. He said it was dangerous for one group's point of view to remain unchallenged, so that, for instance, the enzyme Kornberg was working with might still turn out to be a repair enzyme. At the time, the so-called Kornberg polymerase was presumed by almost everyone to be solely responsible for DNA replication in *E. coli*. In fact, Joel Huberman, a postdoc in the Kornberg group, gave a seminar in the Boston/Cambridge area the following year on the polymerase work. David Botstein was roundly booed by the audience when he asked, "What about the argument that the Kornberg polymerase is merely a repair protein, and the real polymerase is a different protein?" Within a year, however, Paula De Lucia and John Cairns at Cold Spring Harbor had isolated the first *polA* mutant,[1] and the race was on to find additional DNA polymerases. It was soon shown that the Kornberg polymerase (now called pol I) played only a supporting role in DNA replication, but a major role in DNA repair. These events had a profound effect on me. I realized that at a time when Sydney Brenner was pointing out that the cell devoted perhaps several hundred genes to encode the enzymes necessary to synthesize the side chains of tRNAs (many of these

JEFFREY H. MILLER 193

side chains being of limited value), many people in the field actually believed that the cell devoted only a single gene/protein to preserving the fidelity of replication of the entire bacterial genome. Jim (together with the experimental work of several groups) taught me the enduring lesson that the prevailing dogma of a field is always open to challenge and that competition is good for science.

Sometimes Jim could be a little Delphic when offering advice. Once, Jan Pero, a graduate student in Jim's group who was one year ahead of me, encountered Jim going the opposite way on the Biolabs stairway, and said to him that she wanted to discuss what thesis project to do. Jim continued walking up the stairs and after about five steps stopped, looked down at Jan, and said, "Lambda." And continued on. However, there was nothing ambiguous about Jim's advising me to go to Cold Spring Harbor, or subsequently to get involved in writing scientific books for Cold Spring Harbor Laboratory, and that advice led me down adventurous paths.

COLD SPRING HARBOR

When Jim was beginning to rebuild Cold Spring Harbor Laboratory, he wanted to enhance the summer research program. He thus enticed students and more established researchers to spend the summer at this hallowed retreat that was so important to the development of molecular biology. When he invited me to come down and do my experiments there for the summer of 1968, I readily accepted. This was to be the beginning of a long association with Cold Spring Harbor, as I assisted in the Bacterial Genetics course the following summer and was an instructor for the following several summers. In 1976, I again returned to be an instructor, this time together with David Botstein, Ron Davis, and Peter Wensink in a course that was one of the first to have cloning as part of the experiments. My involvement in all of these courses was at the constant urging of Jim, who had a reverence for both Cold Spring Harbor and its course program. In 1997, at a meeting to celebrate the 50th anniversary of the Phage (later to be the bacterial genetics) course, reminiscences from former students of the course included many present-day icons in the field.

Cold Spring Harbor in the late 1960s and the beginning of the 1970s was a far different place than it is now, since it was a much smaller community during much of the year, swelling for the main Symposium in June and a few smaller meetings in the summer, and increasing in size for the summer courses. The number of year-round researchers was very small. John Cairns was the director, handing the reins to Jim gradually during this period. John and his wife Elfie extended virtually unlimited hospitality to all comers. Al Hershey was a permanent resident, as was Barbara McClintock, who once caught me reading her *New York Times* from her lab mailbox and bashed me over the head with the newspaper as she berated me. (I never did that again.) We did become good friends, though.

The Lab was tucked between some very rich village communities, such as Lloyd Harbor and Laurel Hollow, which added to the small-town atmosphere. How small a town was it? Well, in the summer of 1968, Max Delbrück visited for the summer, as did George Streisinger and Julian Davies, among others. Julian was Welsh, and that summer Prince Charles was due to be invested as Prince of Wales. This was a sore point with Welsh nationalists, and to express his opposition to this indignity to the Welsh people, Julian posted signs around the Lab announcing a protest march along Bung-town Road at sunrise on a Sunday. Of course, Julian was kidding. However, the teenage daughter of the Laurel Hollow Police Chief worked as a dishwasher for one of the summer courses. When she brought home one of Julian's bogus posters, her father hit the panic button, and, giving his best imitation of the Sheriff in "Smokey and the Bandit," promptly arrested Julian for incitement to riot. As luck would have it, Jim was out of town, so for a while things got scary, since Julian's immigration visa prohibited him from engaging in political activity. Fortunately, the Judge of Laurel Hollow (Jim Eisenman) was a Trustee of the Lab, so in the end, peace was restored. On another occasion, John Lindsay, the Mayor of New York City, arrived on the Lab beach in a heli-copter, complete with police escort, on one of his regular visits to his brother's house in Laurel Hollow. During this particular summer, one of the summer courses had sev-eral flower children, and I remember the consternation of some of the Lab personnel as Mayor Lindsay's helicopter landed right in the middle of an inescapable cloud aris-ing from those smoking pot. However, apparently oblivious to this, Lindsay and his escort walked right through the cloud to their waiting car, to the relief of everyone.

The Lab operated on a much smaller budget than it does today. The following sum-mer, Jim invited Charley Thomas, then a Professor at Harvard Medical School, to carry out research at the Lab, offering to pay his expenses, expecting him to transport his materials from Boston in perhaps a rented station wagon. Not quite! Sunbathers at the Lab beach were startled by the arrival of Thomas' rented sea plane, and took a long time to respond to the frantic waving of the passengers, before realizing that they had to play the role of the natives greeting Captain Cook and row out to retrieve him and his supplies. When Thomas presented him with the bill, I heard that Jim went ballis-tic. After negotiations, I think the Lab agreed to split the costs with Thomas. Jim seethed. I am told that Jim had his revenge a few years later when he threw Thomas off the Lab's newly installed tennis courts for not wearing whites.

Usually in the summer, there was an evening lecture at 8:00 by an outside speaker. After dinner and before the lecture, the summer students and instructors would play volleyball. Many of the "students" were, in fact, established, highly respected researchers who were switching fields. Thus, in 1969, people like Phil Leder were tak-ing the Animal Virus course. The volleyball games were hotly contested, with nothing more at stake than bragging rights for the evening. I remember Phil Leder and Ethan Signer getting into an argument over an "out" call that carried on for quite some time. Years later, when Burroughs-Wellcome and Genentech were involved in a key trial in England over patent rights, many prominent molecular biologists were paid consul-tants for one side or the other. I couldn't help but note the irony that years before, some of these same scientists competed for the nightly volleyball title, and now they were pitted once again against one another, but this time with hundreds of millions of dol-lars at stake. (I somehow liked it better when it was just volleyball.)

WRITING

Jim was an accomplished writer, as his groundbreaking textbook, *Molecular Biology of the Gene* (Watson 1965) and his historical and autobiographical *The Double Helix*

(Watson 1968) demonstrated. When Benno Müller-Hill and I, along with Julian Gross and Joe Gotts, completed giving the 1970 Bacterial Genetics course, Jim suggested that Benno and I photocopy our experimental notes. After some editing, these could comprise a short lab manual that Cold Spring Harbor would publish. There were a total of 12 experiments. We did this, and after the summer, I joined Müller-Hill's lab as a postdoc. With each revision Jim kept suggesting more experiments, beyond what Benno had agreed on. Jim and I reluctantly dropped Benno from the project (not my proudest moment), which finally resulted in a 62-experiment, 467-page book (Miller 1972). It took me some time to smooth over my relationship with Benno, who has been a good friend and colleague before and after this period. Writing the book was very difficult, since Jim took a personal interest and looked over my shoulder for much of the writing. I spent some time at Cold Spring Harbor or Harvard at several points in 1971, working on the manuscript or correcting the proofs. Jim was a perfectionist and was notorious for making extensive changes in proofs. This book was no exception. Constant revision produced a lot of headaches, but the final product was always improved. I remember Jim putting me in a room at Harvard one evening and not letting me leave until I completed an introduction to a set of experiments. I delivered two pages to him, which he read in his office. He then came back to me and showed me the first page, and then the second. He said, "This page shows you know how to write. This second page is shit!"

He was a tough task master. Someone once said that Jim had the quality of knowing exactly how far he could push each person. With me, he certainly did. He induced me to write a much better book than I ever could have without him, and I am indebted to him for setting a high standard of writing for me to try to reach. I lost 15 pounds during the effort, but the resulting laboratory manual, *Experiments in Molecular Genetics*, published in 1972, was a major success. It represented the first really comprehensive compilation of recipes and protocols used in bacterial genetics, and focused on the lactose system. (Several experiments were contributed by other authors, including Benno, Bill Hazeltine, and Terry Platt.) Jim and I had decided to distribute a strain kit with the manual. For $100, one could purchase 85 items, including several phage lysates. However, supporting the assembly and sale of the strain kit was a major commitment for Jim and Cold Spring Harbor at the time, and Jim deserves a lot of credit. Cold Spring Harbor sold over 350 of the original kits, and several hundred more of a subsequent strain kit. In the early 1970s, this made it possible for many small, out of the way, labs and teaching colleges to acquire a large set of strains that were otherwise inaccessible to them.

Jim was also prominent in pushing for monographs from meetings, and he succeeded in getting Bill Reznikoff and myself to edit *The Operon* (Miller and Reznikoff 1980), based on a 1976 meeting. During the preparation and publication of this and an updated paperback version, Jim played a hands-on role in helping to decide who would write chapters and in reading many of the contributions. His energy for publishing amazed me. It took 20 years for me to get the energy and motivation to write a sequel to *Experiments in Molecular Genetics*. In 1992 Cold Spring Harbor Laboratory Press published the two-volume set, *A Short Course in Bacterial Genetics* (Miller 1992). By now Jim had honed the publishing division of Cold Spring Harbor Laboratory Press into a productive and efficient unit. Nancy Ford was the editor-in-chief, having arrived just as my first lab manual was being completed. She was instrumental in the completion of both the second laboratory manual and a new book I wrote in 1996 with the Cold Spring Harbor Laboratory Press, *Discovering Molecular Genetics* (Miller 1996), a book derived from a course I gave at UCLA that was based on original research papers, my lectures about them, and many of the take-home exams. Again, Jim was supportive and encouraging.

Jim was the great champion of scientific meetings as a vehicle for defining the state of the field and for solving problems and controversies (recall Asilomar). I had already co-organized two meetings at the Lab-owned Banbury Center when I realized in 1989 that the emerging DNA sequence of the *E. coli* genome was being done in a quasi-vacuum and that there was a need to bring together the biologists and geneticists whose work made *E. coli* worth caring about with the sequencers and bioinformatics groups. Whereas yeast had international consortiums, *E. coli* had no organization of researchers that acted as a community. I approached Jim Watson with the idea of holding a Banbury meeting to bring together these groups, and to perhaps start a yearly meeting centered around the *E. coli* genome. (Just trying to get the major players in the *E. coli* genome to agree to a joint conference was very difficult.) Without hesitation, Jim promised to support the meeting, and thus in the late spring of 1990, the Banbury Center hosted an international meeting of some 37 people co-organized by myself, Ken Rudd, Cassandra Smith, and Fred Blattner. There were a number of contentious issues that were at least aired at the meeting, and we agreed to hold a series of international *E. coli* genome meetings, the first being the following year in Wisconsin. Last year, I organized the 10th meeting in this series, now covering all small genomes. This thriving annual international event would never have gotten off the ground without Jim's behind-the-scenes support at the key moment.

CAREER ADVICE

From the time Jim successfully nominated me as a Junior Fellow in the Harvard Society of Fellows (1969–1971), he has made key contributions to my career. After spending a year as a postdoc in Europe, I wasn't sure what to do next. Jim phoned me in Germany, where I was working in Benno Müller-Hill's lab, and asked me to meet him in Geneva the following month. When we met, he pointed out that although there were possibilities for me at Harvard, I should stay in Europe for a while, since it was an important opportunity, and also since it would be beneficial to develop my independence. The Molecular Biology Department at the University of Geneva had some junior faculty positions available, and Alfred Tissières, a long-time friend and colleague of Jim's, was the head of the department. Jim recommended that I apply for the position, and he basically set it up with Alfred to award me the position. I ended up staying in Geneva for 11 years, building up a research group and becoming a full professor. Jim's steering me to Geneva was crucial to my career. Working in Geneva allowed me to develop my own style of science without the extra pressure of the U.S. grant system and the peer pressure to do the fashionable experiment of the day. I was thus able to spend three to four years developing systems to measure the types and locations of mutations caused by mutagens better than anyone had before.

After I returned to the States, to accept a position at UCLA in 1983, I was approached by the publishing firm of W.H. Freeman. They told me that the three authors of their introductory genetics text book, David Suzuki, Tony Griffiths, and Richard Lewontin, had decided to add another author to rewrite a number of their molecular biology chapters. They had asked Jim Watson for some names, and he had recommended me. I joined the team, which later replaced David Suzuki with Bill Gelbart, and thus began a 16-year relationship with W.H. Freeman that lasted through five editions. For most of this time, the textbook *Introduction to Genetic Analysis* (Griffiths et al. 2000) was the largest selling introductory genetics text in the United States and Canada, and unlike the small market manuals and book I wrote before, it really did earn a significant amount of money. As one might expect, I also learned an enormous amount of molecular biology by participating in this book. As Jim told me many years ago, "The best way to learn something is to either teach it or to write a book about it."

Jim's direct impact on my career was still not over. In the mid to late 1980s, he became a member of the Board of Directors of Diagnostic Products, a Los Angeles-based company founded and headed by the late Siggi Ziering, whom Jim had met at a meeting at Cold Spring Harbor. Jim had convinced the company to have a biotechnology unit, and he formed a scientific advisory board and asked me to join, along with Don Ganem, Jonathan Braun, and Owen Witte. I had always been a spectator of the biotechnology sector, but now I was involved, even if in a minor way. The experience I gained from the three years the Board operated emboldened me to form, with Mel Simon and Karl Stetter, a company, now called Diversa (located outside of San Diego) in 1994.

Jim Watson supported my career in many different ways. The so-called Watson-Gilbert group, with associated faculty such as Klaus Weber, imprinted a standard of doing science that has remained with me my entire life as did the training I received in Jon Beckwith's lab. Jim's launching my writing career, as well as setting up my first faculty position, and his introducing me to the biotech world are major contributions. So, during my career I have regarded Jim as a teacher, scientist, publisher, and biotech board head, but most important, for quite some time now, I have considered Jim as a very good friend.

REFERENCES

Griffiths A.J.F., Miller J.H., Suzuki D.T., Lewontin R.C., and Gelbart W.M. 2000. *An introduction to genetic analysis*, 7th edition. Freeman, New York.

Miller J.H. 1972. *Experiments in molecular genetics*. Cold Spring Harbor Laboratory, Cold Spring Harbor, New York.

Miller J.H. 1992. *A short course in bacterial genetics: A laboratory manual and handbook for Escherichia coli and related bacteria*. Cold Spring Harbor Laboratory Press, Cold Spring Harbor, New York.

Miller J.H. 1996. *Discovering molecular genetics*. Cold Spring Harbor Laboratory Press, Cold Spring Harbor, New York.

Miller J.H. and Reznikoff W.S. 1980. *The operon*. Cold Spring Harbor Laboratory, Cold Spring Harbor, New York.

Watson J.D. 1965. *Molecular biology of the gene*. W.A. Benjamin, New York.

Watson J.D. 1968. *The double helix*. Atheneum, New York.

Seems Simple, Very Hard to Do

Mark Ptashne

Memorial Sloan-Kettering Cancer Center

Jim was already on the Harvard scene when I arrived there in 1961. I was a first-year student willing to go anywhere to become Matt Meselson's graduate student, and Matt, influenced by Jim's presence there, had just decided to move from Harvard to Caltech. I didn't pay much attention to organizational matters—including formation of the Committee on Molecular Biology, which in a few years morphed into the full-fledged Department of Molecular Biology—because, I liked to say, I was too busy doing important things. In fact I, like my contemporaries, was trying to survive the scrutiny of the chemists, who had rather a greater role in the early training and approval of molecular biology graduate students than would nowadays be considered healthy. (They, the chemists, were not exactly pushovers—Robert Woodward, E.J. Corey, Frank Westheimer, Dudley Herschbach, E. Bright Wilson.) And so I recommend that you read Paul Doty's description of what he, Jim, and others did, and when, in forming our Department.

By the time I joined as a faculty member, what a Department it was! Small (never more than 12 in all, as I recall), and it included Jim, Matt, Paul, Wally Gilbert, Konrad Bloch, Jack Strominger, and the ever-calming Guido Guiddotti, and those waiting in the wings included Jim Wang, Steve Harrison, Don Wiley, Tom Maniatis, Klaus Weber, and Nancy Kleckner. I don't mean to say that Harvard was uniquely wonderful—think of the Institut Pasteur, the Cambridge (England) Laboratory of Molecular Biology, MIT, and Stanford, for example. Nor can I say that the composition and atmosphere were uniquely a product of Jim's influence. But no one can doubt that his influence was critical.

My recollections are filtered by a selective and somewhat dim memory, but certain aspects stand out. No one had official power: The Chairmanship rotated, and most of us gyrated (inevitably futilely) to avoid it. Pay (so we were told) was strictly by seniority—the longer you lasted the more you got, simple as that. No money was handed out for research—Harvard provided the building but (unless you were a beginning Assistant Professor) little else, and so people were on their own to commune as best they could with the Granting Agencies that later came to play so ominous a role in almost everybody's life. All senior members received equal amounts of lab space, more than the junior professors who were also treated equally among themselves in this regard. Everybody taught the same course load, with some (e.g., Steve, Guido, and Don) heroically taking on extra duties such as running the undergraduate study program. New appointments and promotions were made without regard to field—the goal was to hire and promote people who were doing interesting things.

MARK PTASHNE

François Jacob and Jacques Monod's abstract genetic argument—that prokaryote gene expression is regulated by repressors—rapidly became the persuasive zeitgeist of the 1960s. And, for a good number of biochemists, the isolation and characterization of repressors became the Holy Grail. Mark Ptashne's successful search for, and characterization of, the elusive repressor of bacteriophage λ, work that spanned two decades, can fairly be regarded as the greatest sustained experiment of the last century.

After isolating the λ repressor in 1967, Mark and Nancy Hopkins showed that the protein binds to a specific sequence of bacteriophage DNA. Mark's laboratory elegantly demonstrated that the repressor, with Cro protein, forms a positive and negative feedback system that is at the heart of the decision between the bacteriophages two lifestyles: lysis and lysogeny. Mark writes with brilliant simplicity about this work, without compromising its elegance or sophistication, in his book *A Genetic Switch* (1986, 1992, Blackwell Science and Cell Press).

In a series of more recent papers, Mark's laboratory showed how the principles of gene regulation, as developed in their study of bacteria, apply as well to yeast and higher organisms, including humans. In all of these organisms, simple adhesive surfaces on proteins recruit the protein complex, or complexes, required to transcribe a gene. These ideas, and their application to other regulatory systems, are set forth in the book *Genes & Signals* (2002, Cold Spring Harbor Laboratory Press), written with Alex Gann.

Ptashne received the Lasker Award for Basic Research in 1997, as well as the Gairdner, Horwitz, General Motors, Sloan Foundation, and Charles-Leopold Mayer (Académie des Sciences, Paris) Prizes. He is a member of the National Academy of Sciences and was a founder of the Genetics Institute, a biotech company.

The violin is one of Mark Ptashne's passions. He studied informally at the New England Conservatory of Music in Boston, is said to practice 2–3 hours a day, and owns a Stradivarius and a Guarnerius del Jesu. He has also established a trust fund to provide younger violinists with concert-quality instruments.

Mark Ptashne at Harvard, 1982. (Photograph by Linda Bartlett. Courtesy of Mark Ptashne.)

These egalitarian arrangements provided the backdrop to a rarified atmosphere. The talk was constant, sometimes scatological, and frank—better to put up for scrutiny an untested idea (or even a hoped-for result) than to keep some scientific finding a secret. The good humor was possible because it floated on a bed of seriousness. As long as the rules of openness and generosity were followed, we could even compete with one another. I learned a lot from talking, everyday, to Wally, my competitor in the race to "find the repressor" as we used to say. With a few notable exceptions, most of the important work was done not by postdocs but by students. To reiterate: Jim did not single-handedly gather this group of extraordinary personalities, nor did he alone impose the ethic, but I doubt that anyone would argue that it could have happened without him.

It was inevitable, I guess, that this standard could not be maintained. The field matured, relations between personalities ossified a bit, and so on. A few particularly telling developments transpired after Jim had left for Cold Spring Harbor. I have spoken of the egalitarian nature of Department finances, people applying for, and usually receiving, their own support. But one day, right around the time when money suddenly became harder to come by, the Howard Hughes Medical Institute swept down and gave a substantial sum (a vast sum, it seemed) to Don and Steve. There was a catch: Don and Steve[1] had to set up labs across the river at the Medical School, and spend half their time there. I believe the official excuse was twofold: For some reasons of estate (later modified), Hughes money could go only to medical schools and, more bizarre, the Harvard Medical School "needed this scientific shot in the arm." Two more generous colleagues than Don and Steve cannot be imagined; but this skewing of the financial playing field and their forced abdication of full-time residency were serious blows.

Then as governmental funding got sparse, Harvard (the college) did a remarkable thing: Nothing! Other administrations were alert to the need to provide funds for their scientists—imaginative plans sprung up at the major universities (at MIT, for example) and at medical schools (at Harvard Medical School, for example). Harvard College, part of the world's richest University, went into a bean-counting mode: Embarrassingly low offers were made to outstanding scientists who, of course, went elsewhere. When finally aroused from its dogmatic slumbers, the Harvard Administration acted not by giving funds to the Department, which would have used those funds to hire the best young investigators, but rather by creating an institute for "genomic research" outside the Department, with a director who reports to the Dean.

And the rumors are of more of this to come: Pressures to fuse with departments at the Medical School, an old and destructive idea long fought by the Department; and, equally depressing, talk of gigantic "postgenomic" organizations that will substitute the kind of science that made Harvard what it is with the empty posturing characterized by high organizational efforts and few scientific ideas.

Why have I gone on this long lament? For a simple reason: to pay tribute to Jim. Because, you see, although I can't prove it, I believe that had Jim stayed, Harvard would now be one of the world's premier research (and teaching) institutions. Jim would have done whatever was required—throw tantrums, issue threats, subject the powers that be to ridicule, identify and inspire young scientists, raise money. If you doubt it, consider Cold Spring Harbor. When Jim arrived there, it was an impoverished, mosquito-infested outpost with a fabled past. It is now one of the world's vibrant scientific centers—one of the most highly cited group of scientists in the world; a new graduate school with students equal to those found anywhere; an important publishing house (they published a book I co-authored! [Ptashne and Gann 2002]); a teaching and learning center; a place of architectural beauty and importance. Think of what Jim could have done had he stayed at Harvard.

AN AFTERTHOUGHT

I haven't said much about what Jim did *specifically* at Harvard and at Cold Spring Harbor. It is curiously hard to say just how he exerts his influence. I guess there are too many small matters that in the long run add up: who is hired (or not), which major projects are undertaken (or not), whether to spend money on this or on that, and so on. Jim is simultaneously the least and the most patient individual I know. His impatience can verge on the impetuous: today this must be done (right now), the cure for cancer is this very thing to be explored (right now), and so on. I have met intelligent people who know Jim only slightly and, exposed only to this side of him, think him erratic. But you must sometimes distinguish what he says with what he does and that requires paying attention over a rather long period of time. Whatever the tactics, the strategy is to build, and when it comes to long-range building, Jim is the least erratic person I know.

I did have two writing lessons from Jim when I was a graduate student. (My other teachers in this regard were Matt, Wally, Al Hershey, and, strictly by emulation, François Jacob.) First, Jim made all students in his class write term papers. There was no insistence on thinking up grand new experiments, or devastating some published work. Rather, the goal was to write a few pages clearly enough so "your mother could understand it." Seems simple—very hard to do. Second, I wrote a paper for publication and handed it to Jim (who was sitting at his office) for him to read at his leisure, ponder, and make a comment or two if he felt so moved. He glanced at the first sentence, grimaced, and tossed the paper back with one helpful hint: "unreadable."

REFERENCES

Ptashne M. and Gann A. 2002. *Genes & signals.* Cold Spring Harbor Laboratory Press, Cold Spring Harbor, New York.

Watson at Harvard (1956–1976)

Paul Doty

Harvard University

In retrospect, Jim Watson's arrival at Harvard in the autumn of 1956 was a miracle of unique timing—for Watson, for Harvard, and later for the Cold Spring Harbor Laboratory, which he began building into a world-class research center while still at Harvard.

Three years after the structure of DNA was discovered, little progress had been made in its promised transformation of biology. The Watson-Crick collaboration had ended abruptly, Watson's work with Alex Rich on the structure of RNA was unproductive, and Watson did not fit into the new environment and culture he found at the California Institute of Technology, despite Chairman George Beadle's efforts to make it attractive to him. Watson was looking for a new base.

Prior to 1954, Harvard's efforts to create a critical mass for biochemistry in Cambridge had failed. In the late 1940s, President Conant[1] tried to bring Carl and Gerty Cori[2] from Washington University to establish a biochemistry department. However, the plans failed because with the gender bias of those times, it was not possible to provide a proper appointment for Gerty Cori. In 1951, Edwin Cohn,[3] who had established a pioneering laboratory for blood proteins in the Medical School, was encouraged to move to Cambridge and create a biochemistry department in the unused north wing of the Biolabs. His manner of proceeding created such opposition that, combined with his declining health, the effort was stillborn.

Suddenly, a convergence of events in 1954 created a more promising outlook. The Chemistry Department awoke to the new opportunities in biochemistry by attracting Konrad Bloch[4] and Frank Westheimer[5] from the University of Chicago. My own laboratory (in the Chemistry Department) was becoming a substantial center for the study of nucleic acids and proteins. The molecular approach to biology was gaining a foothold in the Biolabs, the home of the Biology Department. George Wald's[6] work on the molecular basis of vision and his popular biochemistry course were having an impact. John Edsall,[7] the most prominent scientist in Cohn's laboratory, moved to the Biolabs where he continued to direct the undergraduate program in Biochemical Sciences and pursue protein research. Finally, McGeorge Bundy[8] became Dean of the Faculty of Arts and Sciences. My friendship with him had primed him with the need for a major redirection of biological resources if Harvard were to play a proper role in this new frontier.

That Watson might be the much-needed lynchpin in this redirection became evident after getting to know him in the summer of 1954 at Woods Hole, Massachusetts, and during visits to my lab. With Bundy making evident a display of interest in Watson, a seminar in the Biolabs was quickly arranged for October 1954. Jim's low voice

203

PAUL DOTY

Paul Doty, a member of the Harvard Faculty for nearly 45 of his 83 years, has been a fast and firm friend to Jim. The pair remained on close and friendly terms during the entire "Molecular Wars"—a period of a decade or so when Jim was forcing the Biology Department, against its will, into the molecular era. Without Doty's advice and support, Jim could not have prevailed, or at least it would have taken him a lot longer to do so.

Paul Doty is a biophysical chemist whose research focus has been on the structure and functioning of nucleic acids and proteins. Best known is his work on chain separaton and renaturation of DNA, including the conditions under which the original base-paired structure is restored. Over the course of his long career, he has supervised nearly 70 students and 85 postdoctoral fellows, many of whom have had glittering research careers of their own and now occupy positions of influence and authority. Much of the mentoring was shared between Doty and his wife Helga, who was also a molecular biologist. Their family home near their Kirkland Place laboratory was a welcome retreat for many, including Jim Watson.

Doty has had a long and active involvement in public service and activism in nuclear arms control. He served several presidents in official and advisory roles and was in part responsible for inducing the Soviet Union to negotiate the 1972 Antiballistic Missile Treaty.

In 1974, Doty established the Center for Science and International Affairs at Harvard and served as its Director (half-time) until 1985; it has grown to more than 100 members.

and tendency to talk to the blackboard were an obvious handicap, as were rumors of his occasional displays of immaturity and of arrogance above the Harvard norm. This could have provided the basis of a rejection but for the much more positive tone of the letters replying to the search committee's inquires. For example, Fritz Lippman,[9] a companion in the "confidential" style of lecturing, replied "Since he has plenty to say, people will get close." According to hearsay, the Department's deliberations were contentious, but, with strong backing from George Wald and Ernst Mayr,[10] he was offered a five-year appointment as assistant professor beginning July 1, 1955.

Watson accepted on condition that he could take the sabbatical leave that normally accompanied such appointments at the outset rather than near the end as was usual. This seemed a wise choice. He needed time to map out a coherent research program for a group rather than focusing on just his own, space had to be adapted, grant proposals made, and equipment ordered. Moreover, he could take leave of Caltech and return to the other Cambridge to interact again with Crick on the central issue of how information flowed from DNA to the protein it encoded. The Department had no objections, perhaps welcoming a delay in the inevitable "molecular wars" that were rushing forward.

RESEARCH AND TEACHING

Despite little training in chemistry or biochemistry and lackluster research in the two years following the DNA structure, Watson bravely chose to enter the highly competitive and mushrooming arena of protein synthesis and information transfer from

Forty Years of the Double Helix Celebration. From left: Paul Doty, Tom Maniatis, Jim Watson, Wally Gilbert. (Photograph by Margot Bennett. Courtesy of the James D. Watson Collection, CSHL Archives.)

DNA. This step highlighted two traits that were to be displayed repeatedly in the future: his readiness to take risks and his commitment to work exclusively on major problems. In doing so, he succeeded in establishing a major research center in the heartland of the rapidly developing molecular biology. It attracted a continuous flow of talented graduate students, postdoctoral fellows, and later outstanding colleagues, including Wally Gilbert and Mark Ptashne.

The research focus was on the structure of RNA-containing ribosomes where protein synthesis takes place, the identification of the minor RNA component (messenger RNA) that carries the code from the DNA to the ribosomes, and factors that restrict the stretch of DNA that is copied into the messenger RNA. The output of the group soon reached the level of its leading competitors and then continued on to several seminal advances.

The atmosphere of the lab reflected Watson's young-man-in-a-hurry outlook. He energized the group by keeping alive the competitive circumstance in which they worked. The researchers had great independence, but Watson's attention was proportional to the quality and promise of their work. Once-a-week or twice-a-week seminars stimulated broad participation and gave Watson a forum for displaying the high standards that criticism should meet, often at the expense of hurt feelings.

Publications coming from the lab seldom included Watson's name as an author. For him, it was a luxury that his DNA discovery allowed, but one that other young professors could ill afford until their own reputations were well enough established to assure continuing research grants. While researchers often welcomed this display of the independence under which they worked, it meant that the printed record failed to reflect Watson's real contributions.

Counseled by others and myself, Watson improved his lecturing as he developed his own style.[11] He gradually spoke louder, established eye contact with the audience, and exposed his own way of thinking. Before long, he was conveying the inside view of the burgeoning molecular biology revolution for all comers to see, replete with anger, ambition, and excitement. As he preferred teaching undergraduates, his classes increasingly recruited students to work as assistants in his lab and on occasion to take up molecular biology as a career. For example, Nancy Hopkins, now a professor at MIT, followed this course.

MOLECULAR WARS

In the late 1950s, Harvard, like most research universities, was divided over how to accommodate the rising tide of molecular biology, which even then was feared to replace much of the traditional structure and resource base of classical biology and redirect the research priorities of many chemistry departments. In a first step at the organizational level, the small collection of biochemists in the Chemistry and Biology Departments in 1954 were able to form the Committee on Higher Degrees in Biochemistry that enabled them to select incoming graduate students, create a graduate curriculum, and award master and doctorate degrees. John Edsall became the first chairman, followed by Konrad Bloch, and by Jim in 1960–1963. In 1965, its name was changed to include Molecular Biology.

The encroachment of molecular biology into classical biology was vividly personalized by the contest between Jim and Edward Wilson. Wilson, a naturalist devoted to the study of ants, was appointed assistant professor in the same year as Jim. Their initial animosity is indelibly preserved in Wilson's autobiography (Wilson 1994). Fortunately, time has healed the breach (see essay by Edward Wilson in this section). In 1958, the Biology Department, stimulated by a Stanford tenure offer to Wilson, decided to promote him to tenure. When the request for an Ad Hoc Committee, which advises the Dean and the President on tenure appointments, reached Bundy, he insisted that it should address tenure for both Jim and Wilson. Despite the Biology Department's earlier decision to postpone consideration of Watson for tenure, Bundy's insistence that there would be no more tenure appointments until both were addressed together carried the day. The Biology Department on further reflection agreed. The Ad Hoc Committee approved both promotions.

With this promotion now allowing Jim to join in the meetings of tenured professors, he had a proper base from which to try to transform the Biology Department. He did not proceed with a light touch. He tabulated the years remaining before retirement for all department members and targeted every upcoming appointment. Wilson describes department meetings as having an "edgy formality like Bedouin chieftains gathered around a disputed water well." With the support of the other molecularly inclined members—Edsall, Wald, and Levine[12]—the transformation began. Early successes included Walter Gilbert[13] and Matthew Meselson,[14] but there were failures too: David Hubel[15] and Seymour Benzer were not to be moved from their current locations.

WATSON'S WRITINGS

By the early 1960s, the molecular biology revolution was in full force: It needed a tribune. Watson responded. His teaching—with its insistence on incorporating the latest findings each year—prepared the way for the revolution's first textbook. Three years in the making, it appeared in 1965: *Molecular Biology of the Gene*. It was pathbreaking in multiple ways: its devotion to the molecular basis of biology, its emphasis on the structure and interaction of molecules, its reliance on graphic colored diagrams of nearly every concept, and its use of riveting summarizing sentences for section headings. Through four editions over a 23-year span, the book pioneered the establishment of molecular biology as a discipline sturdy enough to restructure biology itself.

As molecular biology matured, its frontier evolved from the mechanism of individual processes such as protein synthesis to address the entire detailed workings of the eukaryotic cell at the molecular level. Later, Watson stimulated and joined a group effort led by Bruce Alberts, one of my most remarkable former graduate students, to create a new approach to the molecular biology of higher cells. *Molecular Biology of the Cell* first appeared in 1983 and reached its fourth edition in 2002, weighing in at eight pounds. The several editions have now passed the million mark in sales.

As the establishment acknowledged, the enduring effect of the discovery of the DNA structure—Watson sharing the Lasker Award and the Nobel Prize in 1962—Watson decided that the way this massive tectonic shift came about needed documentation at the personal level. In 1962, he began writing his own recollections, aided greatly by the many letters to his mother that she had preserved. It was a naked exposé of how he felt at the time, his raw ambition, his awkward manners, but most of all his intense perseverance and his skill in making his collaboration with Francis Crick work. By 1965, several drafts were shown to Crick and Maurice Wilkins. Their displeasure led to some changes, but they fell far short of what was wanted. A review of part of the draft by Houghton Mifflin found it too likely libelous to proceed. Eventually, the final draft of *The Double Helix* was submitted to Harvard University Press and judged suitable for publication. Upon hearing of this progress in securing publication by a prestigious press, Crick and Wilkins shifted into high opposition employing a well-known lawyer to threaten President Nathan Pusey[16] with libel if publication proceeded. When Pusey asked my opinion, I failed to make a clear choice. I felt sympathy for my friend Crick and alarm at a possible legal suit. But the changes he and Wilkins now wanted would defeat Jim's intent to record how he felt at the time. Pusey forced a retraction of the Press's agreement. In 1968, the book was published by Atheneum in New York. It evoked passionate approval and fierce dissent. His portrayal of X-ray crystallographer Rosalind Franklin infuriated feminists and others. However, as its sales passed the million mark with translations into 22 languages, *The Double Helix* became the most popular account ever of a scientific discovery. Over the years, Crick's intense objections slowly faded.

1968

The publication of *The Double Helix* produced enough excitement for one year, but there was more to come. Jim's lab was thriving. Mark Ptashne, then a Lecturer following his being a Junior Fellow in Harvard's Society of Fellows,[17] and Walter Gilbert, a young physics professor switching to molecular biology, were on the crest. They had just demonstrated in two different systems the first clear mechanism of how a gene is turned on and off in molecular terms. Jim continued to promote a competitive climate in his research group, insisting that it could only be a boon to research. In another area, his own group had isolated a protein that was key to activating RNA polymerase to transcribe a gene into mRNA, which would then carry the instructions to the protein synthesizing apparatus. This too was propelled by competition.

The expansion of biochemistry and molecular biology had now reached a point, due in no small part to Jim's efforts, that justified forming a department within the Faculty of Arts and Sciences. That little more accommodation would be forthcoming from the Chemistry Department was brought home by its refusal to offer a tenure position to Gobind Khorana (later a Nobel Prize winner for chemical synthesis of DNA) on the basis that repetitive molecular structures were not at the leading edge of chemistry. With John Edsall's help, I made the pitch to the Dean for departmental status and won the vote of approval from the Faculty of Arts and Sciences. The Department of Biochemistry and Molecular Biology came into full operation in the fall of 1968.

It might have been expected that with department status and the likelihood that he would follow me as chairman, Jim would find this an adequate platform on which to build Harvard's biological future. But that was not to be. Jim was becoming restless, sensing that Harvard might not expand enough to fulfill his vision of the role it should play in the new biology. Since 1948, Jim had developed a romantic attachment to the Cold Spring Harbor Laboratory on the North Shore of Long Island. Although financially impoverished, its summer courses and conferences in a rustic setting had become a magnet for cutting-edge biologists and students aware of the biological explosion that was to come. Jim participated more and more in its summer programs and became a member of the board. In 1967, the Laboratory faced a crisis with the resignation of its Director and failing finances. Fearing CSHL's bankruptcy, Jim offered to become Director on a part-time basis if Harvard would continue his full-time salary; and he would continue with his Harvard obligations unchanged. It was a daring departure for him and a test of Harvard's flexibility. Believing that if the Laboratory became stabilized at its current size, it could be managed by a part-time Director or that its failure to recover would end the experiment, I argued with the Dean to accept the arrangement. Furthermore, it was evident that Harvard research students would benefit by summers at the Laboratory. After all, it might grow into a Harvard annex such as Dumbarton Oaks[18] in Washington. Harvard approved. Early in 1968, the experiment began with many doubting it could succeed. Ed Wilson commented to friends that "I wouldn't put him in charge of a lemonade stand," but in his 1994 autobiography, he graciously admitted error and praised what developed.

There was one more climax to come in this full year. Jim's much recorded preoccupation with the fairer sex was already legendary. His focus was on youth, brightness, and class. Part-time Radcliffe[19] students as well as full-time women assistants or researchers always enlivened his lab. However, this broad acquaintance base did not seem to translate into committed relationships. Hence the surprise when Jim was suddenly smitten with a Radcliffe junior half his age who had been working in his office. His long-term strategy of first carefully casing the field had paid off. In March 1968, Elizabeth Lewis and Jim were married and a most successful and enduring partnership was launched.

WINDING DOWN AT HARVARD

Viewed from Cambridge, the 1968 deal whereby Jim had divided responsibilities as Director at CSHL and Department member at Harvard had the appearance of working. Jim taught mainly in the major introductory course for seniors and graduate students. He maintained the dynamic pace of his lab. And he continued his push for enlarging Harvard's role in the new biology. What were not so evident from Cambridge were the vast changes he was orchestrating at CSHL. Within two years, the moribund and failing institution he adopted had an operating budget of $1 million and this was soon to double. Adroitly wooing wealthy neighbors, gifts of adjacent real estate and endowment monies began to roll in. His vision of building a major institution where larger efforts than possible in an academic structure could be set up in record time was taking shape. With this came the delight for him and his wife Liz of leaving their imprint on every aspect of the expansion, in particular the architecture and design of the campus that was to come (see William Grover's essay in Section IV).

Despite this new devotion, Jim made one final effort to bring to Harvard a concentrated effort on what he saw as the next goal of the new biology, i.e., to unravel the workings of animal cells at the molecular level. For this he saw the molecular biology of tumor viruses as an entering wedge that would embrace an attack on cancer itself. To this end, he undertook a massive campaign for Harvard to build a separate laboratory dedicated to animal cell biology. He initiated the plan, reached agreement on its location, and engaged the architects. Consistent with what drew him to CSHL was the concept of having this as a unit independent of the departmental structure, with a director reporting directly to the Dean. The result was a grant proposal to the National Cancer Institute for nearly $6 million. The key was to bring in a world-class Director. Howard Temin,[20] then at The McArdle Institute, Madison, was the choice. In addition, a promising young assistant professor ready for tenure, Klaus Weber, was to play a major role. Alas, Temin declined largely in order to preserve the promising career that his wife Rayla (a population geneticist) had at Wisconsin. Without clear leadership in view, the grant was denied (1974), and Jim's hope for leaving a visible legacy and a basis for his continued engagement with Harvard died. The Watsons with their two young sons moved from a house on Kirkland Place near the Biolab and my own home in the fall of 1974. Jim took academic leave of Harvard for 1975–1976 before resigning at the end of that year.

Meanwhile, his vision at CSHL was materializing through the most crucial gift to the CSHL, the Banbury estate of 50 acres and an endowment of $8 million. Twenty-five years later, CSHL has become transformed into a world class center for molecular biology—awarding Ph.D. degrees, operating at a $100,000,000 annual level, and rating first in the number of research papers in molecular biology most often quoted.

REFERENCES

Alberts B., Bray D., Lewis J., Raff M., and Watson J.D. 1983. *Molecular biology of the cell*. Garland, New York.

Watson J.D. 1965. *Molecular biology of the gene*. W.A. Benjamin, New York.

Watson J.D. 1968. *The double helix*. Atheneum, New York.

Wilson E.O. 1994. *Naturalist*. Island Press/Shearwater Books, Washington, D.C.

Structure of Small Viruses

F.H.C. Crick and J.D. Watson

Reprinted, with permission, from *Nature*, vol. 177, pp. 473–475.

of which has its atoms arranged in definite (relative) positions in space.

All known plant viruses consist of two chemical components only : protein and ribonucleic acid. It seems likely that there is a general plan for their relative positions and that the majority of the protein lies on the outside of the virus, surrounding a central core composed largely, if not entirely, of ribonucleic acid. This arrangement is well established for only two viruses—the spherically shaped turnip yellow mosaic virus (by Markham[4]) and the rod-shaped tobacco mosaic virus (by both the Tubingen[5] and Berkeley groups[6])—but we believe that it is likely to apply to all simple viruses. That is, the protein component of a round virus is a spherical shell, and of a rod-shaped virus, a cylindrical shell. Our hypothesis is that in both cases these shells are constructed from a large number of identical protein molecules, of small or moderate size, packed together in a regular manner. Our hypothesis may apply, though in a slightly different form, to the ribonucleic acid component. This is discussed in more detail later.

STRUCTURE OF SMALL VIRUSES

IT is a striking fact that almost all small viruses are either rods or spheres. The purpose of this article is to explain this observation by means of the following simple hypothesis : a small virus contains identical sub-units, packed together in a regular manner. It has been suggested before[1] that viruses are constructed from sub-units ; but the idea has not previously been described in precise terms or put forward as a general feature of all small viruses.

We believe that there is conclusive evidence for this hypothesis in two cases and suggestive evidence in a number of others. As most of the present evidence comes from the plant viruses, we shall restrict our discussion to these, except for a few remarks on animal viruses at the end of the article.

Plant Viruses

Notice first that all plant viruses which have been studied carefully are extremely regular in their shape and size[2]. In electron micrographs their dimensions are constant. One particle of turnip yellow mosaic virus, for example, is the same size as another, to within the errors of measurement. Moreover, the 'spherical' viruses have shapes very close to that of a sphere—there seem to be no ellipsoidal plant viruses. All cases where they have appeared as flattened spheres have been shown to be due to the surface tension caused by drying prior to electron microscope examination. In good photographs there are sometimes suggestions that the 'spheres' are more nearly regular polyhedra, which, as we shall see, is what one might expect.

The great regularity of plant viruses is shown even more strikingly by their ability to form crystals (or paracrystals) which give good X-ray photographs[3], often with reflexions extending to small spacings. From this we can infer that a very high degree of order exists within such viruses, and that, to a resolution almost at the atomic level, one virus particle appears identical, or at least very similar, to all its sister virus particles. A plant virus can thus be considered a 'molecule' in the sense used by protein crystallographers—an entity, the major part

Tobacco Mosaic Virus

This rod-shaped virus is the best studied and we shall therefore consider its structure in detail.

Tobacco mosaic virus contains 94 per cent protein and 6 per cent ribonucleic acid[7]. The characteristic particle, which is closely connected with the infectivity, has a 'molecular weight' of about 45 million, a length close to 3000 A. and a diameter of about 170 A. The early X-ray work[3] showed clearly that this particle is made up of sub-units of some sort. More recently it was realized that the basic feature of the structure is its helical nature[8]. The protein part of the virus is constructed from a large number of structurally equivalent sub-units (small globular proteins) set in helical array about the central axis. The pitch of the helix is 23 A. The number of sub-units per turn is more difficult to establish—the most probable value (Franklin, R. E., and Holmes, K. C., personal communication) gives a molecular weight for the sub-unit of about 20,000.

A very similar value is suggested by the chemical evidence. Harris and Knight[9] first examined the carboxyl end-groups of the polypeptide chains, and found that the virus particle had about 2,500 terminal groups, all threonine. This suggested that the virus contains 2,500 identical polypeptide chains, an idea which has been further strengthened by the recent work of both the Tubingen[10] and Berkeley[11] groups, who have identified the terminal three residues at the carboxyl end of this polypeptide chain.

Some additional feature is obviously needed to determine the length of the protein shell, and we would guess that in the intact virus this is controlled by the length of the ribonucleic acid core. This would explain why rods of indefinite length are produced when undenatured protein sub-units are re-aggregated in the absence of ribonucleic acid[12]. Moreover, when the re-aggregation occurs in the presence of ribonucleic acid, it is reported by Fraenkel-Conrat and Williams[13] that rods of 3000 A. in length occur very frequently.

The structure of tobacco mosaic virus, then, is based on a helix, or, in other words, it has a screw axis—in this case[8] a non-integer screw axis. This symmetry axis implies that all the protein sub-units in the body of the virus have the same environment. The same contact points between neighbouring sub-units are used over and over again as we move along the helix. This feature is the clue to the general principle which we can apply whenever, on the molecular level, a structure of a definite size and shape has to be built up from smaller units; namely, that the packing arrangements are likely to be repeated again and again—and hence that the sub-units are likely to be related by symmetry elements.

So far we have been mainly concerned with the protein, and have neglected the ribonucleic acid component of the virus. Is that, too, made up of sub-units? The ribonucleic acid content of tobacco mosaic virus is rather low, and not more than four nucleotides can be associated with a given protein sub-unit. Now if all these groups were identical, the analytical composition of the ribonucleic acid would be based on the number 4, which it certainly is not[14]. Moreover, the ribonucleic acid is probably connected with the genetic properties of the virus, and so its fundamental unit must contain a much larger number of nucleotides.

This does not mean, however, that ribonucleic acid sub-units do not exist, since it is possible that the ribonucleic acid core contains a number of identical strands systematically interacting with the protein shell. The important consideration is that the packing arrangement should be repeated over and over again; and this can be done if the symmetry of the ribonucleic acid is the same as the symmetry of the protein and if the symmetry applies only to the sugar-phosphate backbone and not to the sequence of bases. It remains to be seen whether this type of arrangement can be established experimentally.

Spherical Plant Viruses

We have seen that the rod-shaped helical form of tobacco mosaic virus represents a natural way of constructing a large container from identical much smaller building blocks. The question we must now ask is whether the protein shell of the spherical viruses is likewise constructed by a regular aggregation of one type of small protein molecule, and, if so, how this is done. Unfortunately, there has been, to our knowledge, no systematic chemical search for the presence of sub-units in spherical viruses and so we must rely almost completely on crystallographic evidence.

It has been shown in two cases—bushy stunt virus[15] and turnip yellow mosaic virus[16]—that spherical viruses crystallize in a unit cell which has the shape of a cube; but unfortunately the X-ray photographs did not establish whether the symmetry also was cubic. This is important because, as has been pointed out by Dr. Dorothy Hodgkin[1] and Dr. Barbara Low[1], if the lattice possesses true cubic symmetry so must the virus particle, since there is only one particle in the primitive unit cell.

It has now been clearly established by Caspar (see following communication) that the unit cell of bushy stunt virus has cubic symmetry, and that, in this particular case, the virus has an even higher symmetry than the unit cell. Though this evidence applies to only one virus, we expect that further investigation will show that many small spherical viruses have cubic symmetry, for the reasons given below.

Now a virus possessing cubic symmetry must necessarily be built up by the regular aggregation of smaller asymmetrical building bricks, and this can be done only in a very limited number of ways. Since viruses are made of protein and ribonucleic acid, both

Table 1. THE THREE POSSIBLE CUBIC POINT GROUPS FOR A SPHERICAL VIRUS

Crystallographic description	No. and type of rotation axes present	No. of asymmetric units	Platonic solid with these symmetry elements
23	3 2-fold 4 3-fold	12	Tetrahedron
432	6 2-fold 4 3-fold 3 4-fold	24	Cube Octahedron
532	15 2-fold 10 3-fold 6 5-fold	60	Dodecahedron Icosahedron

The number of sub-units will be the same as, or a multiple of, the number of asymmetric units

of which contain asymmetric carbon atoms of one particular hand only, those symmetry elements (mirror planes and centres of symmetry) which turn a right hand into a left hand are impossible. Thus we can only have rotation axes, and for cubic symmetry this limits us to only three different combinations of symmetry elements.

Each of these three classes must contain at least four three-fold axes and three two-fold axes, arranged as for a tetrahedron. The first class contains no additional type of axis, while the second and third have four- and five-fold axes, respectively. Such an arrangement of symmetry elements is known as a 'point group', in contrast to a space group which applies to a regular arrangement extending to infinity. In Table 1 are listed the three cubic point groups possible for virus particles and also the regular polyhedra which have these symmetry elements (among others). Notice that in all these point groups the minimum number of asymmetric units must be a multiple of 12.

Three further points must be made to prevent misunderstanding. First, it is possible to arrange sub-units in other ways to produce a spherical shell, but the symmetry will not be cubic, and as they are less likely we shall not discuss them further here. Second, the asymmetric unit, upon which the symmetry elements act to build up the spherical shell, may consist of several identical sub-units joined together in some unsymmetrical fashion. This occurs quite often in protein crystals and would not be unexpected. Nor need the sub-unit be a single protein molecule in the chemist's sense of a unit joined together by chemical bonds. Several different protein molecules may aggregate to form the asymmetric unit. Third, our predictions concern the symmetry elements present in a virus particle, not its exact shape. However, this is likely to be approximately spherical, and may, under high resolution, appear polyhedral or perhaps with bumps on, like a rather symmetrical mulberry. Both these forms have been seen in electron micrographs.

It is not easy to explain in a short space why there are so few ways of building a spherical shell, but the reader can soon convince himself that it is difficult by trying to draw identical shapes which completely cover the surface of a tennis ball. It is impossible, for example, to do this entirely with hexagons, even if their shape is irregular. The point is very well stated in D'Arcy Thompson's "On Growth and Form"[17], in which we find "the broad, general principle that we cannot group as we please any number and sort of polygons into a polyhedron, but that the number and kind of facets in the latter is strictly limited to a narrow range of possibilities". The reason is essentially a topological one.

From the present X-ray evidence we are unable to distinguish the respective contributions of the protein and the ribonucleic acid, so we cannot be sure whether the cubic symmetry is perfect and applies strictly to both of them. We cannot tell whether the protein sub-units contain identical sequences of amino-acids, or whether the ribonucleic acid sub-units (if they exist) have identical sequences of nucleotides. It should not be very difficult, by end-group analysis, to decide whether the protein components are all approximately equal. By analogy with tobacco mosaic virus we would guess that this will be found to be the case. With the ribonucleic acid component, however, the problem is more difficult than it was in the case of tobacco mosaic virus, as the number of nucleotides per sub-unit is certainly much larger. (This follows from the higher percentage of ribonucleic acid[7] and the much smaller number of protein sub-units.) Only with a more detailed understanding of the ribonucleic acid core is the problem likely to be settled.

Animal and Other Viruses

For animal viruses we are handicapped because there is no X-ray evidence available so far. However, it is now becoming clear[2] that many of the smaller animal viruses, such as poliomyelitis and the various encephalitic viruses, are morphologically very similar to the spherical plant viruses. Not only are they of similar size (approximately 300 A. diameter); but it has recently been shown[18] that poliomyelitis virus also contains ribonucleic acid and can form crystals which appear as regular as those produced by the plant viruses. We thus think it very probable that cubic symmetry also extends to these animal viruses, and that the soluble antigens[19] (of about 120 A. diameter) frequently observed in infected cells are related to the sub-units normally used in the assembly of the final infective virus.

We also see no reason why our hypothesis should not be valid for viruses containing deoxyribonucleic acid rather than ribonucleic acid. Although the structure of bacteriophages is usually more complex than the smaller viruses discussed here, the fact that their heads appear polyhedral suggests that ideas of this general type may apply to them, too. On the other hand, it is less likely that they will be relevant to the structure of the larger viruses like vaccinia.

Conclusion

We can now describe our hypothesis in a more general manner. We assume that the basic structural requirement for a small virus is the provision of a shell of protein to protect its highly specific packet of ribonucleic acid. This shell is necessarily rather large, and the virus, when in the cell, finds it easier to control the production of a large number of identical small protein molecules rather than that of one or two very large molecules to act as its shell. These small protein molecules then aggregate around the ribonucleic acid in a regular manner, which they can only do in a limited number of ways if they are to use the same packing arrangement repeatedly. Hence small viruses are either rods or spheres. The number of sub-units in a rod-shaped virus is probably unrestricted, but for a spherical virus the number is likely to be a multiple of 12. Every small virus will contain symmetry elements and in favourable cases these can be discovered experimentally

We believe that this hypothesis is likely to apply (in this form or a simple variant of it) to all small viruses which have a fixed size and shape.

F. H. C. CRICK
J. D. WATSON*
Medical Research Council Unit for the
Study of the Molecular Structure of
Biological Systems,
Cavendish Laboratory,
Cambridge
Jan. 23.

* On leave from the Biology Department, Harvard University, and supported by a grant from the National Science Foundation, U.S.A.

[1] Among the more important references are Hodgkin, D. C., *Cold Spring Harbor Symp.*, **14**, 65 (1950). Low, B., in "The Proteins", **1**, 235 (Academic Press, New York, 1953). Schramm, G., *Z. Naturforsch.*, **2b**, 112, 249 (1947).
[2] Williams, R. C., *Cold Spring Harbor Symp.*, **18**, 185 (1953); "Advances in Virus Research", **2**, 184 (Academic Press, New York, 1954).
[3] Bernal, J. D., and Fankuchen, I., *J. Gen. Physiol.*, **25**, 111, 147 (1941).
[4] Markham, R., *Disc. Farad. Soc.*, **11**, 221 (1951). See also Bernal, J. D., and Carlisle, C. H., *Disc. Farad. Soc.*, **11**, 227 (1951), and Schmidt, P., Kaesberg, P., and Beeman, W. W., *Biochim. et Biophys. Acta*, **14**, 1 (1954).
[5] Schramm, G., Schumacher, G., and Zillig, W., *Nature*, **175**, 549 (1955).
[6] Hart, R., *Proc. U.S. Nat. Acad. Sci.*, **41**, 261 (1955).
[7] Knight, C. A., "Advances in Virus Research", **2**, 153 (Academic Press, New York, 1954).
[8] Watson, J. D., *Biochim. et Biophys. Acta*, **13** 10 (1954). Franklin, R. E., *Nature*, **175**, 379 (1955).
[9] Harris, J. I., and Knight, C. A., *Nature*, **170**, 613 (1952); *J. Biol. Chem.*, **214**, 215 (1955).
[10] Schramm, G., Braunitzer, G., and Schneider, J. W., *Nature*, **176**, 456 (1955).
[11] Niu, C. I., and Fraenkel-Conrat, H., *Biochim. et Biophys. Acta*, **16**, 597 (1955); *J. Amer. Chem. Soc.*, **77**, 5882 (1955).
[12] Schramm, G., and Zillig, W., *Z. Naturforsch.*, **10b**, 493 (1955).
[13] Fraenkel-Conrat, H., and Williams, R. C., *Proc. U.S. Nat. Acad. Sci.* **41**. 690 (1955).
[14] Markham, R., and Smith, J. D., *Biochem. J.*, **46**, 513 (1950).
[15] Bernal, J. D., Fankuchen, I., and Riley, D. P., *Nature*, **142**, 1075 (1938). Carlisle, C. H., and Dornberger, K., *Acta Cryst.*, **1**, 194 (1948).
[16] Bernal, J. D., and Carlisle, C. H., *Nature*, **162**, 139 (1948).
[17] Thompson, D'Arcy, "On Growth and Form", 737 (2nd edit., Camb. Univ. Press, 1952).
[18] Schaffer, F. L., and Schwerdt, C. E., *Proc. U.S. Nat. Acad. Sci.*, **41**, 1020 (1955).
[19] Polson, A., *Nature*, **172**, 1154 (1953). Polson, A., and Selzer, G., *Biochim. et Biophys. Acta*, **15**, 251 (1954). Hampton, J. U. F., *Biochim. et Biophys. Acta*, **18**, 446 (1955).

Unstable Ribonucleic Acid Revealed by Pulse Labelling of *Escherichia coli*

Francois Gros, H. Hiatt, W. Gilbert, C.G. Kurland,
R.W. Risebrough, and J.D. Watson

Reprinted, with permission, *Nature*, vol. 190, pp. 581–585.

UNSTABLE RIBONUCLEIC ACID REVEALED BY PULSE LABELLING OF ESCHERICHIA COLI

By Drs. FRANCOIS GROS and H. HIATT

The Institut Pasteur, Paris

Dr. WALTER GILBERT

Departments of Physics, Harvard University

AND

Dr. C. G. KURLAND, R. W. RISEBROUGH and Dr. J. D. WATSON

The Biological Laboratories, Harvard University

WHEN *Escherichia coli* cells are infected with *T* even bacteriophage particles, synthesis of host proteins stops[1], and much if not all new protein synthesis is phage specific[2]. This system thus provides an ideal model for observing the synthesis of new proteins following the introduction of specific DNA. In particular, we should expect the appearance of phage-specific RNA, since it is generally assumed that DNA is not a direct template for protein synthesis but that its genetic information is transmitted to a specific sequence of bases in RNA. It was thus considered paradoxical when it was first noticed[3] that, following infection by the *T* even phages, net RNA synthesis stops even though protein synthesis continues at the rate of the uninfected bacterium. This could mean that DNA sometimes serves as a direct template for protein synthesis. Alternatively, net RNA synthesis may not be necessary so long as there exists the synthesis of a genetically specific RNA that turns over rapidly. This possibility was first suggested by experiments of Hershey[4], who, in 1953, reported that *T*2 infected cells contain a metabolically active RNA fraction comprising about 1 per cent of the total RNA. Several years later, Volkin and Astrachan[5] reported that this metabolic RNA possessed base ratios similar, if not identical (considering uracil formally equivalent to thymine), to those of the infecting *T*2 DNA. By 1958 they[6] extended their observation to *T*7 infected cells, where again the RNA synthesized after phage infection had base ratios similar to those of the phage DNA.

During these years, evidence[7] accumulated that the sites of much, if not all, protein synthesis are the ribosomal particles, and it was thought most likely that ribosomal RNA was genetically specific, with each ribosome possessing a base sequence which coded for a specific amino-acid sequence (one ribosome–one protein hypothesis). Direct verification of this hypothesis was lacking, and its proponents[8] were troubled by the fact that, except for phage-specific RNA, it was impossible to find any correlation within a given organism between the base ratios of DNA and RNA. Moreover, there was no evidence that phage-specific RNA was ribosomal RNA.

Nomura, Hall and Spiegelman[9] have recently discovered that following *T*2 infection there is no synthesis of typical (see below) ribosomal RNA and that the phage-specific RNA sediments at a slower rate (8*s*) than ribosomal RNA (16*s* and 23*s*). The genetic information for the synthesis of phage-specific proteins does not reside in the usual ribosomal RNA. Instead, if we assume that the synthesis of phage-specific proteins also occurs on ribosomes, then the phage-specific RNA might be viewed as a 'messenger' (to use the terminology of Monod and Jacob[10]) which carries the genetic information to the ribosomes. Furthermore, unless we postulate that there exist two different mechanisms for protein synthesis, there should also exist within uninfected normal cells RNA molecules physically similar to the phage-specific RNA and having base ratios similar to its specific DNA.

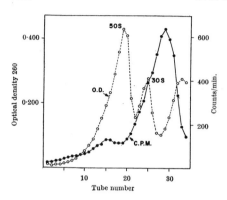

Fig. 1. Sedimentation of pulse-labelled 10^{-4} Mg²⁺ extract. 1 ml. of a crude extract labelled by a 20-sec. pulse of ¹⁴C-uracil and made in 10^{-4} M Mg²⁺ and 5×10^{-3} *tris* buffer (pH 7·4) was carefully layered on top of a 24-ml. sucrose gradient (5–20 per cent) in a Spinco SW25 swinging-bucket tube. It was spun 2 hr. 45 min. at 25,000 r.p.m. at 4° C. The tube bottom was then punctured and 10 drop samples taken to measure 2600 Å. absorption (2 drops) and the radioactivity in 5 per cent trichloracetic acid precipitates (8 drops). All points were counted to at least 1,000 counts

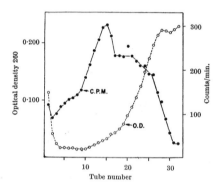

Fig. 2. Sedimentation of pulse-labelled 10^{-4} Mg²⁺ extract, long run. An extract as in Fig. 1 run for 11 hr. at 25,000 r.p.m., 15° C., on a sucrose gradient. Drop collection and radioactivity measurements were made as described in Fig. 1

Here we present evidence that RNA molecules physically similar to phage-specific RNA exist in normal *E. coli* cells and that, under suitable ionic conditions, they are associated with ribosomal particles.

Experimental plan. Most (80–85 per cent) RNA in actively growing *Escherichia coli* cells is found in ribosomal particles composed of 64 per cent RNA and 36 per cent protein[11]. There are two sizes[12] of ribosomal RNA, 16s (molecular weight $= 5·5 \times 10^5$) and 23s (molecular weight $= 1·1 \times 10^6$). The 16s RNA is derived from both 30s and 50s ribosomes, while 23s RNA is only found in 50s ribosomes. The other principal (10–15 per cent) form of RNA in *E. coli* is soluble RNA (now more appropriately called transfer RNA), which functions in the movement of activated amino-acids to the ribosomes. At least 20 (one for each amino-acid) different transfer RNA molecules exist[13], all of which have molecular

weights about 25,000 and sedimentation constants of 4s.

Collectively, ribosomal and transfer RNA comprise at least 95 per cent of *E. coli* RNA. Thus messenger RNA, if present, can amount to at most only several per cent of the total RNA. Now if the messenger were stable, only a corresponding fraction of newly synthesized RNA could be messenger RNA; the great majority of new RNA being the metabolically stable ribosomal and transfer RNA's. If, however, messenger RNA is turning over (as is suggested by the original Hershey experiments) then a much larger fraction of newly made RNA must be messenger. For example, if the messenger functions only once for the synthesis of a single protein molecule, its lifetime might be only several seconds. In this event, if we look at the RNA synthesis occurring during a very short interval, then most of the newly synthesized RNA would be messenger even though this fraction may comprise only 1 per cent of the total RNA.

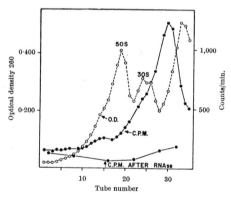

Fig. 3. Sedimentation of T2-infected 10^{-4} Mg²⁺ extract. An extract in 10^{-4} Mg²⁺ of cells infected with T2 at a multiplicity of 20 and labelled with phosphorus-32 between the second and fifth minutes after infection. Run as in Fig. 1. Several samples were treated with ribonuclease (10 γ/c.c.) to determine the background of label not in RNA

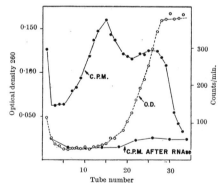

Fig. 4. Sedimentation of T2-infected 10^{-4} Mg²⁺ extract, long run. An extract as in Fig. 3 run for 11 hr. at 25,000 r.p.m. 20° C. Measured as in Fig. 1

We have therefore exposed *E. coli* cells to short pulses (10–20 sec. at 25° C. where the time of generation is about 90 min.) of radioactive RNA precursors (^{32}P or ^{14}C-uracil), rapidly chilled the cells with crushed ice and $M/100$ azide, prepared cell-free extracts by alumina grinding, added deoxyribonuclease at 5γ/ml., and examined the newly made RNA using the sucrose-gradient centrifugation technique[14]. In some experiments ^{14}C-uracil was given to cells of a pyrimidine-requiring mutant (*B*148) which was briefly starved (30 min. at 25° C.) for uracil. No difference has been seen between the properties of RNA labelled in these two ways. Starved cells incorporate more radioactivity, and they were used in most of the experiments reported below.

Results. Radioactive uracil (or phosphorus-32) is incorporated in RNA within several seconds after addition of the isotope. The RNA labelled by 10–20 sec. pulses is stable at 4° C. in cell-free extracts where ribonuclease and polynucleotide phosphorylase are

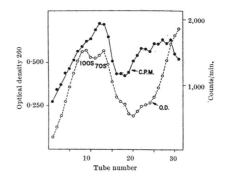

Fig. 7.   Sedimentation of *T*2-infected 10^{-2} Mg^{2+} extract. An extract in 10^{-2} *M* Mg^{2+} of cells infected with *T*2 and labelled with phosphorus-32 from the second to the fifth minutes after infection. Run on a sucrose gradient in 10^{-2} *M* Mg^{2+} for 2 hr. 45 min. at 25,000 r.p.m.   Drop collection and radioactivity measurements as for Fig. 1

not active. Traces (1γ/ml.) of ribonuclease degrade it under conditions where RNA in ribosomes is untouched. This suggests that it exists less protected than bound ribosomal RNA. Similarly, addition of phosphate permits the polynucleotide phosphorylase[15] in the cell extract to degrade preferentially pulse-labelled RNA. Our experiments thus as a matter of routine avoid the use of phosphate buffers.

Figs. 1 and 2 show how RNA labelled by a 20-sec. exposure of uninfected cells to ^{14}C-uracil sediments in a sucrose gradient. The cell-free extract contains 10^{-4} *M* magnesium ions in which 30*s* and 50*s* ribosomes predominate. The majority of the radioactivity is not associated with ribosomes but moves with a 14–16*s* peak. There is also RNA which moves more slowly, in addition to a faster forward moving at 70*s*. The slower sedimenting fraction shows up more clearly in the longer centrifugation shown in Fig. 2. Here a sharp 14–16*s* component is seen together with material sedimenting at 4–8*s*. Figs. 3 and 4 illustrate experiments with extracts from *T*2 infected cells exposed to phosphorus-32 from 2 to 5 min. after infection. They are similar, if not identical, to Figs. 1 and 2. Both have a major 14–16*s* component, a slower trailing fraction, and about 10 per cent of the material moving at 70*s*. The 70*s* component can be purified by three 1-hr. centrifugations at 40,000 r.p.m. with 10^{-4} *M* magnesium ions to concentrate the faster-moving ribosomes of Fig. 1. Fig. 5 shows the purified ribosomes consisting largely of 50*s* particles together with a now visible 70*s* component. The radioactivity, however, sediments at 70*s* ribosomes.

Still more label is attached to 70*s* particles when extracts are made in 10^{-2} *M* magnesium ions or when additional magnesium ions are added to 10^{-4} *M* extracts. Figs. 6 and 7 again illustrate the parallel appearance of normal and phage-infected extracts. About 30 per cent of label sediments with the 70*s* and 100*s* ribosomes, with the specific activity of 70*s* ribosomes generally greater than that of 100*s* ribosomes. When slightly lower concentrations of magnesium ions are used to give similar amounts of 30*s*, 50*s* and 70*s* ribosomes, label is specifically associated only with 70*s* particles and no label is in 50*s* ribosomes. The radioactivity sedimenting about

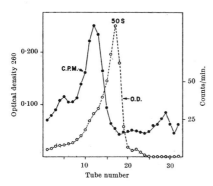

Fig. 5.   Pulse-labelled active 70*s* ribosomes in 10^{-4} Mg^{2+}. An extract of cells labelled with a 20-sec. pulse of ^{14}C-uracil, made in 10^{-4} *M* Mg^{2+}, was purified by three 1 hr. centrifugations at 40,000 r.p.m. in 10^{-4} *M* Mg^{2+}, 5×10^{-3} *M* tris (pH 7·4). The re-suspended pellet was run as for Fig. 1

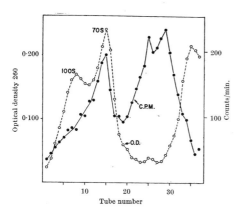

Fig. 6.   Sedimentation of pulse-labelled 10^{-4} Mg^{2+} extract in 10^{-2} *M* Mg^{2+}.   Magnesium was added to the 10^{-4} Mg^{2+} extract of Fig. 1 to bring it to 10^{-2} *M* Mg^{2+}. The sample was then run on a sucrose gradient in 10^{-2} *M* Mg^{2+}, 5×10^{-3} *M* tris, for 2 hr. 45 min. The measurements were made as described for Fig. 1

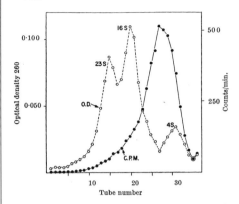

Fig. 8. Sedimentation of pulse-labelled RNA. An extract of cells labelled with a 20-sec. pulse of ^{14}C-uracil was treated with 0·5 per cent sodium lauryl sulphate ('Duponol') and then extracted three times with phenol. The RNA was then precipitated three times with alcohol and finally resuspended in 10^{-3} acetate buffer (pH 5·1). The RNA was run on a sucrose gradient, containing 10^{-3} acetate (pH 5·1) and M/10 sodium chloride, for 10 hr. at 25,000 r.p.m., 4° C. The drop collection and radioactivity measurements were made as described for Fig. 1

30s shows a very broad peak (20–40s) and it is probable that high concentrations of magnesium ions cause the 14–16s material either to aggregate or to assume a more compact shape.

Purified RNA, prepared by sodium lauryl sulphate ('Duponol') and phenol treatment of 20-sec. pulse extracts, sediments as shown in Fig. 8. Again the pattern is identical to that of labelled RNA from $T2$ infected cells (Fig. 9). Most newly synthesized RNA has a sedimentation constant about 8s; there is no appreciable synthesis of typical 16s or 23s ribosomal RNA. Since much new RNA in crude extracts moves at 14–16s, we considered the possibility that pulse-RNA is more sensitive than ribosomal RNA to degradation during the phenol extractions. Sodium lauryl sulphate (0·5 per cent) alone was therefore added to labelled crude extracts. This detergent treatment[12] both separates RNA from protein and completely inhibits action of the latent ribonuclease[16] release upon ribosome breakdown. When such

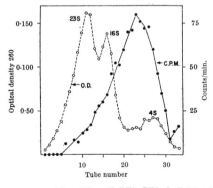

Fig. 9. Sedimentation of $T2$-specific RNA. RNA of cells infected with $T2$ and labelled with phosphorus-32 between the second and fifth minute, prepared and run as described for Fig. 8

treated extracts were run in sucrose gradients, the results were identical to those with phenol-prepared RNA.

The turnover of pulse-RNA is seen in chase experiments in which an excess of cold uracil is added after a 10-sec. ^{14}C-uracil pulse. After 15 min. at 37° C., all the label in crude extracts leaves the 14–16s component and is incorporated in the metabolically stable ribosomal and soluble RNA. In our kinetics experiments, the 16s RNA molecules always become labelled before appreciable labelling of 23s RNA molecules; likewise the 30s ribosomes become labelled before the 50s ribosomes. Since the base ratios of 16s and 23s chains are identical[17], it is likely that the 23s molecules form from two 16s chains.

Discussion. Our pulse experiments show that uninfected cells contain unstable RNA with sedimentation constants and attachment properties similar to those of $T2$-specific RNA. It is tempting to believe that these unstable molecules convey genetic information and are 'messenger' RNA. Complete homology with phage-specific RNA, however, will be demonstrated only if the base ratios of pulse-RNA are those of DNA. Unfortunately, in *E. coli*, the DNA base ratios do not differ greatly from ribosomal RNA, and as yet the base ratios of *E. coli* pulse-RNA are not precisely known. But we do have preliminary results (Hayes, D., and Gros, F., unpublished results) from *Staphylococcus aureus* which indicate an RNA component rapidly turning over and possessing DNA-like base ratios. Moreover, in yeast, there is also reported an unstable RNA resembling DNA in base composition[18]. We thus believe that our current measurements with *E. coli* will extend this fact and rule out the possibility that pulse-RNA is a precursor sub-unit from which ribosomal RNA is built up.

A messenger role for pulse-RNA fits nicely with its specific attachment to 70s ribosomes, the sites of protein synthesis[19]. Our experiments reveal two types of attachment. In one, the labelled RNA moves reversibly on or off 70s ribosomes depending on the concentration of magnesium ions. The second type of attachment binds pulse-RNA irreversibly to 'active' 70s ribosomes. These are 70s ribosomes which do not break apart with 10^{-4} M magnesium ions and which Tissières et al.[19] have shown to be the principal, if not sole, site of *in vitro* protein synthesis. They can be washed several times with 10^{-4} M magnesium ions without losing their ability to act in protein synthesis, and so they must have their genetic RNA firmly attached. It is reassuring that they can contain pulse-RNA. At least two stages, one reversible, the other not, thus exist in active 70s formation.

So far as we can tell, pulse-RNA, when associated with ribosomes, sediments at exactly 70s or 100s. Many experiments show that the label sediments neither faster nor slower than ordinary ribosomes. We find it hard to believe that the 14–16s RNA component which exists in 10^{-4} M magnesium ion extracts can combine with 70s or 100s ribosomes without altering their rate of sedimentation. Another possibility is that with 10^{-2} M magnesium ions, the 14–16s component assumes a more compact configuration similar to that of the RNA in a 30s particle. It could then associate with a free 50s ribosome to form a 70s ribosome which is transformed to an active 70s ribosome.

In conclusion, we state our findings: bacteria contain an RNA component turning over rapidly which is physically distinct from ribosomal or soluble (transfer) RNA. This fraction behaves, in its range of sedimentation constants and its attachment to ribosomes in high magnesium ion concentrations, exactly as does the phage-specific RNA made after T2 infection. Furthermore, it is associated with the active 70s ribosomes, the site of protein synthesis.

Our working hypothesis is that no fundamental difference exists between protein synthesis in phage-infected and uninfected bacteria. In both cases typical ribosomal RNA does not carry genetic information, but has another function, perhaps to provide a stable surface on which transfer RNA's can bring their specific amino-acids to the messenger RNA template.

These experiments were initiated when F. Gros was visiting the Biological Laboratories (May–August 1960). The pyrimidine-requiring strain B148 was kindly provided by Dr. Martin Lubin. The financial support of the National Science Foundation and the National Institutes of Health is gratefully appreciated.

[1] Cohen, S. S., *Bact. Rev.*, **13**, 1 (1949).

[2] Koch, G., and Hershey, A. D., *J. Mol. Biol.*, **1**, 260 (1959). Kornberg, A., Zimmerman, S. B., Kornberg, S. R., and Josse, J., *Proc. U.S. Nat. Acad. Sci.*, **45**, 772 (1959).

[3] Cohen, S. S., *J. Biol. Chem.*, **174**, 271 (1948).

[4] Hershey, A. D., Dixon, J., and Chase, M., *J. Gen. Physiol.*, **36**, 777 (1953).

[5] Volkin, E., and Astrachan, L., *Virology*, **2**, 149 (1956).

[6] Volkin, E., Astrachan, L., and Countryman, J. L., *Virology*, **6**, 545 (1958).

[7] Zamecnik, P. Z., *The Harvey Lectures* (1958–59), 256 (Academic Press, New York, 1960).

[8] Crick, F. H. C., *Brookhaven Symposia in Biology*, **12**, Structure and Function of Genetic Elements, 35 (1959).

[9] Nomura, M., Hall, B. D., and Spiegelman, S., *J. Mol. Biol.*, **2**, 306 (1960).

[10] Jacob, F., and Monod, J., *J. Mol. Biol.* (in the press).

[11] Tissières, A., Watson, J. D., Schlessinger, D., and Hollingworth, B. R., *J. Mol. Biol.*, **1**, 221 (1959).

[12] Kurland, C. G., *J. Mol. Biol.*, **2**, 83 (1960).

[13] Berg, P., and Ofengand, E. J., *Proc. U.S. Nat. Acad. Sci.*, **44**, 78 (1958). Tissières, A., *J. Mol. Biol.*, **1**, 365 (1959).

[14] McQuillen, K., Roberts, R. B., and Britten, R. J., *Proc. U.S. Nat. Acad. Sci.*, **45**, 1437 (1959).

[15] Grunberg-Manago, M., Ortiz, P. J., and Ochoa, S., *Science*, **122**, 907 (1955).

[16] Elson, D., *Biochim. Biophys. Acta*, **27**, 217 (1958). Spahr, P. F., and Hollingworth, B., *J. Biol. Chem.* (in the press).

[17] Spahr, P. F., and Tissières, A., *J. Mol. Biol.*, **1**, 237 (1959).

[18] Yčas, M., and Vincent, W. S., *Proc. U.S. Nat. Acad. Sci.*, **46**, 804 (1960).

[19] Tissières, A., Schlessinger, D., and Gros, Françoise, *Proc. U.S. Nat. Acad. Sci.*, **46**, 1450 (1960).

COLD SPRING HARBOR

Section IV photograph: *Jim Watson (1969). (Courtesy of James D. Watson Collection, CSHL Archives.)*

An Emotional Attachment

BUNGTOWN ROAD, THE MAIN THOROUGHFARE of Cold Spring Harbor Laboratory, runs from Route 25A through the Laboratory before making a sharp left-hand bend by Airslie, the Director's house. It is a road walked each year by thousands of meetings participants as they make their way to the wine and cheese parties, held on Airslie's lawn. Very few of the scientists can imagine, as they walk along the broad black-topped road with its tidy borders, mowed grass, and manicured trees, what a wild, unkempt, but still beautiful place it was when Jim Watson first came to Cold Spring Harbor in 1947. Twenty years later, the grounds were still "...disorderly and delightful with cover, vibrant with birds and animals. Bungtown Road...in early spring...[became] a narrow culvert whose flowered walls were a mass of head-high brambles and rhododendrons." It is not surprising, then, that Jim fell immediately under the spell of the beautiful location. He found equal satisfaction in the reductionist style of doing science proselytized by Max Delbrück, Salvador Luria, Al Hershey, and the Phage Group. However, he had to wait 20 years for an opportunity to join these esthetic satisfactions together by promoting beautiful science in an even more beautiful place.

In 1947, two separate institutions shared the southwest shore of Cold Spring Harbor: the Biological Laboratory and the Department of Genetics of the Carnegie Institution of Washington. The former had been founded in 1890 as a summer school for biology teachers while the latter was established in 1904 and was originally called the Station for Experimental Evolution. It was the Biological Laboratory that was host to the annual Symposia on Quantitative Biology and to the summer courses, of which the Phage Course was one. The two institutions were independent of each other, although for much of the period between 1904 and 1964, they had the same Directors. Even so, the two institutions were careful to remain financially independent of each other. The result was predictable; while the Department of Genetics flourished under the wing of the Carnegie Institution, the Biological Laboratory led a hand-to-mouth existence and for many years existed on the charity of a local group, the Long Island Biological Association.

At the time of Jim's first visit, Milislav Demerec, originally a *Drosophila* geneticist who had moved to bacterial genetics, was the Director of both institutions. On Demerec's retirement in 1960, separate Directors were appointed, but a crisis soon arose. Through the latter part of Demerec's tenure, the finances of the Biological Laboratory had worsened, and in 1962, there was a potential catastrophe when the

Carnegie Institution declared that it was withdrawing its support for the Department of Genetics, then housing Barbara McClintock and Al Hershey. On hearing that the proposed solution was to amalgamate the two institutions to create the Cold Spring Harbor Laboratory, the two Directors promptly decided to resign or retire. John Cairns stepped into the breach, and over the next five years, against great odds and at great personal cost, he brought the new Laboratory on to a more even keel. In 1966, he had done all he could and tendered his resignation.

Jim had visited Cold Spring Harbor almost every year since 1947 and joined the Board of Trustees in 1965. The full story of how he came to be Director is told in the first two contributions to this section, although these accounts differ markedly from each other. Certainly Jim's love of the place was a key factor, but so was his desire to start a major new project focusing on cancer research. The key to unlocking the cellular mechanisms underlying cancer was, he thought, to be found in tumor viruses. These viruses had very small numbers of genes—an important fact in the days before gene cloning and DNA sequencing—yet could convert normal cells into cancer cells. Joe Sambrook was recruited from Renato Dulbecco's laboratory and he formed the nucleus of the Tumor Virus Group working on viruses such as SV40, polyomavirus, and adenovirus, while other groups, for example, in cell biology, studied the cellular process of transformation. This was a very vigorous area of research that sparked the development of methods to map the patterns of gene expression of DNA tumor viruses, to construct genetic and physical maps of the viruses, and, in 1977, to the Nobel Prize-winning discovery of RNA splicing.

By then, Jim had already set his sights on other areas of research. By the late 1960s, he was seeking funds to promote a Cold Spring Harbor program in neuroscience, and in 1970, the Alfred P. Sloan Foundation made a substantial grant to support summer courses in neurobiology. Year-round neuroscience research began in 1978 with a project to develop monoclonal antibodies against neurons in the leech brain. However, the neurobiology group broke up in 1984, and there was a hiatus of some seven years until the Beckman Neuroscience Center opened and a new era of research began, focusing on the genetic underpinnings of learning and memory.

Jim expanded science at Cold Spring Harbor in other directions too. He enthusiastically adopted Ira Herskowitz's[1] suggestion that yeast genetics become part of the Laboratory's research portfolio. Herskowitz had phoned Jim to tell him of the exciting work being done on the cassette model for mating-type interconversion and urged him to make use of the empty space in Davenport (later Delbrück) laboratory. That the space was used for courses during the summer months was not a deterrent, and within a short while, the first mating-type gene was cloned. Delbrück laboratory was home also to a fledgling Plant Molecular Biology Group which, working on the molecular analysis of transposable elements in maize, had close intellectual ties to the yeast research. Jim pursued funding for plant research and was eventually successful in attracting a large grant from Pioneer Hi-Bred International to use recombinant DNA techniques to modify maize.

If Jim's intellectual acumen was rapidly expanding and diversifying science at the Laboratory, nowhere was his hand more physically evident than in the buildings and grounds. While some, including Barbara McClintock, bemoaned the loss of the overgrown shrubbery and the appearance of well-kept lawns that attracted Canadian geese, Jim argued that a physically attractive institute was essential to maintain the sanity of the scientists and to stimulate the generosity of potential benefactors. The former would enjoy the beauty while the latter would feel that here was a well-established, prosperous institute that would do a good job with their money. Liz, Jim's wife, played a key role in ensuring that the older buildings were restored authentically and elegantly and painted in the colors appropriate for their period. The campus changed even more drastically through an extraordinary building program that began with an addition to James laboratory and continued with Grace Auditorium (1986) and the Dolan Hall and Beckman Neuroscience buildings (1989).

Between 1968 and 1993, when Watson stepped down as Director and became President of the Laboratory, the annual income rose from $633,000 to $44,800,000, and by all measures, the Laboratory had become one of the world's great research institutions.

Cold Spring Harbor, 1958–1968: The Years between Demerec and Watson

John Cairns

Hollygrove House, Charlbury U.K.

Jim Watson and I did not overlap in our scientific careers, but we do share one experience, that of being Director of Cold Spring Harbor Laboratory, albeit under rather different circumstances. Here I shall give some background to Jim's more recent achievements—that is to say, write of what went on at Cold Spring Harbor in the ten years before he became Director. That was a tumultuous time in the Laboratory's history, a time when it was not clear what, if anything, the future held for the institution. I preceded Jim—my tenure as Director began in 1963 and ended in 1968—and it is a period in my life that I am not likely to forget. Mary Tudor claimed that when she died the word "Calais" would be found carved on her heart. When I had coronary bypass surgery in 1999, I was surprised that the surgeon did not see the words "Cold Spring Harbor" carved on mine.

TWO INSTITUTIONS, TWO DIFFERENT WORLDS

First, some early history. The Biological Laboratory had been established on the southwestern shore of Cold Spring Harbor in 1890, as an outpost of the Brooklyn Institute of Arts and Sciences, which each summer organized biology courses run by the first Director, Bashford Dean. But the nature of the Biological Laboratory changed with the appointment of Charles Davenport as Director in 1898. Following the rediscovery of Mendel's work in 1900, Davenport became an enthusiastic Mendelian and promoted Mendelian studies in the United States, and in 1904, he persuaded the Carnegie Institution of Washington[1] to establish a Station for the Experimental Study of Evolution at Cold Spring Harbor and to construct a handsome Italianate building to house it. So, Davenport became the first Director of what was later renamed the Department of Genetics of the Carnegie Institution of Washington, which continued to be funded quite independently of the Biological Laboratory.

In the absence of a regular income, the fortunes of the Biological Laboratory fluctuated precariously. A crisis arose in 1923 when the Brooklyn Institute of Arts and Sciences withdrew its support. The Village of Laurel Hollow, home to the Laboratory, is, however, one of the richest regions of the richest nation in the world, and the crisis was overcome when a group of wealthy neighbors came together to form the Long Island Biological Association (LIBA), which took over running the Biological Laboratory. These two institutions, run by LIBA and Carnegie, coexisted for some 50 years.

JOHN CAIRNS

After graduating with a medical degree from Oxford in 1946, John Cairns worked first as an intern and then for two years as a bacteriologist. His first experience of research was at the Walter and Eliza Hall Institute, Melbourne, where John spent two years working on influenza virus with financial support from the British Colonial Office. In return, he was obliged then to spend the next three years working in Entebbe, Uganda. In 1955, John returned to Australia to take up a research position at the newly founded John Curtin School of Medical Research, Canberra, where he worked on the genetics of influenza and vaccinia viruses.

While on sabbatical in Al Hershey's laboratory in 1960, John used autoradiography to determine the length of the T2 bacteriophage DNA molecule. Later, back in Australia he produced his famous autoradiographs of *E. coli* chromosomes complete with replicating forks. In 1974, he was elected to the Royal Society on the basis of this work. He left Australia in 1963 to become Director of Cold Spring Harbor Laboratory and continued working on DNA replication. For several reasons, John long felt that the Kornberg enzyme (DNA polymerase I) was unlikely to be the catalyst of DNA replication in *E. coli*. In late 1968, he and Paula de Lucia isolated a mutant (*polA*) that had less than 1% of the normal polymerase I activity and yet was viable. The name of the mutant—a play on de Lucia's first name—was suggested by Julian Gross, who taught the Bacterial Genetics course at Cold Spring Harbor. It was from the polA strain that pol III, the enzyme that is truly responsible for DNA replication was later isolated. For articles on Cairns' work, see *Illuminating Life: Selected Papers from Cold Spring Harbor 1903–1969* (ed. J.A. Witkowski, Cold Spring Harbor Laboratory Press [2002]).

For the ten years that John and his wife Elfie lived at Cold Spring Harbor, Airslie, the Director's house, was open to a constant stream of visitors. To stay there was to enter a world of English good manners, sharp wit, scientific gossip, music, and much laughter. There was always plenty to talk about. John was a keen observer of the scientific scene, a funny and mordant raconteur, a knowledgeable but indifferent pianist, and a fund of information and anecdote about music—especially opera. No person who visited Airslie could be bored or ill-at-ease.

In 1973, John moved from Cold Spring Harbor to the Mill Hill Laboratories of the Imperial Cancer Research Fund and from there, in 1980, to the School of Public Health, Harvard. He retired in 1991 and returned with Elfie to live near Oxford.

The combination in many ways provided the best of all possible worlds. The Carnegie Institution of Washington was an ideal employer. For, although its salaries were not conspicuously generous, all research expenses were paid and its staff was therefore spared the endless round of grant applications that torments most scientists today. So Carnegie provided the scientific environment, while LIBA provided the environs—life on a country estate that offered the staff virtually rent-free housing within a short walk of the laboratories, plus the buildings in which to run summer meetings and courses. On top of this, the local community, through its high taxes, provided the staff (who did not have to pay those taxes) with free education for their children in the excellent local school system.

To outsiders, it must have seemed inconceivable that such an admirable institution could ever go into a decline. But in the late 1950s, it suffered a fall from grace and ended up nearly being lost forever. The story is the common one of a conflict between the interests of individuals and the interest of the institution where they work. What was unusual here was the fact that no one seemed willing to step in and halt the decline. Although it had been trying to put its affairs in order, the Laboratory was by 1963 effectively bankrupt. Barbara McClintock[2] told me that in the spring of 1963 auditors from the National Institutes of Health paid a site visit that ended with the threat of possible prison sentences and the certain withdrawal of all federal support if the finances were not quickly put in order.

THE HISTORY OF MY OWN INVOLVEMENT

Before going on to explain how this parlous state of affairs came about, I should explain how I came to be Director. In 1960, I had come from Australia to Cold Spring Harbor, with my wife Elfie and our three children, to spend a sabbatical year working with Al Hershey,[3] who together with Barbara McClintock and Berwind Kaufmann[4] constituted the Carnegie's Department of Genetics. Like others before us, we found that in those days the North Shore of Long Island and its schools were a kind of earthly paradise. Each year, the families who lived at the Laboratory could enjoy both the heady delights of the summer program when the site is awhirl with visitors and the magic of the long winter recess when silence returns and the animals in the woods come out of hiding.

Like most visitors, we made no attempt to understand the labyrinthine details of the organization. I did not even think to ask why "Cold Spring Harbor" used to have

Barbara McClintock and John Cairns, 1989. (Courtesy CSHL Archives.)

one director but now, in 1960, had two; happily, it was none of my business. Later, when it did become my business, I had to keep reminding myself that, to judge from my own example, temporary visitors have little sympathy for the plight of the director. Indeed, before the site became affluent and embarked on the modern style of fiercely driven research, most visitors tended to rejoice in all the makeshift measures and manifest decay, perhaps as proof of their own otherworldliness.

In 1962, I returned from Australia for the Symposium on Animal Viruses, and it was then that Paul Margolin (a bacterial geneticist and one of LIBA's scientists) asked, out-of-the-blue, whether I would like to be the next director. Until that moment, I did not even know that Cold Spring Harbor needed a new director. Anyway, being unsure about my own feelings on the matter, I checked with the three other staff members—Edward Umbarger (another bacterial geneticist), Al Hershey, and Barbara McClintock. Two were in favor. The exception was Hershey who, typically, said that he did not care who became director and added that no one in their right mind would want the job. Shortly afterward, Jim Watson and Max Delbrück each pressed me to take it on. So it did not come as a total surprise when a short letter came to me in Canberra in October 1962, from Francis Ryan (a bacterial geneticist, working at Columbia University), asking if I would be willing to be the director. Apparently, a new organization, with Edward Tatum (Rockefeller Institute) as chairman, was being set up to manage as one unit the two existing Laboratories. Two weeks later, Ryan sent me an outline of what was planned.

> A number of Universities including the Rockefeller, Princeton, and Pennsylvania have agreed to form a corporation to manage the laboratories at Cold Spring Harbor as a single unit... . The Board of Trustees of the Long Island Biological Association has agreed to deed their buildings and properties to the new organization; the Carnegie Institute has agreed to lease their facilities and to assign Al Hershey and Barbara McClintock, who are remaining on the Carnegie staff, to work under the auspices of the new organization....The National Science Foundation has made a site visit to the laboratories and indicated that large-scale long-term support in the form of a research contract will be forthcoming upon the appointment of a suitable director.

Three months later, in January 1963, a letter came from Tatum officially offering me the Directorship. I accepted. Shortly afterward, Tatum wrote again to say that they would try to find some way of covering at least the cost of our airfares, and he added: "With the thought of adding to your general background information on C.S.H., I am sending you separately all the material I have available, including copies of the documents relating to the new C.S.H.L.Q.B." Regrettably—and, as I realized later, characteristically—Tatum failed to send the promised documents and failed to tell us that our moving expenses would be covered. Thinking that we would have to pay, we arranged to sell our house in Canberra and auction most of its contents.

I was not able to take the obvious precaution of paying a short visit to Cold Spring Harbor, because I had applied for a Resident Alien Visa and such a visa does not allow a visit to the United States until you formally enter as a future resident. Instead, I had to rely on the apparent enthusiasm of the existing staff and the urgings of Delbrück and Watson. That all was not quite well in the earthly paradise we had enjoyed in 1960 was evident from a letter from Ryan. He wrote to tell me that there were financial difficulties, including "an annual deficit of several tens of thousands of dollars a year," but he said that a Ways and Means Committee had been formed, consisting of Arthur Pardee (Princeton University), Harry Eagle (Albert Einstein College of Medicine), and Philip Handler (Duke University), and he cheerfully added that "it is their task to find private money to meet this deficit."

We arrived in Cold Spring Harbor late in the evening of Saturday, June 1, a few days before the XXVIII Symposium on the "Synthesis and Structure of Macromolecules" was to begin. Having no inkling of what was in store for us, I was shocked to find that I had walked into a situation of scarcely credible horror. LIBA's members had not yet approved the transfer of its land and buildings to the new organization, The Laboratory of Quantitative Biology (LQB). I discovered that the laboratory was in debt to the tune of about 50% of its annual budget and had only enough cash in hand to pay its maintenance staff for the next two weeks. Furthermore, the buildings were in a desperate state of disrepair, and the main sewage system was happily discharging onto the lawn in front of one of the laboratories. Finally, I was staggered to find that the Trustees were so ignorant of the financial predicament of the Laboratory that Barbara McClintock had had to tell Tatum, just before we arrived, that he would have to get a grant if I were to be paid the $15,000 salary I had been promised.

How had a world-famous institution that had played a key role in the development of the new worlds of molecular biology and molecular genetics come to such a pretty pass? One afternoon, during a gap in the middle of the Symposium, we had the first full meeting of the new Board of Trustees and I slowly began to understand what had been going on. To my surprise, most members of the Board were people who, as far as I knew, had had little connection with the Laboratory. It almost seemed as if LQB had been designed to fail and that I was to be the scapegoat. That vague impression (which would become much stronger in the next few weeks) was reinforced when the Board made it clear that they did not want to hear from me until their annual meeting at the end of the year. As it turned out, this was the only occasion on which the Chairman of the Board would visit the site during my five years as director.

THE HISTORY OF THE PRECEDING FIVE YEARS

For many years, the balance between the two organizations—LIBA and Carnegie's Department of Genetics—had been adroitly managed by Milislav Demerec[5] who was Director of both. However, this happy arrangement could not continue beyond 1960 when he passed Carnegie's mandatory age for retirement. Unfortunately, LIBA could not provide him with laboratory space. He therefore conceived of the following plan. He would get federal support so that LIBA could build a large extension of its main laboratory (James laboratory), and at the same time he would recruit a new staff member who, after a year as Assistant Director, could take over Directorship of the "BiLab," as it was called. That would free him of all administrative responsibilities and allow him to retire into a laboratory where he could hope to stay on almost indefinitely. However, his application to the National Science Foundation for money to build the year-round laboratory was turned down on the grounds that he was hugely underestimating the cost. He therefore increased the estimate (from $90,000 to $140,000) and applied to the National Institutes of Health. They offered to meet half the costs but, knowing their man, stipulated that construction should not begin until a source had been found for the other half. These negotiations were going on just before Demerec's compulsory retirement from Carnegie, so there was no time to waste. He therefore disregarded the injunction by the National Institutes of Health and started construction on the assumption that the additional $70,000 would turn up, sooner or later.

Demerec also went ahead with the other half of the plan. In 1959, Arthur Chovnick, a 34-year-old *Drosophila* geneticist from the University of Connecticut, was appointed to be Assistant Director. And in the following year, Demerec announced to the startled Board of LIBA that he had officially promoted Chovnick to the position of Director of the BiLab and had given him the job of supervising the construction of the new laboratory and finding the money to pay for it. I have often wondered what I would have done if I had been in Chovnick's shoes, being appointed without the approval of my Board of Trustees and stuck with a program of someone else's design that was going to bankrupt my institution. I think I might even have tried to accelerate the bankruptcy in the hope that LIBA's activities would be taken over by a federal agency, for this was the post-Sputnik era when President Kennedy was increasing the federal funds for science by a factor of ten.

I do not know what Chovnick's underlying plan was, but I do know some of the things he accomplished during the next two years. He completed the extension of James laboratory and renovated two of LIBA's buildings (Nichols and Hooper). He inaugurated a new three-week summer course on Animal Cells and Viruses, and a summer program for undergraduates. He managed to repel the challenge by the town of Oyster Bay to dredge the harbor and build a marina on the sandspit.[6] He extricated the BiLab from a questionable but lucrative project to test the effects of LSD on volunteers from the surrounding community, financed covertly by the CIA. Most importantly, he changed the way the BiLab published its Symposia by bringing in a new editor, Leonora Frisch, and by subcontracting the printing and binding and handling the marketing and sales in-house. This resulted in a lasting improvement in the quality of the Symposium volumes and changed a moderate annual expense into a sizeable net profit. It was this profit that was to save the life of LQB during my first winter as Director.

Unfortunately, these achievements were overshadowed by the cost of the James extension which was roughly $100,000 more than the sum provided by the grant from the National Institutes of Health. So LIBA suddenly found itself in debt and unable to meet its commitments. In 1962, after just two years as Director, Chovnick returned to his life in research at the University of Connecticut, and Edward Umbarger took over as Acting Director. With Chovnick's departure, the year-round activity of the BiLab was reduced to two groups, under Margolin and Umbarger, working on the genetics and biochemistry of amino acid synthesis in *Salmonella typhimurium*.

Berwind Kaufmann had become Acting Director of the Carnegie's Department of Genetics but he was due to retire. A search was undertaken for a new Director, but it soon became apparent that nobody wanted the job—to be director of just one of the two institutions at Cold Spring Harbor was a hopeless proposition. Carnegie, rebuffed, considered closing down its half of the Cold Spring Harbor enterprise and moving Hershey and McClintock elsewhere. If that had come to pass, I do not think that "Cold Spring Harbor" would have survived. But Hershey and McClintock insisted that they wanted to stay where they were and that encouraged LIBA's Board of Trustees to look for some new authority that could preside over both halves.

One obvious thought was that CSH should be managed by the consortium of universities, Associated Universities, Inc., which runs various federal scientific institutions.[7] According to Barbara McClintock, Tatum and Ryan arranged a meeting with representatives of the consortium but effectively scuppered any possible deal by insisting that the Association would have to put at least $2 million into a rescue plan. Not surprisingly, the offer was turned down, and this then left Tatum and Ryan free to set about assembling an entirely separate group of academic institutions. Eventually, eight institutions agreed to join, most of which (in particular, The Rockefeller University) were not members of Associated Universities. At Carnegie's insistence, each of the eight institutions promised to contribute $25,000 to get the LQB going, but by the time I arrived, they had decided to renege on this promise.

THE SUMMER OF 1963

The annual summer Symposia[8] are world famous, and the 1963 Symposium, which started a few days after we arrived, proved to be the saving of the LQB. Go into any science library in the world and you will see that the 1963 volume—*The Synthesis and Structure of Informational Macromolecules*—is more tattered and torn than any of the others. In its day it was nothing less than an account of everything known about molecular biology, and 1963 was exactly the right moment for a résumé. Since there were not yet any textbooks on molecular biology, the Symposium volume became a best-seller. Together with a long-overdue doubling in price (from $4 to $8), it was to give LQB a profit of about $50,000 during the following winter. Without this, we could not have survived.

Many of the people at the 1963 Symposium asked me about my plans for the Laboratory—as if I had any plans at that stage. Complete strangers would accost me and insist on telling me what they thought was the solution to LQB's problems. (Like Dustin Hoffman's drunken advisor in "The Graduate," who thought the secret of success lay in plastics, their solution was the one word money—money that would be raised, not by them or me of course, but by some all-powerful third party.) What I hoped was that one of them would clear up the mystery surrounding the creation of LQB. Several people suggested that the plan might be to let LQB collapse so that it could be then taken over by The Rockefeller University. One of these was the electron microscopist, Robley Williams, and he volunteered to leave the Symposium early so that he could talk to his friend Detlev Bronk, the President of the Rockefeller Institute. A few days later, Williams called me from Berkeley and told me that Bronk had simply said "The time is not ripe," an answer that hardly relieved my sense of insecurity. Like Macbeth, I felt I was a bear tied to a stake and must stay the course.

Using my family as unpaid labor, I set about trying to make LQB look slightly less rundown in the cheapest way possible, which was to mow the lawns; by the end of my Directorship, there was no stretch of grass that I had not had to mow at some time or other. Interestingly, all the nonscientific staff happily joined in our efforts to save money. I remember the cook for the summer dining hall rejoicing in the fact that he had fobbed off on the summer visitors a bouillabaisse made out of free fish heads obtained in a local market. Thanks to such measures, we were able to struggle through from one week to the next. However, six weeks into my time as Director, I felt I had to send for help. Francis Ryan appeared to be the most active member of the Board of Trustees, and so I telephoned him at Columbia University and asked if he would be willing pay us a site visit, after which he and I could discuss the situation and decide what should be done.

The Death of Francis Ryan

So it came to pass, on the morning of July 6, that Francis and I started our tour of LQB, inspecting the rotting leaking buildings and stepping through the open sewage on the lawn in front of Jones laboratory. I remember it was a beautiful summer day, permeated with that gentle aroma of decaying woodwork and fermenting harbor mud which, for so many of the world's molecular biologists, still summons up the remembrance of those early days of molecular biology. Francis was horrified by what he saw. Apparently no one on the Board of Trustees (except possibly the two representatives of LIBA) had any idea of the seriousness of our predicament. The moment he got back to Manhattan, he said, he would arrange an urgent meeting with Tatum to discuss what should be done. It seemed that I had picked the right Trustee to be my emissary, and for the first time, I felt a flicker of hope. Two days later, the hope was extinguished. Francis Ryan had had a fatal heart attack. He was only 47. Whether he had got in touch with Tatum I never found out.

The Summer

Mainly for my own benefit, I prepared a rough estimate of the repairs that would be needed to secure all the buildings from further decay and sent my summary to Tatum and Harry Eagle (Ryan's replacement as Vice Chairman of the Board). It did not elicit much of a response. Eagle telephoned simply to say that something must be done, and then quickly hung up before I could make any suggestions. Tatum did not respond.

Later that summer, I visited Caryl Haskins, President of the Carnegie Institution of Washington. I told him that there was a real risk that LQB would collapse within a year and (somewhat disingenuously) that I was concerned about the consequences for Hershey and McClintock. He replied, with great cheerfulness, that I should not worry on that score, Carnegie would support them wherever they wanted to go. It was my impression at the time that Haskins believed Demerec had regularly used Carnegie money to supplement LIBA programs and that proof of this would be the rapid collapse of LQB now that this cross-flow had been blocked off. In fact, for many years, the flow had been in the other direction—LIBA had provided Carnegie staff with virtually rent-free housing but could not afford to maintain the buildings. I returned from Washington knowing that I should expect no help from Carnegie.

Toward the end of summer of 1963, I visited the National Institutes of Health and the National Science Foundation to explore the possibilities for some form of help from the Federal Government. In due course, the promised support from the National Science Foundation came through. But, perhaps as the result of some signal from on high, the National Institutes of Health proposal was vetoed at the last minute even though it had successfully gone through all the official steps for its approval.

THE WINTER OF 1963–1964

The Board of Trustees held its first annual meeting in November 1963 at The Rockefeller University. I described our desperate financial state and our efforts to get help from various federal agencies. To my surprise, there was little reaction. Although I said that it seemed quite likely that LQB would actually run out of money during the winter, the Board decided that it "would not be practical" for the Participating Institutions to give LQB even the interest earned on the money they had supposedly set aside for LQB to use in an emergency. The only suggestion the Board had for raising money was to ask the local community and the wider scientific community for contributions. Since the local community, in the form of LIBA, had not been able to keep the BiLab alive and most members of the scientific community were (in those days) not rich, the suggestion was ludicrous. Moreover, the scientific members of the Board did not appear to be willing to set an example by contributing anything themselves.

The budget we had prepared for the annual meeting included the cost of various absolutely essential repairs, but it was promptly rejected by the Board because it predicted a significant deficit. They demanded that I produce a balanced budget and in the next few weeks, I gave them a revised version that simply omitted all those repairs which we knew we were going to have to carry out, and that allowed Harry Eagle, the Chairman of the Ways and Means Committee, to congratulate me on having solved all our problems.

It is clear from the minutes of the Board meetings during 1963 and 1964 that the Trustees avoided making any decisions that might make them accountable should LQB collapse—that was to be my responsibility, not theirs. My life would have been much simpler if, with the death of Ryan, I had abandoned all hope of getting help from my Board of Trustees. Certainly, my attempts over the next four years to involve the scientific members of the Board of Trustees more closely in LQB's finances annoyed them simply because they could not, or would not, respond.

THE STAFFING AND SCIENTIFIC DEVELOPMENT OF LQB

However much our fruitless interchanges with the Board of Trustees occupied my mind at night, during the day I still had to run the affairs of LQB—reporting the previous summer's activities to the supporting federal agencies, editing all the Symposium manuscripts (at the rate of five a night during the summer months), inviting the speakers for the next Symposium, serving as Principal Investigator for the many grants that would support the next summer program, acting as Laboratory photographer, and so on. But in the summer of 1963 the staffing of LQB was as precarious as its finances. I could not call on McClintock and Hershey for help because they were supported by Carnegie money and were therefore to be left in peace. The scientific staff inherited from the BiLab consisted of Umbarger and Margolin, but shortly after we arrived, Umbarger left for a year at Leicester University in England and then went on to Purdue, while Margolin throughout made it clear that he did not want to be involved in any administrative duties.

Plainly, we needed at least one other scientist on the staff who was prepared to help with the summer programs and would be willing to act occasionally as a kind of handyman around the site Although there were no doubt many versatile scientists in the United States, I did not know them. So I thought back to Australia (where everyone knows how to do everything) and recruited the molecular biologist, Cedric Davern.[9] He arrived in February 1964 and immediately took on the responsibility for the summer teaching programs. As soon as he and his wife were settled in, he became officially the Assistant Director. As Jim Watson will acknowledge, every laboratory should contain at least one Australian.

Up to a point, the summer activities at Cold Spring Harbor were more or less self-sustaining. The summer program was an established activity, assured of support from the federal agencies and therefore not a source of anxiety. The subject for each Symposium, and who should be invited, was decided with the help of outside advisers. The three summer courses, on bacteriophage, bacterial genetics, and mammalian cells, and the National Science Foundation's program for undergraduates, were well-established and could look after themselves, as could the Nature Study Program for children from the local community. For me, perhaps the strangest part of these activities was the duty of arranging the guest lists for the dinner parties organized by the community for the speakers at the Symposium.[10] One hostess complained that the fuss I made about it suggested I thought that some of the hosts might end up marrying their guests and then hold me responsible (the implication being that no one, in their right mind, would want to marry a scientist).

The scale of the summer activities, however, was steadily increasing. In 1961, Chovnick had installed closed circuit TV for the overflow from the lecture hall during the Symposium, and we now found that we had to keep the TV going for all of the meetings. In the next five years, we started two new ventures that were the precursors of much that was to follow later. One was a new course, initiated in 1965 by Delbrück, on the sensory receptors of the bread mold *Phycomyces*. He had always hoped that a detailed analysis of the mechanisms of biology would reveal new laws of physics, but so far molecular biology had failed to upset physics in any way. He was now looking to a simple system that could be thought of as a precursor of the nervous system of higher organisms. The Phage course, which he had started at Cold Spring Harbor 20 years earlier, had trained many of the world's leading molecular biologists, and he hoped to repeat the process and build up a school of molecular neurophysiologists.

Our other new venture also began in 1965. At Jim Watson's suggestion, Gunther Stent and I edited a book of essays, entitled *Phage and the Origins of Molecular Biology* (Cairns et al. 1966) in time for Max Delbrück's 60th birthday in 1966. Previously, Cold Spring Harbor's publishing business had consisted of the annual Symposium volume plus the production of a few broadsheets such as the *Drosophila* Newsletter. With this new book, the Laboratory embarked on a new career that, in subsequent years, was to turn it into a significant publishing house.

There was an increasing need for the LQB to have either some form of endowment or a massive institutional grant for the long-term stability of the institution, but I came to realize that neither I nor the existing Board of Trustees was likely to achieve this kind of support. I decided that I should not try to keep any of the staff who wished to leave, or try to recruit replacements, and soon Margolin, Speyer, and Davern left for more stable positions in other institutions.

Early in 1967, Jim Watson suggested that Ray Gesteland would be the right person to fill the gap left by Davern's departure. Ray had been a graduate student of Jim's at Harvard and was just finishing a postdoctoral year in Geneva and, like Davern, he is the kind of person who can turn his hand to anything. He and his family arrived in August, and he quickly took over much of the administrative burden of the summer program as well as organizing his own laboratory. His coming made my life much easier, and in due course, he was to play a crucial role during the first years of Jim's Directorship.

FINANCIAL RECOVERY

During the five years that I was Director, there had been a gradual restoration of LQB's finances. By the summer of 1964, we had managed to pay off all of LQB's debts, and later we had built up a reasonable cash reserve so that federal auditors were no longer breathing down our necks. This turnabout in the affairs of the Laboratory was achieved largely from within, by a combination of an increased precision in the handling of federal grants, an increase in our charges for room and board, and a substantial rise in book sales. Toward the end of 1964, we were able to start a fund drive that allowed a steady increase of about 20% per annum in our budget for maintenance. By the summer of 1965, it must have seemed to outsiders that the worst was over. LQB's gross annual budget was steadily rising; between 1963 and 1968, it increased about 16% a year, from $290,000 to $620,000 (astonishingly, under Jim Watson, this rate of increase has continued for a third of a century). By 1968, we had carried out perhaps half of the needed repairs to the physical plant (which included a temporary solution to the sewage problem), and had moved our cash-in-hand from debts of about $60,000 to a reserve of some $150,000. Therefore, we had been successful in coping with the short-term problems.

But while the LQB's finances were now in good order, we had no endowment and therefore no way of guaranteeing the salary of any scientific staff. I had friendly discussions with several foundations but was finally told by a representative of the Sloan Foundation that we could never expect to get anything from any foundation until our Trustees were seen to be doing something. As the Trustees had done next to nothing up to that point, I had no hope that they were likely to do anything in the future. So in 1966 I wrote to the Board and asked them to start looking for my replacement.

THE NEXT PERIOD OF TRANSITION: 1966–1968

Almost from the start of my time as Director, Jim Watson had been a regular visitor to our house, and I had gotten him elected as an independent member of the Board of Trustees. He, at least, was deeply concerned with the fate of LQB, and it was he who drafted my letter of resignation. Jim also prepared a document outlining what he himself thought should happen to LQB, for he made no secret of the fact that he had long dreamed of being Director at Cold Spring Harbor Laboratory.

Following the announcement of my wish to resign, the Board created a Search Committee to look for a new director, but for some reason, it never met. The Trustees had already made it quite clear that they believed the difficulties at LQB were attributable to mismanagement on my part and, before that, on Chovnick's part. So they sent in a professional administrator to investigate our management practices. However, the man they chose, Jim Brainerd, concluded that the Trustees and their parent institutions were not closely enough involved with LQB's affairs. Each Participating Institution should be asked to pay up or at least reaffirm its willingness to pay the $25,000 initially pledged, and the Board should meet more often and should hold its meetings in Cold Spring Harbor rather than at The Rockefeller University.

By the summer of 1967, the Board had been further enlarged by the addition, among others, of Bentley Glass (the State University of New York, SUNY). This was quickly followed by a crucial suggestion which, I believe, was the real turning point in the history of LQB. Glass proposed that SUNY should join the list of Participating Institutions. Furthermore, he announced that SUNY would straightaway produce half of the $25,000 which, at the time of the takeover, Carnegie had asked each institution to contribute, and that the remaining half would come the following year. This offer effectively forced the other Participating Institutions to cough up or quit. Over the next two years, therefore, LQB was going to acquire an additional $200,000. Even more importantly, one other crucial change occurred. Walter Page (the representative of LIBA and the kindest of men) succeeded in persuading Tatum that he could not stay on indefinitely as Chairman of the Board. As a result, Norton Zinder replaced Tatum as the representative for The Rockefeller University, and Glass became the new chairman.

This rejuvenated Board now had before it the document, prepared by Watson in the winter of 1966, that outlined the history of the laboratories at Cold Spring Harbor, their contributions to science, and his thoughts about the future of LQB. The purpose of the outline was to serve as the basis for a drive for endowment support from several foundations. Impressed by this buoyant vision of the future, the Board suggested that Watson be the next Director and he accepted. To be sure, the foundations of the Laboratory were much stronger than they had been five years previously, but the continuing survival of the Laboratory was still not a foregone conclusion. Jim therefore was prudent in keeping his Harvard connection as a safety line should things go wrong.

I have tried to describe how Cold Spring Harbor survived a period of great danger and emerge with a reasonable cash reserve, an involved Board of Trustees, and one winner of a Nobel Prize as Director, another on the staff, and yet another in the offing. Whether that happy outcome could have been achieved by a less tortuous sequence of events no one will ever know; history does not allow the testing of alternative pathways.

Writing this article has taken me back to battles I would rather forget. But my account would be misleading if I did not point out that during my five years as Director—forcibly separated from a much-loved life in science and apparently cast by some in the role of fall guy—there was another side to each day: a huge circle of friends and a happy thriving family living in a beautiful environment enriched by the welcoming hospitality of the local community. If I had to single out one event to represent the very best aspect of our time at Cold Spring Harbor, it would be the party held in Airslie House in 1969 on the occasion of Al Hershey's Nobel Prize. During the afternoon, we had endless phone calls from neighbors asking if they would be allowed to join in the celebrations if they brought over several bottles of champagne. As a result, that evening, we had a steady stream of visitors over many hours, and one of the Page sons strained his wrist from opening bottles in our kitchen. I remember thinking that this was the ideal kind of relationship between a scientific institution and its immediate neighborhood—a party done on the cheap but overflowing with goodwill.

REFERENCES

Cairns J., Stent G.S., and Watson J.D., eds. 1966. *Phage and the origins of molecular biology*. Cold Spring Harbor Laboratory, Cold Spring Harbor, New York.

Cold Spring Harbor Symposia on Quantitative Biology. 1963. Volume 28: Synthesis and structure of macromolecules. Cold Spring Harbor Laboratory, Cold Spring Harbor, New York.

Life with Jim

Norton D. Zinder

The Rockefeller University

SCIENCE

It has never been clear to me if I met Jim during graduate school days in the Midwest. The Midwest was the birthplace of bacterial genetics in the late 1940s: There was Josh Lederberg at Wisconsin, Salvador Luria at Indiana and later at Illinois, Sol Spiegelman at Illinois, Cyrus Levinthal at Michigan, and Aaron Novick and Leo Szilard at Chicago. It wasn't until later—after the field had achieved fame—that it was taken over by the large coastal colleges.[1] Jim was with Salvador Luria in Indiana and I was Josh Lederberg's first graduate student. We had meetings at least twice a year, when the latest and freshest new discoveries were always brought to the table. In those early days, there were many. Jim and I should have met then, but I have no memory of it.

I really met Jim at the 1953 Cold Spring Harbor Symposium on "Viruses." I had hoped to be one of the stars of that Symposium. It was the first time I was going to describe bacterial transduction in detail, with definitive evidence that it was the result of a bacteriophage carrying genes from one bacterial cell to another (Zinder 1953).[2] Of course, we all know what happened in 1953. A few weeks before the Symposium, Delbrück sent reprints of the Watson-Crick *Nature* papers (Watson and Crick 1953a,b) on the structure of DNA to the participants. The meeting recognized these findings as extraordinary, as indeed they really were. Jim and I did chat about this and also about the work he had done in bacterial genetics. Frankly, my understanding of structural matters was very limited, but I did recognize the implications of the structure for most genetic problems. Although my paper was well received, I was disappointed by being overshadowed by the Watson-Crick model of DNA.

Jim went off to Caltech and I went to work at The Rockefeller University. I believe we saw each other at the Brookhaven Symposium on "Mutations" in June, 1955. Also, he might have dropped in during the summer at Cold Spring Harbor where I spent a month house (cat) sitting for Al Hershey and lecturing in the Bacterial Genetics course. Conversations with Jim at that time were often very strange; right in the middle of a conversation he'd suddenly think of something else and just walk off (something that still disconcerts people).

At Caltech, Jim and Alex Rich tried to study the structure of RNA using X-ray diffraction, hoping that the structure would be as revealing of the function of RNA as the double helix had been of the function of DNA. Given the different types of RNAs and their lack of significant stable structure, Jim and Alex didn't get very far. Jim was then offered a job at Harvard and set up his first laboratory. It was the era of the messenger

NORTON D. ZINDER

Norton Zinder's long and complex career covers both research and the use and abuse of science in the larger world. His career got off to a flying start when, with his doctoral advisor Josh Lederberg, he discovered the phenomenon of transduction whereby a bacteriophage carries a small amount of DNA from one bacterium to another. This amounts to genetic engineering in nature, and when the recombinant DNA period began, phage were quickly adopted as vectors for carrying more substantive amounts of DNA into bacterial cells. Another fundamental discovery by Zinder's laboratory was the isolation of a bacteriophage using RNA rather than DNA as its genetic material. Zinder immediately saw how to exploit the parallels between the RNA coding for f2 phage proteins and the messenger RNA coding for genes in DNA. This led to a disagreement with Fraenkel-Conrat who claimed to have made a similar observation with tobacco mosiac virus (see Zinder, *Trends Biochem. Sci. 22*: 318–320 [1997]).

Zinder has been indefatigable in his service to biology and science in the public arena. He was Chairman of the Review Committee of the Special Virus Program of the National Cancer Institute. The report was devastating, commenting that only 50% of the program was supportable at some level. Zinder was also a key figure in the recombinant DNA debates, particularly the Asilomar meeting where he, Sydney Brenner, Paul Berg, and Maxine Singer hammered out the first draft of the report. On a more serious matter that still affects us, Zinder served on the National Academy of Sciences Board of Army Science & Technology (BAST) and for nine years was involved with the disposal of the Army's stockpiles of chemical weapons. In addition, Zinder played a key role in the scientific politics that surrounded the Human Genome Project from its inception to its grand finale.

RNA hypothesis and Jim, together with a constellation of stars—François Gros, Howard Hiatt, Alfred Tissières, and Wally Gilbert—did a study of the RNA produced following T-even phage infection (Gros et al. 1961).

I was working at that time on the newly discovered RNA-containing bacteriophage. After Tim Loeb, a graduate student, isolated the male-specific *coli* phages, we purified one and it turned out to contain RNA, the first such phage.[3] The potential scientific convergence of an RNA-containing phage and messenger RNA was obvious. So we studied this small phage, both as a phage and as a potential messenger. During the early 1960s, we showed that we could make the phage coat protein in extracts of bacteria to which phage RNA was added. This was at the same time that Marshall Nirenberg and Gobind Khorana were adding random polynucleotides to the similar cell-free extracts and finding that specific amino acids were incorporated into polypeptides.[4] The genetic code was being resolved. We also had a set of nonsense or chain-terminating mutants that caused premature termination of protein synthesis. These would grow only on certain suppressor strains. We were collaborating with Alan Garen, a bacterial geneticist at Yale, who had isolated the suppressor strains, to find the cellular component that caused suppression.

Then, suddenly and without warning, the Watson laboratory became our major competitor. A paper appeared in *Science* on suppression, submitted by two of Jim's graduate students, Mario Capecchi and Gary Gussin, and without Jim's name, showing that a tRNA serine was responsible for suppression (Capecchi and Gussin 1965). We had found the same result in my New York laboratory, but it could not be repeated at Yale. It was some time before we realized that H.W. Garen's laboratory was next door to Fred Richard's laboratory; they were crystallizing RNase, which was probably floating in the air[5] (Wycoff et al. 1967).

During this period, Watson had an active laboratory of his own for one of the few times in his career. He had a number of excellent students. However, Jim rarely put his name on the papers from the laboratory, although he was totally involved in all of them. Fritz Lipmann,[6] who followed in great detail the discoveries in protein synthesis, once even asked me who these unknown people were. Our two sets of students became friendly enemies and blamed Jim and me for giving away our secrets. I had the feeling we were competing with a ghost and Jim was also somewhat upset about the competition. Keith Porter,[7] an old friend who left Rockefeller to become head of Biology at Harvard, told me that Jim was annoyed that our labs came up with the same results at the same time. I wasn't all that happy either.

The next contest was on the universal start signal for protein biosynthesis. Jim with his infinite sources of information knew that Fred Sanger[8] had isolated a tRNA methionine upon which the methionine was *n*-formylated, so they studied its incorporation into the amino terminus of proteins being synthesized in *E. coli*. We were using the coat protein of bacteriophage for the same purpose. When we compared the amino-terminal peptide of the phage's coat protein with the same peptide from coat protein synthesized in vitro, we found that they differed—the protein made in vitro had an extra formyl methionine group at its terminus. Shortly thereafter, Jim strode into the laboratory and asked me how does protein synthesis begin? When I quickly answered it does so with *N*-formyl methionine, his face dropped and puckered as it is wont to do when surprised. We quickly arranged to share the data and published the results back to back in the *Proceedings of the National Academy of Sciences* (Adams and Capecchi 1966; Webster et al. 1966). Members of both laboratories were disappointed in not being the sole discovers of the universal start signal for all of protein biosynthesis.

With the solution of the whole genetic code by 1966, as well as the determination of most of the special properties of the RNA-containing bacteriophage, the scientific competition between our laboratories ceased. My further interactions with Jim were over matters of scientific politics.

COLD SPRING HARBOR LABORATORY

Milislav Demerec had been at Cold Spring Harbor since the 1920s and directed the two laboratories on the site—the Carnegie Institution of Washington's Department of Genetics and the Long Island Biological Association's Biological Laboratory. In 1960, he retired as Director, but the search for a new Director ran into some difficulties. There were several problems. The first was what to do about the two Laboratories? The Department of Genetics was rich but stingy, and the Biological Laboratory was poor, and the buildings of the latter were in such sad shape that $500,000 in capital expenditures were needed. Another difficulty was that Carnegie did not allow its scientists to apply for outside grants. In addition, Carnegie felt that LIBA, being so poor, would fall into the Carnegie's hands for nothing if it provided no help. I gave them a list of what I believed was absolutely needed to put things right; they turned them down and I turned down the job. Carnegie then withdrew from all responsibility for Cold Spring Harbor, except for supporting Al Hershey and Barbara McClintock.

Instead, a number of universities undertook to contribute funds to create a new institution, the Cold Spring Harbor Laboratory of Quantitative Biology. The institution was an amalgam of the Biological Laboratory and a much reduced Department of Genetics made up of only Al Hershey and Barbara McClintock. Francis Ryan, a *Neurospora* geneticist from Columbia University, was especially active and his early death was a serious setback. The financial condition of the Laboratory was dire, particularly because of the accumulated neglect of the physical plant. John Cairns came as Director in 1963; however, he felt that he had no support from the Board of Trustees, especially Ed Tatum of the Rockefeller Institute, who was chairman of the Board.

I joined the Board in 1967, shortly after Jim had become Harvard's representative (1965). Jim was a supporter of Cairns since he also liked to be associated with rich people. In 1966, Cairns told the Board that he was going to resign, but the Board had already decided that John had to go. At about the same time, Jim prepared a document describing what he thought should be done, and I said to Jim if the job was so easy, why didn't he take it over. To everyone's surprise, he said he would think it over. The next day he accepted the post saying that at first he would spend half the time at Cold Spring Harbor and half the time at Harvard. When the 14 universities created the Cold Spring Harbor Laboratory, they all promised several thousand dollars in emergency money to back up the financial status of the Laboratory. When Jim took over, he called an "emergency" meeting in order to get some funds to do essential repairs so that some of the laboratories could be used. I went to see Detlev Bronk,[9] President of Rockefeller, about the money, and in typical Bronk fashion, he said we would give the whole $5000 because if we didn't no one would. Most of the other institutions were shamed into giving something, usually lesser amounts. Still, Jim had over $20,000 to do with what he needed. Thus began my first term of six years on the Board with Jim. Then money came in from a number of sources—LIBA, the National Institutes of Health, and the National Science Foundation—and Jim started as fast as he could to rebuild the Laboratory. From 1968 until 1976, Jim divided his time between the Laboratory and Harvard. In 1976, he moved down permanently. One of his key moves was to turn the Laboratory to the study of cancer viruses, and from early on, he collected a first-rate scientific staff.

My first round on the Board was from 1967 to 1975, and I had two special roles. One was as Chair of the committee to oversee the promotion of the members of the Laboratory. The other was to try to defuse Jim's resignations—when upset by the Board, he would resign and it was my job to bring him back. Once he walked up and down Bungtown Road during the yearly Symposium and told everyone he met that he had just resigned. He then went down to Airslie, the Director's house, where my wife and his wife were having tea, and told them he was resigning. Marilyn told Liz not to worry, I wouldn't let Jim resign. I arrived a few minutes later, assured Jim all would be well and took him back to the meeting. What was this all about? Across the harbor was a small marina. A local builder wanted to buy it and turn it into a large commercial marina which would destroy the view from the Laboratory. Jim wanted us to buy the marina for some $400,000 which we didn't have. But the Board was persuaded by Jim's resignation and found a way to beg, borrow, and steal the money. Jim got his way and, as often happened, all turned out well. The view was preserved, and over the years, the marina even made the Laboratory money by way of rent. During the next three years, somehow all the buildings were rebuilt (and in good taste with the energetic help of Liz Watson [Watson 1991]) and the Laboratory started to prosper.

My second stint as Trustee was as secretary to the corporation, and I had to certify signatures on checks over a certain amount. Another one of my steady jobs was seeing that nothing happened when Jim decided to blame Rich Roberts for everything and fire him.[10] Rich would call me, and I would call Jim, who usually had calmed down by this time, and within the day Rich was rehired. It used to be said that you hadn't arrived at CSHL until Jim had fired you at least twice. I understand that things are somewhat calmer these days. All in all, the new CSHL Trustees were devoted to the Laboratory and forgave Jim his many similar foibles. First-class science was done, new programs began, scientists flooded to the place, and the Symposia and courses were better than ever. Jim is the only manager I know who succeeded by pure petulance.

RECOMBINANT DNA AND ASILOMAR

The decade of the 1970s gave molecular biology two of its most important techniques: recombinant DNA and DNA sequencing. In addition, it was a decade of very serious political turmoil in many areas, not least in the interactions between science and the public. Jim, needless to say, played a major role in these debates.

At first, there was the concern that many people who were not properly trained in microbiology were starting to handle tumor viruses, a rapidly expanding area of cancer research and one that Jim introduced to CSHL. Under the auspices of the NSF program in molecular biology of the cell, a meeting on biological safety was held at Asilomar, California, in January 1973. At the meeting, Jim was in his negative mood, having just warned the Congress on the dangers of human cloning. Experts at the meeting described how to handle potentially dangerous microorganisms with various forms of physical containment, but the broader question of just how dangerous the tumor viruses in fact were was not answered satisfactorily. Jim in a typical tirade went after Jack Strominger who was working with herpesvirus not far from Jim's Harvard laboratory, warning him to stop or be sued. All calmed down later. The meeting was written up in a book called *Biohazards in Biological Research*, which could be used as the primer for work with infectious organisms (Hellman et al. 1973).

In the mid 1960s, Jim had become interested in using tumor viruses to investigate the molecular mechanisms of cancer in animal cells and even included a chapter on cancer in the first edition of *Molecular Biology of the Gene* (Watson 1965). Later, Jim turned Cold Spring Harbor into a Cancer Center studying the small DNA-containing tumor viruses, and the Laboratory received a five-year, $1.6 million grant, a sign that things were looking up. With the war on cancer set up by Nixon, the National Cancer Board and the Director of the National Cancer Institute became independent of the NIH. Jim was appointed to the Cancer Board. So convinced were the authorities that a cancer virus for humans would soon be found that they built a special containment building on the NIH campus. There was also the special virus cancer program which was budgeted at about 10% of the NCI's budget. It was a contractor program, completely in the control of a few in-house people who distributed large chunks of money to a few favored scientists. As might be expected, it created considerable antipathy in the scientific community. Jim convinced the Cancer Board to set up a review of this program and recommended an excellent committee, with me as chairman. For most of 1973 and part of 1974, the committee wandered from laboratory to laboratory reviewing their programs. It really was a gravy train. Our report suggested a more equitable and open mechanism to distribute the funds to a much larger group of scientists (Culliton 1974). Jim was satisfied with the report, as was the Cancer Board. The old boys program and contract research faded away over the next few years.

Service on the National Cancer board and the 1973 Asilomar meeting were just preludes to what would happen during the rest of the 1970s—the Recombinant DNA war was about to begin. At the Nucleic Acid Gordon Conference in 1973, the participants, primed by concerns raised by Robert Pollack, then a scientist at CSHL, wrote a public letter to the National Academy of Sciences warning of the potential dangers of gene splicing. The Academy formed a committee to look into the matter, with Paul Berg as chairman, and members including Dan Nathans, Richard Roblin, Sherman Weissman, David Baltimore, Jim, and myself. At a meeting in David Baltimore's office at MIT, we decided to write a letter to the scientific community asking them to defer doing recombinant DNA experiments with oncogenic viruses and drug-resistant bacteria and to take extra care with the other experiments (Berg et al. 1974). We also asked for an international meeting to discuss the details of recombinant DNA. This became Asilomar 2. During the meeting, Jim was in his well-known, meeting-laconic mood: He participated while reading the newspaper. He did not object to what was done nor to the redrafting of the letter by Roblin.

The letter appeared in *Science* and *Nature* in July of 1974, and for a brief period, until the February 1975 Asilomar conference, things seemed quiet. Then about 150 scientists from throughout the world came together at Asilomar to discuss their work and how they assessed the potential hazards of different experiments with different organisms (Rogers 1977; Watson and Tooze 1981). A new mechanism for containment—biological containment—was described. The microorganisms used as hosts for recombinant DNA molecules would be modified with special growth requirements so that they could not live outside of the laboratory. This illustrates the principle of being too clever by half. Many people concluded that if we scientists were so worried that we thought special containment was needed, then the situation must be extremely dangerous.

By the time of the conference, Jim had changed his mind about what to do, and when Jim changes his mind, he changes his mind. He was not shy about letting everyone know where he now stood. Josh Lederberg also felt as Jim did, given that there was no evidence for any special dangers beyond those accepted for dangerous naturally occurring microbial pathogens; setting guidelines was impossible; and, most seriously, the guidelines would be codified by the authorities. In contrast, there were others who spoke for stopping all such work immediately, extending the voluntary moratorium called for in the *Science* letter. However, the majority position was that some regulation was needed, and, if this were the case, it would be worth doing it ourselves by attempting to classify the experiments with a sliding level of containment.

On the last night, the members of the organizing committee wrote a summary of what they thought had been the gist of the discussion regarding the containment required for the different experiments with different organisms. When the document appeared, the audience insisted on voting on every sentence, going over the points again that the committee had thought settled. Nevertheless, few changes were made—the committee had found the majority position.

The rest of 1975 was quiet, but in June of 1976, the NIH promulgated official guidelines that were based on the Asilomar document, and things started to collapse. In Cambridge, Massachusetts, hearings were held by Mayor Vellucci of Cambridge on Harvard's plan to build a P3 containment facility. With the aid of some powerful faculty who were part of the Science for the People group,[11] a moratorium was instituted in Cambridge. A science-fiction story by Liebe Cavalieri of the Sloan-Kettering Cancer Institute had appeared in 1976 in the *New York Times* magazine section, describing fulminating infectious cancer due to recombinant DNA. The New York State Attorney General's office asked me who was doing those experiments in New York. The public was becoming unnecessarily alarmed and the politicians were not slow in getting in on the act. In the spring of 1977, a restrictive regulatory bill was introduced into the Senate by Senator Kennedy's Labor Committee, and another in the House of Representatives by Congressman Roger's Commerce Committee. For the next year, many of us, including Jim, would lobby and write to our congressmen to try to soften the rigidity of these regulatory bills. However, we made little progress early on.

Jim did what he does best, giving speeches and writing essays that appeared in CSHL Annual reports and in journals. One, published in the *Washington Post*, was directed to Robert Redford, the movie star and environmentalist (Watson 1978). It asked why he was working to stop our work when in the past, all the molecular biologists tended to be on his side of the environmental movement. Jim concluded that, unfortunately for the truth, such movements had to make all the news bad for maximum effect.

Jim's message to the rest of us was that as long as we persisted in saying that we must protect the public from potential dangers by having specious guidelines for DNA experiments, we were going to be in trouble. But he went on to realize that the real enemies at that time were on the left wing of the scientific community and the environmental lobby ("kooks, shits and incompetents" in one of Jim's memorable phrases) and that if we surrendered, our solid middle would be overwhelmed by the media and the politicians.

We didn't. The academic community was unanimous in opposing New York State's very restrictive Recombinant DNA Bill, as were a few powerful friends of The Rockefeller University, and it was vetoed by Governor Carey. In the U.S. Senate, Senator Nelson of Wisconsin was joined by Senator Moynihan of New York in introducing a substitute amendment for the Kennedy bill. When Kennedy saw that the amendment would win, he withdrew his bill. The House bill was stymied in committee by heavy lobbying and the opposition of the chairman of the full committee, Haley Staggers, a Congressman from West Virginia. Happily, all potentially restrictive legislation came to an end in the period from 1977 to 1978. By late 1978, the guidelines began to be relaxed, a process that has been going on ever since.

COLD SPRING HARBOR LABORATORY FAUX INTERREGNUM

I left the Cold Spring Harbor Board in 1986, which meant that I no longer went out there once a month and now saw Jim only periodically. In 1987, Jim started thinking about releasing some of his duties and finding a new Director for the Laboratory. He asked me to chair a committee to seek a new Director. Also on the committee were

Jim Watson and Norton Zinder at the 1974 Symposium. (Courtesy CSHL Archives.)

Matthew Scharf (Albert Einstein College of Medicine), Jim Darnell (The Rockefeller University), Eric Kandel (Columbia University), and Robert Cummings (a local Trustee and Treasurer of the Laboratory). I called them and we discussed the problem as to how we were to convince any candidate that Jim would eventually really give up total control. At a meeting in my office, we wrote the job descriptions for the President and the Scientific Director. It was fairly easy to distribute the functions of hiring and firing, salaries, and space. Money raising and general Laboratory public relations were to remain with Jim. I then wrote the critical sentence "on a day-to-day basis, the staff were to report to the Director." I then faxed the document to Jim and within the hour received a call from him telling me that he wasn't ready yet and the committee was put on hold for six months. The staff not reporting to him was too much for him to take. I called my colleagues telling them of the success of our committee which would probably never meet again—it didn't.

THE HUMAN GENOME PROJECT

During the mid to late 1980s, the molecular biology community was once again in turmoil. This was provoked by the proposal by several senior scientists that the human genome had to be sequenced (Cook-Deegan 1994). This proposal was even more audacious because the lead federal bureaucracy was not the NIH but the Department of Energy (DOE). With the end of the Cold War, the DOE was looking for some large project to occupy its National Laboratories and decided to promote carrying out this project. Discussions as to whether to proceed roiled the scientific community—NIH vs. DOE, Big Science vs. Little Science, Centers vs. investigator grants, and, above all, the costs. The relevant scientists were split and took different sides on the different issues. Jim was to play a large role in the Program and in doing so revealed all the many aspects, good and bad, of his character. In 1988, Jim Wyngaarden asked Jim to become Director of the National Genome Center, and then that summer, he asked me to Chair the Advisory Committee to the NIH project. At the end of August, there was a general meeting in Spain and almost everybody who was anybody went.

For me, it was an opportunity to discuss the membership of my committee. It seems no one could be appointed until all agreed to serve. There were two holdouts and one disqualification. The two I called when I returned agreed to serve. Mary Lou Pardue, a cytogenetist at MIT couldn't serve as she was a member of the DOE committee. When I saw Nancy Wexler at the meeting, I asked if she would join and she accepted. The meeting also provided me with an opportunity to meet with European genome scientists. In late September, there was a meeting in Switzerland where the Human Genome Organization (HUGO) was formed. It was a strange organization that had the great goal of trying to keep the Genome Project international. Its major problem was that it had no parent organization to nurture it.

In the fall of 1988, the NIH Genome Advisory Committee was named. It was a very powerful committee; its members included Joe Goldstein, Bruce Alberts, David Botstein, Lee Hood, Phil Sharp, Cecil Pickett, Jaime Carbonell, Nancy Wexler, Victor McKusick, and Mark Pearson. On January 4, 1989, the first meeting was held at the NIH. We set up a series of working groups to plan our way forward. These had the advantage that, unlike the main committee, they were not subject to the Federal Advisory Committee rules, which meant that the meetings could be closed. The NIH and the DOE signed a memorandum of agreement, which required that the Advisory Committees should have two-day meetings with a joint meeting on the second day.

At the June meeting, we had reports from all the working groups and planned a retreat at the Banbury Center, Cold Spring Harbor, in August. We were required to meet so that we could formulate a five-year plan to be submitted to Congress. Twenty scientists from the NIH and ten from the DOE were chosen to come. The retreat turned out to be a total war between those who wanted to study genetic diseases and those who wanted to do the infrastructure of the genome. Jim was strongly in favor of the latter. The planned format of the meeting was that I would Chair and lead the discussion of a list of subjects placed on the blackboard. However, we had to fight the fundamental issue before proceeding to details and that took all of the first evening. Those on the medical side were Uta Francke, Francis Collins, Ray White, and Tom Caskey, and those who favored the infrastructure side were Maynard Olson, David Botstein, Shirley Tilghman, and Eric Lander. A hot and heavy discussion ensued. It ran on until Jim signaled me to call a vote. The silent majority, the DOE people, came into play and the vote for infrastructure study won handily.

We then discussed the kind of centers—comprehensive (core and research support) or administrative (core support only). Phil Sharp had chaired the working group that recommended administrative centers only. However, the discussion and the ultimate vote supported setting up a half-dozen comprehensive centers that were to be used as technical outreach in their region. It fell to me to call Phil after the meeting and listen to his fortunately only mild upset.

A key feature was the extension of the *Human* Genome Project to cover sequencing the genomes of *other* organisms that were important genetic systems or that would contribute to the interpretation of the human genome sequence. The model organisms to be studied were *E. coli, C. elegans, D. melanogaster*, yeast, and the mouse. Targets for genetic and physical mapping were set for the next five years. Before sequencing of the human genome began in earnest in about five years, a review would be made of the costs and the efficiency of the technology available. Significant money was to be put into technology development. Finally, the Ethical, Legal, and Social Issues (ELSI) program was established by Nancy Wexler, with a strong committee to oversee any social problems that might develop in the program. Jim and I left the meeting quite content, not realizing what was lying around the corner.

The scientific community was in large measure either neutral or against proceeding with this program, in contrast to the recombinant DNA issue where a substantial proportion of the community was in favor of proceeding. The arguments against the genome projects were that they would consume all the money available, they would distort the doing of science, and there should be no big science in biology. Letters arguing against going forward with the Human Genome Project began to appear in scientific journals and newspapers and were sent to Congress and the NIH. The entire medical microbiology department at Harvard Medical School (35 people) signed a letter to the journal *Science*, written by its Chair Bernie Davis, attacking the Human Genome Project as unnecessary since it was already being done, albeit piecemeal (Davis et al. 1990). The letter claimed the project would take 20% of the NIH budget, thus depleting the pool of money for investigator-initiated research. Three weeks later, an almost invisible erratum appeared changing the number to 2%. Davis wrote to me that he had miscalculated but that it really shouldn't matter. Yet it did matter, as Phil Leder (Harvard Medical School) sent a note to *Cell* saying that we should curb our appetite for money and not ask for $1.5 billion, which was indeed 20% of the NIH budget (Leder 1990). Many individuals believed that this was true, and when their grants were turned down, it was blamed on so much money going to the Genome Project.

Jim and I gave lectures all over the country and were regularly booed, especially by biochemists. I went to the American Society of Microbiology meeting to ask the microbiologists which microbes they wanted to have sequenced first, but most of the discussion was about the petition some wanted to send to Congress to stop the Genome Project. By the time of the June 1990 meeting of the Advisory Committee, the atmosphere was very unhealthy. Jim, who had been negotiating with Congress to obtain our first real budget for the next year, was worried that we would not get it. He threatened to resign at the meeting. Such behavior in the privacy of a CSHL Board meeting can be mitigated but when done at the Advisory Committee meeting with the press present, disaster looms. That year, Jim was sitting next to Cecil Pickett, a burly member of our committee, and right behind them was the door to the room. The plan was that if Jim started to resign, I'd create a diversion by pushing over the pitchers of water that were in front of me and Cecil would escort Jim from the room. But all went well and Congress appropriated the money and was happy with our five-year plan. We approved the sequencing of the *C. elegans* genome through an international cooperation between Bob Waterston (Washington University, St Louis) and John Sulston (Wellcome Trust, Cambridge) with a $300,000 grant to get started. This was to be a proof of principle.

It was at this point that Craig Venter came on the scene. He worked at the NIH and had been testing the new Applied BioSystems Inc. (ABI) fluorescence sequencer. He sent in a grant for $5 million to sequence the so-called expressed sequence tags (ESTs). These are sequences of mRNA which when converted into DNA can readily be sequenced. Having little money and being accused by many of giving it to friends, Jim could not seemingly favor an NIH investigator with that large amount of NIH money. Jim also was pushing for the sequencing of the *complete* genome; ESTs would represent only a small portion of the human sequence. This decision started a feud that would have consquences in the coming years. With other funding, Craig produced several hundred EST sequences. At this point, the NIH decided to patent them even though they were small sequences with unknown functions. Although this decision had major ramifications for the Genome Project, Jim was not consulted or informed. He exploded and thus exacerbated his difficulties with Craig but more importantly with Bernadine Healy, Director of the NIH.

Some time later, we found out that a meeting had taken place at Mount Pleasant, Massachussetts, between Fred Burke, a biotechnology entrepreneur, the scientists Leroy Hood (Caltech) and Craig Venter and other investors such as David Rockefeller. Its purpose was to form a company to take over the Human Genome Project. It didn't get very far. Jim was incensed that, as he saw it, Burke was setting out to sabotage the Project by trying to recruit two of the Genome Project's stars, Robert Waterston and John Sulston. Burke complained to Bernadine Healy that Jim, a federal employee, was interfering in the legitimate operation of an American business. She reopened the issue of Jim's conflict of interest in being Director of both the NIH Genome Center and CSHL, an issue that previous Director Jim Wyngaarden had chosen, prudently, to ignore. One early Saturday morning, I received a phone call from a rather upset Jim; there was an article in *The New York Times* implying that he had many conflicts of interest. Although Healy's own counsel advised that there was no conflict of interest, Jim now felt that he had no choice but to resign and did so. For a year and a half, the project was without a Director until Francis Collins took over. Jim remained in touch with the Genome Project, but I watched from the sidelines. Collins ultimately decided to go ahead and sequence the human genome but progress was very slow.

In December 1997, I received from Jim a fax with the recently distributed planned budget for the Genome Project. He had sent it because he was angry with the planned rate of sequencing and the small amount of money to be appropriated for it. Jim and I were to meet in January at The Rockefeller University, following Eric Lander's Harvey Lecture. We met with Eric in the bar after the lecture to discuss what was going on. What was most disturbing was that by the planned closing date, 2005, only half of the sequence would have been done and that only once. We moved then to put pressure to increase the funding, but failed completely.

That May, I went off to China for a visit. I returned at the end of the month to find several dozen telephone messages from scientists and reporters. One common theme to them all was that I had to calm Jim down as he was giving the Genome Project a bad name. During my absence, Craig Venter had announced that he was setting up a company, Celera, that with the aid of a new sequencing machine designed by Mike Hunkapillar of ABI, would finish the sequence within three years. That he chose to announce this at the Cold Spring Harbor sequencing meeting, the annual gathering of the genome world, added insult to injury. Jim blew his stack over the thought that the Genome Project was going to be taken away from the publicly funded projects, and, as Jim continued to blame Craig for the fact that he had had to resign from the NIH, an explosion was pretty much guaranteed. To obtain the full details, I called Nicholas Wade, a reporter at *The New York Times* to send me his articles. After reading them, I called Jim twice and for an hour each I listened to his famous harangues. I tried to get him to answer the following questions: Would the new procedures work, and, if so, wasn't that what we wanted since Francis Collins was dawdling? Soon Jim and I were at cross purposes which lasted over a year. Whenever we met we just didn't discuss sequencing.

When talking with Craig and Rich Roberts, who chaired Celera's Scientific Advisory Committee, I became convinced that the human genome sequence would be done by this new company. I flew out with them to ABI in California and saw the bread board of the soon-to-be AB3700. When finished, it would produce up to half a million bases of raw sequence a day. At this point, I joined Celera's Scientific Advisory Board as a way to try to get the sequence done in my lifetime.

Now the government consortium decided to speed up all of its endeavors, and the Wellcome Trust in the United Kingdom greatly increased its support of John Sulston's sequencing efforts at the Sanger Centre in Cambridge. New targets were set and the fast machines were bought. It became apparent that even if Craig never put out a line of sequence, the increased activity on the part of what became known as the public sequencing groups might get the job done in about three years.

By the spring of 2000, Celera had five times coverage of human sequence and the public Human Genome Project also had a crude draft of the sequence. With much effort by many people, the two groups agreed to a joint announcement of their success. This was done with much hoopla by President Clinton at the White House and Prime Minister Blair at 10 Downing Street in early June. During the next autumn, the scientific papers were written, but the forced collegiality of the June announcement fell apart over a dispute about data release. In the end, Celera's paper went to *Science* and the public Project's paper went to *Nature*. On February 12, 2001, there was a press conference at the Washington Hilton. Jim and I attended, too happy to be too angry with each other, and peace reigned as Jim took the Watsons and Zinders out to dinner.

EPILOG

James Dewey Watson has made at least three singular contributions to our world: The first was the structure of DNA which changed our thinking about biology for all time; the second was turning Cold Spring Harbor Laboratory into a world-class institution both scientifically and aesthetically; and the third was the creation and building of the Human Genome Project, which, while it would have occurred sometime, his special abilities and talents ensured that it got going sooner rather than later.

I have known Jim for 50 years and hope to have shown in this essay some of his many different faces. Most notorious of these is what Jim calls his calculated madness when he spits vitriol on persons or things. Jim is both right and wrong in the use of the word "calculated"; I don't believe that he actively thinks of what he does during these explosions, but I do believe he has an unconscious mechanism that has calculated that this is how to achieve what he believes is necessary. Jim is notable for saying what he thinks without constraint. We've stayed friends all these years, for I do the same with him. Our relationship has been one of the cornerstones and joys of my life.

REFERENCES

Adams J.M. and Capecchi M.R. 1966. N-Formylmethionyl-sRNA as the initiator of protein synthesis. *Proc. Natl. Acad. Sci.* **55:** 147–155.

Berg P., Baltimore D., Boyer H.W., Cohen S.N., Davis R.W., Hogness D.S., Nathans D., Roblin R., Watson J.D., Weissman S., and Zinder N.D. 1974. Letter: Potential biohazards of recombinant DNA molecules. *Science* **185:** 303.

Capecchi M.R. and Gussin G.N. 1965. Suppression in vitro: Identification of a serine-sRNA as a "nonsense" suppressor. *Science* **149:** 417–422.

Committee on Recombinant DNA Molecules. 1974. Potential biohazards of recombinant DNA molecules. *Proc. Natl. Acad. Sci.* **71:** 2593–2594.

Cook-Deegan R. 1994. *The gene wars: Science, politics and the human genome.* W.W. Norton, New York.

Culliton B.J. 1974. Virus Cancer Program: Review panel stands by criticism. *Science* **184:** 143–145.

Davis B.D. and Colleagues. 1990. Letter: The human genome and other initiatives. *Science* **249:** 342–343.

Gros F., Hiatt H., Gilbert W., Kurland C.G., Risebrough R.W., and Watson J.D. 1961. Unstable ribonucleic acid revealed by pulse labelling of *Escherichia coli. Nature* **190:** 581–584.

Hellman A., Oxman M.N., and Pollack R., eds. 1973. *Biohazards in biological research; Proceedings of a conference held at the Asilomar Conference Center, Pacific Grove California. January 22–24, 1973.* Cold Spring Harbor Laboratory, Cold Spring Harbor, New York.

Leder P. 1990. Can the human genome project be saved from its critics...and itself? *Cell* **63:** 1–3.

Rogers M. 1977. *Biohazard.* Alfred A. Knopf, New York.

Watson E.L. 1991. *Houses for science.* Cold Spring Harbor Laboratory Press, Cold Spring Harbor, New York.

Watson J.D. 1965. *Molecular biology of the gene.* W.A. Benjamin, New York.

Watson J.D. 1978. The Nobelist versus the Film Star. *The Washington Post* (Sunday, May 14). Reprinted, with permission, in Watson 2001.

Watson J.D. 2001. *A Passion for DNA: Genes, genomes, and society.* Cold Spring Harbor Laboratory Press, Cold Spring Harbor, New York.

Watson J.D. and Crick F.H.C. 1953a. A structure for deoxyribose nucleic acid. *Nature* **171:** 737–738.

Watson J.D. and Crick F.H.C. 1953b. Genetical implications of the structure of deoxyribonucleic acid. *Nature* **171:** 964–967.

Watson J.D. and Tooze J. 1981. *The DNA Story: A documentary history of gene cloning.* W.H. Freeman, San Francisco.

Webster R.E., Engelhardt D.L., and Zinder N.D. 1966. In vitro protein synthesis: Chain initiation. *Proc. Natl. Acad. Sci.* **55:** 155–161.

Wyckoff H.W., Hardman K.D., Allewell N.M., Inagami T., Johnson L.N., and Richards F.M. 1967. The structure of ribonuclease-S at 3.5 Å resolution. *J. Biol. Chem.* **242:** 3984–3988.

Zinder N.D. 1953. Infective heredity in bacteria. *Cold Spring Harbor Symp. Quant. Biol.* **18:** 261–269.

CSHL in the Sixties: A View from the Trenches

Ann Skalka

Fox Chase Cancer Center

I had two separate opportunities to become familiar with the laboratories at Cold Spring Harbor before my arrival as a postdoctoral fellow in Hershey's group in 1964. First, in the late 1950s when I was an undergraduate, we came hunting for specimens on biology field trips and, second, as a student in the 1962 CSHL Phage course then taught by Frank Stahl and George Streisinger.[1] The first visit captivated me with the peaceful loveliness of the setting, and the second with the elegance and intellectual satisfaction of the world of phage research. It was therefore with eager anticipation that in 1964, I joined Al Hershey's group in the Carnegie Institution Genetics Research Unit[2] as an American Cancer Society Postdoctoral Fellow. Cold Spring Harbor was still the "Mecca" of the phage world and I felt privileged, indeed, to become a disciple of one of its founding fathers. Perhaps it was this frame of mind that made the modest infrastructure, the substandard housing, and the isolated existence of us year-round inhabitants seem rather insignificant; we lived in what seemed to me a condition of "genteel poverty." And, of course, I was very young.

No one who visits the beautiful and well-cared for buildings and grounds of CSHL these days can imagine its needy condition in the 1960s. My husband and I arrived in the late summer and were put up "temporarily" (with all of our belongings) in a "unit" in Page, a series of unheated, austere motel-like rooms in the location now occupied by Dolan Hall and the adjacent Beckman Building. Our stay in Page was extended into late October, as we waited for our apartment in Hooper House to become available.[3] We were cramped and freezing, and I was sufficiently miserable to complain to our Director, John Cairns, as we met one morning along Bungtown Road. His response was not a promise to speed things along, as I had hoped, but to cheerily offer us some more blankets. Perhaps, I thought, John doesn't feel the cold; he routinely walked around the grounds with shoes on his feet but no socks and only a jacket and long scarf wrapped around his neck. This was one year after he had become Director of the new Cold Spring Harbor Laboratory, formed by consolidating the Biological Laboratory and the Carnegie Institution's Department of Genetics. I was to learn only later what a burden this was.

Those of us supported by Carnegie were shielded from any monetary or other concerns. We had excellent facilities in the Demerec laboratory, and most congenial colleagues, with Hershey's group on the top floor, Joe Speyer, Cairns, and Rick Davern below, and Barbara McClintock on the bottom floor. As we were all immersed in stud-

ANNA MARIE SKALKA

Like most other people who have worked at Cold Spring Harbor Laboratory, Ann Skalka's five years there shaped much of her subsequent scientific career. Arriving in 1964, with an undergraduate degree in biology from Adelphi University and a Ph.D. in microbiology from New York University Medical School, Ann left in late 1969 with a deep knowledge of, and an enduring passion for, bacteriophage λ. For the next eight years, while she worked at the Roche Institute for Molecular Biology in Nutley, Ann worked exclusively on λ. By 1977, when she published her last paper on the virus, all of the principles and most of the details of its molecular biology and genetics had been worked out, and Ann, with many backward glances, turned her attention to retroviruses—a topic that had first interested her as a student in Cold Spring Harbor courses on Animal Viruses and Cells. During the past 25 years, Ann has become internationally known for her work on the virally coded integrase, which catalyzes the integration of retroviral DNA into the host cell's genome.

Since 1987, Ann has been Senior Vice President for Basic Science and Director of the Institute for Cancer Research at the Fox Chase Cancer Center in Philadelphia. Among her honors, she was elected a Fellow of the American Academy of Arts and Sciences in 1994, a Fellow of the American Association for the Advancement of Science in 1996, and a member of the Board of Governors of the American Academy of Microbiology in 1999. The New York Association of Women in Science honored her with its Outstanding Woman Scientist Award in 1985.

ies of one or another aspect of DNA biology, there were many lively discussions about our own research and the latest that had been published in *Nature,* or *Science,* or the *Journal of Molecular Biology.* Members of Hershey's group were investigating various aspects of phage genome structure and function. Eddie Goldberg, Gisela Mosig, Ruth Ehring, and Rudolph Werner were studying T4, and bacteriophage λ was the focus for Phyllis Bear, Betty Burghi, Hershey, and me. We were joined later by Merv Smith, who worked with T5, and Schraga Mackover and Hideo Yamagishi who became attached to the λ team.

All of us were making excellent use of phage genetics and what were, at that time, the most advanced biophysical tools. DNA was fragmented by controlled shear and double-stranded λ DNA was dissociated and the halves separated by density centrifugation. Radioactively labeled mRNAs were isolated and their origins identified by their ability to anneal to physically separated segments of DNA or mutants with known deletions, using the newly developed DNA agarose gels. All of this sounds arcane by today's standards; nevertheless, with mutant DNAs and the new annealing techniques Phyllis Bear and I were able to map the mRNA produced by a "repressed" prophage. Later, in collaboration with Hatch Echols, I provided the first evidence for temporal and genetic control of viral gene expression during the lytic response. This latter work made quite a splash. But it was the discovery with Merv Smith that both T5 and λ form long, multigenome-length DNA molecules during replication—evidence for the "rolling circle model" of replication—that set me on the research path I was to take with me when I left Cold Spring Harbor. The insights gained from these

Ann Skalka, 1980s. (Courtesy of Ann Skalka.)

and subsequent studies of the relationships between the viral and host pathways of DNA recombination, repair, and replication are still relevant today. Indeed, I have of late found myself in a kind of "Hershey" heaven—addressing some of the very same questions I started out with, but with eukaryotic cells and an animal virus.[4]

The year-round staff enjoyed a very warm and congenial after-hours social life in those days as well. I can remember getting together with the Margolins in their cottage across Bungtown Road, where Paul had set up a whole room's display of model trains. A few of us also formed a music group that met weekly at the Goldbergs; Gisela Mosig, Smith, and his wife Barbara played soprano recorders, Ehring and I played altos, and my husband Rudy, a bass. Eddie was our pianist, and his wife, Ariella, served mint tea. Occasionally, a Lab visitor would join us with some other instrument. The group produced quite a happy caterwauling long into the evening; fortunately, there was nobody nearby to complain. To this day, I cannot hear Handel's "Water Music" without being taken back to those fun-filled evenings. On winter days, when there was sufficient snow, we skied on the hill above Page (now occupied by the Adirondack cabins) using a rope tow rigged up to the axle of a wrecked car placed at the top by the longtime friend of the laboratory, Jim Eisenman.

We were, all in all, quite content with our lot. It therefore took me by surprise to read in the 1967 Director's Report that John Cairn's view of the unique and major role of the Cold Spring Harbor Laboratory was to support courses for heterodox disciplines in the making and that its year-round research activities should be thought of as subsidiary. None of us felt the least bit "subsidiary." We all thrived in the combination of quiet isolation most of the year, and the somewhat irritating (although beneficial) invasion of "outsiders" during the summer, when all of the most exciting research was brought to us. In 1966, for example, the Symposium was on the "Genetic Code," and it presented the first complete assignments of codons to amino acids. We were also making some of the most important, fundamental research discoveries of the day. Thus, it was with some trepidation that we learned that in 1967, Cairns would step down as Director to be replaced by the brilliant, but rash and seemingly unpredictable, Jim Watson.

The word went out that Watson considered phage work passé. His new initiatives would be based on neurobiology and on animal virus research as an entrée to the cancer field. This seemed to some of us a premature move, as neurobiology presented an almost impossible challenge and animal virus systems were still quite crude. It was also not good news for me. I was not about to abandon λ phage, as I felt that it still had much to tell us. I had been led to believe that independent support might be forthcoming from the Carnegie Institution to continue my work at Cold Spring Harbor. But my hopes in that direction were soon dashed by Hershey's announcement of his plans to retire and my understanding that the Carnegie assets would then be transferred to CSHL. It seemed clear that the time had come for me to move on. Before I left, however, I prepared for possible future work by taking the Animal Cell Culture and Animal Viruses courses. In addition to meeting wonderful new colleagues, and gaining a somewhat less parochial view of the scientific world, what I learned at these courses would see me in good stead in the late 1970s when I became a retrovirologist.

The first of the animal virus crew to arrive on the CSHL scene was Joe Sambrook. He came with his young family in 1969, seemingly full of enthusiasm and excitement for this new adventure. He was scheduled to move into our Hooper House apartment when we left. I was equally excited about becoming one of the founding members of the newly chartered Roche Institute of Molecular Biology. We felt sorry for Joe, as he too had been put into "temporary" quarters upon his arrival. We were only too happy to let him tour our place in anticipation of his move, and we tried to vacate as quickly as possible.

The move to the Roche Institute was an excellent one for me. I was provided support and the freedom to continue my work with λ and, after a few years, to change the focus of my research to retrovirology. By that time, we had seen the advent of recombinant DNA technology, and my beloved λ provided, at last, an opportunity to attack fundamental problems in animal virus biology with the same rigor that had been possible with phage. It seemed to me at that time that Watson might have gotten rid of his λ people a bit too early, as everybody had begun to clone animal virus genes and λ was the cloning vehicle of choice. Indeed, in 1981, Sambrook, Ahmad Bukhari, and I taught a three-week, CSHL-style recombinant DNA course in Varanasi, India, to be repeated a few years later in Hong Kong with Doug Hanahan and Mary-Jane Gething as co-instructors. Many of the protocols from these courses found their way into the successful laboratory manual, co-authored by Tom Maniatis, Joe Sambrook, and Ed Fritsch, and published by the Cold Spring Harbor Laboratory (Maniatis et al. 1982).[5]

I have returned to Cold Spring Harbor for some meeting or other almost every year since my departure. At first, the visits were very painful. It was hard to see the old familiar buildings and grounds change and to sense the subtle shifts in the social and scientific culture. But few can argue with success, and my visits now are filled with deep admiration for what has transpired over the last 35 years. The CSHL staff of today enjoys tastefully restored or beautiful new buildings, functional research facilities, well-appointed residences, and a carefully groomed and extended campus. The scientific world still beats a path to the door, but no one would any longer consider the year-round CSH researchers "subsidiary," as they are at the forefront of their fields. Jim's decision to emphasize cancer research has been a resounding success and was started by him at exactly the right time. The Cold Spring Harbor Laboratory was an early beneficiary of Nixon's war on cancer, and remains a premier cancer center to this day. For all of this we can justly say BRAVO, Jim!

REFERENCES

Maniatis T., Fritsch E.F., and Sambrook J. 1982. *Molecular cloning: A laboratory manual.* Cold Spring Harbor Laboratory, Cold Spring Harbor, New York.

Director's Report

J.D. Watson

After his appointment to Cold Spring Harbor Laboratory in 1968, Jim Watson's annual Director's Report at first resembled his predecessors', combining news of the year's significant events at the Laboratory with brief, often ominous digressions on the current state of its fortunes. Within a few years, the tone and purpose of Jim's reports changed. As the Laboratory's finances began to improve, there was less need to dwell on the challenges of building renovation and fund-raising, and the reports broadened to include essays written, in Jim's words, "to convey the intellectual excitement then gripping our Lab, if not the world of biology." In these pieces, Jim often addressed scientific advances that had generated controversy in the press. His purpose was unashamed, passionate advocacy for the social benefits of such advances and scornful dismissal of the contrary-minded. He was writing for the kind of thoughtful, inquiring, but not scientifically trained people who lived in the Laboratory's neighborhood and supported it generously with their time and dollars. Knowing their special concerns, he returned frequently in the 30-year span of these essays, to the topic of cancer research, and did so again in 1990 with this elegant summary of oncogene discovery and its implications for cancer treatment.

Director's Report from the Cold Spring Harbor Laboratory 1989 Annual Report.

DIRECTOR'S REPORT

The understanding of cancer as an aberration of the normal processes of cell growth and division has long stood out as a prime, if not ultimate, goal of the world's biomedical research community. When Everest was conquered, we saw the challenge of cancer in terms of that long-sought-after "Himalayan" goal. Now, with time, we see that we are assaulting a more-K2-like peak, where the ice falls ahead pose complexities that even the resolute and strong know may be close to the limits of human endurance.

When I was a boy growing up in Chicago, cancer was only talked about in whispers, a scourge that struck at random and against which we had no medical means of fighting back, particularly if it had spread beyond its point of origin. The only hope had to be the new facts that science would one day discover. After I became a student at the University of Chicago in 1943, I became aware of the research monies given to its Medical School by Albert and Mary Lasker. They wanted the world to have the scientific knowledge that would reveal the real faces of the enemy. Blindly thrashing against a foe that we knew only by name and not by form or substance could only perpetuate our fears. So, the Laskers put real life into the body known as the American Society for Cancer Control, then an assembly of doctors, many of whom were habituated to keeping the truth from their patients. Their efforts transformed this ineffective organization into the American Cancer Society, a national body founded in 1944 that would work for the public good by using the scientific mind, as opposed to the surgeon's scalpel, as the means ultimately to banish cancer from the human vocabulary.

It was in this same year that Avery, MacLeod, and McCarty published their historic paper showing that DNA molecules, not proteins, were the hereditary molecules of bacteria. At that time, very few scientists worked on or were excited by DNA or with RNA, its equally mysterious companion nucleic acid. So the Avery result did not immediately galvanize a then-unfocused biological community into a DNA-dominated mentality. I heard first of Avery's experiments through Sewall Wright's course on physiological genetics that I attended in the spring of 1946, my junior year in college. DNA's potential significance, however, only hit me with a vengeance when I moved on in the fall to Indiana University as a graduate student. There, my first-term courses brought me into the center of the gene replication dilemma: How could genetic molecules with their very great specificities be exactly copied?

Salvador Luria in his virus course excited me about these still very mysterious disease-causing agents, while Hermann J. Muller in his advanced genetics course recounted his life-long odyssey in search of the secrets of the gene. The simplicity of Luria's bacterial viruses (phages) immediately fascinated me, and in the spring of 1949, I started my Ph.D. thesis research in his lab. A year earlier, Luria had become one of the first recipients of the American Cancer Society's (ACS) new research grants. These were very important monies for the fledgling scientific area that later was to be known as molecular biology. The National Science Foundation (NSF) had not yet come into existence and the National Institutes of Health (NIH), much less its National Cancer Institute (NCI) component, had only a minuscule budget for scientific investigators outside its own Bethesda walls. At that time, the ACS did not have its own staff for evaluating grant proposals, a task then given to the Committee on Growth of the National Research Council.

Support of Luria's research by the ACS was not at all surprising. Several types of viruses were known to cause cancer in a variety of animals, and it was natural to think that some human cancers might also have viral etiologies. But in those early postwar years, no one really knew what a virus was, and directly attacking how the cancer-inducing viruses acted was not a realistic objective. Many viruses, including Luria's little phages, contained DNA, and we often speculated that DNA was their genetic component. But there were other viruses that totally lacked DNA and instead had RNA components. Conceivably, both forms of nucleic acid carried genetic information, but there still existed many scientists who suspected that maybe neither DNA nor RNA was a truly genetic molecule. Perhaps there was a fatal flaw to the Avery experiment that no one had yet caught.

General acceptance of the primary genetic role of DNA only came when Francis Crick and I found the double helix. The fact that it had a structure that was so perfect for its self-replication could not be a matter of chance. When I first publicly presented the double helix at the 1953 Cold Spring Harbor Symposium, there was virtually immediate and universal acceptance of its implications. At long last, we had the reference molecule on which to base our thinking about how living cells operate at the molecular level. And the DNA viruses immediately could be viewed in a more approachable fashion. The DNA molecules within them were clearly their chromosomes; and within a year, Seymour Benzer produced a detailed genetic map of the *r*II gene of phage T4 in which the mutant sites along a gene were correctly postulated to be the successive base pairs along the double helix.

Less obvious was whether RNA also could be a genetic molecule. By then, we believed that RNA functioned as an informational intermediate in the transfer of genetic information from the base-pair sequences of DNA to the amino acid sequences in proteins (DNA→RNA→protein). As such, RNA did not need to be capable of self-replication, it only needed to be made on DNA templates. Vigorous proof that RNA also could be genetic molecules came from Alfred Gierer's 1956 demonstration in Tübingen that RNA purified from tobacco mosaic virus was infectious.

Viruses by then had become perceived as tiny pieces of genetic material surrounded by protective coats made up of protein (and sometimes lipid) molecules that ensured their successful passage from one cell to another. At first, we believed that the proteins used to construct their outer coats were the only proteins coded by the viral chromosomes. The enzymes used to replicate their DNA were initially believed to be those of their host cells. This assumption, however, created the dilemma of how the RNA of RNA viruses was replicated if the RNA within their host cells was made entirely on DNA templates. One way out of the dilemma was to postulate that some types of DNA-made RNA were later selectively amplified by RNA-templated RNA synthesis catalyzed by host cell enzymes. By 1959, however, Seymour Cohen's and Arthur Kornberg's labs began to show that phage chromosomes coded for many of the enzymes needed to replicate their DNA. This opened up the possibility that animal viruses also coded for the enzymes that duplicate their DNA. If true, I thought we might have the first real clue as to how viruses cause cancer.

Dissolving the deep enigma surrounding viral carcinogenesis first became a goal of mine when I learned of tumor viruses in Luria's 1947 virus course. A young uncle of mine was then dying of cancer, and it was that fall when I first acutely sensed the need for science to fight back. This desire was rekindled in the spring of 1958 when I was visiting Luria's lab, by then in Urbana. There I heard Van Potter from the University of Wisconsin, Madison, give a lecture on the biochemistry of cancer. From him I first realized that the cells of higher organisms, unlike those of bacteria, needed specific signals to divide. In fact, the majority of cells in our bodies are not dividing but are in an apparent resting state where DNA synthesis is not occurring. A DNA virus infecting such cells would be unable to multiply unless it coded for one or more enzymes that specifically functioned to move their quiescent host cells into the "S" phase of DNA synthesis. Conceivably, insertion of animal viral genomes into the chromosomes of resting host cells would convert them into dividing cells with the signal for DNA synthesis always turned on.

This idea came to me when I was preparing a lecture on cancer to beginning Harvard students whom I was trying to excite with the new triumphs of molecular biology. It was they who first learned of my hypothesis. That viral carcinogenesis might have such a simple answer dominated my thoughts all that spring of 1959. In May, I presented it as my prize lecture for that year's Warren Award of the Massachusetts General Hospital. Francis Crick and I shared the award, and my presentation came after he told an overflow audience how transfer RNA was the "adaptor" molecule he had earlier postulated for reading the messages of RNA templates. Thanks to Mahlon Hoagland and Paul Zamecnik's new experiments, there were no doubts as to whether Francis' ideas were on track. His talk had the virtue of being not only elegant, but also right. On the other hand, my talk had to seem more hot air than future truth. I left the Museum of Science Lecture Hall depressed at the thought that I had appeared at least an order of magnitude less intellectually powerful than Francis. Clearly, I might have given a more convincing talk if I had a plausible hypothesis as to why RNA viruses also sometimes induce cancer. As opposed to the situation with DNA, resting animal cells are constantly making RNA. Conceivably, there were two very different mechanisms through which the DNA and RNA viruses caused cancer. The other possibility was that my idea, although pretty, was just wrong.

During that spring, I started some experiments with John Littlefield, who had been purifying the Shope papilloma virus from rabbit warts. At that time, it was the smallest known DNA tumor virus and we expected its DNA to have a molecular weight of about four million. Surprisingly, using sedimentation analysis, we measured an apparent molecular weight of some seven million, with some molecules of seemingly twice that size that we thought might be end-to-end dimers. Unfortunately, we never looked at them in the electron microscope. If we had, we would have discovered that the Shope papilloma DNA is circular and that the faster-sedimenting molecules were not dimers, but a supercoiled form of the uncoiled simple circle that has a molecular weight of five million. In retrospect, I felt stupid, because earlier I had spent much time arranging for Harvard's Biological Laboratories to get an electron microscope. But, circles were not yet in the air and I never expected to see anything interesting.

Then the only, and not always dependable, source of the Shope papilloma virus was the Kansas trapper Earl Johnson. So, the discovery of a more accessible and even smaller mouse virus was beginning to revolutionize tumor virology. In 1958, Sarah Stewart and Bernice Eddy, working at the National Cancer Institute, opened up the DNA tumor virus field to modern virological methods through being able to propagate Ludwik Gross' "paratoid" virus[1] in mouse cells growing in cell culture. They renamed this virus "polyoma," after its unexpected property of inducing a broad spectrum of tumors following inoculation into immunologically immature newborn mice. Quickly, several molecularly oriented virologists, including Renato Dulbecco at Caltech, Leo Sachs in Israel, and Michael Stoker in Glasgow, took up the polyoma virus system, moving on several years later to the newly discovered, similarly sized monkey tumor virus SV40. Easily workable cell culture systems to study the multiplication of these viruses as well as their cancer-inducing (transforming) properties were in place by the early 1960s. The time had thus come to ask whether these DNA viruses contained one or more specific cancer-inducing genes. So, there was an aura of real excitement permeating our 1962 Symposium on "Animal Viruses." I came down from Harvard and listened to Dulbecco give the closing summary at which the then-young Howard Temin and David Baltimore were much in evidence.

I did not, however, then join in the cancer gene quest. My earlier experiments on papilloma DNA were diversions from a ribosome-dominated lab that unfortunately was still in the dark as to where to go next. But when we found the first firm evidence for messenger RNA in March of 1960, the course of my Harvard lab for the next decade was firmly set. We wanted to understand how messenger RNA was made and then functioned to order the amino acids on ribosomes during protein synthesis. But I continued to emphasize tumor viruses in my Harvard lectures, which eventually formed the basis for my first book *The Molecular Biology of the Gene* (1965). Its last chapter, "A Geneticist's View of Cancer," discussed the DNA and RNA tumor viruses, concluding with the statement that through study of the simple DNA and RNA tumor viruses, we have our best chance of understanding cancer.

My taking on the Directorship here early in 1968 at last gave me the opportunity to get into the DNA tumor virus field. The great era of phage and bacterial genetics research at Cold Spring Harbor was coming to an end and we needed a new intellectual focus as a reason for our existence. Fortunately, that summer, our animal virus course brought to us several individuals who were just starting research with tumor viruses. The lecturer to excite me most was Joe Sambrook, then a postdoc in Dulbecco's Salk Institute lab where he worked with Henry Westphal on the integration of SV40 DNA into the chromosomal DNA of cells made cancerous by SV40. Soon after meeting Joe, I asked him to move here and start a DNA tumor virus lab. He quickly accepted, wrote a successful grant application, and arrived here the following June.

Within several years, Joe was leading a very high-powered group in James lab consisting of Henry Westphal, Carel Mulder, Phil Sharp, Walter Keller, and Mike Botchan whose main purpose was to identify the SV40 gene(s?) that leads to cancer. By then, George Todaro and Robert Huebner, members of the NIH Special Cancer Virus Program, proposed using the name "oncogene" for a cancer-causing gene, and this designation rapidly caught on. Through work here and at several other key sites, including the Salk Institute, NIH, and the Weizmann Institute, the SV40 oncogene(s?) was shown to be identical to the so-called "early gene(s)" that functions at the start of the SV40 replication cycle. This was a most gratifying result, compatible with my brainstorm of a decade earlier that the DNA viral oncogenes function to convert host cells into states capable of supporting DNA synthesis.

Key tools in everyone's analysis were the newly discovered restriction enzymes that cut DNA molecules at precise nucleotide sequences. A given restriction enzyme was used to cut up a viral genome into discrete pieces that could then be isolated from each other by a powerful new ethidium bromide agarose gel procedure developed here by Phil Sharp, Bill Sugden, and Joe Sambrook. Restriction enzymes came to the laboratory when Carel Mulder brought Herb Boyer's *Eco*RI into the James lab and later went on to isolate the *Sma*I enzyme. Soon afterward, Joe Sambrook and Phil Sharp began to use *Hpa*I and *Hpa*II enzymes, whose use was pioneered by Ham Smith and Dan Nathans at Johns Hopkins. More and more restriction enzymes came on line through the efforts of Rich Roberts, who arrived here in late 1972. About 50% of the world's commonly used restriction enzymes were discovered over the next decade in the Roberts laboratory.

By then, James lab was also working with a second DNA tumor virus, a human adenovirus that Ulf Pettersson had brought from Uppsala in 1971. Its life cycle also was divided into an early phase and a late phase, with the genes carrying its oncogenic potential also being "early" genes. A clear next objective was to find and identify the messenger RNAs for proteins encoded by the early and late adenovirus genes. Ray Gesteland's and Rich Roberts' groups in Demerec lab took on this task, which soon began to generate mystifying results. All of the late mRNAs seemed to possess a common terminal segment even though they were encoded by widely separated sequences of DNA. Resolution of the paradox occurred in late March of 1977, when Rich Roberts orchestrated a team consisting of Tom Broker, Louise Chow, Rich Gelinas, and Dan Klessig to their monumental discovery of RNA splicing. Independently, Phil Sharp and Susan Berget, then at MIT, made the same great discovery after initially observing with the electron microscope that the 5′ end of a late adenovirus messenger RNA did not behave as expected.[2]

The discovery of RNA splicing was a once-in-a-lifetime event that completely transformed all of eukaryotic biology, and our 1977 Symposium, where the discovery was first publicly announced, was an occasion of intense intellectual ferment. Afterwards, new implications arose virtually weekly. Among the first was understanding that the T(umor)-antigen-coding SV40 early gene specified two different cancer-causing proteins. They are derived by two different ways of splicing the early SV40 messenger RNA. The once-thought single SV40 T(umor) antigen in fact consists of large (T) and small (t) components, with the main cancer-causing activity due to the large T antigen. Splicing also occurs with the early adenovirus mRNAs, with two of the resulting protein products of the E1A and E1B genes playing essential roles in early viral replication as well as having oncogenic activity.

Now we realize that the subsequent working out of how these tumor virus oncogenes actually induce cancer would have been virtually impossible if the procedures of recombinant DNA had not been discovered in 1973. They have allowed us to study the action of individual oncogenes as well as to prepare the large amounts of highly purified oncogenic proteins needed to study their molecular functioning. We had, however, to wait six long years after Herb Boyer and Stanley Cohen gave us the first generally applicable recombinant DNA procedures until the stringent NIH prohibitions against using recombinant DNA to clone viral oncogenes were dropped. Only in early 1979 could the recombinant DNA era of tumor virology take off.

Not only were the DNA tumor viruses ripe for analysis, but how to think about the RNA tumor viruses was also known. Through work in the 1960s by Harry Rubin, Peter Vogt, and Howard Temin, the defective nature of most RNA tumor viruses had been firmly established. Their replication requires the simultaneous presence of a normal helper virus. In acquiring their cancerous potentials, the RNA tumor viruses had somehow lost part of their own genomes. The way such RNA genomes, be they normal or defective, are replicated was first correctly hypothesized by Howard Temin. In 1964, he suggested that the infecting RNA molecules served as templates to make DNA genomes, which, in turn, integrated as proviruses into host cell chromosomes. Proof came in 1970 when Howard Temin working with Satoshi Mizutani, and independently David Baltimore, discovered within mature RNA tumor virus particles the enzyme reverse transcriptase. Soon the name "retroviruses" became used to encompass all those RNA viruses that replicate their RNA through a DNA intermediate.

Studies on the Rous sarcoma virus (RSV) provided the first deep insights on how the RNA tumor viruses cause cancer. RSV mutants that were unable to transform cells were found by Peter Duesberg and his collaborators to frequently lose part of a specific region of the genome that they called src. Its true nature became known from Mike Bishop's and Harold Varmus' 1976 seminal experiments showing that the sequences within RSV are highly homologous to those of a normal cellular equivalent. This finding immediately suggested that the cancer-causing signals of retroviral genomes have nothing to do with the replication processes of retroviruses. Instead, they originated from illegitimate recombinant events that replaced normal retroviral base pairs with DNA segments bearing cellular genes. A year later, the protein product of *src* itself was isolated and found independently by Ray Erickson and Art Levinson to be a protein kinase, an enzyme capable of adding phosphate groups to preexisting proteins.[3]

Over the next decade, more than 30 additional oncogenes were isolated from RNA tumor viruses. In each case, they closely resemble a normal cellular gene. The proteins these oncogenes encode have seemingly very diverse roles; some are growth factors, others are receptors, many are kinases, and still others code for proteins that bind to DNA and control transcription. Unifying the roles of all these oncogenes, as well as of their normal cellular equivalents, is their involvement in the signal transduction processes that control whether a cell divides, remains quiescent, or becomes terminally differentiated.[4] In normal cells, the functioning of these signal transduction genes is tightly regulated, so that they function only when cell division is needed. In contrast, the functioning of their oncogene derivatives is unregulated and leads to overexpression of their respective protein products. Proto-oncogene is the term now used to designate normal genes that can be converted into oncogenes by mutations or abnormal recombinational events.

We thus see that the oncogenes of DNA and RNA tumor viruses work in fundamentally different fashions. Those of DNA tumor viruses play essential roles in the replication of the viral genomes, with their cancer-causing attributes related to the tricks by which they turn their normal quiescent host cells into factories primed for DNA synthesis. In contrast, the oncogenes of retroviruses play no role in their replication, having arisen by genetic accidents that dissociate growth-promoting genes from their normal regulatory signals.

When they were first found, the question had to be faced whether the oncogenes of retroviruses were essentially laboratory artifacts and not related to human cancer. One way to settle the matter was to devise procedures that directly looked for human oncogenes by asking whether DNA isolated from human cancer cells could convert a normal cell into a cancerous cell. At MIT, Bob Weinberg first convincingly showed that this could be done using the DNA infection (transfection) procedures that Mike Wigler helped to develop while he was a graduate student at Columbia University. By that time, Mike had joined our staff and was focusing on ways to clone the genes that his transfection procedures had functionally introduced into cells. In 1981, Wigler and Weinberg, working with the same cancer cell line, used different cloning procedures to isolate the first known human oncogene. More importantly, this bladder cell oncogene turned out to be virtually identical to the viral oncogene *ras* isolated several years before by Ed Scolnick when he was at NCI. It was just the first of several retroviral oncogenes shown to be a cause of human cancer. Now no one doubts that the study of retroviral oncogenes bears directly on the understanding of human cancer.

The NIH-3T3 cultured mouse cells that Wigler and Weinberg made cancerous by the addition of the oncogenes were later found to be more predisposed to cancer than cells obtained from the organs of living animals. Now we realize that Weinberg's and Wigler's classic experiments would have failed if they had used cells whose growth regulation was more normal. Two years later in 1983, Earl Ruley, here at James lab, showed that the ras oncogene only transforms normal rat kidney cells to a cancerous state when a second oncogene is simultaneously added. In his experiments, either the adenovirus E1A oncogene or the retroviral myc oncogene could complement the activity of ras. At the same time, Helmut Land and Luis Parada working at MIT in Weinberg's lab independently came to the same conclusion: Normal cells do not become fully cancerous through acquiring a single oncogene, but instead they become cancerous progressively, as other oncogenes successively come into action.

When the rush to use recombinant DNA procedures to study oncogenes began, we had to worry whether the research expertise and facilities at Cold Spring Harbor were up to the task. So we brought to James lab in 1980 John Fiddes from the University of California at San Francisco, where he was one of the first serious gene cloners. At the same time, we persuaded Tom Maniatis, who, before moving on to Caltech, had helped develop cDNA cloning as a member of our staff, to introduce a summer molecular cloning course. Started in 1980, this course gave rise in 1982 to the extraordinarily successful cloning techniques book *Molecular Cloning: A Laboratory Manual*, by Maniatis, Fritsch, and Sambrook, which sold over 60,000 copies in its first edition. We also planned and constructed in 1983 a major south addition to Demerec Laboratory aimed at strengthening our facilities for protein chemistry and mutagenesis analysis. Equally important, we realized that we could not successfully exploit the monoclonal antibody procedures discovered in Cambridge, England, by George Kohler and Cesar Milstein in 1975 until we built a further addition to James lab. We had already constructed, in 1970, a south addition for offices and a seminar room and, in 1972, a west addition for virus culture. We needed to use monoclonal antibodies first to purify and then to better define the surfaces of oncogenic proteins. Planning for the north (Sambrook) addition allowed us to get Ed Harlow straight from his Ph.D. at the Imperial Cancer Research Fund (ICRF) Laboratories in London. There he had made monoclonal antibodies against both the SV40 T antigen and the still very mysterious p53 protein, a cellular constituent that David Lane and Lionel Crawford at ICRF had found to bind to the SV40 T antigen.

Upon arriving here, Ed focused on the key adenovirus oncogenic protein E1A to see which proteins it bound. He hoped that by identifying the cellular components with which it interacted, clues would emerge as to how E1A caused cancer. To spot these cellular proteins, he used a monoclonal antibody against E1A to precipitate it from extracts of adenovirus-infected cells. Then, he displayed the resulting precipitate on a gel to see whether proteins in addition to E1A could be detected. In this way, several unknown cellular proteins were found to bind to E1A. What any of them did remained a mystery until in the fall of 1987 a paper was published by Wen-Hwa Lee on the properties of Rb, a newly identified DNA binding protein that helps to prevent cancer. When Rb is absent in a human due to mutations in both of his two genes, retinoblastoma (cancer of the retina) develops. Those individuals who inherit a bad gene from one of their parents are at risk for this cancer, frequently developing retinoblastoma at an early age when a cancer-causing mutation occurs in the remaining good gene. Harlow's lab noticed that the Rb protein had been assigned a size very similar to one of the proteins (105K) that binds tightly to the E1A protein. Hoping that they might be the same, Harlow's lab began a collaboration with Bob Weinberg's lab, one of the three groups that had just cloned the gene. Happily, the two proteins (Rb and 105K) proved to be identical, suggesting that E1A's oncogene potential lies partially in its ability to neutralize the anticancer activity of the Rb protein. I say partially because besides binding to Rb, E1A binds also to several other, still to be functionally identified, molecules, each of which also may be a cancer-preventing (anti-oncogene) protein.

The implication of Harlow's discovery widened with the subsequent finding that the T antigens of SV40 and polyoma also tightly bind Rb, as does an oncogenic protein coded by a papilloma virus that causes warts. Moreover, the once mysterious p53 protein that binds to the SV40 (polyoma) T antigen was shown last year by Arnold Levine and Bert Vogelstein also to be an anti-oncogenic protein. Although p53 does not bind to E1A, it does bind to E1B, a second "early" adenovirus protein that potentiates the oncogenic transformation potential of the E1A protein.

The study of tumor viruses has thus advanced fundamental cancer research more than anyone could have predicted when serious research on them began some three decades ago. The RNA tumor viruses have revealed almost all of the oncogenes known today. Without them, we would largely be in the dark as to the molecular players in the signaling processes that lead to cell division. Equally important have been the insights gained from learning how the oncogenes of the DNA tumor viruses work. The knowledge that they prevent anti-oncogenes from functioning gives us a new way to identify anti-oncogenes and will materially advance our understanding of hereditary predispositions to cancer.

We must remember, however, that the small hyperplastic tumors that result from gain of oncogenes that promote cell growth and division are generally benign. These usually tiny tumors generally only grow to life-threatening size when they become infiltrated (vascularized) by newly growing blood vessels that bring to them the oxygen and nutrients needed for their growth. Douglas Hanahan elegantly showed this through experiments done in collaboration with Judah Folkman. In our Harris laboratory, Doug introduced oncogenes into the germ cells of mice to produce transgenic mice in which these cell-division-signaling genes are expressed in early development as well as throughout adult life. His targeting of the SV40 T antigen to function in the pancreas resulted in large numbers of benign hyperplasmic growths in the insulin-producing islets. Only a small percentage of these benign growths, however, turned into rapidly growing tumors with infiltrating blood vessels. They did so by acquiring the ability to send out angiogenic (blood-vessel-forming) signals that induced neighboring endothelial cells to form new blood vessels. Finding out which molecules carry these signals will soon become a major objective for the coming decade of cancer research. If we could find inhibitors of these angiogenic growth factors, we might have in hand a powerful new way to stop cancers from growing. Most importantly, the endothelial cells that line our blood vessels effectively do not divide in adult life. So, as Judah Folkman has long dreamed, inhibitors of tumor angiogenesis would not necessarily affect the healthy functioning of our preexisting blood vessels.

The truly cancerous cells of solid tumors (as opposed to those of the circulating cells of the blood) also show failure of their normal cellular affinities and spread (metastasize) to many unwanted tissue sites. Our first molecular clue as to the oncogenic changes that create cells capable of metastasis came this past January from the cloning of an oncogene on human chromosome 18 that leads to a final step in the progression of normal colon cells into their highly malignant equivalents. Through a very difficult feat of gene cloning, Bert Vogelstein found that this oncogene codes for a cell membrane protein involved in cell-cell recognition. Over the next few years, the losses of many additional cell-recognition proteins are likely to be implicated in the unwanted spread of tumor cells from their original sites of origin.

At long last, we may thus have the proper intellectual framework to understand most of the more common life-threatening cancers. At their essence are three types of genetic changes: (1) those that make cells divide when they should not, (2) those that lead to the formation of blood vessels that infiltrate into and thereby nourish the growing tumors, and (3) those that modify cell-recognizing molecules in ways leading to losses of their respective cell's ability to recognize their normal cellular partners. We have indeed come a very long way, but there remain myriad further details to unravel about both currently known oncogenes and the many more oncogenes yet to be discovered. Many of these new observations will initially unsettle us and momentarily make us despair of ever being able to have a fair fight against an enemy that so constantly changes the face it presents. But now is most certainly not the moment to lose faith in our ability to triumph over the inherent complexity that underlies the existence of the living state.

Given enough time, and the financial and moral resources that will let those born optimistic stay that way, the odds for eventual success in beating down cancer are on our side.

Jim as a Mentor 1971–1974

Phillip A. Sharp

Massachusetts Institute of Technology

There are scientists that lead by example, i.e., doing experiments , and others that lead by communication, i.e., talking, and then there are a few who lead by directing an organization. Jim has done all three, but he was in the latter category when I was at Cold Spring Harbor from 1971 to 1974.

My interactions with Jim began while I was a postdoctoral fellow at Caltech, making the decision to do additional research as a postdoc before seeking an independent position. In Norman Davidson's lab at Caltech, I had made the transition from chemist to molecular biologist studying plasmid gene structure in bacteria, but I wanted to study gene expression in mammalian cells. This being pre-recombinant DNA, the only system where detailed studies were possible required the use of animal viruses. Thus, I decided to apply to a number of labs for a position, including Jim's at Cold Spring Harbor. I soon learned that Jim did not have a lab at Cold Spring Harbor, at least in the conventional sense, but was Director, part time, and had recruited a number of very good molecular cell biologists and virologists. These included in the molecular area, Joe Sambrook, Walter Keller, Heiner Westphal, and Carel Mulder. Jim called a few days after receiving my letter to offer me a position, and requested an almost immediate response. He was leaving for Europe and told me that he planned to try to recruit a fellow during the trip if I was not going to accept. My answer set in motion my move to Cold Spring Harbor in six months and my initial meeting with Jim.

I arrived at the Lab in July shortly before the beginning of the Tumor Virus course and the annual Tumor Virus meeting. Jim attended many of the lectures during both the course and the meeting, talked about the current research, and suggested that I talk to a number of the more senior scientists around the Lab. Talking with Jim was fun. He would inject an interesting tidbit about the history of molecular biology and gossip about a colleague's romantic interests or cultural pursuits, subjects that added color to the day-to-day conversations. Some of his comments were critical but never mean-spirited. He shared with me several insights into human nature such as "never try to rationalize a colleague's taste in either women or religion." At Cold Spring Harbor, an architecturally beautiful and environmentally sensitive physical setting, Jim created an aura of science first and an interest in people. He was generous with his time to his young colleagues and genuinely interested in their science.

I found Joe Sambrook to be an interesting colleague and began to collaborate with him on studies of the stages of gene expression during SV40 infection and in transformed cells. This research was done in hot competition with George Khoury and Malcolm Martin at the National Institutes of Health. Jim would suddenly appear at the door of my office, usually at about 10 p.m., and ask me about the results as I was sitting at my desk trying to orga-

PHILLIP A. SHARP

Phil Sharp, born on D-Day (June 6, 1944), grew up on a small farm in Falmouth, Kentucky, and attended grade school first at McKinneysburg, then Falmouth, and finally in the newly consolidated Pendleton County High School. In a biographical sketch prepared at the time of the award of his Nobel Prize, Phil wrote:

> The rural background of my childhood made me feel more comfortable attending a small institution in a familiar environment. Therefore, I entered a small liberal arts school, Union College, in the foothills of eastern Kentucky...[which]...in those days it was one of the gateways for the youth from the mountains in the eastern part of the state to emerge into a larger world.

The first stop in the larger world was the University of Illinois, Champaign-Urbana, where Phil earned a Ph.D. for studies on the polymer properties of DNA. During a subsequent postdoctoral fellowship in Norman Davidson's laboratory, he used electron microscopy to study the structure of plasmids of the sex factors and drug-resistant factors of bacteria. In 1971, Phil moved to Cold Spring Harbor Laboratory to begin studies on the molecular biology of animal viruses and mammalian cells that were to take him to fame. He joined the Center for Cancer Research and Department of Biology at the Massachusetts Institute of Technology in 1974. After the discovery of splicing (1977), for which Phil shared the 1993 Nobel Prize with Rich Roberts, his laboratory worked out much of the complex biochemistry involved in the process.

From 1985 to 1991, Phil was Director of the Center for Cancer Research at MIT and from 1991 to 1999, he served as Head of the Department of Biology. In February, 2000, he was named Founding Director of the McGovern Institute for Brain Research, a position he still holds.

Phil Sharp has been honored with numerous awards, including the Gairdner Foundation International Award, General Motors Research Foundation, Alfred P. Sloan, Jr. Prize for Cancer Research, Louisa Gross Horwitz Prize, and Albert Lasker Basic Medical Research Award. He is an elected member of the National Academy of Sciences, the Institute of Medicine, the American Academy of Arts and Sciences, and the American Philosophical Society.

nize my data and plan for the next day. There would be a pause during which insecurity would dry my mouth, and then he would initiate a conversation about experiments or discuss new discoveries he had heard about during his travels. I knew he appreciated our recent results when he sent Joe and me to London for a month to attempt the same experiments on polyomavirus. The experiments did not work, but we had a great time in England. It was during this trip that I traveled to Glasgow to meet Jim Williams who had characterized a number of temperature-sensitive mutants of human adenovirus, a DNA viral system with a large genome where regulation of gene expression might be more elaborate than that of SV40.

My interest in adenovirus came from a new office mate at Cold Spring Harbor, Ulf Pettersson, who had trained with Lennart Philipson in Uppsala, Sweden. Jim had recruited Ulf to the lab because he was both an accomplished young scientist and had experience working with adenovirus. That Ulf and I shared an office was probably not by chance. Our per-

Jane Flint, Terri Grodzicker, and Phil Sharp, circa 1973. (Courtesy CSHL Archives.)

ceptive Director had recognized a match. Ulf was interested in DNA replication in mammalian cells, and adenovirus, which replicated to high levels, was a promising model system. The virus also had elaborate stages of gene regulation and displayed the synthesis of long nuclear RNA, a phenomenon previously reported during expression of cellular genes. The latter observation fascinated me and we soon began to collaborate on the common goal of adenovirus genome structure.

As I joined the Lab in 1971, Hamilton Smith and Dan Nathans published their classic studies defining the biochemistry of restriction endonucleases and their use in the analysis of SV40 molecular biology. In the same time period, Herb Boyer's lab discovered the *Eco*RI restriction endonuclease, which was more specific than the endonucleases from *Haemophilus parainfluenza* and *H. influenza* purified by the Johns Hopkins group. Clearly, Cold Spring Harbor had to incorporate this technology into its research program, which led to a meeting in Jim's office of a number of investigators where this consensus was formed. Shortly thereafter, I combined staining with ethidium bromide and electrophoretic agarose gels of DNA to accelerate the purification of restriction endonucleases. With these enzymes, Ulf and I decided to determine the cleavage maps of adenovirus so that segments of the genome could be used to analyze transcription and replication. Ulf and I collaborated with Carel Mulder and Helio Delius in these experiments and started the preparation of a manuscript to publish our results. It was during this process that I recognized Jim's subtle hand as a Director.

Jim had agreed to communicate the paper to the *Proceedings of the National Academy of Science*. This meant that the paper was not going to be reviewed in the conventional sense. Ulf and I prepared the manuscript and circulated it through collaborators for input and then to colleagues for comments. We then presented the paper to Jim for his consideration. The reply came the next day. Jim said that he would like to contact Al Hershey and ask him if he would look at the manuscript. We readily agreed, not knowing of Al's legendary and formidable ability as an editor. Al asked that we leave the paper in his mailbox and said that he would contact us in a few days. At a subsequent meeting in Al's office, we learned to appreciate the importance of the correct use of each word in the manuscript. Al's office was the ultimate in simplicity—a desk, three chairs, large metal filing cabinets, and a single ashtray, the only object on his desk. Al returned the paper with comments written in red in all of the margins. He edited our logic, our language, and the description of experiments. Each comment was pointed and improved the paper.

This modest affair typifies Jim as a mentor. Jim did not get involved in many details of doing science at this stage of his career. However, he understood greatness in people and arranged for junior colleagues to have access and interact with them. This created a wonderful learning experience. I am grateful to Jim for the things I learned, the friends I made, and the quality of the science I was exposed to during the years I spent at Cold Spring Harbor Laboratory.

From Development of Yeast Cells to Human Brain Hemispheres

Amar J.S. Klar

National Cancer Institute at Frederick

ROUNDING UP THE YEAST GROUP

My first interaction with Jim came in 1977, and although it was long distance, one aspect of his personality was immediately apparent—he makes decisions quickly and acts on them immediately. I returned a call from him just after having given a seminar at the University of California at Irvine. Our brief conversation still echoes vividly in my mind.

"Hello, Dr. Watson; this is Amar Klar."

Abruptly, Jim replied, "Oh, yes, I know you; I know what you do. We are opening a yeast lab to work on mating-type switching. Whatever you need, I will arrange for it. You should realize your appointment has to go through a committee, but I will send you the appointment letter tomorrow. You should sign it and send it back to my Assistant Director, Mr. Bill Udry. Bye."

I didn't even get a chance to say "good-bye" before he had hung up the phone.

Another aspect of Jim's character is that he is determined and he doesn't give up easily. On the day of our phone "conversation" recounted above, Jim had to go to some trouble to track me down. First, he called my postdoc advisor, Seymour Fogel, in the Genetics Department at the University of California at Berkeley. Seymour told him that I was off to give a seminar at the California Institute of Technology and gave him the name and phone number of my host there, Norman Davidson. Right away, Jim made another call, this time to Norman who said, "Amar gave a talk here yesterday, but today he has a presentation at the University of California at Irvine." After securing the name of Rowland Davis, my host at Irvine, Jim called Davis, only to get his secretary, who told Jim that I was in the midst of delivering my seminar. Jim demanded that she deliver his message immediately. He must have been so insistent that the secretary politely interrupted my seminar, and asked me to please call Dr. Jim Watson right away. Jim doesn't like to waste time, and he's very decisive.

The appointment Jim referred to in our phone conversation had, in fact, been discussed before he called me that fateful fall day in 1977. My future colleague, James B. Hicks, then working at Cornell University, had delivered a brief seminar to a half-dozen senior scientists at Cold Spring Harbor Laboratory, trying to persuade them that the Laboratory should start a yeast group consisting of himself, Jeffrey Strathern (who was already working at CSHL as a postdoc), and myself. By the end of the seminar,

Amar J.S. Klar

Amar Klar was born and educated in India and came to the United States to do his Ph.D. with Harlyn Halvorson at the University of Wisconsin. Halvorson was interested in the synthesis of enzymes during the yeast cell cycle and Klar's first paper dealt with *GAL4* and the regulation of galactose catabolic enzymes. From the snow of Wisconsin, Klar moved to the fog of the Bay Area to a postdoctoral position with Seymour Fogel at Berkeley. There, he pursued research on gene conversion and switching of mating types, a topic that was to occupy him for the next few years.

Klar tells in his essay of how he, together with Jim Hicks and Jeff Strathern, formed the "Three Yeastketeers" of Delbrück. It was an auspicious place to be at in an auspicious time. Not only did Cold Spring Harbor have available a full repertoire of molecular techniques, but, more importantly, Barbara McClintock was still active and her heterodox views of genes and genetic elements encouraged the young yeast group to think boldly. Hicks, Strathern, and Klar formed a remarkably productive group, coauthoring—in various combinations—some 30 papers during the period of their collaboration.

All good things must come to an end, and first Strathern, then Hicks, and finally Klar left Cold Spring Harbor, Klar going in 1988 to the National Cancer Institute at Frederick. There he has continued to work on yeast—his interests expanding to cover a wide variety of epigenetic phenomena, with excursions into the genetics of handedness, and the spiraling of leaves on stems that follows the Fibonacci series.

Hicks had convinced the committee that the three of us should come as independent investigators, working together on the topic of yeast mating-type switching. The common baker's yeast has the remarkable property that cells spontaneously alternate in between two sexual cell types, called **a** and α, by heritable but reversible changes at the mating-type locus (*MAT*). How cells differentiate from one to the other form would be the focus of the group.

According to a story Hicks told me later, the committee quickly agreed to his and Strathern's appointment. Then Hicks was asked why I should be in the group. Silence, as Hicks tried to determine what sort of information the committee needed to make a decision. Finally, David Zipser, a bacterial geneticist and senior scientist at CSHL broke the silence and asked what I had done scientifically. So Hicks told the committee about my talk at the CSHL Yeast Conference that summer when I had spoken about my research on budding yeast, particularly my experimental verification of the transposition (controlling/cassette) model. It had been well received—Jim Broach even going so far as to call it a "bombshell," although Seymour Fogel commented that I would never get such a great response in my future presentations. More to the point, I had met both Jim Hicks and Jeff Strathern who appreciated the result and asked me to join the Yeast Group that was to be put together within the year. Jim, Jeff, and I felt an immediate empathy, understanding one another's genetic arguments readily. David Zipser again injected, "I got it." He asked Hicks, "Do you want Klar to join this group because you guys proposed a model and Klar experimentally established it?" Hicks agreed.

But when other senior staff wanted me to visit CSHL for a formal interview, Jim's decisiveness and impatience with wasting time showed when he told the committee members that an interview would be a waste of time because I had already given the

The Yeast Group, circa 1983. From left to right: Amar Klar, Jeff Strathern, Jim Hicks. (Courtesy CSHL Archives.)

best talk at the Yeast meeting. In the absence of any dissenting views, the committee approved my appointment and Watson got on the phone to track me down.

To sum it up: Watson's word is final.

WORKING IN THE YEAST GROUP

My talented colleagues and I pooled our resources, resulting in several joint publications. The success of the group was the direct result of openness, constant discussions, and sharing goals, ideas, and results. Only after our group cloned the *MAT* locus in 1979 (Hicks et al. 1979) did the story become understandable to nongeneticists. This molecular work beautifully confirmed the conclusions arrived at by the classic genetic studies.

Throughout our years of research, Jim Watson was quick to make us feel the importance of our work and supported us, as was indicated when he promoted each of us at a fast pace from Staff Investigator to Senior Investigator and then to a Senior Scientist position in little more than four years. During the first three years, we occupied the Delbrück laboratory where the field of molecular biology was started. Max Delbrück and Salvador Luria had taught the Phage course in this laboratory, and we were excited to work in this historic place. To begin with, we used the laboratory for only nine months of the year; in the other three months, over the height of the summer, it was home to three courses. In the summer of 1980, we rented a shaky trailer and parked it behind the lab for use as a makeshift laboratory. Soon after, an extension to our facility was constructed to provide us with more stable and year-round working conditions. As a result of the success of our group, a couple of years later, still another extension was constructed to accommodate our expansion into plant molecular biology research. Only a portion of the resources required for these additions were covered by our grants. Luckily, Jim Watson was there to support us financially whenever needed by mostly drawing from the Robertson Endowment Fund of the Laboratory. Watson never turned us down for any request, and he was particularly delighted in the expansion of the facility.

As expected from a good administrator, Jim considered his colleagues' suggestions carefully. Feeling confident about the accomplishments of our group, I suggested that he should incorporate the mating-type story in the next edition of his eminent text book, *Molecular Biology of the Gene* (Watson 1965). That edition indeed highlighted yeast studies in not one, but two chapters of the book. Since then, yeast has become an important model organism to study. Jim's foresight was revealed in an earlier edition of the book in which he stated that yeast was poised to become the best eukaryotic experimental system. It did!

WATSON AND CRICK (STRANDS) ARE DIFFERENT

Our group was splintering as each of us began to focus on different aspects of genetics. Both Strathern and Hicks became interested in corn genetics and the molecular biology of transposable elements, while I was more interested in exploring the generalities of the cell-type switching phenomenon and sought to work on some other system where the best tool of biology for groundbreaking studies, i.e., genetics, could be likewise applied. Such a genetics system of mating-type switching of the unrelated fission yeast was developed by European scientists, but it was very confusing even to card-carrying geneticists.

To make better sense of that system, I asked David Beach (from Edinburgh) to join our group for his postdoctoral training. Our cloning and characterization of the *mat1*, *mat2*, and *mat3* loci established the cassette mechanism for mating-type switching in fission yeast as well, despite the fact that mating-type cassette sequences in both yeasts are unrelated. However, major differences exist in the mechanisms of switching and silencing of both systems, which led us to discover new principles of biology. In budding yeast, only the older "mother" cell produces a pair of switched cells, whereas in fission yeast, only one among four grandchildren of a cell switches. I obtained unequivocal evidence from meiotic analysis that some chromosomally borne imprinting event exists at the *mat1* locus which results in a site-specific double-stranded break. Such an imprint during its replication initiates switching by *mat1* gene conversion in only one of the two daughter chromatids, causing one, but never both, of the daughters to switch.

I met with Jim to discuss the idea that the imprint may be strand-specific, which are complementary and not identical by the Watson-Crick model (Watson and Crick 1953). In their single-page paper in 1953, they incorporated a famous understatement of molecular biology, "It has not escaped our notice that the specific pairing we have postulated immediately suggests a possible copying mechanism for the genetic material." Since the phenomenon of gene regulation was not yet discovered, they could not have foreseen that DNA chain differences could result in nonequivalent sister chromatids and hence, nonequivalent sister cells. Jim listened to me intently as I explained our *Strand-Segregation Model*, proposing that inheritance of the specific "Watson" or "Crick" strand from the parental chromosome at *mat1* may confer developmental asymmetry to daughter cells. I presented a genetic test of the model in which a strain engineered to contain an inverted duplication of the *mat1* locus should make both daughters developmentally equivalent, because both daughters would inherit the imprinted strand at *mat1* from the parental cell. Consequently, two cousins among four granddaughters of a cell should switch, as opposed to the one-in-four granddaughter switching observed in standard strains. Barbara McClintock predicted that the experiment had to work because, to her, corn sister chromatids cytologically "looked" different from each other (Klar 1992). Jim's response, as always, was quick and decisive. "How soon can you do this experiment? Could you do it before the Symposium?"

Jim can be impatient, too. It took some time to make the required constructions. Jim was very much interested in the outcome of the experiment. I recall him saying, "If the experiment works, you would be *in*." (To date, I do not know what he meant by "in.") He inquired about its progress so frequently, I started avoiding him.

Finally, I obtained the result we'd been trying to achieve. Excitedly, I stopped Jim during one of his frequent unannounced early morning walks through our laboratory. On a chalkboard presentation of that once-in-a-lifetime kind of result, I explained that a key genetic prediction of our model had been met (Klar 1990), i.e., sister cells had become developmentally equivalent when they are engineered to contain inverted duplication of the mating-type locus. This established the *Strand-Segregation Model* and clearly ruled out all other models suggesting unequal distribution of some other factor to daughter cells.

> Jim likes to keep things simple. He said, "This is well and good, but it's too complicated. How could you explain the conclusion more simply to others?"
>
> I answered, "Tell them that the Watson strand is different from the Crick strand."
>
> Jim got up, mustered a broad grin, and left.

LEAVING COLD SPRING HARBOR

Let me share another story reflecting Jim's quick repartee. Jeff Strathern moved to the National Cancer Institute-Frederick facility in 1984 and Jim Hicks moved to the Scripps Institute at San Diego in 1986. After 10 years at the Lab, in 1988 I decided to move to NCI and join Jeff in Frederick, Maryland.

> Watson asked me to stay and continue my research at Cold Spring Harbor. "Why do you want to move?"
>
> I replied, "It's always good to move and to interact with new colleagues."
>
> His answer: "That doesn't apply to you; your colleagues have moved out, so this is a new environment for you."
>
> I said, "Well, housing is cheaper in Frederick than here."
>
> With a snort, Jim retorted, "It's cheaper because nobody wants to live there!"

WATSON'S INTEREST IN HUMAN HANDEDNESS STUDIES

Having learned two new principles of biology applicable to eukaryotes—that DNA chains can provide the basis for developmental asymmetry and that the developmental decisions through gene regulation can be propagated along with DNA replication through multiple cell divisions—one wonders whether this new knowledge can provide an alternative explanation to hitherto unexplained phenomena where such sophisticated tools of genetics cannot be applied. A case in point is the basis of human handedness. It has been a key "Nature versus Nurture" question for centuries as to why most humans prefer right hand use over left hand use.

Jim's interests are far-ranging and every time I see him, I am struck anew with his interest in important problems. In 1996, I mentioned to Jim during a wine and cheese party that I was also pursuing an answer as to why some people are left-handed. In quick succession, Jim (a lefty) asked several questions.

"Is there genetics involved?"

"Yes," I answered, wondering why he was asking.

"How many genes?"

"One, with two alleles," I said.

"What is the allele frequency?"

"Fifty-eight percent dominant, fully penetrant functional *RIGHT* allele and forty-two percent nonfunctional recessive allele."

"What is your model?"

Excited, I grabbed a cocktail napkin and drew the model on it predicting that a single dominant gene makes a person right-handed by guiding the developmental choice to proceed in a specific direction, analogous to making a choice at a fork in the road. Those carrying the nonfunctional, *random-recessive* allele on both homologs lack the signal for choosing direction and thus have a 50:50 chance of being either right-handed or left-handed. I likened this to the heads or tails outcome of tossing a coin. Before my description of the model was complete, Jim left abruptly without any explanation. I knew him well enough not to be concerned as this is one of his attributes. However, about 20 seconds later, he came back with Bruce Stillman, the new Director of the Lab, in tow. Jim proposed that I give a talk on the etiology of handedness at an upcoming CSHL Symposium on the topic of Brain Function and Dysfunction that Bruce had organized. Soon, we retired for dinner at Blackford Hall, where Jim dominated the conversation, pointing out that handedness has been an extremely important question of biology for a long time and nobody has a good grasp of why or how it develops. He told me jokingly, "If you map the handedness gene, I promise you coverage in *Newsweek* magazine." He also suggested that I should start a biotech company with the name "Left/Right, Inc." to map the locus. He also said other humorous things to make his point, but they should not be printed.

The handedness field is dominated by psychologists and was new to me. "I don't think I'm ready," I protested, to present my work of family history that provided the best evidence for the *Random Recessive Model*. Jim insisted that presenting my work at that Symposium would be the best opportunity to change people's minds. Feeling pressured, I needed reassurance. "I will talk, but if I make a fool of myself, would you protect me?" "Yes!" came the answer. I agreed and Stillman would find a slot for my presentation.

Despite my misgivings, my talk went well. This study was unique in two respects in that (1) it was the only study among hundreds done in the past, where family history was followed for three generations, and (2) it started with both left-handed grandparents. Our key finding was that their right-handed children produce a higher percentage of left-handed (or ambidextrous) children, similar to the percentage of left-handed offspring of the conventional left-handers, and not the lower frequency found with the children of standard right-handers (Klar 1996). These results argued against the standard psychology model that handedness is a learned behavior and instead supported the single-gene model. Our model also genetically explained the baffling phenomenon of discordance in monozygotic twins, as each one of a twin pair with a random recessive genotype has an equal chance of being right-handed or left-handed. Others working on the so-called "complex" traits continue to think that handedness, being a complex trait, should be specified by the interaction of multiple genes combined with environmental influence.

It also turns out that the direction of scalp hair-whorls and handedness are coupled in fascinating ways. Most people in the general public are righties and their hair-whorls coil clockwise (~91%). Interestingly, the lefties and the ambidextrous individuals are equally divided in developing clockwise and anticlockwise whorl rotations. Likewise, individuals with anticlockwise rotation are one-half lefties/ambidextrous and one-half righties. The findings of predominant coupling between handedness and hair-whorl rotation in the general public, and their decoupling in lefties/ambidextrous individuals, establish that handedness and hair-whorl rotation develop from a common genetic mechanism (Klar 2003a). Nature wins, nurture looses!

HANDEDNESS AND PSYCHIATRIC DISEASES

Although handedness remains an interesting puzzle in its own right, our interest is not in finding the cause of handedness per se; rather, we are interested in explaining the partial correlation of handedness with the language specialization of brain hemispheres whereby 97% of right-handers but only 70% of left-handers and ambidextrous individuals develop language in the left side of the brain. Furthermore, the reason for a three-fold increased prevalence of left-handedness in patients with psychiatric diseases of schizophrenia and bipolar affective disorders remains unexplained. Watson knew the importance of handedness and brain hemisphere specialization; he was the Principal Investigator on an $8 million grant to map the locus causing bipolar affective disorder.

Despite thousands of studies conducted to date, the cause of these debilitating diseases and their mode of inheritance remains hotly debated. I have speculated that the handedness gene may have evolved in humans to localize the development of the language center only in the left hemisphere of the brain by a mechanism analogous to the visceral specification where nonrandom DNA strand segregation (Klar 1994) may well be crucial. It is possible that the same genetic mechanism predisposing individuals to left-handedness may at a lower rate cause language development in both brain hemispheres, resulting in illness (Klar 1999).

There are some new findings on the etiology of schizophrenia and bipolar affective disorders apparently involving brain laterality development from studies of affected families carrying chromosome translocations. The strongest evidence for a genetic basis for psychosis consists of a chromosome 1;11 translocation that segregates with the disorders through multiple generations in a large Scottish pedigree. Psychosis in this family is clearly due to genetics as no one without the translocation is diseased. Curiously though, only one half of the translocation carriers are diseased. This result satisfies a key prediction of the strand-segregation model by postulating randomization of the parental Watson and Crick chain segregation due to the translocation. In other words, psychosis develops when DNA chains of chromosome 1 or of 11 are not nonrandomly segregated due to the translocation (Klar 2002). The novel proposal is that a gene is not mutated, nor is an epigenetic process altered by the translocation. This rationale is drastically different from the conventional explanation involving genetic heterogeneity, environmental factors, segregation of modifiers, and variable penetrance of disease-causing mutations or epigenetic alterations at the translocation junction (Klar 2003b; Millar et al. 2003).

During my visit to CSHL in August 2001, Jim, at the prime age of 73, prodded me to map the handedness gene soon. He said, "I want to know the answer now while I can understand it and not later on when I may not."

TO CELEBRATE WATSON IS TO CELEBRATE SCIENCE

It would be hard to find someone more dedicated to science than Jim Watson. Working at CSHL, it was difficult to separate one's personal life from the scientific one; such an integrated lifestyle bothered some, but I benefited greatly from it. Despite the fact we were living and breathing a life of science, we felt that we were part of the family. For example, Jim and his wife, Liz, entertained all of the single or newly married young investigators at an annual Christmas Eve party at his residence.

In all my interactions with Jim, I have been most impressed by his foresight in singling out important problems, and then hiring and betting on younger talents to solve those problems. On behalf of the Yeast Group, I want to thank Jim for his support and encouragement. My own career profited greatly from my association with him and with my colleagues in the Yeast Group. I am fortunate enough to be able to say that Jim does bring out the best in all of us.

REFERENCES

Hicks J.B., Strathern J.N., and Klar A.J.S. 1979. Transposable mating type genes in *Saccharomyces cerevisiae*. *Nature* **282:** 478–483.

Klar A.J.S. 1992. The role of McClintock's controlling element concept in the story of yeast mating-type switching. In *The dynamic genome* (ed. N. Fedoroff and D. Bostein), pp. 307–314. Cold Spring Harbor Laboratory, New York.

Klar A.J.S. 1990. The development fate of fission yeast cells is determined by the pattern of inheritance of parental and grandparental DNA strands. *EMBO J.* **9:** 1407–1415.

Klar A.J.S. 1994. A model for specification of the left-right axis invertebrates. *Trends Genet.* **11:** 302–306.

Klar A.J.S. 1996. A single locus, *RGHT*, specifies preference for hand utilization in humans. *Cold Spring Harbor Symp. Quant. Biol.* **61:** 59–65.

Klar A.J.S. 1999. Genetic models for handedness, brain lateralization, schizophrenia, and manic depression. *Schizo. Res.* **39:** 207–218.

Klar A.J.S. 2002. The chromosome 1;11 translocation provides the best evidence supporting genetic etiology for schizophrenia and bipolar affective disorders. *Genetics* **160:** 1745–1747.

Klar A.J.S. 2003a. Human handedness and scalp hair-whorl direction develop from a common genetic mechanism. *Genetics* (in press).

Klar A.J.S. 2003b. Response to Millar et al. Critique of chromosome 1;11 translocation causing psychosis. *Genetics* **163:** 837–838.

Millar J.K., Thomson P.A., Wray N.R, Muir W.J., Blackwood D.H.R., and Porteous D.J. 2003. Response to Amar J. Klar: The chromosome 1;11 translocation provides the best evidence supporting genetic etiology for schizophrenia and bipolar affective disorders. *Genetics* **163:** 833–835.

Watson J.D. and Crick F.H.C. 1953. A structure for deoxyribose nucleic acid. *Nature* **171:** 737–738.

Big Shoes to Fill, with the Laces Untied

Bruce Stillman

Cold Spring Harbor Laboratory

As a student, I did not anticipate taking Jim Watson's advice or even meeting him. But even in graduate school half a world away in Australia, I unwittingly followed one of the rules for success in science that he presented at the 40th anniversary of the discovery of the double helix in 1993 (Watson 1993). "...you must always turn to people brighter than yourself" was his first rule and I have been fortunate to be able to do so, inside and outside science. And I did this by coming to Cold Spring Harbor Laboratory in 1979 as a postdoctoral fellow.

In Canberra I was advised not to go to Cold Spring Harbor. My graduate advisor, Alan Bellett, opposed the all-consuming, intimidating style of science that Jim and his protégé Joe Sambrook, once also a student in Canberra, had established at the beginning of the 1970s, when Cold Spring Harbor Laboratory became a major center for cancer research and attracted many of the best young scientists of the time. Jim had revived the Laboratory, setting it on a course to study cancer and bringing back its former scientific glory. He recreated an environment that I imagine paralleled the exciting graduate student summers he had spent at Cold Spring Harbor with the likes of Salvador Luria and Max Delbrück. But although Alan was against it, other people I knew in Canberra said "Go to Cold Spring Harbor: That's where the action is." So in the spring of 1979, I arrived to start a postdoctoral fellowship in a new area of science for the Laboratory, adenovirus DNA replication, and found myself, per Jim's first rule, among many people far smarter than I was used to. The place was intimidating enough, but that only challenged me to learn more and work harder, which I know is what Jim wanted of his young postdocs anyway.

It was immediately obvious that I had much to learn, but I was not discouraged. Jim had by then expanded the program of meetings and courses, and it was easy to sit in on lectures and learn from a more illustrious array of teachers than any single graduate course could put together. This opportunity is still available to the graduate students who matriculate in the school that we have appropriately named for Jim Watson.

My arrival as a postdoc was not my first visit to the Laboratory or my first meeting with Jim. The summer before, Jim, Tom Broker, and Ahmad Bukhari had organized the 43rd Cold Spring Harbor Symposium in part to celebrate the silver jubilee of the discovery of the double helix. The Symposium, appropriately on the replication and recombination of DNA, was a remarkable introduction to the world of Jim Watson. I was not supposed to be there, but just before the meeting began, Alan Bellett became

BRUCE STILLMAN

Successions are testing times for any organization, especially when the incumbent is a very hard act to follow. None of the traditional rules for choosing successors has much to recommend it. Hereditary, apostolic, elective—all of these have had their fair share of disasters. Dynastic succession—much out of favor in these democratic times—may be a good option, depending on the quality of the incumbent. If someone has done a poor job in guiding an institution, there is no reason to believe that they would do any better in choosing a successor. If, however, they have guided the institution with wisdom and imagination, there is every reason to believe that their choice will be wise.

When Jim arrived back in Cold Spring Harbor from his stint in Washington as Director of the Human Genome Project, he must have felt that the time had at last come to look around for a successor. The Lab had been running smoothly in his absence and much of the responsibility but little of the power had passed into other hands. Some years before, when Jim had briefly considered stepping down from the Directorship, a number of people had told him that Bruce Stillman was the best person for the job. But Jim then felt that Bruce was too young, that his work would suffer greatly, that he did not have enough experience, and so on. But the truth was that Jim himself was not ready to leave. By 1994, things had changed, and Bruce was the obvious and best choice.

Bruce was born in one of Melbourne's leafy suburbs, Glen Waverley, now highly fashionable, then merely genteel. He completed high school and his undergraduate degree in Sydney. After submitting his Ph.D. thesis to the John Curtin School of Medical Research at the Australian National University, Bruce moved to Cold Spring Harbor Laboratory as a postdoctoral fellow in 1979. He was promoted to the scientific staff in 1981 and, in 1994, was named Director.

Bruce is recognized as a world leader in studies of DNA replication and chromatin structure. His laboratory recently demonstrated how a set of proteins works in concert to duplicate both the basic sequence of DNA as well as silenced states of chromatin. The findings provide the first explanation of how both DNA sequences and their associated states of gene expression are coordinately passed on to future generations of cells.

For his accomplishments, Bruce Stillman has received a number of honors, including election as a Fellow of The Royal Society and, more recently, as a member of the U.S. National Academy of Sciences. In 1999, Bruce was appointed an Officer of the Order of Australia for service to scientific research in the field of molecular biology.

---

unable to travel and I was plucked from my lab bench as his stand-in. Two days later, I arrived at Kennedy Airport at 5:30 in the morning and was in Cold Spring Harbor in time for the first morning session of the meeting. At the first coffee break, I somewhat sheepishly approached Jim who was talking to Arthur Kornberg, the founder of the field, to thank him for accepting an unknown graduate student as a replacement speaker. Jim was very pleased to say hello and welcomed me to the Laboratory. I know now that Jim at meetings prefers to hear a good talk from a new, young scientist than a repeat performance from a Lab head. At that time, Jim reckoned that only scientists under 30 were capable of doing important science.

I have attended every Symposium since, and what a learning experience it has been. Looking back at the topics Jim selected for meetings and also at the people he recruited to teach courses at Cold Spring Harbor, it is clear that these events have significantly influenced science, not just what was done at Cold Spring Harbor Laboratory, but in whole fields of research. Yeast genetics is just one example. Jim's insight was to bring Fred Sherman and Gerry Fink to Cold Spring Harbor for 17 years to teach generations of young people who have become leaders in the field.

Two months went by at Cold Spring Harbor in the spring of 1979 and I still had not passed my thesis defense. Because I had left Canberra the day I submitted my thesis and did not intend to return, it was arranged that Jim and Marshall Horwitz of the nearby Albert Einstein College of Medicine would be on my thesis committee, with one Australian examiner, Jim Peacock, sending in questions by mail. I never found out what those questions were. The thesis exam was short and consisted only of discussion over coffee about what I was going to do at Cold Spring Harbor. Jim was not interested in what I had done, only in what was to come. He has never been one for wasting time and conforming to rules.

Jim would occasionally wander into the laboratory late at night and just stand there, waiting for someone to acknowledge his presence with a short report of what they were doing. This is really how I got to know Jim. He wanted the bottom line, not the details, especially since I was doing biochemistry, which was never high on Jim's list of interesting topics of conversation. But he did like the results. At first, I was jealous of the cell biologists Keith Burridge and Jim Feramisco who briefly occupied the lab down the corridor and had amazing microscope images of the inner workings of cancer cells that attracted Jim's attention. As in the double helix, Jim saw beauty in the actin cables that were disrupted in tumor cells. But the photos did not reveal how things really worked, and Jim wanted to understand that and then move on. Jim's famous textbook, *Molecular Biology of the Gene*, excited me and countless others by his extraordinarily lucid descriptions of complex phenomena and his ability to point out the next important areas on which to work (Watson 1965). The lesson I learned from all this was that clarity of thought opens paths for discovery.

I had to walk up the hill to James (no relation to JDW) lab to do all my tissue culture work, since Demerec did not have sufficient hoods and had no spinner flasks or incubators. Current students and postdocs in the Demerec building may think this strange but I was happy to do it. I took the opportunity to run into the "James gang," those scientists who studied under the watchful eye of Joe Sambrook. James was also where Jim's office was, with its opportunities to discuss science or to hear scientific gossip. And there was plenty of that in James. I still learn important (and not-so-important) gossip from Jim, who tells it with the impishness of an Irishman spinning a yarn. James lab was the center of the Laboratory in those days and my frequent visits there may have had something to do with my eventual appointment as Director of the Laboratory.

In the mid 1980s, I saw at first hand another example of the impact Jim could have on science outside Cold Spring Harbor. The 1986 Symposium on the Molecular Biology of *Homo sapiens* was held in the new Grace Auditorium (built instead of the squash court and gym that Jim has wanted at Cold Spring Harbor for so long and still does not exist). An afternoon session of the meeting was devoted to a discussion of the merits of sequencing the human genome. This was a relatively new idea and Jim was wary

Mike Mathews, Bruce Stillman, and Fred Aselbergs, 1979. (Courtesy CSHL Archives.)

of the proposal by the Department of Energy that its National Laboratories would control the project. He wanted support for the idea that the National Institutes of Health would do so. The discussion was memorable: Many scientists were strongly opposed to science done on the large scale that would be necessary. But Jim knew by then that genome sequencing had to go ahead and already had a vision of how it could be done. He invited colleagues both for and against the idea to debate the issue, and throughout the discussion, he stood silently on the sidelines. Then, at the right moment, he spoke, outlining how NIH should be involved and how he saw the project moving forward. Although he did not change the mind of those who opposed the idea in the first place, he did influence those who supported the project. Soon, a National Academy of Science committee, under the leadership of Jim's long-standing friend Bruce Alberts, recommended support for the project the way Jim had envisioned it. So it was not surprising that Jim was appointed the first Director of the Human Genome Project at NIH and played a key role in defining the scope of the research. Much of what Jim presented at that 1986 afternoon discussion came to be, although I do not think even he could have predicted that the human genome would be completed exactly 50 years after the announcement of the double helix.

Did Jim get involved in the early stages of the genome projects by chance? I think not. Characteristically, he had the vision and saw the path long before most others did and he could not resist bookending his career in experimental DNA science with the double helix on one end and the sequence of the whole human genome on the other. But there may have been an additional reason. By then, he had been running Cold Spring Harbor Laboratory for nearly 20 years. The research was moving along well and, with David Micklos, he had just started the DNA Learning Center, the latest of his major additions to the programs of the Laboratory. Was it time for a new challenge, especially one that did not require him to give up the considerable advantages of being head of Cold Spring Harbor? After all, Jim is restless and always wants to move forward into new areas.

He took on the Human Genome Project in Washington with considerable personal hardship, commuting from Cold Spring Harbor to Washington weekly and working harder than he had for some time. I could see it in his face, especially after a year or two. But it was for the benefit of the entire scientific community. Jim ensured that biology would play a major role in the Genome Project by attracting talented geneticists such as Maynard Olson, David Botstein, and Francis Collins into the project, with Francis succeeding him as Director of the NIH effort. Moreover, his foresight in including ethics and social issues helped gain Congressional support for the project that was essential if it was to succeed. Even after leaving Washington, he tirelessly worked the halls of Congress to ensure increases to the genome budget so that the project would not lose momentum. Few are aware of the behind-the-scene contributions Jim made at critical times to ensure that those he had encouraged to risk their careers on the ambitious project would have the funds necessary to continue at full speed.

The Genome Project taught me another of Jim's lessons. Over the years, and on many issues, I have noticed that Jim knows where he wants to be long before others realize where he is going. He may propose outlandish or extreme positions that I suspect he knows will provoke arguments. But those who argue usually end up compromising with him, thus agreeing to what he wanted in the first place.

Joe Sambrook's departure for Dallas in 1985 and Jim's increasingly frequent trips to Washington meant that he needed help running Cold Spring Harbor Laboratory. He turned to Terri Grodzicker and Rich Roberts who, respectively, became Assistant Director for Academic Affairs and Assistant Director for Research. They were obvious choices if Cold Spring Harbor was to move forward when Jim was unable to give full-time attention to details. With exciting science from Ed Harlow's cancer research lab that demonstrated the first connections between oncogenes and tumor suppressor genes, the Laboratory was in good scientific shape. Rich Roberts ran a laboratory next to my own in Demerec that was always a pleasure to visit because of the attractive technicians who worked there. Like Joe Sambrook, Rich was one of the really smart scientists at Cold Spring Harbor with whom a discussion was always productive. He too nurtured my science at a critical time, and later I worked closely with him on administrative duties in Demerec.

By 1990, I had been at the Laboratory for 11 years and my research had gone well. I was approached about becoming Director of the Virus Laboratory at the University of California, Berkeley, and would have left Cold Spring Harbor in 1991 had it not been for an unexpected lunch. Without my knowledge, Jim had gathered support for my appointment as Assistant Director of Cold Spring Harbor Laboratory, with the understanding that if it worked out, I would succeed him as Director two years later. Jim would then take on the newly created position of President. This complete surprise was sprung over lunch at Jim's ultra-exclusive country club. It was classic Watson, doing the unconventional and changing course in a dramatic way. Victor McElheny's (2003) biography of Jim alludes to considerable prior discussion about the Directorship of which I was completely unaware (and which, from my discussions with Jim, may not have happened exactly as McElheny suggests).

Although profoundly honored by this proposal, I had several concerns. At the age of 37, I was not yet ready to give up research. I had a young family to consider. And how would this arrangement square with the fact that Rich Roberts was running research at the Laboratory? During much of the five weeks I spent considering the Cold Spring Harbor offer, I discussed with Rich his possible continuing role in helping run the lab. But it was not surprising that just before I assumed the Directorship, Rich left to join New England Biolabs where he became Research Director. A year later, he and former Cold Spring Harbor scientist Phillip Sharp won the Nobel Prize for their contributions to one of the greatest discoveries in modern molecular biology. Jim's abrupt change in leadership was complete.

I was warned by many, including Barbara McClintock, who had an inherent suspicion of anyone with the title "Director," that Jim would not yield power at Cold Spring Harbor. But he handed over many of the reins surprisingly quickly. Jim retained responsibility for long-term strategic planning, and initially kept direct oversight of the Laboratory Press, the DNA Learning Center, and the Banbury Center. I ran research and oversaw the program of meetings and courses. From the beginning, Jim gave me a very free hand in hiring scientists and directing research. A new neuroscience program had just gotten under way, something Jim had long desired at Cold Spring Harbor. I quickly had to learn some neuroscience and spent many interesting hours discussing with prominent neurobiologists, particularly Eric Kandel, ideas about how we should proceed. As Director, I had Jim as a valued mentor and I learned from him to have the confidence not to listen to all the advice of trusted colleagues. We had lengthy discussions about the kind of research to be done in the neuroscience center that opened in late 1991. In making the first staff appointments, I would not have had the guts by myself to ignore the advice of prominent neuroscientists to stay out of *Drosophila* genetics as a way of understanding learning and memory. But Jim was prepared to take the chance and I became equally convinced about the power of *Drosophila* behavioral genetics after seeing Tim Tully's flies at Brandeis perform after a memory training session. Jim was right: This was the way to go and it fitted in well with the long history of genetics at Cold Spring Harbor Laboratory.

Jim imparted to me a style of directing science that is uniquely his. Do not be afraid to take bold moves; invest in young people; say yes even if you do not have the resources in hand; and most importantly, on rare but critical occasions, know when to say no. Mentoring colleagues was a talent that Jim had down to a fine art. It is perhaps the most important lesson I have learned from Jim in all our long relationship, and now, knowing how difficult it is, I believe it is one of his most remarkable accomplishments. When he first came to Cold Spring Harbor, many were skeptical about his administrative skills. But he rejuvenated the Laboratory and has since become recognized as one of the best science administrators ever.

From Jim, I also learned to listen to, but not necessarily follow, the advice of Cold Spring Harbor Trustees. If I had taken the advice of our scientific Trustees when we were deciding to establish the graduate school now named in Jim's honor, we would not now have our superb students. The Watson School has been a resounding success, convincing even the most doubting critic that Cold Spring Harbor Laboratory has created yet another unique resource to enhance its academic environment. A reminder of another of Jim's 1993 rules: Take risks (Watson 1993).

Few of those who work at or visit Cold Spring Harbor know how generously Jim and Liz Watson have contributed financially to the success of the many programs here. Much of the artwork that now graces our buildings, many of the annual exhibitions and events that make Cold Spring Harbor an interesting place to be, and numerous other community causes have been generously supported by or donated by the Watsons. When I became Director, they decided to relinquish the beautiful home of 20 years in which they had lived most of their married life. Airslie, a grand and beautiful house at the head of the Sandspit that separates the inner and outer waterways at the head of Cold Spring Harbor, has been home to Directors of the Laboratory since 1943, starting with Milislav Demerec. There was no need for the Watsons to move: As President, Jim continued to have a vital role at the Laboratory and Airslie had been elegantly renovated just before they moved in. But with characteristic generosity, they paid for the building of a new house, Ballybung, and moved there in 1994. To me this was an extraordinary gesture. Only Jim knew, as I now know, that living in a house off the Laboratory grounds is not compatible with the demands of successfully running Cold Spring Harbor Laboratory. As I sit at home in Airslie writing this essay, I feel exceptionally lucky to have Jim as a neighbor and a mentor. He wrote in 1993 that it is good to have someone up your sleeve to save you when you're in deep shit (Watson 1993). Jim has been the one up my sleeve.

There are numerous times in the summer when Jim wanders the grounds of Cold Spring Harbor Laboratory in loafers with untied laces, reflecting the casual atmosphere that typifies the place. No one can fill Jim's shoes, laces tied or untied. On the table next to me is Jim's latest book, *DNA: The Secret of Life* (Watson 2003), one that should rival the success of his earlier description of the discovery of the double helix. In this new book, he makes clear where he wants people and society to go. Once again, Jim Watson is ahead of the pack, and although it may take society a long time to catch up, eventually that will happen and it will be for the good.

REFERENCES

McElheny V.K. 2003. *Watson and DNA: Making a scientific revolution.* Perseus, Cambridge, Massachusetts.

Watson J.D. 1965. *Molecular biology of the gene.* W.A. Benjamin, New York.

Watson J.D. 1993. Succeeding in science: Some rules of thumb. *Science* **261:** 1812–1813.

Watson J.D. 2003. *DNA: The secret of life* (with A. Berry). Alfred A. Knopf, New York.

Just Jim

Michael Wigler

Cold Spring Harbor Laboratory

SAVED BY THE DOUBLE HELIX

In 1962, as a ninth grader, I was in a program for the scientifically gifted. One day, responding to an after-class question, my teacher whispered, lest anyone overhear, that every cell of the body had a complete blueprint for the entire organism. Ridiculous, I thought. First, how could anyone know this to be true? Second, even if it were true, how foolish to burden every cell with all this information. How could the specialized cell know which part of the blueprint it was meant to read? Third, such a blueprint could never be embodied, let alone copied or read.

A strong prejudice formed on the spot: Life was a freakish accident on the planet earth, and no good principles would come by studying it. If the workings of life were a mystery, it was because its designs were so utterly silly that they could not be disentangled through the efforts of rational minds. I vowed that I would waste no more time on Biology.

By the time I had entered twelfth grade, my interest in Physics suffered a similar fate. At the atomic level, the rules of the universe became increasingly capricious, and beyond a certain scale, the rules themselves were forever veiled. Since humans held no interest for me, as any species capable of the death camps and Hiroshima could hardly be worth study, by a process of deduction all that remained was Mathematics. Poetry was to be found there, embedded in design and economy of thought, and its only limits were imagination and the power of mind.

Two years into Princeton, limited by both my imagination and power of mind, and lacking sustaining human relationships, my cognitive world had crumbled, followed soon after by my emotional state. Or perhaps it was the reverse sequence. From that cognitive and emotional rubble, I began a long period of reconstruction. This recovery drew strength from family and friends and from some surprising quarters, including a textbook on molecular biology.

The first step was to recognize that if I were in an existential hell, so was everyone else. This reconciled me to humanity, and one of my early decisions was to help others, should I achieve competence. Pursuit of Medicine seemed logical. Of course, the high life of the mind was no longer an option, and I would have to study Biology.

J.T. Bonner and Edward Cox taught Biology 101, 102. The suggested reading for the first semester included D'Arcy Thompson's *On Growth and Form* (Thompson 1942).

MICHAEL WIGLER

Cold Spring Harbor changes people. From promising to fully fledged, wide-eyed to worldly, and, sometimes, from sensitive to cynical. And these changes can happen rapidly, within the span of a postdoctoral fellowship or even over a summer or two. But Mike Wigler has worked at Cold Spring Harbor for 25 years and has changed imperceptibly, if at all. As he describes in the following essay, all of the adjustments needed to succeed in the Cold Spring Harbor style of science were already in place before he came to the Laboratory. So well-bonded was Wigler to Watsonian laws of behavior and thought that the CSHL created by Jim may be the only place where Wigler's science could have flourished so abundantly.

In 1981, Mike's lab was among the first to isolate the human *ras* oncogene. Two years later, his laboratory identified a form of the gene in yeast, providing a powerful model system to map the *ras* signaling pathway from cell surface to the nucleus. A vivid, if starry-eyed, account of these experiments was published in *Natural Obsessions: The Search for the Oncogene* by Natalie Angier (1988, Houghton Mifflin, Boston).

To discover new cancer genes, Mike, in collaboration with Nikolai Lisitsyn, developed a powerful technique called representational difference analysis (RDA), which detects genetic abnormalities that accumulate in the genomes of tumor cells, including DNA amplifications, rearrangements, loss of heterozygosity, and homozygous deletions. RDA led Mike to the *PTEN* gene, a tumor suppressor gene that is mutated in many kinds of human tumors and in the germ lines of people who inherit a condition (Cowden's syndrome) that predisposes them to breast, thyroid, and other cancers.

More recently, Mike has begun to combine representational approaches of genomic analysis with DNA microarray technology to develop methods for high-resolution scanning of the genomes of cancer cells.

This seemed a heroic but unsuccessful effort to infuse Biology with Science. *The Double Helix* by James Watson was also suggested reading (Watson 1968). This, on the other hand, was an adventure story of the highest order. A brash American had made the biological discovery of the century. Armed with a sharp instinct for significance, an unrelentingly honest eye, and blindness for barriers, Watson had revealed the Great Secret before hardly anyone knew it existed. To carry off the crime, this Hermes needed an Hephaestus, Francis Crick, the accomplice whose wayward genius could be diverted for sufficient moments.

I have always been able to block out the world, and I had the barest awareness of DNA before reading *The Double Helix*. I knew none of the details. My awareness of molecular biology came upon first reading. *The Double Helix* was for me an historical record, a morality play, a great scientific treatise, and an adventure story all at once. It made a deeper impression on me than anything I had read before or since, with the exception of Aesop's Fables (from my early boyhood), the Bible, and Kafka's *The Castle*. The horizons of the possible reopened. The world was not bleak. I just had taken the wrong view.

All this was confirmed in the second semester. The text was the second edition of Watson's *Molecular Biology of the Gene* (Watson 1970). This brave melding of new ideas from chemistry, techniques from physics, and logical reasoning gave proof that a new science had been born. I flew through the pages. The biological "world" was presented as the problems Nature had overcome, with problems in abundance. The laws of physics were the tools Nature used to create herself. Perceiving her problems and her solutions was the human challenge, testing our imagination, resourcefulness, and knowledge of the laws. Each discovery was an adventure story, judged by its relevance to the other stories and by how well it was told.

I took joy that the world had opened, but I was to miss the fun. I was not to partake. My fate was Medical School, my penance for years of closed-minded thinking.

PRELUDE TO A MEETING

No one accepts penance well, especially self-administered, and I never made it through medical school. At the time, there was an irrepressible excitement for all of the biological sciences. Drawn to this excitement in my first year at Rutgers Medical School, I began to experiment, something I had never done before. I discovered, if only for myself, that disrupting the cytoskeleton could inhibit replication of certain viruses and that I could culture nerve cells from the embryonic chick heart. Everywhere I turned I recognized unexplored terrain. But before long, the medical deans at Columbia University, to which I had transferred, discovered something too, that I had been an admissions error.

I made the transition from medical school to graduate school smoothly, completed my graduate work with Bernie Weinstein on tumor promoters, and commenced my work with Richard Axel and Saul Silverstein on gene transfer. But I had neglected to write my thesis and was unable to afford dates with my girlfriend. I woke up, wrote my thesis, and graduated. Suddenly I was a hot property in the job market.

Never having lived more than 40 miles from New York City, I wanted to stay in the area. My family was on Long Island, and my girlfriend lived in Manhattan. Mike Botchan, a friend of Axel and a scientist at Cold Spring Harbor Laboratory, knew and appreciated my work. Mike had done beautiful work, as had other scientists at the Lab, producing discoveries that had the same flavor and rigor as those described in the *Molecular Biology of the Gene*. I recognized the signature. Mike encouraged me to give a seminar at the Lab and meet Jim Watson. But Columbia was also interested in keeping me.

There was no love lost between Columbia and Jim Watson. Columbia was home to Erwin Chargaff, the nucleic acid chemist who discovered the parity rule: the content of G matched that of C, and A of T, in DNA. This was a huge clue to the puzzle, explained by the complementarity of the double helix. Apparently, Chargaff held a grudge. Even in 1974, when I took the required course in biochemistry, one of his colleagues would give one lecture questioning whether the model of the double helix was scientifically sound.

I inferred that an unintended side effect of publishing *The Double Helix*, and the style of science that it spawned, was to radically change the equilibrium between thought, data, and belief. It is undeniable that the results of molecular biologists had *appeal*. The unstated fear of the old guard was the wall that separated what we believed to be true from what we wished to be true would erode. This wall, mortared over centuries with blood, was what made Science strong. I thought that molecular biology was rigorous, but the established forces were very resistant, and as a result, Columbia had remained at the station, very much after the train had departed.

To regain lost momentum, Columbia had hired Sol Spiegelman to direct an Institute for Cancer Research. The Institute was in effect a ghetto for molecular biologists at the College of Physicians & Surgeons, segregated geographically at the Delafield Hospital along Riverside Drive. I viewed it as an oasis, removed from the plodding habits of established scientific thinking.

Sol had established the first practical method of using hybridization to distinguish different nucleic acid species (filter hybridization) and had established the first in vitro self-replicating system, based on RNA phage polymerases and templates, a precursor to the polymerase chain reaction and in vitro evolution. He was an excellent biochemist and had missed by a few months being the first to discover reverse transcriptase.

Sol clearly had great respect for Jim Watson, and the students who had been through Jim's lab at Harvard. But what I think Sol most admired about Jim was that he kept his name off the papers of his students. Don Mills told me this Spiegelman story. One morning, when Don was a lowly technician in Sol's lab, he had an idea for an experiment, which he communicated to a postdoc. This postdoc apparently talked to Sol. Later that afternoon, Sol came to Don and said, "I had a great idea. Try this..."

Despite the almost universal admiration for what Jim Watson had accomplished, charges and innuendos began to flow from many quarters. Jim was prone to uncritical enthusiasms. He was a finisher, not an originator. He set researcher against researcher in an intramural competition to increase productivity. He was obsessed with sex. He had a horribly nasty streak. And maybe he was an anti-Semite.

Of course, none of this was true. But even Botchan, who was exceedingly fond of Jim, set a cautionary note. When I talk to Jim, Botchan suggested, I might not be able to understand him; he mumbles and is often incoherent.

JUST JIM

I did come to Cold Spring Harbor, and sank into my work, which is all I had ever wanted to do. Jim and Liz came to our wedding, and my wife Deedee and I still have the pitcher with the painted pig they gave us as a wedding gift.

Jim did harshly criticize my job seminar, but only after I had been at the Lab for 20 years. His faith was in bright and ambitious young people, and his job was to identify them and stoke their ambitions. From the beginning, Jim supported my work and my ego, unstintingly. I never saw him treat any other scientist differently, or set one against another. Doing science is hard enough. His advice was unerring when from time to time I came to him with the choices that I could not make. When I ran over budget, which I did every year except one, Jim never tried to trim my sails. You have to spend money to bring in money, he explained. Think big. "A Director's job," he once told me, "is to say yes. If I have to say no, then I have failed."

I did find his conversations hard to follow at first, as he leapt from observation to observation, and he did tend to mumble. With time it made more sense, as I did the work to find the thread. There was always a thread, often an interesting and enter-

Celia Frazer and Mike Wigler, 1979. (Courtesy CSHL Archives.)

taining observation about human social organization, or a concealed piece of advice. But I never gave Jim much to work with and never shared Jim's fascination with the blue bloods of Long Island's Gold Coast. ("Always have rich friends," he advised.) After many years, Jim learned that I wasn't a conversationalist. So now he talks to me mainly about tennis, a shared passion. Jim wishes it remembered, he bragged, that at age 75 he could serve at 100 mph.

I never experienced, nor saw, the famous bad temper, except once. It was in a dispute with Columbia over patent rights. Jim could use his anger effectively in a negotiation, and his reputation as a hothead served him well. He explained to me that you have to be judicious when calling someone a "shit," or especially a "little shit." Reserve that for special occasions, he advised.

Jim was often outspoken, though, and this landed him in hot water more than once, most notably when he went to work for the NIH as the first Director of the Human Genome Project. I was very disappointed that he took that assignment—that a great man of science had joined the bureaucracy in Washington. So when I heard the news that he was fired, I was delighted. He had not capitulated.

On that day, as I saw Jim cross the lawn in front of Grace Auditorium, I went up to him to offer my congratulations. For the first time, Jim glared hard at me. Perhaps he misinterpreted my unrestrained joy as schadenfreude. Grimacing, he told me, "This is the worst day of my life."

PRECURSORS

How had I so misunderstood him? This puzzled me for years, until I read a biography of Niels Bohr by Abraham Pais (1991). Niels Bohr was the Danish physicist who at a very young age proposed the first quantum structure of the atom. He was beloved by the Danes, who regarded him as a national treasure and hero. Bohr was the Director of the renowned Institute of Theoretical Physics, where many of the great physicists of the twentieth century were mentored. He was always generous with advice, and his enthusiasm for science irrepressible. And here is a critical detail. Bohr mumbled, and leapt from subject to subject in an apparently unordered manner, so much so that conversations with him were invariably described as difficult to follow. Bohr, later in life, became involved in politics and the role of physics in modern society.

The parallels were unmistakable. Then I recalled from my reading of *The Double Helix* that Jim had spent a brief period as a postdoctoral fellow at Bohr's Institute and had dinner with the great man. This was before Jim's place in History had been secured, and surely Bohr must have profoundly influenced him, perhaps subconsciously.

Like Bohr, Jim viewed himself, and came to be viewed, as a citizen-scientist. He always had an eye for the larger epic, and eagerly moved in a much larger circle of life. He suffered miserably under Bernadine Healy as NIH director, and mourned the loss of the opportunity to serve the nation. He summed up his experience this way: "If you don't like your boss, quit."

I proposed my theory to Jim—that he was influenced by Bohr—but he actively denied the idea, and offered me a much less convincing exemplar of science that he had chosen as a model, George Gamow. Jim's denials of the parallels with Bohr have, I believe, an odd root. One must assume that Bohr, like Jim, was a brilliant man. But Jim does not regard himself as brilliant. Although Jim does recognize his own genius, I am not sure that Jim regards himself as smart. (By the way, imagine Bohr's self-image, surrounded as he always was with wunderkinder.) I have often heard Jim say, "Scientists do not have to be very smart." I take more to heart this saying of Jim's, "If you are the smartest person in the room, then you have failed."

With time, the parallels to Gamow grew on me. I recalled a title on my childhood bookshelves, *One, Two, Three... Infinity*, with its mysterious cover drawing of the mysterious universe (Gamow 1961). Hadn't Gamow, one of the few physicists with an understanding of general relativity, written popular books on the most difficult of scientific subjects? Long before Stephen Hawking's *Brief History of Time* (Hawking 1988), and the spate of popularized science that followed, Gamow tried to make modern physics accessible. Although that effort failed, certainly one of the successes of molecular biology has been its accessibility. And who might have suggested to Jim that he could write a comprehensible memoir?

THE FUTURE

When finally I did meet Jim in the summer of 1978, in the little office in James lab overlooking the harbor, what struck me as peculiar was not that the office was small, not that he mumbled, not the frequent guttural interruptions of speech. No, Jim was intent on the future, and although he could not see it clearly, or verbalize it, he wanted to get there first. He was not in the least embarrassed by not knowing precisely how to get there. Just follow your sense. The future would not hide.

This attitude was strange to me. Science, I had thought, was largely the work of cutting through old myths, slaying the false ideas that bind us. But Jim had a different view. The kind of science he pursued was new entirely. There were no false ideas of any strength to struggle against, because the very objects of our inquiry had yet to be experienced. The struggle was to bring new ideas into existence where none had existed before.

I saw this most clearly during the development of Neurobiology at the Lab. Here was a subject for which we had few conceptual handles. The safe thing to do would have been to focus on the development of the nervous system, where techniques similar to those used throughout developmental biology were yielding some solid results. Jim chose instead Learning and Memory. Jim reasoned, why wouldn't this field yield to the same assault of youthful enthusiasm that had sent other walls crumbling down? So we began with fly genetics, a once promising approach that had since been largely discarded by others. Jim hired Ron Davis and Tim Tully and research in Neurobiology at Cold Spring Harbor was reborn. Jim would have started other initiatives, especially in behavioral genetics, but one's energy does not go on forever.

To bring Neurobiology a home, Jim went to his rich friends, asking them to believe in him. They did, enabling Jim to build a lab up on the hill. If I recall correctly, when the plans for the lab on the hill were in the early stages, Jim wanted four bell towers, not just the single one we currently have. One for each nucleotide, I might have asked. No, he said, there should be one for each of the three great religions, and one for the fourth. Which one is that, I inquired. He replied, "The one yet to be discovered." "If we don't try," I imagine him saying, "we will have failed."

REFERENCES

Gamow G. 1961. *One, two, three...infinity: Facts & speculations of science*. Viking Press, New York.

Hawking S.W. 1988. *Brief history of time: From the big bang to black holes*. Bantam Books, New York.

Pais A. 1991. *Niels Bohr's times: In physics, philosophy, and polity*. Oxford University Press, United Kingdom.

Thompson D.W. 1942. *On growth and form*. Cambridge University Press, United Kingdom.

Watson J.D. 1968. *The double helix: A personal account of the discovery of the structure of DNA*. Atheneum, New York.

Watson J.D. 1970. *Molecular biology of the gene*, 2nd edition. W.A. Benjamin, New York.

Milestones and Mentoring: How Jim Watson Influenced a Scientific Career

Douglas Hanahan

University of California, San Francisco

Perhaps the most unappreciated of Jim Watson's contributions to science by the community at large is the cadre of young scientists that Jim has mentored, both at Harvard and at Cold Spring Harbor Laboratory. Many of them rank among the more influential scientists of their generation, having made important and in some cases historic contributions to knowledge of biological and biochemical principles and mechanisms. I was one of the young scientists whose career was significantly impacted by Jim, and my story may help convey his extraordinary influence as a mentor over a period of some 25 years.

MY EARLY DAYS AT HARVARD

My entrée into biology came in 1975 as an MIT physics undergraduate student who reluctantly took an introductory course in biology, fortuitously taught by Salvador Luria (coincidentally Jim Watson's thesis advisor), based on his still remarkable textbook, *36 Lectures in Biology* (Luria 1975). Luria was inspiring to me, as until then, I had naïvely considered biology a boring categorical science. He conveyed an infectious enthusiasm about a revolution that was unfolding in biology, catalyzed by the technological breakthroughs of recombinant DNA and molecular cloning that were certain to allow access to genes within the genomes of any organism. Feeling that the revolution in quantum physics had matured, if not plateaued, I was drawn to this uncharted new molecular biology and the capability to clone and manipulate genes.

Being in Cambridge in 1975–1976, it was hard to be unaware of another side to the revolution in recombinant DNA—a growing debate about the safety and ethics of cloning genes from humans and other organisms. My first encounter with Jim Watson came in a forum held in the spring of 1976 at the Harvard Science Center. He had come from Cold Spring Harbor to take part in the debate and was pointedly dismissive of those who raised concerns about hypothetical dangers of recombinant DNA technology. I don't recall (nor imagine, now knowing Jim) whether he was diplomatic or particularly logical in his defense of recombinant DNA, but he was determined that we must immediately and aggressively pursue the opportunities afforded by the technology. In the short run, the proponents of recombinant DNA lost their battle. The debate locally led to a ban on DNA cloning in Cambridge, and nationally to a set of guidelines

DOUGLAS HANAHAN

In the early 1980s, Doug Hanahan acquired a jet-black Datsun 280Z. He would typically arrive at James laboratory, unannounced in the middle of the night after a lightning drive down I95 from Harvard and would disappear equally suddenly a few weeks later in a healthy roar of exhaust. The people working in James were quite jealous of both Doug's car and his lifestyle. None of them could possibly afford a vehicle that was so intensely fashionable; and the idea of swinging between places with such complementary virtues as Cold Spring Harbor and Cambridge certainly had its attractions. All this contributed to Doug's reputation, which he did little to discourage, as Playboy of the Northeastern World. But nothing could be further from the truth: Doug was an intensely serious scientist who worked with high efficiency and productivity, even by the demanding standards of the James laboratory.

At Cold Spring Harbor, Doug worked on methods to improve both the efficiency and reproducibility of transformation of *E. coli* by plasmids. Twenty years later, his transformation buffers and strains remain those of choice for most people. After writing his thesis (*The Transfer of DNA between the Genomes of* E. coli *and Mammalian Cells*), Doug began work on animal models of cancer by constructing a series of transgenic mice in which SV40 T antigen is expressed exclusively in the insulin-producing cells of the pancreas. Doug's imaginative exploration of these animals and Jim's involvement at crucial points along the way are described in this essay.

from the National Institutes of Health dictating that cloning mammalian genes should be performed in specialized physical containment laboratories. These policies and politics delayed progress of the revolution in molecular biology and frustrated many, and they profoundly affected my career in an incongruously beneficial way.

During my first 18 months as a graduate student at Harvard, I did "rotations," in the laboratories of Paul Doty in Conant Laboratory (an appendage of the Chemistry Department), and with Wally Gilbert and Matt Meselson in the Biological Laboratories (the "Biolabs"). I took a few courses in biochemistry and molecular biology and was deeply impressed by Jim's brilliant textbook called *Molecular Biology of the Gene* (Watson 1965) which was remarkable for its visual style and conceptual clarity. While little was accomplished in my rotation in Wally's lab, two important seeds were set. First, I assimilated an attitude of the Gilbert laboratory, born in the days when Jim and Wally ran a group together. It was an attitude of scientific self-confidence, of "chutzpah": You should not feel insecure about being a novice in a particular field, despite natural tendencies to veer into scientific areas where you were knowledgeable. Rather, if your work led you into a new field, you should dive in, being prepared to look the novice if not the fool for so doing. Sometimes such naïveté could be a blessing, as you were not burdened by the conventional wisdom (and preconceptions) of the field. The second seed set by my experience in the Gilbert lab involved the insulin gene, as Wally's lab was preoccupied at the time with cloning the rat and human insulin genes in a tense and exciting race with Bill Rutter and his colleagues at the University of California, San Francisco. I was instilled not only with the physiological importance of insulin, but also with the special qualities (and challenges in studying) of the cells that make it, the β cells of the pancreatic islet of Langerhans.

Then, in January 1978, I joined the lab that Paul Doty co-ran with his wife Helga Boedker, deciding that their plan to clone the developmentally regulated collagen genes was ripe. And, with the imminent departure of two postdocs, Hans Lehrach and Anna-Marie Frischauf, I could see the opportunity to play a lead role in the project.

The plan of the Doty laboratory to clone cDNAs for chicken collagen genes in *E. coli* was stalled by the policies of the National Institutes of Health requiring that molecular cloning experiments be performed in special P3 physical containment laboratories. Harvard did not have a P3 lab. Being unable to get access to the newly constructed P3 lab at MIT, Paul Doty turned to his old friend Jim Watson. Cold Spring Harbor Laboratory had built a P3 lab so that its scientists could clone viral genes. Jim approved Paul's request, despite some skepticism from Joe Sambrook, who was himself using recombinant DNA technology to further the Lab's work on DNA tumor viruses. That decision became a milestone for me, leading me into a decades-long association with CSHL and an enduring relationship with Jim. In late January of 1978, Hans Lehrach and I traveled to CSHL with ice buckets of materials, intending to clone a cDNA for chicken collagen.

The P3 containment lab was in a corner of James laboratory, where Joe Sambrook and a group of extraordinary young scientists were studying DNA tumor viruses. The "James gang" included (or was soon to include) Mike Botchan, Robert Tjian, Terri Grodzicker, Ashley Dunn, Yasha Gluzman, and David Lane. The offices were sequestered in a separate wing of the building, and Jim's office was at the far end of the corridor, with a sweeping view over an idyllic scene of small lab buildings, pastoral landscaping, and the inner harbor. I was introduced to Jim shortly after my arrival. Jim encouraged us and was disparaging of the NIH guidelines that had brought us to CSHL.

Working under cumbersome circumstances in the confinement of the small P3 lab, Hans and I made a cDNA library and transferred the recombinant plasmid DNAs into the enfeebled *E. coli* strain χ1776. Hoping to get thousands of colonies, we got only a handful, and none proved to contain the collagen gene. We went back to Harvard empty-handed, where we produced another batch of cDNA, and returned to CSHL. The second visit again ended in failure, with still too few colonies.

It was frustrating to travel from the Doty lab at Harvard to CSHL with our laboriously prepared samples, only to produce a few meager colonies of recombinant plasmids. While waiting for another batch of cDNA, I began to vary the conditions used to render *E. coli* competent for plasmid transformation (involving incubating chilled cells in a solution of calcium and other salts), seeking somehow to improve our miserable yield of clones. I began to incrementally improve the efficiency, and it made a difference. Our third visit to the P3 lab in James lab was successful—we identified a few clones carrying sequences hybridizing to chicken collagen mRNA.

In March of 1978, Hans Lehrach and Anna-Marie Frischauf assumed faculty positions at the European Molecular Biology Laboratory in Germany, and I was left the task of traveling to CSHL by myself, trying to isolate cDNA clones for a second gene encoding another component of trimeric type I collagen. A new graduate student, John

Wozney, joined the project and analyzed cDNA clones in Cambridge while I was at CSHL. I continued working on the transformation of $\chi1776$, eventually improving its plasmid transformation efficiency by 1000-fold, a dramatic difference for precious preparations of recombinant DNA (as they were so often in those days).

BECOMING A NOMADIC GRADUATE STUDENT

I was initially greeted with bemusement and some reluctance by the staff in James lab. Nevertheless, in the course of my visits, I became acquainted with the scientists in the building, which was a hotbed of frenetic excitement, with the unfolding discoveries of RNA splicing and split genes, and the vast frontier of opportunity afforded by gene cloning. I would stop to listen and eventually join in the typically loud and heated debates at the blackboards in the narrow halls of James lab, and in the adjoining suite of offices. I also began to sit in on the weekly James lab "in-house" meetings, where the latest results were presented, often with vehement challenges and criticisms—you had to have self-confidence about yourself and your results or be reduced to emotional rubble. Joe Sambrook was in particular a scathing but often insightful critic, intolerant of sloppy science or unsubstantiated conclusions. Over time as my visits continued, the cool receptions I initially faced from the scientists turned warmer.

A turning point came in late 1979 when there was no longer any need for me to travel to CSHL, since Harvard had finally built a P3 facility in the Biolabs. I was by then getting involved in gene transfer experiments with Botchan, Gluzman, and Mike Wigler. Jim Watson encouraged me to keep coming to CSHL and to spend as much time there as I could. Jim was still predisposed to Harvard and its graduate students (having brought several others down in prior years), and he had by then decided that I had some talent. So did Joe Sambrook, and his encouragement was also very important, given his initial skepticism of me, and his importance as head of James lab and Assistant Director. They offered me a room in one of the old houses converted into postdoc housing, and a modest stipend to supplement my graduate student salary, which was not sufficient to sustain my travel and visits. Somehow, I convinced Paul Doty, my thesis advisor back at Harvard, that continuing to work on gene transfer at CSHL was a good thing, even if it slowed down my progress toward the goals of his lab. This support and encouragement, from Jim, Paul, and Joe, led to a remarkable period, where for four years I was a nomadic graduate student, traveling back and forth from Harvard to CSHL. I commuted in an old station wagon filled with ice chests, lab supplies, some clothes, and my tennis racket.

As the transformation efficiency improved, so did interest in my method for making E. coli competent at DNA uptake, as by then DNA cloning was a breakthrough technology that biologists everywhere sought to employ. Ever-changing formulations of the transformation buffer (dubbed "Liquid Gold" for the color imparted by the cobalt hexamine trichloride) were being sent out to scientists around the world, who were desperate to improve their transformation efficiency so as to enable molecular cloning of genes of interest. While I kept the formulation confidential initially until I had finalized it, I was not sophisticated enough either to patent the formulation or to set up a company that produced Liquid Gold. Instead, in 1983, I published a description of the method and an exhaustive characterization of the parameters of plasmid transforma-

François Jacob at left and Doug Hanahan at right, 1982. (Courtesy CSHL Archives.)

tion of *E. coli* in the *Journal of Molecular Biology*. I also made an *E. coli* strain—DH1—deficient in recombination (a desirable property for gene cloning) and later a mutant derivative of DH1, called DH5, that was widely adopted for use in DNA cloning.

A TRADITION OF TENNIS

Our mutual interest in tennis provided plenty of opportunities for Jim and me to become better acquainted. He would see me in the halls of James lab, or the dining room at Blackford Hall, and invite me to play. We came to know each other during memorable drives through the pastoral surroundings to the blue-blood Piping Rock Club for tennis games on their pristine grass courts, or in poor weather, to an old seaplane hanger housing two clay courts on the edge of Oyster Bay. Jim favored grass and clay, as these surfaces suited his game, and likely made our matches more competitive than they would have been on a faster hard court. Our conversations en route to tennis games were a mixture of profound and inane, of personal and intellectual. The topics ranged from the pedigrees and strange habits of the old wealth in the neighborhood, to the latest science, to his son Rufus' worrisome problems in school, later diagnosed as a perplexing mental illness, to new plans for the Laboratory grounds, to my results, progress, and plans. Although my "progress reports" were brief in the early days, Jim always seemed to know more about what I was doing than I recall telling him.

AN ADVENTURE WITH A VIRTUAL BIOTECH COMPANY

My tangential project on improving *E. coli* transformation led me into another remarkable experience for a mid-phase graduate student—involvement in a biotech company that CSHL was trying to establish. I recall excited statements from Jim about how a human protein, called tissue plasminogen activator (tPA), could have a huge impact on the treatment of heart attacks, if only its gene could be cloned and the protein manufactured in sufficient quantities to treat patients. The CSHL company, called "Cell Biology," was never capitalized, but I became involved with Jim and Joe Sambrook and the rather peculiar CEO, Angus McIntyre, in its sole project. Joe and his collaborator (and later spouse) Mary-Jane Gething were trying to clone the tPA cDNA, and I joined them, helping to produce cDNA libraries. I saw a lot of Joe and Mary-Jane during this period (1982–1983) not only in the lab, but also in the course of memorable meals and fine wines in their apartment behind James lab and a vacation together in the south of France. I particularly recall an almost furtive rendezvous at a Howard Johnson's restaurant in western Massachusetts, to pass over an ice chest of recombinant cDNA that I was to convert into a library. Clones of human tPA were eventually isolated by us in collaboration with Genetics Institute, a company in Cambridge, Massachusetts founded by Mark Ptashne and Tom Maniatis. Our success came within weeks of a parallel success at Genentech, but we lost the race to clone tPA, as played out eventually in the Courts. The saga of this stillborn company was a formative one for me despite being frustratingly close to a success that would have markedly changed all our lives, and the endowment of CSHL.

DEVELOPING ONCOMICE AT CSHL

In 1981, through the support of Jim Watson and Paul Doty, I was appointed (while still a graduate student with no thesis in hand) a Junior Fellow in the Harvard Society of Fellows. This fellowship paid a postdoc-level stipend, reducing a major incentive to complete one's Ph.D. I immediately traded in my old Datsun station wagon for a black Nissan 280ZX equipped with a radar detector, which made the trips from Cambridge to Cold Spring Harbor faster, and more pleasurable. Initially, I continued working on my various ongoing projects. I was, however, ruminating on my charter as a Junior Fellow ("to pursue excellence in intellectual endeavor whatever one's field and wherever such pursuit might take you"), and a new technology struck a chord. Several groups had generated transgenic mice, which seemed to be a logical extrapolation of the gene transfer approaches I had been using with *E. coli* and cultured mammalian cells. I decided that I too wanted to make transgenic mice and that I should wind down my current experiments, write and defend my thesis, and dive in. But where, and how? I never thought of applying to any of the prominent labs successfully making transgenic mice to do a traditional postdoctoral fellowship, which would have been a logical move. Rather, I went to talk to Jim, and I had a conversation that was perhaps the defining moment of my scientific career.

I sat in Jim's office, both of us slouched in Eames chairs—I alternatively looking at Jim or gazing out over the trees at the blue sky and boats in the harbor. I relayed my enthusiasm about setting up a program utilizing the new transgenic mouse technology. We discussed the perception of the time that this was a very difficult technology with uncertain determinants for success, undoubtedly a tough road for a neophyte. I professed optimism despite this somewhat disconcerting perspective. Jim asked me pointedly: Was I ready to focus on setting up this technology, in making it work, and then doing creative science with it? Jim alluded to my multitude of research projects both in Cambridge and at CSHL, which, while interesting, were arguably too broad and too many. I replied that I was prepared to make a commitment. I relayed my most well-developed project idea, which was to use a hybrid oncogene (called RIP-Tag), in which the insulin gene regulatory region (RIP) controlled expression of the SV40 T-antigen oncogene (Tag) that Yasha Gluzman and I had originally planned to deliver into pancreatic islets somatically by viral infection; instead, I would put it into the germ line of transgenic mice. Jim liked the idea, and then pronounced that I should come to CSHL as a staff member and that he would support me in setting up a transgenic mouse program.

Jim went on to predict that I would not be able to get an NIH grant to make transgenic mice, given my lack of experience and the perceived barriers to entry, and therefore he would find funding for me. And so he did, initially from the Robertson Research Fund of the Laboratory and then in the form of a project grant he solicited from Monsanto, which was at that time interested in transgenic organisms (both plants and animals). I went into Columbia University's Medical School for several weeks in early 1983 to be trained by Liz Lacey and Frank Costantini in methods for isolating and reimplanting fertilized mouse eggs, and injecting them with recombinant DNA. The quid pro quo was that I would help them prepare the summer course labs at CSHL for the first Mouse Embryology course, taught in the summer of 1983 by Lacey, Costantini, and the mouse embryologist Brigid Hogan (then of ICRF in London). I practiced the various methods on and off throughout 1983 while closing out my life at Harvard and moving down to Long Island, into an old carriage house under a giant oak tree in Lloyd Neck, beginning a five-year period in full-time residence at CSHL.

By late 1983, I was busy injecting oncogenes into mouse embryos, following up on the project I had described to Jim. In February 1984, my first transgenic mouse was born, carrying a hybrid insulin oncogene, called RIR-Tag; she died 9 weeks later, with red nodules in her pancreas. In early April, a litter of seven mice was born from eggs injected with a similar oncogene, called RIP1-Tag, of which four proved to be transgenic. One female died at 9 weeks of age, again with red lumps in the pancreas. The second female died a few weeks later, having mated and born a litter of pups. I was able to establish a family (formally called RIP1-Tag#2, or RIP-Tag for short) from her progeny; every transgenic mouse inheriting the RIP1-Tag oncogene died suddenly at 9–12 weeks of age with pancreatic tumors, confirming the causality of this viral oncogene, as an agent capable of inducing cancer to arise from cells expressing it de novo in a normal tissue of a mammalian organism. To analyze the phenotype of these mice, I soon faced the necessity of histology. Fortunately, Sue Hockfield, a molecular neurobiologist, had some expertise, and she patiently instructed me. But I started to see a limitation of a great institution so focused on DNA: There was no pathology, no anatomy, no immunology, and little tissue biology.

During the next few months, I continued characterizing the RIP-Tag mice. In February, 1985, I submitted a paper describing the RIP-Tag mice and their pancreatic islet cell tumors, evidently arising via a multistage pathway where other "events" were required, much as inferred for human cancer. I speculated that induction of angiogenesis might be one such event, motivated by the groundbreaking work of Judah Folkman[1] and by the blood red appearance of the islet tumors. My paper was published in

May 1985 as a single-author article in *Nature* (Hanahan 1985). During the 2 years spent learning to make and then producing transgenic mice, I worked alone without collaborators or group members (initially even without technical assistance). My interest in Folkman's work and angiogenesis was to have a profound effect on my research and on Jim's view of cancer.

When I moved to CSHL in 1983, I was housed in a small lab of my own within James laboratory and had an office between Joe Sambrook's and Jim's offices. Jim was on sabbatical in England for the first year, and Joe was Acting Director. Despite Joe's reputation for abrasive critique and intolerance of what he considered sloppy or unfocused science, he was to my mind remarkably charming and effective as Director, defying the predictions of some staff that he would be a tyrant. I saw Joe not only in the halls of James lab, but also at regular dinners that had become a tradition during the cloning of tPA; we had become close friends. Joe seemed ready for the job as Director. I thought Watson and Sambrook were a great team, but I sensed Joe was frustrated at being Assistant Director and ready for a true leadership position (one without Jim not infrequently overruling his executive decisions). And I felt that Jim was spending too much time worrying about landscaping and fund-raising, and not enough time thinking about science, for which he had such amazing intuition when his mind was clear and focused.

En route back from a molecular embryology conference in Germany, I stopped in London to see Jim, and we had lunch. I relayed my impression that Joe was doing a great job as Assistant Director. I proposed that he should step down as Director and become President, leaving him with more time to think about science, giving Joe some space to grow as a leader. Jim barely registered my proposal and brushed it aside. He was not ready. After lunch, I joined Jim as he picked up a suit at Gieves & Hawkes on Saville Row, and I ended up buying a pin-striped suit myself (hardly ever worn I must confess). While the meal, the conversations, and the errand on Saville Row were memorable, my mission was unsuccessful. Jim returned as Director, relegating Joe to his old job as Assistant (to the) Director. In due course, Joe left CSHL to become Chair of Biochemistry in Dallas, to the regret of many, including, in my opinion, both Jim and Joe, and me. (Ten years later, Jim did become President, turning the helm over to Bruce Stillman, who has done an admirable job at managing the ever-growing institution.)

On Jim's return from sabbatical, I would see him regularly. He would appear suddenly in the door of my office, and as his office door was often open in the evenings, I would occasionally stick my head in, and sometimes we would talk. We also continued playing tennis, with conversations during the transit to the courts, and I became a regular guest at dinner parties given by Liz and Jim Watson. Jim would hear of my results, and I would hear from him about all sorts of things, which ranged from banal social gossip to ideas and plans for the Lab, to the vision and then the debates and finally the plan to sequence the human genome. He seemed excited about my work on oncomice, and encouraging, although rarely with specifics.

The years (1985–1988) following the report in *Nature* of the RIP-Tag transgenic mice were meteoric. I met Judah Folkman and initiated a collaboration now spanning 17 years that has centered upon the regulation and functional importance of angiogenesis for tumor development. And Tim Adams, a postdoc in Ed Harlow's group in James lab (who had trained as an immunologist), introduced me to cellular immunology. We collaborated and showed that the RIP-Tag mice expressing the T-antigen neoantigen in the rare islet β cells could be used to study immune self-tolerance and its relationship to autoimmunity. That first step into immunology began what has proved to be an enduring investigation of interactions between oncogenes, neoplastic development, and the immune system. The chutzpah of the Watson-Gilbert lab at Harvard encouraged me in this new field. Rather than hesitating or wilting for my lack of expertise, I dove in, being unafraid of making a fool of myself. This attitude, this mixture of self-confidence, of naïveté (sometimes of critical facts but also of the burdens of conventional wisdom, which can be distracting), and of willingness to ask for help and be patronized as a neophyte by experts, was one of the most important lessons to come from my graduate training. And it had come to me not explicitly, but rather implicitly, distilled initially from the then still-echoing resonance of the ex-Watson-Gilbert lab in the halls of the Harvard Biolabs, and later from its philosophical continuance at the Laboratory on Long Island that Jim Watson revived and reinvented.

CONTINUING INTERACTIONS FROM FARTHER AFIELD AT UCSF

In 1988, I was recruited by Bill Rutter and Bruce Alberts to join the Department of Biochemistry and Biophysics at the University of California, San Francisco. The departure was emotionally complex. Jim wanted me to stay, offering me a likely Hughes position and a new lab to be built on top of the McClintock Building, but he did not pressure me, nor was he angry about my subsequent decision to leave. This lack of friction with Jim was unusual, as many who left the Lab became alienated with Jim in the process. Jim tended to emotionally reject those he cared about when they left. I think that Jim realized I needed to make this move, and our friendship and interactions continued. His parting blow was beating me at tennis shortly before I moved: It was rare for him to beat me even then, but he was inspired that day, and we both remember it. (I left CSHL with more than just my mouse models and a burgeoning research group. I had met Steinunn Baekkeskov when she was a student in the Molecular Cloning course and married her—an especially joyful impact of CSHL on my life.)

In the years following my move to San Francisco, I continued to see Jim during my regular visits to the Lab to attend workshops and conferences. Surprisingly, I left some of these visits with Jim vaguely saddened that his mind was so clearly filled with political frustrations (in particular related to his tumultuous tenure as inaugural Director of the Human Genome Project), as well as with the continuing stress of courting rich people for donations to CSHL and with his plans to build this or remodel that. He didn't seem to be so excited about new scientific results or concepts (at least as evidenced by our conversations). I felt that Jim was not taking full advantage of a precious talent. When he was focused on a field, he had a special intuition for its key biological problems, about what questions were ripe for study, and who was the right person to make them. (I remember Jim's mentoring of Mike Wigler's historic entrée into discovering cellular oncogenes. In my opinion, without Jim's cajoling, almost threatening encouragement, Mike would never have cloned the Harvey Ras oncogene.) Perhaps that special talent was now being diffused by his administrative responsibilities. During the early to mid 1990s, I thought that Jim had lost his passion for science. He talked about neurobiology and the efforts ongoing in the big new neuroscience building he created above James lab. Certainly, he was advocating neurobiology because the brain was an evident grand frontier for the new millennium. He was also motivated, I thought, by being tormented by the decades-long mental illness of his son Rufus, a bright and thoughtful boy, a son whose future was sidetracked by an illness that is still not fully understood, or treatable. For a man so used to stunning success, despite the odds, it was clearly hard to feel powerless to understand much less to solve a wrenching personal problem founded in biology.

A NEW SCIENTIFIC PASSION: ANGIOGENESIS AND CANCER

In the mid 1990s, I observed a wonderful awakening in Jim of a passion for science. Jim became inspired about tumor angiogenesis, the formation of new blood vessels that sustain tumor growth and dissemination. He saw tumor angiogenesis as a fascinating biological process and a potentially revolutionary new target for attacking tumors. Jim had first met Judah Folkman in the mid 1970s, back in his Harvard days, when Judah was starting his work on tumor angiogenesis, then an enthusiastic M.D. overflowing with ideas and observations but lacking the rigors of experimental design and validation so central in Jim's world of bacterial genetics. My sense is that Judah did not make a favorable impression on Jim then. Twenty years later, it was a different story. Judah had founded the field of angiogenesis research, which was growing expansively worldwide, and he had become an innovative, successful experimental scientist.[2]

I like to think that the seeds in Jim's re-acquaintance with Judah and his growing excitement about angiogenesis came in part from me. Judah and I had started collaborating on the analysis of tumor angiogenesis in the RIP-Tag mouse model of cancer, shortly after meeting at a conference in 1986. Jim heard of the first results as they unfolded in 1987–1988 while I was still at CSHL, and then after I moved to UCSF. In the same period (1989) that Judah and I reported on the angiogenic switch in the RIP-Tag transgenic mouse model (Folkman et al. 1989; see also Hanahan and Folkman 1996), Noel Bouck from Northwestern University published a paper showing that a tumor suppressor locus controlled expression of an endogenous angiogenesis inhibitor protein, thrombospondin 1, such that loss of the tumor suppressor down-regulated this angiogenesis inhibitor, thereby facilitating tumor vascularization. This, along with results from the Folkman lab, sparked the realization that endogenous proteins could restrict angiogenesis and that tumors found ways to co-opt them. Judah's lab moved full force into discovering new angiogenesis inhibitors.

During my regular visits to CSHL in the 1990s, I would tell Jim of our progress in studying angiogenesis, and he became increasingly interested, and supportive. He emphatically encouraged my strategic decision in the early 1990s to start using our models to investigate the prospects of angiogenesis inhibitors as therapeutic agents. The field of cancer research, including Judah's lab, was then (and largely still is) vested in the use of tumor transplant models (lumps growing under the skin from inoculated tumor cell lines), which are fast but arguably lacking key characteristics of cancers developing in different organs. I had come to suspect that something important could be learned by investigating our new mouse models of organ-specific, multistage tumorigenesis (even though the experiments took much longer and were much more expensive). Jim then began to proactively ask me about my latest results, rather than waiting for me to offer updates. In 1996, Judah and I published the first paper evaluating angiogenesis inhibitors in the RIP-Tag model of pancreatic islet carcinoma (Parangi et al. 1996). Jim offered to manage the review and submission of the manuscript to *PNAS* and encouraged continuing investigations of anti-angiogenic therapies.

A milestone in Jim's growing passion for angiogenesis came in 1998. In mid March, Judah and I both spoke at a small CSHL conference entitled "Pathways to Cancer." Judah spoke about his lab's discovery of two angiogenesis inhibitors that were embedded in larger proteins and released by proteolysis to become potent inhibitors of new blood vessel growth. The protein fragments were called angiostatin and endostatin, and Judah electrified the audience with experiments showing that these endogenous cellular constituents could regress and in some cases cure transplanted tumors in mice. He predicted that such endogenous inhibitors, being normal constituents of the body, would be less toxic (and possibly more effective) than the pipelines of (typically toxic) chemical inhibitors arising from discovery programs in academia and industry. Jim was sitting in the front row. His excitement about tumor angiogenesis grew from this day into a passion.

A manifestation of Jim's growing inspiration about angiogenesis that had an almost unbelievable impact came six days after the Pathways to Cancer meeting, as a consequence of a dinner conversation Jim had with a *New York Times* reporter, Gina Kolata, at a UCLA symposium. Jim pronounced that Judah would "cure cancer in 2 years." It was another classic in Jim's history of memorable but often disconcerting statements made in public speeches that boldly conveyed his enthusiasm or opinion on some issue, but bordered on the fantastic, the extreme, or even the offensive. Jim believes that such statements are the best way to get people's attention for things that he thinks are important. Coming from a legendary Nobel Laureate, such an extraordinary statement, about a field already generating excitement in the press for its potential in treating cancer, was a reporter's dream. Jim's (private) remark provoked a front page article in *The New York Sunday Times* on May 8, 1998, which propelled Judah into the television evening news and onto the covers of *Time* and *Newsweek*. There was a maelstrom of publicity, a frenzy that cancer was about to be cured in short order by this wonderful new concept. An emotional, even angry, backlash came with the realization that cancer will not be cured with one magic bullet, even if angiogenesis inhibition becomes an enduring part of cancer therapies in the future (as I believe it shall). Jim's prediction has linked Jim and Judah in a strange bond, of impatient public expectation and shared personal passion for angiogenesis inhibition.

Meanwhile, Jim continued to ask about my work on angiogenesis inhibitor therapies in mouse models. Although we still talked about tennis (and occasionally still played), now he wanted to know about the details of the progress, *about the science*. It was invigorating that he cared. Jim's passion continued to grow. He motivated a series of small meetings at the Banbury Conference Center on tumor angiogenesis and anti-angiogenic therapies. He pushed me to do more, and applauded our results, which were revealing subtleties in the effects of angiogenesis inhibitors used at different stages of disease progression. He was exultant about data where my lab mixed two kinase inhibitors targeting distinctive angiogenic signaling circuits, producing dramatic regressions of late-stage tumors. These data (as well as new preclinical results from Folkman's and other labs) suggested that angiogenic therapies could really work if the right anti-angiogenic drugs were used in appropriate (and perhaps significantly refined) treatment regimens, guided by appreciation of the biology of tumor angiogenesis and its complex regulation, not by just applying the traditional designs of high-dose chemotherapy.

Jim increasingly became dissatisfied with the clinical development of anti-angiogenic therapies, as reports appeared in both scientific and lay press that clinical trials of angiogenesis inhibitors (including angiostatin and endostatin) were equivocal, raising doubts about their promise (and Jim's historic prediction). His impatience was founded in his unflagging conviction about the obviousness (to him) of targeting not the genetically deranged and ever-evolving tumor cells but rather their necessary supporters, the endothelial cells composing tumor vasculature. Jim did not waver in his conviction because of these highly publicized setbacks. In a statement I presented on Jim's behalf at a recent (2003) Symposium honoring Judah Folkman's 30 years of angiogenesis research (and 70th birthday), Jim stated: "Your conception, like that of the double helix, is much too pretty not to be true." But Jim was increasingly irritated by the uncertain progress in translating these exciting discoveries about tumor angiogenesis from the laboratory to the clinic, weighed upon both by his still-resounding public prediction that angiogenesis inhibitors would eradicate human tumors and by the increasing frequency that friends and acquaintances were dying (painfully) of cancer.

As his interest had grown in seeing the potential of angiogenesis inhibitors for treating cancer realized, Jim had visited biotech companies developing anti-angiogenic drugs—and left feeling they weren't doing it right. Amid the growing distractions of the impending celebrations and reflections both of the discovery of the double helix 50 years ago and of his 75th birthday, Jim proposed in 2002 to found a new biotech company whose goal was to make a success of anti-angiogenic therapy for cancer. Jim began spending surprising amounts of time and energy promoting his concept for a new angiogenesis company, making time for meetings and travel to New York City and further. It was a wild, arguably crazy idea in a depressing economy, a bad scene for biotechnology ventures in particular, and a particularly bleak time for a subject (anti-angiogenic therapies) viewed in many circles as inflated and unlikely to succeed. Jim was passionate, however, and recruited Judah and myself to join him and several others in starting a company. Jim's new quest is currently still very much a dream, a virtual company with a vision and a plan but little else, and its success far from certain. While it would have been easy to decline to join such an unlikely enterprise in light of the depressing climate for biotech ventures, it was difficult to dismiss Jim when he was this inspired. So often his intuition to charge forward and dive into to a new arena has been right, even in the face of daunting logistical or political barriers (witness the recombinant DNA debate, or an anemic small research lab on Long Island in need of critical care and leadership, or the Human Genome Project). We shall see whether this new venture succeeds, confirming another of Jim's inspirations. But even if not, it has been a special experience to see Jim so excited about science and about using knowledge to tackle an insidious and devastating disease. Jim relayed how someone told him recently that "lightning doesn't strike twice" and that he should not expect another improbable success, but in Jim's mind, it can, and he will.

These milestones, coming at different times and in such different ways, illustrate how Jim Watson has over and over impacted the course of my scientific career, sometimes deliberately, and sometimes not. While the nature of the mentoring has evolved over time, Jim's influence continues, now spanning 25 years since I first sat in his corner office in James lab, thankful for his allowance of an expectedly brief visit to CSHL. It is only in retrospect and reflection that these interactions with Jim, subtle and often unappreciated for their significance at the time, can be seen to represent defining moments in my scientific career, whose course has not been linear, or predictable. Perhaps some day my successes will be viewed as a small part of the legacy Jim Watson has left to science not only in his personal achievements, but as well in those scientists he has in various ways guided and inspired to exceptional accomplishment.

REFERENCES

Folkman J., Watson K., Ingber D., and Hanahan D. 1989. Induction of angiogenesis during the transition from hyperplasia to neoplasia. *Nature* **339:** 58–61.

Hanahan D. 1983. Studies on transformation of *Escherichia coli* with plasmids. *J. Mol. Biol.* **166:** 557–580.

Hanahan D. 1985. Heritable formation of pancreatic beta-cell tumours in transgenic mice expressing recombinant insulin/simian virus 40 oncogenes. *Nature* **315:** 115–122.

Hanahan D. and Folkman J. 1996. Patterns and emerging mechanisms of the angiogenic switch during tumorigenesis. *Cell* **86:** 353–364.

Luria S.E. 1975. *36 Lectures in biology*. MIT Press, Cambridge.

Parangi S., O'Reilly M., Christofori M., Holmgren L., Grosfeld J., Folkman J., and Hanahan D. 1996. Antiangiogenic therapy of transgenic mice impairs de novo tumor growth. *Proc. Natl. Acad. Sci.* **93:** 2002–2007.

Watson J.D. 1965. *Molecular biology of the gene*. W.A. Benjamin, New York.

CSHL in Transition

Ray Gesteland

University of Utah

I went to Cold Spring Harbor Laboratory in 1967 when it was at a nadir, on the ropes. John Cairns, the Director, was performing the Herculean task of holding things together. The near disaster state was obvious when I visited the Lab from Geneva for a job interview. John told me that the Lab could not afford an honorarium for my seminar and instead he gave me a remaindered copy of *Phage and the Origins of Molecular Biology* (Cairns et al. 1966), whose production run had been overestimated. Even this did not discourage me.

I took the position, my first real job, as Assistant Director of the Laboratory because of John. I had met him in 1963 when as a graduate student in Jim Watson's lab, I had weaseled my way into the Cold Spring Harbor Symposium by agreeing to show slides and take candid pictures for the Symposium book. Despite the state of the Lab that John had inherited, his intellect, sense of humor, and sincere friendliness were magnetic. Upon moving to Cold Spring Harbor in August of 1967, my lab was next to John's, and the daily discussions with him covered the complete spectrum: DNA replication, telescopes, photography, sociology, and Lab and funding politics. But the overwhelming influence was the purity of his approach to science; he was a wonderful mentor for a young and undisciplined mind. John Cairns and his wife, Elfie, provided a warm and rich environment for my wife Harriett and me—the cheerful calls from the front porch of Airslie to stop for a beer and a chat on the way home to the Stables, the dinner parties with community and Lab friends, and the special friendship shown to our children.

But Jim Watson also played a key role in my decision to go to Cold Spring Harbor, a decision that was not viewed with equanimity by Harriett, who had not seen the place but had heard of the desperate straits of the Lab and the fact that there was only enough money in the bank to pay salaries for two months. Our arrival in hot and humid August with two young children to be put up in a decaying, non-air-conditioned cabin did not quickly cement the sensibility of the decision. Earlier that summer, Jim had summoned me from Geneva to Paris, where he was visiting, to encourage me to sign on with Cold Spring Harbor rather than accept a more conventional academic job. Jim knew that I had enjoyed my earlier visits to Cold Spring Harbor and correctly sensed that the Cairns and the informal style of the Lab would appeal to me. Besides, I should not worry, although Jim was at Harvard, he "would not let Cold Spring Harbor fail." Clearly, there was the implication that he might step in, and, of course, a year later, in 1968, he did.

When I arrived, the year-round scientific staff was remarkable but miniscule: John Cairns, Al Hershey, Barbara McClintock, and Paul Margolin (who left shortly there-

RAYMOND F. GESTELAND

Ray Gesteland was born and raised in Madison, Wisconsin. He attended the University of Wisconsin and received a bachelor's degree in chemistry and a master's degree in biochemistry, which involved a herd of cows. As Ray tells it: *"I was studying fluoride poisoning, which is a big environmental and agricultural problem near smelters. Unfortunately, instead of dealing with the problem, the people running the smelters would pay off the farmers for the cows that were lost due to fluoride poisoning. I got sick of the work due to the situation, so I bailed to Harvard University in 1961."*

When he arrived at Harvard, everyone warned him: "Whatever you do, don't work for that crazy guy Watson." Nevertheless, Ray completed his thesis project in Jim's laboratory in 1965. After a year and a half in Alfred Tissières laboratory in Geneva, Ray came to Cold Spring Harbor in 1967. As Assistant Director, he was instrumental in maintaining the equipoise of the laboratory during the tempests and vacuums that accompanied the change in Directorship in 1968. And in the subsequent years, when Jim was most of the time in Harvard, Ray administered the Lab with great sensitivity and intelligence.

In 1978, Ray joined the faculty of the Howard Hughes Medical Institute at the University of Utah. He is now Vice President for Research and Distinguished Professor of Human Genetics at the University of Utah.

From his student days in Harvard until now, Ray has been interested in how ribosomes work. Together with his long-time collaborator, John Atkins, Ray has investigated nonstandard decoding, in which ribosomes respond to specific signals in the mRNA by changing the reading frame. Atkins and Gesteland have also identified other types of signals that cause ribosomes to respond to stop codons by inserting either selenocysteine (the 21st encoded amino acid) or the conventional amino acids glutamine or tryptophan.

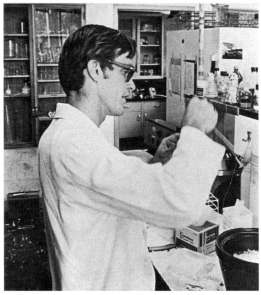

Ray Gesteland, 1974. (Courtesy CSHL Archives.)

after); four postdoctoral fellows: Ann Skalka, Shraga Makover, Rudolph Werner, and Phil Harriman. I was a bit in awe. But undaunted, I decided that what this group needed was an evening in-house seminar series. There seemed to be very little communication among the lab groups—a deficiency that could surely be corrected by a little organization. One Wednesday evening, we assembled for the first in the series of in-house seminars, which was to be given by Barbara McClintock. Barbara talked about her current ideas and experiments—I was amazed but uncomprehending. About ten minutes into the talk, Al Hershey asked a very specific question in true Hershey style: "I must be the only person in the room that does not understand, but what is....." The answer had the general flavor of an anecdotal description of a particular gall on a plant that she passed on her daily walk to the beach. It was clear to her that this answered Al's question. This was not at all obvious to Al. He paused, then asked another question and got a similar kind of response. After one more try, he gave up and walked out. We never got together again. From then on, I left communication to the random, informal style that had worked in its own way for a long time.

This was a different world. I was doing an experiment that required a blender to shear the pili from *E. coli* cells. I went to Al who said "Hmmm—I remember using one once—it must be around here somewhere." After some rummaging, he produced THE Blendor complete with an adhesive tape label stating the amounts of ^{32}P and ^{35}S radioactivity that it had contained when Al's great experiment was done in the 1950s.[1] I could not bear to use it; it went to the museum.

Frankly, I was worried about Jim's role as Director. By the time that he made the decision to leave Harvard, I had learned enough about Cold Spring Harbor to be very concerned about whether his brusque, sometimes brutally honest style could possibly work in the small community of the Laboratory. There was no elbowroom, no escape. How could he possibly be an administrator? How could Jim play the schmoozing and fund-raising role in the Long Island Community that was required for survival of the Lab? Amazingly, Jim grew into the job quickly—not without strain on the staff—not without some administrative chaos—and not without apprehension and puzzlement in the community.

Jim brought a decidedly different style to the destitute Lab. In fact, the Cairns and Watson styles could not have been more different. John, understandably, had the "half-empty" view of the Lab; actually, he would probably have said it was 95% empty. Jim, on the other hand, had the "half-full" view—what the Lab needed was a few bold moves, and boldness was certainly something Jim could provide. Don't worry about the little stuff—Damn the torpedoes! However, stabilizing the financial status was crucial. It was essential to maintain good will and a sense of continuity even though the Lab was financially in serious trouble. Key to providing this stability was Jim Brainerd,[2] our newly appointed Administrative Director, who had a wonderful style and demeanor, coupled with a lifetime of experience in management. His tenure at the Lab was limited as he and his wonderful wife Frances were eager to move to the next phase of their life—retirement.[3]

Recruitment of Bill Udry, Jim Brainerd's successor, turned out to be either a stroke of genius or just good luck. Bill knew his way around Washington and was quickly able to renegotiate the Laboratory's indirect cost rate so that the funds that come attached to grants to cover the infrastructure costs of doing research were greatly increased. Amazingly, Bill also negotiated back payment of these precious unbudgeted funds at a higher rate for the previous five years—a bonanza of uncommitted funds.

Jim's confidence again drove the next scientific move. Jim saw that a logical and financially smart direction for the Lab was to attack cancer through tumor viruses and so, on John Cairns' advice, he recruited Joe Sambrook from Dulbecco's group at the Salk Institute. Joe then persuaded two of the other postdoctoral fellows at the Salk (Heiner Westphal and Carel Mulder) to join him at Cold Spring Harbor. In 1968, Sambrook and Lionel Crawford wrote an application to NIH for a Program Project Grant on SV40 and polyomavirus. This provided funds for renovation and equipping James laboratory and for salaries and running expenses for the new team. Joe arrived at the Laboratory in 1969 and the others followed a few months later after James lab was functional. Hardly was the paint dry on the walls of James when President Nixon ordered NIH to wage a War on Cancer. In quick order, a new and much larger grant application was written to establish a Cold Spring Harbor Cancer Center. Despite the fact that the existing cancer centers were linked to clinical enterprises, the grant was awarded based on the vision and talent of the Sambrook-Mulder-Westphal team. At the end of the first year, a visiting review committee, on seeing the one slim publication, asked "Is this what you have done with the one million dollars?" Jim somehow finessed this, showing his confidence in the new effort, a confidence that was well-founded as the group became very productive and the mainstay of the future of the Laboratory. Again, Jim's confidence and his decisiveness and his willingness to take chances had paid off handsomely.

Jim's management style at Cold Spring Harbor was simple in one sense, yet subtle and complicated in another. The outward, public style had a strong component of intimidation: "You will do it my way or you will be relegated to the folks whom I ignore." But underneath that caustic and seemingly spontaneous veneer was a carefully thought out and responsive approach that was very skilled and effective. So, on the one hand, he was very loyal to those he liked—if the situation called for it, he would be the first person there to offer help. On the other hand, he could move quickly when the situation called for action. A brash postdoc from Boston came down for the summer to do experiments in Demerec laboratory. After two weeks, the folks in the adjacent labs had had their fill. Jim, with no hesitation, told the visitor that he had offended everyone and that he should pack his bags, and get out immediately. Perhaps the scientist learned from this experience for he went on to be highly successful in both academic and commercial science. Whether he was ever restored to Jim's good graces is more problematic.

Jim's successes in science and science management had a very important underpinning—his scientific intuition. This was one of the first and most lasting of lessons from being in his lab. When Jim was writing the first edition of *Molecular Biology of the Gene* (Watson 1965), he would bring chapters to us graduate students and postdocs in the lab for comments. He asked me to look at the chapter that dealt with ribosomes and protein synthesis. The writing was rough but the concepts were clear. "Ribosomes move along mRNA in a 5´ to 3´ direction." I tactfully pointed out to Jim that he had obviously made a simple error—surely he must have seen recent papers showing that ribosomes in fact moved from 3´ to 5´. Alex Rich and Howard Dintzis, using different approaches, both reached the same conclusion. Jim's retort: "3′ to 5′ doesn't make any biological sense. They must move in the same direction that RNA is made. Don't worry, by the time the book comes out someone will show that it is really 5′ to 3′." I had no reason to think that Jim had really read these papers in detail, let alone that he had understood the technical details from which he might have been able to judge the merits of the conclusion. But, of course, Jim was right.

Why has Watson had such a remarkable effect on molecular biology? To me, the fundamental reason is his uncanny intuition and, more importantly, the boldness and confidence to act on his intuitions—his strokes of genius. This was manifest in many different ways, often not subtle, often not sensitive, and not always with success but overall with remarkable effect on five decades of a new science.

REFERENCES

Cairns J., Stent G.S., and Watson J.D., eds. 1966. *Phage and the origins of molecular biology*. Cold Spring Harbor Laboratory, Cold Spring Harbor, New York.
Watson J.D. 1965. *Molecular biology of the gene*. W.A. Benjamin, New York.

Cold Spring Harbor and Recombinant DNA

Tom Maniatis

Harvard University

It was July 1976, a typical hot and humid summer evening in Cambridge. The site was City Hall, in a room that had the feel of a Civil War era courtroom, an impression enhanced by the absence of air conditioning. Students and Cambridge activists were hanging from the balconies armed with signs scrawled with anti-recombinant DNA slogans. Scores of makeshift fans were frantically waving to fend off the oppressive heat. It could have been the Scopes trial, but the occasion was a Cambridge City Council hearing on recombinant DNA, called to determine whether Harvard University should be issued a permit to build a biological containment facility. I was standing in

Harvard scientists at the debate on recombinant DNA in City Hall, Cambridge, Massachusetts. Rick Losick at far left; Tom Maniatis, third from left; and Carl Wu, second from left in front of Tom Maniatis. (Photograph by Rick Stafford. Used with permission.)

THOMAS MANIATIS

There are, presumably, "golden ages" in all disciplines, periods when new knowledge is acquired at a rapid rate, and every new fact discovered or process understood leads to new questions. There was a golden age in molecular genetics through the 1950s and early 1960s that famously came to an end in the late 1960s when it seemed to many that all of the big ideas had been explored and that only mopping up of insignificant details was left. But just a few years later, a new golden age was initiated by recombinant DNA techniques and DNA sequencing.

Tom Maniatis was one of those fortunate scientists who was in the right place at the right time to mine the first and many of the richest nuggets of this new golden age. Trained in molecular biology at Vanderbilt University, in 1971, he moved as postdoctoral fellow to Mark Ptashne's laboratory at Harvard. Ptashne was continuing to anatomize the λ operator and Maniatis joined him in using restriction enzymes to dissect the functional components of the operator. Maniatis by heroic means determined the sequence of 33 (out of 100) bases of the leftward operator and no fewer than 74 base pairs of the rightward operator—all before the development of the chemical and dideoxy sequencing methods (1975).

At about the same time, recombinant DNA methods, in particular cDNA cloning, made it possible do molecular analysis of eukaryotic genes, and Maniatis and his colleague Argiris Efstratiadis were among the first to take up the challenge. At that time, they had to select tissues that made large amounts of a protein so that there was a good chance of finding cDNA clones, so they chose chorion and globin genes. For the next ten years, globin genes in a variety of species were subject to detailed scrutiny.

Maniatis moved from bacteriophages to mammals just as the recombinant DNA controversies were getting under way, and the research he wanted to do—making cDNA libraries of mammalian genes—was a target for opponents of genetic engineering. The recombinant DNA Luddites in Cambridge forced a city-wide ban on such experiments and Maniatis's research career was in danger of grinding to halt. However, as Maniatis recounts in his essay, Jim gave him a safe haven at Cold Spring Harbor where he succeeded in making full-length cDNA clones.

Maniatis returned to Harvard via a four-year stay at Caltech. By now, he was acknowledged as one of the leaders in recombinant DNA technology, and with Jim's encouragement, he began teaching with Ed Fritsch a Cold Spring Harbor course on molecular techniques. In turn, this led—again with Jim's encouragement—to a techniques manual, *Molecular Cloning* (1982, Cold Spring Harbor Laboratory). This had the same impact on laboratory research worldwide as Jim Watson's *Molecular Biology of the Gene* (1965, W.A. Benjamin) had on biology teaching.

the balcony, a recently appointed Assistant Professor in Biochemistry and Molecular Biology at Harvard, not much older than the students around me. In fact, I was in full uniform—long hair, jeans, and Birkenstock sandals. It was fortunate that the students did not know that I was the enemy; my future research at Harvard depended on building the laboratory in question. I saw the same bitterness and anger in the faces of students that I had seen in numerous antiwar demonstrations I had attended.

The meeting was instigated by George Wald, a Harvard biology professor, a group of left-wing scientists (Science for the People) led by Jonathan King at MIT and Jonathan Beckwith at Harvard Medical School, and Mayor Vellucci, who was repeatedly elected by his East Cambridge constituency by exploiting their contempt for Harvard. In fact, the Mayor once threatened to turn Harvard Yard into a city parking lot, and he took every opportunity to torture the University. George Wald was a Nobel Laureate and well-known anti-war activist. Science for the People was an outgrowth of the anti-war movement, and their political activism was directed against the misuse of science for weapons development and for the scientific justification of social inequities and racism. Now its political tactics were directed toward the hazards of recombinant DNA. Jonathan King conjured up images of plagues and slow death due to the release of recombinant bacteria from the Harvard labs into Cam-

George Wald speaks at the First Parish in Cambridge, Massachusetts, 1976. (Photograph by Rick Stafford. Used with permission.)

bridge sewers. I was a political neophyte but could see that the anti-recombinant DNA coalition had an agenda that went far beyond the question at hand. It was a circus-like atmosphere with the students hatefully giggling and cheering as Mayor Vellucci put one Harvard administrator or professor after another in their place. After hours of testimony and another meeting, a moratorium on recombinant DNA work in Cambridge was declared. I left the hall after midnight knowing that my "temporary" residence in Cold Spring Harbor would continue indefinitely. As the crowd poured onto the street outside, I ran into Jonathan King, and I confronted him about his statements on slow death. He looked me in the eye in a most patronizing manner and explained that this was a political issue and he had to use political tactics. I then asked him how he could justify using his scientific credibility to distort the truth for political objectives (a charge Science for the People often made of others). He turned and walked away. At that moment, I felt very grateful that Jim Watson had given me a place to continue my research safely removed from Cambridge.

When I arrived at the Harvard Biolabs in the fall of 1971 for postdoctoral studies in Mark Ptashne's lab, Jim Watson was in transition from Harvard to Cold Spring Harbor, so I did not see much of him. In fact, we were never introduced, although I would occasionally be on the receiving end of a microscopic nod when we passed in the hall. When I finished my postdoctoral studies on bacteriophage λ operators, I was appointed to a junior faculty position in the Department of Biochemistry and Molecular Biology, but by then Jim had moved full time to Cold Spring Harbor. While finishing my postdoctoral studies, I collaborated with Argiris Efstratiadis, an M.D. and at that time a graduate student in Fotis Kafatos' lab, to develop cDNA cloning methods. At the time, "Arg" was working out conditions for the synthesis of full-length double-stranded cDNA and I was measuring the size of the reaction products by denaturing gel electrophoresis. Our goal was to establish a method for cloning full-length cDNAs. However, the recombinant DNA moratorium in Cambridge made all of this effort pointless. I was therefore delighted when Jim Watson provided me with the opportunity to continue the cDNA cloning work at Cold Spring Harbor.

The evening I arrived at Cold Spring Harbor Laboratory, I attended a party for a departing staff member at Terri Grodzicker's apartment. As I approached her walkway, I could see Jim bounding down Bungtown Road in the distance with his characteristic gait. He stumbled toward me, almost knocking me down to welcome me to the Lab. Originally, I was to be in James lab, but Jim nervously told me that there was a change in plans—I would be in Demerec. Later I learned that Joe Sambrook was furious that Jim had offered me space in James without asking (Joe considered me another one of those Harvard—). Rather than wasting energy on a relatively minor issue, Jim conceded and quickly found a room for me in Demerec. I later observed or heard of numerous conflicts between Jim and Joe, who had a remarkably constructive love/hate relationship. Each was a gifted administrator in his own way. Joe was "hands-on" and able to focus on details, while Jim concentrated on the big picture. Most of the time their talents synergized; sometimes they mixed explosively. However, it was clear that they had enormous respect for each other. Although my relationship with Sambrook was off to a rocky start, I grew to admire his intellect, organizational skills, leadership ability, and even his unique character. I became close friends with Mike Botchan, a postdoc in Joe's lab, and through that friendship gradually established a good relationship with Joe, although he often referred to me (and others) by nicknames that do not bear repeating here.

As I settled into Demerec, I quickly became aware of Jim's method for "encouraging" hard work at the Lab. He would roam from one end of the grounds to another at all times of day and night, sometimes stopping to ask how things are going, most of the time just sticking his head in to see who was around. In fact, nothing had to be said. The mere presence of Jim was sufficient pressure to work hard. Another purpose of the late night visits was to acquire and disseminate the latest scientific gossip. Jim seemed to know everyone and everything, so he was a valuable source of information. Jim attended nearly every seminar at the Lab when I was there, as well as talks of selected speakers at the numerous conferences. He would stand quietly at the back of the room, scanning the crowd for interesting faces, sometimes reading the *The New York Times* as he stood. I concluded that he had an incredibly effective editing compartment in his brain, which filters out masses of detail and trivia from scores of talks and generates a clear understanding of the most important results presented. Jim is also good at hunting down people with the most interesting results at meetings, and quickly extracting the essential information. His favorite time of attack was at breakfast, bursting into the room, quickly scanning the crowd for the right face, and then making a beeline for the person of interest. He used this method not only to point people in the right direction, but also to identify the most creative and able young scientists in their fields. I found it amusing to watch the body language (including my own) of people in Jim's presence at meetings. The increase in anxiety level is palpable when Jim approaches.

I remember running into Jim on Bungtown Road the morning Gek Kee Sim (a graduate student in my lab) and I had successfully cloned the first full-length globin cDNA. Jim was delighted, his investment in my lab paid off. As my stay at the Lab changed from temporary to semipermanent, my family moved into the Firehouse, on the second floor, downstairs from Rich Roberts and his family and upstairs from Terri Grodzicker. Although I had a temporary appointment, and five people were crammed into a small laboratory that used to be a kitchen, I spent almost two years at the Lab. It was a formative time in my career. With no administrative or teaching responsibilities, I could devote full time to my lab work and students, and the meetings provided me with a broad perspective in biology. I also had the time to read and think in ways that would not have been possible at Harvard. I never asked Jim why he offered me a place at the Lab, but whatever the reason, I am very grateful.

Toward the end of my time at the Lab, it became clear that it would not be easy to return to Harvard to continue my work, and the space crunch at CSHL made it difficult to build a group there. Thus, when I was offered a position at the California Institute of Technology, I decided to take it. My decision was made easier by the fact that I was recruited in the winter during a blizzard on the East Coast, and I visited Pasadena on a rare sunny day with no smog. Jim was not happy with my decision to move to Caltech; he thought I should remain at the Lab or return to Harvard. As a last minute effort to change my mind, Jim invited me to Christmas dinner with him and Liz and David Dressler, a faculty member at Harvard. Jim and David teamed up to paint the bleakest picture of life at Caltech. I had already made my decision so the evening was exhausting. I later realized that there were many reasons for Jim's dislike for Caltech. His time there was during his post-DNA depression, his work on RNA structure did not go well, and he was frustrated by the lack of available women. Fortunately, my time at Caltech was wonderful. I truly enjoyed the scientific atmosphere and collegiality. It was also one of the most productive phases of my scientific career.

Based on the work started at CSHL, we made rapid progress after arriving at Caltech. I was fortunate to attract an outstanding group of students and postdocs who systematically established cloning methods, including the construction and screening of genomic DNA libraries. The primary objective of my lab was to understand the mechanisms of globin gene regulation, and an entire range of the latest recombinant DNA and molecular biology methods was being employed. This included the introduction of cloned genes into cultured cells, the result of collaboration with Richard Axel's lab at Columbia University. After my narrow escape from Cambridge, my lab was one of the few places in the world where the entire armamentarium of recombinant DNA methods was being practiced. Jim knew this, and asked me to organize a course at CSHL on Molecular Cloning of Eukaryotic Genes in the summer of 1980. In those days, the courses were used as catalysts to accelerate the growth of emerging fields. Jim expanded the course offerings to include virtually every interesting area of biology, from yeast genetics to cell biology to neurobiology. He had an uncanny ability to predict emerging new directions in biology and to identify the best instructors willing to teach intensive three-week courses. The Molecular Cloning course replaced the RNA Tumor Virus course taught the previous year by Nancy Hopkins from MIT. Nancy agreed to help with organizing the Molecular Cloning course, and Ed Fritsch, a postdoctoral fellow in my lab, and I taught it, with much support from the year-round people in James laboratory.

In the second year, Doug Engel, with whom I had worked with closely at Caltech, replaced Nancy. Prior to the first year, Ed and I organized all of the protocols used in my lab into a nascent lab manual, and prepared lab exercises and reagents. As with other CSHL courses, the pace of the Molecular Cloning course was intense: lab from early morning to late at night, an excellent schedule of guest lectures in the afternoon, and late-night pizza and beer to discuss the results of the day's work. Late-night sessions included an endless battle of off-color jokes delivered by Mark Ptashne (guest lecturer) and Malcolm Gefter (student) and midnight swims at the Robertson Estate pool. The students left exhausted, but with a sophisticated understanding of molecular cloning as well as practical lab experience. Among the students in the first Molecular Cloning course was Bob Waterston of human and mouse genome sequencing fame.

At the end of the first year of the course, Jim urged me to use the course lab manual as the basis of a cloning manual for publication by Cold Spring Harbor Laboratory Press. Among Jim's many achievements at Cold Spring Harbor was the rejuvenation of the Press. Jim viewed the cloning manual as the beginning of the next generation of lab manuals modeled after the highly successful bacteriophage genetics manual written by Jeffrey Miller (1972). Considering all of the pressures of running a lab at Caltech, along with teaching and chairing an NIH study section, I was not eager to take on additional commitments. However, Jim wisely recruited Joe Sambrook to join the effort. Jim knew that Joe is an excellent writer and that he is highly organized and gets things done. In addition, Joe could facilitate interactions between Caltech and the publications office at Cold Spring Harbor. Nancy Ford, Director of Publications, and Doug Owen, who prepared the text for publication, also helped us tremendously. Transforming the manual from a collection of recipes to a coherent concept-based text was an enormous undertaking. A major plus was the fact that all three of us were "hands-on" in the lab. Joe had pioneered the use of restriction enzymes to create physical and genetic maps of viral DNA, and he was using a variety of recombinant techniques in his lab to study DNA tumor viruses. I was still working in the lab, so Ed and I were veterans at cDNA and genomic cloning. Together, the three of us had personally used virtually every procedure described in the manual. We were also steeped in the biology that underlies the technology. Joe and Ed had strong backgrounds in DNA and RNA tumor viruses, respectively, while my postdoctoral studies provided a solid foundation in bacteriophage genetics and molecular biology.

At the time, recombinant DNA technology was at an early stage so relatively few people were able to access the methods. We therefore labored to present in-depth descriptions of the biology underlying the protocols so that readers could learn to troubleshoot. It is hard to imagine now, but in 1980, kits for virtually every method were not available, and the vast majority of reagents necessary for the work had to be prepared by the investigator. When we were writing the cloning manual (Maniatis et al. 1982), we (at least I) did not realize the impact it would have on biomedical science. I felt that the manual would be used primarily to introduce new students and postdocs to recombinant DNA work in established labs, greatly facilitating the training of beginners. However, the real impact was on hundreds of investigators in a broad spectrum of biology, from medicine to molecular evolution. These people had no training in molecular biology, and they did not have access to labs that could teach them. Little did we know that our painstaking efforts to write a clear and understandable text with each protocol would prove to be so important. For years afterward, I was approached at conferences by investigators from virtually every field of biomedical science to tell me how the manual had transformed their research. I believe that Jim knew this when he urged us to undertake the project, and like most of Jim's initiatives, it was a win-win situation for everyone. An important plus was that sales of the manual contributed to the success of Cold Spring Harbor Laboratory Press and brought significant revenues to the Lab.[1] The success of the manual is an example of Jim's unique ability to make things happen. His success is based on an extraordinary intuition that allows him to see things clearly before anyone else. In addition, he has an unusual ability to identify the right people for the job, and phenomenal powers of persuasion.

Two of Jim's unusual managing techniques deserve mention here. First, when dealing with the Board of Trustees, he threatened to resign if he didn't get his way (of course, as far as I know he never came close to resigning). Second, if he didn't like how staff members behaved he fired them on the spot. For example, Jim fired Joe Sambrook several times during Joe's tenure as Scientific Director of the Lab, and even postdocs were fired many times (in particular, Mike Botchan). However, to my knowledge, Jim never really fired anyone. For example, one of my students was returning from New York late one evening with her boyfriend, and they sped through Oyster Bay. They were pulled over by an Oyster Bay policeman and the boyfriend was rude to him. After receiving a call from the chief of police, the next morning Jim stormed into my office and demanded that I fire the student for jeopardizing the Lab's relationship with the local community. I listened quietly, then informed the student of Jim's anger and threat. I didn't fire her, and Jim did not comment on her continued presence at the Lab. However, his message was clearly understood.

During the past 20 years, I have interacted with Jim as a member of the Board of Trustees at Cold Spring Harbor, at numerous CSH conferences, and during his frequent visits to Cambridge. His intense interest and passion for people and science have continued unabated, and he is always thinking of new and exciting projects.

He has also developed a real passion for tennis, playing several times a week. I too am an avid tennis player and was astonished the first time I hit with Jim. Although his style is a bit unorthodox, he hits with great intensity and accuracy. As with his other activities in life, he is highly selective in choosing partners; he now rarely hits with anyone of lesser skill than a professional or an NCAA champion. I believe he actually hit with Boris Becker at Wimbledon in recent years.

Jim has had an enormous impact on the lives of countless young scientists. At Harvard, Jim established the most exciting and productive molecular biology group of its time. His textbooks in molecular and cell biology introduced thousands of students to the revolution in science in a clear and readable way. He transformed Cold Spring Harbor from a poorly endowed, mostly summer research institute into a dominant force in a broad spectrum of biomedical disciplines from yeast genetics to neuroscience. I am grateful to Jim for rescuing me from Cambridge in 1975, for making the cloning manual possible in 1980, and for his friendship and advice.

REFERENCES

Maniatis T., Fritsch E.F., and Sambrook J. 1982. *Molecular cloning: A laboratory manual.* Cold Spring Harbor Laboratory, Cold Spring Harbor, New York.

Miller J.H. 1972. *Experiments in molecular genetics.* Cold Spring Harbor Laboratory, Cold Spring Harbor, New York.

Origin of Concatemeric T7 DNA

J.D. Watson

Reprinted, with permission, from *Nature New Biology,* vol. 239, No. 94, pp. 197–201, October 18, 1972.

(Reprinted from Nature New Biology, Vol. 239, No. 94, pp. 197–201, October 18, 1972)

Origin of Concatemeric T7 DNA

J. D. WATSON

The Biological Laboratories, Harvard University, and the Cold Spring Harbor Laboratory

The observed concatemers of T7 DNA are consistent with replication schemes resulting in double-helical molecules with 3′ ended tails. Right-ended and left-ended molecules can then join to form dimers which on further replication similarly form larger concatemers.

THE replication pattern of T7 DNA at first site appears disarmingly simple. Initiation begins at an internal site 17% from the left end with replication proceeding in both directions to give rise first to an eye-shaped intermediate containing a replicating bubble, then to a Y-shaped form, and finally to two unit length daughter molecules (Fig. 1)[1,2]. Given the simple way the original infecting molecules replicate, we might expect that subsequent cycles of DNA replication would also generate unit length DNA molecules. Later in infection, however, most newly synthesized T7 DNA is present in concatemers of length two, three, four times . . . that of the original parental molecule[3-5]. With time these concatemers break down to unit length molecules that become incorporated into mature virus particles.

Equally puzzling has been the fact that the two ends of the T7 molecule are genetically equivalent, containing the same sequence of about 260 base pairs at both ends of the molecule[6]. At first, this finding prompted the suggestion that circular intermediates could be generated by limited digestion with exonuclease. Attack of infecting T7 molecules by an enzyme like Escherichia coli exonuclease III would convert them into forms with sticky ends like those of phage λ ; these would be expected to circularize the moment they are formed. But when Wolfson, Dressler, and Magazin[1,2] found that the first cycle of T7 replication did not appear to involve a circular form, the significance of the redundant ends became again an open question.

I shall show that consideration of linear replication in terms of our knowledge of the enzymology of DNA replication leads to the expectation that the replication of linear molecules necessarily generates concatemers which are integral multiples of the mature viral chromosome. For this process to occur, terminally repetitious sequences are prerequisite.

Growth within Replication Bubbles

Electron microscopy of the replicating bubbles reveals three main states[7] (Fig. 2). In the first category (a) all the DNA within the bubble appears double-stranded, including the regions immediately adjacent to the growing forks. The second group (b) comprises bubbles with one single-stranded section always located next to the growing fork. In the third group (c) there are two single-stranded sections, one at each growing fork and always situated in trans. Failure to observe the two single-strand regions in cis orientation confirmed the prevailing belief that the two chain ends (5′ and 3′) at each replication fork must elongate in different ways, with spurts of 5′–3′ growth going before the 3′–5′ growth in the complementary strand. Delius et al.[8] have directly proved that the 5′ ends abut onto the single-stranded portions of replicating T4 DNA. All such single-

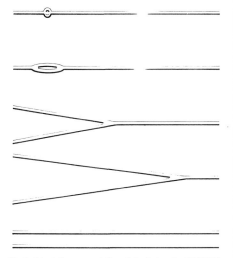

Fig. 1 Schematic representation of the first cycle of T7 DNA replication.

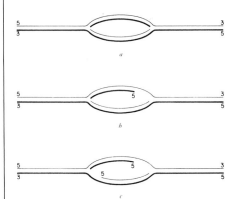

Fig. 2 The strandedness of DNA within replicating bubbles.

stranded sections probably reflect that growth in the 3'–5' direction lags behind the 5'–3' elongation in the adjacent chain.

Daughter-strand Initiation

The problem of how the replicating bubbles come into existence is far from solved. The work of Brutlag *et al.*[9,10] suggests that the enzyme RNA polymerase sometimes starts the process by the 5'–3' synthesis of a short section of complementary RNA. After some fifty-one hundred ribonucleotides have been laid down, the RNA polymerase falls off, allowing a DNA polymerase molecule to add deoxynucleotides to the RNA chain. This generates a mixed RNA–DNA chain with the RNA section at the 5' end. Later the terminal RNA portion is removed by a specific enzyme, conceivably one like *E. coli* ribonuclease III ; this enzyme can digest the RNA component of DNA/RNA hybrids without causing any cleavage of DNA strands[11].

Discovery of a key role for RNA polymerase in the initiation of some DNA synthesis may help to explain the paradox that no known DNA polymerase can initiate synthesis of new DNA chains. All require a primer chain containing a free 3'OH group[12–14].

Use of Okazaki pieces

The apparent 3'–5' growth in the absence of any known enzyme that adds mononucleotides to 5' ends can be explained by one or more short strands being synthesized in the 5'–3' direction ahead of the main 5' ended daughter strand[15–17]. Such chains may grow backward from the growing fork until they are joined onto the main daughter strand by polynucleotide ligase. Strong support for this hypothesis was obtained by Okazaki *et al.*[17], who found that much newly synthesized DNA is first found as part of chains of 500–2,000 bases. Unless such Okazaki fragments arise artefactually by nuclease attack during extraction from cells, their existence must mean something important. Hence, the hypothesis is that they help resolve the dilemma of 3'–5' growth.

Initiation of Okazaki Fragments

How the Okazaki fragments themselves are initiated is completely uncertain. The growing tip of the 5'–3' oriented daughter strand might temporarily come loose and bridge the replicating fork by pairing to several bases on the opposing template strand[12,13,18]. The tip would then grow backward, eventually to meet and join the 5' end of the 3'–5' oriented daughter strand (Fig. 4). If an endonuclease cut occurred at

the fork before joining, an Okazaki fragment would be generated and the 5'–3' daughter strand could continue to grow along its original template. As chain elongation proceeds, bridging and cutting would repeat itself many times. This hypothesis (currently called the "knife and fork" model)[13] automatically explains the presence of a single-stranded region on one side of many growing forks. As soon as bridging occurs, these should disappear, starting from the growing fork. Internal single-stranded sections are, however, almost never observed[7], but this may only be because once a bridge connexion has been made, subsequent backward growth occurs too rapidly to be easily caught in the middle.

The knife and fork model also predicts that denaturation of replicating molecules should yield growing tips which spontaneously form hairpin loops. Such loops have been looked for during T7 multiplication by Barzilai and Thomas[19]. Initially they thought they had such evidence when they found that the supposedly single-stranded T7 DNA obtained after alkali denaturation frequently contained double helical sections. However, further experiments revealed that the double helical components were much larger than expected, occasionally the size of unit length T7 DNA molecules, and not short double helical tips attached to much longer single-stranded molecules. Furthermore, in pulse-chase experiments they do not show the expected short half-life. Conceivably they arose by a reaction pathway like that described by Weiss where a combination of exonuclease and ligase action (artefactually?) cross-links opposing strands of double helices.

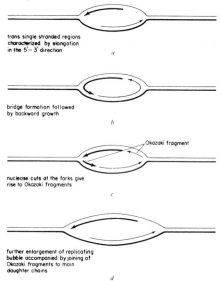

trans single stranded regions characterized by elongation in the 5'–3' direction

a

bridge formation followed by backward growth

b

Okazaki fragment

nuclease cuts at the forks give rise to Okazaki fragments

c

further enlargement of replicating bubble accompanied by joining of Okazaki fragments to main daughter chains

d

Fig. 3 Knife and fork model for the bidirectional growth of a replicating bubble.

The alternative possibility must thus be considered that Okazaki fragments also start by the synthesis of short RNA chains onto which deoxynucleotides begin to grow. RNA polymerase has a high affinity *in vitro* for single-stranded DNA and, in the presence of ribonucleoside triphosphates, catalyses the synthesis of short RNA chains. In contrast, if the templates are double helical DNA, much longer chains are made before the RNA polymerase molecules dissociate from their respective DNA-nascent RNA chain complexes.

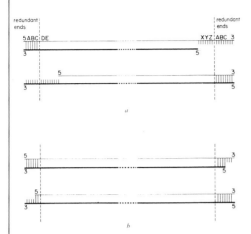

Fig. 4 Complementary single tailed products of the duplication of a terminally redundant DNA molecule; in (a) the tails are longer than the redundant section, whereas in (b) the tails are shorter than the redundant section.

RNA polymerase may therefore frequently bind to the single-strand DNA found within replicating forks. After binding, if the *in vivo* reaction proceeds like that *in vitro*, short RNA chains will be made that serve as primers onto which deoxynucleotides can add.

Completion of Replication

While 5′–3′ oriented growth should proceed smoothly to the end of its template, I see no simple way for 3′–5′ growth to reach the 3′ end of its template. This dilemma holds for both the knife and fork model and the RNA polymerase initiation mechanism. Consider first what would happen with the knife and fork scheme as 5′–3′ replication proceeds towards the template end. After a bridging and cutting event near (but not at) the end, there will be a spurt of 5′–3′ growth until the 5′ template end is reached and the parental strands separate. As soon as this happens, further bridging becomes impossible and we are left with a 3′ ended single-stranded tail projecting from one end of each daughter double helix. One of each pair of daughter helices will have a tail on its left end, the other half on its right end (Fig. 4).

We get the same result if an RNA primer does the job. Even if RNA polymerase can attach to the extreme 3′ end of its DNA template, the resulting 5′ terminal RNA section will soon be enzymatically digested away, leaving a daughter double helix with a 3′ tail. Again half of these molecules will have left-ended tails, the other half right-ended tails.

If such daughter molecules were to replicate further, they would again produce 3′ tailed progeny double helices. Most important each such cycle of replicating would produce smaller and smaller progeny molecules. We might thus conclude that neither of the above proposals for 3′–5′ growth can be right. However, the existence of concatemers is a strong argument that either one or both of these schemes are correct. Or if the true mechanism remains to be discovered, it also will be characterized by failure to complete growth on the 3′ template ends.

Effect of Redundancy

The realization that 3′–5′ growth may not go to completion immediately allows us to propose a function for the terminally repetitious base sequences at the end of T7. For their presence means that the two 3′ ended tails produced by the replication of an original T7 DNA molecule will have com-

plementary sequences that spontaneously will base pair to each other to produce a hydrogen-bonded linked dimer. The exact structure of such molecules will depend on the relative length of the free tails compared with that of the redundant sequence. If both tails are longer than the common sequence, then gapped molecules are produced containing single-stranded sections (Fig. 5). These can quickly be filled in by the action of a 5′–3′ directed DNA polymerase. Ligase can then join the adjoining chains to yield a covalently bonded double helical dimer.

In contrast, if the tails are shorter than the redundant stretch, then linked molecules will be produced which have two protruding internally located 3′ ended tails. Their conversion into a covalently bonded dimer may involve the action of the T7 specific exonuclease[21]. This enzyme, the product of gene 6, resembles *E. coli* exonuclease III in that it only works on double helical DNA. It differs, however, in that it works from the 5′, not the 3′ end. One of its functions may, therefore, be to eat away sufficient 5′ ended nucleotides so that 3′ ended internal tails can snap back onto the main helical axis. Alternatively it might function before dimer formation, cutting away a sufficient number of 5′ terminal nucleotides that are stronger than the redundant bits. As before, we conceive the final joining process to involve DNA polymerase as well as ligase.

After their formation, dimers should replicate, as such, beginning at one or both of its initiation sites. The end result in either case will be two daughter dimers each with one 3′ ended tail. These, also, will tend to stick to each other and a concatemer of four times the unit length will emerge. We thus see that concatemers are an immediate product of the replication of linear DNA molecules that have redundant ends—that is, as long as there is no way to run 3′–5′ growth all the way to the end of the template. So the fact[22] that not only T7, but also P22, T4 and T1 have both redundant ends and concatemeric intermediates, is a strong argument for our basic premise about 3′–5′ growth.

Unique 5′ Terminal Nucleotide Sequences

All T7 DNA isolated from mature T7 particles has unique 5′ ended groups[23]. This fact, first shown by Weiss and Richardson, means that the concatemers are cut at very specific points when they give rise to mature DNA. As a result, all the used strands have AG at their 5′ end while TC is the 5′ terminal sequence of the r strand. Because the method for sequence determination starts with an alkaline phosphate treatment, they had no way of seeing whether any 5′ terminal triphosphate groups are present in mature T7 DNA. They only could conclude that at least one phosphate group was present on each 5′ end. Now that we realize that most, if not all, mature DNA arises from concatemers, we must expect that independent of how RNA chains are initiated, subsequent work will reveal few, if any, 5′ triphosphate end groups.

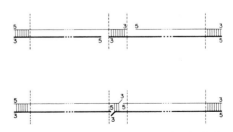

Fig. 5 *a*, Gapped molecule produced by the union of molecules whose tails are longer than the redundant section; *b*, internal tails produced by the union of tails shorter than the redundant section.

3

Unit Length T7 DNA Molecules

Two specific enzymatic breaks, one in each chain, are necessary to start the process of detaching a unit length T7 DNA molecule from a concatemer[24]. They must be located on each side of the terminally repetitious sequence and so staggered that the longer of the two resulting chains has a 5' terminal (Fig. 6). Creation of such cuts will not likely physically separate the two pieces since large numbers of hydrogen bonds will still hold them together. Separation will, however, automatically be set in motion, if at the site of each cut a DNA polymerase begins to add deoxynucleotides to the free 3'OH groups thereby displacing a 5' ended tail. When the growing 3' ends meet somewhere in the middle of the redundant section, there no longer will be any hydrogen bonds holding the fragments to each other and they will fall apart. At this stage both are likely to have 5' ended tails but given the 5'–3' specificity of DNA polymerase these will quickly become part of double helical sections.

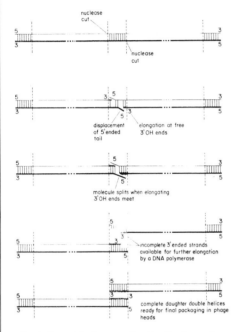

Fig. 6 Proposal for the conversion of a dimeric concatemer into two unit length double helices with unmuted terminally redundant ends.

This highly specific cutting and refilling process can be imagined to occur at each redundant region along a concatemer. Conceivably a complete unit length T7 molecule is produced for every 3' tailed fragment originally used to make up the concatemer. But given the presence of the T7 exonuclease within the infected cells, the concatemeric ends may sometimes have 3' tails. Thus, the fragments produced from the ends might form further concatemers. Alternatively, extensive T7 exonuclease action may cause many concatemers to circularize, in which case all the final products of the cutting-refilling process will be complete unit length molecules.

Still to be worked out is the time couse of appearance of these specific endonucleases. Already there are several strong hints that they appear relatively late in infection. One such indication is the very long length of many concatemers. While until recently attention focused on the more easily studied molecules two–three times the unit length, now it is realized that the longer concatemers are easily lost (or broken) during extraction of DNA from infected cells and that much replicating T7 DNA is present as molecules at least five–ten times the unit length[25]. Furthermore, the addition of chloramphenicol up through the sixth minute of infection prevents concatemer breakdown[24,26]. Thus no cutting enzymes appear to be synthesized until many cycles of T7 DNA duplication have occurred.

Further progress in understanding the cutting process may depend on the isolation of the responsible enzymes. Here much help may come from the use of T7 mutants whose DNA replication process is blocked at the concatemer stage[26–28]. Such mutants fall into two groups, one a group of genes (8, 9, and 10) that code for several of the T7 head proteins, the other a group of two genes (18 and 19) whose function remains unknown. Involvement of the head protein genes suggests some kind of head structure must be formed before the final DNA maturation events occur, a situation thought also to hold for T4 and λ. This requirement may be a way to prevent concatemer breakdown from interfering with the concatemer forming events. Many unwanted (incomplete) chains would be generated if the cutting enzymes began to work before the 3' tailed fragments become covalently joined. Also some device must have evolved to be sure that the cuts on each side of the redundant fragment occur almost simultaneously. For if they do not, the 5' tails, which flip out when DNA polymerase starts to elongate at free 3'OH groups, will grow to at least unit length sizes, only being released when they eventually run into cuts made in adjoining genomes.

Obvious candidates for the products of genes 18 and 19 are the cutting enzymes themselves. Two separate proteins seem likely to be needed in view of the 260 or so base pairs separating the two ends of the redundant region. This number corresponds to a length of almost 1000 Å, a distance not often encompassed by average size proteins. So it makes sense now to look for two enzymes, one responsible for making the cut of the left end, the other which works on the right end.

Experimental Evidence

A thorough examination of T7 concatemers just completed by Schlegel and Thomas[25] supports the general picture presented above. Focusing their attention on the smaller concatemers, they used a variety of chromatographic and enzymatic techniques to show that most concatemers are characterized by both internal and terminal single-stranded regions. Moreover, they showed that many of the unit length T7 molecules found within infected cells have a 3' ended single strand tail protruding from one side only. Many of these latter molecules may be the primary products of the duplication of parental T7 DNA molecules. The fact that the longer concatemers have internal single-stranded regions as well as 3' ended tails suggests that a minute or so may normally be required for the conversion of a hydrogen bonded linked concatemer into a covalently completed concatemer. Further evidence for such "gapped" configurations comes from experiments which show that subdenaturing temperatures break apart most of the concatemers into unit length molecules.

Concatemers with Permuted Ends

Our analysis of T7 DNA replication applies equally well to those phages whose linear chromosomes have permuted sequences. T4, the best understood example, has redun-

4

dant ends which differ from one phage particle to another. As first realized by Streisinger and Stahl, such DNA molecules must arise from much longer concatemers which are cut into "headful" size pieces some time during formation of the mature heads[23-31]. During formation of the headful lengths, the cutting nuclease(s) must not recognize any specific sequences; instead some still unknown spatial factors must fix the site of nuclease action.

The initial process that generates the T4 concatemers must be the same that makes necessary the T7 concatemers, that is, the inability of a $3'-5'$ directed elongation process to reach the end of its template. We should note there that the T4 redundant sections comprise some 1–2% of the T4 genome and so on the average are some ten times longer than those of T7. Formation of their concatemers thus may very often involve extensive cutting away by exonucleases specific for 5' terminated nucleotides.

I thank David Dressler and John Wolfson for discussions, and Charlie Thomas, Gordon Lark, Gisela Mosig, and Ric Davern for their comments on the manuscript. Financial support has been provided by the National Institutes of Health.

Note added in proof. Work just published by Sugino, Hirose and Okazaki (*Proc-US. Nat. Acad. Sci.,* **69**, 1863 ; 1972) indicates that many Okazaki fragments contain 50–100 ribonucleotides at the 5' end.

Received June 5, 1972.

[1] Wolfson, J., Dressler, D., and Magazin, M., *Proc. US Nat. Acad. Sci.,* **69**, 499 (1972).
[2] Dressler, D., Wolfson, J., and Magazin, M., *Proc. US Nat. Acad. Sci.,* **69**, 998 (1972).
[3] Carlson, K., *J. Virology,* **2**, 1230 (1968).
[4] Kelly, T. J., and Thomas, C. A., *J. Mol. Biol.,* **44**, 459 (1969).
[5] Ihler, G. M., and Thomas, C. A., *J. Virology,* **6**, 877 (1970).
[6] Ritchie, D. Q., Thomas, C. A., MacHattie, L. A., and Wensink, P. C., *J. Mol. Biol.,* **23**, 365 (1967).
[7] Inman, R. B., and Schnos, M., *J. Mol. Biol.,* **56**, 319 (1971).
[8] Delius, H., Howe, C., and Kozinski, A., *Proc. US Nat. Acad. Sci.,* **68**, 3049 (1971).
[9] Brutlag, D., Scheckman, R., and Kornberg, A., *Proc. US Nat. Acad. Sci.,* **68**, 2826 (1971).
[10] Wickner, W., Brutlag, D., Schekman, R., and Kornberg, A., *Proc. US Nat. Acad. Sci.,* **69**, 965 (1972).
[11] Robertson, H. D., Webster, R. E., and Zinder, N. D., *J. Biol. Chem.,* **82**, 243 (1968).
[12] Kornberg, A., *Science,* **163**, 1410 (1969).
[13] Richardson, C. C., *Ann. Rev. Biochem.,* **38**, 795 (1969).
[14] Goulian, M., *Ann. Rev. Biochem.,* **40**, 855 (1971).
[15] Gilbert, W., in *Endocrine Systems and Selected Metabolic Disease* (edit. by Netter, F.), **4**, 220 (CIBA, 1965).
[16] Mitra, S., Reichard, P., Inman, R. B., Bertsch, L. L., and Kornberg, A., *J. Mol. Biol.,* **24**, 439 (1967).
[17] Okazaki, R. T., Okazaki, T., Sakabe, K., Sugimoto, K., and Sugino, A., *Proc. US Nat. Acad. Sci.,* **59**, 598 (1968).
[18] Guild, W. R., *Cold Spring Harbor Symp. Quant. Biol.,* **33**, 142 (1968).
[19] Barzilai, R., and Thomas, C. A., *J. Mol. Biol.,* **51**, 145 (1970).
[20] Weiss, B., *Proc. US Nat. Acad. Sci.,* **65**, 652 (1970).
[21] Kerr, G., and Sadowski, P., *J. Biol. Chem.,* **247**, 311 (1972).
[22] Thomas, C. A., and MacHattie, L. A., *Ann. Rev. Biochem.,* **36**, 485 (1967).
[23] Weiss, B., and Richardson, C. C., *J. Mol. Biol.,* **23**, 405 (1967).
[24] Thomas, C. A., Kelly, T. J., and Rhoades, M., *Cold Spring Harbor Symp. Quant. Biol.,* **33**, 417 (1968).
[25] Schlegel, R. A., and Thomas, C. A., *J. Mol. Biol.* (in the press).
[26] Hausman, R., and La Rue, K., *J. Virology,* **3**, 278 (1969).
[27] Studier, F. W., *Virology,* **39**, 562 (1969).
[28] Studier, F. W., *Science,* **176**, 367 (1972).
[29] Sechaud, J., Streisinger, G., Emrich, J., Newton, J., Lanford, H., Reinhold, H., and Stahl, M. M., *Proc. US Nat. Acad. Sci.,* **54**, 1333 (1965).
[30] Shalitin, C., and Stahl, F. W., *Proc. US Nat. Acad. Sci.,* **54**, 1340 (1965).
[31] Streisinger, G., Emrich, J., and Stahl, M. M., *Proc. US Nat. Acad. Sci.,* **57**, 292 (1967).

Printed in Great Britain by Flarepath Printers Ltd., St. Albans, Herts.

335

Jim and the Board: Behind the Scenes

Bayard Clarkson

Memorial Sloan-Kettering Cancer Center

HOW I CAME TO BE A TRUSTEE

I first met Jim Watson in 1968 shortly after he succeeded John Cairns as Director of the Cold Spring Harbor Laboratory of Quantitative Biology (LQB), an entity formed in 1962 by the merger of the facilities of the Carnegie Institution with those of the Biological Laboratory. The Carnegie Institution later sold all its buildings and property to CSHL for a dollar, its Board apparently having decided that other areas of scientific endeavor had a brighter future than genetics. As one might suspect, Jim had some pungent comments about this decision; to paraphrase the mildest, he called their decision "One of the most mind-boggling misjudgments in the history of science."

Frank Horsfall, then the Director of Sloan-Kettering Institute (SKI), had called me to his office to ask if I would be willing to serve as SKI's representative on LQB's Board of Trustees, succeeding Leo Wade. Leo was the Administrative Director of SKI, and for reasons not then apparent to me, he had decided not to renew his appointment as SKI's institutional Trustee on LQB's Board. It is evident from John Cairns' account that despite his heroic efforts during his tenure as Director to save the Laboratory from bankruptcy, its financial footing was still precarious. In retrospect, I suspect that Leo and Frank had come to the conclusion that the Laboratory was a sinking ship and that a rather junior associate member would therefore be quite adequate to represent SKI during LQB's final demise. Horsfall had spent most of his career at the Rockefeller Institute across the street from SKI, and no doubt had been given a decidedly dismal account of LQB's prospects by his former colleague, Edward Tatum, then Chairman of the LQB's Board of Trustees.

PARTICIPATING INSTITUTIONS: BULWARKS AGAINST INSOLVENCY

The LQB Scientific Advisory Committee, headed by Ed Tatum, recruited eight academic institutions—the Rockefeller Institute, Duke University, Albert Einstein College of Medicine, Princeton University, SKI, the Public Health Research Institute, New York University, and Brooklyn College (later switched to The City University of New York). The Long Island Biological Association (LIBA), the local community association that had administered the Biological Laboratory since 1924, was also a member. In 1967, Bentley Glass and Jim Watson persuaded Stony Brook and Harvard to join this group of contributing institutions, followed later by Columbia and Yale.

337

BAYARD CLARKSON

Bayard (Barney) Clarkson's association with Cold Spring Harbor Laboratory began in the same year that Jim Watson became Director, 1968. Barney has served on the Board ever since, first as a member, then Vice Chairman (1980–1986), then Chairman (1986–1992), and now as Honorary Trustee. This was a period of extraordinary change, especially during his Chairmanship when decisions were taken to expand into neurobiology and to build the Neuroscience Center.

Barney is an eminent cancer clinical researcher who trained at Yale University and the College of Physicians & Surgeons of Columbia University. After internship and residencies at New York Hospital, Barney received a Special Lasker Fellowship in Chemical Chemotherapy and he moved to Memorial Hospital. He became a Member of the Memorial Sloan-Kettering Cancer Center in 1984 where he continues to work. For most of his research career, Barney has singled out leukemia for special attention, combining a life-long search for chemotherapeutic agents with molecular analysis of the intracellular signaling pathways that are altered by *BCR/ABL* fusion genes, the primary initial genetic abnormalities in chronic myelogenous leukemia.

In addition to his contributions to Cold Spring Harbor, Barney has played important roles in the American Association for Cancer Research, as President (1980–1981) and Treasurer (2001–). He is also a Trustee of Clarkson University, originally established in 1896 as the Thomas S. Clarkson Memorial School of Technology, in honor of Thomas, an ancestor of Barney's.

Each participating institution was entitled to name one representative to LQB's Board of Trustees (providing it honored its financial pledge), whereas LIBA, because of its long-standing support, was entitled to name two Trustees. The first LIBA appointees to the Board were Walter Page and Robert Lindsay,[1] both of whom were long-time residents in the neighboring community and senior officials at J.P. Morgan, the bank that had traditionally managed the Laboratory's financial portfolio. The Page family was among the most faithful local supporters of the Laboratory. Walter or his father, Arthur, served almost continuously on the Laboratory's Board of Trustees from 1924 to 1986. Older scientists who attended Symposia or participated in summer courses or in research programs during 1950–1970 will surely remember, probably with mixed feelings, residing in the "Page Motel," a complex of crude wooden cabins located in the woods above the Laboratory (now the site of the Neuroscience Center). The most flattering terms used to describe the Motel's accommodations were "spartan," "minimal," or "elemental"; there was no insulation, and in the late fall or early spring, it was often miserably cold. However, there is no record that any of these hardy scientists suffered serious ill effects, and scientific discourse apparently flourished in this primitive and presumably monastic environment.

FORESTALLING BANKRUPTCY

Shortly after my election in early 1968 as an LQB Trustee, I called Roddy Lindsay to find out the real situation at LQB and what to expect. He told me that during his tenure on the Board, the Laboratory had indeed faced imminent bankruptcy with $60,000 in

unpaid bills. To avoid (or at least postpone) bankruptcy, the Board decided to delay paying its outstanding bills until receipts from the sale of the latest Symposium began to
come in. Older readers will fondly recall the annual dark red Symposia volumes. These
were produced long before the plethora of journals appeared in the 1970s; they were
highly valued as the best and most up-to-date collection of reports of important new
advances in the biological sciences. Almost all major libraries and biological institutions
subscribed, as did many individual scientists. Key to the Laboratory's survival, these red
volumes made enough money to pay the outstanding bills and avoid bankruptcy.

Despite John Cairns' valiant efforts to keep the Laboratory afloat, several senior
staff members left what they regarded as a sinking ship, and when Jim took over as

*Jim Watson and Bayard Clarkson in the Hazen Tower at the Neuroscience Center, Cold
Spring Harbor Laboratory. (Goodrich ©1992 Newsday, Inc. Reprinted with permission.)*

Director in 1968, he began with nearly blank slates for both scientific staff and financial resources. Our initial fund-raising efforts were quite puny by today's standards, and accordingly yielded only meager returns. To give one example, early in 1969, Jim was contacted by an elderly, very wealthy former CEO of a major pharmaceutical company. The old gentleman was interested in a recent report from a Canadian laboratory that claimed RNA obtained from planaria (flat worms) that had been trained to respond to certain stimuli could transmit the memory of this training to other worms.[2] When he learned that a Nobel Laureate who knew a lot about DNA and RNA had recently moved into the neighborhood, he wrote Jim to inquire how he might take advantage of this new discovery to improve his own failing memory. In 1969, the Laboratory was still too impecunious to host a formal luncheon, so we invited the old gentleman to my house for lunch, with the intent of informing him about the Laboratory's research programs relating to DNA and RNA. We asked him for $60,000 to help support this research (and incidentally save us from bankruptcy). After a pleasant lunch, Jim made his pitch, skillfully tiptoeing around the touchy issue of whether it was really true that RNA could transfer improved memory capability to an aging human brain. At the end of what I thought was a highly convincing presentation of the importance of further basic research on DNA and RNA, the old gentleman proclaimed that he would be glad to participate as one of the 60 contributors to make up the $60,000. I don't remember whether we even got that $1000!

JIM'S ROLE MODELS

Although I don't know for certain, I suspect the genesis of Jim's reconstruction plan was closely related to his early training and what he had learned from his role models. The Laboratory had been the summer home and workplace where Jim's most influential mentors—Max Delbrück, Al Hershey, and Salvador Luria—gathered in the decades of the 1940s and 1950s. These were Jim's heroes, and, personal eccentricities aside, they were all brilliant, highly imaginative, and creative scientists, and Jim, I believe, hoped to emulate them.

When he first arrived as Director in 1968, Jim still held the view that scientists, at least biological scientists, did their best work at an early age, probably before 30 and certainly before 40, after which they were inevitably sliding on the downslope of their intellectual prowess. (It is ironic and fortunate that Jim himself has provided the best counterargument to this belief!) So in his recruitment efforts, he began looking for young men or women who at least had the potential of demonstrating the brilliance and creativity of his mentors. Only later, when the Laboratory had become much larger, did he recognize the necessity of having a stable constituency of senior investigators to provide scientific and administrative leadership and continuity. In the initial stages of rebuilding, he supervised everything himself, keeping a vigilant eye on the progress of each laboratory, and continuously prodding or modulating research programs he thought were underperforming.

THE 1971 NATIONAL CANCER ACT

In addition to providing bold and imaginative scientific leadership, Jim proved to be an outstanding fund-raiser (although he will tell you he has never even come close to reaching the goals he would like to achieve). At first glance, the late 1960s and early 1970s did not appear to be a very auspicious time for rejuvenating a small, private biological laboratory. The generous postwar federal funding of science that had revitalized research at many leading universities and other institutions was tapering off during Nixon's presidency. This postwar infusion of federal monies had made the participating institutions sufficiently flush to be able to share their largesse and save the Laboratory from extinction. Nevertheless, it would have been foolish to expect more than temporary help from the participating institutions. It was inevitable that sooner or later they would find higher spending priorities of their own, rather than continuing to bail out a neighboring institution, no matter how highly regarded or sentimentally attractive it might be.

Jim's first choice of a promising area on which to concentrate the Laboratory's effort was cancer, and more specifically to use DNA tumor viruses as a means of tackling the genetic basis of cancer (this was in the pre-recombinant DNA days when the genes of mammalian cancer cells were inaccessible). This was a financially as well as intellectually astute choice. Through the prodding of Cornelius (Dusty) Rhoads and other leading scientists, together with influential, public-spirited citizens such as Mary Lasker and Benno Schmidt who were passionately dedicated to conquering cancer, in 1971, Congress and President Nixon declared "War on Cancer." The National Cancer Act was passed, giving the National Cancer Institute and its Director a privileged position at the National Institutes of Health and making new federal monies available for cancer research. The passage of this Act occurred at a very opportune moment for the Laboratory and full advantage was taken in obtaining major grants to launch research programs and to recruit bright young tumor virologists.[3]

JIM'S OUTSPOKENNESS GETS HIM INTO TROUBLE

Jim was also highly successful in motivating leading individuals in the local community to support the Laboratory. He and Liz easily made many new friends and were widely sought after as interesting and delightful dinner guests. Everyone I know in the community is very fond of Liz and Jim, even while sometimes smiling with amusement when he occasionally makes a gaffe or forcefully expresses an opinion some might consider wild or even outrageous. I recall one LIBA meeting in Bush Lecture Hall in the early 1970s that was attended by as many as 100 of the Laboratory's loyal supporters from the local community.

This particular LIBA meeting happened in the midst of a controversy then raging about the wisdom and legality of conducting recombinant DNA research, research that had already been prohibited in Boston. Indeed, because of the ban, several leading molecular biologists from Harvard had already moved temporarily to Cold Spring Harbor to continue their experiments. The lay audience at the LIBA meeting did not fully appreciate all the nuances of the pro and con arguments, but they were left in no doubt as to Jim's opinion when he told them that "The only people against recombinant DNA research are kooks, shits, and Smith girls." There was an immediate buzz of whispers among the audience to find out how many of the ladies present had gone to Smith; as it turned out about half had, including my wife. She and most of the other ladies present had by this time become good friends of Jim's and had become accustomed to his occasional show-stoppers. The majority of this friendly and supportive audience was therefore more amused than offended or even surprised. However, this was not always the case. Sometimes, other audiences composed of strangers unacquainted with Jim's outspoken tendencies were less amused and less forgiving of his uninhibited pronouncements.

JIM THINKS OUT OF THE BOX

I have seldom met anyone who is as candid as Jim in freely expressing both his immediate and considered opinions on topics. Whether one agrees or not, he always has a valid reason behind his opinions, and in my own experience, he has been proven right much more often than not. Jim has a very quick mind and a fantastic memory, and coupled with his proclivity for holding strong opinions on certain subjects, especially anything that might threaten scientific integrity, excellence, or progress, he sometimes gets in trouble voicing sound-bite synopses when the opportunity is lacking to explain his views in greater depth.

Jim is also highly imaginative and prides himself on being able to think out of the box. He is quite capable of formulating enormously elaborate and convoluted hypotheses to try out on his friends and gauge their reaction. Recently I ran into a mutual long-time friend of Jim's and mine the day after Jim had tried at some length to convince us of the validity of his latest theory about the underlying genetic reasons for behavioral differences between fat and lean people. When she saw me, she burst out laughing and said, "The only thing funnier than Jim's hypothesis was the look on your face."

On the other hand, Jim does not hesitate to confront the gaps in his store of knowledge, including things that are common knowledge to clinical scientists. Once at a meeting at the Laboratory's Banbury Center, I almost fell off my chair when Jim asked the speaker, a prominent hematologist, what the hematocrit was; having gone to medical school, I assumed everyone knew that. This illustrates Jim's natural curiosity and his easy willingness to ask questions about things he doesn't know or isn't sure about. Unlike many other bright people who believe they are expected to know almost everything, Jim is never afraid to admit his ignorance; in fact, one of his great strengths is his readiness to ask simple, penetrating questions that demand clear answers.

JIM'S INTERESTS GO BEYOND THE LABORATORY

Jim's initiatives were not confined to scientific research in the laboratory. In 1972, Walter Page and Edward Pulling introduced Jim to their friend, Charles Robertson. After Charlie had carefully scrutinized Jim and the Laboratory to assess his probability of success, in 1973, he gave the Laboratory $8 million plus his own magnificent estate in Lloyd Harbor. Prior to this, the Lab had essentially no endowment, and Charlie's generous gift was invaluable in jump-starting its revival and providing financial stability.

Jim used the estate to establish the Banbury Center as a small conference center for no more than 30–40 participants. The Banbury Center meetings deal not only with scientific (and often controversial) topics in biology, but also with a wide range of science topics of public interest. The main objective was to bring together the best-informed experts in whatever subject matter was under discussion and to try to arrive at a consensus of what was well-established scientific evidence, as opposed to the exaggerated and speculative reports often found in the media. Depending on the topic, the participants might include journalists, legislators, environmentalists, or experts in other disciplines as well as scientists holding opposing views. Over the years, the Banbury Conferences have proved to be a valuable forum for providing decision makers with scientifically up-to-date objective appraisals of what is truly known or still unknown about controversial issues.

Jim's concern about making sure that the public has access to the best science led him to implement a series of lectures for the Laboratory's neighbors. Given in the Grace Auditorium by distinguished scientists in many different fields, these lectures help also to make the neighbors realize that the Laboratory is a resource for them and an institution of which they should be proud. Additionally, concerts given in Grace Auditorium by celebrated performing artists help to bring the staff and the community together to enthusiastically support the place. I think it is fair to say that almost none of these new programs would have been started without Jim's inspirational ideas and perseverance.

JIM AND THE BOARD OF TRUSTEES

I think that Jim would be the first to recognize that the strong support of the Trustees and Members of LIBA, later called the Cold Spring Harbor Laboratory Association (CSHLA), is a key element in what he has been able to do. Individual Lay Trustees were selected by a Board Nominating Committee while Scientific Trustees were formally proposed by their Institutions. In reality, the Scientific Trustees were usually pre-selected by Jim and only subsequently formally approved by their institutions and the Lab's Board. The Individual Trustees, drawn largely from local communities, were equally supportive in many other ways such as providing advice on budgets, investment portfolios, property acquisition, community relations, industrial relations, commercial applications, legal issues, and fund-raising campaigns. The Board was small enough (25 and later 35 members) that everyone got to know everyone else. The Board meetings were almost always harmonious and interesting, and although differing views were often expressed, I can hardly recall a single instance of acrimony or occasion in which a consensus or reasonable compromise was not reached.

Because the full Board only convened biannually, a small Executive Committee of the Board met together with Jim and his Senior Administrative Staff more frequently, usually monthly, to handle day-to-day matters that required Board input or decisions. Jim was as effective in selecting good administrators as he was in choosing top scientists, so Board members had the relatively easy and pleasant task of working with members of the staff who were almost invariably both able and congenial. Jim was both inspirational and demanding in his pursuit of excellence. If a scientist or administrator failed to perform adequately or showed a serious character flaw, he did not hesitate to fire the person. In a few instances, the issues leading to dismissal were highly charged and potentially extremely embarrassing and harmful to both the individual and the Laboratory. Jim invariably handled these difficult situations with great discretion and sensitivity. Because only one or two Board members were privy to the full stories, most people are unaware of how Jim agonized over these difficult decisions, especially if they involved people he was fond of.

The only exceptions I can recall to the otherwise tranquil Trustee meetings were a few occasions in the early years of Jim's Directorship when the Lab's financial position was still rather precarious. In each instance, the controversy was precipitated by Jim's determination to buy additional properties in the neighborhood that he felt were essential to preserve the Lab's beautiful setting and to allow its future expansion. On one such occasion, Jim insisted we buy the small, rather inconspicuous marina across the harbor that had recently been put up for sale. A developer had already made an offer, and his plan to greatly enlarge the marina would have destroyed the natural beauty of the harbor. The asking price was not great, but the problem was that there were no reserve funds at all for this contingency. The more conservative Lay Trustees led by Walter Page, Ed Pulling, and Bud Galston objected—they had been taught all their lives that expensive new ventures should not be undertaken if one wasn't sure where the money was to come from. Jim exploded. He threatened to resign if the Board refused to buy the marina and stormed out of the room. We all looked at each other when we grasped the gravity of the situation—now what do we do? Jim Darnell, the Rockefeller Trustee and an old friend of Jim's, finally set the proper tone. I don't recall his precise words, but he began "We must remember what this man has done for this place...". Once Darnell had broken the ice, Bruce Alberts and I believe that all of the other Scientific Trustees persuaded the other Trustees that we had no choice but to buy the marina; we would simply somehow have to find the money. So the Board capitulated and Jim won this battle, but only by making his dramatic threat to resign—over a marina! The sequel to this episode is instructive. Jim was, of course, right in insisting it was important that the beauty of the Lab's setting on the harbor be preserved. Once the Lab took possession of the marina, it was not allowed to expand, and moreover, over the years, it has returned a nice rental income to supplement the Lab's programs.

Walter Page later warned me not to embark on costly projects without prior assurance of adequate funding. But almost in the same breath he confessed that in his lifelong experience, Cold Spring Harbor Laboratory seemed to be a unique exception to this rule—somehow, somewhere the money was usually found to keep up with Jim's ambitious ideas. In fact, probably my own most important contribution to the Laboratory's success was to recruit David Luke to the Board. David agreed to serve as Treasurer and to head a major and highly successful fund-raising effort and later succeeded me as Chairman.

ALL'S WELL THAT ENDS WELL

In the 30-odd years since Jim became Director in 1968, the Laboratory has more than fully regained its former illustrious stature to become one of the superpowers of biological research in the world. If I were to pick two main themes to encapsulate Jim's success in rebuilding the Laboratory, the first would be his uncompromising insistence on scientific excellence and total integrity, together with his intolerance of sloppy science or any kind of dupery. The second major theme contributing to the Lab's successful revival was Jim's clairvoyance in focusing on important, timely, and solvable biological problems, and persevering with these even if advances were not immediately forthcoming. Walter Page was right: The Lab is an exception, but it would not be so without an exceptional leader.

Vision, Innovation, Breadth, and Strength

David L. Luke III

Locust Valley, New York

In the late 1960s, Cold Spring Harbor Laboratory was a long-established institution with a fairly narrow scientific focus. It had a limited and somewhat uncertain financial capacity, and it lacked a positive or clearly defined plan for participation in what would become the exciting and important field of modern genetics and molecular biology. Jim Watson, 40 years old when he became Director of the Laboratory in 1968, was well known for his personal scientific prowess and had a Nobel Prize, but the needs of the institution were much broader than his background had prepared him for, and it was fair to wonder what lay ahead.

My acquaintance with the Laboratory developed suddenly and unexpectedly in 1985. I knew of it from a distance, but my first introduction came from Barney Clarkson, a leading cancer researcher at Memorial Sloan-Kettering. Barney, an old and close friend, served on the Laboratory's Board of Trustees and talked with great enthusiasm about the institution. He told me that he had agreed to become the Board's next Chairman but on condition that an individual with more experience in general management and financial matters would serve with him. The person he had in mind for this role was me. I accepted with enthusiasm: The invitation was a wonderful fit with my growing fascination with the field of genetics and, given my professional interests, its applications in plant science.

When I arrived as the new Treasurer and Board Member in 1986, Jim's 18 years of leadership had already produced good progress in meeting some of the Laboratory's most pressing and immediate needs. His warm relationship with Charles Robertson had resulted in a welcome addition to the Laboratory's endowment and the wonderful gift of the Banbury property, which was to become an important foundation for the Lab's program of courses and meetings. With support from Oliver and Lorraine Grace, a handsome new auditorium had been constructed. However, the Lab was getting ready for much more. Jim's constant message was, "We can't afford to stand still!" I believed this too and was fully prepared to comply as long as we had sound plans for carrying out our programs and meeting our objectives. The Board was equally supportive.

I had not known Jim before joining the Board, but his relationships with Ed Pulling and other community leaders had prepared him for working with Board members who were not scientists. An early objective after my arrival was the creation of a responsible and balanced budget that covered all annual expenses including depreciation. But we soon began to plan major new projects that would become the heart of the first capital fund-raising campaign in the Lab's history, the Second Century Campaign. When the Campaign began in 1987, the initial target was $44 million, and when we concluded four years later, we had raised a total of $52 million. This paved the way for a great increase in the Lab's depth and breadth of activity. During the early 1990s, a new neuroscience program focusing initially on genes affecting the formation of memory was undertaken and located in the new Beckman Neuroscience Center. Dolan Hall was built to provide on-campus, overnight lodging for attendees of the meetings program. The DNA Learning Center was established in a newly acquired building to give high school students and teachers classroom exposure to modern biology.

For fund-raising, we established a strong Campaign committee, which was expected to meet regularly to hear reports from all involved, including Jim. He was an active and effective participant and did his full share of the work. He was more comfortable in soliciting some individuals than others, but when occasionally we had to press him, he would willingly support others who took the lead with a particular prospect.

The momentum and success of the Second Century Campaign instilled the feeling that not only could we not afford to stand still, but we didn't really have to: Our operating budgets were in balance, we were exceeding our capital campaign targets, and we began to look ahead with pride and confidence.

I became Chairman of the Board of Trustees in 1992. During the early 1990s, government support for science began to flatten, no longer increasing each year as it traditionally had. I began to feel that we should seek new ways to help ourselves through our own efforts, specifically, by considering the revenue potential of intellectual property opportunities from our own research. The federal government was beginning to emphasize translational research, so the timing seemed right. To avoid the charge of focusing on profit for profit's sake from research, we decided to designate a component of our endowment as the Science Fund. Any proceeds from our intellectual property were to go directly into this fund, which at the direction of our Board, was to be used solely for the support of future research at the Laboratory. In other words, we would recycle any fruits of today's research directly into support for tomorrow's research.

As we contemplated this idea, I wondered how Jim and others might view it. Several prestigious and highly respected large universities had apparently turned their backs on the chance to commercialize their intellectual property, and we seemed to be among the first academic institutions to consider actively codifying and pursuing our potential. I was therefore very pleased that after a full discussion, Jim and the Board enthusiastically endorsed the program. It quickly became a great success.

By the mid to late 1990s, the Laboratory had increasing financial resources and was able to create steadily more buildings and more comprehensive facilities. Yet the Board and executives recognized that the most important asset of the institution was the creative intellectual talent of our research staff. Jim felt that it was vital to be able to constantly stimulate and reinforce this key asset, and that the best way to do so would be a program that, each year, brought some of the world's best and brightest young minds to the Laboratory as graduate students, to interact with our research staff. We also felt that there was the possibility of establishing a model of graduate student education that differed from those of the major schools of science. Part of this difference was the goal of granting Ph.D. degrees in roughly four years, rather than the six to seven years that had become the norm elsewhere. As we reviewed the idea of establishing a graduate school of our own, it seemed more and more logical. However, we had one problem. As plans developed, I felt strongly that the school should have an appropriate name and concluded that it should be the "Watson School of Biological Sciences." In discussion with a number of our Trustees, including some who were in senior scientific positions in other universities, I found nothing but great enthusiasm for this suggestion. There was, however, one exception. When the subject was raised with Jim Watson, the answer came firmly back "Not in my lifetime!" We decided not to accept this and persisted until we had at least an initial reluctant acceptance.

To make certain that the new School was financially self-sufficient, we decided to raise an endowment of $32 million to support the initial phase of the School's life. That objective was fully met in June of 2002. Before and after the School's development, our scientific Trustees and other distinguished scientists reviewed and critiqued its design and progress. They were, and remain, enthusiastic supporters. In a recent review of a training grant application, a National Institutes of Health committee gave the School an exceptionally favorable appraisal, remarking, "We simply don't give marks this high to anyone anymore!" With the passage of time, Jim has become very much involved with the School. I have always felt that he is as much an educator as a scien-

David Luke (center). Dorcas Cummings Lecture, May 1993. (Courtesy CSHL Archives.)

tist, and his keen interest has led him to want to interview every single applicant to the School. I believe that he is now as proud to have his name associated with the School as we are to have it there.

The success of the Laboratory is related in many cases to its outstanding scientific and educational programs. Equally important, however, has been the emphasis Jim has always placed on the importance of really bright young people with the energy and motivation to be highly innovative. The Lab has seldom locked itself into indefinite continuation of employment of scientists, making possible the nimble pursuit of new areas of endeavor and opportunity. As I have watched other highly respected institutions trying to change in order to pursue new priorities, I have felt that Cold Spring Harbor Laboratory has a clear and great advantage—a direct result of Jim's strong feelings about this aspect of managing science.

In this essay, I cannot list all the exceptional scientific programs and other accomplishments of the Laboratory in the period I have known it, nor all the members of its dedicated organization who deserve credit for what has been accomplished. Nor have I mentioned the warmth and cheer that his wife, Liz, brings to so many of Jim's relationships with others. On his appointment, Jim faced very big challenges. No one at the time could have imagined all that would be achieved at Cold Spring Harbor in the subsequent 35 years. His vision of opportunities in science, his energy and willingness to commit himself strongly to chosen objectives, and his respect for the roles and potential contributions of others have ensured that his service at Cold Spring Harbor Laboratory has been of extraordinary value, not just to the institution, but to the wider world of science.

Under the stimulus and leadership of Jim and his team, the Lab now radiates vision, innovation, breadth, and strength.

Portraits: Robertson, Pulling, and Grace

On their arrival at the Laboratory in 1968, Jim and Liz Watson were warmly welcomed into the community by many residents of the three villages surrounding the Laboratory—Laurel Hollow, Cold Spring Harbor, and Oyster Bay Cove. Well-educated, accomplished, charmed by the newlyweds, if sometimes a little disconcerted by Jim's opinions, these individuals responded with generous donations of time, energy, and financial support. This social network was vital to the Laboratory, and to a Director trying hard to strengthen its financial position, and it brought Jim into contact with men and women he came strongly to admire. Jim often marked their passing with sincere and graceful tributes in the Laboratory's Annual Reports, of which these are excerpts.

CHARLES S. ROBERTSON (1905–1981)

Charles Sammis Robertson, through his several gifts to this Laboratory, changed radically our nature, giving us the capacity again to do science at a level with the best and allowing us to escape out of a long cycle of physical decay that had been badly accentuated in the early 1960s upon the decision of the Carnegie Institution of Washington to discontinue support for its Genetics Program at Cold Spring Harbor.

We met first in the summer of 1972, soon after the death of his beloved wife, Marie. They had married in 1936, quickly assembling a large parcel of land in Lloyd Harbor that overlooked the waters of Cold Spring Harbor and that had for almost 200 years been farmed by members of his mother's family, the Sammises...

Upon his wife's death, Charles Robertson became concerned over the long-term future of his house and property... He came to us with the hope that, as an academic institution, we might utilize well his land and buildings... It was an offer too wonderful to believe, or to consider even momentarily turning down, and we eagerly joined the Robertson family to set up a separate corporate entity to be called the Robertson Research Fund. On June 14, 1977, the Banbury Meeting House was formally dedicated, with Francis Crick giving the first lecture.

From the beginning of his formal association with us, Charles Robertson displayed an active interest in our Neurobiology Programs and early expressed the desire to help us further expand studies on the biological basis of behavior. Toward that objective, in 1977 he set aside further income from the Banbury Foundation to create the Marie H. Robertson Fund for Neurobiology.

In all his dealings with me and other members of the Laboratory, Charles T. Robertson was the perfect benefactor, modest, yet highly intelligent and desirous of further learning, graciously serious, but always with a sense of humor, and deeply loving and loyal to those individuals and institutions that he admired. His coming into our lives was a marvelous, unexpected gift, his delight and interest in the programs he helped make possible was a joy, and his passing this spring an occasion of deep sadness and reverence.

EDWARD PULLING (1898–1991)

Edward Pulling...was a truly remarkable man whose career embodied the virtues of education, family life, and devotion to service for the public good. In his dual roles, as a Trustee of this Lab and as Chairman of the Long Island Biological Association, he played an invaluable role in the Laboratory's achievements over the past two decades. My wife and I will always remember the gracious way Ed and his wife Lucy brought us into their world when we arrived in this community in the summer of 1968...

In 1969, Ed assumed the chairmanship (of LIBA), a position he was to hold for 17 highly effective years. Soon the LIBA membership was doubled to nearly 500 families, and conditions were created for the subsequent holding of major fund drives...

A mere chronicling of the LIBA fund drives does not adequately reflect the many important gifts to the Lab itself that came in large measure through his actions. I particularly remember Ed tracking me down in California in late June of 1972 to arrange a date when Charles S. Robertson would make his first visit to the Lab and have lunch at Osterhout Cottage where Liz and I were then living. This was the most important lunch ever held at the Lab, initiating the subsequent measures which led to the creation of the Robertson Research Fund and the Banbury Center. Ed's enormous enthusiasm for the Lab was also the major factor leading the Doubleday Trust to give us the Doubleday shares that made possible the creation of the Doubleday professorship for advanced cancer...

In his passing, we have lost an extraordinary force for enlightenment and decency.

OLIVER RUSSELL GRACE (1909–1992)

In his 82 years, Oliver lived at least three lives: He was a dedicated and loving husband and father, a successful businessman, and a generous and thoughtful philanthropist. It was in this last capacity that the Laboratory and I initially became acquainted with him. My first visit with him was in 1977, soon after he and his wife Lorraine moved to Oyster Bay. They had long been friends with Franz and Betty Schneider who brought us all together for a Sunday lunch at the Piping Rock Club. The Schneiders knew of Oliver's dedication to cancer research and wanted to interest him in our Laboratory, of which Betty was then a Trustee. (Oliver had helped to form the Cancer Research Institute [CRI] in 1953 and personally supported several programs that are now integral to the CRI operation.) Later, his fiscal, intellectual, and moral support would help make possible the substantive changes that have so enlarged this Laboratory's potential to promote science.

This long-standing interest in cancer research prepared Oliver for a call in the early 1980s from his friend Ed Pulling. Pulling was the Vice Chairman of our Board as well as Chairman of the Long Island Biological Association, our community support group then mounting a drive to raise funds for a new auditorium in which to hold our ever-swelling meetings. Oliver liked the plans and soon made the major gifts making possible the Oliver and Lorraine Grace Auditorium, with its imposing outside terrace carved out of the hillside to the north. Later, he supported the Laboratory in other ways, most notably in establishing the Oliver R. Grace Professorship for Cancer Research... He joined the Laboratory's Board of Trustees in 1983 and immediately became one of its most active members, later serving as the Board's secretary as well as a member of the Board's committees.

Everyone who knew him well remembers Oliver Grace as a man of integrity, intelligence, discipline, and compassion. From his family life, to his Wall Street transactions, to his philanthropy with the Cancer Research Institute and Cold Spring Harbor Laboratory, Oliver Grace lived up to the Latin motto of his ancient Irish lineage: *Concordant Nomine Acta*—"Our deeds bear out our name."

A Morning on the Porch

Jim Eisenman

In 1953, the Cold Spring Harbor Laboratory, then named the Long Island Biological Association, and the Carnegie Institution Department of Genetics (both directed by Milislav Demerec), contracted with my wife Jan and me to sell a small piece of their upland. That same year, James Watson and Francis Crick published a paper suggesting a structure for DNA, noting gently, at the end, that this structure might function in the replication of the genes of all living things (Watson and Crick 1953). Fifty years later, this historic understatement continues to reverberate around the world and none doubt that it will continue to do so for the next fifty.

By the early 1960s around the Lab, the phrase "Watson and Crick" was heard so often that it had become part of the white noise, along with the bird songs and distant train whistles. To me at least, having never met either gentleman, it was simply a phrase describing an important event that abruptly changed the direction of things— until, that is, I met the Watson part of the phrase one sunny morning (a guest from Harvard and not yet married), sitting on the edge of John and Elfie Cairns' porch at Airslie, the Laboratory Director's residence.

Around the Cairns house, the minds were always nimble and Jim Watson seemed to fit right in. The first sight of a person whose name precedes him always requires the undoing of preconceptions. For a start, I had thought both the phrase's individual components were British. But here sat an American (up front certainly, although not prototypical), helping John with a current problem that defied solution—the Laboratory's uncertain finances and its inability to get the attention of a local resident named Sherman Fairchild, an enormously successful founder of two high-tech corporations bearing his name. I knew Fairchild a bit through the legal world, but Jim had a fresh angle on making an approach to him: a mahogany speed boat towing seven perfect, long-limbed ladies on golden water skis would trace graceful arcs in Sherman's lagoon at the northeast end of the harbor. I noted the fact that John, new to balance sheets, but one of the fastest learners in town, had already told Jim about the Laboratory's endemic fiscal problems. I also filed away the recognition that sitting here on the porch was a mind with a fresh approach to the most important, difficult, and disliked chore in all academia—fund-raising. Now, 54 years later, looking at what the mahogany boat gambit and other such activities have brought in, Cold Spring Harbor Laboratory can be respectably compared with the eight colleges and universities of the Ivy League in the United States, remembering that Jim was for many of years a sole practitioner in a field new to him, with one telephone and one pencil, working on behalf of an institution in which he was also responsible for the extraordinary quality of the science. Those eight great institutions, meanwhile, were sustained by large professional teams of fund-rais-

JAMES EISENMAN

When Jim Watson's predecessor as Director, John Cairns, arrived at the Laboratory with his wife Elfie in 1963, they became fast friends with Jim and Jan Eisenman, near neighbors in Laurel Hollow. The couples had much in common: teenaged children, a love of the outdoors, intellectual curiosity, and a generally exuberant approach to life. Jim Eisenman had graduated from Brown as an engineer and had seen wartime service in the Merchant Marine before qualifying as a lawyer in 1948. Always fascinated by science and technology, he founded a patent law firm and worked directly with collaborators on a number of inventions. He was also the Village District Judge in Laurel Hollow for more than 20 years, with a jurisdiction that extended to the Laboratory and was exercised more than once by the exploits of staff members. With the encouragement of John Cairns, Jim became involved with the Long Island Biological Association, a group of neighbors who provided strong and important support of many kinds for the Laboratory in the local community. He was a vital part of the Association for more than 30 years, serving as its Treasurer from 1966 to 1989. In that capacity, he worked closely with Jim Watson and was much involved in the early years of Jim's Directorship as efforts were made to put the Laboratory on a sound financial basis. In this essay, written during his final illness and almost certainly incomplete, Jim Eisenman recalls his first meeting with Jim Watson, the opening encounter in a relationship of strong mutual respect that extended for almost 50 years. Jim Eisenman died on November 16, 2001.

ers, dedicated departments, seasoned presidents, fawning alumni, and accumulated years of experience.

Going back to that day on the porch, the next topic of conversation had to do with a book Jim was writing—an esoteric scientific tract, I assumed, except that the curious name, "Rosie," came up several times. "Rosie," I would learn later, was Rosalind Franklin, a young, skillful British scientist, soon to die, ever aloof to collaboration, but who figured hugely in the discovery of the structure of DNA. The problem was libel (false defamation expressed in writing, a young lawyer would say). Well, this was my area of expertise and I piped up "Fear not, no matter what, truth is a complete defense," speaking more loudly than usual. Elfie Cairns, a virtual library of knowledge (and looking out for my welfare, I know), quickly drew me aside to tell me that black and white were not always the colors of libel law, at least in England. If one's motive was not up to the purity of one's statement, then watch out for the process server. Also, she told me, England had always been a favorite forum for libel suits because the plaintiff did not have the burden of proving an untruth. Rather, the defendant (curiously) is handed the burden of proving his own truth (offset only by the rule that the loser pays the whole tab). This was tricky stuff for a lawyer already in over his head and I hurried back to the conversation to put on the record (as we say) the pile of exculpatory phrases that are the essence of the lawyer's trade. I was too late. The conversation was now about a quixotic poet from Greenland's north slope.

The weeks that followed brought no clarity, just ever more frequent allusions, printed and spoken, to Jim's forthcoming book. "Unheard of in science." "A brash

Jim Watson, Ahmad Bukhari, and Jim Eisenman, 1979. (Courtesy CSHL Archives.)

undertaking." "A time bomb." "Science will never be the same." "Wow." "Ouch." And finally, one idea that turned me pale—the proposed title, "Honest Jim"! Nobody could use a dumb title like that without inviting a lawyer to rummage in his locker. However, *The Atlatic Monthly* prepublished the book serially, under the perfect title: *The Double Helix*.

Before that, in 1966, on the lawn behind Blackford Hall at the Lab, one of Jim's long-limbed ladies would jump out of a birthday cake for the other name in the famous phrase: Francis Crick. The affair, to celebrate Francis' 50th birthday, was orchestrated by Ric Davern, the Assistant Director of the Lab and a scientist from Tasmania, a wonderful guy who went far fast in U.S. academia but died too soon. He had a problem and came to me with it, I think, because I was the local judge in those days. Rick had a persuasive and powerful way with words (he once warned me that "There's an asp in that tub of lard") and explained his problem: The inside of the cake had limited space and would not accommodate both clothes and limbs. He guessed, however, that Watson and Crick wouldn't call the Constable over an animated birthday cake. He was correct, of course, and Francis got on fine with the long limbs.

I cannot tell when the tensions, suspected or otherwise, subsided after either event, particularly the book's. Fortunately, the curves were asymptotes. But even after 54 years, Jim still faces only forward, abruptly changing the direction of certain things, animate and inanimate, and accelerating the speed of many others, motivated always—I like to think—by the still suspect notion that truth is a complete defense.

REFERENCES

Watson J.D. and Crick F. 1953. Molecular structure of nucleic acids. *Nature* **171:** 737–738.

An Architect at the Lab: Some Personal Recollections

William Grover

Centerbrook, Connecticut

Great places are created by passionate individuals. Jim Watson's passion for Cold Spring Harbor Laboratory is evident in the remarkable place it has become since he became its Director in the early 1970s. The Lab was nicely rustic before then—a memorable and historic village that charmed the many brilliant scientists who came there each summer to exchange ideas. I recall, however, that it was rather rundown and overgrown with vines, like a summer camp gone to seed. Jim recognized the importance of this unique scientific community, and as Director, he encouraged architecture and landscape that would keep the place beautiful for its neighbors, but unconventional and inspirational for those who lived and worked there.

Jim Watson and Bill Grover at the cornerstone laying for the Neuroscience Center and Dolan Hall, 1989. (Courtesy CSHL Archives.)

357

WILLIAM GROVER

After Jim became Director and the Laboratory grew richer, a surprising side of Watson emerged: a builder-cum-landscape artist with an obsessive determination to make the Laboratory as beautiful as it was scientifically renowned. Jim was trenchant in his view that to be successful, an institution had to look the part, so despite occasional grumbling from the research staff that more money seemed to be spent on trees than experiments, an era began in which the face of the Laboratory changed dramatically. Older structures were imaginatively renovated and dramatic new buildings were placed provocatively among the Victorians on the harbor shore. Jim's chief accomplice in this serious and consuming work was Bill Grover, senior partner at Centerbrook Architects and Planners, located across Long Island Sound in the Connecticut village of the same name. A former industrial designer at General Motors, Grover had gained his Master's degree from Yale and begun a practice with Charles Moore, then Dean of Architecture at the University. This essay describes the partners' first encounter with Jim, provoked by the Watsons' delight in Moore's Californian Sea Ranch, where they had stayed on their honeymoon. The bold renovation of Airslie that followed was the beginning of a partnership that has produced a series of strikingly successful buildings, each resulting from Grover's sensitive interpretation of Watson's strongly voiced vision. Jazz musician, sailor, and artist, Bill Grover has placed an indelible stamp on the village of science.

When Jim and Liz were married, they honeymooned in California and happened to stay at the Sea Ranch on the coast north of San Francisco. Architect Charles Moore and his partners had recently designed a handsome ten-unit, barn-like condominium on the edge of the ocean cliffs there and the Watsons were intrigued by its simplicity and the way it fit smoothly into the strong landscape. Subsequently, they discovered that Moore had become the Dean of the Yale School of Architecture, just across Long Island Sound from Cold Spring Harbor. They called his office in Essex, Connecticut, to see if he would be interested in designing the renovation of Airslie House[1] for them. I was one of several young architects working for Moore at that time who were about to be put out of a job because Richard Nixon had cut off funds for the Department of Housing and Urban Development projects that had been our livelihood. When we made our first visit to the Lab, Moore's bankruptcy seemed imminent and I think Jim may have liked the fact that we appeared to be tense and anxious as we toured Airslie. Our architectural practice, which later became Centerbrook Architects, ultimately survived, in no small part because of the projects offered us by Jim and Cold Spring Harbor Laboratory. Jim has managed to keep us not only tense and anxious, but also excited and enthusiastic for the last 26 years. Below are just a few of my recollections of working with Jim.

THE CURVE OF THE AIRSLIE DRIVEWAY

No other client of mine has ever spent as much time considering and refining the curve of a driveway. At our first design meeting, Jim, Chuck Moore, Jack Richards,[2] and I spent most of an afternoon with a garden hose articulating and marking out the exact line of that curve. I realized then that every detail of our work for Jim was going to be subject to very serious scrutiny, before, during, and after construction.

Beckman Neuroscience Center courtyard. (Photograph by Andrew Garn. Courtesy CSHL Archives.)

PAINT COLORS

Colors don't look the same on a color chart as they do on a wall. The number of colors we tried on the interior walls of Airslie must have exceeded 100. We would select a range of colors, order a quart of each, and paint a section of wall. Jim and Liz would consider the color and each would suggest a variation. More colors would be obtained and applied until an acceptable hue was decided upon. Jack Richards deplored the idea of wasting unused paint so he mixed the remainders of all the sample quarts together and painted the whole attic with the resulting greenish brown.

THE POSSIBLE INFLUENCE OF THE MOVIE "SLEEPER" ON THE DESIGN OF JONES LAB

When it came time to renovate the historic Jones lab into a state-of-the-art neuroscience lab, we proposed to restore the original wood shell of the building and construct within it four shiny aluminum laboratories with rounded corners to make them clearly different and up-to-date compared to the 1895 structure. When the project (our first attempt at a laboratory) subsequently won an important national design award, Jim suggested that the design was not original and that we had borrowed the idea from the "Orgasmatron" in Woody Allen's movie "Sleeper." Creativity, Charles Moore once told me, is not revealing one's sources.

Grace Auditorium. (Photograph by Andrew Garn. Courtesy CSHL Archives.)

GETTING THE ARCHITECT'S ATTENTION

The presentation of our initial design concepts to Jim usually gets a quick and thoughtful response. A young architect in our office had stayed up late finishing a model of the proposed renovation of Blackford Hall. When we presented the model to Jim and Jack, Jim announced: "That's shit! If you can't do better than that, I'll get another architect"! After the young man and I left the meeting, Jim apparently asked Jack: "Do you think I got their attention?" The young architect left Centerbrook soon afterward and is currently building houses in Ecuador. I'm still here, but Jim's initial responses never fail to get my attention.

THE COLORS OF DAVENPORT

For many years, Davenport, the wonderful Victorian house on Route 25A was painted white (dusted with highway dirt). When it came time for a renovation of the building, Liz asked me what color I thought it should be painted. I suggested an archeological investigation. Scraping down through layers of old paint, she found that it had originally been painted in a variety of Victorian colors of tan, red, and green. Liz and Jim obtained a book of original Victorian paint schemes and selected colors that Davenport was most likely to have been painted. When the painting began, there was apparently some objection by one or more members of the CSHL Board of Trustees who thought it would be too expensive to paint it in multiple colors and therefore it should remain white. The story goes that Jim offered to resign as Director if the colors he and Liz preferred were not implemented. I was told that the Board backed off, and Jim later paid for the added cost out of his own pocket.

RIDING IN THE LAB BUICK

When we would meet at the Lab to discuss architectural projects, Jim often drove us to lunch in an exceedingly large, dark green Buick station wagon. I was flattered, the first time, when others from the Lab graciously insisted that I ride in the front seat with Jim. I soon realized that they were acting out of self-preservation rather than deference to my professional stature. Jim would drive at variably high and low speeds while discussing the projects—his mind clearly not on the task of driving. He also didn't notice that the windshield wipers were operating on a bright sunny day in July. No one in the car commented on this so I didn't either.

SPEED LUNCHES

Did you ever notice that by the time the person who immediately follows Jim in the Blackford cafeteria line takes a seat, Jim is nearly finished eating his lunch?

THE HOLLY TREE INCIDENT

The landscape and appearance of the Lab is one of Jim's greatest interests. The location of every tree and shrub is of significance to him. One late afternoon as he walked home from his office in James Annex, he noticed a man on a backhoe digging a hole to plant a holly tree near Page-Delbruck Laboratory. He advised the operator that the tree would look better about 5 feet west of the proposed location. When the operator protested that the architect and Jack Richards had established the exact location, Jim insisted in no uncertain terms, and showed exactly where he wanted the tree to go. Not wanting to argue with Jim, the backhoe operator began digging where Jim had indicated. A few scoops down he hit a buried 15,000-volt primary electrical line which, with considerable fireworks, melted a chunk out of the backhoe shovel and shut down electrical service to most of the Lab. This experience may have tempered Jim's (and the backhoe operator's) enthusiasm for excavation, but it has not cooled his interest in the precise location of plant material.

There are more stories...but I'll save them for another time.

The passion that Jim and Liz have for good design, and their insistence on it, have made Cold Spring Harbor Laboratory a truly great and memorable place to work, live, and visit. I share those passions, and the Watsons are among my most treasured collaborators. I continue to be delighted with any challenge they may offer. Few architects have ever been as fortunate.

GENOMES

Section V photograph: *The announcement of the draft sequence and initial analysis of the human genome (February 12, 2001, Press Conference, Capitol Hilton, Washington, D.C.) (From left to right) Eric Lander, Bob Waterston, Jim Watson, Francis Collins. (Photograph by Bill Branson, NIH. Printed, with permission, courtesy of the National Human Genome Research Institute.)*

Managing the Genome

THE 1986 COLD SPRING HARBOR SYMPOSIUM was titled, with true Watsonian flourish, "The Molecular Biology of *Homo sapiens*" at a time when many would have thought that the subject hardly existed, let alone there being enough hard facts to sustain a five-day meeting. However, Jim was certainly correct when he wrote of "...our newfound ability to study ourselves at the molecular level," and much of the meeting was occupied with the molecular studies of human DNA through mapping, cloning, and sequencing of genes.

None of these were easy to do at that time. Finding human disease genes by using restriction-fragment-length polymorphisms as genetic markers had had its first successes only two years earlier and required heroic efforts in both finding families and carrying out the subsequent linkage analyses. Moving from a mapped position to a cloned gene was no less heroic, and no one had yet succeeded, although hunters of the genes for cystic fibrosis, Huntington's disease, and Duchenne muscular dystrophy were fast closing in on their targets. And DNA sequencing, although routinely using Sanger or Maxam-Gilbert methods, was limited to fairly short tracts. It still required a major commitment of resources and chutzpah on the part of an investigator to tackle sequences longer than a few kilobases. To think of tackling something of the size and complexity of the human genome seemed both foolhardy and harebrained. By the end of the Symposium, this had changed. Jim had organized a "consciousness-raising" discussion about what large-scale DNA sequencing might achieve, and participants left the meeting with the idea that sequencing of *genomes* might be possible and that there were some people who planned to do it!

Jim was not the first or even an early proponent of sequencing the human genome. The first discussions had taken place at the University of Santa Cruz at a time when Robert Sinsheimer had hoped that a Human Genome Project could capture funding intended originally for a new telescope in Hawaii. He convened a small meeting attended by Wally Gilbert, David Botstein, Lee Hood, Sydney Brenner, John Sulston, Bob Waterston, and Ron Davis—people whose names were to reappear frequently throughout the long saga of establishing the Human Genome Project. The meeting concluded that a Human Genome Project was not only desirable, but doable. Sinsheimer's estimate of the cost was $5 million (1984 dollars) per year for up to 20 years. But, even at this bargain price, a Human Genome Project proved unattractive to the donor who was interested in stars rather than genes. However, in the nick of time, an unlikely angel appeared on the scene—the United States Department of Energy (DOE).

The DOE had a long-standing interest in human genetics because of its need to determine the mutagenic effects of radiation on humans. Believing that sequencing genomic DNA might be a way to do this, Charles DeLisi, then head of the Office of Health and Environmental Research at DOE, convened a series of meetings in 1986 that led the DOE to reassign some 1987 funding to a genome project.

Meanwhile, the National Institutes of Health (NIH), the federal institute that would have seemed the natural home for a Human Genome Project, seemed oblivious to the discussions at Santa Cruz and DOE, in part because these early meetings had been restricted to a small coterie of scientists. In September, 1985, Renato Dulbecco was the keynote speaker at the dedication of a new laboratory at Cold Spring Harbor and used the occasion to argue that the best approach to cancer was to determine all the genes involved by sequencing the human genome. His address reached a far greater audience when it was published as a perspective in *Science* in March, 1986.

At the last moment, Jim inserted a discussion on sequencing the human genome, led by Paul Berg and Walter Gilbert, into the 1986 Symposium program on Saturday, June 3. The auditorium was packed as Berg outlined what was meant by a Human Genome Project, and it was filled with drama as Gilbert began to write numbers on the board, showing that such a project would cost $3.5 billion. There was a heated exchange as the discussion was opened to the audience. Many argued that the money could come only by cutting investigator-initiated grants, that the work was too boring, that it wasn't science, and that no one would want the results. There were other, less-emotive arguments advanced in the following months. Bob Weinberg, for example, wanted to know how the sequence was to be interpreted. If he were to be offered the 200,000-base sequence of the retinoblastoma gene, he could not imagine "...what help this would prove in solving the important problems surrounding the function of this gene and its encoded protein."

Despite the largely negative response, the idea of a Human Genome Project had taken hold and Jim, Berg, and Gilbert soon began to urge Jim Wyngaarden, the Director of NIH, to take up the cause. As Wyngaarden describes in his contribution to this book, he needed little encouragement and soon arranged for a series of reports that recommended setting up a Human Genome Project under the NIH. By the summer of 1988, all that was needed was to find a project director. The issue came up during a meeting held by the Office of Technology Assessment when Watson commented that "I instinctively believe that one person should be in charge of it who understands the scientific issues and who is not chosen purely to be an administrator." A little later, Watson asked John Sulston whether, from his experience mapping *C. elegans*, he believed that the Genome Project required one person in charge, who would "...live and die for the thing."

> Sulston: "It seems to me rather appalling...He's [the director of the project] admin-sitrating (sic) this huge empire. Do you really want to see that?"
>
> Watson: "I think someone has got to do it."
>
> Sulston: "You would like to do it."
>
> Watson: "Well, I couldn't think of a job I'd like less (laughter)....But I just have a

feeling that someone has to keep track of the whole thing over a long period of time with a certain degree of intensity..."

These early protests not withstanding, Jim's strong statements that the project had to be run by a scientist and not a bureaucrat left him with few options when Wyngaarden offered him the job. The doubts expressed by E.O. Wilson when Watson became Director of Cold Spring Harbor Laboratory had long been laid to rest by Watson's subsequent success, but becoming a federal official was rather different. It was immediately clear that NIH had never had a Director like Watson, who, used to being a benevolent autocrat in his own domain, insisted on impressing his goals and ethos on the Human Genome Project. His declarations on the societal implications of the Human Genome Project, his extension of the project to include other organisms, and his stipulation that the sequencing data be freely available irrevocably determined the style of the project.

Jim continued to deploy that "certain degree of intensity" whenever he felt that the project was under attack. At one meeting where two critics—Bernard Davies and Don Brown—spoke, Watson told Brown to stop being "mystical" about traditional investigator-initiated projects funded by RO1 grants. When Brown responded that it wasn't appropriate for "...someone in the Genome Project to demean RO1s," Jim replied in characteristic fashion: "That is pure crap."

It was, perhaps, inevitable that Jim's determination to call a spade a spade eventually led to him falling afoul of bureaucratic conventions. His insistence that the human genome should be in the public domain, coupled with his determination that the project should go ahead with the best people, led to a confrontation with an entrepreneur, Fred Bourke, and Bernadine Healy, director of NIH and Jim's boss. Jim Wyngaarden and Robert Cook-Deegan describe the episode more fully in their contributions to this book, but the end result was that Jim resigned in April, 1992.

Although Jim's tenure ended in acrimony, there is no doubt that Wyngaarden made exactly the right choice in taking him on. Although there were many other scientists who could have taken on the task, none had the panache, political clout, and commitment to see the job through without the reward of personal aggrandizement. Jim had always believed that structure was the best and perhaps only key to understanding how things work. He saw that the Human Genome Project would enlighten the entire sweep of human biology and behavior in the same way that his discovery of the DNA structure had illuminated the inner workings of single cells. As Jim put it in 1989 "How can we not do it? We used to think our fate was in our stars. Now we know, in large measure, our fate is in our genes."

Dr. Watson Goes to Washington

Bradie Metheny

Washington Fax

It's been more than 20 years, but I still remember how James Dewey Watson looked and moved while sitting at the witness table before the House Appropriations Health Education and Welfare Committee (HEW). There were nine other distinguished scientists sitting at that table with him, but Watson is the only one I remember in great detail. A few straggles of hair lay mussed on the great head. His nose was screwed up, his face intent with impatience. His eyes darted about inventorying everything and everyone in the room. If they asked him a question, I knew his lack of attention would result in an embarrassing moment for all concerned.

I had not met Jim Watson until the night before when a group of America's most eminent scientists, among them several other Nobel Laureates, gathered in Washington, D.C., to testify the next day before two special congressional hearings, one in the House and one in the Senate. My job was to coordinate this pick-up group of novice advocates for science in their efforts to educate Congress on the needs of America's life science enterprise.

Watson was late arriving for the dinner meeting the first night. Mahlon Hoagland,[1] who was President of the Worcester Foundation for Experimental Biology,[2] championed the gathering and had been selected as spokesperson. He and Lewis Thomas, president of the Memorial Sloan-Kettering Cancer Center, found themselves defend-

M. Goldstein (left) and Bradie Metheny (right) at the Banbury Center meeting on "Funding for the Decade of the Brain," November, 1992. (Courtesy CSHL Archives.)

BRADIE METHENY

Some people are movers, happier to work behind the scenes, whereas others are shakers, best stirring the pot, and some, like Jim, are both, adjusting their tactics to suit the occasion. Bradie Metheny is a mover *par excellence*. For more than 30 years, he has worked in the area of science policy in Washington, trying to help scientists and leaders within the federal government develop rational and productive policy. One of his best known roles was as coordinator of the Delegation for Biomedical Research, an informal group of eminent scientists and Nobel Prize winners. Metheny planned strategy, prepared testimony, conducted educational forums, and arranged special hearings to help convince members of Congress of the need to secure federal support for research in the biomedical sciences.

Metheny has been a reporter and editor in both broadcast and print journalism, a radio show host, TV writer/producer, and a consultant and executive of numerous programs and projects in public relations, public information, and governmental affairs. As a science policy writer, he contributes to a variety of publications nationally and founded *The Washington Fax*, a daily subscriber-based electronic science policy news and information service.

Metheny has been described as a "...robust, affable, optimistic Missourian. Direct, honest, and politically savvy," ideal characteristics for having to shepherd scientists who know where to go in their own field, but who might get lost on the Hill.

ing Watson against harsh charges from the others in the group—that he was a "loose cannon," and "he couldn't be trusted not to go his own way against the best interests of science." Hoagland and Thomas, by the sheer strength of their combined wills, quelled the dissenters and had everyone on track with cogent points clear in their minds by the time Watson arrived. My confidence, on the other hand, was badly shaken. I had no idea how I would tell a distinguished Nobel Laureate to be quiet if the occasion should arise.

When, the next morning, the late Rep. William Natcher,[3] chairman of the new HEW Subcommittee, said in his rich Kentucky drawl: "Dr. Watson," the moment I'd dreaded was at hand. Watson was gawking about the room. All too slowly for my comfort, he turned to the Chairman and began, without delay, to lay out succinctly and articulately the clear relationship between research and education, and how important a part of the continuum of science these are. I remember taking a deep, satisfying, and audibly relieved breath.

I would have only one more anxious moment that first time I met Jim. The day after the congressional hearings, we were to meet with President Jimmy Carter's science advisor, Frank Press, in the cabinet room at the White House. Press was detained, and the ten or so scientists were spread around a huge table in that very prestigious and elegant room. It was quiet. There was no conversation. Somewhere within earshot a no-doubt ancient and venerable clock was ticking. Whether these world-class scientists were as much in awe as I was, I can only speculate.

The silence continued, the scientists' eyes fixed upon the papers before them. From the corner of my eye, I saw Watson move and lean back in his chair, raising his feet slightly off the floor. My imagination galloped away with my fear that Watson was going to lean yet further back and put his feet on the table. I quickly rose to forestall him, as did my assistant Shelly Lauzon. But by the time we had stood up, Watson had shifted in his chair and simply stretched his legs out under the table, settling back to continue the wait.

Later that evening, after the last scientist was safely on a plane, we did an assessment of the event, and we felt good. The scientists and the politicians had come face to face, and learned from each other. The first steps toward trust and respect had been taken. "And the loose cannon didn't fire," Shelly noted, stirring our collective relieved laughter. "In fact, he was really good," she added, almost in a whisper. The rest of us nodded or uttered our various forms of "yep."

Watson was responsive, articulate, and straightforward in his responses to congressional questions, views, and discussion. If he believed, as did many scientists at the time, that it was beneath him to talk with senators, congressmen, members of the administration, and their staffs, he didn't let it show. For the 10 years I served the delegation, I was always able to call on him for advice or testimony, and he always made himself available. Other than Dr. Michael DeBakey and four or five others, the scientific community in the late 1970s wanted no part of "lobbying" Congress or the Administration. The "Delegation for Basic Biomedical Research," as this group of scientists was soon dubbed, emerged very early in the game of scientists going to the Hill.

Although Watson was thought to be a "loose cannon," nothing he did or said was in any way destructive. In fact, it was just the opposite, and a rapport developed between Watson and the politicos on the subcommittees. It took me a while to understand that his effectiveness with politicians was a result of his gutsy and straightforward responses to their questions. They needed to know what was fact and what was fiction, and Watson told them what he believed to be true regardless of the impact of his remarks.

But during these early days of the delegation, I also was aware that, for some reason unclear to me at the time, Watson was a controversial man in the scientific community. Back then I knew little about science, its culture, and its personalities. I had not seen firsthand the members of that distinguished club get into a "snit" and take up sides against one of its own. Among the scientific community, loyalties are blood thick, tenacity to opinion is unshakable, and memories are long. At the time of the first visits of the Delegation to Capitol Hill, I had yet to witness the division of the community over the David Baltimore–Thereza Imanishi-Kari case,[4] or hear about the battering of Ludwig Gross over the idea that cancer is caused by multiple viruses.[5] Nor did I know about "Judah Folkman's War" over his idea of using anti-angiogenesis drugs as a weapon in the war against cancer.[6] To be a scientist requires intelligence most of us are only smart enough to recognize, a confidence so deep-rooted that one's opinion can be changed only by the strongest evidence, and a skin so thick that it can't be lashed by words or deeds.

Hoagland would say later he had never seen the scientific community as divided about an incident as it was over Watson and his book *The Double Helix* (1968, 1980). The book was Watson's effort to "tell of the long struggle to decipher the structure of DNA," wrote Walter Sullivan of the *New York Times* in his article "A Book That Couldn't go to Harvard." Sullivan got to the crux of the turmoil when he wrote "The book tells the story in highly personal terms, describing the idiosyncrasies of the principals, their quarrels, and friendships."

Gunther Stent (1980) in his essay in *The Double Helix*, writes that a draft Watson circulated among the persons mentioned in his story "evoked some severe criticism, on the grounds, not so much that Watson's account was historically inaccurate or self glorifying, but that it was gratuitously harmful in its characterization of, or off-hand remarks about, many people." A number of members of the scientific community thought Watson was "unfair" to his collaborator Francis Crick and cruel to Rosalind Franklin, a crystallographer who worked in Maurice Wilkin's laboratory at King's College in London. Hoagland describes the book as an innovative and unique approach to laying out, with an attempt at complete honesty, the venture to find the structure of DNA. He thought Watson accomplished this goal for the book well. But many, at the time, did not.

The book was not the only ghost always present and waiting to be summoned up at those early delegation appearances before Congress. There was Watson's position that the Nixon War on Cancer would neither deliver to science its aspirations nor deliver to the American people its promise of a cure. It was Nixon's contention that the nation could declare war on cancer, throw money at the problem, and win victory in 10 years. Watson didn't believe this for a moment and opposed the effort vocally. Unlike the Kennedy "moon project," where a lot of basic research had been done by Robert Goddard and others before him, Watson was of the opinion that science didn't know enough and had not done enough basic research to fulfill the political promise of curing cancer.

Here Watson, all by himself, climbed up to sit in the hot seat. There were those in science who looked on the "War on Cancer" as an opportunity to get more federal money funneled into basic research, thus remedying the unbelievable short supply of funds, particularly in the life sciences. Watson was so opposed to the War on Cancer that when his teacher, mentor, and friend Salvador Luria asked him to speak at the dedication of MIT's newly formed Cancer Center, which Luria would direct, Watson used the occasion to restate his opposition. The event sparked one of the few times I heard voices raised by Delegation members during the 10 years I served them. Luria and Watson got into a heated discussion of the incident, requiring Lew Thomas to bang the table and admonish, "Now both of you behave." The room settled down and Mahlon Hoagland got everyone back to business. Hoagland somehow always created an atmosphere that allowed this group of highly opinionated people to speak their minds as they believed necessary and yet get across the expert information they were there to present, and with an eloquence only this distinguished body of dedicated souls could produce.

While everyone who served on the Delegation brought the valued perspective of a working scientist, Watson, Baltimore, Hoagland, and Thomas, and perhaps one or two others, brought the additional experience of running an institution—worrying about budgets and raising money to keep the bench scientists at work. This perspective was valued by members of Congress, as well as members of the Administration, in understanding the reality of what is required in the way of resources to keep the scientific enterprise strong and growing.

The Nixon Administration, however, was not fond of Watson. Here was a Nobel Laureate who for some reason, and despite his detractors, was believed in many quarters, and he was attacking one of their showpieces. For his part, when questioned by a member of Congress, Watson didn't pull his punches, but stayed out of the partisan political muck. He did this by clearly articulating his answers based on sound thinking and reasoning why the War on Cancer could not be won in 10 years. His answers were so soundly thought out, they were near impossible to refute. Once, Senator Birch Bayh, a Democrat from Indiana and a strong supporter of the National Institutes of Health, whose wife Marvel was then a cancer victim, asked Watson whether he thought we could win the war, and Watson gave his usual assessment. Bayh responded, "Doctor, I do so wish I didn't believe you."

I was always amazed at Watson's style of delivery in response to congressional questioning. I came to believe that he was so confident of the reasoning behind his answers he intentionally allowed the pause that once terrified me in order to allow us to watch him search his mind for just the right word to convey his thoughts accurately.

What Watson and the professional politicians grasped in this very early stage of scientific-political interaction, what took the rest of us longer to catch onto, is how important his interaction really was to the welfare of the scientific enterprise and ultimately to the nation. Even more important was the realization that this working relationship had to be based on total honesty, or science and society would both suffer greatly. Too many of us at this early stage had our eyes on the funding and not on the long road yet to be traveled together by scientists and politicians.

Although Watson was one of the best known of the Delegation, he was not the only heavy contributor to its achievements. Truth be known, I had the best job yet to exist in science advocacy. I had a squad of highly intelligent and articulate individuals who cared greatly about the American scientific enterprise and, in particular, about the opportunities that must be created for the creative, bright young minds on their way into the culture of science. Watson, along with Baltimore, Berg, Thomas, and later Harold Varmus, had a specific feel for how the federal government worked. They had knowledge of its system, tolerance of, if not full respect for, the federal practitioners of governing, and an instinct for how they as statesman from science could reach in and make an impact. After Hoagland retired, it was Watson and Baltimore who carried the water for science.

In 1987, Watson was exactly where he should have been with the experience, political access, and courage to do a tough job: getting the Human Genome Project underway.[7] The study of human genetics had been sputtering along since just after World War II, mostly in the Atomic Energy Commission where people were interested in mutations and where they came from. In about 1985, Charles DeLisi, Director of the Office of Health and the Environment in the 10-year-old Department of Energy, placed a small amount of money in his budget for the purpose of getting the Genome Project on the public policy agenda. But by this time, as with any new scientific field, genomics was not the territory of just one house of science. The NIH budget had been increasing, and Ruth Kirchstein, who was then Director of NIH's National Institute of General Medical Sciences (NIGMS), claimed that NIGMS was the main funding source for genetics research at NIH (although there was some dispute about the figures).

Even so, no one at this stage of the game, including NIH, grabbed the ring of leadership. Stifling the initiative was the huge cloud of the project's enormity and, at some level, awareness of the ethical, legal, social, and economic tentacles that would have to be dealt with beyond the science. Nevertheless, Jim Wyngaarden was increasingly in favor of a role for NIH and began the slow process of setting up committees to report on the desirability or otherwise for NIH to get involved with human genome sequencing. Bits and pieces about the complexity, scope, and importance of the Genome Project began leaking from the Office of Technology Assessment, where Robert Cook-Deegan was heading up a congressionally requested study that ultimately would be titled "Mapping Our Genes—Genome Projects: How Big? How Fast?" Even before the report was due to be issued formally in 1988, it seemed obvious that there had to be a far-reaching vision and strong central leadership for the project. The Question was Who? Where? How?

On the Hill, the discussion was bouncing from one congressional committee to another with little being done to establish a direction or a track for the project to run on. Watson was concerned about the project and lack of leadership. We discussed the fact that we likely could shorten the time to get the project focused by getting Rep. Natcher, whose subcommittee was now called Labor, Health, and Human Services, Education and Related Agencies, to take an interest.

I believed Mr. Natcher's subcommittee could take a leadership position, direct substantial funds into the project and, indeed, jump-start a Center for Genomic Research at NIH without further action by a congressional authorizing committee. This feat was possible due to special sections of Public Health Law that allowed funds to be appropriated for projects if those projects were within the NIH mission, where Watson and I believed genomic research belonged. Jim was willing to take a chance and try my interpretation of the situation. I called Natcher's office to request an appointment for Watson. At the same time, Natcher asked me to get him one or two experts he could talk with about AIDS. I arranged for David Baltimore, who co-chaired the Committee on a National Strategy for AIDS out of the National Academy of Sciences and the Institute of Medicine, to accompany us.

The meeting involved Natcher; the late Rep. Silvio Conti of Massachusetts, the subcommittee's chief Republican; Massachusetts Democrat Joe Early, a member of the subcommittee and an NIH champion; and Baltimore and Watson. Baltimore agreed to bring together a group of experts for a hearing on the AIDS issue. Watson asked Mr. Natcher if the subcommittee would be appropriating funds for the Genome Project. Natcher asked Watson what he thought was required. As I recall, Watson said $30 million. Natcher said the committee would certainly consider the request, but NIH Director Jim Wyngaarden would have to indicate he wanted the money.

Shortly after the meeting, Watson and I met with Wyngaarden. Watson in his direct fashion asked the NIH Director if he and NIH intended to pick up leadership of the Genome Project. If NIH was not going to assume that leadership, Watson said he would put his influence behind the DOE effort. Wyngaarden didn't miss a beat, assuring Watson that NIH was going to pick up leadership of the Project. Within weeks, Watson was named Director of the NIH Human Genome Project. Work began that required all of Watson's skills, and perhaps a few of his faults, to plow through the intrigue and weave of institutional, national, and international politics.

Who better to step into this political Donnybrook where high ethical ideals and unassailable honesty must be the norm than this Irish Catholic boy, who grew up in a working-class Chicago household where books, birds, and FDR were the bedrock of dinner table discussion? Forming saleable ideas became a mark of success in the Watson household and second nature to Jim Watson. Selling ideas is part of Watson's heritage. He uses conventional methods when possible, but he is not opposed to using outrageous or controversial propositions to get his ideas considered, whether on the lab bench or in a science policy debate.

Watson knows who he is and how he is regarded. He knows his own intelligence and that his record of achievements will ensure that his ideas—even the ones he frames in the most outrageous, attention-grabbing fashion—will get serious consideration. He seems at ease being viewed at times as controversial or difficult. Watson is a deliberate, self-assured man. In his book, *A Passion for DNA: Genes, Genomes, and Society* (Watson 2000 and 2001), he expresses the seriousness of his commitment to truth, even as an undergraduate:

> You were never held back by manners, and crap was best called crap. Offending somebody was always preferable to avoiding the truth, though such bluntness did not make me a social success with most of the classmates.

REFERENCES

Stent G.S. 1980. The DNA double helix and the rise of molecular biology. In *The double helix: A personal account of the discovery of the structure of DNA* (ed. G.S. Stent), pp. xi–xxii. W.W. Norton, New York.

Sullivan W. 1980. A book that couldn't go to Harvard. In *The double helix: A personal account of the discovery of the structure of DNA* (ed. G.S. Stent), pp. xxiv–xxv. W.W. Norton, New York.

U.S. Congress, Office of Technology Assessment (OTA). 1988. *Mapping our genes: The genome projects—How big? How fast?* OTA-BA-373 Appendix B, pp. 180–186. U.S. Government Printing Office, Washington, D.C.

Watson J.D. 1968. *The double helix: A personal account of the discovery of the structure of DNA.* Atheneum, New York.

Watson J.D. 1980. *The double helix: A personal account of the discovery of the structure of DNA* (ed. G.S. Stent). W.W. Norton, New York.

Watson J.D. 2000, 2001. *A passion for DNA: Genes, genomes, and society.* Cold Spring Harbor Laboratory Press, Cold Spring Harbor, New York.

Jim Watson and the Human Genome Project

James B. Wyngaarden

Durham, North Carolina

In June 1986, while attending a meeting of the European Medical Research Council in London, a British colleague asked what I thought of Charles DeLisi's[1] announcement that the U.S. Department of Energy (DOE) had committed $2 billion to launch a human genome sequencing project. My inquirer was clearly both astonished and envious of the way such endeavors could be initiated in the United States. Nothing like this could happen in Britain. My reaction to his statement was one of alarm at what appeared to be an attempt by DOE to usurp leadership of a major theme of biological research in which the National Institutes of health had primogenitor seniority.

Genetic research had been fundamental to the mission of the NIH since its inception. NIH had supported programs in bacterial, phage, yeast, animal, and human genetics since the 1950s. The deciphering of the genetic code by Marshall Nirenberg and his colleagues had brought NIH its first Nobel Prize in 1968.[2] Identification and sequencing of structural genes of interest were common events in the intramural programs of almost all NIH Institutes and constituted major themes of extramural grants programs, especially those of the National Institute of General Medical Sciences (NIGMS). By 1986, there was a growing awareness of the possibility of sequencing entire human chromosomes, and a few editorials and workshops had addressed the topic, including the formidable technical challenges involved. Ruth Kirschstein, the Director of NIGMS, was tracking these genomic developments for NIH and keeping me informed. In addition, the Howard Hughes Medical Institute was holding a conference on gene mapping and sequencing the next month (July 1986). However, the reported DOE pronouncement was a blockbuster! My mental reaction was "Not on my watch." If a massive gene mapping and sequencing program was to be initiated, the NIH was going to be *the* major player.

The structure of NIH and its budgetary process did not enable its Director to assign substantial funds to a new genome sequencing endeavor. DOE could not have done that either, but rumor had run ahead of reality.[3] NIH budget activities went through multiple internal planning steps and several layers of departmental and Office of Management and Budget (OMB) reviews before presentation to the Congress. Frequently, two years elapsed from first stages of internal planning at individual Institute and NIH Director levels to actual appropriation by the Congress and signature by the President. NIH would need to address the policy issues raised by the DOE initiative promptly if it was to compete effectively for leadership in the field of gene sequencing!

James B. Wyngaarden

A native of Grand Rapids, Michigan, Jim Wyngaarden completed undergraduate work at Calvin College and Western Michigan University and earned his M.D., *cum laude*, from the University of Michigan Medical School.

Before becoming Director of the National Institutes of Health in 1982, Wyngaarden had a long career in academic medicine at Duke University and the University of Pennsylvania Medical School. As a young researcher at Duke, Wyngaarden established a laboratory to study the regulation of purine biosynthesis and the production of uric acid. He was a member of a team that pioneered the use of allopurinol, a drug originally developed as an anticancer agent, for the treatment of gout. Together with William Kelley and Edward Holmes, Wyngaarden formed a trio that led the way nationally in the purine field for more than 20 years, while also serving as Chairman of the Department of Medicine for his last 15 years at Duke.

Wyngaarden coauthored the standard and classic textbook *The Metabolic Basis of Inherited Disease* with John Stanbury and Donald Fredrickson (his predecessor as Director of NIH). First published in 1960 as a single volume with 1477 pages, the latest (8th edition, under other editors) is now published in four volumes, totaling 6338 pages.

After seven years as Director of NIH, Wyngaarden worked as Associate Director of Life Sciences in the White House Office of Science and Technology before returning to Duke as Director of the Human Genome Organization and Vice Chancellor for Health Affairs.

Wyngaarden has received numerous honors, awards, and special recognition, including serving on the President's Science Advisory Committee and the President's Committee for the National Medal of Science. In 1974, he was elected to the National Academy of Sciences and served as Foreign Secretary of the Academy from 1990 to 1994. He was elected to the Royal Swedish Academy of Sciences in 1987. He has received honorary degrees from many institutions including the University of Michigan and Tel Aviv University, Israel.

On returning from London, I discovered that most NIH Institute Directors were disinterested in a genome project. They saw little merit in systematic sequencing of long stretches of DNA compared with focusing on specific genes of known function, especially those relevant to the mission of their own institutes. Their positions were similar to those of many leading scientists who held the view that more information would be gained if sequencing went hand in hand with other lines of investigation, such as genetics and biochemistry.[4] Ruth Kirschstein convened a group whose report to me essentially proposed leaving any massive sequencing effort to DOE. Nevertheless, they recommended that NIH focus the October meeting of the Director's Advisory Committee (DAC) on the genome project to determine the attitude of the scientific community. Privately, several Institute Directors expressed intense opposition toward any centralized organization of genome sequencing activities within NIH, fearing emasculation of their own programs, and additional competition for funds. Several also expressed serious reservations about NIH undertaking a large targeted project that would require top-down management. In their view, such an approach was contrary to the culture of NIH.

The October 1986 DAC meeting included presentations by such renowned scientists as David Botstein, Charles Cantor, and David Baltimore. Support for a genome project was mixed. There were reservations about NIH getting into "big" or "managed" science and concerns over the adequacy of existing databases to handle the magnitude of new data that might be generated.[5] Given the realities of securing funds for a genome project, it was clear that a great deal of work on consensus building lay ahead if we chose to compete for a leadership position in the sequencing effort. I knew from experience that success would be determined by the appropriations process in the Congress, rather than by policy persuasion within the Administration. But how was NIH to achieve the consensus necessary to influence the appropriations process? And within NIH, where were we to find the time, energy, and enthusiasm to address a potential genome project amidst the enervating AIDS-related issues and other controversies that dominated the agenda?

An opportunity to put a toe in the door arose toward the end of the fiscal year 1988 budget hearings before the House Appropriations Subcommittee (held in February and March, 1987). In his concluding remarks, Chairman William Natcher asked me to send him a report on what NIH would do with an additional $700 million, in $100 million increments, beyond the sums requested by the Administration. After requesting $250 million for additional research project grants, and $150 million for other programs dear to the hearts of Institute Directors, I asked for $30 million for genome research in the fifth $100 million increment. Following my testimony, several members of the House and Senate Appropriations Subcommittees met informally with members of the Delegation for Basic Biomedical Research (a group of Nobel Laureates very influential with the Congress). At that meeting, they were briefed by Jim Watson and David Baltimore on additional funding requests for AIDS and other topics. Jim spoke specifically to encourage the $30 million add-on for genome research.

The House responded to Watson's and my requests by appropriating $30 million for genome research. The Senate was more parsimonious, and appropriated only $6 million. At the conference, they split the difference and Congress eventually approved $18 million. After Gramm-Rudman-Hollings recisions,[6] $17.2 million was appropriated to NIGMS for genome research in fiscal year 1988. This was an important event, involving the first money ever specifically appropriated to NIH for genome research. However, it did not mark a departure from traditional practices of awarding research funds by peer review of (relatively) small, investor-initiated research project grant applications.

Meanwhile, the National Academy of Sciences (NAS) was also addressing the desirability of a coordinated effort to map and sequence the human genome. Its Board on Basic Biology (BOBB) convened a meeting on August 5, 1986 (just two months following the European MRC meeting in London), which included 15 invited participants, one of whom was Jim Watson. The consensus was that an appropriate first goal was to develop a physical map of restriction fragments of the human genome (and possibly others) that might benefit a later large sequencing effort.

In January 1987, the Committee on Life Sciences (a subcommittee of the BOBB) appointed a 15-member Committee on Mapping and Sequencing the Human Genome, which included Jim Watson and five others who participated in the August 5 meeting. Bruce Alberts served as chairman. The influential report of the NAS, *Mapping and Sequencing the Human Genome* (1988), published one year later, concluded, "Acquiring a map, a sequence, and an increased understanding of the human genome merits a special effort that should be organized and funded for this purpose." It recommended a rapid scale-up to $200 million per year of additional funding for a special effort over the "next two decades." It also recommended that "a single federal agency serve as the lead agency for the project," but left open which agency this should be. Some members favored DOE because of their an early advocacy of the project, and because of their experience in managing large-scale tasks. Others, including Watson (Roberts 1988), were said to be adamantly opposed to a central role for DOE. The main argument against DOE was the lack of credible external peer review. Most of the committee members favored NIH.

With the publication of the NAS report, this country's most authoritative scientific body had reached an indispensable consensus, but grass roots support in the life science community was spotty. Mail received at NIH was predominately negative, often stridently so. The reservations were many. Some were primarily financial: Writers feared that funds would be diverted from project research. Others were philosophical and involved fears that NIH was moving toward centrally managed science, away from investigator-initiated proposals. Still others feared a deleterious influence upon graduate training and that "mindless sequencing" would replace original inquiry. Important scientific opinion leaders, including David Baltimore, were not persuaded that NIH should undertake a large, directed genome project.

On February 29, 1988, I convened an Ad Hoc Advisory Committee on Complex Genomes in Reston, Virginia, to assess the prospect of mapping and sequencing complex genomes, particularly the human genome. The biomedical research community, and the majority of the NIH research Directors, strongly favored an informal program of peer-reviewed research grants similar to that which was producing rapid progress in molecular biology and genetics. A new philosophical approach of the type envisioned by the NAS Committee would require a new organizational structure at NIH, which in turn would require departmental approval and congressional concurrence in the form of funds appropriated for a defined program. In 1988, the NIH Director had no authority to shift funds appropriated to individual Institutes or to create a major new organizational entity. Congressional action depended not only on testimony by the NIH Director, but also on testimony of individual Institute Directors and nongovernmental witnesses from the scientific community and the general public. The Reston meeting brought together senior NIH staff (including four Institute Directors), an 18-member advisory committee (which included Jim Watson), and about 20 additional university and federal participants. Since I wanted very much to gain David Baltimore's support, I asked him to chair the meeting. After two days of intense discussion, the committee recommended a "systematic, centrally coordinated" initiative, and developed a set of guidelines that included stringent peer review during all stages of the project. They also unanimously endorsed my proposal "to establish an Office of Human Genome Research, headed by a new Associate Director within the Office of the Director of NIH." In a letter of transmittal accompanying the final report, David Baltimore later stated, "I trust that this document can serve as the basis for NIH to develop a vigorous program to exploit the opportunities in Genome Analysis that have arisen in the last few years."[7]

As the meeting ended, a group of participants asked to meet with me. Realizing that NIH would need an internationally renowned leader of towering reputation if it was to secure lead-agency status in the federal genome project, and the resources to achieve the goals of the program, they had caucused and identified Jim Watson as that person. The prospect thrilled me immediately.

I had first met Jim Watson in the fall of 1963, when he visited François Gros[8] at the Institut de Biologie-Physicochemique in Paris, where I was spending a sabbatical year from Duke University. His penetrating intellect made a lasting impression on me. I next met Jim in late 1986 or early 1987 in Don Fredrickson's[9] office at the Howard Hughes Medical Institute. Some time after that, Jim came to see me in my office at the NIH, where he blasted me for not showing more leadership on genome sequencing. This meeting was in part responsible for the request from NIH, via the Assistant Secretary for Health, to the NAS to make recommendations concerning mapping and sequencing of the human genome, which in turn stimulated the Reston meeting. But despite my awareness of Jim's mercurial personality, I had no reservations about him being the right person for this job. When I met with him, no persuasion was necessary. Jim had already secured approval from the Cold Spring Harbor Laboratory Trustees to take the position, provided he could divide his time between Cold Spring Harbor and Bethesda.

Jim Watson officially became Associate Director for Human Genome Research at the NIH on October 1, 1988. The budget for genome research in fiscal year 1989 (which began the day of Jim's appointment) was $27.5 million, and still a part of the appropriation to NIGMS. Jim's new office would provide policy guidance, identify meritorious research topics, and promote development of new technologies. In addition, at his initial press conference, Jim announced that 3% of genome funds would be devoted to studies of ethical, legal, and social implications of human genome research. This was a master stroke that caught everyone by surprise (it had not been discussed with anyone, including me), but one much admired by the press, the public, and the Congress. This initiative became known as the ELSI program.

The conditions and arrangements that enabled Jim's appointment were unusual, perhaps unprecedented (but so was Jim!). Unfortunately, they had within them the seeds of future trouble under a different NIH Director. Jim would be a part-time Associate Director, giving NIH 1–2 days per week in Bethesda. He would continue as Director of Cold Spring Harbor Laboratory (CSHL) on Long Island, but would recuse himself from any grants related to the Human Genome Project. His holdings in various companies were reviewed by NIH legal counsel and not found inappropriate. However, even before Jim arrived to begin working, there were allegations of conflicts of interest because of the relationship between CSHL and a for-profit company. These allegations were investigated by the NIH Division of Management Survey and Review, and dismissed.

During the months between Reston (February 1988) and the October appointment, NIH (with Jim's involvement) concluded a memorandum of understanding with DOE concerning definitions, goals, and guidelines of the Genome Project. It also established a joint advisory committee, and an interagency working group, and agreed upon joint sponsorship of meetings and workshops. Jim established cordial relationships with DOE, and together with Jim Decker, David Galas, and others at DOE developed a joint NIH-DOE genome newsletter.

Jim recruited Elke Jordan[10] to serve as Director of the Office of Human Genome Research to oversee its day-to-day management. On November 1, I first mentioned to Jim and Elke the possibility of evolving the "Office" into a "Center" which would in effect be a mini-institute with its own appropriation and council. In my judgment, this upgrade might become feasible when the budget for the program reached $50 million. The administration had accepted my request for $100 million for fiscal year 1990 (which would begin October 1, 1989) and congressional hearings would take place in early 1989. Until then, the office was largely a policy, planning, and coordination unit with a small operating budget; the bulk of genome money was still a component of the NIGMS appropriation.

The first meeting of the newly appointed Program Advisory Committee on the Human Genome took place on January 3–4, 1989, under the chairmanship of Norton Zinder. Jim, Elke, and other speakers described the goals of the program, the functions of the office, and activities in various other institutes. Data repositories and management were reviewed in detail. Representatives of DOE, the Howard Hughes Medical Institute, the National Science Foundation, the Department of Agriculture, and the new Human Genome Organization (HUGO) described their activities. Others summarized related genome endeavors in Japan, the United Kingdom, and the European community. The second day focused on training issues and ethics.

I anticipated that the Congress would act favorably on the President's request for a substantial increase in the budget for human genome research at NIH. Accordingly, I prepared a proposal to convert the Office to a Center, which I submitted to Dr. Otis Bowen, Secretary of the Department of Health and Human Services on January 4, 1989. I knew that the Secretary could create a new Institute (or Center) at the NIH on his own authority, although this had occurred only once before when Secretary Calabresi created the National Institute of Environmental Health Sciences in 1960. I hoped that Secretary Bowen would act on this request before January 20, when the Reagan Administration and Bowen's appointment would end, but that did not happen.

In April 1989, after serving for more than seven years as Director of NIH, I announced my intention to resign, effective in August. The new Secretary of the Department of Health and Human Services, Dr. Louis Sullivan, asked me if there was anything special I would like to see accomplished before I left, and I cited the pending request for Center status for the Office of Human Genome Research. Secretary Sullivan approved the request on June 22; the Center became a reality on October 1, 1989 (the first day of fiscal year 1990), and Jim Watson was appointed its first Director. This development removed the program from its temporary location in the Office of the Director, NIH, and gave the unit independent status equivalent to that of a small institute. The appropriation request, not yet voted on by Congress, was amended by OMB to transfer $99.1 million from the budget of NIGMS and $0.9 million from the budget of the Office of Director to create an appropriations request of $100 million for the new National Center for Human Genome Research (NCHGR). The actual appropriation turned out to be $59.5 million, but the Center was in place.

In December, Jim Watson invited me to a dinner at a Bethesda restaurant for members of the Human Genome Advisory Committee. After dinner, Jim rose to make a few remarks and I discovered that I was the guest of honor. Jim retraced the several steps I had taken that led to the creation of the Center for Human Genome Research and said he wanted to recognize me for having made "all the right decisions." I was stunned, but I deeply appreciated Jim's remarks, which more than sufficed to remove the lingering hurt of that earlier day in my office. But that was part of what I found so fascinating about him. I have never seen Jim Watson in an apathetic mood!

Watson's initial emphasis was on mapping large stretches of DNA in the human genome and model species—on creating both genetic and physical maps. The initial mechanism was the traditional investigator-initiated research project grant, awarded by NIGMS. But in early 1989, Jim floated an idea to carve up the genome by giving individual countries responsibility for specific chromosomes (Dickson 1989). As with his ELSI proposal, there had been no internal discussion of this idea, but his proposal presaged a pattern of policy evolution by pronouncements that made for lively times in handling public and scientific reaction. At times, this habit seemed almost playful on Jim's part. Was Watson serious or pulling a leg?

In July, the Genome office announced it would create special laboratories or centers to pursue mapping or sequencing of the human genome. Watson envisioned that eventually half of the Project's budget would go to such centers, rather than to investigator-initiated science. Centers would be created not just in universities but in companies as well. "If we go along the way NIH usually does, it could easily take 100 years to get the sequences," Watson told *Science* magazine (Roberts 1989). Although it was not clear how such centers would be structured, the reaction of leading advisors was one of apprehension. Centers were not in good repute among basic scientists. There were major concerns about peer review, accountability, quality, and ongoing evaluation, as well as doubts concerning an adequate concentration of genome-related grants in one location to constitute a center. Watson and Jordan listened. The request for applications was quietly shelved and redrawn. The NIGMS then established seven centers at U.S. universities in support of large-scale high-resolution maps of human chromosomes 4, 7, 11, and X, as well as of the mouse chromosome. Pilot sequencing projects were initiated in model organisms, including *E. coli*, yeast, *C. elegans*, and mycoplasma. And in its first year (fiscal year 1990), the ELSI program became the largest Federal benefactor of research on social and ethical implications of research technologies.[11]

In April 1990, NCHGR published a five-year scientific plan, setting out goals for genetic and physical maps, DNA sequencing, model organisms, informatics, ELSI issues, research training, technology development, technology transfer, and international cooperation.[12]

In testimony to the U.S. Congress on the Genome Project budget and his plans for the program, Jim Watson performed masterfully. Committee members were in awe of him, and they treated him with well-deserved respect and careful attention. Jim spoke clearly and informatively without condescending to his scientifically naïve listeners. They grasped the general concepts and the overall goals and enthusiastically backed them where it counted—with authorizations and appropriations. During the first five years of the Genome Project (as Office and Center), the NIH genome budget annually exceeded that of the DOE program by twofold. Under Watson's relentless drive and passionate leadership, NIH became the de facto lead agency. Without Jim Watson, it may not have happened.

Jim had fixed ideas of where and how he wanted to lead the genome mapping and sequencing program. Predictably, these led to controversies. Others wished he had put more resources into gene function and biology, and small centers. But his two greatest battles were elsewhere, one scientific and one philosophical, even ethical.

The first involved disagreement over cDNA sequencing, which Watson regarded as insufficiently rigorous science often involving portions of genes of unknown functions, and a diversion from the loftier goal of direct DNA sequencing. Sequencing cDNAs represented a cheap and easy way to identify expressed genes that could be used in genetic mapping. He vigorously fought its leading proponent, J. Craig Venter (then at NIH, later the founder of The Institute for Genomic Research and Celera). DOE, France, the United Kingdom, and Japan all embraced cDNA sequencing. Nevertheless, critics also conceded that Watson's "single-mindedness and doggedness" was responsible for much of the progress recorded in these early years (Paul Berg, quoted in *Nature*; Anderson 1992).

The second controversy grew out of the first but was distinct from it. It concerned the attempt by NIH to file for patents covering nearly 3000 cDNA sequences obtained by Craig Venter. Watson stood for international collaboration, open sharing of sequence information, and open access to databanks. The decision to seek cDNA patents was made by Dr. Bernadine Healy who had become Director of NIH in April 1991. The philosophical differences between Watson and Healy were irreconcilable and became increasingly bitter and public. Their relationship, prickly from the beginning, deteriorated further, and soon they were communicating by way of the news media (Anderson 1992; Greenberg 1992). Healy became interested in potential conflicts of interest in Watson's hybrid NIH–Cold Spring Harbor position and concerned about the propriety of some of Jim's stock holdings (which had been explored in 1986 and reviewed annually without identification of a conflict). The final straw apparently was a complaint by a financier, Frederick Bourke, who had written to Healy raising ethical concerns about Watson. Bourke charged that Watson had attempted to use Glaxo, a British company in which his family held some stock, to intervene in some way to persuade a British scientist (John Sulston) from going to work for him in a planned Seattle sequencing company (Roberts 1992). The Department of Health and Human Services considered conducting an investigation of the charges, but never did so. What is known is that Jim Watson had helped to persuade the Wellcome Trust to start supporting sequencing in the United Kingdom in a big way, and this had made it more difficult for someone like Bourke to recruit top genome scientists from Britain.[13] Jim Watson was no longer enjoying his role at NIH and had been considering leaving his position sometime in the fall. This last event caused him to advance the date and he resigned on April 10, 1992.

The slings and arrows of outrageous fortune aside, Jim Watson stands (in Norton Zinder's apt comment) as a Colossus astride the Human Genome Project (Cook-Deegan 1994). He is probably the only person who could have held together "...an often fractious amalgamation of researchers, bureaucrats, politicians, and foreign partners that made the project go (Palca 1992)." Five years after Jim's departure, Donna Shalala, Secretary of HHS, elevated the NCHGR to the National Human Genome Research Institute. In an additional few years, high-resolution maps were constructed for all human chromosomes, and the sequence of the human genome was virtually deciphered. Credits belong to many players—NIH, DOE, numerous centers in the United

States, England, France, and other countries, and a galaxy of scientists in the United States and abroad. But it was Watson's talents and will that crafted, launched, and guided the nascent programs. In a career spanning 50 years, he had played an insuperable role in the patrimony of both DNA structure and the human genome sequence. There is a remarkable symmetry to his achievement. It will never be repeated.

REFERENCES

Anderson C. 1992. Watson resigns, genome project to change. *Nature* **356:** 549.

Cook-Deegan R. 1994. *The gene wars: Science, politics, and the human genome,* p. 161. W.W. Norton, New York.

Dickson D. 1989. Watson floats a plan to carve up the genome. *Science* **244:** 521.

Greenberg D.S. 1992. Exit Watson, the genome chief. *The Lancet* **339:** 980.

Mapping and Sequencing the Human Genome. 1988. National Academy Press, Washington, D.C.

Palca J. 1992. The genome project: Life after Watson. *Science* **256:** 959.

Roberts L. 1988. Academy backs genome project. *Science* **239:** 725.

Roberts L. 1989. Plan for genome centers sparks a controversy. *Science* **246:** 204.

Roberts L. 1992. Why Watson quit as project head. *Science* **256:** 301.

The Colossus of Codes

Robert Cook-Deegan

Duke University

I have never seen Jim Watson in a dispassionate mood. His relentless intensity generates the funnel cloud surrounding him, and it is not hard to trace his path because it leaves a broad, sometimes bloody, swath. I will follow one such path through the early history of the Human Genome Project. Some of the interpretations below are no doubt off the mark, and where that is the case, I hope Jim and others will correct them.

A biography of Jim Watson will have to treat him as a scientist, a writer, a science administrator, and an institution builder. He is also a political figure, and I will focus on his political role in the genesis of the Human Genome Project, because that is how I came to know him.

Jim was a Famous Scientist starting at age 23, and he never had to curry attention or worry much about money. He lived fully aware of how his mythology preceded him, and what effect it had on others. Indeed, who among us has not watched him stoop down to untie a shoe or reach up to muss his hair just before a meeting an important personage? This cultivated eccentricity, playing to his public persona, is part of his charm, although disconcerting to observe the first few times.

Jim used that source of power extensively as Director of the National Institutes of Health's genome program. I will concentrate on his role from 1986 to 1992, as the Human Genome Project changed from being an idea to becoming a project funded by governments and not-for-profit organizations around the world. I will then turn to two specific decisions he made that illustrate the law of unintended consequences: His threat to resign as Director of the then National Center for Human Genome Research (NCHGR), in order to bolster its appropriation, and his decision not to pursue cDNA sequencing at the Center. Like many political choices, these proved momentous—but mainly in retrospect. At the time, they were but two of hundreds of decisions made in the tumult of everyday planning for the Genome Project.

Jim's initial role was as a consensus builder. Given that Jim is mainly famous for being brutally honest and deliberately iconoclastic, this may seem an odd role. But it is not. Jim was an early enthusiast for a concerted effort to map and sequence the human genome, and he did many things, both on stage and off, to promote it. The crucial missing ingredients in early discussions of the genome project were a coherent vision and technical consensus. Jim's main role was to set forces in motion to achieve the elusive consensus.

Jim himself often points to the importance of his meetings with members of Congress, but I think these had little or nothing to do with the appropriations process—the lifeblood of federally funded research—for either the NIH or the Department of Ener-

ROBERT COOK-DEEGAN

Robert Cook-Deegan is one of a rare species: a physician with research experience who has become a public policy expert. After qualifying in medicine in Colorado, he studied oncogenes with Ray Erikson and then went to Washington in 1982 as a congressional science fellow. In the five years he spent at the congressional Office of Technology Assessment, he developed an interest in bioethics and in 1988–1989, became Acting Director of the congressional BioMedical Ethics Advisory Committee. Bob was the Project Director for the very influential OTA report (1988, Government Printing Office, Washington, D.C.), *Mapping Our Genes? Genome Projects: How Big? How Fast?* The opportunity then arose to join the newly established National Center for Human Genome Research, under Jim Watson's leadership, an attractive opening at a time when Jim had adopted what for many was the surprising position that a substantial proportion of the Human Genome Project's funding should be allocated to consideration of the ethical, legal, and social issues raised by gene mapping and sequencing. Cook-Deegan's experiences at the Center, discussed in this essay, seeded a continuing interest in the ethical controversies provoked by genome science and resulted in a highly regarded book, published in 1994 by W.W. Norton and Company, entitled *The Gene Wars: Science, Politics, and the Human Genome*. He remains professionally engaged with these issues as an investigator at the Kennedy Institute of Ethics, Georgetown University, and Director of the Center for Genome Ethics, Law, and Policy at Duke University, and has established a Human Genome Archive at the National Reference Center for Bioethics Literature at Georgetown University that contains his files and interview transcripts.

R. Rose (left) and Robert Cook-Deegan (middle) at the Banbury Center meeting on "Funding for the Decade of the Brain," November 1992. (Courtesy CSHL Archives.)

gy (DOE). When I first questioned the House and Senate staff most directly responsible for the initial funding of the U.S. Genome Project, for example, they barely remembered meeting with Jim until he was formally part of the NIH. Indeed, when he did interact directly with members, it did not always go well, as we shall see. His role as an "inside" player on Capitol Hill was far less important than his many actions in forging consensus among prominent molecular biologists and thereby influencing science administrators, such as NIH Director James Wyngaarden, who had a direct role in the budget process.

Two actions deserve particular mention. It was Jim who invited Paul Berg and Walter Gilbert to chair an impromptu discussion of the Human Genome Project at Cold Spring Harbor during the June 1986 Symposium on "Molecular Biology of *Homo sapiens*." Rumors of the DOE genome project had by then begun to circulate, but for many attending the Symposium—which assembled the pantheon of human molecular genetics—the session was the first open exposure to the notion, and it broadened discussion from a small cadre of politically attentive leaders to a much larger audience of NIH-supported researchers. Perhaps most important, however, was Jim's role in engaging the National Academy of Sciences in the debate (National Research Council 1988).

It was Jim who lobbied the National Research Council (NRC) to do a study and then secured funding from the James McDonnell Foundation to support the work of the resulting NRC committee on mapping and sequencing the human genome. It is worth dwelling on this, because it signals sophistication about political process that is rare among scientists, administrators, and for that matter, politicians. People who want to get things done tend to equate progress with direct control. They generally marshal resources, link arms with allies, and hit the Hill and the executive branch to lobby for what they want. This can work, but often it is viewed, correctly, as self-interest or self-promotion. It is the rare person willing to give away power and trust in process, but that is what it means to turn to the National Academies. I believe the main explanation for the funding of genome projects in the United States, Europe, and Japan after 1988 was their scientific credibility, which grew substantially from the NRC study.

The NRC Committee on mapping and sequencing the human genome drafted a coherent plan that was credible precisely because it was not controlled by NIH or DOE. Bruce Alberts, who later became President of the National Academy of Sciences in no small part because of his role on the NRC Committee, chaired the Committee. A parallel DOE Advisory Committee, whose recommendations were similar (except the one saying DOE should run the project) had little authority or credibility because its composition and process were controlled by DOE and the national laboratories. The main difference was not the scientific plan, but independence and systematic process.

Jim became the founding Director of the Office for Human Genome Research in October 1988 because he was the most obvious leader. A year later, the Office became the National Center for Human Genome Research (NCHGR). When I first heard rumors that he might be picked to lead the NIH genome effort, I photocopied and sent him a section of Wallace Stegner's (1982) biography of John Wesley Powell. Like Jim, Powell was a famous scientist who founded and directed a federal mapping effort, in Powell's case the U.S. Geological Survey. Powell, whose Washington mansion on Massachusetts Avenue is now the Cosmos Club, became famous for exploring the Grand Canyon, despite having lost an arm in the Civil War Battle of Shiloh. Like Watson, he had written a wildly popular book about his adventures. And like Jim, Powell was not just a scientist, but also a representative of science to the general population. In another, eerie, parallel, both Watson and Powell were forced out of Washington over the politics of exploiting natural resources—in Powell's case, water, and in Watson's case, the commercial value of genomic sequence data.

Stegner dwells at some length on Powell's conflict with Senator William "Big Bill" Stewart, a case study in science's collision with other political interests. Powell was revered in scientific circles, but his position of power came a cropper at the hands of Senator Stewart, a lawyer from Nevada who had made his name selling water to mine operators and defending the claims of the Comstock (silver) Lode claim holders. (Stewart also for a short while employed a certain Samuel Clemens as his personal secretary, years before Clemens achieved fame as Mark Twain.) Powell believed strongly in a coherent plan to distribute water in the semi-arid regions of the American West, and he opposed unplanned development. Sale of western lands in the public domain was frozen pending completion of Powell's survey, and he wanted to do a large and thorough survey. This caused conflict with the interests of mine owners, ranchers, farmers, and others chomping at the bit to develop the west. Senator Stewart was the tool of these interests, and through hearings and press announcements, he accused Powell of misusing public funds, womanizing, and other misdeeds. Politics as a blood sport is not new in Washington.

The genomic juggernaut may now seem to have been unstoppable, but at the time, it felt vulnerable. The appropriations process each year included squabbles about how much funding NIH and DOE should get for their respective genome projects, and which agency should "lead" the project. In spring 1990, the NIH budget priority was preserving investigator-initiated grants (RO1s), the antithesis of the very large center-based genome grants. The House trimmed $36 million (of $108 million requested) from NIH's genome program. Watson and his deputy director, Elke Jordan, had a stormy meeting with Chairman William Natcher's chief appropriations staffer, Michael Stephens, and Watson threatened to resign. Watson's protests were duly noted, and Stephens later acknowledged that Watson's making a stink did increase the NCHGR budget that year (it was ultimately almost $90 million). Watson's tactic worked, but it also set the stage for his later undoing. Natcher, a prim southern gentleman, acquired a distaste for Watson, and let NIH Director Bernadine Healy know that she could have Watson's head anytime she wanted it.

This Salome option mattered a year later, when Watson and Healy collided over patent applications for cDNA fragments (expressed sequence tags, or ESTs) being sequenced by J. Craig Venter in NIH's intramural research program. The Watson-Healy contretemps extended for a year of quote-to-quote combat in newspapers until March 1992, when Watson resigned from NIH. On the surface, Healy was concerned about Watson's financial holdings and possible conflicts of interest. Watson was indeed unusual among NIH Center or Institute Directors in that he was distinctly part-time, and most of his income came from Cold Spring Harbor Laboratory, his book sales, and his investments, not his federal job. The waiver he needed to continue as a federal employee and NCHGR Director, however, had been repeatedly granted in past years. Moreover, according to Michael Astrue, then chief counsel to the Department of Health and Human Services, the waiver Watson needed was no different from waivers

NIH-DOE Genome meeting at the Banbury Center, 1989. (Top row) Uta Francke, Mark Guyer, Francis Collins, Robert Moyzis, Jaime Carbonell, Jim Watson, Tony Carrano, Maynard Olson, Ray White, Sheldon Wolff, David Lipman, Mark Pearson, David Botstein, Elke Jordan. (Center row) Benjamin Barnhart, Norton Zinder, Leonard Lerman, Diane Pabst. (Front row) Charles Cantor, Shirley Tilghman, Mary-Lou Pardue, Tom Caskey. (Courtesy CSHL Archives.)

granted to many senior officials, including Healy herself. Watson could probably have weathered the storm of spring 1992 and remained as NCHGR Director. However, with Natcher in the debit column, Jim's situation was much more precarious than if he had had a strong champion on the Hill.

My impression is that Jim never relished the NIH job. His heart was always in Cold Spring Harbor. He spent as little time in Washington as he could, and his federal responsibilities were much more a duty than real fulfillment. He was fully aware that his role was to stand over the NIH part of the Genome Project, leaving the day-to-day operation to the permanent NIH staff. When Norton Zinder called him the Colossus, it was an apt image. The Colossus of Rhodes, the famed statue of Helios, stood for 56 years and then broke at the knees in an earthquake; the Colossus of Codes lasted 4 years, from October 1988 to March 1992. At least Jim was not sold for scrap metal like his Greek counterpart.

Jim's decision not to fund cDNA sequencing had less direct impact on his personal life, but a huge impact on the course of genomics throughout the world. From the very beginning, there was ambiguity about whether cDNA sequencing would be part of the Human Genome Project. Responding to a question at the June 1986 Cold Spring Harbor Colloquium, Wally Gilbert said, of course, one would start with sequencing cDNAs, but that eventually it would be simple and easy enough to do a total genomic reference sequence. The DOE and European Community programs included a cDNA sequencing component, and cost estimates prepared for the 1988 OTA report "Mapping Our Genes" included $20 million for mapping and then sequencing human genes (via cDNAs) in the first five years, as a prelude to large-scale genomic sequencing (OTA 1988). Including cDNA sequencing, however, always raised several issues. First was a question of fairness. Those working in small laboratories were quite concerned that large sequencing groups would have first crack at all the juicy bits of the genome if they did cDNA sequencing. Second was concern about getting distracted from completing the genomic sequence, because the natural tendency would be to characterize genes as they became known, and follow their trail to biological function (and sometimes to practical diagnostic and therapeutic use), rather than staying focused on completing a reference genomic sequence.

The *C. elegans* model was quite appealing, where the two major centers (which became the Sanger Centre in Cambridge, U.K., and Washington University in Saint Louis) did physical mapping and sequencing, but left classical genetics and functional characterization largely to the larger academic research community. This is the model that Jim chose, as the nematode project was always close to his heart, including its "open source" style and concerted management. The spirits of John Sulston and Bob Waterston hung over the human genome, and it made sense at the time.[1]

Who would have guessed that the gap would be filled by private capital? The ruckus over EST patents brought forth two major private cDNA sequencing ventures. Randy Scott in California followed the EST patent controversy and his company Incyte began cDNA sequencing as a pathway to discovering human genes. Wallace Steinberg also read about Craig Venter. Steinberg was an "angel" investor who lured Craig into forming the not-for-profit The Institute for Genomic Research (TIGR), and then tapped Bill Haseltine to run Human Genome Sciences (HGS), a for-profit company that would extract commercial value from the sequence data. It did not quite work out as planned, as TIGR soon dropped human EST sequencing and turned to microbes. HGS developed its own prodigious sequencing capacity and began to identify and then characterize human genes systematically, starting with those having signal sequences, transmembrane domains, DNA-binding motifs, and other sequence-based indicators that the corresponding proteins were tantalizing targets for pharmaceutical development. TIGR and HGS later parted company, but the historical pathway from Jim's no-cDNA-sequencing decision to the formation of TIGR and HGS is clear. Other companies, such as Hyseq, Sequenom, SmithKline Beecham (later part of Glaxo SmithKline), Amgen, Millennium, and many other firms also mounted substantial cDNA sequencing programs. All this was long before Celera re-ignited a public-private debate about total genomic (not cDNA) sequencing.

The decision not to include cDNA sequencing was not Jim's decision alone, but it did fall on him more than anyone else to make the call. In the event, the main "public domain" EST and cDNA sequencing effort at Washington University was ultimately paid for by Merck, a private firm. That effort was announced in September 1994 and began to release data in February 1995. The National Cancer Institute began its Cancer Genome Anatomy project in 1996 to do public domain cDNA sequencing, and then worked with other NIH Institutes to build the Mammalian Gene Collection. But in the early years of the Genome Project, 1989 through 1994, cDNA sequencing was excluded from NCHGR funding as a matter of policy. Bill Haseltine has told me on several occasions that the capital for his company, HGS, would not have been available in 1992 and 1993 if NIH had had a major cDNA sequencing effort under way, and it seems doubtful that Incyte would have turned to cDNA sequencing if it had had to compete with a big public sector program. Pharma and genomics firms would surely have done substantial gene sequencing, but it would have started years later, and built on, rather than competed with, a public domain cDNA sequencing effort.

This topsy-turvy decision making points to the incredibly intricate public-private research and development mutualism in genomics, but it also highlights how poorly our tools for research and development planning predict the decisions that matter most, and how little we really know about how public funding for science works its way to practical application, including commercial development.

More than a decade later, I believe it is still impossible to tell whether all the investment in private cDNA sequencing brought benefits sufficient to outweigh its inefficiencies—duplication and leaving most information about human gene sequences in private, proprietary databases for many years where the huge international academic health research enterprise could not get full access to it. Jim's decision had an enormous effect on private capital markets by inducing investment in several startup first-generation genomics firms from 1992 to 1994. Those firms, in turn, generated the first hoofbeats in a genomic stampede from 1996 to 2000 that stopped only with the chastening of capital markets in 2001 and 2002.

At the end of year 2000, more than 70 publicly traded genomics firms were valued at over $96 billion,[2] although their value has since plummeted. At least 430 startup companies, and several dozen established pharmaceutical, biotechnology, and agricultural research and development firms have committed billions of dollars a year to genomics for several years. Much of that investment might have happened anyway, but at the crucial historical branch point, for three or four years the largest public funding source, NIH, decided to focus on *genomic* sequencing and leave gene sequencing to others. With the door open to capturing the commercial value of sequence data one gene at a time, private sector cDNA sequencing efforts took off. The quality of Jim's decision thus remains very much in doubt, but its importance does not. Right or wrong, it was a big decision.

It is utterly unfair to evaluate decisions through the retrospectoscope, and my point here is not to render a harsh historical judgment. It is, rather, to point out that even the greatest scientists with the best of intentions and the most elaborate network of scientific gossip in the world—and Jim's network is still unrivaled—cannot fully predict the consequences of their decisions. In all senses of the words, great men make big decisions. Sometimes they get them right; sometimes wrong; and sometimes, as in this case, we have to wait decades to know.

REFERENCES

National Research Council. 1988. *Mapping and sequencing the human genome.* National Academy Press, Washington, D.C.

Stegner W.E. 1982. *Beyond the hundredth meridian: John Wesley Powell and the second opening of the west.* University of Nebraska Press.

U.S. Congress, Office of Technology Assessment (OTA). 1988. *Mapping our genes: The genome projects—How big? How fast?* OTA-BA-373 Appendix B, pp. 180–186. U.S. Government Printing Office, Washington, D.C.

Jim and the Japanese Human Genome Project

Kenichi Matsubara

DNA Chip Research, Inc., Japan

COMING ACROSS TO THE HUMAN GENOME

I have been privileged to live through a wonderful period in the development of biology: As a student, I witnessed the discovery of the double helix and the decoding of genetic codes, I participated in research using recombinant DNA techniques and DNA sequencing technology, and I have worked for genome sequencing efforts in Japan.

The latter had far more to do with politics than with science, and it was not my first experience of the differences between those two worlds. In 1975, I attended the Asilomar meeting on recombinant DNA as one of only two participants from Japan. My connection with the recombinant DNA technology was inevitable as Paul Berg's 1972 paper reported ligation of SV40 with a bacterial plasmid (λdv) which I had discovered while doing a postdoc with Dale Kaiser at Stanford University (Matsubara and Kaiser 1968). Subsequently, I was a member of the Japanese recombinant DNA technology guideline start-up committee and also of the Japanese version of the U.S. Recombinant DNA Advisory Committee.[1]

In these committees, I was soon frustrated by the lack of enthusiasm for DNA-based work and by the slow development of the life sciences and industry in Japan. People did not understand the importance of recombinant DNA, nor did they see that their own research could be extended by genetic engineering, an approach to biology that would lead to an entirely new style of research, as well as the development of a new industry, biotechnology. However, years later, these same people underwent a metamorphosis, and flew to recombinant DNA like moths flying toward a light. This experience influenced me later, in 1990, when I saw the coming of human genome sequencing. I thought then that I could do something for Japanese biologists to encourage them to recognize, accept, and adopt swiftly this second big technological wave that would change the course of life sciences and biotechnology.

I GET DRAWN INTO THE DEBATE ON THE HUMAN GENOME PROJECT

In the spring of 1987, I was one of organizers of a workshop on molecular biology of hepatitis B virus at Cold Spring Harbor Laboratory. While I was there, I had a conver-

KENICHI MATSUBARA

Kenichi Matsubara received his Ph.D. from the University of Tokyo, and he carried out research at Kanazawa and Kyushu Universities and then at Harvard and Stanford in the United States. It was while he was at Stanford with Dale Kaiser that Matsubara came to the 1968 Cold Spring Harbor Symposium on the "Replication of DNA in the Microorganism." He and Kaiser presented a paper on "λdv, an autonomously replicating DNA fragment" (Matsubara and Kaiser, *Cold Spring Harbor Symp. Quant. Biol. 33:* 769–775 [1968]), later to achieve fame (as λdvgal) as a component of the first recombinant DNA molecules made by Jackson, Symons, and Berg in 1972. Matsubara returned to Japan in 1968 as an Associate Professor at Kyushu University, and in 1975, by now a full Professor at Osaka University, he participated in the Asilomar Conference and went on to be a fellow in the Department of Biophysics at Princeton. Matsubara returned to Osaka University Institute of Molecular and Cellular Biology and then became a Professor at the Nara Advanced Institute of Science and Technology in 1997. As he describes in his essay, Matsubara has long been interested in genomics and his work in promoting a genomics approach to biology in Japan, although long and arduous, has borne fruit.

sation with Jim Watson. He said that he was planning to run a human genome sequencing project in an international consortium and he asked me if I would help in encouraging Japanese participation. I said yes, but I knew that it would be tough going, as Jim must have known from his past participation in AMBO, an Asian version of EMBO. Jim had collaborated with Itaru Watanabe, the founder of the Japanese Molecular Biology Society in trying to establish AMBO, but they had failed. Their lack of success was typical of the difficulty of bringing about change in the Japanese science community.

In November of that year, some 30 people assembled at Lake Montreux near Geneva to discuss the human genome initiative, and they agreed to initiate international efforts to promote genome sequencing. The attendees started the Human Genome Organization (HUGO) (McKusick 1989) for international coordination, but details of how the work would be distributed and coordinated, and political issues resolved, were not addressed, leaving the program to individuals in the participating countries. Three Japanese scientists were invited to the meeting: Nobuyoshi Shimizu, Tasuku Honjo, and myself. After the meeting, we discussed what to do and decided to organize the Japanese Human Genome Project. I was asked to take the lead, but I was reluctant to do so since I had no experience of human genome analysis. At that time, I was working on human liver cancer problems and hepatitis B virus. I knew also that it would be very difficult and time-consuming to start up a project in Japan, taking time that I would prefer to use for my research.

I took on the responsibility, however, partly because of my seniority—I was the oldest and had served on a number of committees for promoting Japanese science—and partly because of my concern that Japan might replay its failure to adopt a new technology. Anyway, it was a matter of Chance and Necessity. I promised myself that I would take it on only until the Japanese Human Genome Project was under way. However, there was no guarantee that anything would happen; all I had was optimism.

TALKING TO SCIENTISTS AND BUSINESS

As soon as I got back from the Lake Montreux meeting, I initiated two activities: talking to scientists and talking to science policy makers. In 1987, there was a limited number of scientists in Japan working on human molecular biology, and these people were too junior in the Japanese community to exert a strong influence to start up the project. They vowed, however, to collaborate and help wherever possible. A group of senior people of my generation, including Hiroshi Yoshikawa, Michio Oishi, Mitsuaki Yoshida, and Asao Fujiyama, volunteered to form a core group to promote the project. Senior scientists from the field of medical science readily understood the importance of the Human Genome Project and supported our activities. Without their help, the Japanese Genome Project would not have been born.

I had numerous discussions with scientists and reporters and gave lectures for the human genome initiative to many societies and meetings. The highlight was a discussion in the 1989 general assembly of the Japanese Molecular Biology Society at Sendai. Some 500 people participated, and there were fierce discussions as to whether we needed such a project, how to overcome the possible diversion of our precious research money, and how to avoid making slaves out of young scientists doing monotonous sequencing jobs (much the same issues as those facing Jim in the United States). I promised that I would work for a completely new funding source, and for a new contract system in which one could hire technicians, although neither of these existed in Japan at that time. Both of these promises were fulfilled, fortunately, in parallel with development of the Human Genome Project.

Talks with industry people were even more difficult. They had been living in a community in which they defined themselves as people who did manufacturing, but not people who did science. They kept saying that they would "discover" good ideas for manufacturing, but would not carry out research on their own ideas. There were some people in the industry sector who showed interest in the Human Genome Project, but none of them could commit themselves.

Fund-raising was almost impossible in Japan because of prohibitive regulations for organizing a nonprofit corporation through which we could collect tax-deductible monies, or run a public fund-raising project like the Telethon in France.[2] So, I had to turn to public monies. However, Japanese society lacks opportunities for scientists and politicians and science policy makers meet routinely to discuss important matters. Nor do we have an organization like the National Research Council in the United States, which can carry out authoritative and independent studies of important scientific issues.

So, despite the support from the scientific community, I was unable to set up an all-Japan planning and steering committee for the Human Genome Project. It was clear to me that close collaboration between SAN (industry), KAN (bureaucrats), and Gaku (scientists) was badly needed but was going to be hard to achieve.

TALKING TO GOVERNMENT OFFICERS

Talking with government officers was the only way left for me. These officers are called "directors," and they are in charge of bottom-up matters. They listen to appeals, and discuss and do surveys, and if they find the matter important to Japan, as well as relevant to their own agency, they will write a proposal with budget requests. The proposals will be later adjusted within the agency and reviewed by the Ministry of Finance for a budget in the following year. However, these directors cannot formulate an all-Japan, interagency proposal.

There are five agencies whose activities are related to life sciences or their applications, and I had to contact them one-by-one. Of these, the Ministry of Health and Welfare (MHW), the Ministry of Industry and Trade (MITI), and the Ministry of Agriculture, Forestry, and Fishery (MAFF) showed no interest in the Human Genome Project. (Later, MAFF started a Rice Genome Project in a framework essentially similar to that of the Human Genome Project.) The Science and Technology Agency (STA) could give support, but provide a grant for just one international meeting!

This left only the Ministry of Education, Science, Culture, and Sports (Monbusho). Directors there understood the importance of the human genome effort, and allocated a 200 million yen grant for preparatory studies, which began in the winter of 1988. I used this grant to invite people to discuss the development of a Japanese human genome program, to survey the relevant activities in the United States and Europe, and to start recruiting and training the scientists who would be needed for the program.

At the same time, we started to push for a recommendation by the Science Council of Monbusho that it would support the Human Genome Project. This was essential since almost all major activities in Japan are based on such recommendations. While I was engaged in these activities, making slow but steady progress, Jim's letter arrived.

JIM'S LETTER

During the conversation at Cold Spring Harbor, Jim had promised to come to Japan on an appropriate occasion, possibly around the fall of the year (1987), to talk to administrators about the Human Genome Project. We discussed the Japanese problems and the possible influences that he could have on them.

In the summer of 1989, however, after a HUGO meeting at Moscow which I was not able to attend, he sent me a letter, telling me that he would not come. And that was not all. He also wrote that there would be no data disclosure to Japan if Japan did not participate in the human genome efforts. A little later, a revised letter followed. I suspected that he might have been ill-informed or misled during the Moscow meeting about the Japanese efforts. This letter was widely distributed, although it was addressed to me as "personal." As would be expected, Jim's remarks stirred up a variety of sentiments and discussions. Many reporters rushed toward me, expecting an argument between Japan and the United States, and some of my colleagues expected the same.[3]

OUR OLD TIMES

This is the moment for me to say something about Jim and myself. I have known him since I was doing a postdoc at Harvard from 1964 through 1967, where Jim's office, decorated by tens of empty wine bottles, was located on the same floor. Since then, we have had occasional contacts, including the period when I translated *Molecular Biology of the Gene* (Watson et al. 1987) into Japanese (Watson et al. 2001).

The days at Harvard were pleasant and full of joy, personally and scientifically. I had married Midori shortly before, and I was exposed, for the first time, to the East Coast campus atmosphere. Perhaps everybody there shared the same feeling; most of them were young and were eager to do something good in science. Molecular biology was also young and vigorous. Everyone in the field was active, friendly, and collaborative. Jim and Wally (Gilbert) collaborated closely, jointly leading a relatively large group of people.

They often organized seminars given by distinguished guests, and there were frequent presentations for thesis defenses. Jim used to sit in the center front row in the lecture hall, facing toward us (i.e., showing his back to the speaker), and made critical and interesting comments as to the background of the topic, its implication, its impact, and the direction for the future. An example of a typical Jim comment: "scissors and paste can never make a good thesis" when a graduate student was sweating for his second trial for thesis defense. (Of course, there were no word processors then, only Xerox machines). Wally, on the other hand, with his pipe or cigar between his teeth, loved to discuss technical problems, creating vigorous discussions.

Jim, as a successful Director of the Cold Spring Harbor Laboratory in later days, seemed never to lose this attitude to science. One early summer morning in the late 1980s, he phoned me at Osaka University Institute for Molecular and Cellular Biology where I was acting as Director. Jim was visiting Japan, and he asked if he could come to visit to learn about our science. Of course I said yes! He gave a nice talk about cancer and his thoughts around the topic to people who packed the lecture hall, despite the short notice. He told me later over lunch at my home that it was like "oxygen" for him to be with scientists again, having been circled by business people for several days in Japan.

I must make some remarks about Jim's textbook, *Molecular Biology of the Gene*. One day, months ahead of the publication, Jim called upon me and asked me to translate it into a Japanese edition. I had translated Bruce Alberts' (1983) textbook of *Molecular Biology of the Cell*, and Jim knew it had been well-received. I did the translation, with much pleasure, and naturally, the book enjoyed a big success as it should, and did, everywhere in the world. English speakers may not have noticed, but Jim's sentences are about twice as long as Bruce's, although without losing clarity. But it was a bit burdensome for the translator.

THE GAIATSU

As I read Jim's letter, it made me think that, on the one hand, he was trying to show U.S. Congressmen, with whom he was negotiating, that there would be no free ride for Japanese scientists. On the other hand, in addressing Japanese industry people and officers, he was trying to give *Gaiatsu*. Gaiatsu is the mighty pressure coming from a foreign country, to which the Japanese policy-making process has often been subjected. A typical example was the opening of the Japanese ports for trade after the demands made by Matthew Perry in 1853, exactly 100 years before the Double Helix. Perry's Gaiatsu induced the collapse of the Tokugawa regime then in power.

Jim's letter had no influence upon Japanese biotechnology people as they didn't see its relevance to what they were doing, but the government administrators with whom I had been talking understood its implications. The letter was another demonstration of Jim's deep thinking and his commitment to the Human Genome Project, combined with his unique personality. I sent back a reply to Jim, telling him simply that we were working hard for the Japanese Human Genome Project—there was no need for alarm. Looking back now, however, I can see that Jim's letter played some role in catalyzing the speedup of the Japanese genome efforts.

THE MONBUSHO HUMAN GENOME PROGRAM

In 1989, the recommendation "Promotion of human genome program in universities" was approved, and based on this recommendation, Monbusho made a grant of 700 million yen a year for five years (Roberts 1989). We set forth four subprojects: human genome analyses and disease gene hunting, cDNA research, technology developments including analyses of model organisms, and informatics. Two percent of the grant was ear-marked for ethical, legal, and social issues studies. Monbusho set up a Center for Human Genome Analyses in the University of Tokyo, which has become the true center of excellence in genome sequencing and genome informatics. As noted earlier, when I took responsibility for promoting a Japanese Human Genome Project in 1987, I decided that once that was done, I would return to research. However, people asked me to take care of the Monbusho project, and my second term of ordeal started. In 1991, STA arranged to start a grant for human genome analyses, and in 1995, project money to run human genome sequencing was allocated. In the same year, the Japan Society for Promotion of Sciences (JSPS) associated with Monbusho also started support for sequencing. I was asked again to take care of these activities, permitting the coordination of the Monbusho and STA activities.

MORE SEQUENCING EFFORTS

Soon things were going well, and Japanese sequencing teams contributed to sequencing of human chromosomes 21 and 22 (Dunham et al. 1999; Hattori et al. 2000). However, it was clear in 1995 that our contribution to the total sequencing efforts of the human genome would be small, if not marginal. Monbusho, although supportive of the Human Genome Project from the beginning, was reluctant to take up the large-scale sequencing job, since it was spending some 100 billion yen per year for all categories of scientific research grants at that time. They said they would have to cut down budgets for school children's lunch if they were forced to do more sequencing! From 1995 through 1999, I arranged to issue an urgent appeal to the Science and Technology Council, organized a resolution by 20 major DNA researchers in Japan, and also made another proposal to a MITI committee. All these were calls for strengthening sequencing activities in Japan. I worked all possible avenues to find our super-helper. I was called the GENOMU MAN.

   A new Director at STA pushed for a larger sequencing center within STA, with a budget of about 8 billion yen to be attached to Riken. However, the Director General in charge of budget and financial affairs at Riken bluntly told me "It's not what Riken wants. It is a nuisance that you bring in unwanted jobs." When the budget negotiation for the fiscal year 1998 was done, I was surprised to see that while 8 billion yen was certainly allocated to Riken, only 800 million yen was assigned to human genome sequencing. I went to the office of Koji Omi, a Congressman who had worked for the Science and Technology Promotion Act. Upon listening to me, he telephoned the Director General in STA in charge of the Riken genome center plan, and said "Hey, the leader of Japanese Human Genome Project is in front of me and he says he is unhappy. I request that you re-examine the budget." The Riken Genome Center plan was put back on the tracks, and in middle of 1999, they celebrated the opening ceremony of the new building.

Sequencing efforts in Japan, in the ten years of development, yielded fruits that include analyses of human chromosomes 21 and 22 (in combination, 6% of the total sequences). There have been several other contributions to international sequencing consortia, such as the weed *Arabidopsis* (24%), yeast (2.3%), and *B. subtilis* (31%). In microbes, complete sequencing of the genomes of blue-green algae *Cynecocystis, E. coli, E. coliO157*, and the hyper-thermophile *Crenarchaeon* has been done, and there is the continuing Rice Genome Project. In addition, there is a comprehensive collection of mapped expressed sequences from the worm *C. elegans*. However, even as we entered the twenty-first century, the Japanese community in large part, including business people, does not understand the implication of human genome analyses. There have been some sporadic genome-related projects in agencies that did not participate in the original program, but these activities, unfortunately, were not coordinated with other efforts. They were designed not for the good of Japan, but for the good for the agencies, a behavior typical of budget competition among agencies.

THE LIFE SCIENCE SUMMIT

In the summer of 2000, when the draft sequence of the human genome was released, people in Japan suddenly faced up to the implications of decoding the genome, and learned, at the same time, that the Japanese contribution to the international consortium was 6%, compared with 67% from the United States and 22% from the United Kingdom. They realized that they might become losers in the growth of new life sciences and in the new businesses based on informatics and intellectual property rights. A chorus took place: "We are at the edge of crisis. While we have been dreaming that we were strong in manufacturing, we missed the race in information technologies. Now, we are missing the race in biotechnology. We must catch up!"

A meeting called the Life Science Summit was convened, and hundreds of business leaders attended. Keidanren, the league of industry leaders released a report asking for large governmental investments for strengthening technology developments, including biotechnology. In answer, the then Prime Minister Keizo Obuchi initiated the so-called Millenium Project in which 64 billion yen was allocated for biotechnologies. People jumped to genomics, in the hope that they would participate in genome-based drug discovery. Thus, Japan looked to have awakened from its long sleep and recognized the importance of the human genome efforts.

EPILOG: WHAT COULD WE DO AFTER ALL?

The "awakening," however, did not come from a change in the attitude of people toward science. They are still far from accepting the idea that science is fundamental for the well-being of society. There are no concerns that more and more money is being spent even though there are still major problems in the administration of Japanese science, especially the governmental systems in which I struggled. All my experiences were exactly what I saw in the 1970s and1980s, and what I wanted to avoid at the time when I took on the Japanese Human Genome Project. Nothing has changed in 20 years, and I am afraid that everything will continue as before.

I want to close on an optimistic note and mention the cDNA research that has been going on since 1988. This has been a success and could be a model for future developments. When the idea of cDNA research came up in 1988, I pushed it forward, as it was clearly interesting science. I formulated two subprojects: one for full-size cDNA collections and the other for expression profiling. I am pleased to see that both of these lines of work have developed into mainstream activities of functional genomics, although at the time when we initiated the project, only a few people were thinking about the post-sequencing era. For the next decades, the growing biological databases and their efficient application will lead to a new style of life science which we may call Information Biology. It will be a playground for the younger people following us. I am pleased to see that genome biology has been accepted and recognized as indispensable in scientific communities and that the scientists performing sequencing are no longer regarded as job slaves or maniacs or in a wasteful race for data-throughputs that insults thoughtful people.

I have been amazed for years to see how a single person like Jim can succeed in one area after another. The discovery of the DNA double helix; the writing of *The Double Helix* (1968); the textbooks; the unparalleled Directorship at Cold Spring Harbor Laboratory; and the charismatic leadership in the science community—all these have come from his ability to concentrate and focus on what is at hand. But above all, these accomplishments have made me realize what a unique talent he has to know what needs to be done and to act on it.

REFERENCES

Alberts B., Bray D., Lewis J., Raff M., Roberts K., and Watson J.D. 1983. *Molecular biology of the cell*. Garland Publishing, Inc., New York and London.

Dunham I., Shimizu N., Roe B.A., Chissoe S., Hunt A.R., Collins J.E., Bruskiewich R., Beare D.M., Clamp M., Smink L.J, et al. 1999. The DNA sequence of human chromosome 22. *Nature* **402:** 489–495.

Hattori M., Fujiyama A., Taylor T.D., Watanabe H., Yada T., Park H.S., Toyoda A., Ishii K., Totoki Y., Choi D.K., et al. 2000. The DNA sequence of human chromosome 21. *Nature* **405:** 311–319.

Matsubara K. and Kaiser A.D. 1968. Lambda dv: An autonomously replicating DNA fragment. *Cold Spring Harbor Symp. Quant. Biol.* **33:** 769–775.

McKusick V. 1989. The Human Genome Organization: History, purposes and membership. *Genomics* **5:** 385–387.

Roberts L. 1989. Japan boosts genome research. *Science* **246:** 439–440.

Watson J.D. 1968. *The double helix: A personal account of the discovery of the structure of DNA*. Atheneum, New York.

Watson J.D., Hopkins N.H., Roberts J.W., Steitz J.A., and Weiner A.M. 1987. *Molecular biology of the gene*. The Benjamin/Cummings Publishing Company, Inc., Menlo Park.

Watson J.D., Hopkins N.H., Roberts J.W., Steitz J.A., and Weiner A.M. 2001. *Molecular biology of the gene*. Japanese translation, Denki University Press, Tokyo.

James D. Watson and the ELSI Years

Nancy S. Wexler

Columbia University

Only one individual could have set up and funded the Ethical, Legal, and Social Issues (ELSI) program of the Human Genome Project: Jim Watson. His first act as the new Director of the Human Genome Project at the National Institutes of Health was to announce at his first press conference—without discussing it with anyone—that he was setting aside a significant percentage of the Human Genome Project budget to address the impact on people and society of having our genome in hand.

In Cambridge, Massachusetts, Jim Watson's home before moving to assume the Directorship of Cold Spring Harbor Laboratory in 1976, the clamor between town and gown had been particularly outspoken. Jim Watson and others had called for a moratorium and organized a retreat at the Asilomar Conference Center in California to consider the issues and develop procedures and safeguards for proceeding with recombinant DNA research. Eventually, these careful deliberations at Asilomar of both the realities of science and the necessity of social and civic responsibility gave all involved—town and gown—confidence to end the moratorium.

Still, the idea of the social responsibility of scientists that was inherent in the Asilomar recommendations was anathema to some molecular biologists. Fifteen years later, they had visions of "Asilomar revisited" and resisted having their Human Genome Project slowed down, or even derailed, by a few whining, self-righteous, scientifically uneducated ethicists. Into this new maelstrom of misunderstanding stepped the intrepid Jim Watson. His scientific and "molecular" credentials were impeccable and no one could accuse him of being an interloper, a troublemaker, or a "soft scientist." He had both leverage and the vision to go with it.

Robert Williamson and Nancy Wexler at the 1986 Symposium on Molecular Biology of Homo sapiens. *(Courtesy CSHL Archives.)*

NANCY S. WEXLER

In 1984, Nancy Wexler became President of the Hereditary Disease Foundation, a non-profit organization founded by her father in 1968 for the investigation of causes and cures for Huntington's disease. Her mother had died from this hereditary, untreatable, and fatal brain disorder. Nancy graduated from Radcliffe with an A.B. in Social Relations and English and received her Ph.D. in Clinical Psychology in 1974. She later became Executive Director of the Congressional Commission for the Control of Huntington's Disease and Its Consequences. In 1979, she learned of the world's largest family with Huntington's disease living along the shores of Lake Maracaibo, Venezuela, and began a continuing study of many thousands of people affected by and at risk for Huntington's disease in this community. Nancy's unique personal and professional expertise in the ethical aspects of gene identification resulted in an invitation from Jim Watson to join the Joint NIH/DOE Ethical, Legal, and Social Issues Working Group (ELSI) of the National Center for Human Genome Research (NCHGR), which she chaired from 1989 to 1995. She is now Higgins Professor of Neuropsychology in the Departments of Neurology and Psychiatry of the College of Physicians & Surgeons at Columbia University.

I had the good fortune to watch Jim in action first hand. On October 1, 1988, Jim was officially appointed as NIH Associate Director in charge of the Human Genome Project—an enormous job under the aegis of the newly established Human Genome Center at the NIH. In those early days, the Center was not yet a Division or an Institute at the NIH, but it did have an official Program Advisory Committee (PAC). Jim's first move was to select Norton Zinder as the first head of that PAC. Norton was one of the scientists who, in 1974, had called for a temporary ban on certain types of genetic engineering research until the scientific community could assess the risks associated with that research and come up with suitable guidelines for carrying out this work. Norton made certain that his PAC took seriously its mandate to create guidelines and procedures for the mammoth job ahead.

Three weeks after Jim assumed office, one of the first major organizational meetings for human genome research took place at the Hotel Sidi Sider in Valencia, Spain. The prospect of shaping such a critical endeavor—as well as the balmy Mediterranean weather—helped organizer Santiago Grisolía attract many luminaries.

One evening after dinner in Valencia, while I was sitting on the veranda of the hotel, I saw Jim and Norton staring at me. I had a sense that something was up. It turned out that Norton and Jim were in the process of filling the last position on the PAC and wanted to know if I would be interested in taking it. I was a psychologist, genetic researcher, and part of the team that, in 1983, had found a DNA marker linked to the gene for Huntington's disease—the first such success. I was President of the Hereditary Disease Foundation and connected to health advocacy groups as well as to academia. I also had a one-in-two chance of inheriting Huntington's disease from my mother, who had died of the disease 10 years earlier, so I could represent the voice of families contending with genetic disease. And I would be the sole woman on the Committee.

Interested? Of course...I was honored! I wanted to run around the hotel shouting for joy! Thanks to Jim, Norton, and the astonishing members of the Committee, those years were some of the most amazing of my life. Everyone took very seriously our mission to guide and craft the most ambitious science project in history—the discovery of our genetic essence.

Each member of the PAC chaired a working group that would delve into the details of a particular area: genetic mapping, physical mapping, sequencing, informatics, and others. As the Department of Energy (DOE) directed its own independent but complementary Human Genome Project, most working groups were funded and administered by both the NIH and the DOE. Norton and Jim asked me to join Victor McKusick as a co-chair of the Joint NIH-DOE Working Group on ethics. Victor is a giant in the field of human genetics, and the prospect of co-chairing with him was a bit intimidating. Moreover, I reminded Jim and Norton, I wasn't an ethicist. But they wanted the working group also to include the ethical, legal, and social implications of mapping and sequencing the human genome. Jim was adamant that he did not want, in his words, "the usual suspects" for the inaugural ELSI group. He *did* want outspoken, thoughtful individuals who would not be afraid to work outside the envelope, and I was privileged to be able to work with an extraordinarily talented team of Committee members.

In the beginning, some observers described the Human Genome Project as the first "Big Science" Project since the Manhattan Project. This onerous comparison with the endeavor that created the atomic bomb served only to emphasize the necessity for openness and transparency in this new science venture.

The secrecy believed mandatory for the bomb's creation and deployment permanently altered the public's unquestioning trust in science and scientists. Science would need to proceed differently. Many scientists would insist, and most importantly, Jim Watson would insist. He understood that mankind could not obtain such revolutionary knowledge without exercising the greatest care in studying the unique ramifications of this knowledge on humanity itself. The molecular and the societal must proceed hand in hand.

With one stroke of the pen, Jim created the largest international budget in history for examining the ethical, legal, and social implications of science. Some observers sniped that he had created the ELSI program and funded it so generously only to deter criticism of the Human Genome Project. Sometimes his well-known hostility to political correctness in all its guises was interpreted as resistance to ELSI issues in general; surely he was just trying to buy off critics of the Project, or bribe them, or silence them. Indeed, some critics of the Human Genome Project were fearful of being bought off. They did have moral quandaries about accepting ELSI funding—they were concerned that taking ELSI money was tantamount to supporting the science. They feared that any criticisms they might raise in the future about genome research—especially if these concerns emanated from research conducted with ELSI funding—would be met with derision and skepticism or be ignored by the genome community. But it is true that funding from the ELSI program was without strings. Criticism and suggestions were genuinely welcome.

Doubt, disparagement, and criticism from some quarters never lessened Jim's own commitment to the ELSI cause. For one thing, he and Norton realized that they would be criticized whether or not the program existed. More basically, he was a bold and decisive leader. He was never afraid to put forward an idea just to provoke a response—for example, his suggestion at the beginning of the Human Genome Project that the mapping and sequencing projects be divided up by chromosomes, with each chromosome assigned to particular groups. Since the work would be so overwhelmingly difficult and time-consuming, perhaps specific countries could take responsibility for certain chromosomes. When leaders in the former Soviet Union heard about this idea, they protested to the State Department that they wanted to be assigned chromosome number one, since it was the biggest. Others complained that the entire idea was unworkable. But back then, it was as good an idea as any. It got everyone talking and arguing and coming up with something better, if only to one-up the Human Genome Project. Jim was not concerned that an idea might hurt his reputation but was interested in getting the job done as fast and as accurately as possible.

Jim realized that the involvement of different countries would induce the governments of those countries to help pay for the project. The expertise of each country working in a synergistic mode was critical because the Project was so vast. In almost all research applications to the Human Genome Project, a section on how such collaborations and data-sharing would occur was mandatory. In many applications, a section on ELSI issues was also required.

Jim was quick to realize that many on Capitol Hill, particularly Congressman David Obey, Chair of the House Appropriations Committee, seriously questioned the political, economic, psychological, and social impact of having our genome in hand. Obey mandated that the Genome Center provide policy options aimed at preventing the possible misuses and abuses of genetic testing and, at one time, suggested slowing down the funding for genome research until the ELSI issues were sorted out—an unrealistic idea, as Obey himself knew. It was impossible to reverse the science that was already well-launched.

Vice President Al Gore shared many of these same concerns. I was with Jim one afternoon when he testified before the then-Senator Gore. When Gore questioned the societal impact of acquiring this potentially dangerous knowledge, Jim was quick to describe the ELSI program. Following Jim to the microphone was the head of the DOE's Human Genome Project program. When Gore asked this gentleman how much he was setting aside for ELSI, he stammered, "No set amount." Gore reprimanded him, "Don't you think you ought to?" And so Jim influenced even the DOE's three percent set aside for ELSI! And then Al Gore persuaded Jim Watson on the spot to raise his funding percentage to five percent!

Organizational trees in Washington, D.C. get pretty complex pretty fast, and ours was no exception. Both the NIH and the DOE had their own Human Genome Projects, and each of these Projects quickly developed internal ELSI programs for their granting operations. The staff directors of these internal ELSI programs also served as staff to the Joint NIH-DOE ELSI Working Group. This is how we were fortunate to acquire the ethicist and philosopher Eric Juengst as the first Director of the NIH ELSI branch. Eric's move from the shelter of two major bioethics centers, the University of California, San Francisco, and the Hershey Medical Center in Pennsylvania, into the pit of government politics and the internecine politics within the Human Genome Center (which, frankly, held a mixed view of ELSI's potential), showed a truly intrepid spirit. His intelligent, calm, humorous championship of the goals of ELSI was responsible for much of its success. He was joined as deputy director by Elizabeth Thompson, a nurse with extensive training in genetics and genetic counseling. On the DOE side, where the ELSI mandate was even more of an anomaly than on the NIH side, the program was admirably served by Michael Yesley and Daniel Drell.

The Working Group's first meeting took place at the NIH in Bethesda in September, 1989. Since no group like ours had ever existed at the NIH or the DOE, we had no precedents. Most critical was our decision at that first meeting to tackle the development of policy. We worked hard to develop a formidable research agenda. We could choose to either delegate this agenda to the outside research community or strive to do some of it ourselves, particularly in areas in which we perceived great urgency. We were also eager to take on a challenge not typical within the confines of the NIH or DOE—the development of social policies. This decision entailed creating task forces, holding workshops, commissioning reports, and other activist activities. The following description of our research agenda is taken from Jonathan Beckwith's autobiography, *Making Genes, Making Waves: A Social Activist in Science* (2002):

1. Fairness in the use of genetic information. This included issues of insurance and employment discrimination.

2. The impact of genetic information on the individual, including issues such as stigmatization and psychological responses.

3. The privacy and confidentiality of genetic information.

4. The consequences of HGP for genetic counseling.

5. The influence of genetic information on reproductive decisions.

6. The impact of introducing genetics into mainstream clinical practice.

7. The historical analysis of the misuses of genetics in the past and their contemporary relevance.

8. The influence of commercialization of the products of the HGP.

We also encouraged the development and funding of educational materials covering this new genetics geared to the general public as well as medical audiences.

We established a Task Force on Insurance, co-chaired by Tom Murray and Jonathan Beckwith, two of the first ELSI Working Group members, and assembled a group of experts, including representatives from the health and life insurance industries, with a primary interest in health insurance. Then, as now, many people were uninsurable for medical coverage because they suffered from or were at risk for a genetic disease. Having Huntington's disease in the family, for example, makes one by definition uninsurable. There was a sea change in this task force when the Clinton administration took over in 1992 and began pushing for universal coverage in health care. We had been arguing that since virtually all diseases have a genetic component, all of us will have some genetic disorder that will make us uninsurable when the human genome is deciphered and the genome of every individual is available to insurance companies. When Hillary Rodham Clinton learned this, she immediately understood the profound import of this information and used this logic to promote health care reform.

A major accomplishment of the ELSI Working Group involved protecting workers' entitlements. The Americans With Disabilities Act of 1990 prohibits discrimination against people who are currently disabled, have a history of disability, or give the appearance of being disabled and are discriminated against, even if they are not, in fact, disabled. We thought that these provisions should be protective not just of symptomatic individuals, but also of people who carry an abnormal gene for an illness that will appear in the future, like Huntington's disease; people who are asymptomatic carriers of a disease that may appear in their children, like cystic fibrosis; or people at risk for genetic disorders. When we appealed to the Equal Employment Opportunity Commission (EEOC) to include these groups in the legislative regulations that they were currently drafting for implementing the bill, we were told that these provisions had nothing to do with genetic diseases—that their genes are individuals' own responsibility.

This lack of understanding of elementary genetics was appalling, and we began an educational campaign at the commission. We also appealed to Senator Tom Harkin, the originator of the bill, who was very sympathetic to our cause and understood the issues immediately. In the end, the change in administration in Washington saved us again. The Clinton administration appointed a new EEOC Commissioner who was very responsive and receptive. The new regulations specifically included—and still include—an example of a person who tests positive for colon cancer as one case of an individual protected by the American With Disabilities Act. Bob Cook-Deegan and Mark Rothstein, who by this time had joined the working group, did heroic labor to obtain these regulations, and their good efforts have since been rewarded by important judicial decisions.

One of the first crises confronting the fledgling ELSI Working Group involved carrier-testing for people who had mutations in the gene causing cystic fibrosis. This gene had just been discovered in 1989, one of the first to be found using recombinant DNA techniques. There are many mutations in this gene, with a deletion accounting for the majority of them. As one in twenty-five Caucasians carries a gene with one of these mutations, many groups—researchers and clinicians alike—pressed to make a carrier-screening test rapidly available to the public. However, certain subtleties made genetic counseling problematic. Not all of the mutations had been discovered, so a "negative" result would not take into account mutations not yet uncovered. Could investigators teach both clinicians and their patients to make this important qualification, especially since genetic education and knowledge of probability theory were often not well taught either in medical school or to the general public? Was partial, possibly misleading, information necessarily better than no information at all?

Cystic fibrosis cannot be treated *in utero*. Once a pregnancy has ensued, abortion is the only option for prevention. But parents were often not told. They were merely advised to get genetic testing. Nor were they offered carrier testing prior to pregnancy when the results, obviously, would allow more options. And then there was the question of insurance. The nadir of this aspect of the imbroglio occurred when an HMO agreed to pay for carrier-testing for a fetus. When the company learned from the test that the child would be born with cystic fibrosis, it informed the couple that its responsibility stopped with the test alone. If the couple chose to continue with this pregnancy, the insurance company would not pay for the subsequent medical care of the affected child. The public outcry at this HMO for forcing a couple to have an abortion for financial reasons finally persuaded it to reverse its position. The case served as an early wake-up call to everyone in the field: The new genetic testing would be fraught with complexity and dilemma.

Many thoughtful people proposed pilot projects for designing the best way to introduce the new cystic fibrosis screening measures to the public. Suitable educational materials could be developed. The problem of false negatives could be addressed. And all of these measures could serve as a model for testing many other genetic diseases. But this ambitious pilot-testing program for cystic fibrosis would have a hefty price tag. Who would pay? The Cystic Fibrosis Foundation was deeply committed to finding treatments and cures for the disease; it did not see prevention as part of its mandate. Moreover, some Cystic Fibrosis Foundation members felt that any such expansion of their mandate would be an insult to those living and contending with the disease. This position was understandable. Less understandable were the program managers at the NIH's National Institute of Diabetes, Digestive, and Kidney Diseases, who said that genetic testing was not within their purview. They only did "hard science" with the aim of curing cystic fibrosis, pure and simple, and they had no stops along the way. They would not fund pilot projects on cystic fibrosis testing. The National Institute of Child Health and Human Development was equally disinterested.

We at the ELSI Working Group felt otherwise. We thought pilot projects that investigated in a scientific and reliable way how best to deliver and receive such critical testing information were *not* ancillary to our mandate. They were, in fact, its sine qua non. We brought this recommendation to the PAC for its approval. At that time, when the Project was new and all such matters were handled in something of an ad hoc fashion, the procedure was for the Committee to approve our recommendations before either the NIH or the DOE Human Genome Project programs could write the checks. There followed an extraordinary and lengthy debate regarding pilot projects for cystic fibrosis. Norton Zinder thought the idea theoretically sound, but he was concerned that it would eat up the ELSI budget. Norton said, "Once the camel puts its nose under the tent, Nancy, you'll see, it will take over." Phil Sharp, a PAC member from MIT said, "How can we engage in mapping and sequencing the human genome without attending to its impact on people themselves? I vote for it!"

Approval was granted by the Committee, but Norton Zinder was right: We would have to have help coping with the camel. No problem! Jim announced that the fledgling ELSI program and Human Genome Project alone should not have to assume the burden of total funding. He sent Elke Jordan, Deputy Director of the National Center for Human Genome Research, and Eric Juengst to take his concerns to all the Institutes that had any kind of mandate for cystic fibrosis. Simply put, they could not be responsible scientific citizens without attending to the impact of having the cystic fibrosis gene cloned and available for testing. Jim insisted that they join us in a collaboration. Suddenly, all the other Institutes discovered that policy and clinical practice were part of their mandate after all!

Many Institutes had been allergic to considering that the societal ramifications of their scientific research were part of their remit. But Jim Watson changed that attitude, not by haranguing or pontificating, but by being in the vanguard and showing everyone that ELSI issues are fundamental. They are a fact of life now, and we have no real choice about addressing them. The CF Pilot Testing Projects were so successful that when genes predisposing to breast cancer were discovered, pilot projects were de rigueur. Today, almost all Institutes of the NIH have some ELSI component.

Some genome scientists have complained that the ELSI program has never produced universal insurance coverage or enacted privacy laws. Progress and change take time. In our society, the appropriate legislative corrections may be more difficult to accomplish than mapping and sequencing the genomes of all the human and model organisms combined. At least in the scientific arena, there is the will and motivation to do the work. The sociopolitical and economic forces resisting change are of Himalayan magnitude, but change is happening slowly, nevertheless, sometimes state by state, sometimes at the federal level.

The main reason ELSI issues are on the world's radar screen is the advocacy of Jim Watson. Before Jim stepped in, it was unprecedented to include, at the inception of a science project, be it large or small, a simultaneous commitment to investigate and attend to the societal ramifications of this science. Jim's unique contribution was to put ELSI concerns smack into the midst of the molecular biological agenda. He changed the psychological mind-set, the ethos and nature of the conversation. He created the expectation that this conversation should occur. Most people now accept that these two forces can and must coexist and complement each other.

Jim was indefatigable in his pursuit of the goal of mapping and sequencing the genomes of human and model organisms. He was on the road constantly, meeting with members of Congress, speaking before academic institutions, professional meetings, corporate executives—speaking to whomever he thought would lend a receptive ear or persuade a resistive stance. On some of these occasions, I accompanied him to explain the ELSI program. I particularly remember two occasions, one in Dallas, Texas, one in Ann Arbor, Michigan.

In Dallas, we were attending the annual meeting of a professional society. The hotel overlooked the grassy knoll where President Kennedy had been assassinated. I had never seen the site before, and now it seemed almost surreal—those horrific memories etched in the bland Texas sunshine. I turned away from the window with a chill and walked into a huge auditorium filled beyond capacity with men and women who wanted to hear Jim Watson speak. And he did not let them down. With a combination of personal charm and an elegant elucidation of complex science, Jim explained the work of the Human Genome Project as only he could. He promised that funding for the Human Genome Project would not compete with these society members' own funding, that so-called "Big Science" would not overwhelm "little science."

In audience after audience, city after city, any remaining resistance melted away as Jim promised each group to sequence their particular favorite organism or model system, be it plants, yeast, worms, flies, or mice. Any genes shared across species are likely to be important. Experiments could be carried out on these model systems that could not be performed on humans. At every stop, there were converts.

At the University of Michigan in Ann Arbor, Jim shared the stage at the Rackham Auditorium with Francis Collins, a number of others, and myself. High school and college students arrived in droves by bus from as far away as Flint and Kalamazoo, filling all the red plush seats and spilling into the aisles and the back of the auditorium. Even the foyer behind the auditorium was jam-packed. Fire marshals were summoned and with stern faces began clearing out the overflow. Finally, under the Rackham's ceiling of celestial blue studded with gold stars, Jim regaled the group with tales of DNA and girls and the Human Genome Project and girls, much to the raucous enthusiasm of the audience. At the end, students crushed around Jim, seeking his autograph on their well-worn paperback copies of *The Double Helix*, their programs, their biology texts, anything.

Over the course of the six years that I was Chair of the Joint NIH/DOE ELSI Working Group, each of the other working groups initially established to set policy or start work had gradually been absorbed into the National Center for Human Genome Research as a branch, or had fulfilled its mission and disappeared. The Joint NIH/DOE ELSI Working Group was the only one that maintained itself, even grew and created an independent mission statement, operating procedures, and rotation schedule. We met quarterly and the Task Forces met even more often. We had achieved a semi-autonomous existence. We had a substantial budget and reasonable independence from the administration of the Genome Center. Jim approved our foray into policy—a highly unusual activity within the NIH confines at that time.

Those of us who had joined the initial working group in 1989 began to rotate off the board in the mid 1990s. In 1995, Lori Andrews succeeded me as chair and Troy Duster became co-chair. With the full support of Jim Watson, the work continued—until certain cataclysms rocked us.

Jim became outraged by the attempts of Bernadine Healy, then Director of the NIH, and Craig Venter, a molecular geneticist in the NIH intramural research program, to patent regions of the human genome. Craig had purchased some of the first gene-sequencing machines and had proceeded to sequence ESTs, or "expressed sequence tags." Each of these snippets of DNA is part of an individual gene, but no one had any notion about the rest of the respective gene, its utility, or its function. Preexisting patents on thousands of ESTs could potentially block all manner of research into the details and uses of specific genes, once these genes were finally isolated. Even more damaging, a preexisting EST patent could block research on a gene as a drug target.

Characteristically, Jim was vocal in his negative opinion of this patenting tactic. He was galled that Craig and the NIH were laying claim to vast stretches of the human genome without doing the hard labor of mining and developing the genes. Craig and the NIH's appeal to the U.S. Patent Office to gain ownership threatened to destroy the careful international collaborations Jim had worked so hard to put in place. Jim's infamous characterization of Craig's EST achievement—"any monkey could do that"—earned him considerable enmity in high places. Bernadine Healy could not appreciate Jim's quixotic force and made his position untenable. So he resigned.

In the contest between Jim Watson, the ultimate antibureaucrat, and the NIH, a government bureaucracy of considerable proportions, all of us sided with Jim. Jim actually won—with the patent office, which eventually denied the claims, with scientists, and with the public. And the NIH lost the invaluable services of one of the great forces in twentieth-century science.

Francis Collins replaced Jim as Director of the Genome Center, which then quickly became a formal Institute of the NIH. A physician and molecular geneticist, Francis was a pioneer in developing many of the early recombinant DNA techniques of gene finding. As part of a large collaboration, Francis and his group were co-discoverers of the gene for Huntington's disease. The Collins group also discovered the genes causing cystic fibrosis, neurofibromatosis, breast cancer, and others. As a physician, Francis took care of patients dying from these diseases. He also had a personal, intense, and active interest in ELSI issues—attending many of the Working Group meetings and becoming an articulate interpreter of the ELSI challenge to Congress, to other scientists, and to the public. Francis felt that the funding should be consolidated in programs within the NIH Genome Institute and began building a strong program within the newly constituted Institute, particularly by hiring Kathy Hudson as Assistant Director for Policy Coordination, NHGRI. Both the extramural and intramural ELSI grant programs were strengthened, and the ELSI programs remain vibrant at the NIH and DOE today. The old ELSI Working Group was reduced to one meeting annually. Lori, Troy, and the other members chose to resign in 1996, and the group disbanded.

Jim never was and never will be afraid to push against "politically correct" boundaries in any direction. He believes passionately in a woman's right to choose whether or not to have a baby and not be pushed around by outside forces, particularly by the state or the church. In his mind, it is the woman's prerogative to have a baby she knows will develop a genetic disease, and she should not be sanctioned by the government or insurance companies or other commercial or state entities. On the other hand, if a woman wants to terminate that fetus because she knows what will befall her child, or if she wants to terminate that fetus for any reason whatsoever, that should also be her prerogative, with no negative repercussions. No government or company or social organization or individual should prevent her or make her feel guilty or harass her.

When the recombinant revolution began, scientists and the public considered only the potential of changing somatic cells. Any treatments and cures would be directed at non-germ-line cells, therefore creating the fix for only one generation. Noting the frequency with which Mother Nature surprises us, this restriction seems only prudent.

The advent of Dolly, the cloned sheep, was a revelation that cloning could work. We then discovered that Dolly had the short telomeres of her elderly mom, and died prematurely. We discovered that gene therapy aimed at curing one disease creates another: The virus suited like a Trojan Horse to carry in normal genes for one disease unfortunately makes its home in another gene which, when its doors are opened, causes a leukemia.

These are important cautionary tales. Nevertheless, during the ELSI era, Jim also began talking and thinking about the scientific and ethical possibilities of germ-line gene therapy. His willingness to consider such arenas where others fear to tread may be part of his instinctive desire to disturb the status quo, scientifically and otherwise. Jim has never been one to shy away from controversy. He does not have a reflexive, hostile reaction to germ-line gene therapy. Jim understands that correcting a genetic abnormality in an embryo of a few cells is technically more straightforward than trying to fix trillions of cells in the adult or where the site of action is hard to reach, like the brain. Unlike many other public figures, his distaste for political correctness and all it entails gives him the liberty to entertain and discuss these ideas. Not a religious person, he has no sanctimoniousness about the sanctity of the germ plasm as something untouchable. He sees it in "draft" form. If his discovery of how DNA physically replicates itself and passes on information to the next generation enables the leading strand to educate the lagging strand and to protect us from suffering, Jim is willing, at least, to contemplate it.

I am deeply indebted to Jim for all of his discoveries, his creation and championship of ELSI, his elemental force, and—most particularly—his friendship.

REFERENCES

Beckwith J.R. 2002. *Making genes, making waves: A social activist in science.* Harvard University Press, Cambridge.

SECTION VI

EDUCATION

Section VI photograph: *Maynard Olson summarizing the Symposium, The Genome of* Homo Sapiens, *June 2, 2003. (Photograph by Jan Witkowski. Courtesy CSHL Archives.)*

COMMUNICATING SCIENCE

IT IS UNLIKELY THAT THOSE WHO LISTENED to Jim's first student lecture—given at Caltech where he moved after Cambridge—would have held out much hope that he would become a great educator. By his own admission, it was "dreadful," but he used its failure to think of ways to improve the "coherence if not actual zing" of the remaining lectures in the series.[1] Nevertheless, Jim's style of presentation does not seem to have been any better by the time he had his job seminar at Harvard in January, 1955. It cannot have been an easy talk, reporting as he was on the highly speculative scheme, devised by Leslie Orgel and himself, in which a single-stranded RNA molecule was synthesized on a double-stranded DNA template.[2] This involved some rather improbable chemistry, with RNA being synthesized in an anhydride form. Fortunately, the Biology Department had few chemists to pose awkward questions. However, Jim spoke in a "...low voice that only occasionally made it to the back of the lecture hall."[3] The chairman of the search committee, John R. Raper, an authority on sexuality in fungi, was sufficiently concerned to write to several scientists asking what they thought of Jim's lecturing skills. Fritz Lipmann's response was succinct and to the effect that if Jim had interesting things to say, the students would come to hear him.[4]

This was indeed the case. The Harvard student body published an annual review of lecturers and, despite repeated references to the need for Harvard to provide him with a microphone, Jim's lectures were highly rated, even before the added luster of his 1962 Nobel Prize.[5] Lecturing was made more difficult because there was no textbook covering a young field that had not yet moved beyond the research laboratory. Jim resolved to write the textbook he wanted and in the style he believed was needed. As Keith Roberts describes in his essay in this section, the book, *Molecular Biology of the Gene*, was unlike any previous textbook in biology in its style of writing and design. Not content with giving "facts," Jim conveyed the excitement of the new field, intent on converting students to think about biology in molecular terms. It was a sensation, leading to a major revision of the style of science textbooks.

The science textbook was not the only genre that Jim revolutionized. The phrase "scientific autobiography" on a dust jacket has been known to put readers to sleep even before opening the book; the autobiographies were often self-congratulatory and written to portray the scientist-author in the manner of Arrowsmith or Gottlieb,[6] seekers of natural truths, untainted by the whims and wiles of ordinary people. *The Double Helix* changed that view of scientists forever. It covered just the period of the discovery, and Jim wrote as though he was living the experience and not in the manner expected of a Harvard professor. Controversial even before publication—the principal players in the story threatened to sue and Harvard's President Nathan Pusey forced Harvard Press to drop the book—*The Double Helix* is a fast-moving, opinionated memoir in a style more to be expected of a roman-à-clef than an autobiography. Hugely successful, never out of print and translated into 22 languages, it continues to arouse strong passions, especially for Jim's characterization of Rosalind Franklin. Brenda Maddox's recent biography of Franklin gives a comprehensive, balanced, and readable account of Franklin's life and work.[7]

Jim's enthusiasm for books continued and has been a major part of his intellectual life. He went on to co-author two more very successful textbooks, *Molecular Biology of the Cell* and *Recombinant DNA*, the latter opening with the undeniable statement that "There is no substance as important as DNA." And in *The DNA Story*, he and John Tooze collected materials relating to the recombinant DNA debates of the 1970s that showed with devastating clarity how much the debate was driven by hysteria and politics.

Jim's move to Cold Spring Harbor provided him with new opportunities, for now he had his own meetings program and publishing house. He soon expanded the number of meetings and courses held each year. This was regarded as a mixed blessing by the year-round staff who, for many years, had to relinquish their laboratories for three months to accommodate the summer courses. Charles Robertson's gift of his Banbury estate in 1976 enabled Jim to develop it as a conference center for small discussion meetings. And Jim provided the means and support for David Micklos to create the DNA Learning Center, where students as young as eighth graders (14 years of age) learn genetics and carry out laboratory experiments.

Just as Jim built upon the existing meetings program at Cold Spring Harbor, so he developed a vigorous publication program on the financial base provided by the sale of the annual Symposium volumes. Jim used the meetings as the sources for books, often on topics that no commercial publisher would consider but for which there was a scientific need. Many were published in the Cold Spring Harbor Monograph series as definitive accounts of the current state of an area of research. In large part, the financial freedom to cover recondite topics came from sales of laboratory manuals, the first of which was Jeffrey Miller's *Experiments in Molecular Genetics*.[8] Its successors have become the most respected and widely used source of technical information in molecular biology.

The Laboratory was slow to join the rush to publish new scientific journals, chiefly because of possible conflicts of interest and accusations of favoritism. But after much debate, *Genes & Development* was launched in 1987. By any objective criteria, *G&D* has been a success. It attracts a steady flow of good papers, ranks among the most highly cited journals in biology, has a reputation for editorial probity, and, to everyone's relief, has made a return on its investment in the past few years. Other journals have followed.

In 1995, Jim articulated his vision of a graduate school for the Laboratory. It would be highly selective, offer a unique curriculum designed to train communicators of science not just investigators, and graduate its students in four years rather than the average seven. The Watson School of Biological Sciences enrolled its first class in October 1999 and awarded its first Ph.D. in May, 2003.

Many think that Jim's Cold Spring Harbor has made as great a world-wide impact through its education programs as through its science.

The Pied Piper at Harvard

David Botstein

Stanford University School of Medicine

There was a time, not really so long ago, when careers in academic research and the teaching of undergraduates were inseparable. In 1959, when I began college, we thought of the undergraduate years as a time to find an interesting career that suited what talents we had; we took courses and sought out faculty hoping to learn about science at the leading edge. My teachers and mentors, even in the most elementary courses, were the active scientific leaders in the physics, chemistry, and biology of the time (including such luminaries as R.V. Pound, George Kistiakowsky, Konrad Bloch, William Lipscomb, and my tutor, Boris Magasanik).[1] Even so, the Harvard professor of that era who probably had the most to do with drawing undergraduates (including myself) into the study of modern biology was Jim Watson. Jim seemed particularly motivated to teach undergraduates and was evidently willing to take us seriously. He had a strong influence on my choice of career, even though, having started as a physics major, I never actually took a course from him.

It is commonly assumed that to be influential, undergraduate college teachers must be spellbinding lecturers, capable of making virtually anybody interested, at least for an hour, in their subject. It was only after I heard Jim lecture in his introductory biology course that I began to appreciate that charismatic leadership could be attained by means other than entertaining scholarly lectures. In 1961, only five years after he joined the Harvard faculty as an Assistant Professor (and eight years after the publication of the double-helix structure), Jim Watson was, for the undergraduates and graduate students alike, the most attractive and effective intellectual leader among the biology faculty. Yet the best that can be said of his lectures was that they were unpredictable. Jim spoke very quietly, and directly to the blackboard, much of the time. Jim's lectures did not travel smoothly along well-predetermined paths; directed random walks would be a better description. He was easily distractable, and his legendary mannerisms also distracted us. He larded his lectures with tidbits of gossip about scientists, which, although sometimes entertaining, added little or nothing to the flow of ideas or arguments. Yet he acquired a following among students the like of which I have not seen since. Students flocked to his courses and those he recommended; they signed up to study the molecular sciences (then mainly chemistry) and to work in laboratories then being established in the brand-new field called "molecular biology."

To what can one attribute Jim's success as an intellectual motivator, if not scintillating lectures? It was not his books, which came later (the immensely successful undergraduate textbook *Molecular Biology of the Gene* was published in 1965 and the best-selling *The Double Helix* was published in 1968) and it was not the Nobel Prize,

DAVID BOTSTEIN

David Botstein holds an undergraduate degree from Harvard (1963) and a Ph.D. from the University of Michigan (1967) for work on the synthesis and maturation of bacteriophage P22 DNA. Genetic and biochemical analyses of this phage and its hosts were to be the mainstay of Botstein's laboratory during his early years as a faculty member at MIT. By the late 1970s, however, Botstein had moved into yeast genetics, after taking the Cold Spring Harbor Yeast course in 1971. In 1980, he made a dramatic entry into mammalian genetics by describing a general method for linkage mapping of the human and other large genomes. This work laid the theoretical groundwork for cloning the first human disease genes, including those for Huntington's disease, Duchenne muscular dystrophy, and cystic fibrosis. In turn, the success of cloning clinically important human genes was one of the key arguments advanced for the Human Genome Project.

Initially, however, Botstein had real doubts about the value of the Human Genome Project, particularly when the costs of the Project seemed likely to reach billions of dollars. As a member of the National Academy committee chaired by Bruce Alberts, Botstein argued persuasively that the knowledge and skill necessary to tackle the human genome would be best gained by sequencing smaller, simpler genomes, such as the fruit fly and yeast. These model genomes were added to the Project, and Botstein, by then working at Stanford, became a leader of the international team that successfully sequenced the yeast genome in the early 1990s.

Since then, Botstein has become interested in the global aspects of genomic organization and expression and in the disorder that diseases like cancer inflict on the genome. He is exploring how data obtained from parallel mass screening methods (such as DNA microarrays) can be efficiently collated, integrated, and mined. Recently, Botstein has been been appointed as Director of the Lewis-Sigler Institute for Integrative Genomics at Princeton University. In 1981, Botstein was elected to the National Academy of Sciences and was President of the Genetics Society of America in 1997.

Botstein's style of lecturing is exactly the opposite of Jim Watson's: forceful, didactic, linear, and very loud. One is left in no doubt as to what Botstein believes and thinks should be done.

---

which was awarded in 1962, after Jim's influence at Harvard was well-established. Jim was, in the interval between 1956 and 1962, not yet a celebrity.

I have come to believe that Jim's intellectual appeal had two aspects. One was the content of his message, which was that the obvious, indeed the only productive scientific path forward in biology, was through the study of the biological macromolecules—DNA, RNA, and protein. These were the actors in the central dogma of the new biology, and the DNA structure provided its intellectual foundation. As undergraduates, we were easily converted: The arguments for this point of view were persuasive, and of course they have more than stood the test of time. By teaching an introductory biology course, Jim quickly became the most visible advocate for the molecular approach to biology among the faculty.

The second aspect of Jim's appeal to students was the iconoclastic and aggressive way in which this message was conveyed to the classical academic biology establish-

David Botstein holding forth at the Human Genome Project debate at the 1986 Symposium. Wally Gilbert listens. (Courtesy CSHL Archives.)

ment, then dominated by zoologists, botanists, and evolutionists. Jim enjoyed the role of *enfant terrible*, all the more because he knew he was right, and evidence of that rightness was accumulating day by day. The message became, in Jim's hands, a crusade. Possibly most exciting to the nonbiology undergraduates (and maybe the most galling to the biology establishment) was the idea that the new molecular direction would bring to biology the rigor and sophistication of "hard" physical science. There was no more potent emblem for this than the presence of Wally Gilbert, then an Assistant Professor of Physics and regarded as a highly promising theoretician, in Jim's lab, where he could be seen running ultracentrifuges and thinking about how DNA information might be turned into proteins.

The combination of an open, attractive new field, complete with a deduced, empirically verifiable (as opposed to revealed) truth, led by a charismatic figure who pulled no punches ("Honest Jim") in a charge against an entrenched academic establishment, was irresistible. This was, after all, the time of President Kennedy's "New Frontier," the Peace Corps; it was the dawn of the idealistic youth rebellion of the 1960s. It was significant, I think, that Jim was not that much older than the undergraduates. He was an active participant in the student social scene and regularly dated undergraduate Radcliffe women. It was also a time when the prospects for the future for academic physicists and mathematicians were becoming much less certain. It is no wonder that so many of my peers, especially those initially attracted to physics, ended up committed to study molecular biology in one of the handful of graduate programs recommended by Jim.

With the publication of *Molecular Biology of the Gene*, Jim expanded his audience well beyond Harvard. This enormously successful text reflected both of the aspects that made Jim so influential at Harvard. First, the message was presented clearly, concisely, and directly, with astonishing scholarship but utterly without the standard academic trappings. This book presented a radical new model for biology textbooks. Here there was no mumbling; readers could easily grasp, with no distractions, Jim's total command of the entire body of knowledge of molecular biology. Second, "Honest Jim," the *enfant terrible* and in-your-face iconoclast, was embodied in the book by unhedged opinions about which ideas and findings were important and which methods were useful, and even predictions about which fields of study were fertile and how they might be likely to develop. Jim put into his textbook, edition after edition, his own very latest understanding, sometimes based on breathtakingly little evidence but always guided by astonishingly accurate intuition. It mattered little when he occasionally guessed wrong. Jim's direct style in the book, as at Harvard, succeeded in conveying the promise and excitement of the molecular biology to an audience of students looking toward their own futures, each trying to decide where to place bets. The package was completed upon the publication of *The Double Helix*, in which the gossipy and contentious "Honest Jim" side became available, undiluted with molecular detail, to a wide audience outside Harvard and, indeed, outside academia. With the two books representing the two aspects of his appeal, Jim Watson sold an entire generation of students (including many not initially headed for scientific careers) on molecular biology.

Jim Watson's place in scientific history was, of course, secure after the publication of the DNA structure in 1953. What he accomplished in his research at Harvard, while by no means unimportant, was secondary, in my view, to what he accomplished by his teaching. He encouraged a generation of young people to join the molecular biology church. By taking up the Directorship of the Cold Spring Harbor Laboratory, Jim moved permanently from the role of researcher to the role of impresario of science. At Cold Spring Harbor, the crusade was institutionalized. The meetings and courses served the need to illuminate the path forward for professional scientists; the DNA Learning Center was established to bring the word to younger students and the public at large.

The culmination of Jim Watson's influence was, without doubt, the Human Genome Project. Highly controversial when first proposed, this became, quite naturally, the Holy Grail of molecular biology. Jim's advocacy and leadership bore the usual dual trademarks of his remarkably effective style. There were scientific arguments and judgments, leavened by strong (but not infallible) intuition about what made scientific sense. There were big victories here for science: Jim's advocacy of the eukaryotic model organisms was a key judgment, as was the decision to allot a fraction of the funding to ethical, legal, and social issues. "Honest Jim" was to be found here as well, gossiping about the players in the genome game, holding forth about the politics of science inside the Beltway, and trying to entrain the whirlwind of nationalism by suggesting that each first-world nation should commit itself to sequencing particular human chromosomes. As always, Jim was generous with his opinions, and rarely pulled any punches. Jim's tenure as Director of the National Center for Human Genome Research at the National Institutes of Health was an edgy performance. Whenever Jim got up to talk, it was unclear whether we were going to hear some great scientific insight, or some marginal item of gossip.

The Genome Project was, of course, a big success, even though some of Jim's plain talk inevitably resulted in a somewhat premature end to his Directorship of the Center. Nevertheless, as with the undergraduates at Harvard, Jim's combination of scientific direction and personal charisma (now considerably augmented by his celebrity) had got Jim the result he wanted: There was no longer any serious question about the logic and wisdom, if not the execution, of genomic sequencing. And, of course, once again, what he wanted was good for science and for us all.

REFERENCES

Watson J.D. 1965. *Molecular biology of the gene*. W.A. Benjamin, New York.
Watson J.D. 1968. *The double helix: A personal account of the discovery of the structure of DNA*. Atheneum, New York.

There Is More Yet to Come

Arnie Levine

Institute for Advanced Study, Princeton

In the late 1980s when fraud in research was much in the air, the National Institutes of Health mandated that every university with an NIH-funded training grant should provide a course for its graduate students about the ethics of doing science. Courses on this subject popped up across the United States, and the subject matter and approach to these issues took many forms. At Princeton University, where I was Chairman of the Molecular Biology Department, we decided to supplement the discussion of ethics, notebook keeping, and life in the laboratory with topics rarely discussed with graduate students such as "How do you choose a research problem when you are first setting up your lab?" We all thought it would be more interesting to pair faculty members with our graduate student class so that they could compare different styles and approaches.

So it was on one Wednesday evening session of this course that John Bonner and I arrived to talk with the students. Clearly, John and I were very different. John had been a Harvard undergraduate and graduate student. He came to Princeton for his first position and stayed to become Chairman of the Biology Department, the position he held when I arrived in 1968. John is cultured and sophisticated and has a broad respect for and knowledge of biology, organisms, and ecosystems. In contrast, I was an undergraduate at the State University of New York at Binghamton where I first saw the double helix. After my doctorate, working with viruses at the University of Pennsylvania, I was a postdoctoral fellow at Caltech carrying out research with bacteriophages. While I was there, I got to know Max Delbrück quite well and benefited from his strong opinions. I was a product of my times, a confirmed reductionist, a lover of model experimental systems, dedicated to the concept of strong competition between laboratories and a seven-day-week work ethic. This is what Delbrück taught us.

John Bonner spoke to the students first. He said he arrived at Princeton in a classical Biology Department and chose to work on *Dictyostelium discoideum*, a slime mold, because the organism had a wonderful and complex life cycle, it was beautiful, the cells in colonies form complex structures requiring cell communication, and it gave him a chance to study whole organisms in their ecosystem. Furthermore, at the time, very few people worked in this area of research and so there was little or no competition. John went on to point out that he had spent a lifetime in this endeavor and he still found it fascinating and filled with wondrous research problems. John indeed had made a big impact upon this field and was well known in the academic community.

It then became my turn. I came to Princeton and had chosen first and foremost to work with SV40 because it was simple, i.e., it had six to eight genes and yet it could

ARNOLD J. LEVINE

Twenty years ago, Arnie Levine led a team that discovered p53, a powerful tumor suppressor that plays a critical role in the progression of many different types of human cancer. For this and subsequent discoveries, Levine has received many honors, including election to the National Academy of Science in 1991 and to the Institute of Medicine in 1995. In 2001, he was awarded the first Albany Medical Center Prize in Medicine and Biomedical Research and, in the same year, the Alfred Knudson Award in Cancer Genetics from the National Cancer Institute.

Brooklyn-born, Levine received a B.A. from the State University of New York at Binghamton in 1961. Resisting his parents' fervent wish that he become a physician or a dentist, Levine went to graduate school at the University of Pennsylvania and was awarded a Ph.D. in 1967. After postdoctoral work at Caltech, Levine moved to Princeton as an Assistant Professor and in 1976 became a full Professor of Biochemistry. In 1979, he left Princeton to Chair the Department of Microbiology at Stony Brook, but then he returned to Princeton in 1984 as the Chair of the Department of Molecular Biology. In 1998, he was appointed President of The Rockefeller University, a position he occupied for four years before moving to his present position—that of Professor of Pediatrics and Biochemistry at the Robert Wood Johnson Medical School of the University of Medicine and Dentistry of New Jersey.

Levine was a postdoctoral fellow when he first met Jim and, as this essay describes, the relationship between them has been maintained for nearly 25 years.

cause cancer in hamsters. I wanted to know which gene caused cancer and how. I chose SV40 because many laboratories were gearing up to work on this model organism, so lots of information would become available rapidly. In the same year, Jim Watson had come to Cold Spring Harbor and hired Joe Sambrook, who set up James lab to work on SV40 and was then joined by Heiner Westphal and Carel Mulder from the Salk Institute and Walter Keller from NIH. In the years before molecular cloning, the DNA tumor viruses provided a system to allow reductionist answers to questions about the workings of eukaryotic genes. What was true for a simian virus in hamsters would lead to understanding cancer in humans. We had grown up in the early times of molecular biology, and all of these assumptions were to us clearly justifiable and maybe even correct.

As the students interrupted us and began to challenge our philosophies, I could not help but realize that John Bonner, the white-collar scientist, and myself, the blue-collar scientist, were replaying the dominant theme happening at many universities. Namely, the replacement of classical biology with molecular biology, with a concurrent real loss of something, as well as gaining a new way to do biology. Ever since 1953 and the realization that the structure of DNA taught us how DNA might duplicate itself and encode information, Watson, Crick, Delbrück, and others captured a generation of reductionists for biology.

I had learned that lesson well from 1966 to 1968 as a postdoctoral fellow at Caltech—meeting often with Delbrück. Two of my closest friends at Caltech, Rolf Knippers and Martin Heissenberg, were German and were adopted by Max. Martin worked in Max's lab and I would get included on occasion in Max's activities and sermons.

Rudy Jaenisch (left) and Arnie Levine (right) at the Genetic Manipulation of the Mammalian Ovum and Early Embryo meeting, Banbury Center, 1984. (Courtesy CSHL Archives.)

I was well prepared then, in the summer of 1967, to travel from Pasadena to Aspen to attend a course in Pathobiology. It had not escaped my attention that the first lecture was to be given by James Watson. I cannot say I remember much about the content of the lecture that day, but after the lecture, about noontime, I went up to ask Jim a question. After patiently waiting my turn, Jim had clearly lost patience with the young crowd around him and he suggested we all go to a bar he had found called Gelena Street East for a beer and a sandwich. We all followed Jim and over a beer, Jim began describing a book he had written about the discovery of the double helix. It was clear that this was a topic Jim wanted to talk about and I recall his particular glee in reciting the first line of the book "I never met Francis Crick in a modest mood." I had a terrific time with Jim Watson in Aspen, and we did eventually get around to talking about science, in particular what were the big questions that needed to be solved.

By the summer of 1968, I had gotten a job at Princeton and set up my lab to study SV40 DNA replication. In the fall of 1968, I was surprised to get a call from Jim inviting me to give a seminar at Harvard. He had seen my published papers from my post-doctoral work on ϕX174 and remembered me. I came to Harvard, had a terrific time talking with lots of people, and gave my seminar at 4:00 p.m. Jim sat in the front row (I was very nervous) and read a newspaper most of the time. I had gotten used to Delbrück's behavior at seminars (he would walk out) and so I went on as best that I could. I was especially surprised when Jim asked a question at the end. I went out to dinner with him at the Harvard Faculty Club and was simply amazed that he was paying attention to me. I learned that when Jim decides you are okay, he is loyal, helpful, friendly, and fun to be with.

During my first year at Princeton, Jim commuted between Harvard and Cold Spring Harbor and set up the DNA tumor virus group led by Joe Sambrook. By the summer of 1969, the first Tumor Virus course was held at Cold Spring Harbor and I was a student in that course. Those three weeks were my introduction to Cold Spring Harbor in the hot and humid summertime with no air-conditioning except in the labs. The rooms in decrepit Williams House were small, damp, moldy and were shared with human and nonhuman inhabitants. But we were never in our rooms. Lectures were given in the morning and evenings by a host of invited speakers. Laboratory experiments were carried out in the James lab all afternoon, with late night visits to take some data points or do cell culture work. My lab mate was Walter Keller, who later joined the James lab group, and it was really good that he was such a talented experimentalist. Jim Watson and Joe Sambrook had the bright idea that the students, in their spare time, would write up the lecture notes and find the appropriate references, and the collected notes would become the first edition of a Cold Spring Harbor publication called *The Molecular Biology of Tumor Viruses* (Tooze 1973). I remember Walter Keller and I struggling after a lecture by Paul Black of Massachusetts General Hospital on the changes in carbohydrate composition of transformed cells. We were clearly DNA-RNA people and did not have a lot of faith that carbohydrates held the secret to our understanding of cancer. But we wrote the first draft of a chapter. Jim refers to this in the Foreword of the book when he is explaining why the book was not published until 1973 stating "If we were to be of real value to many...we [realized] that the scope of the book [should be] widened" (see Tooze 1973). John Tooze, the editor of the 1973 edition, refers to it as the second edition (see Tooze 1973).

At the end of the Tumor Virus course, the first Tumor Virus meeting was held at Cold Spring Harbor. I was invited to give a talk, this time on SV40 DNA replication. I spoke in the evening in Bush Auditorium packed with people, a projector, and a giant screen high on the wall. The pointer was a very long pole and when you held it, even with both hands, the audience could see you shaking. Sambrook started the field out with very high standards, tough questions, competitive juices, and occasional shouting. I noticed Jim did not read his newspaper. Through the years, the Tumor Virus meetings evolved into DNA and RNA Tumor Virus meetings, but they were always highly competitive blue-collar science meetings where postdoctoral fellows got a chance to speak for 12 minutes with 3 minutes for questions. When Cold Spring Harbor faculty or postdoctoral fellows talked, it was clear that Joe and Jim had them practice and they were polished. However, I will never forget the year Yasha Gluzman's[1] postdoctoral fellow somehow slipped through the net of practiced talks. He started his talk by describing the isolation of colonies of cells that he said looked just like a fried egg. He then put up an overhead picture of his drawing of a fried egg with the yolk in the center. Everyone laughed. Jim and Joe who had been watching on closed-circuit TV in the James Library were down at Bush before the talk ended. Whoever that postdoctoral fellow was heard it loud and clear from Jim and Joe that this was unacceptable. I don't know what happened to him but I never saw him in the James lab again.

In the early 1970s, Jim invited me to teach the Animal Virus course and the Tumor Virus course at Cold Spring Harbor, which I did for three years. This was Jim's style—he would select young course instructors whom he liked and trusted. It was a terrific experience for me, with invited lecturers, a lab course, and getting to know Jim and the James lab group. It was exhausting, fun, and very informative, a chance to hear from the best people in the world. Jim commonly came to lectures and my only disagreements with him were over how much money we were spending on parties—he didn't like the idea that we celebrated both the 4th and the 14th of July, but we were quite an international group. One of the summers my wife and children came for two days before leaving for air-conditioning and better food. I did have a hard time explaining to Jim why my wife did not think that a summer at Cold Spring Harbor was a great vacation spot (if you're not a scientist).

In the late 1970s, Jim asked me to join the Board of Trustees at Cold Spring Harbor, and over the years I became the institutional representative for Princeton, Stony Brook, and then Princeton again. On the Board, I saw an entirely new side of Jim. He was bold, had great visions for Cold Spring Harbor, and seemed to have a new project for every Board meeting. The financing of these projects never seemed to trouble him. Either Jim or someone would raise the money. Over the years, this resulted in a tremendous expansion and a truly beautiful renovation of Cold Spring Harbor Laboratory. From the perspective of my first visit in July of 1968, the Laboratory of today is certainly a totally different place. What has remained the same, however, is that it continues to be a center for the molecular biology revolution.

Jim accomplished this because he very rarely, if ever, accepted a "no, we cannot do this" from his Board. Even in the hardest of financial times, Jim led and everyone, businessman or scientist, followed with smiles, perhaps strained. For a while, I ran the tenure committee for the Board when Cold Spring Harbor granted a "rolling five" year contract. Jim's dealings with me in this capacity were similar—Jim knew what he wanted and the best thing to do was deliver it. The Cold Spring Harbor of today is truly Jim's creation.

In 1984, I went back to Princeton University to Chair a new Department of Molecular Biology. In the early 1970s, Princeton had a terrific young Department of Biochemistry. It had grown up in both the Chemistry and Biology Departments at Princeton, and the faculty were split into two different buildings on the campus. Jim Watson led an outside visiting committee to look at the Department and make recommendations to the University Administration. Over dinner the second night, the faculty, the University President, and the Dean of the Faculty met with Watson's committee. Jim in his characteristically blunt fashion told the President that Princeton had "the best young biochemistry department in the nation" and if he did not build us a new building for research, we would all leave. Not much room for negotiation and Jim was never asked to be on this committee again. We did not get a building and everyone left. Five years after I left, the same President offered a new building and the creation of a new Department of Molecular Biology. Upon my return, we had a new building going up and lots of positions open.

After some discussion of which new faculty members we wanted to recruit, we decided to see if Mike Wigler at Cold Spring Harbor would move to Princeton. Mike was a Princeton undergraduate in mathematics and was a terrific researcher. Wigler visited Princeton a few times and it began to look serious. I knew that because I got a phone call one day from the President of Princeton. He told me that a wealthy Princeton alumnus from Long Island had called and wanted to know why we were trying to get Wigler to leave Cold Spring Harbor—he was important to their effort and we should leave him alone. I suspect, but never found out, that Jim was behind this. I asked the President what he wanted me to do. He said "you obviously have the right guy, let's hire him." Wigler declined our offer and stayed at Cold Spring Harbor. I got a phone call from Jim who asked me to come down and visit with him. When I went into Jim's office, he closed the door and I was accused of being a traitor to the Lab. I think I spent about one hour in Jim's office, and if I didn't—it sure felt like it. When I left Jim's office the first person I ran into was Joe Sambrook, who took one look at me and started laughing. Joe said he could tell that I just had a meeting with Jim because he had gone through several such meetings himself and knew what it was like.

I did not go back to Cold Spring Harbor for a couple of years. When I did return to give a talk at a meeting, I was a little nervous about my reception. Much to my delight, Jim and I picked up our conversation as if nothing had happened. It was terrific to hear Jim's latest plans for neurobiology at Cold Spring Harbor and to discuss the beginnings of the genome project.

The career and science of Jim Watson have had an extraordinary impact on the generation of scientists who grew up in the field in the 1960s. In 1953, we saw the structure of the genetic information, and it predicted a mechanism for duplication and a mechanism for information storage. By the late 1950s, the experimental evidence for semiconservative DNA replication confirmed the first prediction. By 1961, new approaches for elucidating the genetic code were discovered, and the second prediction of that original paper was confirmed.

While Jim Watson and Francis Crick clearly gave us the foundation for the revolution in biology, Jim went on to put his imprint upon the style of the science that we would all be doing (this was clearly in evidence in *The Double Helix* [Watson 1968]), and he put in focus the big questions of the day. He molded Cold Spring Harbor Laboratory into a place where scientists learn, meet, and communicate. There are scientists who made a major contribution when they were young and then sat back and enjoyed the impact of their work, but Jim continues his leadership of the field. Anyone who has heard Jim give one of his several lectures of the past ten years on the genome project or evolutionary theory and fat people knows that Jim likes big and often controversial ideas. Anyone who has had a private lunch or dinner with Jim knows that his public statements can be just the tip of the iceberg and that there are many more ideas yet to come.

REFERENCES

Tooze J., ed. 1973. *The molecular biology of tumor viruses* (Foreword by J.D. Watson, pp. xvii–xviii). Cold Spring Harbor Laboratory, Cold Spring Harbor, New York.
Watson J.D. 1965, 1968. *The double helix: A personal account of the discovery of the structure of DNA.* Atheneum, New York.

What I Have Learned from Jim

Bruce M. Alberts

National Academy of Science

You have been called honest Jim; moral, indignant Jim; impatient, excited Jim; visionary, romantic Jim—and even outrageous, outspoken, Jim. For someone seemingly born with the genes for a reticent disposition, you have come an amazingly long way in your 75 years.

A keen observer of human behavior, with a sharp focus on the many fallibilities and incongruities that produce a large reservoir of gossip, you are deeply interested in people. Perhaps that is why you noticed me as a 22-year-old first-year graduate student at Harvard who had attempted, with the overconfidence of youth, to explain the molecular basis for much of genetics. My predictions of mechanisms ranged from the initiation of DNA replication to homologous genetic recombination—all in a paper of about 25 pages.

I had based my speculations on what I had learned as a Harvard undergraduate in Paul Doty's laboratory about DNA renaturation (now known as DNA hybridization) and the structure of single-stranded nucleic acids (Fresco and Alberts 1960; Marmur and Doty 1961). Like all of my contemporaries, I had been inspired by your 1953 discovery (with Francis Crick) of the DNA double helix—a discovery then only eight years old (Watson and Crick 1953). But I had falsely concluded from that remarkable breakthrough in our understanding of living organisms that biological systems would turn out to be not only elegant, but also relatively simple. As a corollary, both my fellow graduate students and I believed that—with some careful thinking guided by a few elegant experiments—scientists should be able to predict all of the basic genetic mechanisms from a few fundamental principles. At any rate, this was the underlying assumption of my term paper.

It is now 40 years later, and biological systems have turned out to be enormously more complex than any of us ever anticipated. Most cellular reactions are controlled by large multiprotein machines whose behaviors can only be dissected through a decade or more of careful in vitro experiments (Alberts 1998). These machines have evolved over billions of years through long pathways of mutation followed by natural selection, and their final structure is partly an accident of history. Thus, although each is a very cleverly engineered device, few have turned out to be even roughly predictable—to the great frustration of two generations of theoretical biologists. Thus, what I first learned from you was both inspiring and somewhat misleading. But your interest and encouragement made such a great impression on me as a graduate student that I still remember the details of our conversations.

BRUCE M. ALBERTS

In 1978, with *Molecular Biology of the Gene* in its third edition (1976, W.A. Benjamin) and clearly a success, Jim Watson conceived the idea of a new textbook designed to integrate traditional cell biology with the ideas and techniques of molecular biology. Among the authors he recruited, all young, none with previous experience of textbook writing, was Bruce Alberts, whom he had first known as a Harvard graduate student. Bruce had been recently appointed a Professor at the University of California, San Francisco, Medical School after ten years at Princeton, where he had become an authority on the molecular analysis of protein complexes involved in chromosome replication. The book he and his colleagues created, *Molecular Biology of the Cell* (1983, Garland), published in its fourth edition in 2002, has achieved iconic status. Bruce was awarded an American Cancer Society Lifetime Research Professorship in 1980 and named Chair of the UCSF Department of Biochemistry and Biophysics in 1985. Since 1993, he has been President of the National Academy of Sciences and Chair of the National Research Council, the principal operating arm of the National Academies of Sciences and Engineering. Alberts has long been committed to the improvement of science education, actively participating in projects such as City Science, for the improvement of science teaching in San Francisco elementary schools; the National Science Resources Center, working with teachers, scientists, and school systems; and the National Academies Committee on Science Education Standards and Assessment.

I was flattered by your reaction to my paper. Your enthusiasm for the then-novel idea that DNA polymerase starts at the 3′ end of a single-stranded DNA template, using a hairpin helix as the primer, led to my attending your group meetings as an outsider from the Doty lab. There I became fascinated with the thesis project of your student John Richardson, who was studying the DNA-binding properties of *E. coli* RNA polymerase (see Lionel Crawford's essay in Section III). John had shown that, even though this enzyme binds to specific DNA sequences inside the cell, it also binds much more weakly to any DNA sequence. Later, this finding would provide the inspiration for the project that I designed for my postdoctoral year in Geneva, Switzerland, aimed at developing DNA-affinity chromatography.

But my pursuit of DNA-affinity chromatography would only come after I had become thoroughly disillusioned with repeated attempts to predict biological mechanisms from first principles. The attempt to confirm some of the predictions in my paper with highly focused experiments formed the basis for my research for a Ph.D. degree. Not surprisingly, these were frustrating years. To guess at a mechanism and then perform an experiment that only makes sense if that mechanism is correct is a low-yield, high-risk strategy for any biologist.

Quite unexpectedly, I failed my initial thesis exam in 1965. This shock, coming after four years of research, forced a complete rethinking of my approach to science. My postdoctoral year in Geneva was delayed by six months by the need to retake my exam. This gave me plenty of time to plan a very different approach to biology. In the end, I decided to try to develop a method that would provide important new information independent of any theory: I would attempt to make a chromatography column out of DNA. This DNA-affinity column would hopefully attract all of the many proteins in a

An early author meeting for the first edition of Molecular Biology of the Cell *at Fort Hill, Cold Spring Harbor, circa 1979. From left to right: Gavin Borden (the publisher), Jim Watson, Bruce Alberts, Martin Raff. (Courtesy of Keith Roberts.)*

crude cell extract that normally bind to chromosomes, allowing me to purify these proteins away from the vast excess of other proteins that function elsewhere in the cell. Studies of subsets of these purified proteins might then lead to a detailed understanding of genetic mechanisms, independent of any speculative theories.

Fortunately for me, you spent your sabbatical in Geneva with Alfred Tissières, who was also my official postdoctoral advisor. Despite your 1962 Nobel Prize, you were very accessible, frequently strolling from room to room to listen to the latest results from each postdoc in Tissières' large laboratory and provide advice. You seemed to believe that my approach was too much like "Swedish science," meaning that it focused on developing a method, instead of being a direct attack on an important biological mechanism.

Because my previous five years at Harvard had been all imagined biology with very little in the way of results, I persisted nevertheless. By the end of my year in Geneva, a promising technique called DNA-cellulose chromatography was born. In 1969, this method would allow my new laboratory at Princeton to discover and characterize the first "single-strand DNA-binding protein," a central part of the multiprotein, DNA replication machine (Alberts and Frey 1970).

In early 1966, on a train from Geneva to St. Moritz for the traditional lab ski week, we all finally discovered what had helped to motivate your sabbatical. Typed copies of individual chapters designed for a new book magically appeared, passing from seat to seat and from car to car. These were draft chapters from *The Double Helix*. Beautifully written, we were amazed by each chapter and couldn't stop reading. I especially remember my delight in encountering your humorous description of the young Josh Lederberg at the start of what would become Chapter 20: A brilliant scientist with the "godlike quality of each year expanding in size," perhaps eventually to "fill the universe" (Watson 1968).

You were unmarried in 1966 and interested in beautiful, intelligent younger women. My wife Betty and I were quite amused to be recruited as escorts in St. Moritz to aid in your search for romance. Betty will always remember how kind you were to her when she broke her leg at the end of that ski week. And by the time my postdoctoral year was over, I felt that the three of us had become friends.

The Double Helix served as a centerpiece for the first course that I taught as a beginning Assistant Professor at Princeton in 1968. By then, your recently published book had been universally acknowledged as great scientific history and it had also triggered a widespread debate about the motivation of scientists. Were we mostly motivated by a search for fame and Nobel Prizes, as some had read into your autobiography? If so, were our motivations no more admirable than those of our contemporaries seeking fortunes in the world of business? The possibility was disturbing to me and to many Princeton graduate students. For years, my annual required graduate school course on "the physical chemistry of macromolecules" therefore began by having the students read and discuss *Priorities in Scientific Discovery* by R.K. Merton (1957) and *Motivation Reconsidered: The Concept of Competence* by R.W. White (1959), along with *The Double Helix*.

From many deliberations of this kind, I have concluded that most scientists are driven by the challenge of solving important problems—and by the deep pleasure derived from the feeling of competence that comes from surmounting them (White's "competence principle"—as also experimentally demonstrated with chimpanzees). This view was derived directly from the challenge of your book, and it has provided me with a critical lens for viewing both science and the broader world of humanity.

Much later, I would discover a brief paragraph that much more elegantly expresses what I finally concluded about human motivation after struggling with the challenge that you had raised. It was written by Herbert A. Simon (1916–2001), a Nobelist in Economics and a distinguished member of the National Academy of Science.

> Man is a problem-solving, skill-using social animal. Once he has satisfied his hunger, two main kinds of experiences are significant to him. One of his deepest needs is to apply his skills, whatever they may be, to challenging tasks—to feel the exhilaration of the well-struck ball or the well-solved problem. The other need is to find meaningful and warm relations with a few other human beings—to love and be loved, to share experience, to respect and be respected, to work in common tasks (Simon 1965).

In the early 1970s, I was appointed to be the Princeton representative on the Cold Spring Harbor Board of Trustees. I was therefore in a good position to follow the amazing transformation that you produced at the Cold Spring Harbor Laboratory as its Director, the position you assumed in 1968. Never satisfied with what you had already accomplished, you continually pushed for new buildings and new scientific programs. Once, when the Board turned down a particularly expensive request, you gave us ten minutes to change our mind. Then you left the room, saying you would otherwise resign. The Board—headed by a distinguished New York banker—of course acquiesced, and the Laboratory continued to prosper with you as its visionary leader.

The same type of stubborn, forward-looking vision—clearly exhibited by your own science and by all that you have accomplished at Cold Spring Harbor—also proved to be critical for establishment of a successful Human Genome Program at the National Institutes of Health. As a key member of the study committee that I chaired at the National Academy of Sciences in 1987–1988, and later as the Program's first Director, you saw clearly what most of the scientific community could not see—that such a special program, if properly defined and structured, would greatly accelerate progress in all of biology (National Research Council 1988).

My many interactions with you have taught me something very important about leadership. Successful new initiatives generally originate from the inspiration and energy of one or a few individuals, not from a general consensus. One can expect that, at the start, any bold new idea will seem unreasonable to most people. Therefore, an unreasonable persistence will often be required to move society forward.

After time passes, and a bold new idea has proven to be successful, most people will insist that the once-ostracized idea had been obvious all along. In this way, we trivialize the entire history of human achievement. And we mislead the next generation of young people into thinking that the only ideas worth pursuing are those that make sense to the majority. Hopefully, the terrific success of Cold Spring Harbor Laboratory's Dolan DNA Learning Center, which you started as a bold new idea in 1987—plus the many related educational efforts that it and other outreach efforts by scientists have spawned for students around the nation—will help to dispel this debilitating myth for the next generation.

I cannot end this brief essay without emphasizing the tremendous part that you have played in producing a new generation of textbooks in cell and molecular biology. The *Molecular Biology of the Gene* appeared in 1965, just as I was completing my Ph.D. at Harvard. How I wished it had come out years before when I was an undergraduate! I might then have understood many aspects of cell chemistry—for example, the logic of deriving the specificity of molecular interactions from the sum of many weak noncovalent bonds—a great deal earlier than I had (Watson 1965). So when you phoned in early 1978 to invite me to be one of your co-authors on a new type of textbook that you had invented—*Molecular Biology of the Cell*—I immediately accepted.

Had you provided me and the other four authors (Martin Raff, Keith Roberts, Julian Lewis, and Dennis Bray) with a more realistic estimate of the time that would be required from each of us to write the first edition of this book, it is unlikely that any of us would have agreed to begin. What was advertised as an effort requiring only two summers turned out to involve an exhausting series of book meetings that required more than 365 12-hour days from each author. These extended over Christmas, Thanksgiving, and many other missed family occasions. But once again, you had it exactly right. The time had indeed come to unify the traditional discipline of cell biology (then based mostly on light and electron microscopy) with the exploding newer discipline of molecular biology (based on biochemistry and genetics). *Molecular Biology of the Cell*, published in 2002 in its fourth edition, will have sold more than a million copies before the fifth edition appears (Alberts et al. 1983, 2002).

Because of your two major textbooks, extending over 40 years, an enormous number of scientists have greatly expanded their view of biology. I include here all of the authors, who have learned an enormous amount about both biology and clear writing through the privilege of working with you and with each other on these important education projects.

To summarize, Jim, I have learned many important lessons from my close interactions with you over the years. First, to expect elegance and simplicity from biological mechanisms (even if the simplicity part was wrong); second, to view the motivations of my fellow scientists as noble ones, based on a search for understanding and a feeling of competence; third, that leadership works best if it is bold and does not always seek consensus; and—last but not least—how to think about biology much more conceptually and broadly.

For my entire generation of cell and molecular biologists, it has been a great ride, and I thank and congratulate you for the many roles that you have played in making it possible.

REFERENCES

Alberts B. 1998. The cell as a collection of protein machines: Preparing the next generation of molecular biologists. *Cell* **92:** 291–294.

Alberts B.M. and Frey L. 1970. T4 bacteriophage gene 32: A structural protein in the replication and recombination of DNA. *Nature* **227:** 1313–1318.

Alberts B., Bray D., Lewis J., Raff M., and Watson J.D. 1983. *Molecular biology of the cell*. Garland, New York.

Alberts B., Bray D., Lewis J., Raff M., and Watson J.D. 2002. *Molecular biology of the cell*, 4th edition. Garland, New York.

Fresco J.R. and Alberts B.M. 1960. The accommodation of noncomplementary bases in helical polyribonucleotides and deoxyribonucleic acids. *Proc. Natl. Acad. Sci.* **46:** 311–321.

Marmur J. and Doty P. 1961. Thermal renaturation of DNA. *J. Mol. Biol.* **3:** 585–594.

Merton R.K. 1957. Priorities in scientific discovery. *Am. Sociol. Rev.* **22:** 635–659.

National Research Council. 1988. Mapping and sequencing the human genome. National Academy Press, Washington, D.C. http://www.nap.edu/books/0309038405/html/index.html.

Simon H.A. 1965. *The shape of automation for men and management*. Harper and Row, New York.

Watson J.D. 1965. *Molecular biology of the gene*. W.A. Benjamin, New York.

Watson J.D. 1968. *The double helix: A personal account of the discovery of the structure of DNA*. Atheneum, New York.

Watson J.D. and Crick F.H.C. 1953. Molecular structure for nucleic acids: A structure for deoxyribonucleic acid. *Nature* **171:** 737–738.

White R.W. 1959. Motivation reconsidered: The concept of competence. *Psychol. Rev.* **66:** 297–333.

On Drawing Molecules

Keith Roberts

John Innes Centre

THE MBoG YEARS

Why the old lady was thwacking me so aggressively with her rolled umbrella was not, at that point, at all clear. Fresh from England, I had just gotten off the bus in front of the YMCA on Massachusetts Avenue. It was a crisp cold day, and I was cheerful, looking forward to some real lab experience at Harvard. And that was when she struck. It was early 1964, Kennedy was dead, Jim Watson had been in the news following the 1962 Nobel Prize, and I had reached the inevitable conclusion that I would never get a

Keith Roberts taking a summer "Rhino" picture, Harvard Biolabs, 1964. (Courtesy of Keith Roberts.)

KEITH ROBERTS

A recurrent theme in Jim Watson's careers as educator, as institutional leader, and in particular—recollecting how the double helix emerged—as a scientist has been an appreciation of the visual. For Jim, the harmony between function and structure, whether it be biological, architectural, or graphic, is both rich and resonant. This is best exemplified in his textbooks, starting with *Molecular Biology of the Gene* (1965, W.A. Benjamin), which changed the publishing landscape by looking, as well as being, unique. The chief architect of the transformation was Keith Roberts, the book's illustrator in its first three editions, who in addition to his work as a scientist and author, is celebrated for his artistic contributions to books such as *Molecular Biology of the Cell* (1983, Garland) and *Introduction to Protein Structure* (1991, Garland). After gaining a Ph.D. in biochemistry at the University of Cambridge, he moved to the John Innes Centre in nearby Norwich where for 16 years he was Head of the Department of Cell Biology. He is currently Associate Research Director and his science focuses on the functional architecture of the plant cell wall. His other interests include science education in schools—he is the founder of the Norfolk-based Teacher-Scientist Network—and his family-owned restaurant, *Tatlers*, in Norwich.

good feel for research at Fison's Fertilizer Research Station at Levington, near Ipswich. A positive response to my impertinent request to come and work instead in Jim's lab before I went to University, seemed heaven-sent. But it turned out that the Brits had arrived in force just before me, or rather their music had. When the old lady did finally stop, I learned not only that I was a degenerate follower of the Rolling Stones, but that mop hair cuts and leather jackets were the very attributes of Satan himself. With hindsight, I realize I should have been flattered.

After one night at the Y, the next day I found my new home, a generous cooperative house in nearby Bigelow Street, and I was now ready to pass between the imposing rhinos on guard outside and find Jim's lab in the Biolabs. I could never have imagined how key elements of my future would be mapped out in the next few months. To start with, I was put to work with Wally Gilbert,[1] learning to pour plates, streak out *E. coli*, and to do β-galactosidase assays. My plates usually ended up with a sprinkling of alien growths, even though Wally's, covered in cigar ash, were invariably sterile. But I got there in the end, and without having to learn to smoke.

I can't really remember the details of how I switched from Petri dishes to pencils, doing drawings for Jim, who was then writing the first edition of his first textbook, *Molecular Biology of the Gene* (MBoG) (Watson 1965). Jim has a great eye, don't get me wrong. I greatly admired some stunning drawings he had just bought by Maillol, the great French sculptor, whose skills as a draughtsman are sadly underrated, and he has since put together a large, eclectic but discerning art collection. Even Jim, however, would admit that his drawing ability fell way short of his talents elsewhere. His solution was to try and get his secretary, Sara Malkames, to do the illustrations. Keen on Sara, I offered to help, since I was also enthusiastic about drawing and just marginally better than her. But Jim, as I remarked, does have an eye, and I was soon transferred nearer to Jim's office, and Sara, to work on the drawings.

The walk from Bigelow Street to the Biolabs was special. Every morning I took a slight detour just to walk through the recently built Carpenter Centre for the Visual Arts, using the S-shaped ramp that rose up and penetrated Le Corbusier's building, connecting Prescott St. on one side of the block with Quincy St. on the other. I still harbored ambitions to be an architect and the pull of this building every morning only just lost out to the pull of Jim's lab. Years later in 1984, Gavin Borden, the founder of Garland Publishing and the man behind Jim's later textbook, *Molecular Biology of the Cell* (Alberts et al. 1983), coincidentally gave me a copy of volume 31 in the Le Corbusier Archives he had published. This contained facsimiles of all of the architectural drawings for this remarkable building.

It was clear, even at my tender age, that MBoG was a different sort of book. Jim's really important innovation was concept headings. These short didactic statements organized the division of the text into bite-sized and digestible sections, each of which needed one or two illustrations to clarify, extend, or illuminate the text. This innovation, together with my youth and naivety, meant that there were no real constraints, and we could focus on the sort of figures that would match the style of the text. I was unaware of how unusual such an illustration program was. At the time, most textbooks at this level relied heavily on two main sources, comparable figures from other books (often directly stolen, but usually modified a tad to avoid copyright problems), and original figures and illustrations from the scientific journal literature, usually relatively unmodified. In Jim's case, there weren't any really comparable books and very little in the way of conceptual journal figures, so most of the illustrations for MBoG were generated from scratch.

It took me a while to develop a *modus operandi*, particularly as the publisher had offered the use of a color, in our case a golden ochre, which was also a radical departure for this sort of textbook. In those pre-digital days, each layer of the drawing, the black, the grays, the lettering, the full color, and the screened color, had to be drawn in enlarged form in black Indian ink on separate transparent sheets, usually Kodatrace. Each of these would then be used to make a separate plate for the printing process. This was a labor-intensive process that was hard to correct and hard to proof, and it was done in a professional New York-based graphics studio, much of it by a skilled and engaging man called Bill Prokos. My job was to generate a single drawing, including the color, which he could use as an accurate template for this production process. I had just gotten into the swim of things on that first trip when it was time to return back home to start my degree.

Jim's generosity and faith made a permanent mark on my life. We all respond and do better when someone believes in you, and Jim has a remarkable knack of getting the very best out of people. I had borrowed the airfare from my parents, and somehow Jim managed to pay me enough to allow me to fly home just before term started, to pay my parents back the loan, and still have a great social life in Cambridge. I explored the area on an old Harley-Davidson belonging to an architectural student in the Co-op house. He never rode it himself, but kept it parked raunchily in front of his window simply to gaze at each day. I had no licence, no helmet, and no insurance. But nothing could spoil the noise and thrill of riding that thing around. It was only years later, back in Norwich, that I finally, and legally, bought a Triumph to rediscover that experience before giving it to my first research student, who rode off to Germany on it with his

Ph.D. Evenings at the Brattle Cinema in Harvard Yard allowed me to get up to speed with the complete oevres of Humphrey Bogart and Ingmar Bergman, an experience rendered somewhat surreal by the tradition that the whole audience chanted the complete script of every movie. The Co-op house, where by this time I had painted two large murals, also organized trips and parties. The Newport Folk Festival with Dave van Ronk, Pete Seeger, Jim Kweskin, and Bob Dylan was helping shape my musical tastes. And Jim came gallantly along to a couple of the house parties, embracing youthful Bohemia in his stride.

My return to start life in Cambridge, U.K. was quite a comedown after Cambridge, U.S., only partially relieved by the frisson of receiving early call-up papers from the U.S. military just before I left. I was on an immigrant visa and President Johnson's Gulf of Tonkin resolution was leading to rapid mobilization for the war in Vietnam. Safe in England, I worked on and off during term time and holidays on the drawings before returning with my girlfriend the following summer to work in the lab again, this time as an assistant with Benno Müller-Hill who, together with Wally Gilbert, was closing in on the *lac* repressor. The first edition of MBoG finally appeared in that summer of 1965. There was of course a party to celebrate, held jointly with Albert Lehninger whose small, lucid text on bioenergetics was being published in the same series at the same time. At the party, I made my first and only attempt to stand on a skateboard. When I set off, I wasn't sensitized to poison ivy, but afterward, at the bottom of the hill, I assumed I was.

THE MBoC YEARS

My involvement with Jim and MBoG lasted another 11 years. I spent numerous holiday periods back in the United States, at Cold Spring Harbor Laboratory, helping to generate the illustration programs for subsequent editions in 1970 and 1976, help that was generously credited by Jim. Now that I had my Ph.D., I was much better qualified to get my head round the scientific concepts and I was becoming more skilled at the conceptual illustrations, particularly as the third edition increasingly covered more cell and developmental biology. But Jim's creative energy never stops and the ink was barely dry on the text of the third edition of MboG (Watson 1976) before he had successfully conspired with Gavin Borden of Garland Publishing to generate a new textbook, one that would take a conceptual approach to the molecular basis of cell biology. Seemingly oblivious that this project threatened financial ruin for his small private business (which, at that point, was publishing the holograph manuscripts of James Joyce), Gavin was seduced. As were in turn all of the authors of what became, after a gestation of nearly 8 years, *Molecular Biology of the Cell* (MBoC) (Alberts et al. 1983).

The illustrations for MBoC were conceived from the outset by Jim as a coherent visual story that would parallel the written text. For the first two editions, published in 1983 and 1989 (Alberts et al. 1983, 1989), we worked under the same constraints as in MBoG—a single color and multiple final separation drawings done in New York—until the digital revolution in printing finally released us in the 1990s. With the third edition came full color and a productive, sustained collaboration with Nigel Orme, a talented local graphics artist (Alberts et al. 1994). Our friendship and collaboration had started earlier, when I recruited him, on the strong recommendation of a mutual friend, to work with me on another Garland book—*Introduction to Protein Structure*, by

Carl Branden and John Tooze (1991). I wanted to get away from the conventional com-
puter-drawn molecular models of protein structure, and Nigel's wizardry with color
pencils had helped translate my sketches into fantastic, evidently hand-drawn structures in strident colors. They created a real impact and he was rapidly co-opted onto
the MBoC team, learning his way around Adobe Illustrator and Quark Express from
scratch, and becoming an integral part of the project.

Jim's first meeting for the authors of MBoC was held at a house he then had on
Martha's Vineyard and the second, at Fort Hill, a huge estate just around the headland
from Cold Spring Harbor (see photo in Bruce Albert's essay). Although his day-to-day
involvement with MBoC declined after that, his enthusiasm for the project and its conceptual basis was crucial. Even on the third edition, he still lined up gamely on the
Abbey Road zebra crossing for the book's back cover photograph (Alberts et al. 1994).
It was Jim who, together with Gavin Borden, established the successful framework for
writing the book. All the writing and drawing were to be done during extended times
when we all lived together communally, doing nothing but talking, writing, drawing,
eating, and dreaming about the book. Various encampments were established for the
process over the years in London, New York, San Francisco, France, Norwich, Woods
Hole, and Santa Cruz, but the base camp was now Bruce and Betty Alberts's congenial
house, an Edwardian artists' studio in St. John's Wood, just behind the Abbey Road
recording studio in London. This textbook creation model is being recreated on Cold
Spring Harbor Laboratory's Banbury Center site.

By the time I moved from MBoG to MBoC, I had assembled a rough and ready but
pragmatic set of five rules of science textbook illustration that had evolved from my
engagement with Jim's work on MBoG. They seem pretty obvious and simplistic to me
now, but it constantly amazes me when I look at the seemingly endless stream of biol-
ogy-related textbooks, how few of them have thoughtful and coherent illustration programs, properly integrating with and enhancing the text. Take color as an example.
Lubert Stryer's *Biochemistry*, a 1975 classic, instantly and very early set the gold standard for clear, simple drawings, with their sparse, intelligent use of pure process colors (Stryer 1975). They are inspirational, perfectly conveying the links between molecular architecture and biological function. Few books have matched this achievement,
and it illustrates my first rule: Illustration programs need to be unified or consistent
throughout the book. This means not only line weights, typefaces, and scale, but also
the consistent use of symbols, for example, for ATP or a ribosome, throughout the
book. My second rule is that a figure should tell only one story, as economically as possible. Readers should get the general gist of a figure within a few seconds with labels
kept to the minimum needed for understanding what the parts or processes are. My
third rule is to pay attention to scale. On the one hand, I like to show molecules
involved in a process, for example, with roughly the right relative sizes. It's not always
possible, but it certainly helps. On the other hand, many drawings and photos are of
"real" things and thus scale bars are immensely helpful in relating schematics or
micrographs to sizes in the real world. My fourth rule relates back to color. Much of
this is subjective, but it contributes to the overall feel and coherence of a text if a clear,
simple palette of colors is used. Don't use color where it's not needed and use the
brightest or strongest colors only for emphasis. (This may seem obvious, but nevertheless the use of color in most recent biology texts in the United States is entirely gra-

tuitous.) My last rule is to think carefully about ways in which figures can do something other than tell a story—link, reinforce, remind, revise, summarize, or just simply add a welcome touch of light relief.

With hindsight, I am absolutely certain I would never have been involved in drawing many thousands of molecules and cells over nearly four decades if Jim had not had faith in me from the beginning. It is also probably true that without the example of Jim's scientific enthusiasms for molecular and cell biology, I would not have made the precise career choice I did.

THE DOUBLE HELIX

I want to move now from the general to the particular, from the diaspora of images of DNA that surround us today, back to just one image, the ur-DNA, the original Watson and Crick drawing of the DNA double helix. This simple drawing in the first *Nature* paper (Watson and Crick 1953) was the first time the world caught a glimpse of the double helix. And bear in mind too that, unless they made arrangements to see the

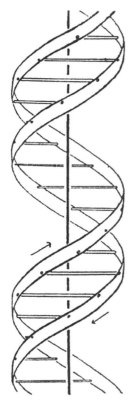

physical model that Watson and Crick had built in Cambridge, this model was all they would see for a year and a half until a more detailed version was presented, as promised, in a paper in the *Proceedings of the Royal Society, A* (Crick and Watson 1954). More or less at the same time, Crick's popular article appeared in the *Scientific American* (Crick 1954) with a photo of their small Perspex axis/wire model. In this respect, it is extraordinary how little was made explicit in a paper that after all was presented under a *Nature* heading of "Molecular Structure of Nucleic Acids." It is also remarkable how little attention this crucial illustration has received; perfect in its context and the basis of all our subsequent ubiquitous DNA iconography.[2]

Indeed, considering the number of words lavished on the history of the DNA discovery, discussion of the drawing is notable by its absence. Jim doesn't mention it at all in *The Double Helix* (Watson 1968) and only recently does he note, in passing, in *Genes, Girls, and Gamow* (Watson 2001) that it was Francis Crick's wife, Odile, who actually did the drawing, probably with input from Francis. As far as I'm aware, Crick has not commented directly on either the drawing itself or its origins, except indirectly in his *Nature* review in 1974 where he says "The structure is produced like a rabbit out of a hat, with no indication as to how we arrived at it. No dimensions are given (let alone coordinates) except that the base pairs were 3.4 Å apart and that the structure had 10 base pairs in its repeat" (Crick 1974). A large version of part of the drawing can be seen pinned to the wall behind the model in the famous picture of Watson and Crick posing with the model, taken for the student newspaper *Varsity* by Anthony Barrington Brown on May 21, 1953, just less than a month after the *Nature* paper had appeared.

DNA double helix from Nature paper, April 25, 1953, p. 737. Drawing by Odile Crick. (Reprinted, with permission, from Nature.)

This tiny line drawing, rapidly produced in the few days while the manuscript was being typed by Jim's sister, has great iconographic significance. Part of its wonder is that the figure just pops up out of nowhere, with no obvious precedents. Only the "demonstration model" existed at the Cavendish, with its cumbersome retort-stand axis and intrusive clamps. Jim insists that their "paper was entirely conceptual" and that they therefore never did do a proper drawing of the molecule, as opposed to the model. Neither did they do an "end-on" view of the helix to show the base pairs because they were unsure of the precise details of the sugar-phosphate backbone, and in any case, this would have required "a commitment to detail that couldn't be made because of uncertainty about the helix diameter. There was a wobble factor of perhaps 18 to 21 Å." With a similar discovery two years earlier, the protein α-helix, things were very different. Here, Pauling and his colleagues presented a detailed graphical representation of a ball-and-stick atomic model, seen as a side-on projection that showed the exact positions of all the atoms and the intramolecular hydrogen bonds. It then took decades before the simplifying genius of Jane Richardson reduced β strands to arrows and the α-helix to a simple flat ribbon. This conceptual simplification was exactly what had been done to the DNA backbones in the line drawing.

So what did it tell us? What meanings could it carry? Surprisingly, for so few lines, quite a lot. The two intertwined sugar-phosphate backbones are shown as flat ribbons around the dyad fiber axis in the center. The line of the fiber axis is not really part of the model, and has clearly come from the central, dominating, physical rod at the heart of the demonstration model, required to support the rest of the structure. It performs a real function in the drawing, however, cleverly articulating which base pairs are behind, and which are in front of, the central axis. In other words, it helps the three-dimensional presentation. Both helices are right-handed. The two backbones are antiparallel, as indicated by the two small arrows. The base pairs are shown connecting each backbone at right angles to the fiber axis, creating a tenfold screw axis. The pitch of the helix and its overall dimensions, while not indicated by a scale bar, can be derived easily from the three critical dimensions given in the text, a Z repeat of 3.4 Å, a radius to the phosphorus atoms of 10 Å, and a structural repeat of the helix after ten residues. In fact, the drawing conveys, in clear and simple graphical form, most of the key points made in the text.

What it doesn't tell us, however, is also revealing. As Crick points out, the key omission is atomic detail, the precise coordinates. Although these were measured from the "demonstration model," there was a vagueness about the angles, with the result that the helix diameter was never very precisely established. Although the figure of 20 Å is stated in the text, the physical model, at least from the photos, looks much fatter, nearer 24 Å in fact, whereas the drawing is clearly thinner with a diameter of 18 Å measured in relation to the stacking of the base pairs. (The clever redrawing, with added base letters, used in *The Double Helix* [Watson 1968] has been carefully recalibrated back to exactly 20 Å.) The base-pair details are not shown either, because more than one way existed for numbering atoms in the bases. It was not even easy to reconstruct them, and to see how they would fit in and stack. It became clear later that in the physical model, they were too far from the axis, and that really there is no room for the hole down the center for the retort stand. In no real sense, however, is the drawing "wrong." The paper, as Watson and Crick acknowledged, was purely conceptual— a hypothesis, an idea, not a result. And the drawing had to balance the presence of the key elements of a new structure, with the absence of enough robust data to pin it all down, as there had been with the α-helix. "This figure is purely diagrammatic... .," the paper exclaims, as the drawing perfectly captures all the conceptual points of the proposed structure in its simplicity.

What exactly is this slight figure—a diagram, a model, a structure, an analogy? It's certainly not a molecular model in the sense of the beautiful van der Waals drawing done later by Maurice Wilkins, and neither is it a drawing of the molecule itself. It couldn't be thrown away once the detailed molecular structure was finally pinned down in the 1980s, since it had residual explanatory power. The whole idea of models in science is complex, that much I did gain from Mary Hesse's lectures on the philosophy of science when I finally got to Cambridge University and started my degree. Her examples were exclusively from the physical sciences, but I feel certain that there are more intriguing and richer examples to explore in the life sciences. The paper was conceptual, and the figure was "purely diagrammatic"—just the same, in fact, as the bulk of the drawings in the textbooks Jim was involved in.

My own view is that the drawing is really a metaphor, a rich and imaginative device with intrinsic meaning quite far removed from the DNA structure itself, yet a central ingredient in the structural hypothesis of the *Nature* paper. It was the very first conceptual drawing of a macromolecule, and it paved the way for all the later molecular simplifications that were needed to make our increasingly complicated codex of structures more accessible. I would love to hear Odile Crick's recollection of how it was all done, and in my view, she deserves a prize too!

REFERENCES

Alberts B., Bray D., Lewis J., Raff M., and Watson J.D. 1983. *Molecular biology of the cell.* Garland, New York.

Alberts B., Bray D., Lewis J., Raff M., and Watson J.D. 1989. *Molecular biology of the cell,* 2nd edition. Garland, New York.

Alberts B., Bray D., Lewis J., Raff M., and Watson J.D. 1994. *Molecular biology of the cell,* 3rd edition. Garland, New York.

Branden C. and Tooze J. 1991. *Introduction to protein structure.* Garland, New York.

Crick F.H.C. 1954. The structure of the hereditary material. *Sci. Am.* **191(4):** 54–61.

Crick F.H.C. 1974. The double helix: A personal view. *Nature* **248:** 766–769.

Crick F.H.C. and Watson J.D. 1954. The complementary structure of deoxyribonucleic acid. *Proc. R. Soc. A* **223:** 80–96.

Stryer L. 1975. *Biochemistry.* W.H. Freeman, San Francisco.

Watson J.D. 1965. *Molecular biology of the gene.* W.A. Benjamin, New York.

Watson J.D. 1968. *The double helix: A personal account of the discovery of the structure of DNA.* Atheneum, New York.

Watson J.D. 1976. *Molecular biology of the gene,* 3rd edition. W.A. Benjamin, Menlo Park, California.

Watson J.D. 2001. *Genes, girls, and Gamow: After* The Double Helix. Oxford University Press, Oxford.

Watson J.W. and Crick F.H.C. 1953. Molecular structure of nucleic acids: A structure for deoxyribose nucleic acid. *Nature* **171:** 737–738.

Education by the Sea Shore

Jan Witkowski and John Inglis

Cold Spring Harbor Laboratory has long been one of the elite biomedical research institutions, and although research remains its primary task, five of its six Divisions focus on science education rather than investigation. All five Divisions originate in decisions Jim Watson made in the 1980s and 1990s to expand and broaden the Laboratory and give specific individuals the responsibility for directing these new programs.

One of Jim's great skills is the ability to select people to do a job, and then leave them alone (by-and-large) to get on with it. This freedom is fun and exciting, as those who direct the educationally oriented Divisions have found, but with it comes the assurance of having to take responsibility if things do not go right. Let there be incompetence, folly, or failure to seize the moment, and Jim leaves no doubt about his feelings. (It used to be said that you hadn't arrived at Cold Spring Harbor until Jim had fired you at least twice.)

Education was the foundation of the Laboratory's humble origins as a summer school for biology teachers. The Brooklyn Institute for Arts and Sciences was founded in 1823 as the Brooklyn Apprentices' Library Association, but as times changed, its mission and its name changed too. By 1890, part of the Institute's purpose was to promote science through further training of teachers. The aims of the summer school were "(1) to furnish a place of general biological instruction and (2) to offer an opportunity for investigation to advanced students." The Brooklyn Institution turned to the North Shore of Long Island as the site for its Biological Laboratory, influenced no doubt by the beauty of the coastline and the gift of land from John D. Jones. The first students were taken in the summer of 1890 and the prospectus offered courses in systematic zoology, botany, and bacteriology. These courses continued into the 1940s (with Experimental Surgery, Experimental Endocrinology, and Marine and Fresh Water Zoology in the curriculum), but it was the Phage Course begun by Max Delbrück and Salvador Luria that established the "modern" era of teaching at Cold Spring Harbor.

MEETINGS AND COURSES

The Laboratory has been the site of the annual Cold Spring Harbor Symposia on Quantitative Biology since 1933. For the first nine years, the topics had largely to do with biophysics, but when the post-War Symposia resumed in 1946, genetics became the dominating theme for the next 20 years. Between 1951 and 1966, the Symposia were the occasions on which the latest data on molecular genetics were presented, and the participants' lists from those meetings read like a Who's Who of molecular biology. Yet despite the success of the Symposia and their importance to the economy of the Laboratory, the meetings program was not expanded almost certainly because of the poor food, miserable accommodations (no air-conditioning), and overcrowded lecture hall, even after Bush Auditorium was built in 1953.

But as Jim Watson pointed out in his 1969 Annual Report, the world of molecular biology had grown enormously in the numbers of scientists and in the range of topics studied. If the Laboratory was to continue to develop as the communications center for molecular biology, Jim concluded that " [it can do so]...only by greatly expanding the number of meetings and courses held each year." He set about doing so with vigor. By 1986, there were 12 meetings each year that filled Bush Lecture Hall to overflowing. In that year, Grace Auditorium was opened, and once again, the Laboratory had an auditorium to match the intellectual quality of its meetings. In 1933, the founder of the Symposia, Reginald Harris, had asked participants"...to give special consideration to theoretical and controversial aspects, that the discussion may be both significant and creative..." As a result, discussion periods at the Symposia are not for the faint-hearted. The front-row seats tend to be occupied by heavyweights who are not shy to ask questions the speaker does not want to hear. Jim used to sit there, but in recent years, he has discovered an alternative place, halfway down, in the right gangway, not against the wall but leaning forward, unavoidable and unmistakable, especially in his favorite yellow sweater. A disconcerting sight, surely, for the less experienced. Pressure from other events means that Jim now attends less frequently, but he still presides over the proceedings through a wonderful portrait by the Australian artist, Lewis Miller, close to the podium, and any speaker who had an interesting tale to tell can still expect to find Jim close by at coffee time with a penetrating question or a speculation of his own.

Meeting participants lounging on Blackford lawn at the Genome Meeting, May 19, 2000. (Photograph by Jan Witkowski. Courtesy CSHL Archives.)

The Yeast Course class of 1982. Gerry Fink is jumping and Fred Sherman is crouching to his left. Jim Hicks is behind Fink's left shoulder. (Courtesy CSHL Archives.)

GRACE AUDITORIUM AND BEYOND

David Stewart, Executive Director of Meetings and Courses

During the 1970s and 1980s the courses taught at the Laboratory increased in number, overseen by Terri Grodzicker,[1] who combined the roles of research scientist and Assistant Director for Academic Affairs. There were 4 courses in 1968 and no fewer than 25 in 1993. That year, it was clear that the meetings and courses program had reached a turning point—there were still some weeks available in the year for further expansion, but management of the program was needed not only on a day-to-day, but also on a long-term basis.

Jim recruited me in 1993 to direct the meetings and courses program and I have continued to enlarge the meetings program and to increase the range of topics by introducing biotechnology conferences in the winter months—now there are almost 20 meetings each year. One of the reasons that persuaded me to come to Cold Spring Harbor was Jim's enthusiasm to reach beyond the confines of Grace Auditorium electronically. When we met in Cambridge in 1994 for an informal interview, Jim was already talking about using satellite broadcasting across the United States and the world. During my first years here, I accumulated a thick file of possibilities, but the technology was too expensive. However, the advent of Internet broadcasting led to the introduction in 2001 of Web-based video archives of the regular meetings and culminated in the live broadcast of a 2003 *Biology of DNA* meeting to more than 50 countries. Jim's enthusiasm for the electronic distribution of meetings' content contrasts with his own aversion for computers. He still writes everything longhand, and it was a day to remember when he gave his first PowerPoint presentation, on June 4, 2003, in St. Louis.

> David Stewart is an Edinburgh-trained geneticist who graduated from Cambridge with a Ph.D. in biochemistry. Before joining Cold Spring Harbor Laboratory, he worked at a small private company in the United Kingdom developing affinity methods for purifying proteins and using rational drug-design techniques to develop synthetic ligands that interact specifically with proteins.

BANBURY CENTER

In 1976, Jim eagerly seized the opportunity to create a new style of meeting for Cold Spring Harbor. The local philanthropist, Charles Robertson,[2] gave his 45-acre estate in Lloyd Harbor to the Laboratory. Instead of building laboratories in such a lovely place, Jim suggested that the estate be used as a conference center for small discussion meetings, along the lines of the Ciba Symposia in London. These meetings are for only 24 invited participants, and the presentations are published, together with edited transcripts of the discussions. The garage for the Banbury estate was converted into the Conference Room, and Francis Crick formally opened the Center in June 1977.

Banbury meeting in session. (Photograph by Jan Witkowski. Courtesy CSHL Archives.)

The first Director of the Banbury Center was Victor McElheny, who had been science correspondent for *The New York Times* and the *Washington Post*. Jim saw that environmental cancer and risk assessment were important topics and, he hoped, likely to attract funds from the National Cancer Institute and other federal bodies. Unfortunately, this proved not to be case; although McElheny held important meetings and published widely cited proceedings, it was not possible to sustain a program as narrow as that originally planned. Gradually, the program changed under subsequent directors, first Mike Shodell, and then Steve Prentis, who came from Elsevier in England to run both Banbury Center and the Publications Department. Jan Witkowski expanded the Banbury program and the Center now holds more than 20 meetings each year on topics as varied as *Genetic Enhancement of Athletic Performance, Green Tea and Cancer, RNA Metabolism and Fragile X*, and *Can a Machine Be Conscious?* It has an international reputation as the place to go to learn the latest news and to thrash out the problems.

THE COUNTRY ESTATE

Jan Witkowski, Executive Director of Banbury Center

After Steve Prentis's tragic death in March 1987, Jim recruited me (also from England but at the time learning to wear cowboy boots in Houston) to direct the Banbury Center. It was immediately clear to me that Jim's flair for identifying important (and often controversial) issues in science, and his unparalleled range of contacts, would ensure that the Banbury Center was an entertaining place to be. One can never quite be sure what will happen when Jim is around. Banbury meetings are closed to encourage communication of unpublished results, and Jim's low tolerance for bullshit is often evident just before lunch. On one occasion, a speaker was droning on, refusing to acknowledge first hints and then direct requests from the session chair to come to a close. At last, Jim could bear it no longer and burst out (I have forgotten the exact words but the tenor is correct): "Shut up, R****, we can't stand it anymore."

The most valuable time at Cold Spring Harbor meetings is the time *not* spent in the sessions. Much communication goes on informally during coffee breaks, and there is the traditional wine and cheese party on the lawn of Airslie during meetings on the main campus. The equivalent at Banbury meetings is the pre-dinner cocktail by the grandfather clock in the lobby of Robertson House. Jim uses these occasions to pin down speakers who have not made themselves clear, or to encourage those whose work he thinks has potential. These must be unnerving encounters for the unsuspecting. All who know Jim know that he thinks a lot during conversations, and when he thinks, he stops talking. It may be for only 10 or 15 seconds, but each second seems like a minute. Encouraging him to speak by offering a word or phrase doesn't help—Jim will respond and then lapse into silence again as he resumes his train of thought. Jim seems to have a list of targets in his mind, and constantly looks out for people higher on the list than his current companion. So, during the pauses, or even in mid sentence, Jim will wheel away in pursuit of someone else with whom he has more interesting business.

Banbury Center was in difficult financial straits in its early years, but Jim's conviction that such a place was needed, together with support from the Laboratory's scientists, kept the Center going. That so many participants say that their Banbury Center meeting was the best meeting that they have ever attended is a testament to Jim's belief in the power of education—in Banbury's case, of scientists educating each other.

Jan Witkowski has a B.Sc. in zoology and a Ph.D. in biochemistry. His scientific research interest was Duchenne muscular dystrophy, and he continues to do research in history of science. He is a coauthor with Jim Watson of the book *Recombinant DNA* and editor-in-chief of *Trends in Biochemical Sciences*.

THE DOLAN DNA LEARNING CENTER

The training program for science teachers that was the foundation for the Dolan DNA Learning Center (DNALC) began in 1985. David Micklos, then the Laboratory's Director of Public Affairs, realized that it was necessary to introduce DNA literacy in the middle school and high school classroom if children were to become adults with the skills and information to make informed decisions about genetic technology. It was clear, however, that traditionally trained teachers lacked what was needed to impart this knowledge, so David developed a curriculum for this purpose. This led in 1988 to the creation of the DNALC, the world's first science center devoted entirely to genetics education of the public, and especially of young people. The Center's national and international impact has been remarkable, and it has been a model for similar programs throughout the world.

Dave Micklos, Jeff Diamond, Greg Freyer, and the DNA Vector Vans, 1987. (Courtesy CSHL Archives.)

An Experiment in (DNA) Education

David Micklos, Executive Director of Dolan DNALC

Jim hired me in 1982, because he knew it was time "to explain ourselves better to the outside world." As Jim Watson is correct in saying, I was hired to do public relations and development, but got too interested in education while he was away on sabbatical in 1984. During that time, I spent spare moments in the Rich Roberts' lab, where I hatched a plan with postdoctoral fellow Greg Freyer to develop a simple set of experiments that would allow high school students to get their hands dirty with recombinant DNA.

By the time of Jim's return from England, we had managed to raise $60,000 to begin to equip six local school districts for DNA experimentation, and we conducted our first training workshop in summer 1985. Jim supported my moonlighting, I think, because he knew it was time for the Laboratory to take the lead in fostering "DNA literacy" among the general public, just as it had led the way with professional scientists. This was a bold move at a time when high-level scientists, here and elsewhere, were expected to concentrate solely on their research.

By the summer of 1986, we had a spiffy "Vector Van," loaded to the ceiling with pipettes, centrifuges, and water baths, which we took on a nationwide training tour that ended at the University of California at Davis. The next year, we acquired a second Vector Van and in summer 1987 held workshops in 14 locations around the country. In addition to the Van, we had equipment stashed at several locations around campus. We operated the fusion of public affairs, development, and education out of what is now the Meetings Office on the main floor of Grace Auditorium.

By this time, it was clear to Jim that the education program had to conform to his dictum of organizational evolution: "You get bigger, or you get smaller." So he determined that we should take over an abandoned school on Main Street and convert it into a DNA museum. Of course, none of us really understood what this might entail, and I braced myself to answer tough questions when this proposal was brought to the Board of Trustees for discussion. But then, David Botstein, the outspoken Professor of Genetics at MIT, rose to champion the proposal—and the scientific Trustees fell in strongly behind him.

Luckily, we had some key support among the Laboratory's local Trustees. David Luke worked behind the scenes to help us obtain a major grant from the Josiah Macy Foundation, while Mary Jeanne and Henry Harris provided the key gift to help pay for the first six-month's lease. Helen Dolan's early participation on the education committee would later result in vitally important support for expansion.

So, in the fall of 1987, we began to renovate the neo-Georgian brick building, constructed in 1925 as the first modern elementary school in Cold Spring Harbor Village. In the following spring, we conducted the first "lab field trips" in which students used restriction enzymes to cut viral DNA and separated the fragments by electrophoresis, or inserted an antibiotic resistance gene into bacteria. Thus, we became the first place in the world to conduct these experiments with large numbers of students. Since that time, more than 100,000 students have performed these experiments at the Center without mishap, proving the relative safety of DNA methods. Soon, I was driving a 24-foot truck back and forth between Washington, D.C., loading and unloading pieces of an exhibit borrowed from the Smithsonian Institution. For a time, I had to crawl on all fours under exhibitry to get to my office. But then all was in place for the official opening of the DNALC in September 1988.

Then, just as I was entertaining visions of grandeur—with me at the helm of three CSH Departments—Jim lowered the boom. At a lunch that has made me leery of business lunches to this day, Jim gave me a choice: "Dave, you can run public affairs and development, or you can run the DNA Center, or you can hand in your resignation."

In retrospect it was lunacy that I opted to give up my nice office in Grace Auditorium for a basement office at the DNALC—moldy, cramped, and subject to periodic flooding from the boy's bathroom above. Within months, I was wondering if I had made the right choice. I was overextended, and Jim matter-of-factly reminded me, "We can forget about you pretty quickly over there on Main Street."

In fact, Jim never forgot about me. He did for me no more and no less than he has done for a hundred others: He opened doors and let me walk through them. And he never took an ounce of credit for focusing me on a vision I could not have seen with my own eyes alone.

David Micklos did a masters degree in science writing before coming to Cold Spring Harbor to head the Public Affairs and Development Departments in 1982. In 1985, he began to train high school teachers to clone genes, and started the DNA Learning Center in 1988. He is co-author of *DNA Science* and *Laboratory DNA Science*, and won the 1990 Charles A. Dana Award for Pioneering Achievement in Education.

THE WATSON SCHOOL OF BIOLOGICAL SCIENCES

For many years, the Laboratory has run a joint Ph.D. program in genetics with Stony Brook University and has been involved in multiple other graduate programs as well. Students do their course work at Stony Brook and their research in laboratories at Cold Spring Harbor. The program is very successful and benefits both institutions, but Jim felt that there was every reason for Cold Spring Harbor to begin its own doctoral program, not least because he wanted to institute a four-year course. The Watson School of Biological Sciences admitted its first students in 1999 and granted its first Ph.D. in 2003.

Watson School of Biological Sciences. Jim Watson (in hat), Winship Herr, Dean, to his left, with staff and students outside Urey Cottage, May 2003. (Courtesy CSHL Archives.)

Educating the Scientists of the Future

Winship Herr, Dean of Watson School of Biological Sciences

It happened one Saturday morning in early November 1995. As I sat on the side of the Plimpton Conference Room dutifully listening to the President's report to the Board of Trustees, I began to focus on Jim Watson's description of his "Vision 2000." He had four goals—one piqued my interest: Cold Spring Harbor Laboratory should establish a graduate school and What! "I think Winship Herr should chair a subcommittee of the Board of Trustees to investigate the feasibility of such a graduate program." And so it was that I began an adventure in which I have dedicated the past seven and a half years to what became the Watson School of Biological Sciences. I marvel to this day at Jim's amazing ability to figure out what makes people tick and to push just the right buttons.

Eighteen months later, the Board of Trustees decided to go ahead with an application to the New York State Education Department for accreditation and authority to grant doctoral degrees in the biological sciences. It then became imperative to actually put together a doctoral curriculum. Here, I was stymied with how to get the right faculty input into its design. I did not want it to all be done at meetings of senior faculty, nor did I want it to become unwieldy. Here, at a meeting, Nouria Hernandez had a brilliant idea. She suggested that I offer an open invitation to all the faculty to attend a series of weekly teas to discuss the new graduate school. In this way, only those who were interested would come, making for productive discussions.

Indeed, it worked out spectacularly well and, owing to the diverse nature of the faculty of the Laboratory—research and nonresearch faculty—having graduate school experiences from around the world, an innovative program was assembled. A first year in which courses and laboratory rotations were separated into different phases was designed, with the initial fall term representing an intensive course curriculum to teach the students scientific reasoning and logic as well as communication skills and ethics. We also took advantage of what the Laboratory had to offer by having the students teach at the Dolan DNA Learning Center and take one-week-long intensive courses taught by outside instructors but at the lovely Banbury Center. And we placed a heavy emphasis on mentoring, particularly by designing a two-tier mentoring program in which each student has both research and academic mentors.

Jim did not come to those organizational teas, but of course he had his input. If there is one defining principle of the Watson School curriculum, it is that it should take no longer than four years to learn how to do science and obtain a doctorate in the biological sciences. And where did that idea come from? Jim, of course! Indeed, I will never forget being alone with Jim in his office—how many of us have had the same experience?—when he wanted to know why he had seen a reference to a four-year to four-and-a-half-year degree program. He made it clear to me that it was a four-year program and if anyone thought differently to send them to him. I never did and from that day on it was always just a "four-year program."

Over the years, Jim has been extremely devoted to the School, which can have its pluses and minuses! Every year, Jim has met with many—in some years nearly all—of the students coming to interview at the Laboratory, often disrupting each student's schedule by spending well over the allotted 30 minutes. And then of course he always had an opinion, with which I generally concurred. My most nerve-wracking times with the School have, however, been when Jim's opinion did not match that of the faculty—me included. He would hound me unmercifully trying to get me to make an offer. But when all was said and done, whether he won or not, we would celebrate together the success in recruiting an outstanding class of students.

And then there is the quintessential Jim in the off-hand hallway discussion. After Cold Spring Harbor Laboratory was accredited to grant the Ph.D. degree in September 1998, I was appointed Dean of the School. At that time, I ran into Jim on the first floor of the Beckman Building and he asked me if I now planned to resign as the Laboratory's Assistant Director. He argued that I would not be able to be both Dean and Assistant Director. At the time, I was unsettled by the discussion. I felt that I was being shunted aside from the mainstream of the Laboratory power center! It was only over three years later that I realized how right he was and I asked Bruce Stillman to relieve me of my duties as Assistant Director. Of course, Jim was on the phone the next day to congratulate me on having finally come to my senses!

Nearly eight years have gone by. Perhaps most special for all of us involved was just last May, indeed May 13, 2003, when the first Watson School student, Amy Caudy, defended her Ph.D. dissertation after about three-and-a-half years in the School. I look forward to celebrating with Jim and all the others who have been involved with this lovely adventure the many more Ph.D.s to come.

Winship Herr did his Ph.D. with Wally Gilbert, with whom Jim had had a joint laboratory at Harvard. He came to Cold Spring Harbor in 1983 for his postdoctoral studies and began research on transcriptional regulation. From 1994 to 2002 he was Assistant Director.

PUBLICATIONS AND COLD SPRING HARBOR LABORATORY PRESS

Publishing at Cold Spring Harbor began in 1933 with the volumes reporting the proceedings of the Symposia and, in a period when there were few journals, many breakthroughs in molecular genetics were announced at these Symposia. The income from sales of the Symposium volumes was an important source of revenue. But with the exception of *Phage and the Origins of Molecular Biology* (published in 1966 as a celebration of Max Delbrück's 60th birthday), the Laboratory published nothing other than the Symposium volumes until Jim became Director in 1968. He arrived at Cold Spring Harbor as an innovative, successful author. He had grown up with books, believed strongly in their importance, and had robust opinions about how they should look, what should be in them, and how they would sell.

Authors meeting at the Writing Center, Meier House. From left to right: Nipam Patel and Nick Barton (authors), Michael Zierler (developmental editor), and Alex Gann (senior editor). (Photograph by Miriam Chua.)

In only his third Director's Report, in 1970, Jim was musing on what the molecular biology literature really needed: a way of finding journal articles easily (anticipating Medline by a year); short intelligent reviews (six years before the first *Trends* review journal); and textbooks containing the newest research, written by young scientists, not out-of-touch teaching professionals. Jim's manifesto for future publishing at Cold Spring Harbor was plain: monographs on topics that also made good meetings; manuals on techniques taught in the Laboratory's courses; books that would excite students; and a quicker way of disseminating information from the Symposium.

In the 1970s and 1980s, the books published from the Laboratory were small in number but hugely influential: monographs that crisply summarized entire research fields and manuals that brought the techniques of the new biology to an ever-expanding community. The 1982 *Molecular Cloning* manual by Tom Maniatis, Ed Fritsch, and Joe Sambrook was a landmark in recombinant DNA technology, selling over 60,000 copies. In Annual Reports throughout these years, Jim reflected on the very real concerns of a small, entrepreneurial publisher: pricing, low or high; controlling costs; enforcing deadlines; reaching breakeven levels of sales. There was rueful acknowledgement that commercial publishers might do things differently. But the same Reports proudly recorded the achievements of the small Publications Department as

---

NEVER AT REST

John Inglis, Executive Director of Cold Spring Harbor Press

By the 1980s, Jim Watson had recognized that with the quickening pace of molecular biology research, journals now had more influence on research than books. The success of *Cell* had shown that a top-flight journal could also make money. Proposals for new journals had been discussed over the years, including an idea of Jim's for a neuroscience journal that would have preceded *Neuron*. But good journals reject many more papers than they accept. Would authors wounded by the editorial process blame the Laboratory—or worse, Jim himself—rather than the anonymous peer reviewers? In late 1985, Steve Prentis came to run the Banbury Center with, in addition, a proposal for a new journal that would focus on the molecular analysis of embryonic development. The project was much debated, but in the end, the financial and social risks were accepted and a plan was made to launch *Genes & Development* in early 1987. The community responded with a flood of submitted papers. Tragically, Steve died in a car accident just as the first issue was being published, and Laboratory scientist Michael Mathews stepped in to become Executive Editor. Very soon came the predicted test: a paper from a towering figure in the field that was outside the scope of the journal. For that reason it was declined, quickly, politely, and without review. Outraged, the author, an old friend of Jim's, immediately called him. The future of the journal hung in the balance. Jim was disturbed but declined to intervene. Its editorial independence assured, the journal flourished. It now ranks among the handful of truly influential journals in molecular biology.

With the Laboratory steadily growing and the prospect of a human genome project on his mind, Jim decided to reduce his very direct role in the publishing program and recruited me to be its Executive Director in 1987. As well as the new journal, the program's output then consisted largely of the proceedings or abstracts of meetings held at the main campus and at the Banbury Center, and manuals from some of the Cold Spring Harbor courses. I was excited by the prospect of expanding this scope and building on the program's reputation for quality.

The Laboratory's conference participants, course instructors, and staff are still the reservoir of potential editorial talent that Jim first tapped 30 years ago. Our audience has expanded far beyond working scientists and also embraces college students, the general public, and children of middle and high school age. But Jim continues relentlessly to prompt and goad, challenging himself and others to think hard about better ways of teaching students and scientists just what they need to know, no more and no less. For the Press editors, lunches with Jim remain entertaining, stimulating, occasionally baffling occasions, filled with ideas for new books, gossip, questions, a sharp interest in the financial details, and always the challenge to do things right.

John Inglis has a degree in Zoology and a Ph.D. in immunology from Edinburgh Medical School. He began his publishing career as an Assistant Editor of *The Lancet*, and before coming to Cold Spring Harbor in 1987 was the founding editor of *Immunology Today* and managing editor of the *Trends* journals.

it grew from a corner of the Nichols Building into its own home in Urey Cottage, producing more books, and selling steadily more copies. Jim's 1976 Annual Report acknowledged the "highest quality advanced books in biology" being produced by Nancy Ford and her staff.

Cold Spring Harbor Laboratory Press was officially born in 1988 as an operating division of the Laboratory. Now housed at the Woodbury campus, and with a staff of more than 45, offices in San Diego and Oxford, England, and an international sales program, the Press publishes five journals, a variety of electronic and online media, and 15–20 new books each year.

LEARNING FROM JIM

Jim has influenced and guided scientific education in its widest range—from high school student to the professional, and in forms as varied as journals, books, courses, and meetings. One thread runs through all this—Jim's apparently never-ending knowledge of not only what is hot now, but what will be enduring. And he has definite ideas about what *should* endure and uses the meetings, courses, and books to inspire the science that makes it so.

ENDNOTES

SECTION I • ORIGINS

Renato Dulbecco—*Phage Days in Indiana*

1   Bacteriophages lose infectivity during exposure to ultraviolet light and are no longer able to form plaques when plated on bacterial lawns. Nevertheless, bacteria infected with a combination of several inactivated phage particles can produce viable offspring. This phenomenon, which Salvador Luria called "multiplicity reactivation," is easily explained today by intracellular complementation and recombination between the DNAs of the infecting phage particles. In 1947, Luria's interpretation was that the phage genome consisted of several discrete pieces that could reassort in bacteria infected with lethally irradiated phages. When Jim joined the laboratory, Luria asked him to find out whether multiplicity reactivation also occurred in bacteria infected with bacteriophages that had been inactivated by X-irradiation.

2   Dulbecco's sharp-eyed observation, puzzling at the time, is now well understood. In bacteria, photoreactivation is the first defense against DNA damage caused by ultraviolet light. The process is catalyzed by a single protein—photolyase—which captures the energy of a single photon of visible light and uses it to split the damaging pyrimidine dimers created by exposure of DNA to ultraviolet light.

3   In the late 1940s and early 1950s, the research groups of Frank Putnam and Lloyd Kozloff, working in Earl Evans' department at the University of Chicago and Ole Maaløe (Copenhagen) used radiolabeled isotopes to trace the origins and follow the fate of bacteriophage proteins and nucleic acids during infection of bacteria. The state of the field was summarized by Kozloff at the 1953 *Cold Spring Harbor Symposium* and in *Phage and the Origins of Molecular Biology* (1966, Cold Spring Harbor Laboratory).

4   The Rover 2000TC was the sportiest of the P6 line of cars produced by the Rover Car Company between 1963 and 1977, a period in the English car industry marked by takeovers, government-inspired mergers, union intransigence, and financial fragility. The Rover 2000TC like many cars of its vintage was elegant, badly put together, and mechanically unreliable.

Gunther S. Stent—*Quiz Kids*

1   The *Quiz Kids* was produced between 1940 and 1953 in NBC's Merchandise Mart studios in Chicago, generally under the sponsorship of Miles Laboratories, makers of Alka-Seltzer.

2   Born and educated in sleepy Adelaide, South Australia, William Lawrence Bragg came to England in 1909 with his father William Henry Bragg, a mathematician, and graduated two years later from Trinity College, Cambridge, with first-class honors in physics. The younger Bragg is most famous for his law on diffraction of X-rays by crystals, a "theory which makes it possible to calculate the positions (of diffracted X-rays) for all dispositions of crystal and

photographic plates." He made this discovery in 1912 during his first year as a research student in Cambridge. Bragg discussed his ideas with his father, who held the Chair of Physics at Leeds and who turned his sons' ideas to practical use by constructing an X-ray spectrometer that could be used to analyze many different types of crystals. The collaboration between father and son, which earned them jointly the Nobel Prize for Physics in 1915, led many people to believe that the ideas were those of Bragg's father—a distortion that gnawed at William Lawrence for many years.

3   William Lawrence Bragg went on to become director of the Cavendish Laboratory, where Jim Watson and Francis Crick, relying on data obtained by the X-ray diffraction techniques that Bragg had pioneered, later worked out the structure of DNA. (For more details, see Phillips, D., William Lawrence Bragg. *Biograph. Mem. Fellows Roy. Soc. 25:* 75–143 [1971].)

4   André Lwoff, the Director of the Institut Pasteur, was to French geneticists as was Max Delbrück to American. Apart from charisma, however, the two men had little in common. Delbrück, quantitative and skeptical, sent his remarkable group of converts and disciples far and wide; Lwoff, an observational and avuncular scientist, gathered his colleagues into the shelter of the Institut Pasteur. Lwoff's most remarkable discovery was to show that bacterial viruses such as λ may exist in a noninfectious form (the lysogenic prophage) that is passed, much like a bacterial gene, from one generation of bacteria to the next. Under certain conditions, the prophage could be induced to replicate and to infect other host cells. Always a social philosopher, Lwoff thought of lysogeny as a form of harmony and lytic replication as anarchy.

As for the other people in *Le Grand Patron*'s attic:

Elie Wollman investigated how genes are transferred from male to female bacteria by using a kitchen blender to disrupt the cell pairs at different times during conjugation. He and Jacob found that the genetic markers of the donor cell enter the recipient in a specific order and hence were able to map the relative location of genes on the donor chromosome.

Alvin Pappenheimer showed that induction of β-galactosidase activity in *E. coli* required de novo synthesis of the protein. *Melvin Cohn* identified β-galactosides which were inducers of enzyme activity but were not substrates for the enzyme. These discoveries killed off any residual notions that induction was due to "adaptation" of the preformed enzyme and led *François Jacob* and *Jacques Monod* to propose a series of new concepts, those of messenger RNA, regulator genes, operons, and allosteric proteins.

5   In 1950, Max Perutz and John Kendrew were having difficulty in interpreting the patterns of X-ray diffraction of crystals of myoglobin and hemoglobin. They had been forced by the power of Francis Crick's arguments to abandon Patterson synthesis as a method to obtain the structure of the proteins; isomorphous replacements were still several years into the future. Under these circumstances, it is perhaps not surprising that Bragg chose to talk about work that was done by Linus Pauling, at a distance of eight thousand miles from Cambridge.

Seymour Benzer—*Some Early Recollections of Jim Watson*

1   Max Delbrück, a rigorous and systematic thinker, nevertheless believed that experiments could (and perhaps should) accommodate just enough flexibility to detect the unexpected. This he called the principle of limited sloppiness.

2   In the 1940s, Albert Kelner, while measuring the effect of temperature on killing of bacteria exposed to ultraviolet irradiation, noticed that spores of *Streptomyces* were more resistant to

killing if they were exposed to light from a laboratory window. A few months later, Renato Dulbecco observed the same effect in bacteria infected with phages that had been exposed to lethal doses of ultraviolet light.

3 Seymour Benzer's own taste in food is highly eclectic, to say the least. Jonathan Weiner, in his biography of Seymour, describes gastronomical adventures in the Benzer fruit fly laboratory at Caltech in the late 1960s:

> Benzer's graduate students and postdoctoral fellows "worked in the middle of the night, rambling from fly room to fly room in Church Hall and sampling—sometimes vomiting—an assortment of snacks; haggis, century eggs, fish lips, all of which Benzer insisted on sharing whenever he and his students paused for what he called "tearing a herring." (From Weiner 1999.)

> François Jacob describes Benzer's lunchtime diet while he worked at the Pasteur Institute. "Every day... he brought some unusual dish—cow's udder, bull's testicles, crocodile tail, filet of snake ... which he simmered on his Bunsen burner."

> At home in the 1960s, Benzer's first wife Dotty watched him eat caterpillars, duck's feet, horse meat, chicken brains, and snails.

4 Paul Weiss was Chairman of the National Science Foundation Board that awarded Jim a Merck Postdoctoral Fellowship to work in Copenhagen.

5 Mary Adeline Delbrück (nee Bruce) married Max Delbrück in August 1941 in Pasadena. Manny has related that Max took one week off from his experiments to get married. He could not wait to get back to Cold Spring Harbor, where they spent their honeymoon—most probably in Room 1 of the Page Motel, to which they returned for many subsequent summers. Manny, a Californian who had grown up in a British environment on Cyprus, could match Max in energy and *joie-de-vivre* and could easily outstrip him in wit and humor. Jim Watson was much taken with Manny, writing in *Genes, Girls, and Gamow* (2002, Knopf) about "a wife like Manny, whose Scottish good looks went well with a free-spirited mind that sought out friends with novel backgrounds and viewpoints."

SECTION II • CAMBRIDGE

Introduction—*Talking and Thinking*

1 Watson J.D. and Maaløe O. 1953. Nucleic acid transfer from parental to progeny bacteriophage. *Biochim. Biophys. Acta* **10:** 432–442.

2 Maddox B. 2002. *Rosalind Franklin: The dark lady of DNA*, p. 142. HarperCollins, New York.

3 Watson J.D. 1968. *The double helix: A personal account of the discovery of the structure of DNA.* Weidenfeld and Nicolson, London.

4 J.D. Bernal and D.C. Hodgkin had obtained the first X-ray diffraction pictures of a protein, pepsin, in 1934, whereas W.T. Astbury and F.O. Bell did the same for DNA in 1938.

Avrion Mitchison—*Jim's Cool Reception among the British Geneticists*

1 Haldane, who visited the Soviet Union in the late 1920s, had by the start of World War II become a committed Marxist, not just in politics, but also in the philosophy of science and in its experimental practice. It was clear to Haldane "that (if we had embraced communism earlier), we should have found it easier to accept relativity and quantum theory, that tau-

tomerism would have seemed an obvious hypothesis to organic chemists, and that biologists would have seen that the dilemma of mechanism and vitalism was a false dilemma." Haldane's commitment to Soviet communism, so complete and all-encompassing at the time of his run-ins with Ronald Fisher, was not to last. After several years of futile struggle to reconcile dialectical materialism and Lysenkoism with Darwinian evolution and Mendelian genetics, he renounced communism and all its baggage.

2   Heinz Hopf, a German mathematician (1893–1971), developed a series of theories about the behavior of one-dimensional dynamical systems. He showed that changing the value of a single parameter can affect a system so substantially that it becomes destabilized. The critical point where the system dynamics change is known as Hopf bifurcation.

3   Jim Watson had had a brush with plasmagenes when, as a graduate student at Indiana, he had written a paper for Sonneborn on the work of the German geneticist, Franz Moewus, who had claimed remarkable discoveries about sexuality in *Chlamydomonas*. Moewus' results could not be repeated and his work was eventually rejected. Av Mitchison's uncle, J.B.S. Haldane, had been the first to be suspicious of Moewus' results.

Francis Crick—*Our Work on Virus Structure*

1   For a recent detailed account of early work on TMV, see *The Life of a Virus: Tobacco Mosaic Virus as an Experimental Model, 1930–1965* (by Angela N.H. Creager. [2002, The University of Chicago Press, Chicago and New York]).

2   George Beadle and Edward Tatum shared half of the Nobel Prize in 1958 (the other half went to Joshua Lederberg) for their discovery that each gene directs the synthesis of a specific polypeptide. Beadle summarized the one gene:one enzyme hypothesis as follows: "Each of these thousands of gene types has, in general, a unique specificity. This means that a given enzyme will usually have its final specificity set by one and only one gene" (Beadle, *Chem. Rev. 37*: 15–96 [1945]).

3   Alfred Mirsky, a biochemist at Rockefeller, was unconvinced of the claim that DNA was the sole genetic material. For years after Oswald Avery's discovery, Mirsky doggedly pointed out the difficulty of assuring that Avery's DNA preparations were not contaminated by minute quantities of protein.

4   Rollin Hotchkiss, who joined the Avery lab at Rockefeller in 1946, refined the purity of the DNA of the transforming factor and also showed that the purified DNA contained transforming genes other than those involved in the rough to smooth transition. Hotchkiss was something of a poet as well as a good scientist. His poem "The Night Before Crickmas" is printed in Section II of this book.

5   In May 1951, Pauling wrote a celebrated series of papers describing the structural motifs of proteins at the atomic level. The most important of these motifs was the α-helix—a helical chain of amino acids held in place by hydrogen bonds (Pauling et al., *Proc. Natl. Acad. Sci. 37*: 205–212 [1951]).

6   Of the 20 or so amino acids used to construct proteins, 19 can exist in left- and right-handed versions, called D and L, that are mirror images of one another. A protein constructed entirely of D-amino acids would be the mirror image of a protein constructed of L residues. However, virtually all proteins synthesized in cells are constructed entirely of L-amino acids and lack mirror symmetry.

7   For a historical review of the early work on virus structure, please see Morgan (*Trends Biochem. Sci. 28*: 89–90 [2003]).

[8] Don Caspar's discovery of the icosahedral symmetry of tomato bushy stunt virus (BSV) was made in October, 1955, based on X-ray precession patterns recorded from virus crystals he had grown in Cambridge and older crystals made by Fred Bawden and Bill Pirie at the Rothamsted Agricultural Experimental Station. Bawden and Pirie told him that (ca. 1948) they had given crystals of both BSV and turnip yellow mosaic virus (TYMV) to Harry Carlisle at Birkbeck College. In November 1955, Caspar went to Birkbeck (where Rosalind Franklin and Aaron Klug were busy with TMV) to search through Carlisle's refrigerators where, to his satisfaction, he found the crystals. Caspar has described subsequent events as follows:

> After I had found these crystals in Carlisle's refrigerator, I met with Rosalind in her new office. I was keen to take the TYMV as well as the BSV crystals back with me to Cambridge to try to establish if TYMV had the same icosahedral symmetry that I had just identified for BSV. Rosalind declared that the TYMV crystals would stay at Birkbeck. She had been considering possible independent projects for Aaron Klug since he had already taken a keen interest in the mathematical analysis of diffraction by objects with icosahedral symmetry following my description of the diffraction evidence I had obtained for icosahedral symmetry in BSV. Analysis of the structure of the TYMV crystals that I had found at Birkbeck was a natural choice for him. In hindsight, it is difficult to conclude how well-formulated Rosalind's ideas were at the time of our meeting regarding the future of TYMV crystallographic studies at Birkbeck, but the bottom line was disappointingly clear to me: I was not to take the TYMV crystals I had found in Harry Carlisle's refrigerator back to Cambridge.
>
> While I was talking to Rosalind, I was leaning with my left elbow on the lab bench where she prepared her TMV specimens. As the prospect of leaving without the TYMV crystals loomed unavoidable, I smelled burning. Rosalind had a Bunsen burner on her lab bench with a small pilot light, to avoid having to relight it every time she needed to use it to seal a TMV specimen. I had leaned my shoulder over this burner and was burning a neat hole in the sleeve of my jacket—the jacket of the new charcoal grey suit I had just purchased in Cambridge and was wearing for the first time. By time I returned to Cambridge that evening, I was in a foul mood.
>
> Don Caspar, personal communication

[9] In the early 1950s, Lady Adrian was a Justice of the Peace and presided over a court in Cambridge dealing with minor infractions of the law. She was a descendant of the philosopher David Hume and was the wife of Edgar Douglas Adrian who shared a Nobel Prize with Sherrington for work on transmission of nerve impulses.

Gerald Roland Pomerat—*One Day in the Cavendish (April 1, 1953)*

[1] Watson J.D. 1968. *The double helix: A personal account of the discovery of the structure of DNA.* Atheneum, New York; Crick F.H.C. 1988. *What mad pursuit: A personal view of scientific discovery.* Basic Books, New York.

[2] Kohler R.E. 1991. *Partners in science: Foundations and natural scientists 1900–1945.* University of Chicago Press, Illinois.

[3] Warren Weaver was a physicist and mathematician who in 1932 took charge of the Rockefeller Foundation's Natural Sciences Division. The Foundation's earlier interests were primarily in medicine and public health, but about 1930, it began substantial funding of the sciences. Weaver coined the term"molecular biology" to describe the programs that he initiated at the Foundation.

[4] de Chadarevian S. 2003. The making of an icon. *Science* **300:** 255–257.

[5]   Bragg W.L., Kendrew J.C., and Perutz M.F. 1950. Polypeptide chain configurations in crystalline proteins. *Proc. Roy. Soc. A* **203:** 321–357.

[6]   Phillips D. 1971. William Lawrence Bragg. *Biograph. Mem. Fellows Roy. Soc.* **25:** 75–143.

[7]   Todd A. 1990. A recollection of Sir Lawrence Bragg. In *The Legacy of Sir Lawrence Bragg* (ed. J.M. Thomas and D. Phillips), pp. 95–96. The Royal Institution of Great Britain, London.

[8]   Kemp M. 2003. The *Mona Lisa* of modern science. *Nature* **421:** 416–420.

Sydney Brenner—*Jim and Syd*

[1]   In 1953, Brenner was doing his D.Phil. with Sir Cyril Norman Hinshelwood in the Physical Chemistry Laboratory at the University of Oxford. Hinshelwood, a chemist who won the 1956 Nobel Prize for Chemistry, was interested in tackling biological topics, e.g., bacterial growth, as problems in chemical kinetics, a strategy that did not find much favor with bacteriologists. This was not the sort of research that Brenner wanted to do, but he nevertheless completed his doctorate in 1954. Brenner drove to Cambridge in April, 1953, to see the DNA model (Brenner S., *My Life in Science* [2001, BioMed Central, London]).

[2]   Brenner and Francis Crick were colleagues for many years in the MRC Laboratory of Molecular Biology, Cambridge, and worked closely together until Crick went to the Salk Institute, La Jolla, in 1977. They are now reunited—Brenner has been Distinguished Research Professor at the Salk Institute since 2000.

[3]   Boris Ephrussi was a French geneticist who was interested in developmental and biochemical genetics. He and George Beadle carried out early work—linking the synthesis of pigments in the *Drosophila* eye to particular mutations—that led to Beadle and Tatum developing the one enzyme:one gene theory. Ephrussi also carried out important research in yeast genetics, in particular studies of the *petite* mutants caused by mutations in mitochondrial DNA.

[4]   Princess Margaret, Queen Elizabeth's sister, was well known for her colorful life and was the least likely of all the Royal family to feel the need for a scientific advisor.

[5]   Melina Mercouri was a Greek actress who starred in many films. She is best known for her portrayal of a vivacious prostitute in *Never on Sunday*, directed by her husband, Jules Dassin. She protested the military takeover of Greece in 1966 and was stripped of her Greek citizenship. When democracy returned, she was elected to the Greek Parliament and became Minister of Culture and Sciences. Jules Dassin films included *Rififi*, a classic heist film. His directing career suffered a severe setback during the 1950s after he was accused of being a communist and was blacklisted by Hollywood. He went to live and work in France.

[6]   Alan Hodgkin shared the 1963 Nobel Prize in Physiology or Medicine with his colleague Andrew Huxley for their work on nerve conduction using single giant axons from the squid. His and Huxley's names are enshrined in the Hodgkin-Huxley equations that describe the ion fluxes during the propagation of an action potential. (The third recipient of the 1963 Nobel Prize was John Eccles.)

1953 SYMPOSIUM

[1]   Lawrence Bragg, Director of the Cavendish Laboratory.

[2]   In the early to middle 1950s, Aaron Bendich (1917–1979) worked on chromatographic fractionation of purified DNAs used to transform *Haemophilus*.

3 Erwin Chargaff and his colleagues found "regularities" in the base composition of DNA, which "reflected the existence in all DNA preparations of certain structural principles." In particular, for double-stranded DNA, they showed that the ratios of A:T and G:C were close to unity, independently of the species of origin of DNA. This discovery, which became the first of Chargaff's four "parity rules," was essential for the development of the double-helix model of DNA.

4 Leo Szilard (1898–1964) was a Hungarian physicist who developed the theory of nuclear chain reactions and later campaigned for nuclear disarmament. For a few years in the early 1950s, Szilard ran a biology laboratory at the University of Chicago and published papers on phenotypic mixing in bacteriophages.

SECTION III • CAREER SCIENTIST

James D. Watson—*Remembering Delbrück*

1 Emory Ellis ran a bacteriophage laboratory at Caltech in the late 1930s. It was here that Delbrück learned to work with bacteriophages. He and Ellis carried out a crucial study, "the one-step growth experiment," which established that growth of phage involved three processes: adsorption, growth within the infected bacterium, and finally, lysis of the bacterium with concomitant release of progeny phages (Ellis and Delbrück, The growth of bacteriophage. *J. Gen. Physiol. 22:* 365–384 [1939]). Delbrück later described bacteriophages as "a fine playground for serious children with ambitious questions" (Delbrück M., Experiments with bacterial viruses [bacteriophages]. *Harvey Lect. 41:* 161–187 [1946]).

Alexander Rich—*Does DNA Form a Double Helix?*

1 Francis had completed his long-delayed Ph.D. thesis and was spending a postdoctoral year working on the three-dimensional structure of ribonuclease with David Harker at the Polytechnic Institute of Brooklyn.

2 Max Perutz has described his emotions when he first saw the result of introducing a heavy atom (mercury) into a crystal of hemoglobin:

> As I developed my first X-ray photograph of mercury haemoglobin my mood altered between sanguine hopes of immediate success and desperate forebodings of all possible causes of failure. I was jubilant when the diffraction spots appeared in exactly the same position as in the mercury-free protein, but with slightly altered intensity, exactly as I had hoped. (Perutz M.F., *Protein Structure: New Approaches to Disease and Therapy* [1992, Freeman, New York].)

3 In the spring of 1954, George Gamow, with help from Jim Watson, set up the RNA Tie Club to promote the exchange of ideas and information about the genetic code. Jim suggested that the membership should be limited to 20, one for each amino acid. Gamow was alanine, Jim proline, Crick tyrosine, Brenner valine, and Rich arginine. Gamow designed a tie which Jim then had made by a haberdasher in Los Angeles. Gamow wrote to Jim in great glee in November saying the tie was wonderful and he would wear it at the next meeting of the National Academy of Sciences. Other regalia included a tie pin emblazoned with a three letter abbreviation of the bearer's amino acid. The Club had its own letter head and slogan ("Do or die, or don't try"), and the officers included Optimist (Jim), Pessimist (Crick), and Lord Privy Seal (Rich). Others, whose membership in the Club is more puzzling, included Edward Teller (leucine), Richard Feynman (glycine), and Erwin Chargaff (lysine). Several important papers were circulated to members, including Crick's Adaptor Hypothesis. For more details, see J.D. Watson, *Genes, Girls, and Gamow* (2002, Knopf).

4   Christa Mayr, the elder daughter of Ernst and Gretel Mayr. For more information about Jim's relationship with Christa Mayr, see J.D. Watson, *Genes, Girls, and Gamow* (2002, Knopf).

5   Severo Ochoa and Arthur Kornberg shared the 1959 Nobel Prize in Physiology or Medicine for the discovery of enzymes that catalyzed the synthesis of nucleic acids. However, the Ochoa/Grunberg-Manago enzyme had rather unusual properties. Not only did it use diphosphates as substrates, but it did not need a template and could catalyze the synthesis of an RNA when only one ribonucleoside diphosphate was provided as substrate. Instead of a template-dependent RNA polymerase, the enzyme eventually turned out to be polynucleotide phosphorylase, which usually catalyzes the breakdown of RNA rather than its synthesis.

6   Peter J. Pauling, son of Linus, was a lecturer in physical chemistry in the Department of Chemistry at University College London from 1958 to 1989. He died April 23, 2003, in his 72nd year.

7   Julian Huxley (1887–1975) was a prolific essayist, committed evolutionist, prominent atheist, and the brother of the novelist Aldous Huxley. His paternal grandfather was the biologist T.H. Huxley. After graduating from Oxford, Julian Huxley taught at Rice University, Houston, but returned to England during World War I. He was the first director of UNESCO and a founder of the World Wildlife Fund. For further information, see C.K. Waters and A. van Helden, eds., *Julian Huxley—Biologist and Statesman* (1992, Rice University).

Joan Steitz—*Flowers and Phage*

1   In 1956, Alfred Gierer and Gerhard Schramm were one of three groups of scientists to provide definitive proof that the RNA of Tobacco Mosaic Virus is autonomously infective. This was the first evidence that RNA was not just a passive intermediary between DNA and protein but was capable of self-replication and of storing genetic information independently of DNA. For more details on the discovery of infectivity of TMV RNA, see A.N.H. Creager, *The Life of a Virus: Tobacco Mosaic Virus as an Experimental Model, 1930–1965* (2002, University of Chicago Press).

2   The idea that a short-lived courier molecule was required to transpose the information in genes into protein originated the late 1950s in *le Grand Patron*'s (André Lwoff's) attic at the Institut Pasteur. The conventional wisdom of the day dictated that ribosomes were preprogrammed to synthesize specific proteins. However, the Paris group with Art Pardee had obtained results that could best be explained if a labile RNA ferried information from the gene to uncommitted ribosomes. The crucial experiments to confirm the messenger RNA hypothesis were carried out in Matt Meselson's lab at Caltech and Jim Watson's lab at Harvard. Both laboratories were able to show that bacteria contained a new class of RNA molecules that were rapidly synthesized, became associated with ribosomes, and then were rapidly degraded. Wally Gilbert has described how the Harvard experiment was done:

> We sought an unstable intermediate molecule that could carry the information from DNA to the cytoplasmic factories, the ribosomes, which synthesized the proteins. The three of us [Francois Gros, Wally Gilbert, and Jim Watson (holding the stopwatch)] did the experiments together—one shaking a large flask of bacteria, one holding the stopwatch, and one pouring in 20 mC of radioactive phosphate to label the RNA for 20 seconds before the litres of culture were poured over ice. We worked day and night throughout the summer. We were seeking an elusive target, which many people did not believe existed, and which we would often compare, when speaking to each other, to the search for the neutrino. (Gilbert, *Nature 421:* 315–316 [2003].)

The experiments in Pasadena were finished sooner than those in Harvard and were perhaps more elegant. In today's climate, they would certainly be published first. However, in the early 1960s, friendship and camaraderie were more important than they now are, and Jim was able to persuade the Pasadena group to delay publication. Both papers appeared together in *Nature* a few months later (Brenner et al., *Nature 190:* 576–581 [1961]; Gros et al., *Nature 190:* 581–586 [1961]).

3   Walter Paranchych isolated R17 from the sewage of Philadelphia (Paranchych and Graham, *J. Cell. Comp. Physiol. 60:* 199 [1962]).

4   The Brouhaha between Nathan Pusey and Jim was caused by *The Double Helix*. Originally, Jim intended that the book would be published by Harvard University Press. But, on reading the manuscript, the Press decided that it would be wise to obtain the written consent of people who might feel that they, their colleagues, or relatives had been harshly treated by Jim. These people turned out to include Francis Crick, Rosalind Franklin's family, Maurice Wilkins, and most unfortunately for Jim, Linus Pauling. It was Pauling's outraged letter to Pusey that led to Harvard's decision not to publish the book and to the ensuing and long-running contretemps between Pusey and Jim.

Benno Müller-Hill—*On the Edge: My Time in Jim Watson's Lab*

1   By the end of 1961, Jacob and Monod, like Benno Müller-Hill, had concluded that the repressor must be a protein. "The RNA repressor was based on completely stupid reasons" said Jacob. Looking back a few years later, Monod said "the repressor couldn't be anything other but protein...because of its capacity to recognize structures" (H.F. Judson, *The Eighth Day of Creation: Makers of the Revolution in Biology* [expanded edition], p. 546. [1996, Cold Spring Harbor Laboratory Press, Cold Spring Harbor, New York]).

2   The repressor eluded capture by biochemists for so long because it is present in such meager amounts. Normally, only about 10 molecules of the protein are present in each bacterial cell.

3   *lacI* is the gene in *E. coli* that encodes the Lac repressor. The *lacI* mutants isolated by Benno Müller-Hill specifically block translation of full-length repressor protein. In the absence of active repressor, the cells express the *lac* genes constitutively.

4   The repressor controls the expression of a group of genes concerned with transport and metabolism of the sugar lactose. In the absence of lactose, the repressor binds to a target region of DNA (the operator) and prevents expression of the genes. In the presence of an inducer such as lactose or a molecule with a similar shape, the repressor is remolded into a form that can no longer bind to DNA. Two good ideas enabled Gilbert and Müller-Hill to isolate the repressor: They used a mutant form of the repressor that bound the inducer more tightly, and they used a radioactive inducer (IPTG) to search for the repressor in extracts of bacteria. As Müller-Hill and Gilbert had hoped, the mutant repressor snared the inducer in a tight embrace, and the radioactivity, acting like a sonar beacon, allowed them to purify the IPTG:repressor complex from the mixture of cell proteins.

5   The experiment could not work in the absence of CAP/CRP protein, which guides RNA polymerase to the "correct" promoter site for initiation of transcription.

6   A λ lysogenic strain of *E. coli* that overexpresses Lac repressor.

7   The book, *Genes, Girls, and Gamow* is published in the United States by Alfred Knopf (2002). It had been previously published in slightly different form in the United Kingdom by Oxford University Press (2001).

8   Charles Davenport became Director of the Biological Laboratory at Cold Spring Harbor in 1898 and immediately began to build a minor scientific empire. In 1904, he persuaded the

Carnegie Institution of Washington to establish a Station for Experimental Evolution there, adjacent to the Biological Laboratory grounds, with Davenport as Director. The Carnegie scientists studied heredity and breeding. By 1910, Davenport's interest had shifted to human genetics. In a classic case of tragically misinformed science, Davenport established the Eugenics Record Office at Cold Spring Harbor, again with himself as Director.

Alfred Tissières—*When Ribosomes Were King*

[1] The Molteno Institute, in the Center of Cambridge, near the Cavendish Laboratory was established in 1921 to carry out Research in Parasitology. The Molteno family, who paid for the new building, were farmers in South Africa with an interest in animal diseases. In 1953, the work of the Institute had expanded to include plant viruses, under the direction of Roy Markham, a biochemist who specialized in viral nucleoproteins. Markham was the person to whom Jim Watson was formally assigned during his time in Cambridge. Salvador Luria used Markham's name to persuade Paul Weiss, the Chairman of the Merck Fellowship Board, that Jim was moving to Cambridge (specifically, to the Molteno) to continue his biochemical studies rather than to work exclusively on the structure of DNA. Markham acquiesced willingly in the charade. Nevertheless, Roy Markham was the person to whom Jim turned for advice in late January 1953, when details of the Pauling-Corey triple-stranded model of DNA became available. Markham, to Jim's great relief, confirmed that Pauling had made a disastrous error—the phosphates were not ionized as they must be for DNA be an acid.

[2] This work culminated in 1959, when Alfred Tissières and Jim showed that ribosomes consist of two components, one heavier than the other (Tissières et al., *J. Mol. Biol. 1:* 221–233 [1959]).

[3] What Alfred Tissières does not mention is his important role in establishing reliable cell-free protein synthesizing systems. In the summer of 1959, at a Gordon conference, he heard about Paul Zamecnik and Mahlon Hoagland's success at Massachusetts General Hospital in establishing these systems and wanted to use them to test whether his ribosome preparations were functional. Tissières and David Schlessinger found that cell-free systems made according to Zamecnik's protocol were unreliable, and they set about optimizing the preparation. From their earlier work, they knew that low concentrations of Mg^{2+} were required to hold ribosomes together. So, by the simple expedient of optimizing the Mg^{2+} concentration, Tissières, Schlessinger, and François Gros were able to generate preparations that worked reproducibly with high efficiency (Tissières et al., *Proc. Natl. Acad. Sci. 46:* 1450–1463 [1960]). It was their preparations rather than Zamecnik's that Marshall Nirenberg and Johann Matthaei used in their classic experiments to crack the genetic code.

Lionel V. Crawford—*It Smells Right...*

[1] The Shope papillomavirus causes giant skin tumors, which on the faces of cottontail rabbits can look like horns or beards. The particular batch of papillomas used by Jim Watson and John Littlefield were collected by Earl Johnson, a rabbit hunter, in the harsh Kansas winter of 1958–1959. The Watson and Littlefield paper, published in 1960, shows that double-stranded DNA extracted from the purified viral particles consisted of two components that sediment at different rates. Jim and John Littlefield drew the logical conclusion that the virus preparation must contain DNA of two different sizes, and they speculated that the smaller component might be derived from defective viral particles. Although their observations were accurate, their conclusions were wrong. Shope papillomavirus contains only one DNA

molecule that can exist in two forms: a closed-circular, supercoiled molecule that sediments rapidly, and a nicked circular slower-sedimenting form. In the 1960s, the Crawfords (Lionel and Elizabeth) worked imaginatively and intelligently for several years on the physical properties and structure of the two forms of circular DNA. However, as Lionel points out, it was Jerry Vinograd's group at Caltech that finally worked out the relationship between hydrodynamic behavior and topological properties of supercoiled DNA.

2 Keith Porter moved from The Rockefeller University in 1961 to become Chair of the Biology Department at Harvard. A diminutive man, he was one of the giants of cell biology and established standards for how electron microscopy should be done. It reflects highly on Elizabeth Crawford's skills as an electron microscopist that she was allowed to use one of Porter's precious instruments. It might also have helped that she had worked at the Cavendish. Keith Porter died in 1997 at the age of 84.

3 Julian Davies was born in Wales and still retains a dilute Welsh accent. Trained as an organic chemist, he switched to molecular microbiology in 1962 when he joined Harvard Medical School. During a long career in both academia and industry, his research has focused on various aspects of microbial ecology, chiefly on studies of antibiotics, and antibiotic resistance. He was elected as a Fellow of the Royal Society in 1994. Davies was a frequent visitor to Cold Spring Harbor in the late 1960s and early 1970s and was famously the organizer of a protest march that went wrong (see Jeffrey Miller's essay in Section III).

4 John Richardson was a Ph.D. student with Jim Watson, working on factors involved in termination of transcription of prokaryotic genes.

Edward O. Wilson—*Excerpt from* Naturalist

1 Francis Crick, in his book *What Mad Pursuit* (1988, Basic Books) tells an anecdote about the use of Watson-Crick.

> Fortunately, people...recall that there are two characters called Watson and Crick [but] are not sure which is which. Many's the time I've been told by an enthusiastic admirer how much they enjoyed my book—meaning, of course, Jim's. By now, I've learned that its better not to try to explain. An even odder incident happened when Jim came back to Cambridge to work in 1955. I was going to work in the Cavendish and found myself walking with Neville Mott, the new Cavendish Professor. "I'd like to introduce you to Watson," I said, "since he's working in your lab." He looked at me in surprise. He said "Watson? I thought your name was Watson-Crick."

Jeffrey H. Miller—*Growing Up Around Jim*

1 Paula De Lucia and John Cairns isolated *polA* mutants that grew normally under conditions where DNA polymerase I was nonfunctional. They concluded that DNA polymerase I is not the primary enzyme required for DNA replication in *E. coli* (De Lucia and Cairns, *Nature 224:* 1164–1166 [1969]). See "DNA Synthesis and the Case of the Missing Enzyme" (p. 303) in *Illuminating Life* by J.A. Witkowski (2000, Cold Spring Harbor Laboratory Press).

Mark Ptashne—*Seems Simple, Very Hard to Do*

1 Don Wiley and Steve Harrison, distinguished structural biologists, were studying the complex viral structures used by influenza, AIDS, ebola, and herpes simplex viruses to bind to cell surfaces and enter cells.

Paul Doty—*Watson at Harvard (1956–1976)*

[1] James Bryant Conant, a chemist and President of Harvard University (1933–1953), was responsible for the organization of the nation's civilian scientific effort in the development of new weapons in World War II.

[2] Carl and Gerty Cori received the 1947 Nobel Prize for Physiology or Medicine for their work on the biochemical pathway by which glycogen is broken down into glucose in liver and muscle. As part of this work, they also elucidated the molecular defects underlying a number of genetically determined glycogen storage diseases.

[3] Edwin Cohn, who died in 1953, worked together with John Edsall at Harvard Medical School on the solubility of proteins in various media, on their sizes and shapes, and on their molecular changes under various conditions.

[4] Konrad Bloch shared the 1964 Nobel Prize in Physiology or Medicine for discoveries concerning the mechanism and regulation of the metabolism of cholesterol and fatty acids.

[5] Frank Westheimer, a physical organic chemist, invented molecular mechanics and photoaffinity labeling and pioneered the application of pseudorotation to phosphate ester chemistry.

[6] George Wald, a Professor of Biology, had been on the Harvard faculty since 1935. In 1967, he was to share the Nobel Prize for Physiology or Medicine for his work on the role of vitamin A in vision. Once a hero to many students for his passionate opposition to the Vietnam War, Wald, in the 1970s, became a vocal, and at times illogical, contributor to the debate on recombinant DNA.

[7] John Edsall's expertise was in the chemistry and structure of blood and muscle proteins.

[8] McGeorge Bundy was National Security Adviser, first to President Kennedy and later to Lyndon Baines Johnson. As President of the Ford Foundation, he facilitated a large grant for the founding of the Center for Science and International Affairs, established by Paul Doty.

[9] Fritz Lipmann's discovery of coenzyme A explained how it could be transmitted through the cell in the form of a label, activated 2-carbon compound (acetyl-coA). For this work, he shared the 1953 Nobel Prize in Physiology or Medicine with the English biochemist Hans Krebs. Lipmann had emigrated to the United States in 1939, working first at Cornell, then Harvard, and then Massachusetts General Hospital (Boston) (1941–1957). In 1957, he moved to The Rockefeller University, continuing research on high-energy phosphate compounds, until his death in 1986.

[10] Ernst Mayr is best known for clarifying how a new species forms and adapts to changes in its environment. A winner of the Crafoord Prize, he has been described as "the greatest living evolutionary biologist."

[11] The 35th annual *Confidential Guide*, which contains students' assessments of faculty performance says of Jim Watson:

> Watson in spite of a soft highpitched voice that could barely be heard, received unanimously favorable comments. His precise lectures included valuable points not found in the readings with regard to contemporary biological research.

The following year, Watson warned students in the Bio2 class "that if they were looking for a thorough, well-organized biology course, they had better look elsewhere." The 38th Confidential Guide states "Watson, who has yet to master the art of speaking clearly and loudly, had a lot to say, and delivered what were generally considered the ten most valuable lectures in the course. Last year's audience urged that future listeners be sure to get in the first two rows when Watson approaches the podium."

12 Paul Levine, who worked on *Chlamydomonas*, was one of a group whose interests were cellular rather than organismic.

13 Wally Gilbert taught theoretical physics at Harvard from 1956 to 1964, when he was appointed as an Associate Professor of Biophysics. In the mid 1970s, he and Alan Maxam developed a method of DNA sequencing that relied on base-specific chemical cleavage. For this, Gilbert shared the 1980 Nobel Prize for Chemistry with Fred Sanger and Paul Berg.

14 Trained in physics and chemistry (with Linus Pauling at Caltech), Matthew Meselson, together with Frank Stahl, used equilibrium density centrifugation to show that the replication of DNA is semiconservative. For details, see Frederic Lawrence Holmes, *Meselson, Stahl and the Replication of DNA: A History of "The Most Beautiful Experiment in Biology"* (2001, Yale University Press). Since 1963, Meselson has been concerned with chemical and biological defense and arms control (see M. Meselson, ed. *Chemical Weapons and Chemical Arms Control.* [1978, Carnegie Endowment for International Peace]).

15 David Hubel, an expert in information processing in the visual system, moved to Harvard in 1959, but to the Medical School rather than the Biolabs. Hubel shared the 1981 Nobel Prize in Physiology or Medicine with Torsten Wiesel and Roger Sperry.

16 Nathan Marsh Pusey, President of Harvard from 1953 to 1971, gained national prominence for his defense of universities and academic freedom during the McCarthy Era. Whatever modicum of trust existed between Jim Watson and Pusey evaporated in the heat surrounding the University's refusal to publish *The Double Helix*. Pusey died at the age of 94 in 2001.

17 The Harvard Society of Fellows provides young scholars with an opportunity to pursue their studies in any department of the University, free from formal requirements.

18 Dumbarton Oaks is a Federal-style house in the Georgetown section of Washington, D.C., that was given to Harvard University in the early 1940s by Mildred and Robert Woods Bliss. The gardens and the collections of Byzantine and Pre-Columbian art are open to the public.

19 Radcliffe was a women's college, closely associated with Harvard. By the time that Jim and Elizabeth Lewis met, Radcliffe students received Harvard diplomas signed by the presidents of both institutions. The two schools eventually merged in 1999.

20 In 1975, Temin shared the Nobel Prize in Physiology or Medicine with Renato Dulbecco and David Baltimore for discoveries concerning "the interaction between tumor viruses and the genetic material of the cell."

SECTION IV • COLD SPRING HARBOR

Introduction—*An Emotional Attachment*

1 Ira Herskowitz was Professor of Genetics at the University of California, San Francisco. He died April 28, 2003 of pancreatic cancer at the age of 56.

John Cairns—*Cold Spring Harbor, 1958–1968*

1 The Carnegie Institution of Washington was founded in 1902 by Andrew Carnegie "to encourage, in the broadest and most liberal manner, investigation, research, and discovery, and the application of knowledge to the improvement of mankind." Carnegie made his huge fortune from iron and steel; in 1901, his personal wealth was estimated to be $500 mil-

lion. He was a great philanthropist—it is estimated that he gave away some $350 million. His initial donation to the Institution was for $10 million.

2   Barbara McClintock carried out her undergraduate and graduate work at Cornell University, and she was an instructor and subsequently a research associate in botany at Cornell University. McClintock spent six years at the University of Missouri before moving to the Department of Genetics, Carnegie Institution of Washington, at Cold Spring Harbor in 1942, where she spent the rest of her career. McClintock was the third woman elected to the National Academy of Sciences (1944) and the first female President of the American Genetics Society (1945), and she received many prizes, most notably the National Medal of Science, 1970; the Albert Lasker Basic Medical Research Award, 1981; and the Nobel Prize for Physiology or Medicine, 1983. Barbara McClintock died on September 2, 1992.

3   Al Hershey graduated from Michigan State University in 1930 and received his Ph.D. from the same institution in 1934. Hershey moved to Washington University School of Medicine in 1934 where he worked with an authority on bacteriophage. In 1950, Hershey joined the staff of the Carnegie Institution of Washington's Department of Genetics at Cold Spring Harbor. Hershey was Director of the Genetics Research Unit formed after the Carnegie disbanded the Department of Genetics in 1962 until his retirement in 1974. He was elected a member of the National Academy of Sciences in 1958 and received the Albert Lasker Award in 1958 and shared the 1969 Nobel Prize for Physiology or Medicine with Max Delbrück and Salvador Luria. He died on May 22, 1997.

4   Berwind Kaufmann was a *Drosophila* geneticist and a Director of the Carnegie's Department of Genetics at Cold Spring Harbor for two years (1960–1962). Kaufmann was a coeditor with Milislav Demerec of *The* Drosophila *Guide; Introduction to the Genetics and Cytology of* Drosophila melanogaster (1940, Carnegie Institution of Washington), which began as a cyclostyled newsletter in 1940 and went through many editions; the last, with revisions by Allan Spradling, was published in 1996.

5   A Yugoslav-born geneticist, Demerec came to Cold Spring Harbor in 1923 and was Director of both the Biological Laboratory (appointed 1941) and Carnegie's Department of Genetics (appointed 1943) until his retirement in 1960. Originally a *Drosophila* geneticist, Demerec turned to bacterial genetics in the 1940s. He and his daughter Zlata mapped the genes of the *trp* pathway in *Salmonella* using transduction (see essay by Norton Zinder in Section IV) and showed that the order of these along the chromosome was the same as their order in the pathway.

6   Cold Spring Harbor is an inlet running north-south from Long Island Sound which runs east-west. I hope that the Sandspit, which separates the inner harbor from the Sound, still remains a place for insights, escapades, and assignations. For it was part of the coming of age for the generations of scientists who, in days gone by, paced back and forth along its length. Jim Watson later repulsed a proposal to develop a commercial marina in the inner harbor.

7   Associated Universities Inc. (AUI) is a consortium of nine universities in the northeast: Columbia University, Cornell University, Harvard University, The Johns Hopkins University, Massachusetts Institute of Technology, the University of Pennsylvania, Princeton University, the University of Rochester, and Yale University. Founded in 1946, the AUI manages several large-scale projects, including the National Radio Astronomy Observatory, and, from 1947 to 1998, Cold Spring Harbor's neighbor, the Brookhaven National Laboratory.

8   These Symposia had an unusual origin. In 1924, Charles Davenport, the first Director of the two organizations, sloughed off the endless round of fund-raising onto his son-in-law Reginald Harris, by making him the Director of the BiLab, so that he himself could retreat into the comforts of Carnegie. Like Wotan's plan to beget a son who would steal the gold to pay back the cost of building Valhalla, Davenport's scheme was not entirely successful. Although Har-

ris did have time to invent the summer Symposia in 1933, and it was thanks to the Symposia and its summer courses that the BiLab acquired its worldwide reputation, he died after a short illness caused by overwork in 1936. And as for Davenport, a latter-day Captain Ahab, he caught pneumonia while rendering down the head of a killer whale he had decapitated with the view to presenting its skull to the Cold Spring Harbor Whaling Museum (of which he was Curator and Director) and died in terror as the vision of this whale came at him from the bottom of the bed. It makes me wonder if the Fates have something terrible in store for every Cold Spring Harbor Director.

9   John Cairns knew Ric Davern from Australia, where Davern, a molecular biologist, worked for a government laboratory. Davern had been a postdoctoral fellow with Matt Meselson and had demonstrated that the RNA synthesized after phage infection was unstable, unlike the host's ribosomal RNA, which was stable (Davern and Meselson, *J. Mol. Biol. 2:* 153–160 [1960]). In 1967, Davern left Cold Spring Harbor for the University of California at Santa Cruz.

10   These dinner parties are one of the established customs associated with the Symposia. Beginning in 1954, members of the Long Island Biological Association invited meeting participants to have dinner in their homes. Some 30 dinner parties are held on the Sunday evening of each Symposium.

Norton D. Zinder—*Life with Jim*

1   All of the people mentioned by Norton Zinder were eventually to migrate from the Midwest to one or other coast: Lederberg to Stanford and then to The Rockefeller University, Luria to MIT, Spiegelman and Levinthal to Columbia, Novick to the University of Oregon, and Szilard to Washington, D.C. and then La Jolla.

2   Zinder joined Lederberg in 1948 and completed his Ph.D. in 1952. Lederberg had just begun using *Salmonella*, and Zinder attempted to demonstrate recombination using different *Salmonella* strains. He found evidence of recombination, but only one marker was transferred, suggesting that some mechanism other than conjugation was involved. Zinder went on to show that markers could be transferred between cultures even when these were separated by a filter, showing that something—a "filterable agent"—was passing between the cultures. Lederberg gave an account of these findings at the 1951 Cold Spring Harbor Symposium. This was a key event for Zinder as Harriet Ephrussi-Taylor suggested that his results could be explained by a phage carrying a piece of DNA. Zinder went back to Wisconsin and soon showed that this was the case (Zinder and Lederberg, *J. Bacteriol. 64:* 679–699 [1952]). Transduction was the key tool in the fine-structure genetic mapping of *Salmonella* carried out by Demerec and Hartman at Cold Spring Harbor.

3   The phage was isolated by Tim Loeb, a graduate student at The Rockefeller University who asked Zinder whether there might be male-specific phages for *E. coli*. Zinder said ""yes" and Loeb went off to a raw sewage plant in New York City for samples. He isolated two phage: f1, which was a DNA phage, and f2, which was the first RNA phage.

4   Marshall Nirenberg and his colleague Heinrich Matthaei were the first to show that synthetic polynucleotides could be translated into polypeptides; polyuridylic acid led to the formation of polyproline. Nirenberg and Gobind Khorana shared the 1968 Nobel Prize in Physiology or Medicine with Robert Holley, who was the third recipient for his sequencing of alanine transfer RNA.

5   Fred Richards is an X-ray crystallographer at Yale University and with Hal Wyckoff and collaborators, they solved the structure of ribonuclease-S. This was the third protein structure to be determined by X-ray diffraction of crystals.

6 Fritz Lipmann shared the 1953 Nobel Prize in Physiology or Medicine with Hans Krebs. Lipmann's citation was for "his discovery of co-enzyme A and its importance for intermediary metabolism." Lipmann came to Cold Spring Harbor for meetings and celebrated his 80th birthday at the 1979 Symposium.

7 Keith Porter was one of the first to use the electron microscope to study cell and tissue structure. He developed a microtome for cutting the thin sections needed for the electron microscope. Porter was involved in a prolonged controversy over his conception of a "microtrabecular lattice" of fine fibers in the cytoplasm that directed many cellular functions.

8 Fred Sanger is known for three things in particular: His extraordinary modesty, determining the amino acid sequence of insulin (Nobel Prize for Chemistry, 1958), and developing the dideoxy method of DNA sequencing (Nobel Prize for Chemistry, 1980, sharing half with Walter Gilbert. Paul Berg was recipient of the other half for studies of the biochemistry of nucleic acids).

9 Detlev Bronk, a neurobiologist, was also President of the National Academy of Sciences. It is from the Bronk's family farm that the New York City borough derived its name.

10 Rich Roberts came to Cold Spring Harbor in 1972, from Harvard, as a nucleic acid chemist. He took up the newly discovered restriction enzymes, and his laboratory played a key role in the early development of recombinant DNA techniques by isolating and freely providing many new restriction enzymes. Roberts was also an early advocate of the use of computers in molecular biology. He shared the 1993 Nobel Prize in Physiology or Medicine with Phil Sharp for his part in the discovery of RNA splicing.

11 To placate Science for the People—a left-wing group of community activists, based in Boston—the Cambridge City Council set up the *Cambridge Biohazards Committee* to inspect laboratories and review containment procedures, all in the name of protecting the community.

Ann Skalka—*CSHL in the Sixties: A View from the Trenches*

1 The Cold Spring Harbor Phage course began in 1945, taught by Max Delbrück and Salvador Luria, and based on a course that Delbrück had developed at Vanderbilt University. The course ran for 26 successive years.

2 When the Carnegie decided to close down its Department of Genetics at Cold Spring Harbor, Al Hershey and Barbara McClintock refused to move. Instead, the Carnegie created a Genetics Research Unit consisting of just Hershey and McClintock, with Hershey as Director.

3 Cold Spring Harbor Laboratory is on the site of a small whaling station that was active from 1836 until about 1860. By the 1880s, the site had been abandoned and the buildings were derelict. Hooper, an attractive clap-board house with a shingle roof, was one of the original buildings, built about 1835. Barbara McClintock's apartment was in Hooper. Page Motel was in stark contrast. Built in 1955 and extended in 1959, it provided spartan accommodation for meetings and course participants. The Motel was demolished in 1987 to make way for Dolan Hall and the Beckman Neuroscience Center.

4 "Hershey heaven"—Alan Garen quotes Hershey as saying that heaven is "Having an experiment that works, and getting to do it over and over again."

5 In 1980, Cold Spring Harbor Laboratory held a laboratory course, taught by Tom Maniatis, Ed Fritsch, and Joe Sambrook, on the Molecular Cloning of Eukaryotic Genes. The protocols used in the course were thoroughly tested and published as *Molecular Cloning: A Laboratory Manual* (1982, Cold Spring Harbor Laboratory Press). It created a cloning revolution by giving scientists access to what had been almost mystical knowledge, restricted to just a few laboratories. There have been other manuals for molecular genetics but none with the impact of the first edition of *Molecular Cloning*.

James D. Watson—*Director's Report, 1989*

1   Ludwik Gross is a Polish-born cancer researcher who, while working as a full-time doctor in New York and without research support, discovered the first mammalian leukemia virus—the RNA-containing mouse leukemia virus. His results ran counter to then prevailing orthodoxy and were initially widely held to be erroneous, even fraudulent.

2   Splicing is an important feature of gene expression. Most genes (except in bacteria) contain regions, called introns, which do not encode any of the sequence of the protein that the gene specifies. After the DNA has been copied into messenger RNA, these regions are excised by special enzymes. The resultant pieces of RNA are then joined up (spliced) by other enzymes to form the functional messenger. The pieces of RNA are sometimes joined together in varying order and thus give rise to a family of related proteins (splice variants).

3   Kinases are enzymes that introduce phosphate groups ($-PO_3$) into specified points in proteins. Such phosphorylation, as it is called, can engender large changes in the properties and activity of the protein and is an important factor in control of metabolism.

4   Signal transduction is the process by which an event at the cell exterior, most often the binding of a molecule (hormones, such as insulin, are familiar examples) to a receptor on the cell surface, sets in train reactions within the cell. The attachment of the triggering substance to its receptor is pictured as releasing a signal on the inside of the cells to start the required sequence of events.

Douglas Hanahan—*Milestones and Mentoring*

1   Judah Folkman postulated in the early 1970s that continued growth and progression of tumors required enhanced blood supply, that "successful" tumors must secrete factors to stimulate formation of new blood vessels, and that angiogenesis inhibitors would therefore be powerful therapeutics.

2   The turning point in Judah's career came when he resigned as Surgeon-in-Chief at Children's Hospital of Harvard Medical School, to focus full time on developing a successful research program (R. Cooke, *Dr. Folkman's War: Angiogenesis and the Struggle to Defeat Cancer* [Foreword by C.E. Koop] [2001, Random House, New York]).

Raymond F. Gesteland—*CSHL in Transition*

1   For one of the classic papers of molecular biology, see Hershey and Chase (*J. Gen. Physiol. 36:* 39–56 [1952]). See "The Hershey-Chase Experiment" (p. 201) in *Illuminating Life* by J.A. Witkowski (2001, Cold Spring Harbor Laboratory Press).

2   Jim Brainerd, who was appointed as Assistant Secretary/Treasurer of the Laboratory by the Trustees, came from a position at the American School in Beirut. He worked at Cold Spring Harbor for only two years before retiring first to Menlo Park in California and then Borrego Springs. He was succeeded in late 1971 by Bill Udry, who previously was CEO of the Eye Research Institute, Bethesda. Bill was the Administrative Director of the Laboratory until 1984, when he took a position as Senior Vice President at the New York Institute of Technology on Long Island.

3   Gesteland visited the funky desert community of Borrego Springs, between San Diego and the Salton Sea, and discovered that the Brainerds in their "retirement" became the heroes of the town, having raised funds for and promoted the Anza Borrego Preserve and a new church.

Tom Maniatis—*Cold Spring Harbor and Recombinant DNA*

1   It is not clear whether Jim realized what a boon *Molecular Cloning* (Maniatis et al. 1982, Cold Spring Harbor Laboratory, Cold Spring Harbor, New York) would be to the Laboratory's finances. Joe Sambrook tells how he was working very late one night in his office in James on the third draft of the Manual. Jim appeared in his doorway and asked what he was working on. After Joe told him, Jim responded with a snort, said "Well it won't sell anyway," and disappeared.

Bayard Clarkson—*Jim and the Board: Behind the Scenes*

1   Walter Page was Chairman of the Laboratory's Board from 1980 to 1986. Robert ("Roddy") Lindsay served as Treasurer from 1959 to 1963, but he resigned because of increasing business demands at J.P Morgan.

2   In the 1960s, James V. McConnell published experiments showing that planaria could undergo classical conditioning training, using an electric shock and light. Planaria are cannibals and McConnell found that if he chopped up trained planaria and fed them to untrained planaria, the latter learned the task more quickly. Later, he found that RNA extracts from trained worms injected into untrained worms were just as effective. These results led to a fad for working on macromolecular memory in pigeons and rats. The field fell into disrepute when better controlled experiments were performed (Greenspan, *Curr. Biol. 13:* R126–R127 [2003]).

3   President Richard M. Nixon launched the "War on Cancer" on December 23, 1971, when he signed the National Cancer Act. The preamble to the Act declared "...that a great opportunity is offered as a result of recent advances in the knowledge of this dread disease to conduct energetically a national program against cancer." One of the most significant administrative changes was to have the Director of the National Cancer Institute (NCI) submit the NCI's budget estimate directly to the President. The most controversial was the establishment of 15 new centers that were to combine clinical and fundamental research. (The Act is available online at http://www3.cancer.gov/legis/1971canc.html.)

William Grover—*An Architect at the Lab: Some Personal Recollections*

1   Airslie House has been the official residence of the Director of Cold Spring Harbor Laboratory since 1943.

2   A general contractor with his own firm in the Huntington area, Jack Richards was first hired by Jim in 1969 to construct the James Office building. The relationship quickly flourished, based on Jack's willingness to provide quality work and Jim's respect for Jack's taste and technical knowledge. Appointed to the staff of the Laboratory in the early 1970s, Jack served as Director of Buildings and Grounds until shortly before his death in 2000.

SECTION V • GENOMES

Bradie Metheny—*Dr. Watson Goes to Washington*

1   Mahlon Hoagland had carried out research on protein synthesis with Paul Zamecnik at the Massachusetts General Hospital. They worked out the step of amino acid activation required for protein synthesis and showed that a soluble RNA (later called transfer RNA) became

associated with amino acids prior to be incorporated into protein. Hoagland describes that biochemists like Zamecnik and himself were a breed apart from the molecular biologists like Watson and Crick. It was only when Jim visited them that they found that Crick had already postulated, on theoretical grounds, the existence of their soluble RNA (Hoagland M., *Toward the Habit of Truth: A Life in Science* [1990, W.W. Norton, New York]; Hoagland, *Trends Biochem. Sci. 21:* 77–80 [1996]).

2   The Worcester Foundation for Experimental Biology was founded in 1944 by Hudson Hoagland, Mahlon's father, and Gregory Pincus of the contraceptive pill fame.

3   William H. Natcher was elected to the U.S. House of Representatives in 1953 and served until his death in 1994. He made Congressional history by not missing a roll call or vote in over 40 years. Natcher was a staunch supporter of biomedical research and the NIH and was able to direct large sums of money to NIH. The large conference center on the NIH campus in Bethesda is named the Natcher Building.

4   Thereza Imanishi-Kari was accused by a postdoc, Margaret O'Toole, of manipulating results obtained in a collaborative project with David Baltimore. After a prolonged controversy that involved the Secret Service, Imanishi-Kari was cleared of any wrongdoing. The affair was notorious for the vehemence with which it was pursued and the passions it aroused (D.J. Kevles, *The Baltimore Case: A Trial of Politics, Science, and Character* [2000, W.W. Norton, New York])

5   In 1951, Ludwig Gross isolated a virus that causes leukemia in mice. This led to a renewed interest in viral causes of human cancers, and human viral oncology became a major program of the National Cancer Institute in the 1960s and 1970s (see essay by Norton D. Zinder in Section IV).

6   Judah Folkman proposes that the development of a blood supply to a tumor is a critical step in the progess of a cancer and that substances such as endostatin that stop angiogenesis should be effective in controlling cancers. There have been some spectacular successes but the treatment has yet to be widely accepted (R. Cooke, *Dr. Folkman's War: Angiogenesis and the Struggle to Defeat Cancer* [Foreword by C.E. Koop] [2001, Random House, New York]).

7   See Robert Cook-Deegan's essay in Section V and his book, *The Gene Wars: Science, Politics and the Human Genome* (1994, W.W. Norton).

James B. Wyngaarden—*Jim Watson and the Human Genome Project*

1   Charles DeLisi was head of the Office of Health and Environmental Science within DOE. DeLisi thought that sequencing the human genome would be of value in understanding the genetic damages caused by high-energy radiation.

2   The Nobel Prize for Physiology or Medicine was shared in 1968 among Robert Holley, H. Gobind Khorana, and Marshall Nirenberg and was awarded for "interpretation of the genetic code and its functions in protein synthesis."

3   In an article in *Science* entitled "*Proposal to sequence the human genome stirs debate*," Roger Lewin reported that DOE spent over $2 billion through the years on energy-related effects on human genetics. This may well be the basis of the rumor circulated at the MRC meeting in London. (Lewin, *Science 232:* 1598 [1986].)

4   Maxine Singer, cited in Lewin (*Science 232:* 1598 [1986]).

5   *The Human Genome.* Proceedings of the 54th meeting of the Advisory Committee to the Director, National Institutes of Health, Oct. 16, 17, 1986. Department of Health and Human Services, March 1987.

6 Faced with ever-increasing budget deficits, in 1985, Congress enacted the Balanced Budget and Emergency Deficit Control Act, which was known as Gramm-Rudman-Hollings—named after the Senate authors of the original bill (Senators Phil Gramm of Texas, Warren Rudman of New Hampshire, and Ernest F. Hollings of South Carolina). Gramm-Rudman-Hollings established "maximum deficit amounts." If the deficit exceeded these statutory limits, the President was required to issue an order reducing all nonexempt spending by a uniform percentage.

7 Ad Hoc Program Advisory Committee on Complex Genomes, Report to the Director, National Institutes of Health, Reston, Virginia, February 29–March 1, 1988.

8 In 1963, François Gros was one of Jim's chief collaborators in experiments undertaken at Harvard in the summer of 1960 to identify mRNA (Gros et al., *Nature 190:* 581 [1961]).

9 In 1986–1987, Donald Frederickson was President of the Howard Hughes Medical Institute. He was a Director of the National Institutes of Health and a leading genetic researcher on the links between fats and heart disease. Frederickson died in 2002 at age 77 of an apparent drowning.

10 Elke Jordan was responsible for establishing the infrastructure of the Human Genome Project at NIH. In 1989, she became deputy director of the National Center for Human Genome Research, which launched the Human Genome Project in 1990. She managed early pilot projects on sequencing the genomes of yeast and nematodes and administered the grants to develop the technology that would eventually map and sequence the human genome.

11 Foreword, Annual Report I–FY 1990. National Center for Human Genome Research, National Institutes of Health, Public Health Service, Department of Health and Human Services.

12 A five-year plan for the Human Genome Project. National Center for Human Genome Research, National Institutes of Health, Public Health Service, Department of Health and Human Services, 1990.

13 In a later interview Jim Watson said: "He [Bourke] and Leroy Hood had considered forming a private company, based in Seattle, to sequence the human genome. Through patenting key genes they hoped to effectively dominate the commercial exploitation of the human genome... . When I learnt that Bourke was trying to move [Bob] Waterston and [John] Sulston to Seattle, I worried that the NIH might lose its most successful genome-sequencing effort, and the UK government might abandon large-scale genome research." (http://www.wellcome.ac.uk/en/genome/geneticsandsociety/hg13f005.html)

Robert Cook-Deegan—*The Colossus of Codes*

1 Robert Waterston, an American, and English-born John Sulston were both, at different times, postdoctoral fellows in Sydney Brenner's *C. elegans* group in Cambridge, U.K. Waterston's return to Cambridge on sabbatical sparked a collaboration with Sulston that produced in 1989 a physical map of the worm genome, followed in 1998 by the complete DNA sequence. Both scientists were early and vital recruits to the Human Genome Project and Jim Watson looked to them for technical and conceptual leadership when human sequencing began in earnest in the early 1990s. After many years at Washington University in St. Louis, where he headed the Department of Genetics and the Genome Sequencing Center, Bob Waterston became Chair of the Department of Genome Sciences at the University of Washington School of Medicine in January 2003. John Sulston was the first Director of the Wellcome Trust Sanger Institute in Cambridgeshire, stepping down in 2000 to continue his laboratory studies on the worm. He was knighted for services to genome research in 2001 and shared the Nobel Prize for Physiology or Medicine in 2002 with Sydney Brenner and Robert Horvitz.

2   World Survey of Genomics Research, http://www.stanford.edu/class/websites/genomics/entry.htm.

Kenichi Matsubara—*Jim and the Japanese Human Genome Project*

1   The National Institutes of Health set up a Recombinant DNA Advisory Committee (RAC) in 1974. The NIH rules on using recombinant DNA technology were published in 1975: "These guidelines include a comprehensive description of facilities and practices intended to prevent unintended release or inadvertent exposure to either genetically modified organisms or recombinant DNA. Compliance with the guidelines is mandatory for investigators at institutions receiving NIH funds for research involving recombinant DNA."

2   The Telethon, a 30-hour entertainment show on television, is run by the Association Française contre les Myopathies to raise money for research on neuromuscular disorders. It raised 91,546,548 euros ($107,000,000) in 2002.

3   Jim was arguing primarily that Japan contribute funds for supporting HUGO, which at that time was expected to play a major role in coordinating sequencing efforts in different countries. Jim wrote that $300,000 was an appropriate contribution for a "great nation." (Roberts, Watson versus Japan. *Science 246:* 576, 578 [1989].)

SECTION VI • EDUCATION

Introduction—*Communicating Science*

1   Watson J.D. 2001. *Genes, girls, and Gamow: After* The Double Helix, p. 73. Oxford University Press, Oxford.

2   Watson J.D. 2001. *Genes, girls, and Gamow: After* The Double Helix, p. 110. Oxford University Press, Oxford.

3   Watson J.D. 2001. *Genes, girls, and Gamow: After* The Double Helix, p. 127. Oxford University Press, Oxford.

4   Watson J.D. 2001. *Genes, girls, and Gamow: After* The Double Helix, p. 137. Oxford University Press, Oxford.

5   Harvard Reviews.

6   Lewis S. 1925. *Arrowsmith*. Harcourt Brace and Co., New York.

7   Maddox B. 2002. *Rosalind Franklin: The dark lady of DNA*. HarperCollins, London.

8   Miller J.H. 1972. *Experiments in molecular genetics*. Cold Spring Harbor Laboratory, Cold Spring Harbor, New York.

David Botstein—*The Pied Piper at Harvard*

1   R.V. Pound, a Professor of Physics at Harvard, successfully confirmed the gravitational red shift of light in response to gravity. Pound also was instrumental in the development of nuclear magnetic resonance to study molecular structure.

George Kistiakowsky, Professor of Chemistry at Harvard University, had worked in the Manhattan Project in the later stages of World War II, designing the triggering devices used to detonate the atomic bomb.

Konrad Bloch, Higgins Professor of Biochemistry in Harvard's Chemistry Department, along with Feodor Lynen, won the Nobel Prize in Physiology or Medicine in 1964, two years after Jim Watson, for studies on the regulation of the metabolism of cholesterol and fatty acids.

Bill Lipscomb, a Professor of Chemistry, studied the three-dimensional structures of enzymes and the effects of allosteric shifts. Lipscomb was awarded the Nobel Prize in Chemistry in 1976.

Boris Magasanik moved from Harvard in 1960 to become Professor of Microbiology at MIT, where he studies regulation of bacterial genes involved in metabolism of lactose, histidine, and nitrogen.

Arnie Levine—*There Is More Yet to Come*

[1] Yakov ("Yasha") Gluzman worked in the Tumor Virus Group in James laboratory from 1977 to 1990, first as a postdoctoral fellow and finally as a Senior Scientist. After leaving Cold Spring Harbor, Yasha worked for Wyeth-Ayerst Research in Pearl River, New York. In 1996, at age 48, he was the victim of a gruesome and highly publicized murder committed by his estranged wife and her cousin.

Keith Roberts—*On Drawing Molecules*

[1] After majoring in chemistry and physics at Harvard, Walter Gilbert obtained his Ph.D. in physics at Cambridge University, where he first met Jim Watson. He became an Assistant Professor at Harvard and during the late 1950s and early 1960s taught courses in theoretical physics. In the summer of 1960, Gilbert joined Jim Watson and his colleagues in ultimately succcessful attempts to identify messenger RNA. He found the experimental work exciting and has continued research in molecular biology ever since. Gilbert and Watson ran a joint lab at Harvard that was enormously influential in the development of molecular biology. In the mid 1960s, with Benno Müller-Hill, Gilbert isolated the *lac* repressor, the first example of a genetic control element. With Allan Maxam, in the mid 1970s, he developed a method for rapid chemical sequencing of DNA. He remains interested in the making of useful proteins in bacteria and in the structure of genes and the evolution of DNA sequences. With Paul Berg and Fred Sanger, Gilbert was awarded the Nobel Prize in Chemistry in 1980.

[2] Martin Kemp provides an entertaining review of the use of images of the double helix in art in "The *Mona Lisa* of Modern Science" (Kemp, *Nature 421*: 416–420 [2003]).

Jan Witkowski and John Inglis—*Education by the Sea Shore*

[1] Terri Grodzicker came to Cold Spring Harbor in 1972 and switched from research on the *lac* operon and bacteriophage λ gene regulation to adenovirus and SV40. In 1986, she became Assistant Director for Academic Affairs and since 1989 has been the editor of the journal *Genes & Development.*

[2] Charles Sammis Robertson's family had lived in Lloyd Harbor since the 18th century and owned an extensive estate in the region, although this had been sold by the end of the 19th century. Robertson graduated *magna cum laude* from Princeton, and met Marie Hoffman whose family, the Hartfords, had established the Great Atlantic and Pacific Tea Company. Charles and Marie bought some 45 acres of land in Lloyd Harbor and built a small mansion. In 1973, Robertson established the Robertson Research Fund with a gift of $8 million. Jim had written in the 1968 Annual Report that "...I dream an angel will appear soon." Charles Robertson was that angel.

Bibliography—James D. Watson

Watson J.D. 1950. The properties of X-ray-inactivated bacteriophage. I. Inactivation by direct effect. *J. Bacteriol.* **60:** 697–718.

Maaløe O. and Watson J.D. 1951. The transfer of radioactive phosphorous from parental to progeny phage. *Proc. Natl. Acad. Sci.* **37:** 507–513.

Watson J.D. 1952. The properties of X-ray-inactivated bacteriophage. II. Inactivation of indirect effects. *J. Bacteriol.* **63:** 473–485.

Watson J.D. and Maaløe O. 1953. Nucleic acid transfer from parental to progeny bacteriophage. *Biochim. Biophys. Acta* **10:** 432–442.

Watson J.D. and Hayes W. 1953. Genetic exchange in *Escherichia coli* K12: Evidence for three linkage groups. *Proc. Natl. Acad. Sci.* **39:** 416–426.

Ephrussi B., Leopold U., Watson J.D., and Weigle J. 1953. Terminology in bacterial genetics. *Nature* **171:** 701.

Watson J.D. and Crick F.H.C. 1953. A structure for deoxyribose nucleic acid. *Nature* **171:** 737–738.

Watson J.D. and Crick F.H.C. 1953. Genetic implications of the structure of deoxyribonucleic acid. *Nature* **171:** 964–967.

Watson J.D. and Crick F.H.C. 1953. The structure of DNA. *Cold Spring Harbor Symp. Quant. Biol.* **18:** 123–131.

Crick F.H.C. and Watson J.D. 1954. The complementary structure of deoxyribonucleic acid. *Proc. Roy. Soc. A* **223:** 80–96.

Watson J.D. 1954. The structure of tobacco mosaic virus. I. X-ray evidence of a helical arrangement of sub-units around the longitudinal axis. *Biochim. Biophys. Acta* **13:** 10–19.

Rich A. and Watson J.D. 1954. Some relations between DNA and RNA. *Proc. Natl. Acad. Sci.* **40:** 759–764.

Rich A. and Watson J.D. 1954. Physical studies on ribonucleic acid. *Nature* **173:** 995–996.

Crick F.H.C. and Watson J.D. 1955. The configuration of the nucleic acids. *Inst. Lombardo Sci. Lett.* **89:** 52–66.

Watson J.D. 1955. Biological consequences of the complementary structure of DNA. *J. Cell. Comp. Physiol.* **45:** 109–118.

Crick F.H.C. and Watson J.D. 1956. The structure of small viruses. *Nature* **177:** 473–475.

Watson J.D. 1957. X-ray studies on RNA and the synthetic polyribonucleotides. In *The chemical basis of heredity* (ed. W.D. McElroy and B. Glass), pp. 552–556. Johns Hopkins Press, Baltimore, Maryland.

Crick F.H.C. and Watson J.D. 1957. Virus structure: General principles. In *Ciba Foundation Symposium on the nature of viruses* (ed. G.E.W. Wolstenholme and E.C.P. Millar), pp. 5–13. Little, Brown, Boston, Massachusetts.

Koshland Jr., D.E., Simmons N.S., and Watson J.D. 1958. Absence of phosphotriester linkages in tobacco mosaic virus *J. Am. Chem. Soc.* **80:** 105–107.

Tissières A. and Watson J.D. 1958. Ribonucleoprotein particles from *Escherichia coli. Nature* 182: 778-780.

Nomura M. and Watson J.D. 1959. Ribonucleoprotein particles with chloromycetin-inhibited *Escherichia coli. J. Mol. Biol.* **1:** 204–217.

Tissières A., Watson J.D., Schlessinger D., and Hollingworth B.R. 1959. Ribonucleoprotein particles from *Escherichia coli. J. Mol. Biol.* **1:** 221–233.

Watson J.D. and Littlefield J.W. 1960. Some properties of DNA from Shope papilloma virus *J. Mol. Biol.* **2:** 161–165.

Rich A., Davies D.R., Crick F.H.C., and Watson J.D. 1961. The molecular structure of polyadenylic acid *J. Mol. Biol.* **3:** 71–86.

Gros F., Hiatt H., Gilbert W., Kurland C.G., Risebrough R.W., and Watson J.D. 1961. Unstable ribonucleic acid revealed by pulse labeling of *E. coli. Nature* **190:** 581–584.

Gros F., Gilbert W., Hiatt H., Attardi G., Spahr P.F., and Watson J.D. 1962. Molecular and biological characterization of messenger RNA. *Cold Spring Harbor Symp. Quant. Biol.* **26:** 111–132.

Risebrough R.W., Tissières A., and Watson J.D. 1962. Messenger RNA attachment to active ribosomes. *Proc. Natl. Acad. Sci.* **48:** 430–436.

Kurland C.G., Nomura M., and Watson J.D. 1962. The physical properties of chloromycetin particles. *J. Mol. Biol.* **4:** 388–394.

Tissières A. and Watson J.D. 1962. Breakdown of messenger RNA during in-vitro amino acid incorporation into proteins. *Proc. Natl. Acad. Sci.* **48:** 1061–1069.

Watson J.D. 1963. Involvement of RNA in the synthesis of proteins. In *Les Prix Nobel en 1962*, pp. 155–178. Nobel Foundation, Stockholm, Sweden.

Watson J.D. 1963. Involvement of RNA in the synthesis of proteins (adapted from Nobel Lecture, December 1962). *Science* **140:** 17–26.

Watson J.D. 1964. The synthesis of proteins upon ribosomes. *Bull. Soc. Chim. Biol.* **46:** 1399–1425.

Watson J.D. 1964. The replication of living molecules. In *Light and life in the universe* (ed. S.T. Butler and H. Messel), pp. 295–340. Shakespeare Head Press, Sydney, Australia.

Watson J.D. 1965. *Molecular biology of the gene.* W.A. Benjamin, New York.

Cairns J., Stent G.S., and Watson J.D., eds. 1966. *Phage and the origins of molecular biology.* Cold Spring Harbor Laboratory of Quantitative Biology, Cold Spring Harbor, New York.

Watson J.D. 1966. Growing up in the phage group. In *Phage and the origins of molecular biology* (ed. J. Cairns et al.), pp. 239–245. Cold Spring Harbor Laboratory of Quantitative Biology, Cold Spring Harbor, New York.

Watson J.D. 1966. Life's molecules take shape. *New Sci.* **32:** 424, 425, 428.

Gussin G.N., Capecchi M.R., Adams J.M., Argetsinger J.E., Tooze J., Weber K., and Watson J.D. 1967. Protein synthesis directed by RNA phage messengers. *Cold Spring Harbor Symp. Quant. Biol.* **31:** 257–271.

Watson J.D. 1968. *The double helix: A personal account of the discovery of the structure of DNA.* Atheneum, New York.

Eigner J., Watson J.D., Haselkorn R., Signer E., Fraser D., and Echols H. 1968. Letter: Boycott Chicago! *Science* **162:** 511.

Watson J.D. 1969. Looking after molecular biologists. Director's Report in the Annual Report of Cold Spring Harbor Laboratory.

Watson J.D. 1969. Letter: DNA helix. *Science* **164:** 1539.

Watson J.D. 1970. Communicating the frontiers of science. Director's Report in the Annual Report of Cold Spring Harbor Laboratory.

Watson J.D. 1971. Moving toward the clonal man: Is this what we want? *Atlantic Monthly* **227:** 50–53.

Watson J.D. 1971. The conquest of cancer—How to use money and resources wisely? Director's Report in the Annual Report of Cold Spring Harbor Laboratory.

Watson J.D. 1972. The cancer conquerors. Who should get all that new money? *The New Republic* **166:** 17–21.

Watson J.D. 1972. Origin of concatemeric T7 DNA. *Nat. New Biol.* **239:** 197–201.

Watson J.D. 1972. On being an entrepreneur of science. Director's Report in the Annual Report of Cold Spring Harbor Laboratory.

Watson J.D. 1973. Escalating the war on cancer. *Science Year: A World Book Science Annual*, pp. 24–32.

Watson J.D. 1973. When worlds collide: Research and know-nothingism. *The New York Times Op-Ed*, March 22.

Watson J.D. 1973. Tumor viruses—A route to Mt. Everest of cancer. Director's Report in the

Annual Report of Cold Spring Harbor Laboratory.

Berg P., Baltimore D., Boyer H.W., Cohen S.N. , Davis R.W., Hogness D.S., Nathans D., Roblin R., Watson J.D., Weissman S., and Zinder N.D. 1974. Letter: Potential biohazards of recombinant DNA molecules. *Science* **185:** 303.

Watson J.D. 1974. Getting realistic about cancer. Director's Report in the Annual Report of Cold Spring Harbor Laboratory.

Wason J.D. 1975. The dissemination of unpublished information. In *Frontiers of knowledge: The Frank Nelson Doubleday Lectures*, pp. 158–175. Doubleday, New York.

Watson J.D. 1975. Have molecular geneticists become intellectually passé? Director's Report in the Annual Report of Cold Spring Harbor Laboratory.

Watson J.D. 1976. A massive miscalculation—The "dangers" of recombinant DNA. Director's Report in the Annual Report of Cold Spring Harbor Laboratory.

Watson J.D. 1977. An imaginary monster. *Bull. At. Sci.* **33:** 12–13.

Watson J.D. 1977. In defense of DNA. *New Republic* **170:** 11–14.

Watson J.D. 1977. Molecular biologists and political realities. Director's Report in the Annual Report of Cold Spring Harbor Laboratory.

Watson J.D. 1978. Trying to bury Asilomar. *Clin. Res.* **26:** 113–115.

Watson J.D. 1978. The case for expanding research into DNA. *N. Z. Vet. J.* **26:** 182.

Watson J.D. 1978. The Nobelist vs the film star. *The Washington Post,* Sunday, May 14. D1–D2.

Watson J.D. 1978. The Ninth Feodor Lynen Lecture: In further defense of DNA. *Miami Winter Symp.* **15:** 1–12.

Watson J.D. 1978. Standing up for recombinant DNA. Director's Report in the Annual Report of Cold Spring Harbor Laboratory.

Watson J.D. 1979. DNA folly continues. *New Republic* **180:** 12.

Watson J.D. 1979. The DNA biohazard canard. *Time Magazine,* January 31.

Watson J.D. 1979. Let us stop regulating DNA. *Nature* 278: 113.

Watson J.D. 1979. Academic thinkers and the real world. Director's Report in the Annual Report of Cold Spring Harbor Laboratory.

Watson J.D. 1980. Sixth Daniel C. Baker, Jr. Memorial Lecture. Induction of cancer by DNA viruses. *Ann. Otol. Rhinol. Laryngol.* **89:** 489–496.

Watson J.D. 1980. Maintaining high-quality cancer research in a zero-sum era. Director's Report in the Annual Report of Cold Spring Harbor Laboratory.

Watson J.D. and Tooze J. 1981. *The DNA story: A documentary history of gene cloning.* W.H. Freeman, San Francisco, California.

Watson, J.D. 1981. Striving for excellence. In *Excellence: The pursuit, the commitment, the achievement,* pp. 32–39. Corporate Affairs Department of LTV Corporation, Dallas, Texas.

Watson J.D. 1981. Cancer is a solvable problem. Director's Report in the Annual Report of Cold Spring Harbor Laboratory.

Watson J.D., Tooze J., and Kurtz D.T. 1982. *Recombinant DNA: A short course.* Scientific American Books, New York.

Baltimore D., Berg P., Bloch K.E., Brown D.D., Kornberg A., Nathans D., Smith H.O., Watson J.D., and Thomas L. 1982. Letter: Plea to the scientific community. *Science* **216:** 1046.

Watson J.D. 1982. Academic scientists become entrepreneurs. Director's Report in the Annual Report of Cold Spring Harbor Laboratory.

Alberts B., Lewis J., Roberts K., Watson J.D., Bray D., and Raff M. 1983. *Molecular biology of the cell.* Garland Publishing Inc., New York.

Watson J.D. 1983. Introduction: Double Helix 35th Anniversary Conference. *Nature* **302:** 651–652.

Watson J.D. 1984. Creating new life. *Omni,* May, vol. 6. Interview.

Watson J.D. 1984. Setting priorities for the future. Director's Report in the Annual Report of Cold Spring Harbor Laboratory.

Watson J.D. 1985. Moving on to human DNA. Director's Report in the Annual Report of Cold Spring Harbor Laboratory.

Watson J.D. 1986. From understanding to manipulating DNA. In *The positive sum strategy: Harnessing technology for economic growth* (ed. R. Landau and N. Rosenberg), pp. 213–225. National Academy Press, Washington, D.C.

Watson J.D. 1986. A Human Genome Project. Director's Report in the Annual Report of Cold Spring Harbor Laboratory.

Watson J.D. 1987. Minds that live for science. *New Scientist,* May 21, pp. 63–66.

Watson J.D. 1987. Honesty and decency in scientific research. Director's Report in the Annual Report of Cold Spring Harbor Laboratory.

Watson J.D. 1988. Working for the government—The Human Genome Project gets going. Director's Report in the Annual Report of Cold Spring Harbor Laboratory.

Watson J.D. 1989. The DNA gold rush (Jan.) *Research* **9:** 7.

Watson J.D. and Jordan E. 1989. The Human Genome Program at the National Institutes of Health. *Genomics* **5:** 654–656.

Watson J.D. 1989. A room with a view...For a few dollars more. *BIOtechnol. Education* **1:** 3–5.

Watson J.D. 1989. The science for beating down cancer. Director's Report in the Annual Report of Cold Spring Harbor Laboratory.

Watson J.D. 1990. The Human Genome Project: Past, present and future. *Science* **248:** 44–49.

Watson J.D. 1990. Bragg's foreword to *The double helix*. In *The legacy of Sir Lawrence Bragg* (ed. J.M. Thomas and Sir D. Phillips), pp. 111–113. The Royal Institution, London.

Watson J.D. 1990. First word. *Omni,* vol. 12, pp. 6–7.

Watson J.D. 1990. The Human Genome Project and international health. *J. Am. Med. Assoc.* **263:** 3322–3324.

Watson J.D. 1990. Letters to the editor: Genome Project maps path of diseases and drugs. *The New York Times,* Saturday, October 13.

Watson J.D. 1990. Looking ahead—The next one hundred years. Director's Report in the Annual Report of Cold Spring Harbor Laboratory.

Juengst E.T. and Watson J.D. 1991. Human genome research and the responsible use of new genetic knowledge. *J. Int. Bioethique* **2:** 99–102.

Watson J.D. 1991. Salvador E. Luria (1912–1991). *Nature* **350:** 113.

Watson J.D. 1991. Salvador E. Luria (13 August 1912–6 February 1991). *Proc. Am. Philos. Soc.* **143:** 681–683.

Watson J.D. 1991. Genes and the legacy of psychiatric illness. *The decade of the brain,* Spring, vol. 2, issue 2.

Watson J.D. 1991. The impact of the Human Genome Project. Beckman DU Symposium, April 10, Arnold and Mabel Beckman Center, Irvine, California.

Watson J.D. 1991. Too many noughts. *Nature* **350:** 550.

Watson J.D. 1991. The human genome initiative: A statement of need. *Hosp. Pract.* **26:** 69–73.

Watson J.D. 1991. In pursuit of the genetic grail. In *Chronika: A celebration of science* (ed. R.A. McCabe et al.), pp. 94–95. Athens College, Greece.

Watson J.D. 1991. Moving forward with the Human Genome Project. Director's Report in the Annual Report of Cold Spring Harbor Laboratory.

Watson J.D. and Cook-Deegan R.M. 1991. Origins of the Human Genome Project. *FASEB J.* **5:** 8–11.

Watson J.D. 1992. Tribute to the memory of Dr. Harry Eagle (1945–1992). *Einstein Q.* **10:** 66–67.

Watson J.D., Gilman M., Witkowski J.A., and Zoller M. 1992. *Recombinant DNA*, 2nd edition. Scientific American Books, New York.

Watson J.D. 1992. Early speculations and facts about RNA templates. In *The RNA world* (ed. R.F. Gesteland and J.F. Atkins), pp. xv–xxiii. Cold Spring Harbor Laboratory Press, Cold Spring Harbor, New York.

Watson J.D. 1992. Funding sources for research: Federal and corporate. Director's Report in the Annual Report of Cold Spring Harbor Laboratory.

Watson J.D. 1993. Why Britain's science cannot be sold short. *The Mail,* March 21.

Watson J.D. 1993. Initial implications of the double helix. Introductory issue, April 25. *Structure,* p. iii.

Watson J.D. 1993. Looking forward. *Gene* **135:** 309–315.

Watson J.D. 1993. Succeeding in science: Some rules of thumb. *Science* **261:** 1812–1813.

Watson J.D. 1993. Building our science, preserving our environment. Director's Report in the Annual Report of Cold Spring Harbor Laboratory.

Watson J.D. and Sher G.S. 1994. Does research in the former Soviet Union have a future? *Science* **264:** 1280–1281.

Watson J.D. 1994. Foreword. In *The polymerase chain reaction* (ed. K. Mullis et al.), pp. v–viii. Birkhäuser, Boston, Massachusetts.

Watson J.D. 1994. Toward a biological understanding of human nature. President's essay in the Annual Report of Cold Spring Harbor Laboratory.

Watson J.D. 1995. Values from a Chicago upbringing. In *DNA: The double helix—Perspective and prospective at forty years* (ed. D.A. Chambers). *Ann. N.Y. Acad. Sci.* **758:** 194–197.

Watson J.D. 1995. The Human Genome Project—Ten years later. President's essay in the Annual Report of Cold Spring Harbor Laboratory.

Watson J.D. 1996. Genes and politics. President's essay in the Annual Report of Cold Spring Harbor Laboratory.

Watson J.D. 1997. A laboratory for tough risk-takers. President's essay in the Annual Report of Cold Spring Harbor Laboratory.

Watson J.D. 1997. Genes and politics. *J. Mol. Med.* **75:** 624–636.

Watson J.D. 1997. Good gene, bad gene: What is the right way to fight the tragedy of genetic disease? *Time Magazine*, p. 86, Winter 1997–1998.

Watson J.D. 1998. Alfred D. Hershey: Hershey heaven. *The New York Times Magazine*, January 4.

Watson J.D. 1998. Afterword. Five days in Berlin. In *Murderous science. Elimination by scientific selection of Jews, Gypsies, and others in Germany, 1933–1945* (by B. Müller-Hill), Cold Spring Harbor Laboratory Press, Cold Spring Harbor, New York.

Watson J.D. 1998. Lessons for our new graduate school. President's essay in the Annual Report of Cold Spring Harbor Laboratory.

Watson J.D. 1999. All for the good: Why genetic engineering must soldier on. *Time Magazine* **153:** 91.

Watson J.D. 2000. *A passion for DNA: Genes, genomes, and society*. Cold Spring Harbor Laboratory Press, Cold Spring Harbor, New York.

Watson J.D. 2001. The human genome revealed. *Genome Res.* **11:** 1803–1804.

Watson J.D. 2001. Foreword. The human genome revealed, 2001. In *The human genome* (ed. C. Dennis and R. Gallagher). Palgrave Press, United Kingdom.

Gershon E.S., Kelsoe J.R., Kendler K.S., and Watson J.D. 2001. A scientific opportunity. *Science* **294:** 957.

Watson J.D. 2001. Rules for graduates. In *A passion for DNA: Genes, genomes, and society*, pp. 127–129. Cold Spring Harbor Laboratory Press, Cold Spring Harbor, New York. (U.S. paperback edition.)

Watson J.D. 2001. The pursuit of happiness. In *A passion for DNA: Genes, genomes, and society*, pp. 235–238. Cold Spring Harbor Laboratory Press, Cold Spring Harbor, New York. (U.S. paperback edition.)

Watson J.D. 2001. The human genome revealed. In *A passion for DNA: Genes, genomes, and society*, pp. 239–244. Cold Spring Harbor Laboratory Press, Cold Spring Harbor, New York. (U.S. paperback edition.)

Watson J.D. 2001. *Genes, girls, and Gamow: After* The Double Helix. Oxford University Press, United Kingdom (also published by Knopf [2002] in the United States).

Watson J.D. with Berry A. 2003. *DNA: The secret of life*. Alfred A. Knopf, New York.

INDEX*

*Page references in bold denote biographical sketches of contributing authors. The "n" following a number indicates end-note number.